So lernst du mit Green Line

Introduction

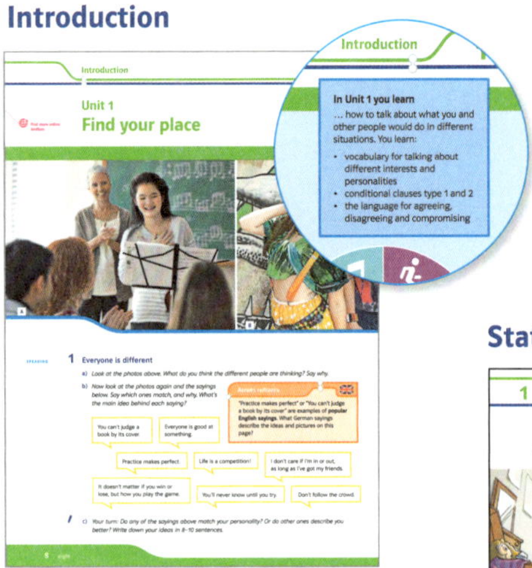

Die ersten beiden Seiten stimmen dich auf das Thema der Unit ein. In der blauen Kompetenzbox siehst du, was du in dieser Unit lernen wirst.

Die roten Dreiecke zeigen dir, dass du hinten im Diff pool z. B. Hilfen und leichtere oder weiterführende Aufgaben findest.

Stations

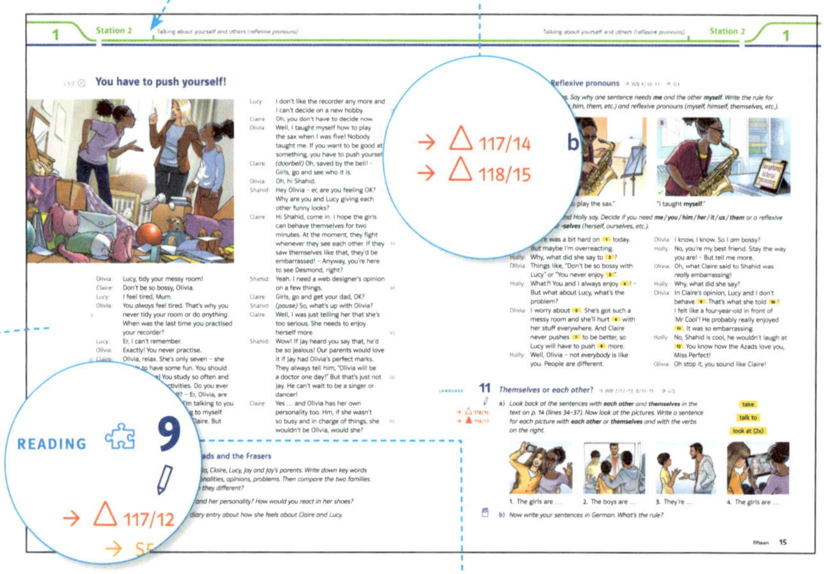

In den beiden Stations jeder Unit findest du deinen neuen Lernstoff, tolle Texte und passende Aufgaben.

Die Aufgaben mit dem Puzzle-Symbol unterstützen dich besonders dabei, deine Lernziele zu erreichen und helfen dir bei der Vorbereitung der Unit task.

Unit task

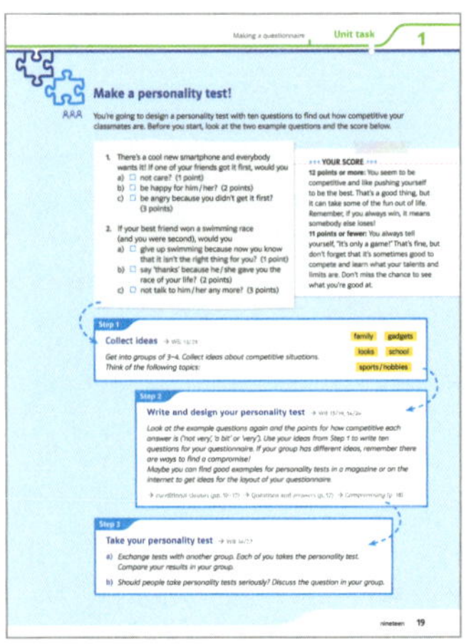

Und so kommt zum Schluss alles zusammen. Anhand dieser großen Unit-Aufgabe kannst du deine neu erworbenen Fähigkeiten schrittweise überprüfen und festigen und dabei auf kreative Weise zeigen, was du nun kannst.

Story

Hier findest du lustige und spannende Geschichten mit interessanten Aufgaben.

Action UK!

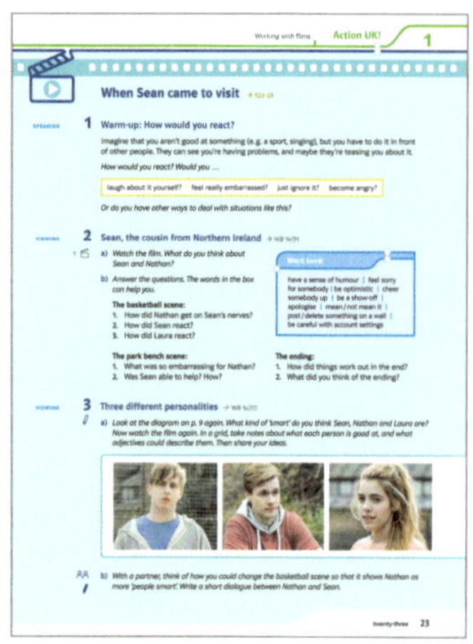

Und auf diesen Seiten gibt es tolle Filme aus Greenwich!

Text smart

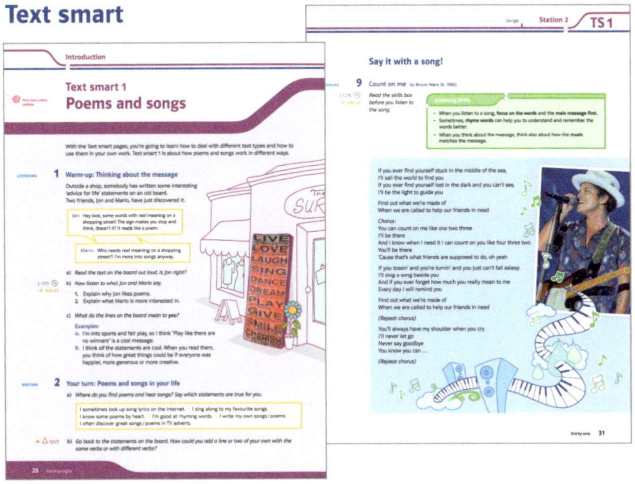

Auf den neuen *Text smart*-Seiten lernst du, wie du mit authentischen Texten (z. B. Sachtexten, Erzählungen, Songs und Gedichten) umgehst und sie im Anschluss für deine eigenen Arbeiten nutzen kannst.

Across cultures

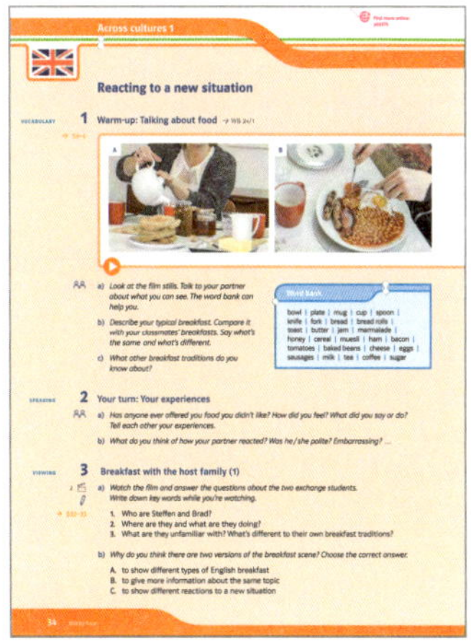

Vergleiche auf diesen Seiten deinen Alltag mit der Alltagskultur in Großbritannien und lerne, mit verschiedenen Begegnungssituationen umzugehen.

Diff pool

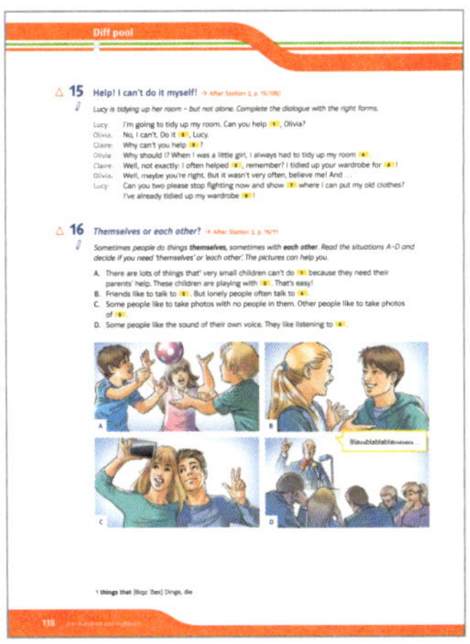

Skills

Grammar, Vocabulary

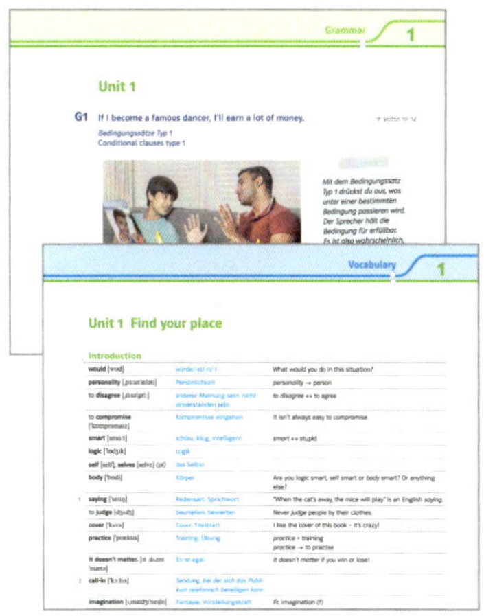

Im hinteren Buchteil stehen dir hilfreiche Anhänge zur Verfügung. Achte auf die Verweise in den Units, die dir sagen, in welchem Anhang du nachschlagen kannst.

Symbole

→ △ 132/1	Verweis auf leichtere Aufgaben / Hilfen im Diff pool	✎	Schreiben (geschlossen / einfach)
→ ▲ 132/2	Verweis auf anspruchsvollere Aufgaben im Diff pool	✎	Schreiben (offen / kreativ)
→ WB 7/4	Verweis auf eine Übung im Workbook	S1/14 ◎	Verweis auf die Schüler-CDs im Workbook (Audio)
→ G2	Verweis auf die Grammatik im Anhang	L1/19 ◎	Verweis auf die Lehrer-CDs (Audio)
→ S2	Verweis auf die Skills im Anhang		Verweis auf die Lehrer-DVD (Film)
	Partnerarbeit		Code auf www.klett.de eingeben und Zusatzmaterial nutzen
	Gruppenarbeit		Übungen, die die Unit task besonders vorbereiten
	Hier entsteht ein Produkt für dein Portfolio.		Across cultures

Green Line 3 für Klasse 7 an Gymnasien in Baden-Württemberg

Herausgeber: Prof. Harald Weisshaar, Bisingen

Autorinnen und Autoren: Carolyn Jones, Beckenham; Jon Marks, Ventnor; Prof. Harald Weisshaar, Bisingen; Alison Wooder, Ventnor sowie Jennifer Baer-Engel, Göppingen; Cornelia Kaminski, Fulda; Elise Köhler-Davidson, Exeter

Beratung: Paul Dennis, Lahnstein; Cornelia Kaminski, Fulda; Nilgül Karabulut, Aachen; Hartmut Klose, Seevetal; Antje Körber, Merseburg; Jörg Nieswand, Berlin; Jörg Schulze, Dresden

Für besondere Unterstützung danken wir herzlich den Schülerinnen und Schülern des **Gymnasiums Hechingen**.

Zusatzmaterial für Schülerinnen und Schüler zu diesem Band:

Workbook + Audio-CD + Übungssoftware	978-3-12-834138-5
Workbook + Audio-CD	978-3-12-834135-4

sowie eine Reihe von abgestimmten *English Readers*

1. Auflage 1 6 5 4 3 2 | 2022 21 20 19 18

Alle Drucke dieser Auflage sind unverändert und können im Unterricht nebeneinander verwendet werden.
Die letzte Zahl bezeichnet das Jahr des Druckes.

Redaktion: Michael Mattison; Anette Mohamud; Martina Reckart; Lektorat editoria: Cornelia Schaller, Fellbach
Herstellung: Anita Bauch; Anne Leibbrand

Gestaltung: Petra Michel, Essen
Umschlaggestaltung: know idea, Freiburg; Koma Amok, Stuttgart
Illustrationen: Peer Kramer, Düsseldorf; jani lunablau, Barcelona
sowie Christian Dekelver, Weinstadt *(Karten)*; Denise Drews, Zürich *(Time line)*
Satz: Satzkiste GmbH, Stuttgart
Reproduktion: Schwaben-Repro, Stuttgart
Druck: Mohn Media Mohndruck GmbH, Gütersloh

Printed in Germany
ISBN 978-3-12-834130-9 (fester Einband)
ISBN 978-3-12-834131-6 (flexibler Einband)

Green Line 3

von
Carolyn Jones
Jon Marks
Harald Weisshaar
Alison Wooder
Jennifer Baer-Engel
Cornelia Kaminski
Elise Köhler-Davidson

herausgegeben von
Harald Weisshaar

Ernst Klett Verlag
Stuttgart · Leipzig

Inhalt

Legende

- Kompetenzaufgabe
- Across cultures
- Across cultures
- ‹ › fakultativ

Unit 1

Find your place

Find more online: 8mf5cm

A

B

SPEAKING

1 Everyone is different

a) *Look at the photos above. What do you think the different people are thinking? Say why.*

b) *Now look at the photos again and the sayings below. Say which ones match, and why. What's the main idea behind each saying?*

Across cultures

"Practice makes perfect" or "You can't judge a book by its cover" are examples of **popular English sayings**. What German sayings describe the ideas and pictures on this page?

- You can't judge a book by its cover.
- Everyone is good at something.
- Practice makes perfect.
- Life is a competition!
- I don't care if I'm in or out, as long as I've got my friends.
- It doesn't matter if you win or lose, but how you play the game.
- You'll never know until you try.
- Don't follow the crowd.

c) *Your turn: Do any of the sayings above match your personality? Or do other ones describe you better? Write down your ideas in 8–10 sentences.*

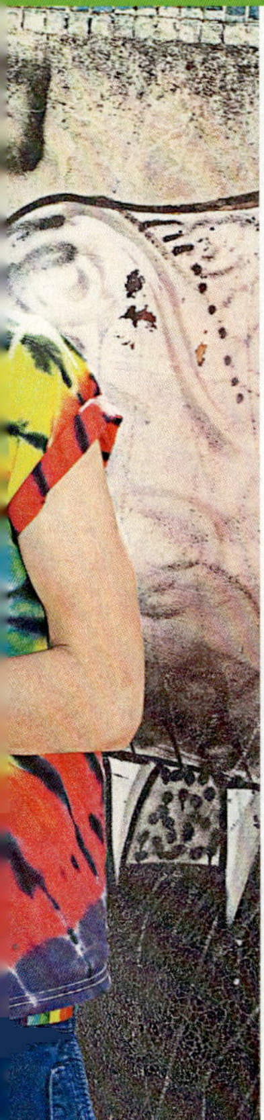

C

In Unit 1 you learn

… how to talk about what you and other people would do in different situations. You learn:

- vocabulary for talking about different interests and personalities
- conditional clauses type 1 and 2
- the language for agreeing, disagreeing and compromising

D

LISTENING **2**

A radio call-in → WB 2/1

a) *Before you listen, look at the diagram above. What do you think a 'body smart' person could be good at? And the other seven kinds of 'smart'? Talk about your ideas in class. The phrases in the box can help you.*

L 1/1–3 → S19–21

b) *Now listen to a radio call-in. What's the subject today? Who are the callers?*

c) *Listen again. What do the callers say about these things?*

their talents / what they're good at | their doubts about themselves | what they've learned about themselves

Useful phrases

A body smart / picture smart / music smart / logic smart / … person
… is good with his / her hands / body / imagination / …
… is good at doing / showing / using / creating / explaining / teaching / …
… knows how to use … / play … / talk … / communicate / compete / …
… is creative / imaginative / confident / …
… likes to … / needs to … / feels … / understands … / …
A … smart person would probably be a good teacher / doctor / …

SPEAKING **3**

Your turn: Your kind of 'smart' → WB 2/2

→ 114/1

With a partner, talk about what kind of smart you both are. Use the vocabulary on these pages for ideas.

L1/4

I want to be the lead dancer!

Jay: Hey, look at this. A boy left school at 15 and became a millionaire!

Shahid: His family were already rich, right?

Jay: No, it says that he lived with his mother in a small flat. At the age of 11, he just thought: "If I learn HTML, companies will pay me to design their websites." So that's what he did.

Shahid: Well, only a few people get that kind of success so young. Everyone would be a millionaire if it was so easy. But it isn't.

Jay: Well, I wouldn't feel so stressed out if I had a million pounds.

Shahid: Why, what's the matter?

Jay: I got an e-mail today. I didn't get the lead part in that dance show. "You can be a backing dancer," they told me. But I want to be the *lead* dancer! If I don't get a lead part soon, I'll never become rich and famous!

Shahid: Jay, relax. If you practise a lot, you'll get a lead part one day. But you can't be serious about becoming rich and famous. Money doesn't grow on trees; you have to *work* for it!

Jay: That's the point. I can't train often enough because Mum and Dad always want me to focus on school. If they believed in my talent, they would support me.

Shahid: They're sure you'll get a good job one day if you get better marks now. They wouldn't worry if they didn't care. And you *are* a bit laid-back. Anyway, you know you can't leave school until you're 18. If you just dropped out now, you wouldn't have any choices later.

Jay: That's easy for you to say! Yesterday I saw your picture on a magazine again! You make easy money as a model just because you look good. If I didn't have to go to school, I'd go to London and be a model too!

Shahid: But I do modelling just for fun! I'd be stupid if I just relied on my looks, so that's why I'm studying for a career in IT. If I make the right plans now, I'll have more choices later. And if *you* make the right choices, you'll find your place too.

READING

1 Jay and Shahid: Plans and dreams

a) *What are Jay's plans for the future? And Shahid's?*

b) *Say what Jay's different problems are. The words on the right can help you with your answers.*

c) *What advice do you have for Jay? Discuss your ideas with a partner.*

compares himself with …

wants to be / have …

can't wait to be / have …

his parents always …

LANGUAGE

2 Find the rule: Conditional clauses type 1 and 2 → WB 3/3–4 → G1–2

a) *Look at the examples for **conditional clauses type 1** and **type 2**. What's the difference in meaning between the two types? Answer the questions.*

Type 1: If you **practise** a lot, you **will get** a lead part one day.
Type 2: If they **believed** in my talent, they **would support** me.

Q1: Does Shahid think Jay will practise a lot?
Q2: Does Jay think his parents believe in his talents?

b) *Look at the examples in a) again. What verb forms do you need in the **if-clause** and the **main clause**?*

c) *Go back to the text about Jay and Shahid. Collect all sentences for **type 1** and **type 2**. Make a grid.*

conditional clause type 1	conditional clause type 2
…	…

LANGUAGE

3 If I learn HTML … → WB 3/3–4 → G1

→ △ 114/2
→ ▲ 114/3

*Read the news report about David Karp. What were David's thoughts at the different times before and during his career? Finish his sentences and make **conditional clauses type 1**.*

Tumblr founder **David Karp** has just sold his New York business to Yahoo for $1.1 billion. He began learning HTML at the age of 11 and soon started to design websites for businesses. "I always used a deep voice when I was on the phone so people didn't know how young I was!" he says. Karp dropped out of school at the age of 15 and developed Tumblr, the social network company, in the bedroom of his mother's small flat. In 2009, he was named Best Young Tech Entrepreneur by Business Week.

Example: **1.** Companies will pay me to design their websites if I **learn HTML**.

go back to school | not know how young I am | learn HTML ✓ | sell my business | have more time for my business ideas | live at home for the first years | win awards and be rich

1. Companies will pay me to design their websites if I …
2. If I drop out of school, I …
3. But if I don't succeed, I …
4. If I use a deep voice on the phone, people …
5. I'll save money if I …
6. If my business is a big success, I …
7. I'll have more than a billion dollars if I …

LANGUAGE

4 Chatroom posts: What would *you* do in Jay's shoes? → WB 3/5 → G2

→ △ 115/4
→ ▲ 115/5

a) *In a chatroom, Jay has asked other young people for their advice about his problems. Read their advice for him. Put the verbs in the right form:* ***simple past*** *or* ***would / wouldn't*** *+* ***infinitive.***

→ △ 115/6

b) *In a group, think about different problems. Then think about what kind of advice you would give in a chatroom for the different problems. Use* ***conditional clauses type 2****.*

Examples:
- If my best friend **told** others all my secrets, she **wouldn't be** a friend any more!
- If I **were** you, I **wouldn't worry** about how rich my friends are. Are they friends because you like them or because they have money?

calum13_leedsboy September 4, 20:05
If I 1 (be) you, I 2 (not be) sad about the backing part. I 3 (be) happy if I 4 (have) a backing part in a dance show, but I never get ANY parts!

koolkatie14_cardiff September 4, 20:08
You 5 (not feel) so stressed out if you 6 (not think) about your brother and his modelling job so much. But it sounds like you think about it A LOT!

jjm_uk14 September 4, 20:50
It sounds like you want to give up just because you didn't get the lead part this time. But you're only 13! If every dancer 7 (give up) so quickly, nobody 8 (ever become) a star!

skater4ever15 September 4, 21:14
It sounds like your parents don't know how good you are. If they 9 (know) about your talent, maybe they 10 (find) a way for you to have time for school AND for practising. So SHOW them!

LANGUAGE

5 A successful young fashion designer → WB 4/6–7

→ △ 115/7
→ ▲ 116/8
→ ▲ 116/9

Ivy Francis is only 19 and has already become a rich and successful fashion designer. How would her life be different if she wasn't rich and successful? Make ***conditional clauses type 2.***

Example: **1.** If I **didn't get** so nervous before big shows, I'**d sleep** better.

not travel so often | know who liked me for me and not for my money | sleep better ✔ | not make a lot of money | not be famous | have more time for sports | not get to know lots of great places

1. If I didn't get so nervous before big shows, …
2. My team and I would have more time for family and friends if …
3. But if I didn't travel so often, …
4. If I didn't work so hard, …
5. People wouldn't say hello to me if …
6. I couldn't buy what I wanted if …
7. If I didn't have a lot of money, …

MEDIATION

6 A German talent show

→ △ 116/10
→ ▲ 117/11
→ S18

You've made an English friend on a social network. She's going to take part in a talent show on German TV, but the information she's received for her audition is in German. You can help her: Send her a short message in English with the main points.

Sing dich zum Star!

- Wähle einen Song aus und bereite ihn gut vor. Achtung: Wenn du einen sehr bekannten Song auswählst, musst du auch sehr gut sein! Die Jurymitglieder hören solche Songs ständig. Du wirst einen besseren Eindruck machen, wenn du einen Song auswählst, der nicht in der aktuellen Hitparade ist.
- Wenn du viel übst, hast du schon viel gewonnen. Denn stell dir vor: Wenn du an deinem großen Tag auf der Bühne stehen und den Songtext vergessen würdest, würdest du dich ganz schön blamieren.
- Bitte denke auch an dein Äußeres. Du möchtest einen guten ersten Eindruck machen!
- Wenn du unter 18 bist, muss eine erwachsene Begleitperson dabei sein.

LISTENING

7 < A song: Holiday > Madonna

L1/6

Holiday, celebrate

If we took a holiday
Took some time to celebrate
Just one day out of life
It would be, it would be so nice

Everybody spread the word
We're gonna have a celebration
All across the world
In every nation

It's time for the good times
Forget about the bad times
One day to come together,
to release the pressure
We need a holiday

If we took a holiday
Took some time to celebrate
(Come on, let's celebrate)
Just one day out of life
It would be, it would be so nice

a) *How would Jay celebrate if he took a holiday for one day? Finish this sentence for him:*
Jay: If I took a holiday for one day, I'd …

b) *Your turn: What would be a special holiday for* ***you****? Finish the sentence in a) for yourself.*

WRITING

8 Your turn: If I …

→ WB 5/8–9

Finish the sentences on the right with your own ideas.

If I get bad marks in the next English test … | If I were better at … | If it rains tomorrow … | If I had more time for … | If my friends were …

L1/7

You have to push yourself!

Olivia: Lucy, tidy your messy room!
Claire: Don't be so bossy, Olivia.
Lucy: I feel tired, Mum.
Olivia: You *always* feel tired. That's why you never tidy your room or do *anything*. When was the last time you practised your recorder?
Lucy: Er, I can't remember.
Olivia: Exactly! You never practise.
Claire: Olivia, relax. She's only seven – she needs to have some fun. You should do the same! You study so often and have so many activities. Do you ever really *enjoy* yourself? – Er, Olivia, are you listening to me? I'm talking to you but I feel like I'm talking to myself.
Olivia: Of course I'm listening, Claire. But isn't this about Lucy?
Lucy: I don't like the recorder any more and I can't decide on a new hobby.
Claire: Oh, you don't have to decide now.
Olivia: Well, I taught myself how to play the sax when I was five! Nobody taught me. If you want to be good at something, you have to push yourself!
Claire: *(doorbell)* Oh, saved by the bell! – Girls, go and see who it is.
Olivia: Oh, hi Shahid.
Shahid: Hey Olivia – er, are you feeling OK? Why are you and Lucy giving each other funny looks?
Claire: Hi Shahid, come in. I hope the girls can behave themselves for two minutes. At the moment, they fight whenever they see each other. If they saw themselves like that, they'd be embarrassed! – Anyway, you're here to see Desmond, right?
Shahid: Yeah. I need a web designer's opinion on a few things.
Claire: Girls, go and get your dad, OK?
Shahid: *(pause)* So, what's up with Olivia?
Claire: Well, I was just telling her that she's too serious. She needs to enjoy herself more.
Shahid: Wow! If Jay heard you say that, he'd be so jealous! Our parents would love it if Jay had Olivia's perfect marks. They always tell him, "Olivia will be a doctor one day!" But that's just not Jay. He can't wait to be a singer or dancer!
Claire: Yes … and Olivia has her own personality too. Hm, if she wasn't so busy and in charge of things, she wouldn't be Olivia, would she?

READING **9** **Compare two families: the Azads and the Frasers**

→ △ 117/12 → S5–6

a) *Make a grid with columns for Olivia, Claire, Lucy, Jay and Jay's parents. Write down key words about the different people's personalities, opinions, problems. Then compare the two families. How are they the same? How are they different?*

→ △ 117/13

b) *What do you think about Olivia and her personality? How would you react in her shoes?*

c) *Imagine you're Olivia. Write a diary entry about how she feels about Claire and Lucy.*

→ S11–14

LANGUAGE

10 Find the rule: Reflexive pronouns → WB 6/10–11 → G3

a) *Look at the pictures. Say why one sentence needs* **me** *and the other* **myself***. Write the rule for object pronouns (me, him, them, etc.) and reflexive pronouns (myself, himself, themselves, etc.).*

"Nobody taught **me** to play the sax."

"I taught **myself**."

→ △ 117/14
→ △ 118/15

b) *Read what Olivia and Holly say. Decide if you need* **me / you / him / her / it / us / them** *or a reflexive form with* **-self** *or* **-selves** *(herself, ourselves, etc.).*

Olivia: Claire was a bit hard on 1 today. But maybe I'm overreacting.
Holly: Why, what did she say to 2 ?
Olivia: Things like, "Don't be so bossy with Lucy" or "You never enjoy 3 ".
Holly: What?! You and I always enjoy 4 ! – But what about Lucy, what's the problem?
Olivia: I worry about 5 . She's got such a messy room and she'll hurt 6 with her stuff everywhere. And Claire never pushes 7 to be better, so Lucy will have to push 8 more.
Holly: Well, Olivia – not *everybody* is like you. People are different.
Olivia: I know, I know. So I *am* bossy?
Holly: No, you're my best friend. Stay the way you are! – But tell me more.
Olivia: Oh, what Claire said to Shahid was *really* embarrassing!
Holly: Why, what did she say?
Olivia: In Claire's opinion, Lucy and I don't behave 9 . That's what she told 10 ! I felt like a four-year-old in front of 'Mr Cool'! He probably really enjoyed 11 . It was so embarrassing.
Holly: No, Shahid is cool, he wouldn't laugh at 12 . You know how the Azads love you, Miss Perfect!
Olivia: Oh stop it, you sound like Claire!

LANGUAGE

11 *Themselves or each other?* → WB 7/12–13, 8/14–15 → G3

→ △ 118/16
→ ▲ 119/17

a) *Look back at the sentences with* **each other** *and* **themselves** *in the text on p. 14 (lines 34–37). Now look at the pictures. Write a sentence for each picture with* **each other** *or* **themselves** *and with the verbs on the right.*

take
talk to
look at (2x)

1. The girls are …

2. The boys are …

3. They're …

4. The girls are …

b) *Now write your sentences in German. What's the rule?*

L 1/9 ⊙

An interview with Ayla

Holly and Olivia have interviewed Ayla Bayram, a Year 12 student at TTS and the school's best runner.

Holly: Hi Ayla. How are you?
Ayla: I'm fine, thanks.
Holly: Thanks for your time.
Ayla: No problem!
Holly: Er, you had the fastest time in the mini marathon last year. But have you ever run in a *real* marathon?
Ayla: I've never run in a real marathon, no. But two months ago I ran in a half marathon. It was great!
Olivia: Are you going to run in this year's mini marathon?
Ayla: I haven't decided yet. But I'm still 17 *this* year, so maybe I should run!
Olivia: And have you ever won any awards?
Ayla: Yes, I have. I won the 'Best Maths Student' award when I was 14 years old. But I haven't won any sports awards so far – sorry!
Olivia: Have you ever had an accident?
Ayla: Oh, I've already had *lots* of accidents! Two years ago I had one at the mini marathon: I fell and broke my arm!
Olivia: Can you describe how you felt?
Ayla: Well, it was strange: During the race I felt fine, but *after* the race it really, really hurt.
Holly: Oh, I've never broken anything.
Ayla: Lucky you!
Olivia: I've never broken anything either, but I twisted my ankle last year. Ouch!

READING

12 Match the parts

1. Ayla has never run
2. She finished
3. Ayla broke her arm
4. Olivia twisted her ankle
5. Ayla ran
6. Holly has been

a) lucky; she hasn't broken anything yet!
b) last year.
c) in a real marathon before.
d) with the fastest time last year.
e) at the mini marathon two years ago.
f) in a half marathon two months ago.

LANGUAGE

13 Signal words → WB 9/16–17 → G4

Find these signal words in the text. Which ones go with the simple past and which ones with the present perfect simple?

when I was … | last … | never | so far

ever | after … | yet | … ago | already

LANGUAGE **14**

Questions and answers → G4

→ △ 119/18

Make questions and answers like the examples. Use the present perfect simple and the simple past.

Example: Have you ever been to England? – Yes, I have. I was in London last …
Have you ever seen a famous actor? – No, but I saw a pop star when I …

LANGUAGE **15**

Simple past or present perfect? → WB 10/18–19 → G4

→ △ 119/19
→ ▲ 120/20

Luke wrote his cousin Jan in Cracow an e-mail about a funny basketball game.
Put the verbs in the simple past or the present perfect simple. First look for signal words.

I 1 (never/see) a basketball game like the one I 2 (see) yesterday. It 3 (be) so embarrassing! First, one reporter almost 4 (become) sick in front of the camera and 5 (go) to find the toilet! "Er, er, we're so sorry: This 6 (never/happen) before!" the other reporter 7 (say). After that it 8 (get) worse. Before the game the star player 9 (tell) a reporter: "I 10 (give) the crowd a great show in every game so far, and I can do that in this game too!" He 11 (be) right: Ten minutes later, he 12 (lose) his shorts when a player from the other team 13 (pull) too hard! And then, just when I thought, "I 14 (already/see) too many embarrassing things today," a strange man 15 (run) onto the court with no clothes on!

LANGUAGE **16**

My success

Read what Ian, a successful dancer, says about his life. Use the words and phrases to make sentences in the simple past or the present perfect simple.

1. I | never | be | a show-off, but | I | have | a lot of success in life!
2. When | I | be 16, I | be | fed up with life in a small town.
3. I | believe | in my talents as a dancer and | drop out | of school.
4. Five years ago | I | move | to London.
5. And | I | never | look back | on my old life.
6. In London | I | start | my career as a backing dancer.
7. At the beginning | I | enter | lots of auditions.
8. Two years later | I | get | my big chance.
9. I | dance | in 20 different shows so far.
10. I | not be | in the big shows yet, but | I | just | receive | an interesting offer. Life is great!

WRITING **17**

My favourite … → WB 11/20–21

Look for information on the internet about your favourite sports team or sports person.
Then write a short text about what this team or person has done. Try to answer these questions.

- Why is this team / person famous?
- What has this team / person done this year?
- Why has it been a special year for this team / person?

How to compromise

In the classroom, with friends, at home – it's normal to agree, to disagree and to try to find a compromise. This page can help you to practise typical discussion situations.

Yes, you've got a point. I've never thought about it like that. – OK, I've got an idea: Why don't we …

1 The language of compromising → WB 12/22

Make a grid with the headings below. Then add the phrases in the box to your grid under the right heading:

- Asking for an opinion
- Making a suggestion
- Agreeing
- Disagreeing
- Finding a compromise

Useful phrases

Why don't we …? | I don't think that's a good idea. | Yes, we should do that. | Can we meet halfway? | How do you feel about …? | I've got an idea. Can we …? | You've got a point but … | No, I don't mind doing that. | What do you think about …? | I don't think we can do that. | If we did it this way, we could … | It would be better to …

2 Listening: Finding a compromise

L1/11–12 → S19–21

a) *Listen to this family as they try to agree about something. Then answer the questions:*

1. What does Matt want to do? 2. What problems do his parents have with the idea?
3. How does Matt feel misunderstood? 4. What compromise do they find?

b) *Listen again. Which phrases from Ex. 1 did they use? Make a list.*

c) *What do you think about how the conversation ended? Who do you think is happiest about the decision?*

3 Role plays → WB 12/23

In groups of three, choose one of the situations below. Write a discussion with phrases from Ex. 1 and decide which role each of you will play. Act out the conversation.

→ △ 120/21
→ S17

1. You want a tattoo. Your parents disagree.
2. Your best friends don't agree with the guest list for your birthday party.
3. You have a great idea for a fun day with friends. But your friends have other ideas.
4. You've got a new hobby. Your friends think it's a bad idea.

Make a personality test!

You're going to design a personality test with ten questions to find out how competitive your classmates are. Before you start, look at the two example questions and the score below.

1. There's a cool new smartphone and everybody wants it! If one of your friends got it first, would you
   a) ☐ not care? (1 point)
   b) ☐ be happy for him / her? (2 points)
   c) ☐ be angry because you didn't get it first? (3 points)

2. If your best friend won a swimming race (and you were second), would you
   a) ☐ give up swimming because now you know that it isn't the right thing for you? (1 point)
   b) ☐ say 'thanks' because he / she gave you the race of your life? (2 points)
   c) ☐ not talk to him / her any more? (3 points)

+++ **YOUR SCORE** +++

12 points or more: You seem to be competitive and like pushing yourself to be the best. That's a good thing, but it can take some of the fun out of life. Remember, if you always win, it means somebody else loses!

11 points or fewer: You always tell yourself, "It's only a game!" That's fine, but don't forget that it's sometimes good to compete and learn what your talents and limits are. Don't miss the chance to see what you're good at.

Step 1

Collect ideas → WB 13/24

Get into groups of 3–4. Collect ideas about competitive situations. Think of the following topics:

family | gadgets | looks | school | sports / hobbies

Step 2

Write and design your personality test → WB 13/25, 14/26

Look at the example questions again and the points for how competitive each answer is ('not very', 'a bit' or 'very'). Use your ideas from Step 1 to write ten questions for your questionnaire. If your group has different ideas, remember there are ways to find a compromise!
Maybe you can find good examples for personality tests in a magazine or on the internet to get ideas for the layout of your questionnaire.

→ conditional clauses (pp. 10–12) → Questions and answers (p. 17) → Compromising (p. 18)

Step 3

Take your personality test → WB 14/27

a) *Exchange tests with another group. Each of you takes the personality test. Compare your results in your group.*

b) *Should people take personality tests seriously? Discuss the question in your group.*

S 1/4–10 L 1/13–19

Hang out with us instead!

A Jay was bored and fed up. "Am I the only person in the world who just wants to have a bit of fun on a Saturday afternoon?" he thought to himself. He felt bad about an argument with Luke. They couldn't agree about anything these days. "What was our fight about?" Jay couldn't even remember. "If Dave was here, he'd solve the problem in a moment," he thought. Dave was always able to find a compromise. But Dave now lived in Cornwall. For a moment, Jay thought about Holly, Olivia and Gwen. "Maybe we could do something together," he thought. But then he was sure he didn't need a 'girls day' today. Well, Jay wasn't allowed to go out anyway: He was in trouble with his parents for bad marks at school, and so he was grounded until next Friday. What a life!

"But I need to get out of this flat now!" he told himself. "My parents are out, so why not?" He felt a bit bad because they trusted him, but it made him crazy to stay at home all day. So he put on his trainers and left. "Freedom!" he shouted. He already felt much better.

B Jay walked towards the park and thought about the next dance show – he was sure he could get the lead part next time. When Jay reached the park, he saw them. Finn and Max.

Two of the coolest boys at school. They were two years older and part of the in-crowd. They looked so cool with their skateboards. They were laughing about something. "About me?" Jay hoped not. As he came closer, he felt a bit nervous, but he didn't need to: The boys were very friendly to him.

"Hey Jay!" said Finn, the blond boy. He was the in-crowd's 'boss'.

"He knows my name?!" Jay thought.

"Hey, what's up?" asked Max.

Jay wasn't sure how to answer. *Nothing* was up – that was the problem.

"We're going to go down to the high street for some coffee. Do you want to come with us and hang out?" Finn asked.

"Hanging out with the cool blokes. Luke will be so jealous!" he thought. But Jay tried to act cool and not show how excited he really felt. "Sure. I've got an hour before I need to be somewhere else," he told them.

C When they were all in the café, Jay started to relax a bit. Finn and Max were friendly and asked Jay a lot of questions. "I can't believe they're interested in me," he thought.

"Your brother is the model with the cool clothes, right?" Finn asked.

"Yeah, that's him," Jay answered.

"All the girls think he looks great," Max added.

"I don't see it myself," Jay answered, and they all laughed. They chatted about films and video games and found they liked the same things. Jay told them about his problems with Luke, and how he missed Dave. Finn and Max understood.

"Jay, you need some new friends," Finn said. "Your old friends are boring. Hang out with us instead!"

Stop and think:

What's going through Jay's head?

D "Your brother Shahid isn't just a model, he's a DJ too," Max said.

"Yeah," Finn added, "he's got some really cool mixes. We're planning a big party for next Saturday, for cool people."

"So," Max added, "would you be able to borrow Shahid's laptop? Just for the night?"

"He'll never lend it to me," Jay said.

"Hey Max, maybe you were right. Jay isn't cool enough for us," Finn said.

Not cool enough? Before he could stop himself, Jay said, "Wait! Er, Shahid is going to be away next Saturday. He's got an overnight modelling job in Manchester."

"Great! You can just borrow his laptop and he'll never know!" Max said.

"So come to our party with the laptop – but without your boring friends," Finn said.

"Well …," Jay didn't know what to say.

"Max wasn't sure about you, but I think you're cool. I'll give you my mobile number. Text me later if it's yes or no," Finn added.

Stop and think:

What would you do in Jay's shoes?

E Back home, Jay didn't know what to do. Were his old friends really so boring? Were his new friends really friends at all? And how could he go behind Shahid's back like that? Jay had to decide. Finally, he texted Finn these words: **cu on saturday. WITH the laptop.** ☺

F Jay had an awful week. Shahid knew Jay didn't feel so great, but he thought it was because of his bad marks. Shahid had more time for Jay than usual and told him about his conversation with Claire at Olivia's house. "It's funny. Now I know that not all families are the same." Shahid treated Jay like an adult – and Jay only thought about his plan to take Shahid's music. He felt bad. But it was too late to change things now. Before he knew it, it was Saturday evening and Jay was at Finn's front door. Finn opened the door, smiled, and grabbed the laptop out of Jay's hands.

G At the party, Shahid's music sounded fantastic. His brother was a great DJ! Everyone was dancing, but nobody was interested in Jay. "And I'm wearing my coolest outfit!" he thought. Finn and Max ignored him too. But suddenly, three pretty girls came up to Jay. He smiled at them.

"Ohh, poor baby. Have you lost your mummy, little boy?" one of them asked, and everyone laughed.

Jay felt so stupid. "Where's Luke when I really need him?" Jay asked himself. He really missed his friend.

Then, the music suddenly stopped. People started to leave. "What a stupid party!" some of them said. "No music, no party. Let's go!" others shouted. Jay then knew that something was very wrong.

"Hey Jay," Finn shouted. "Max dropped the laptop and now it's dead. So now we haven't got any music!"

"Yeah, thanks for nothing," Max added. "If your brother made real money as a model or DJ, he could buy something better than this piece of junk here!"

They didn't notice that Jay was white with anger. And they didn't care. Jay grabbed his brother's laptop, ran out the door, and ran all the way home.

Back in his room, he saw that Finn and Max were right: The laptop really was dead! It didn't work – at all. What would his brother do when he came home? Jay had one night to think about it. "And this is going to be one very long night," he knew.

SPEAKING

1 Your reaction

a) *What do you think about Jay's story? Share your ideas.*

b) *What kind of trouble have your brothers / sisters / cousins / friends got into before? Was it big trouble, or not so big? Maybe some of the phrases in the box can help you.*

Useful phrases

- One of my friends always gets into trouble for telling lies / making nasty comments / …
- My friend / cousin breaks the rules at home / at school / in our team / …
- There's always trouble when …
- I know somebody who always goes too far to be the best / to be popular / …
- He / She likes to start fights / tease people / …

READING

2 Understanding the story → WB 15/28–29

→ S5–6

a) *Which of the themes on the right are important in the story? Say why.*

Example:
Jay really wants to be popular. That's important for the story because … That's why he …

b) *With a partner, think of good headings for parts A–G of the story.*

Word bank

Nouns:	the in-crowd | peer pressure | freedom | fun | excitement
Verbs:	fit in | go behind somebody's back | lie to somebody
Adjectives:	lonely | cool | popular | new | old | confused | boring | honest

SPEAKING

3 Role play: Turning points in the story

→ S7

a) *First read the skills box. Then find the other turning points for Jay in the story.*

b) *Choose one of the turning points from a). Now imagine that Jay is having a video chat with Dave about what to do at one of the turning points. What advice would Dave give him? How would Jay react to Dave's advice? Write a short dialogue for them.*

c) *Now act out your dialogues in class with your partner.*

Reading skills

A **turning point** is a part of a story where a character must make a decision about what to do next. The decision can be good – or bad – for the character and for others.

Example: In Part A you find the story's first turning point. Jay was grounded but decided to leave the house anyway. Good or bad idea?

WRITING

4 What happens next? → WB 15/30

→ △ 120/22
→ S11–14

a) *When Shahid comes back from his modelling job in Manchester, Jay needs to tell him about his laptop. How do you think Shahid will react? Collect ideas and write an ending to the story. Exchange texts with your partner and give each other feedback.*

b) *Now compare your texts with the two different endings on p. 287.*

When Sean came to visit → S22–23

SPEAKING

1 Warm-up: How would you react?

Imagine that you aren't good at something (e.g. a sport, singing), but you have to do it in front of other people. They can see you're having problems, and maybe they're teasing you about it.

How would you react? Would you …

laugh about it yourself? | feel really embarrassed? | just ignore it? | become angry?

Or do you have other ways to deal with situations like this?

VIEWING

2 Sean, the cousin from Northern Ireland → WB 16/31

1 **a)** *Watch the film. What do you think about Sean and Nathan?*

b) *Answer the questions. The words in the box can help you.*

Word bank

have a sense of humour | feel sorry for somebody | be optimistic | cheer somebody up | be a show-off | apologise | mean / not mean it | post / delete something on a wall | be careful with account settings

The basketball scene:

1. How did Nathan get on Sean's nerves?
2. How did Sean react?
3. How did Laura react?

The park bench scene:

1. What was so embarrassing for Nathan?
2. Was Sean able to help? How?

The ending:

1. How did things work out in the end?
2. What did you think of the ending?

VIEWING

3 Three different personalities → WB 16/32

a) *Look at the diagram on p. 9 again. What kind of 'smart' do you think Sean, Nathan and Laura are? Now watch the film again. In a grid, take notes about what each person is good at, and what adjectives could describe them. Then share your ideas.*

b) *With a partner, think of how you could change the basketball scene so that it shows Nathan as more 'people smart'. Write a short dialogue between Nathan and Sean.*

LISTENING

1 The saxophone lessons → WB 18/1

L 1/20

a) *Listen to the conversation between Helen and her mum. Then answer the questions.*

1. What's the problem between Helen and her mum?
2. Why does Helen's mum think that it's important to practise?
3. What compromise do they reach?

b) *What do you think is good or bad about the compromise between Helen and her mum? Give reasons for your opinion.*

c) *With a partner, act out a conversation with a different compromise. You can use one of these ideas or think of your own compromise:*

Helen will pay for part of the lessons. | Helen will do extra work around the house to help pay for the lessons. | Helen will continue with the lessons, but will do some extra practice for four weeks.

VOCABULARY

2 Different kinds of smart

a) *Kim and John spent the day together in Lonchester. Read what they say about their day.*

Kim:
The day in Lonchester was fantastic. It's a cool place. It was my first time here, but every underground in every city is almost the same. You just follow the colours and numbers! I found a great place for lunch – not where all the tourists go. I watched some children our age and then we went where they went. I didn't go to Lonchester to hang out with tourists! John wanted to go to the harbour, but the first street looked like trouble so we took a different street, turned right, then left, then right and got there safely. I asked a few people and then we got a free tour of one of the ships!

John:
I really enjoyed our day in Lonchester. 625,000 people live there, but more than 1 million people work there. It's the home of a huge biscuit company. It took us 37 minutes to get there by underground. In the afternoon the trains leave every hour, always at half past. A famous person designed the train station. We ate lunch at 12 o'clock and it only cost £3. The harbour was interesting because about 20 ships arrive and depart every day. It's the second biggest harbour in the south of England. You can't really take tours of the ships, but we got one! Kim just asked. I didn't know that was possible.

b) *What's the difference between 'street smart' and 'book smart'? Make a grid and put in examples from the text.*

c) *Are you more like Kim or John? Explain why you think so. Compare your ideas with a partner.*

LANGUAGE

3 What will the future bring?

*Use the prompts to make **conditional clauses type 1**.*

Example: 1. If I practise a lot, I'll play in front of a big audience[1].

practise play

study become

drop out never succeed in life

push oneself play

save open

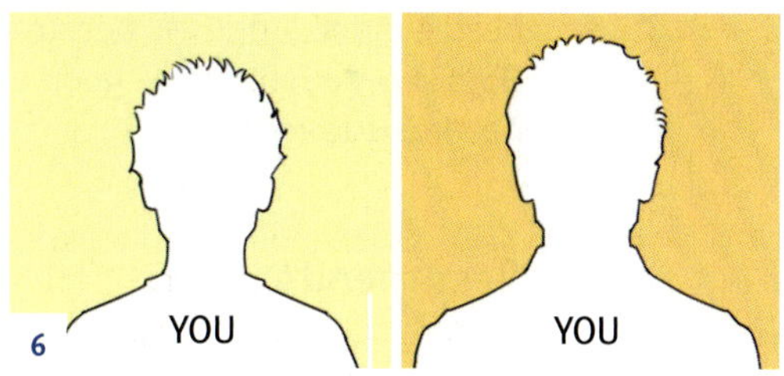

?? ??

LANGUAGE

4 Why I can't go to the school dance → WB 18/2a)

*Jack is angry because he's been grounded and can't go to the school dance. Fill in the correct verb forms to make **conditional clauses type 2**.*

1. If I ___ (not be) grounded, I'd go to the school dance. I love to dance. 2. If I had better marks, I ___ (not be) grounded. It's so boring here at home. 3. If I ___ (pay) attention at school, I ___ (have) better marks. I'd really like to succeed. 4. If I ___ (enjoy) class more, I ___ (pay) attention[2]. But it's so hard. 5. If we ___ (not have to) learn so much grammar, I ___ (enjoy) class more. Cars would be an interesting topic for class. 6. If English ___ (be) easier, we ___ (not have to) learn so much grammar. Who needs grammar? 7. If we ___ (compromise) and made German and English the same, English ___ (be) so much easier. 8. German isn't as hard as English. I bet if I ___ (ask) my teacher, she ___ (disagree) with me.

So you see – it's all because of English. That's why I can't go to the school dance!

1 audience [ˈɔːdiəns] Publikum | **2 to pay attention** [ˌpeɪ əˈtenʃn] aufpassen

WRITING

5 I'm sorry

You're staying with a family in Greenwich for six weeks. Yesterday you broke one of the family's rules. Write a short letter to the parents and apologise for what you did wrong. Which rule did you break? Here are some ideas:

you missed a family dinner | you got home late | you didn't do your jobs around the house

Start like this: Dear Jack and Diane, I'm sorry that I …

LANGUAGE

6 Talking about each other → WB 19/2c)

Read what two teenagers say about boys and girls. Decide if you need an ***object pronoun*** *(me, him, her, etc.) or a* ***reflexive pronoun*** *(myself, himself, herself, etc.).*

A. What boys think about girls

"I look at 1 once in the morning and that's enough, but girls are always looking at 2 ! I guess they don't believe in 3 enough and always worry what other people think of 4 . And girls aren't good with secrets. For example, if my sister tells 5 a secret, I never tell anyone else. But if I tell 6 a secret, she can't keep it to 7 . So girls, well, I don't really trust 8 . And they think they know everything too. I don't need a girl to judge 9 because I can judge 10 . Boys know what they're good at and they don't need girls to tell 11 ."

B. What girls think about boys

"Boys don't know how to behave 12 ! I'd never forgive 13 if I acted like a boy. They just don't understand – if you say something mean, you aren't just hurting the other person, you're also hurting 14 because then people don't like 15 . Once I was in big trouble and I couldn't help 16 so I really needed someone to save 17 . A boy walked by but I couldn't even persuade 18 to help 19 . So a girl has to rely on 20 . But sometimes if I'm sad, my brother tells 21 jokes and that really cheers 22 up."

LANGUAGE

7 Best friend?

Read about Sarah's problems with her friend Nina. Complete the text with the correct tenses: ***simple past*** *or* ***present perfect****.*

I'm so fed up with Nina. She says she's my best friend, but she always behaves like she can do everything better. Wait – I'll give you an example. Last week at school I 1 (feel) really optimistic about our Maths test. I 2 (study) a lot at the weekend, but then Nina 3 (tell) me, "If you don't push yourself more, you'll never get marks as good as mine." I have to tell you this: The worst mark Nina 4 (ever get) was a B. After Maths Nina said, "I'll meet you in the cafeteria for lunch!" But during lunch break she 5 (hang out) with Julia and 6 (ignore) me! I 7 (be) stressed out about Nina for three weeks! But I feel a little better today because I 8 (listen) to a radio call-in last night. A caller said she always relies on herself. She doesn't need other people to feel happy. So this is my decision now: I'll chill out about Nina and I'll enjoy myself without her! I think it's time for some new friends!

WRITING

8 Follow or don't follow the crowd → WB 19/3

a) *Choose one of the cartoons and describe what you can see.*

Crying is cool now.

b) *What do you think the cartoon's message is? Do you agree with it? Explain why or why not. The phrases in the box can help you.*

c) *Write a comment about one of the cartoons.*

Start like this: I think you should always try to be … / Peer pressure can make you … / It doesn't matter if everybody else …

Useful phrases

In my opinion, the cartoon's message is … | I think the cartoon wants to show that … | The cartoonist wants us to think about … / wants to make fun of … | I agree / don't agree with the cartoon's message because …

MEDIATION

9 Role play: Your place somewhere else

You're a scout[1] and want to take part in an international summer camp. The biggest one in Japan[2] is too expensive – more than €4,000! On the internet you've found another one in the Netherlands[3] – it's only €335 (plus the train ticket), and you want to persuade your parents to let you go there. Read the text and look up new words in a dictionary. Then act out a role play in German. One of you is the child and one of you is the father / mother.

The 10-day Jamborette in the Netherlands is organised for scouts aged 10–17 years old and their leaders. There will be groups from all over Europe as well as India, Russia, Ghana, Egypt, Turkey, Israel, the USA and Canada.

The Jamborette is very much like a normal summer camp. Each group has its own campsite to set up its tents. You won't have to go shopping for food during the camp, because we'll give you the food and drink for every meal. However, you'll have to prepare it yourself, so don't forget to bring cooking gear like pots, pans and stoves!

The Jamborette is held in Recreatiegebied Spaarnwoude, a nature reserve located between Amsterdam, Haarlem and Velsen. This reserve has many hiking routes, a mountain bike track, swimming lakes and even a ski slope and a climbing wall. The Programme Team of this year's Haarlem Jamborette is working on organising a challenging, active and varied programme: Aqua (water), Trail, Hikes, Sports, Arts & Crafts and Jambotours (culture).

1 **scout** [skaʊt] Pfadfinder/-in | 2 **Japan** [dʒəˈpæn] Japan | 3 **the Netherlands** [ˈneðələnz] die Niederlande

Find more online: zd28me

Text smart 1
Poems and songs

With the Text smart pages, you're going to learn how to deal with different text types and how to use them in your own work. Text smart 1 is about how poems and songs work in different ways.

LISTENING

1 Warm-up: Thinking about the message

Outside a shop, somebody has written some interesting 'advice for life' statements on an old board. Two friends, Jon and Mario, have just discovered it.

Jon: Hey look, some words with *real* meaning on a shopping street! The sign makes you stop and think, doesn't it? It reads like a poem.

Mario: Who needs real meaning on a shopping street?! I'm more into songs anyway.

a) *Read the text on the board out loud. Is Jon right?*

L1/22 → S19–21

b) *Now listen to what Jon and Mario say.*

1. Explain why Jon likes poems.
2. Explain what Mario is more interested in.

c) *What do the lines on the board mean to **you**?*

Examples:
A: I'm into sports and fair play, so I think "Play like there are no winners" is a cool message.
B: I think *all* the statements are cool. When you read them, you think of how great things could be if everyone was happier, more generous or more creative.

WRITING

2 Your turn: Poems and songs in your life

a) *Where do you find poems and hear songs? Say which statements are true for you.*

I sometimes look up song lyrics on the internet. | I sing along to my favourite songs. | I know some poems by heart. | I'm good at rhyming words. | I write my own songs / poems. | I often discover great songs / poems in TV adverts.

→ △ 121/1

b) *Go back to the statements on the board. How could you add a line or two of your own with the same verbs or with different verbs?*

Say it with a poem!

READING **3**

Happy Poem by James Carter (b. 1959)

S1/12 L1/23

Happy as a rainbow
Happy as a bee
Happy as a dolphin
Splashing in the sea

Happy as bare feet
Running on the beach
Happy as a sunflower
Happy as a peach

Happy as a poppy
Happy as a spoon
Dripping with honey
Happy as June

Happy as a banjo
Plucking on a tune
Happy as a Sunday
Lazy afternoon

Happy as a memory
Shared by two
Happy as me …
When I'm with you!

Read the first verse (the first four lines) of the poem. Explain why you think things like a rainbow or a dolphin can be 'happy things'.

READING **4**

The structure of poems: Some basics

→ S7, 15

Read the skills box and then read the rest of 'Happy Poem'. After that:

1. Say what the rhyme scheme is.
2. Copy the poem into your exercise book.
3. Read the poem out loud and mark the words or syllables you need to stress.

Reading skills

Poems which rhyme have a **rhyme scheme**. **AABB** and **ABAB** are very typical; so is **ABCB**:

Roses are red,	(A)
Violets are blue.	(B)
I like poems,	(C)
What about you?	(B)

But the rhyme scheme isn't everything! For the rhyme to work, a rhyming poem must have a **rhythm** with the same **stress** in each line:

Happy as a **rain**bow
Happy as a **bee**

WRITING **5**

Your turn: What makes you happy?

a) *Do all the things in the poem mean happiness for you too? Discuss with your partner.*

→ S4

b) *What makes you happy? Make a mind map with happy words. Your partner does the same. Then compare your mind maps. Are some things the same, or very different?*

→ △ 121/2

c) *Now change the happy poem with your own happy words, e.g. from your mind map.*

d) *Recite your version of the poem to the class. Explain why you changed it the way you did.*

READING

6 Understanding poems → WB 20/1

S1/13 L1/24 → S7, 19–21

a) *Your reaction: Close your eyes and just listen to the poem. Then answer questions 1 and 2. Tell the class what you think. (The phrases in the box can help you.)*

1. Describe how the poem makes you feel and why.
2. What could the poem be about?

The Arrow and the Song
by Henry Wadsworth Longfellow (1807–1882)

I shot an arrow into the air,
It fell to earth, I knew not where;
For, so swiftly it flew, the sight
Could not follow it in its flight.

I breathed a song into the air,
It fell to earth, I knew not where;
For who has sight so keen and strong,
That it can follow the flight of song?

Long, long afterward, in an oak
I found the arrow, still unbroke;
And the song, from beginning to end,
I found again in the heart of a friend.

Useful phrases

- The poem makes me feel …
- I'd describe the atmosphere as …
- The language in this poem is … while the other poem sounds …
- I think the poem is about …

Tip

When you read poems, don't forget to always **read them out loud** to yourself. This gives you a feeling for a poem's **rhythm** and **atmosphere**.

b) *Now divide yourselves up into pairs or small groups. Each pair/group looks at lines 1–4, 5–8 or 9–12. Decide together what your verse is about exactly. Then share your results with the class. Which groups have the same ideas?*

READING

7 Taking a second look

→ △ 121/3

a) *In the 'Arrow' poem, it would be possible to say some things in a more direct way. In your group, rewrite some of the sentences from the poem with simpler, more direct words to show that you understand what they mean.*

Example: I breathed a song into the air. → I sang a song out loud.
→ I sang a song so that others could hear it.

b) *What kind of lines do you like better: the simpler lines or the original ones? Does the original language make the poem special? If yes, how?*

WRITING

8 Your turn: Your idea of friendship

These are two key lines in the poem (lines 11–12):

And the song, from beginning to end,
I found again in the heart of a friend.

Write 6–8 lines about what you would like to find in your friends' hearts. What do you think they'd like to find in your heart?

Say it with a song!

LISTENING **9**

Count on me by Bruno Mars (b. 1985)

L 1/25

→ S19–21

Read the skills box before you listen to the song.

Listening skills

- When you listen to a song, **focus on the words** and the **main message first.**
- Sometimes, **rhyme words** can help you to understand and remember the words better.
- When you think about the message, think also about how the **music** matches the message.

If you ever find yourself stuck in the middle of the sea,
I'll sail the world to find you
If you ever find yourself lost in the dark and you can't see,
I'll be the light to guide you

Find out what we're made of
When we are called to help our friends in need

Chorus:
You can count on me like one two three
I'll be there
And I know when I need it I can count on you like four three two
You'll be there
'Cause that's what friends are supposed to do, oh yeah

If you tossin' and you're turnin' and you just can't fall asleep
I'll sing a song beside you
And if you ever forget how much you really mean to me
Every day I will remind you

Find out what we're made of
When we are called to help our friends in need

(Repeat chorus)

You'll always have my shoulder when you cry
I'll never let go
Never say goodbye
You know you can …

(Repeat chorus)

READING

10 Understanding the song

a) *How do you like the song? Do you think the music matches the message? Why?*

b) *"You can count on me like one two three" (line 7): Which of the definitions below matches that line from the song the best? Or have you got other ideas?*

A. "Like one two three" means that friends are as basic and important as the most basic numbers.

B. It's just a play on words: The singer sings "Count on me" and then he really *counts* the numbers "one, two, three".

C. "Like one two three" means you'll be there to help your friend as fast as possible.

D. …

c) *Which words / phrases in the song have the same meaning as these definitions?*

1. If you feel you can't help yourself out of a difficult situation, you're ___.
2. In difficult situations, people learn their limits. After that they know ___.
3. If you'd do anything for someone, then you'd ___ for him / her.
4. If you need a strong person to go to with a problem, then you need a ___.

→ △ 122/4

d) *Finish these lines with your own words and ideas about what **you** would do for a friend:*

1. If you ever find yourself stuck …
2. When you cry …
3. You can count on me when …
4. If you ever forget …

VOCABULARY

11 What makes a song catchy?

a) *What makes a song catchy? Talk to your partner about the ideas on the right. Have you got more ideas?*

You can dance to it. | You can't keep your feet or hands still! | It's easy to sing along to. | You hear some of the words over and over again. | It makes you feel happy. | You can't get it out of your head for a long time because the melody is so great. | …

b) *How catchy is **your** favourite song? Say which statements in a) match your song.*

→ S3

c) *In the word bank you can see typical words for two popular themes in pop songs:*

1. Don't give up! / You can do it!
2. Happiness

With a partner, use these words (or your own) to write 2–4 lines for a song in one or both categories. Make sure the lines rhyme.

Word bank

1. 'Don't give up!' songs:
fight | win | lose | survive | fall down | stand up | die | champion

2. 'Happiness' songs:
fun | dream | sun | free | smile | laugh | party | friends | forever

12 Poem and song options → WB 20/2, 21/3–4

→ △ 122/5

a) *Look at the following options. In class, talk about what could be difficult about each.*

b) *Now choose one of the options for yourself or for you and a partner.*

S 1/14 L 1/26

Option A:
Read the poem below. Think of reasons why the friend went away. Write the story behind it.

Untitled poem
by Langston Hughes (1902–1967)

I loved my friend.
He went away from me.
There's nothing more to say.
The poem ends,
Soft as it began –
I loved my friend.

Reading skills

Poems which don't rhyme at all or have any clear structure like ABAB are called **free verse** poems. And sometimes, a poem can be somewhere in between, like the one you see on the left. The freer a poem is, the more important it is to **decide for yourself where the stress should be**, and where **a pause** could make it better or more interesting.

Option B:
First look at the photos in exercises 3, 8, 9 and 11. Explain how they match the different songs/ poems/topics in those exercises. Now look at this photo. Find a song to go with it. Explain your choice.

Option C:
Find a song with an interesting story. Present it to your class: Talk about the lyrics, the music, the rhymes, the atmosphere. (If you like, you can also compare the original with a cover version.)

S 1/15 L 1/27

Option D:
Read this poem out loud over and over until you know it by heart. Then recite it to the class. Make sure you know which words you really want to stress to give more feeling.

A smile (author unknown)

A smile is quite a funny thing,
It wrinkles up your face.
And when it's gone,
You'll never find
Its secret hiding place.

But far more wonderful it is
To see what smiles can do.
You smile at one,
He smiles at you,
And the smile makes two.

Find more online: p5357h

Reacting to a new situation

VOCABULARY

1 Warm-up: Talking about food → WB 24/1

→ S3–4

A

B

a) *Look at the film stills. Talk to your partner about what you can see. The word bank can help you.*

b) *Describe your typical breakfast. Compare it with your classmates' breakfasts. Say what's the same and what's different.*

c) *What other breakfast traditions do you know about?*

Word bank

bowl | plate | mug | cup | spoon | knife | fork | bread | bread rolls | toast | butter | jam | marmalade | honey | cereal | muesli | ham | bacon | tomatoes | baked beans | cheese | eggs | sausages | milk | tea | coffee | sugar

SPEAKING

2 Your turn: Your experiences

a) *Has anyone ever offered you food you didn't like? How did you feel? What did you say or do? Tell each other your experiences.*

b) *What do you think of how your partner reacted? Was he/she polite? Embarrassing? …*

VIEWING

3 Breakfast with the host family (1)

2

→ S22–23

a) *Watch the film and answer the questions about the two exchange students. Write down key words while you're watching.*

1. Who are Steffen and Brad?
2. Where are they and what are they doing?
3. What are they unfamiliar with? What's different to their own breakfast traditions?

b) *Why do you think there are two versions of the breakfast scene? Choose the correct answer.*

A. to show different types of English breakfast
B. to give more information about the same topic
C. to show different reactions to a new situation

VIEWING

4 Breakfast with the host family (2) → WB 24/2

a) *Watch the film again. Group A focuses on Reaction 1; Group B focuses on Reaction 2. Then answer the questions.*

1. Describe what's difficult for Steffen.
2. How does Steffen react?

b) *Think of possible headings for the two different reactions.*

Word bank

say sth nice | say the wrong thing | make somebody angry | upset somebody | make somebody feel better | be rude | try something new | show interest | show gratitude | be polite | be impolite | feel embarrassed

c) *Talk to a partner from the other group about the two reactions. Explain which one is more appropriate. What would you do in Steffen's situation?*

d) *Look at the two stills from the film. Match the phrases in the box below to each scene. Then sort them into more polite and less polite phrases. Make a grid.*

A

B

I usually drink milk but I'll try some tea. | Thank you. This looks interesting! | I'm sure English tea is nice too. | I don't eat hot food this early. | I can't eat that much in the morning. | I never drink tea. I'm not used to it. | I'm surprised. It's a very big plate of food. | What is it? I don't think I can drink it! | I'm not sure if I can eat it all but I'll try. | I don't want breakfast.

SPEAKING

5 Role play

→ S17

In your group from Ex. 4, work with the film script and rehearse your scene. Learn your lines by heart and act out your scene to the class.

Unit 2
Let's go to Scotland!

Find more online: r5xe6j

A Dunnottar Castle near Aberdeen

SPEAKING

1 Pictures from Scotland

a) *Describe the photos above. Which one would most make you want to visit Scotland? Explain why. The words in the box can help you.*

b) *Imagine you're on holiday in Scotland. What do you think you can do there? Share your ideas in class.*

Word bank

beautiful landscape | an old castle | historic houses | busy places | modern buildings | traditional clothes | a popular festival | amazing coastline | go hiking / climbing / mountain biking | go shopping / sightseeing | visit museums

SPEAKING

2 Your turn: Present your country

a) *Your exchange partner would like to know more about Germany. You want to send him / her some photos to show what Germany is like. What kind of photos would you choose? Write down your ideas.*

b) *With your partner make a 'Top 5' list of photos about Germany. Present your results to the class. Give reasons for your choice.*

Modern Glasgow

In Unit 2 you learn

… how to describe a place and the reasons for visiting it. You learn:

- vocabulary for talking about places and things to do
- how to talk about actions which started in the past and continue into the present
- how to talk about past activities in progress
- how to use passive forms
- how to make a text more interesting

Ben Nevis (1,344 m)

D The Edinburgh Fringe Festival

E Going out in Edinburgh

LISTENING 3 Ideas about Scotland → WB 25/1–2

a) *Think of what you've read or seen about Scotland before. What do you think is 'typically Scottish'?*

L 1/28–30 → S19–21

b) *Listen to three Scottish teenagers – Jean, Stuart and Carol – talking about typical ideas about Scotland. Match the speakers with the ideas in the box.*

haggis | Scottish accents | tartan clothes / kilts | bagpipes | Scottish independence | the Loch Ness monster

Across cultures

Scotland became part of the UK in 1707, but the **relationship between England and Scotland** has often been difficult. In September 2014, the people in Scotland had the chance to decide in a referendum if they wanted to become independent. 55 % voted against it, so Scotland is still part of the UK. Scotland has its own **national symbols**, like the flag and the thistle. Do you know any German national symbols?

c) *Listen again and note down what the speakers say about the different topics.*

→ △ 123/1

d) *Your turn: What are typical ideas about Germany? Do you think they're true? Explain why or why not. Share your ideas with a partner.*

L1/31

A new Holly?

Gwen and her parents are going to spend their next holiday in Scotland with Gwen's uncle and aunt and their son Ethan. Gwen has invited Holly and her sister Amber to come too.

Holly: Hi Gwen.

Gwen: Hi Holly. You're wearing orange and blue.

Holly: Yes. So?

Gwen: What happened to pink?

Holly: Pink is *old* Holly. New Holly isn't into pink any more.

Gwen: Your backpack is still pink.

Holly: Yes, I know. It isn't that old so I can't throw it away yet.

Gwen: Sounds good. Oh, I got your message. No problem with your mum, then.

Holly: No, she says it's fine if we go to Glasgow with you. But are you sure it's OK with your parents and your uncle and aunt?

Gwen: Yes, I'm sure. We've been planning things. It's going to be a fantastic holiday.

Holly: Yes, right.

Gwen: What's the matter? You haven't been talking about the trip much. Aren't you excited?

Holly: Yes, I am, but it's Amber. She hasn't been talking about anything else since you invited us.

Gwen: That's good, isn't it?

Holly: Yes, but she thinks she's going to be the boss of the whole trip, just because she's older than me.

Gwen: That's just a typical big-sister little-sister thing. And she's been telling you what to do for years, hasn't she? I didn't think it was a big problem for you.

Holly: I know, but it's been getting worse. I don't remember why we invited her.

Gwen: Yes, you do. She's the same age as my cousin Ethan. They'll be great friends, I'm sure.

Holly: Did you know she's been chatting with him online?

Gwen: No, I didn't. How long has she been doing that?

Holly: They've been sending each other messages since the weekend, and he's been sending her photos of himself and his band.

Gwen: Ooh … I think they really *are* going to be good friends! That means we can spend much more time alone. It'll be so much fun!

READING

→ △ 123/2
→ S5-6

1 Understanding the text → WB 26/3

a) *Answer the following questions about the text.*

1. How is 'new Holly' different from 'old Holly'?
2. What's Holly's problem with her older sister?

b) *Can you understand how Holly feels? Explain why or why not.*

LANGUAGE

→ △ 123/3
→ ▲ 124/4

2 What have people been doing? → WB 26/4 → G5

a) *Which sentences in the text tell you what different people have or haven't been doing? Write them down and underline the verb forms.*

Examples: Ethan **has been sending** Amber photos of himself and his band.
You **haven't been talking** about the trip much.

b) *The new tense is the* ***present perfect progressive****. How do you make this tense? When do you use it?*

LANGUAGE

→ △ 124/5
→ ▲ 124/6

3 Find the rule: *for* or *since*? → WB 27/5 → G5

a) *Look at the two sentences below. What words and phrases are used after* ***for*** *and* ***since****? Compare them and explain when you use each preposition.*

1. Gwen has been looking forward to the trip to Scotland **for a long time**. 2. Her uncle and aunt have been living in Scotland **since 1996**.

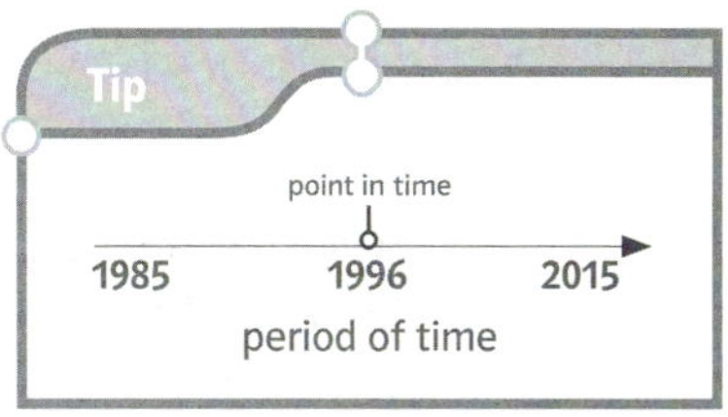

b) *Write the sentences from a) in German. Explain what is different.*

LANGUAGE

→ △ 125/7
→ ▲ 125/8

4 Did you know?

a) *Complete the sentences with the* ***present perfect progressive*** *and* ***for*** *or* ***since****.*

1. People ___ (look) for the Loch Ness monster ___ 1933. Loch Ness is now one of the most popular tourist attractions in Scotland.
2. Scotland ___ (produce) whisky ___ more than 500 years. It produces about 150 million litres per year.
3. Edinburgh ___ (organise) the Fringe Festival every year ___ 1947. It's the largest arts festival in the world.
4. The Scottish National Party ___ (campaign) for Scottish independence ___ more than 80 years. Today it's the biggest party in Scotland.
5. People in Scotland ___ (play) shinty ___ Celtic times. It's a team game and it's similar to hockey.

b) *Your turn: Tell your partner interesting facts about yourself. Use the* ***present perfect progressive*** *and* ***for*** *or* ***since****.*

Example: I've been playing football since I was six years old / for eight years.

LANGUAGE

5 Chat with Ethan → WB 28/6–8

*Amber is having another smartphone chat with Ethan. Complete their chat with **for**, **since** and the verbs in the **present perfect progressive**.*

How long **1** (you live) in your new house?

Only **2** six months, but it's starting to feel like home.

What's the area like?

It's a nice quiet street. But not when my band is practising! We **3** (practise) a lot these last weeks because we've got some important gigs soon.

How long **4** (you play) together?

5 four years, but it feels much longer.

Amazing!

Did I tell you that I'm also in another band? It's a traditional Scottish band with just bagpipes and drums.

That's so cool! How long **6** (you play) the bagpipes?

7 I was about seven. They were bigger than me when I started! Oh, you know what? During your visit, there's going to be a festival at a castle near Glasgow, and both my bands are going to play. We **8** (plan) the festival **9** weeks now.

☺☺☺ I can't wait!

LISTENING

6 < A song: Flower of Scotland >

L 1/34

O flower of Scotland
When will we see your like again
That fought and died for
Your wee bit hill and glen
And stood against him
Proud Edward's army
And sent him homeward
Tae think again

The hills are bare now
And autumn leaves lie thick and still
O'er land that is lost now
Which those so dearly held
And stood against him
Proud Edward's army
And sent him homeward
Tae think again

Those days are passed now
And in the past they must remain
But we can still rise now
And be the nation again
That stood against him
Proud Edward's army
And sent him homeward
Tae think again

Across cultures

As part of the UK, Scotland's official **national anthem** is *God Save the Queen*. There are several unofficial anthems too, because Scotland has its own football and rugby teams. One of these anthems is the song *Flower of Scotland*. It's about Robert the Bruce – he defeated the English King Edward and his soldiers in 1314.

L1/35

Is that made with meat?

"I hope you're all hungry!" said Kirsty, Gwen's aunt. "We've prepared haggis for you!" It was the girls' first day in Glasgow. Kirsty brought a plate with a large brown object on it to the table. Then she brought some bowls of vegetables.

"Is that made with meat?" asked Holly as she saw the haggis.

"Yes," said Kirsty. "It's made with meat and ..."

"I'm a vegetarian," said Holly. "Sorry, I forgot to mention it. I'll just have the vegetables."

"Holly has been a vegetarian since she was ten," said Amber. "She likes to be different."

Ethan laughed, and the others smiled. Holly started to feel embarrassed.

"That's why she always wears pink," Amber went on. "You can see her in her pink jacket with her little pink backpack from a mile away."

"I don't wear pink any more. Haven't you noticed?" said Holly in a cold, quiet voice.

"I like your new house," said Gwen as she tried to change the subject. "When was it built?"

"We think it was built about 150 years ago," said James, Gwen's uncle. "There are thousands of houses like this in Glasgow, but some of them have been pulled down."

"I love your Glasgow accent," said Amber and looked at Ethan. "It sounds so musical."

"I like your London accent too," said Ethan. "What's it like to live there?"

"It's great," said Holly. "I like ..."

"She's got me to look after her," said Amber. "I tell her and her friends about all the cool places to go. I teach them how to be cool."

Ethan laughed again, but nobody else did. Holly stared at the table in front of her.

"Let's play a game," said James and gave Amber a strange look. "I'll tell you something about Glasgow, and our guests must say if it's right or wrong. OK, one: Most of the world's whisky is produced in Glasgow."

"Wrong!" said Holly. "Most of the world's whisky is produced in Scotland, but not in Glasgow."

"Correct!" said James. "Two: No ships have been built here since the 1990s."

"Wrong!" said Holly. "The shipbuilding industry isn't that important any more, but some ships are still built here."

"Correct again!" said James.

"I showed Holly how to find things out on the internet," said Amber quickly. "That's how she knows all this stuff."

Everybody looked at Amber. Then Kirsty said, "More haggis anyone?"

READING

7 Big sister – little sister

→ S5–6

a) *How does Amber react to what Holly says? Find examples in the text.*

Example: Amber says embarrassing things about Holly, e.g. lines 15–17: "Holly has been a vegetarian since she was ten. She likes to be different."

→ S17

b) *Explain why Amber is behaving like this. What advice would you give her? Make notes and act out a dialogue between you and Amber.*

LANGUAGE

8 Find the rule: Passive forms → G6

*Look for **passive forms** in the text and collect them in a grid like this. Find the rule about how the passive is made in different tenses. What verb forms do you use?*

Simple present			Simple past			Present perfect		
Subject	**'to be'**	**Past participle**	**Subject**	**...**	**...**	**Subject**	**...**	**...**
Haggis	is	made	The house	was				

LANGUAGE

9 Hogmanay

*Write sentences in the **simple present passive**.*

Example: 1. In Scotland, the last day of the year **is called** Hogmanay.

1. In Scotland, people call the last day of the year Hogmanay.
2. They celebrate this event with street parties.
3. At midnight, they ring bells and set off fireworks.
4. Then people hold hands and sing 'Auld Lang Syne'.

LANGUAGE

10 Famous Scots → WB 29/9–10

a) *A lot of important inventions and discoveries in the past were made by Scots. Use the words and phrases to make sentences in the **simple past passive**.*

Example:
first sheep | clone | Scottish scientists
→ The first sheep **was cloned** by Scottish scientists.

1. raincoat | invent | Charles Macintosh
2. Penicillin | discover | Alexander Fleming
3. first steam engine | build | James Watt
4. Sherlock Holmes | create | Sir Arthur Conan Doyle
5. first television station | start | John Logie Baird

b) *Find information about three other famous Scots. Make notes about them as in a). Then exchange your results and make sentences from your partner's notes.*

→ △ 125/9

Tip

In passive sentences you can use **by ...** if you want to say **who** did something.

LANGUAGE

11 Facts about haggis → WB 29/11

→ △ 126/10
→ ▲ 126/11

*Complete the text with passive forms: **simple present**, **simple past** or **present perfect**.*

A traditional haggis **1** (make) from a sheep's stomach filled with sheep's heart and other parts of the animal, but there's vegetarian haggis too. It **2** (usually eat) with mashed potatoes and other vegetables, but you can also find it as a burger with chips, in a pasta sauce or as a pizza ingredient. Most of the world's haggis **3** (make) in Scotland, but it **4** (probably not invent) there. Some say that it **5** (bring) to Britain by the Romans. Others think it came from Scandinavia. Haggis **6** (sell) around the world, but some people say it isn't healthy. That's why it **7** (ban) in the USA since 1971.

LANGUAGE **12** ## Active or passive? → G6

a) *Look at the two sentences. Use the phrases on the right to explain why one sentence is* ***active*** *and the other is* ***passive****. Write down the rule.*

1. My mother makes the best haggis in Scotland.
2. Haggis is made from a sheep's stomach.

important who does the action

not important or clear who does the action

b) *Look at these examples. Say why the passive is or isn't used.*

1

2

3
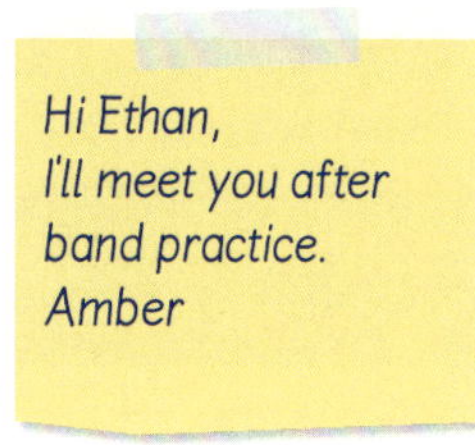

4

LANGUAGE **13** ## In Mary King's Close → WB 30/12

Holly and Gwen are planning their trips to different places in Scotland. They've found this information about a popular sight in Edinburgh. Put the active sentences into the passive, where possible. Decide if you need the by-agent.

Hundreds of years ago, people built very high houses in Edinburgh. They stood on dark and narrow streets or 'closes' which led off from the main street. Sometimes they named a close after a person who lived there, like Mary King. Over the centuries people have told many stories about Mary King's Close. One of the most famous is about a little girl called Annie – she died there in 1645. People have seen her ghost many times since. She isn't scary, but she always looks sad. That's why visitors leave so many toys behind for her.

WRITING **14** ## Glasgow is amazing! → WB 30/13, 31/14

a) *Look at the short text from a website about Glasgow. What kind of language does it use? How does it try to get the reader's attention?*

Do you know that Glasgow is famous for its shipbuilding industry? Titan Clydebank is a shipbuilding crane and it has become one of the most amazing tourist attractions in Glasgow. Are you brave enough to climb up to the top? Fantastic views across Glasgow are waiting for you …

→ △ 126/12 **b)** *Find another Glasgow sight, attraction or event on the internet. Use your ideas from a) to write 2–3 sentences about it. Try to get the reader's attention.*

L 2/2–3 ◎

Holly's blog

Hi everyone! Time for a new update. We've been so busy these last days. Got lots of news for you. Hope you like my latest pics …

I thought the biggest lake in Scotland was Loch Ness, but it's actually Loch Lomond (in fact, it's the biggest lake in Britain). I took this while we were waiting for a boat trip. I know: typical tourists! 😕

Gwen and I made some new friends! We were walking past their field when they came over and started to follow us. I don't think we have cows like this down south.

The Highland Games are held everywhere in Scotland (even in the Lowlands). I've just found some photos on the internet – what was this guy doing?! Any ideas?

I was looking for souvenirs when I discovered these. Just because Loch Ness was too far away to visit didn't mean I couldn't see the monster! Isn't she cute?

Will & Kate came to visit Glasgow – really! I tried to take a pic, but too many people were standing in front of me. So here's an internet photo of Balmoral Castle, the Royal Family's Scottish home. Not much bigger than Ethan's house! 🙂

They really love dancing here! We saw this while we were walking around Glasgow. Nice kilts, gentlemen! Did you know that each clan has its own tartan? I'd really like to know what they wear – or don't wear – under those kilts!

READING **15**

How much do you know about Scotland?

a) *Think of ten questions you can ask about Scotland. Use the information from Holly's blog and from what you've heard in this unit so far. Write down your questions on a piece of paper.*

Examples: What's the Scottish word for 'lake'?

b) *Now divide your class up into two groups. Take turns to ask each other your questions from a). For each correct answer your group gets one point. Make sure that nobody asks the same question twice!*

LANGUAGE **16**

Find the rule → WB 32/15 → G7

Which sentence matches which diagram?

1. The men **were** danc**ing** in the street when it started to rain.
2. At 10:30 a.m. Holly **was** talk**ing** to her mother on the phone.

A. 9:30 → 10:30

B. simple past ↓ past progressive →

LANGUAGE **17**

What were they doing? → WB 32/16, 33/17–18 → G7

→ △ 126/13
→ ▲ 127/14

a) *Gwen and the others went to Edinburgh for a day. What was everyone doing there?*

Example: At 10:00 a.m. the friends were walking up to Edinburgh Castle.

10:00 a.m. – the friends – walk up to Edinburgh Castle | **1:30 p.m.** – Amber – have vegetarian haggis for lunch | **3:15 p.m.** – Gwen and Holly – go on historic tour of city | **3:15 p.m.** – Ethan and Amber – listen to bagpipe player on High Street | **5:30 p.m.** – Holly – look for souvenirs in shop | **7:00 p.m.** – everyone dance at a ceilidh | **9:00 p.m.** – all of them – sleep on train to Glasgow

→ △ 127/15
→ ▲ 127/16

b) *What else was happening on their visit to Edinburgh? Match Holly's comments.*

1. We met some of Ethan's friends 2. Amber almost lost her mobile 3. I was taking some selfies 4. I found these model bagpipes 5. Gwen and I were dancing at the ceilidh	when while	a) I was looking for souvenirs. Cute, eh? b) the lights went out. c) we were walking up to the castle. d) a man in a big tartan hat walked behind me. e) we were waiting for the train to Edinburgh.

WRITING **18**

Your turn: Write your own travel blog → WB 33/19, 34/20–21

→ S11–14

Write a travel blog about a funny or interesting holiday or trip. Find pictures on the internet or draw the places/scenes. Think of interesting texts to go with the pictures. Make sure you also use the past progressive.

How to write a persuasive text

When you write a text to persuade other people to do something, e.g. visit a particular place or attraction, it's important to make your text interesting and to grab your reader's attention.

1 Criteria for a good persuasive text

→ S5–6

Look at the ideas on the right. Find examples for these criteria in the text. Compare your results with a partner.

talking to the reader personally | local tips | longer sentences with linking words | humour | an interesting final sentence | strong adjectives

You can't get further from London!

Well you can, but not in the UK. Did you know that the Shetland Islands are further north than any other part of Scotland? These beautiful islands offer great things to do and see for people of all ages.

Explore fascinating museums which tell the story of life on the islands from Roman times to the present day. One of the most interesting is the Shetland Crofthouse Museum in Dunrossness. Here you can feel what it was like to live on the islands in the 1870s.

If history isn't your thing, our islands offer a lot of exciting outdoor activities. Take a boat trip along the amazing coastlines or improve your climbing skills at one of the spectacular cliffs. But please make sure you reach the top! After your personal adventure, you can relax and visit our tiny, world-famous Shetland ponies.

Probably the best reason to visit the Shetland Islands is to meet the people. Our islands may be small but we have big hearts! So come and see us – and leave everything behind …

2 Strong adjectives → WB 35/22

a) *Strong adjectives can help you to make your text livelier and more interesting to read. Copy the grid. Then fill in the words on the right. Sometimes they fit in more than one category.*

small	good	nice	big
tiny			

amazing | large | beautiful | exciting | huge | fascinating | tiny ✓ | fantastic | spectacular | interesting | wonderful

b) *Find more adjectives for each category and add them to your grid.*

3 Write your own text → WB 35/23

→ S11–14

Choose one of these tasks. Write a short text and make it as interesting as possible. The criteria from Ex. 1 and the strong adjectives from Ex. 2 can help you. Then exchange your texts and give each other feedback.

- Write an advert to persuade tourists to visit your home town.
- Write a text for a flyer about a festival or other event which you enjoyed.

Visit Scotland!

A friend of your family has a house in Scotland and he wants to rent it out to families for their holidays. He asks you to help him with a travel brochure about the region where his house is.

Step 1

Get organised → WB 36/24

Get into groups of 4–5 and decide which part of Scotland you're interested in. This can be a city, an island or any other part of Scotland – but people should want to visit this place for a holiday. (The map at the back of the book can help you.)

→ Introduction (pp. 36–37) → Holly's blog (p. 44)

Step 2

Find information about your place → WB 36/25

Collect ideas about what you're going to put in the brochure. Include lots of interesting things to do and see in and around your place, and useful information (e.g. public holidays, transport, etc.). Agree on who's going to find out about what. You can use the information in this unit and do some research on the internet. Remember to include things to do for people of ***all*** *ages.*

Step 3

Organise the information → WB 37/26

a) *Now organise your information. What order should it be in? Does it cover all the important points? Have you found interesting pictures?*

b) *Try to find good examples for brochures in a travel agency or on the internet. How are texts and pictures arranged on the pages? Discuss your ideas of how you want to design your brochure.*

Step 4

Write your brochure

Write your part of the brochure. When you've finished all your parts, put them together to make the brochure.

→ present perfect progressive (pp. 38–40) → passive forms (pp. 41–43) → Writing a persuasive text (p. 46)

Step 5

Present your brochure

Put the brochures on tables around the classroom. Then have a look at the other groups' brochures. Which region would you like to visit? Give reasons for your choice.

S1/20–23 L2/5–8

I don't believe in ghosts!

SPEAKING

1 Before you read

Have you ever been in a dangerous situation, or maybe someone you know? What happened? How did you or this other person feel? Share your experiences with a partner.

A "That last song from Ethan's band was really good," said Gwen. "I liked the part with the bagpipes. I've never heard that in a rock song." It was the end of the festival. The sky was getting dark and people were starting to go home. "Do you want to have a look round the castle? My parents won't be here for another hour."

"OK," said Holly. "If it's still open. I don't know when it closes."

They walked to the castle entrance. It was free to go in on the day of the festival, and there was nobody in the ticket office. They came through some big empty rooms with stone walls. Suddenly the lights went out.

"I can't see!" said Holly.

"Welcome to my world," said Gwen and laughed. "Don't worry, I'll get us back to the entrance."

Gwen took Holly's hand, led her back to the entrance hall and tried to open the door. It was locked.

"I'll call Amber," said Holly, and took her phone from her pocket. "Oh, there's no signal. Maybe because of the thick stone walls."

"Perhaps there's another way out. Let's find out."

Stop and think:

How do you think Holly and Gwen can get out of the castle?

B "We've been going round in circles," said Holly. "We're at the door for the museum again." She was using her mobile phone as a torch.

"Did you hear that?" said Gwen. There was a strange sound coming from another part of the castle. It sounded like a wounded animal.

"Yes, I heard it," Holly whispered. She was starting to feel scared. The noise came again, louder this time.

"Come on," said Gwen. "Let's find out what it is. I don't believe in ghosts!"

They went through some more rooms and then through a door into a tower. A little moonlight was coming through a small window.

"The sound is coming from above us," said Gwen.

The stairs going up the tower were very old, and some of them were missing. When they carefully climbed up the noise got louder. The stairs ended at an old wooden door.

"What do you think is in there?" Gwen asked in a nervous voice.

"There's only one way to find out," said Holly, and pushed open the door.

Stop and think:

Who or what do you think is behind the door?

C At first it was too dark inside the room, but then Holly saw something moving on the other side.

"Amber!" Holly shouted.

Amber stopped crying and looked up. "Holly! Is it really you?"

"What are *you* doing here?" Holly asked.

"I came up here to get a better view of Ethan's band. But look at the floor!"

There was no floor between the door and the other side of the tower, where Amber was sitting. "It started to fall down when I was walking across it," said Amber.

Then Holly noticed a sign on the door: DANGER! KEEP OUT!

A cracking sound came from where Amber was sitting.

"Oh no!" said Amber. "Now I think this part of the floor is going to fall too."

Holly realised they didn't have much time. "Got a knife?" she asked Gwen.

"I've got a little knife on my key ring."

Holly took the knife from Gwen, and quickly took the pink backpack off her back. She cut the backpack into long pieces and tied them together to make a rope. "Here, catch!" Holly shouted and threw the rope across to Amber. "Hold onto the rope," she said. "I'll tie it to the door."

Amber caught the rope. Then there was a big crack, and the floor started to fall into the tower. Amber screamed and went down together with pieces of old wood. When she hit the side of the tower, she cried out in pain.

"Are you OK?" shouted Holly, as she held onto the rope as hard as she could.

"Yeah, I'm OK," came a very scared voice from below.

"I don't think we can pull her up," said Gwen. "She's too heavy."

Then they heard somebody shouting from below.

"It's Ethan!" said Gwen.

"I've been trying to find you since the end of the gig," he called up, as he climbed the stairs. "A man let me into the castle to look for you and ..." He came through the door, and realised what was happening. "I think the three of us will be enough," he said, and took the end of the rope.

D "Nothing broken," said the doctor. "You can go home. And next time you see a sign that says KEEP OUT maybe you should do what it says."

Amber was sitting on a stone wall outside the castle. Holly, Gwen, Ethan and Gwen's parents were all looking at her.

"Thanks for saving my life," Amber said.

"You're welcome," Holly answered.

"I've been saying some stupid things, and I'm really sorry about it. I don't know why I've been doing it. Maybe it's just because I'm your big sister and I always think I have to show that. Please let's be friends again."

"Yes, let's be friends," Holly said with a smile. "You see, we love each other really," she said to the others.

"I'll buy you another backpack," said Amber. "But not pink."

"No, definitely not pink," said Holly.

SPEAKING

2 Your reaction

Which parts of the story did or didn't you like? Explain why.

READING

3 Understanding the story → WB 38/27–28

→ S5–6 **a)** *Describe the picture. Which part of the story does it show? Sum up what happens before and after the scene in the picture.*

b) *For each part of the story, write down what the characters feel. How does this match what you talked about in Ex. 1?*

READING

4 The climax of the story

→ S7

a) *Read the information in the skills box. Explain where the climax in this story is.*

b) *Do you think the climax is realistic? Give reasons for your opinion.*

Start like this:
I think the climax is realistic because the castle is very old and dangerous. /
I don't think it's realistic because …

Reading skills

The **climax** is the main turning point in a story, when the suspense is highest. At this point the main character usually gets in a difficult situation and changes in some way, e.g. becomes stronger and more confident.

c) *With a partner, think of ideas for a different climax. Then present them to the class. Give feedback about how realistic your classmates' ideas are.*

SPEAKING

5 Role play: An interview with Holly and Amber

→ △ 127/17
→ S17

a) *A reporter for the local newspaper wants to interview Holly and Amber about what happened. In groups of three, think of what questions you'd like to ask the two girls and what answers they could give from their perspective.*

b) *Each of you takes the role of one of the characters – the reporter, Holly or Amber. Practise the interview. Then act it out in class.*

WRITING

6 Write an extra scene for the story → WB 38/29

→ S11–14

a) *Use your ideas from Ex. 5 to tell what happened to Amber* **before** *Holly and Gwen found her. Say why Amber went into the castle and climbed up the tower. Describe how she felt when she was trapped.*

Start like this: "Where on earth did all these people come from?" Amber tried hard to see Ethan and his band, but she soon gave up. Then she had an idea …

b) *Get into groups of 3–4. Read your extra scene to the other group members. Which version do you like best? Try to improve it if you can. Then present your group's version to the class.*

MEDIATION

7 A Scottish legend: The spider

L 2/9
→ S18

a) *You're collecting interesting facts and stories about Scotland because you want to convince your parents to spend your next family holiday there. Listen to the legend about Robert the Bruce and make notes about what happens. The following words and phrases can help you:*

Robert the Bruce | fight the English | hide in a cave | spider's web | not give up

b) *Now sum up the legend in German for your parents, and say why it makes Scotland interesting for you.*

How times change
→ S22-23

SPEAKING

1 Warm-up: Helping out in the neighbourhood

Have you ever helped out in your neighbourhood, e.g. done the shopping for someone, read books to an elderly person, etc.? Tell your partner about your experiences. Who did you help? What did it mean to that person and what did it mean to you?

VIEWING

2 Scotland is famous for its inventors
→ WB 39/30

3

a) *Watch the film. Look at the stills and find headings for the two parts. Sum up what happens in each part.*

b) *What Scottish inventors does Alva talk about? Choose from the list and match the inventors with the correct invention.*

1. Alexander Graham Bell
2. John Henry Holmes
3. Robert Hooke
4. John Logie Baird

a) tin can telephone
b) light switch
c) television
d) telephone

SPEAKING

3 Old vs. new

a) *The film shows one example of how communication has changed over time (rotary phone vs. smartphone / internet). What other inventions (old vs. new) do you know about? Look at the categories below for ideas.*

transport | free time | music | travel | media

b) *Your turn: "Scotland is famous for its inventors." What's your region / town famous for? Write 4–5 sentences.*

LISTENING

1 Landscapes → WB 41/1

L 2/10

a) *Listen to the description of a landscape and draw it in your exercise book. Then compare your picture with those of a partner. Is anything missing?*

b) *Find a picture of a landscape or a city and describe it to your partner. Your partner must draw the picture. Compare it to the original picture.*

VOCABULARY

2 How I've changed

a) *Complete the article with the missing words.*

vegetarian | definitely | discovery | independent | invent | realise | independence | worry | confident

When I look back at when I was little, I can't believe that I was like that. I played with toys and my mum chose my clothes for me. But since about last year I've **1** a new 'me'. That's when I **2** that I wanted to be my own person. It was a spectacular **3**! I babysit and earn some of my own money now so I don't need my parents as much. I've **4** become more **5**. That means I can buy my own clothes and I make more of my own decisions. I've become a **6** too. My dad has been calling me **7**. I like how that sounds. Sometimes they still **8** about me and I have to show them that they can trust me. So in some ways, **9** is like a job – you have to work for it and work at it. So at the moment, I feel more like an adult than a 14-year-old.

b) *Use the text in a) as an example and tell a partner how you've changed. Which of your hobbies / friends / interests have changed? Why? Because of age? peer pressure? parents? …*

VOCABULARY

3 Boring!

Make this e-mail more interesting. Use the ideas on the right to replace the words and phrases in blue.

at home here | whisper | a shower of stars | world-famous | huge | amazing | fascinating | billions of | go round in circles | traditional clothes

Dear Sue,
Edinburgh is so nice! I love it. I really feel like I've been living in this city forever. Well, sometimes I still get lost in the old part of the town. I start walking and then I come back to the same place where I started.
Edinburgh is a very old city. Sometimes you can still see people in typical Scottish clothes, like the kilts. The city is full of fun things to do. Edinburgh Castle is known around the world and every August there's a very big arts festival here.
The landscape is nice here too. If you go to the top of Calton Hill at night and look up, it feels like you're under lots of stars and they're falling down on you. If you tell your friends about this, please try to say it very quietly. I don't want too many tourists here – just me!
Best,
Lilian

LANGUAGE

4 Berlin then and now

Use the words and phrases below to make sentences in the ***present*** *or* ***past passive****.*

Example: 1. The oldest church in Berlin was built in 1230.

1. The oldest church in Berlin 2. In a survey, Berlin 3. 150 years ago, there were no cars so everything 4. In the 1800s, industry was growing and a lot of machines 5. Berlin is very popular and every year its sights 6. The 'currywurst', a popular street food dish[1], 7. Today, to make extra money, many flats 8. The fall of the Berlin Wall	+ pull visit invent celebrate rent out build vote produce	+ by Herta Heuwer. the most 'fun' city in the world. by horses. to tourists. in 1230. by millions of tourists. in Berlin. at the Brandenburg Gate each year.

LANGUAGE

5 Only in Scotland

Practise this dialogue with a partner. Where possible, change the active sentences to passive and the passive sentences to active to make the dialogue sound more natural.

Alan: The concert[2] last night was enjoyed by lots of people. But a storm interrupted[3] our gig. The weather really disappointed us.
David: Oh, that doesn't matter. The storm was just ignored by most of us.
Alan: Was the rain kept out by the roof?
David: Most of it! Raincoats were put on by a lot of people.
Alan: Were they rented out?
David: Yeah, they usually do that at concerts. What's going on at the Highland Games tomorrow?
Alan: Some people have planned a bagpipe contest. And there's a new contest where thistles are walked on. Sounds dangerous!
David: Well, now we can say the Scots invented thistle-walking!
Alan: And listen to this, this is great. The thistle-walking contest is judged by the winners of the bagpipe contest. Funny, isn't it?!
David: Yes, you only find that in Scotland!

1 dish [dɪʃ] Gericht; Speise | **2 concert** ['kɒnsət] Konzert | **3 to interrupt** [ˌɪntə'rʌpt] unterbrechen; stören

LANGUAGE

6 Time for a change → WB 41/2

a) *Complete the text with **for**, **since** and the verbs in the **present perfect progressive**.*

Dear Mum and Dad,
You **1** (give) me the same pocket money **2** three years! Don't you think it's time for a change? Remember: I **3** (not wear) nappies[1] **4** I was about two. Think of all the money you **5** (save) **6** then. And I **7** (not grow) as much **8** I turned 15 so I don't need many new clothes. And you must agree: My behaviour[2] **9** (improve) these last few months. I **10** (not produce) whisky in the garage **11** six weeks now. Just joking! But I **12** (rent out) my tablet to friends to earn some extra money. And I **13** (think) about you too. It's unhealthy to stay the same. You **14** (do) the same thing **15** three years! So really I'm just trying to help you. We can both look forward to a change next month, right?
Love, Jack

b) *What have you been doing for a long time? Which things would you like to change in your life and why?*

LANGUAGE

7 At the ceilidh

*Look at the pictures and make sentences. Use the **simple past** and the **past progressive**.*

Start like this: 1. They were having dinner when …

1

have dinner | ring

2

20:00 | dance at ceilidh

3

sing | go red[3]

4

kiss[4] | take photos

1 **nappy** [ˈnæpi] Windel | 2 **behaviour** [bɪˈheɪvjə] Verhalten | 3 **to go red** [ɡəʊ ˈred] rot werden | 4 **to kiss** [kɪs] küssen

CABULARY

8 Visit Edinburgh! → WB 42/3–4

In small groups, choose one of the attractions below and design a brochure for it. The intros and the words can help you.

The Edinburgh Ghost Tour

You don't believe in ghosts? Well, then you haven't been to Old Town Edinburgh yet! Get yourself ready for …

scary | to scream | castle | to cry | close | trick | surprise | frightening | dead …

Animals in the city

Cities aren't just for people! Come to Edinburgh City Farm and spend a fantastic day with …

creature[1] | cuddly[2] | be a farmer for a day | to milk | to meet | sweet | new friends …

MEDIATION

9 Let's celebrate!

You're on an exchange in England and you've been trying to explain the German tradition of 'Fasching'. You've found this website and show it to your host brother. Tell him about it.

Fasching, Fastnacht, Karneval

In Süddeutschland, Bayern und Österreich wird diese besondere Zeit des Jahres „Fasching" oder „Fastnacht" genannt, in der Mitte und im Norden Deutschlands heißt es „Karneval". Die Traditionen und Bräuche[3] sind unterschiedlich, aber die Umzüge[4] und Feiern finden überall zur gleichen Zeit statt (vom 11. November bis einen Tag vor Aschermittwoch[5]). In Deutschland wird schon seit Jahrhunderten gefeiert, aber es heißt, dass auch die Römer schon Karneval kannten.
Manche Leute feiern Fasching, um den Winter zu beenden. Andere wollen viel feiern, bevor die Fastenzeit[6] vor Ostern beginnt. Und alle, die feiern, wollen ganz schön laut sein. Sie singen, machen Musik, lachen, laufen durch die Straßen und tanzen. In manchen Gegenden gibt es sogar Schulferien um diese Zeit!

1

„Seit Juni arbeiten wir an unserem Wagen für den Karnevalsumzug in Köln[7]."

2

„In meinem Dorf tragen wir seit 200 Jahren die gleichen Masken[8] und Kostüme."

3

„Meine Maske wurde schon von meinem Großvater und meinem Vater getragen!"

1 **creature** ['kriːtʃə] Lebewesen | 2 **cuddly** ['kʌdli] knuddelig | 3 **custom** ['kʌstəm] | 4 **parade** [pə'reɪd] | 5 **Ash Wednesday** [ˌæʃ'wenzdeɪ] | 6 **Lent** [lent] | 7 **Cologne** [kə'ləʊn] | 8 **mask** [mɑːsk]

Find more online: e439my

Text smart 2
Factual texts

Text smart 2 is about factual texts: texts with useful facts and information. You're going to deal with different kinds of factual texts and learn what their features are, how to understand them and how you can write them yourself.

SPEAKING

1 Warm-up: Where to find information

a) *Read the boy and the girl's dialogue. How would* ***you*** *look for the same information?*

A: You're looking for cooking information for your mum? Here?
B: Well this is a library, and libraries have books!
A: Sure, but it's all on the internet, isn't it? Let's have a look …

b) *Your turn: Think of more situations when you need factual information on a topic. Where do you find it? What media do you use? Say why.*

VOCABULARY

2 Different kinds of factual texts

Match the situations on the left with the correct factual text on the right.

1. If you want to know the meaning of a word,
2. If you need basic information about something,
3. If you want to make a cake,
4. If you want to know about important news,
5. If you want to know how to do / make something,
6. If you need an answer to a question that lots of people have asked before,

a) you look for it in an FAQ.
b) you read / watch / listen to a news report.
c) you read a dictionary entry.
d) you follow a recipe for it.
e) you read a reference article.
f) you need to follow the instructions.

SPEAKING

3 Before you read

a) *Look at the next page. What do you expect from the text when you read the headline and look at the photos?*

b) *Say what you already know about hedgehogs. Have you ever seen one?*

Reading skills

A difficult text becomes easier once you **know something about the topic** before you read:
- First, think of your own experiences.
- Also think of what questions on the topic you'd like to ask, and try to collect useful vocabulary.
- And remember: You already know ways to deal with new words (→S10), so don't worry!

What do the instructions say?

S 1/28–31
L 2/15–18

Hedgehog over-wintering instructions

Before the winter months, many young hedgehogs try to eat a lot so they will survive hibernation. If you see a large hedgehog, you can help it by putting out some cat or dog food and water. If it is smaller, looking ill or behaving in an odd way, you should take it to your nearest wildlife hospital for a full examination.

If hedgehogs are too small to make it through the winter period alone, it is necessary to feed and clean them until their weight builds up and they are ready for release in the spring. This takes up a lot of the valuable space we need at the hospital to treat other wild animals. How YOU can help:

1. Take care of a small hedgehog until around mid-April, when the frosts are usually over.
2. Keep it in a warm area such as a shed or spare room. It will need an area where it can sleep and wander round a little bit without getting lost or stuck (they can fit into VERY small spaces). It is essential to keep it warm and active to avoid hibernation; it is too small and WILL NOT survive!
3. Give the hedgehog a container to sleep in. Leave it in the run area so that it can come out when it wants. This bed should contain shredded newspaper (NOT OFFICE PAPER – IT CUTS THEIR NOSE AND FEET), dry leaves or hay.
4. Line the run area with newspaper so you can clean it out daily. Just take up the top sheets of newspaper; that leaves it nice and clean underneath. Always make sure the layer of newspaper on the floor is thick enough to soak up any urine or water.
5. Hedgehogs must have fresh food daily and they MUST have fresh water at all times! The best food to give them is tinned cat or dog food.
6. We will give you a weight chart for each hedgehog. You MUST weigh it at least once a week to make sure it is gaining weight.
7. Only handle the hedgehog when you clean or weigh it. Hedgehogs are wild animals which MUST remain fearful of humans!

As soon as the hedgehog reaches the target weight of about 750g, you should contact us so we can release it back into the wild.

READING

4 Understanding the text

→ △ 128/1

a) *Match these German words with English words in the text.*

Winterschlaf | überleben | vermeiden | Dosenfutter | Schicht aus Zeitungspapier | zunehmen | menschenscheu | aufsaugen | Auslauf | aktiv halten

→ S5–6

b) *Now say what the text is about and what the main parts are.*

c) *In the text, find out the answers to these questions. Give line numbers.*

1. When should you take a hedgehog to the wildlife hospital?
2. Where can you keep a hedgehog?
3. What happens when small hedgehogs go into hibernation?
4. Why do you have to use a lot of paper?
5. What is the wrong kind of paper, and why?
6. What is the best food for hedgehogs?
7. When can you release the hedgehog back into the wild?

READING

5 The language of instructions → WB 43/1

→ △ 128/2
→ S12

Read the skills box. Then make a grid with these two categories:

1. **Steps**
2. **Phrases**

*Now go back to the hedgehog text and fill in your grid. (Write a heading for **all seven** steps in the text.)*

Reading skills

Most **sets of instructions** have these typical features:

1. **Steps:** There are usually **clear steps** which you follow one after the other (Step 1, Step 2, etc.). Sometimes, these steps have **headings**.
2. **Phrases:** You often find **imperative** phrases like "Give the hedgehog …", "Keep it in …", etc.
For **very important information**, instructions often include words and phrases like "Make sure …", "You / It must …" or "Never …".

WRITING

6 Write a 'Hedgehog over-wintering FAQ'

→ △ 128/3
→ ▲ 128/4
→ S11–14

Internet FAQs ('Frequently Asked Questions') are popular for quick answers to popular questions. You can often find information more quickly in an FAQ than in a long text.

Use the information in the text to write an over-wintering FAQ for people who find a hedgehog in their garden and want to help it. Write 4–5 questions and answers for your FAQ.

Example from an FAQ about guinea pigs as pets:

Q: Can I feed my guinea pig treats?

A: Yes, but make sure they're special treats from the pet shop – they have to be good for their teeth. Don't feed them sugar or honey; that's really bad for their teeth.

Tip

When people write FAQs about a special topic, they write questions for what **most people** will want to know. Then they write **helpful** answers with lots of facts and information.

Didn't you hear? It was in the news!

SPEAKING

7 Warm-up: Your news and where you get it

a) *What kind of news are you interested in: local / world / sports / celebrity / school news?*

Example: A: All I need is sports results and maybe some local news too.
B: I'm interested in celebrity news. I want to know all about my favourite stars!

b) *Where do you get your news from: the TV, the internet, your smartphone, …?*

READING

8 What makes a news report a news report?

→ S5–6, 12

a) *Read the two texts below and then answer these questions: 1. What are they about? 2. Which text is a news report and which is a blog post? Say why you think so.*

OMG, GET YOUR TISSUES OUT! katie13_bristol February 12, 2017

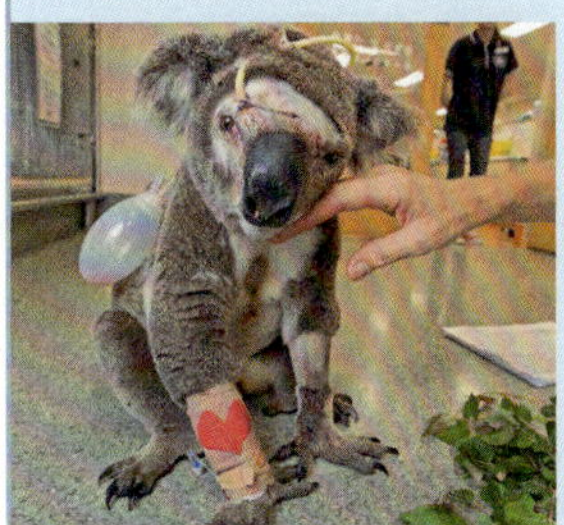

Have any of you heard about the poor koalas who are dying in the Australian bush fires?!?! OMG, I've never seen anything so sad! LOOK at this photo of a poor koala with injuries on its face and arms!!! 😟😟😟 The poor little guy just looks sooooo helpless and it BREAKS MY HEART! 💔💔💔 At least this one was saved. But I'm not sure if people down there are doing enough to help the OTHERS! Time for me to cry AGAIN … 😭😭😭

Koalas: Cute but helpless in deadly bush fires

Moondarra State Park, Australia — by Dave Kovak, 10 February 2017

Every year, the extremely hot and dry summers in south-eastern Australia lead to deadly bush fires with loss of human life. But while most people are rescued before it's too late, thousands of animals aren't so lucky and die in the flames. But some animals are lucky, like this koala who was found by volunteer firefighters in Moondarra last week. The confused, helpless and thirsty koala was found on the roadside and taken to an animal shelter. His paws were badly burnt, but workers at the shelter are sure that he will soon be able to return to the bush.

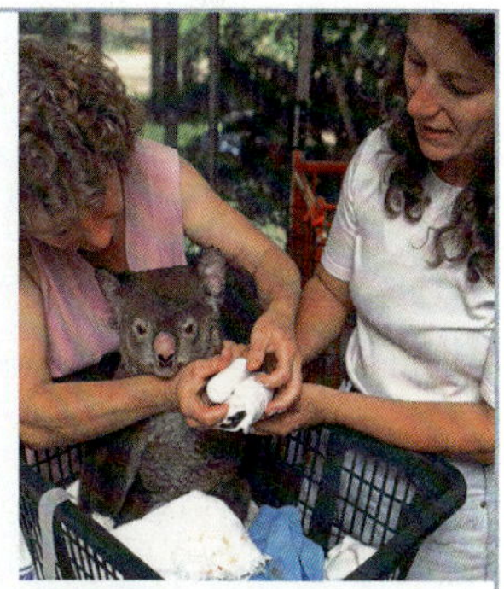

b) *Read the skills box. Write down examples of **facts** and **passive forms** you can find in the news report.*

c) *Go back to the blog post. Which statements are opinions and not facts? What are typical phrases for opinions?*

→ △ 129/5

d) *Turn some of the **opinions** about the koalas in the blog post into **facts**. The skills box and the news report can help you.*

Reading skills

- A **headline** needs to give **important information** so the reader knows what the article is about straight away.
- News reports focus on **facts**. Writers' opinions don't belong in the news.
- News is **not** written in emotional language.
- News reports often use **passive forms**.

SPEAKING S1/32–33 L2/19–20 → S12

9 Before you read

The news report below already has a headline. But the headlines in the box also match the report, as you will see. Which headline interests you the most? Which gives you the most information?

A. Every nine hours a rhino is killed for its horn
B. Elephants and rhinos on the brink of extinction
C. The biggest ever global wildlife protest
D. We are the only hope for elephants and rhinos
E. Illegal poaching of elephants and rhinos still going on

Tip

When you read texts, always look for **useful phrases** to learn by heart. Use them again and again **for your own texts**.

No elephants in ten years?

by Ben Pulsford Friday, 3 October 2015

An elephant and two rhinos that still have their impressive tusks and horns

Illegal ivory

People all over the world will take to the streets tomorrow to march for the future of elephants and rhinos. The Global March for Elephants and Rhinos aims to bring attention to how many of the Earth's giants are killed by poachers for their tusks and horns.

Every nine hours a rhino is killed for its horn (that's around three every day), to be used in traditional Asian medicine. An elephant is killed for its ivory tusks every 15 minutes. This means that 100 elephants are killed every day. The ivory is used to make ornaments and objects such as piano keys. Although international trade in ivory was banned in 1989, illegal poaching is still going on.

If the killing goes on like this, there is a danger that both species will become extinct within ten years. Removing the animals' tusks or horns is also extremely violent and is sometimes done while the animals are still alive.

The march will be the biggest ever global wildlife protest; people in 100 cities across the world will take part. In the UK, official marches are taking place in London, Birmingham, Bristol, Liverpool and Edinburgh. Organisers hope that if enough people take part, those in power will do more to save elephants and rhinos before it's too late.

Jo from 'Action for Elephants UK' says: "Elephants and rhinos are on the brink of extinction because of poaching, and they have no voice of their own. We are their only hope."

Source: www.firstnews.co.uk

SPEAKING

10 Your reaction

After you read the report on p. 60, say what you think about the news report and how it makes you feel. The words in the box can help you.

Useful words and phrases

Phrases: I can't believe that people … | The article makes you think more about … | I hope more people will change … | Why do people …?

Adjectives: cruel | awful | sad | hopeful | …

READING

11 Understanding the text → WB 43/2

a) *Go back to the different headlines in Ex. 9 and answer these questions:*

1. Now that you've read the article, which headline do you think matches the report best?
2. Why do you think the reporter chose a different heading?

→ △ 129/6

b) *All the phrases in the box on the right are from the news report. Can you write a sentence with each?*

→ △ 129/7
→ S18

c) ***Mediation:** Your little brother has seen the photos of the elephant and the rhinos and wants to know what the article is about. Give him the main ideas in German.*

before it's too late (line 15) | on the brink of extinction (line 16) | there is a danger that … (line 9) | those in power (lines 14–15) | a / an … is killed for its … (lines 4–5)

READING

12 Comparing texts: Instructions and news reports → WB 44/3–4

How is the text about elephants and rhinos different from the text about hedgehogs on p. 57? Make lists of what is the same and what is different. Share your ideas.

WRITING

13 Options: Write your own text

→ △ 129/8
→ S11–14

With a partner, choose option A or B and write your text together.

Option A: Write a set of instructions

a) *The hedgehog text is one example of a **set of instructions**. What other kinds (e.g. software manuals) have you read?*

b) *What kind of step-by-step instructions could you write? For what? Think of something useful. Here are some ideas to talk about:*

how to make a great breakfast for your family | how to plan a theme party | how to play a game

c) *Present your instructions to the class.*

Option B: Write a news report

a) *The elephant text is one example of a **news report**. What other kinds of news reports have you read in the last days / weeks?*

b) *What kind of news would you like to write about? Has something interesting happened? Here are some ideas:*

celebrity news (awards / love stories) | sports news (game results / big events) | school news | funny news

c) *Present your news report to the class.*

Find more online: xu3yx2

Making small talk

SPEAKING

1 What went wrong? → WB 47/1

→ S17 **a)** *Read the skills box about small talk.*

b) *Now talk about the cartoon with a partner. What went wrong?*

Speaking skills

Small talk is a friendly way to get to know someone or to talk to someone you don't know well. It's **light** conversation; no serious topics! Follow this pattern:

A asks a question.
B answers, then asks A another question.
A answers, then asks B another question. …

- Be a good talker **and** listener. (Don't hog the conversation!)
- Show interest in your partner: Ask questions.
- When you answer questions, offer more information than just 'yes' or 'no'. But not too much information!

"I just said how are you – I didn't think you'd get on the bus to tell me."

SPEAKING

2 A game: Keep the ball bouncing → WB 47/2

a) *With your partner, choose one of these situations.*

There's a new girl at school. | It's your first day at the sports club. | A new boy has moved into the house next door.

→ S15–16 **b)** *Now make small talk with the person in the situation from a). Each pair needs a small ball. Every time you ask a question, bounce the ball to your partner. Which pair can keep their ball bouncing the longest?*

Useful phrases

Hi. You're new here at / in …, right? | What do you think of …? | What's different about …? | Do you miss anything from …? | Are you enjoying …? | Have you ever …? | Why don't we …? | Have you tried …? | You should … | I've got a great tip: Check out the … I'm sure you'll like it. | Do you feel like hanging out? | If you have any questions / If there's anything you need, just let me know.

I'm … / My name is … | I feel (a bit) nervous / worried / excited / … | That's cool, cheers! | Can you tell me more about …? | I'd like to … | Do you have any favourite places to hang out? | What was that you mentioned about …? | Sorry, I didnt catch what you just said about …

VIEWING

3 At a party

4 🎬

a) *Watch the film. Read the conversations below and then decide which one matches each of the stills. Explain why.*

→ S22–23

1. Girl: It's interesting to compare different countries, isn't it?
   Steffen: Yes, you're right. Have you ever been on a student exchange?

2. Girl: Do you miss anything from home?
   Steffen: No, not really!

b) *Look at the skills box in Ex. 1 again. Then watch (00:38–01:24) and say what goes wrong in the conversation between Steffen, Julie and Nina.*

c) *Now watch the rest of the film. Discuss how Steffen improves his small talk skills.*

d) *Watch (02:18–03:09) again and take notes of the different phrases Steffen uses to keep the ball bouncing.*

WRITING

4 Writing a film script

a) *Work in groups of 3–4. Look at the situations in Ex. 2 again and choose one of them.*

b) *Read the skills box. Write the script for a short film scene about your situation.*

→ S11–14

c) *Act out your scene to the class. Maybe you can also film each other's scenes.*

Writing skills

Stage directions: Only write what you can see or show in a film. You **can't** see a person's thoughts, but you can give hints at a person's feelings in the stage directions, e.g. when you give instructions for facial expressions.

Dialogues: Keep them short and to the point.

Find more online: 3hx8au

Unit 3
What was it like?

A **Celtic Britain** (500 BC)

B **Roman Britain** (43 AD–410 AD)

SPEAKING

1 Warm-up: What was it like?

a) *Say what you know about your grandparents' lives when they were your age. What was different to your life?*

→ △ 130/1

b) *What's the oldest thing in your house? Describe it in a short text. Then tell the class about it.*

c) *With a partner, talk about what you think life was like a long time ago, e.g. 500 or 1,000 years ago. For ideas, think of places in your town or region: castles, old walls, churches, …*

Useful phrases

- I can imagine it was … when my grandparents were young because …
- Back then, people had / didn't have / could / couldn't …
- So it was easier / more difficult / cheaper / more expensive / nicer / … for them.
- I can't imagine how they … because they didn't have … like we do!

In Unit 3 you learn

… how to talk about what life was like at different times in British history. You also learn to describe historical objects. You learn:

- vocabulary for history
- how to talk about the order of actions (*past perfect*)
- how to give extra information in sentences (*defining relative clauses*)

C **Norman Britain** (1066–1154)

READING **2** **British history: Important periods** → WB 48/1

a) *First, just look at the photos in A–E on pages 64–67. If you 'climbed into' these scenes, what do you think things would feel like or smell like? Explain why.*

Word bank

difficult | cold | wet | happy | exciting | boring | noisy | fun | scary | different | hot | (not) comfortable

Example:
A: I bet it wasn't so comfortable on that beach in all those clothes! Same thing in the Tudor period.
B: Who cares about clothes – what did people do without electricity?

b) *Look at the photos again and read the people's statements on pages 64–67. What do they say about the different periods? Think of the main ideas behind each photo and write a caption for each.*

c) *In small groups, compare your captions and discuss which ones work best.*

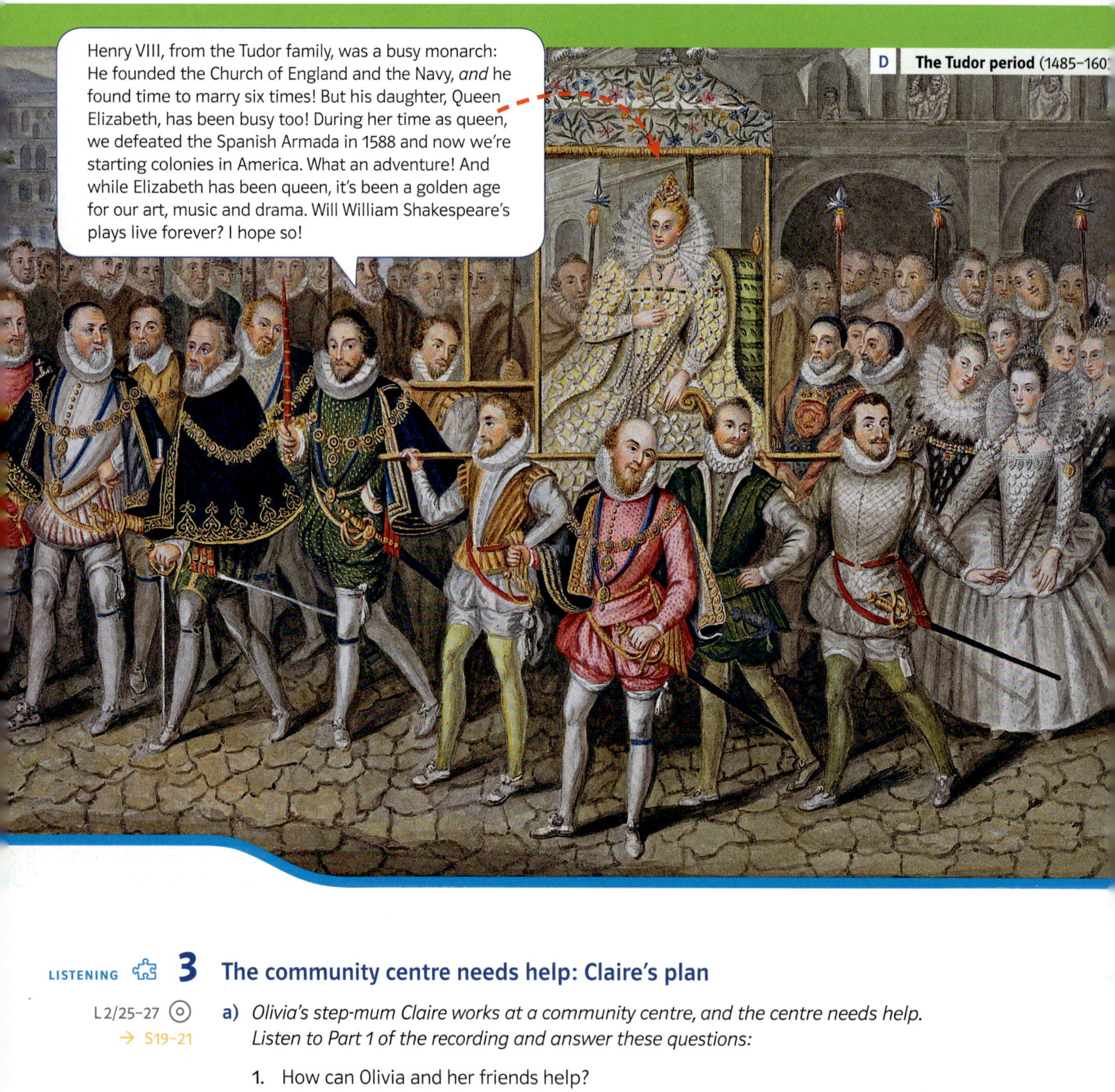

LISTENING **3** **The community centre needs help: Claire's plan**

L 2/25–27

→ S19–21

a) *Olivia's step-mum Claire works at a community centre, and the centre needs help. Listen to Part 1 of the recording and answer these questions:*

1. How can Olivia and her friends help?
2. What do you think of the plan for the calendar?

b) *Now listen to Part 2. Then answer these questions:*

1. Say which students match the five different historical periods and photos on pages 64–67.
2. Say which different objects from the past the speakers talk about. The words on the right can help you.
3. Which historical period is Olivia's group going to do for the calendar?

boots · map · axe · coin · ring · mirror · necklace · knife · belt · sandals · hairbrush

Victorian Britain (1837–1901)

Our cities have become very noisy and smoky, with all the new factories. They're calling it 'the Industrial Revolution'. But the good news is that we have steam trains now, so we can travel more – and faster! This is our first time outside London – the sea air is wonderful! I hope we can soon travel to other countries in the British Empire too, like Canada and India. Life in Queen Victoria's time is very exciting!

F Modern Britain

As I was saying, after World War II, Britain's colonies became independent and Britain became less rich and powerful. But we still had a lot of tradition and history to look back on.

Britain isn't all about history and tradition, is it? What about the fun stuff? Think of all the music that has come out of this country – and is still coming out. We don't need to look back. In a world city like London, you can experience the past, present and future all at the same time!

CABULARY

4 Your turn: Objects in your life → WB 48/2

If you took a photo of yourself with two or three objects which are typical / important for ***your*** *generation's lifestyle, what objects would you show or wear? Say which objects you would choose, and why they're typical for you and people your age. Look at these two photos for ideas or think of these categories:*

clothes / jewellery | free time activities | gadgets

Across cultures

The historical periods on pages 64–67 were all important in **British history**. What historical periods were important or very important for your country's history?

L 2/28

He hadn't finished his game

Olivia: I'm *really* happy that we agreed to do the Tudor period for our calendar page. I'm going to be the perfect Queen Elizabeth!

Jay: Well, we didn't *all* agree. Anyway, who said *you* could be the queen?

Olivia: Well, she was strong and smart – just like me! Do you think she played the saxophone too?

Jay: Don't be silly! Life was boring back then because they hadn't invented all the fun things yet! That's why the Victorians were so much more interesting …

Gwen: Come on, Jay. There are lots of good Tudor characters.

Jay: Yes, but the star is the queen!

Olivia: Of course – it's all about girl power! Before Elizabeth, there had never been a really powerful queen.

Jay: But I'd like to be the star of something!

Holly: Look at this film still from the film *Elizabeth*. You could be Robert Dudley, the queen's favourite. He wanted to marry her …

Jay: No thanks!

Olivia: Don't panic – before Elizabeth became queen she had said, "I'll never marry!" And she never changed her mind!

Gwen: I know, Jay! You can be Walter Raleigh. He helped to found colonies in America, and then he made potatoes and tobacco popular back in England. The English hadn't tasted potatoes before so they were very excited. And as soon as they had tasted them, they couldn't get enough!

Jay: Yes, but who needed *tobacco*?

Holly: Well, what about William Shakespeare? He invented hundreds of famous phrases like "To be or not to be" or "All the world's a stage".

Jay: Stop! I'm a *dancer*, not a writer!

Gwen: OK. I've got the answer. You can be Francis Drake! There's a cool story about him: When the Spanish Armada came to invade England in 1588, Drake was playing bowls. He wasn't worried because he had fought in a lot of battles before. Anyway, he hadn't finished his game so his men had to wait for him. Then, when he was ready, they fought the Spanish – and won!

Jay: What a hero! … But no, I think I'll join the Victorian group. Then I can be the star. Maybe Sherlock Holmes! But wait, he wasn't a real person, was he?

Olivia: Well, do what you want. But let's talk about *my* dress and *my* crown now …

SPEAKING

1 Olivia, Jay and the calendar project

Compare Olivia and Jay's different thoughts and statements about the calendar project.

READING

2 Understanding the text: Match the sentence parts → WB 49/3

1. Before Elizabeth became queen,
2. Life was boring back then because
3. He hadn't finished his game, so
4. People hadn't eaten potatoes before so
5. Before Elizabeth,
6. After Drake had defeated the Armada,

a) his men had to wait for him.
b) she had said, "I'll never marry".
c) he was a hero!
d) there had never been such a powerful queen.
e) they were very excited about new food.
f) they hadn't invented all the fun things yet.

LANGUAGE

3 The past perfect → G8

→ △ 130/2

You use the **past perfect** to show that one event or action happened **before** another one:

This action (↓) happened before this one (↓) in the past.	
After Elizabeth **had decided** not to marry, she never **changed** her mind.	
past perfect (had + past participle)	**simple past**

When actions happened before other ones, sometimes you want to say **why**:

Why did Elizabeth never marry?	Elizabeth's father **had had** six wives, **so** that **was** probably one reason not to marry.
Why was life boring in the 16th century?	Life **was** boring back then **because** they **hadn't invented** all the fun things yet.

Make a diagram to show which actions in each sentence happened ***before*** *and which happened* ***after***.

1. Before the Romans came, the Celts had already been in Britain for a long time.
2. Elizabeth's mother, Anne, had lived in France, so she spoke very good French.
3. After William of Normandy had become king of England in 1066, more and more people learned French.
4. People in Victorian Britain were able to see more and more of their own country after the steam trains had made it quicker and easier to travel.

LANGUAGE

4 The Tudor period: Everyday life in Queen Elizabeth's time → WB 49/4

→ △ 131/3
→ ▲ 131/4

Read the text about the Miller family and put the verbs into the correct form of the ***past perfect***.

Margaret Miller and her brother, Thomas, grew up in Tatley, where the Miller family **1** (have) a home for over a hundred years. Their father **2** (die) when they were very young and their mother **3** (have) five children before them, so life wasn't easy. Before the 1580s, only a few children **4** (be able) to get an education, so the Millers were lucky to go to school. But they were often late when they arrived because they **5** (help) their mother with lots of work at home first. And after they **6** (feed) all the animals and collected the wood, there was no more time for breakfast!

LANGUAGE

5 Simple past or past perfect? → WB 50/5–6

→ △ 131/5
→ ▲ 132/6

After Elizabeth **1** (become) queen, people **2** (have) big parties in the streets. Many (but not all) people in England **3** (be) happy that they **4** (have) a young and very smart queen. When she finally **5** (die) in 1603, she **6** (be) queen for 45 years. She **7** (be) the last of the Tudor monarchs. Most people **8** (feel) that Elizabeth's reign **9** (be) a 'golden age'. William Shakespeare **10** (be) part of that golden age because he **11** (write) so many wonderful plays for England's theatres before he **12** (die) in 1616. 35 plays!

WRITING

6 Write the story about Francis Drake → WB 51/7–8

→ △ 132/7

*Start at picture D, and then find the right order for the rest of the story. Put the verbs in the right form (**simple past** or **past perfect**). Link the events with some of the words on the right.*

after | as soon as | but | because | when | then | so

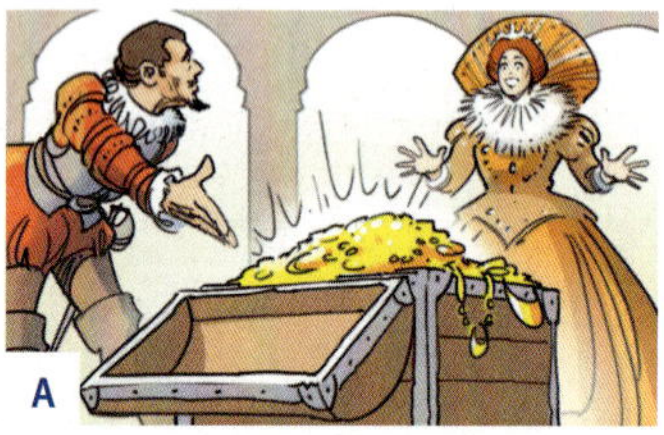
A

in 1580 return to England | waste no time | give queen treasure | queen very happy

B

America | the Spanish attack his ships | make him angry | never forget that

C

in 1588 defeat Spanish Armada | England feel safe again | be a national hero

D

see so many ships as a boy | want to have his own adventures at sea

E

in 1577 sail around world | steal gold / silver | Spanish ships | Spanish hate him

F

on his first big adventure | go to America | sell slaves | capture in Africa before

Start like this: After Francis Drake **had seen** so many ships as a boy, he **wanted** to have his own adventures at sea. Then, on his first big …

SPEAKING

7 Your turn: Funny or interesting things in your life → WB 52/9

→ △ 132/8

What funny or interesting things happened to you in the past? Tell your partner why they happened, what had happened before and what happened next.

"Last January, I stayed with a friend in the mountains. I'd never had a holiday in the snow before and I really loved it. When I arrived, I could smell the wonderful hot meal – his mum had cooked it to welcome me! After the meal, we went out in the snow. But then …"

How to talk about history

For the unit task you're going to present a historical object to your class and you need language to help you with this. This page will give you some useful phrases and help you with a prompt card.

1 Useful phrases for presenting facts and figures → WB 52/10

→ S3–4

a) *The text below is part of what a guide tells a tour group in London. Read what he says, and then put the phrases* ***in bold*** *under the headings in the grid.*

"… Now, we're on Bankside and **in the 16th century** there were four theatres here along the river. In a moment, just around the corner, you'll see the famous Globe Theatre. It **was built in 1599** and it **was used for** all kinds of entertainment – plays, musical events and animal fights. Of course, William Shakespeare wrote and acted here while Elizabeth I **reigned**. He **was born** in Stratford-upon-Avon **in 1564** but **moved to** London as a young man after he had married Anne Hathaway. The diary in my hand probably belonged to Shakespeare himself! – But anyway, it's sad to say that the first Globe **was made of** wood, and when a fire started 400 years ago, the theatre burnt down in just two hours. That was in 1613. It was rebuilt the following year, but pulled down again in 1644–45. The modern Globe was opened in 1997 …"

Prepositions with times and dates	*Descriptions of places / objects*	*Biographical information*	*Typical history verbs*
in 1599	*… was used for …*	*… was born in 1564*	*reigned*

→ △ 133/9

b) *Add these phrases to the right categories in your grid.*

for 200 years | at the beginning of | was worn by | it has invented | was given to | moved to | from 1066 to 1154 | it looks | you can see a / an | at the end of | was brought from

2 Preparing to speak about an object → WB 52/11

→ S12, 17

The prompts on this card are from the same categories as Ex. 1. Use the prompts to write a short speech for a tour guide.

- In this picture, you can see …
- Victorian student / 1890s / writing letter
- quills used for writing / no pens
- made from feathers / difficult to use

L 2/36–37

All's well that ends well

LISTENING

8 Before you read: Where's Jay?

L 2/34–35

→ S18–20

a) *Listen to the recording. What are the friends doing? Why?*

b) *What facts do they learn about the Globe Theatre? Make notes about:*

the building | the audience | the actors

c) *Now read how the story goes on and find out what happens to Jay.*

"The Globe sounds cool," Jay said to Holly and the others. They were late for the start of the tour, and they were walking fast along a dark little road. "The Elizabethans were people who *really* knew how to have fun. You could walk around and shout during the plays, and eat and drink, and there were *animals* there too! How funny!"

The friends turned left into another dark, narrow road and then right into another, walking even more quickly. "I hope you know where we're going," Jay said happily to the others. "I've got no idea! Anyway, did you know that Shakespeare ..." He talked and talked and talked. But then he noticed he was talking to – nobody. Where were the others?! "I'm so stupid!" he thought angrily. "They've turned into another road. I was talking so much, I didn't notice!" Jay turned back, but he soon realised he was passing buildings which he had never seen before. He was in another dark and narrow road. Now he was quite scared. He wanted his friends, but how could he find

Across cultures

The new **Globe Theatre** is one of London's most popular attractions. The theatre was rebuilt very much like the first Globe of Shakespeare's time, and audiences love the special atmosphere there: There's no roof, and you can get very close to the actors!

What special old buildings do you know about? What is special about their history?

people whose phones were all turned off for the tour?

Suddenly, Jay heard a voice and looked round. He saw a man who was talking to a small group of people. He was telling an extremely scary story about a murder which had happened right there in that street! Jay realised he had found another tour group: the Victorian tour. "What luck!" Jay thought excitedly. The guide was talking dramatically about blood and awful crimes and dirt and rats. He could tell stories better and much more excitingly than anyone else that Jay knew. Wow!

The guide suddenly said "Stop!" Everyone stopped and waited quietly. Then they all saw a man that had just entered the street. He was wearing Victorian clothes. He walked past them, slowly and almost silently, like a ghost. A moment later, a woman's voice came from one of the houses. She was screaming loudly and she sounded terribly scared!

Then Jay saw that the 'ghost' had dropped something – his pipe? Jay ran forward and picked it up very carefully. "Perfect!" he thought. "This is exactly the thing I've been looking for. A Victorian pipe I can use for the calendar photo! As Shakespeare wrote, 'all's well that ends well'."

READING

9 What do you think? → WB 53/12

a) *Why do you think Jay enjoyed the Victorian tour so much? What was so interesting?*

b) *Compare what you heard and read about the Globe / Tudor tour and the Victorian tour. Say which one sounds more interesting to you, and why.*

LANGUAGE

10 Find the rule: Defining relative clauses → G9

a) *Look at the text again. Collect the nouns in front of the relative pronouns **who**, **which**, **that** and **whose**.*

b) *Check if the nouns are people or things. When do you use which relative pronoun?*

LANGUAGE

11 Match the sentence parts

→ △ 133/10

1. The man
2. The woman
3. The murder
4. The ghost
5. The people
6. The tour

who / that

which / that

whose

a) had happened in that street was very bloody.
b) heard the story got scared.
c) had just entered the street looked like a ghost.
d) tells us about blood and crime is the Victorian tour.
e) lost his pipe was the murderer.
f) voice they heard was killed.

LANGUAGE

12 Contact clauses → WB 53/13 → G9

a) *Look at the sentences. Is the relative pronoun the subject or the object of the clause?*

1. There are history tours **which** offer special events for kids.
2. It's an event **which** everyone finds exciting.

If the relative pronoun is the object, you don't need it!

> **Tip**
>
> If the word after the relative pronoun is a verb, the relative pronoun must be the subject: S-V-O!

→ △ 134/11

b) *Check the sentences. Say where you don't need the relative pronoun.*

1. Children that are interested in history must go there!
2. There are many things that you can learn.
3. People who like detective stories can help to solve crimes.
4. The props which they use are really cool.
5. And you can take part in a short film which they show on their website later.

LANGUAGE

13 Make one sentence from two

→ △ 134/12
→ ▲ 134/13

Example: The Globe is a famous theatre. I really like it.
→ The Globe is a famous theatre (which) I really like.

1. Last week we went there to see a play. We had just read it in Drama class.
2. Inside the theatre, we were looking for the "seats". We had booked them online.
3. After the play, we talked to the actors. Our teacher had asked them for a workshop.

LANGUAGE

14 Find the rule for adverbs → WB 54/14 → G10-11

a) *Look at the text on p. 72 again.*
What do ***adjectives*** *(slow, quiet) describe?*
What do ***adverbs*** *(slowly, quietly) describe?*
How do you make adverbs?

b) *Find adverbs in the text for these adjectives.*
What can you say about the spelling?

happy – careful – terrible – angry – dramatic

The bus is **slow**. It's going **slowly**.
Your voice is **quiet**. You speak **quietly**.

Tip

A few adverbs are irregular.
good → well
fast → fast
hard → hard

LANGUAGE

15 The Victorian pipe → WB 54/15

→ △ 135/14
→ △ 135/15

Complete the dialogue with the adjectives in the box. Change them to adverbs of manner.

careful | clear | easy | fast | hard | quick | obvious | excited

Jay: What luck that you guys so **1** ignored me on the tour. Otherwise I wouldn't have found this! Look!
Olivia: What's that? A pipe? Wow, let me see it …
Jay: Hey, treat it **2** ! It's very old.
Holly: Why didn't you give it back to the tour guide?
Jay: I was so excited, and I wanted to get back to you guys **3** . I forgot all about it!
Olivia: And you didn't even find us! Well, you can **4** send it back to them now.
Jay: But I don't have the address of the tour company.
Gwen: Come on, Jay. Just check their internet page. The address is **5** displayed there.
Jay: OK, I'll give it back to them *after* the photo shoot, I promise. It'll look great in the calendar photo. I'll look like a real Victorian gentleman! Everyone will clap **6** when they see me.
Olivia: Don't be so sure about that, Jay. I've been working **7** to make my Queen Elizabeth costume more realistic. It's *amazing*!
Jay: I'm sure I'll also find more things to make my costume look more realistic. Just wait …
Holly: Well, you'll have to do it **8** . The photo shoot is tomorrow!

LANGUAGE

16 Adjective or adverb? → WB 54/16, 55/17–19

Complete these online comments about two tours in London.

→ △ 135/16
→ ▲ 135/17

A. "It was a **1** (fantastic) tour of the Globe. The guide explained everything **2** (clear) and told us lots of **3** (interesting) and also **4** (funny) stories. After the tour he also gave us some **5** (good) tips about where to eat **6** (good) and **7** (cheap) near the Globe."

B. "I checked the website **8** (careful) and it looked like the **9** (perfect) history tour by bus. But I was very **10** (disappointed). Most guides work **11** (hard) for their money and are very **12** (nice)! Not our guide. He spoke to us so **13** (rude)! And the bus went past the sights much too **14** (quick)."

Our historical gallery walk

Go for a walk through history! How? Each of you presents a historical object (or a picture of one) to the rest of the class. The best part: You ***are*** *the historical person who presents the object. The best speech along the gallery walk wins! You can be young or old, rich or poor, famous or not famous. Here's an example of things to say in a* ***one- or two-minute presentation*** *about a famous ring:*

"My name is Elizabeth and this is my ring. As you can see, it's made of gold and jewels. When you open it, you can see two pictures: one of me and one of my mother, Anne Boleyn. The pictures were actually a secret nobody knew about: I was only a little girl when my mother died and I never talked much about her. My mother was the second of my father's six wives. He had wanted a son to become the next king. But if you close the ring, you'll see the letters 'ER' – Elizabeth Regina. Elizabeth, the Queen. That's me!"

Step 1

Choose a period, character and object → WB 56/20

Find a photo of your object. Then make notes about what historical period it's from, what kind of object it is, and who it belonged to. This person is the character you'll play. In the grid you can find some example ideas to start with.

→ Introduction (pp. 64–67)

Historical period	Object	Character
Celtic Britain	clothes	a famous person
Roman Britain	weapon	a child
Norman Britain	jewellery	a rich / poor person
Tudor Britain	tool	a king / queen
Victorian Britain	...	...

Step 2

Write a prompt card → WB 57/21

For your card, remember to include these things:

prepositions with times and dates | a description of your object | biographical information | typical history words / phrases

→ Talking about history (p. 71)

Step 3

Make your speech → WB 57/22

Now give your one- or two-minute speech about your object to your classmates. Answer any questions they ask you as a 'historical person'.

→ Talking about history (p. 71) → defining relative clauses (pp. 72–73)

S 2/7–14
L 2/39–46

It's a mystery!

VOCABULARY

1 Before you read: What could go wrong?

Think about what happens at a photo shoot. In a few sentences, describe some things that could go wrong, and say why. Think of the people and things on the right.

models | photographer | other people / things on the set | props | equipment | accidents

A Jim slowly tried to open his eyes but he couldn't look into the lights; they really hurt his eyes. Where was he? In hospital? But why? What had happened to him? He closed his eyes again. He had a really bad headache. "Think!" Jim said to himself. "Try to focus." Slowly, pictures started to come back: Claire … the community centre … historical periods …"OK," he thought, "so I'd just taken some photos for a history calendar. I remember the Victorian picture and the boy – was his name Jay? – who had wanted to be the centre of attention." More memories were now coming back …

B "Quiet, please!" Claire had shouted. "I know you're excited but we need to get organised quickly!" Almost everyone had arrived at the community centre for the calendar photo shoot and everything was in chaos. "This is our photographer, Jim." said Claire. "Do you want to know how you can help him? Be in the right place at the right time and in the right costume! I see a mix of Roman and Norman clothes over there. The Romans and the Normans need to be in their own groups; don't mix up the historical periods!"

C "Where's Holly?" said Olivia. "She can't be late today. I need her now!"

"Well, she isn't your lady-in-waiting in real life!" Gwen said. "I'm sure you can put your dress on by yourself!"

"Yes, but I'll need her in the photo," said Olivia. "How can I look important if nobody is taking care of me? Let's hope she isn't too late or this photo will be a disaster!"

"Drama queen!" said Jay as he walked past the Tudor group. Olivia didn't even hear him; she was still in her own world as the queen. And then the door flew open.

"Sorry I'm late!!!" Holly shouted.

Everyone stopped what they were doing and stared at Holly. It was a shock for everyone. Then they all started talking at the same time. Chaos again. "Oh no!" – "Look at you!" – "What happened?!"

"I fell off my skates and broke my arm," Holly answered and showed them her plaster cast. A few boys and girls had already written their names on it. Olivia was the only quiet one; she didn't say a word.

"Great!" she finally said. "That's going to look really good in the photo! I mean, they didn't even have plaster casts back then!"

"Thanks a lot," said Holly. "My best friend doesn't even ask me if I'm OK!"

D Back in the Victorian room, Jay was having fun in front of the camera. He was a Victorian gentleman, and his partner in the photo was a fine Victorian lady. "Zoom in on me more," Jay shouted, as the girl rolled her eyes.

"Great!" said Jim finally, after he had taken lots of shots. "I think that's the one!"

They all wanted a look at the photos on the camera. "Hey, I look cool!" Jay said.

"You both look cool!" Jim added. "Now, I just need to go out to the car to get some more equipment before I start on the Tudor group. Back in two minutes …"

Stop and think:
What do you think is 'Victorian' about the photo of Jay with the girl on the next page? How do you know? Give examples from the unit or from your own sources.

E "… Would you like a glass of water?" asked the nurse, but Jim wasn't able to focus on anything.

"So, I'd gone down to the car and looked in the boot for my equipment … but after that I can't remember anything. Are they all still waiting for me? I should call Claire – but where's my phone? – Oh, my head! Nurse, could you call the community centre and tell Claire I'm in hospital?" And then he fell asleep again.

F Claire jumped in her car and drove off. The nurse had said that Jim would be OK and Claire was very happy about that. So her problem now was that the Tudor photo had been a disaster! "I just don't understand," she'd said at the time. "Where on earth is Jim? He went out half an hour ago – it's a mystery! I'll just have to try and take the photo myself. – Er, Olivia and Holly, stop fighting! Gwen, please stand still or the photo will be out of focus. And Jay, no photobombing – you're a Victorian!" Finally, everything was quiet and there was a FLASH. They had their photo, Claire hoped.

G "So," Claire finished telling her story to Jim, as he sat in his bed, "that's all I know."

"Show me your photo," he said.

"Oh no, it's awful," Claire answered.

Jim looked. "No, it's fine – maybe a bit dark but I've got some tricks to fix that," he said. "And I can easily edit out the mistakes and crop the photo a bit – it'll be perfect. But I'd still like to know why I'm in hospital."

Stop and think:

What do you think happened to Jim?

H In another part of the hospital, a girl with a broken leg was sitting on a bed. "I was on my bike," she told her parents, "when a man ran out of a building and opened his car boot. You could hear a lot of noise from inside the building so I looked up at the window to see what was happening. The next thing I knew, I had crashed into the man and I was in an ambulance. But who was the man and what happened to him?"

Stop and think:

How many mistakes do you think Jim will have to edit out of this Tudor photo?

VOCABULARY

2 What belongs, what doesn't belong in the scene?

a) *Did any of the problems you mentioned in Ex. 1 come up in the story? Tell the class.*

b) *On the right you see Claire's photo* ***after*** *Jim has improved it. Say which mistakes he has edited out. How has Holly solved the problem with her arm? Explain why these changes were important for the Tudor photo. The word bank can help you.*

Example: Jay had photobombed the Tudor scene as a Victorian!

Word bank

out of focus | wrong period | modern objects | crop / lighten a photo | zoom in on | edit out | photobomb a scene

READING

3 Flashbacks and the order of events → WB 58/23

→ S5–7

a) *First read the skills box. Then find other examples of flashbacks in the story.*

b) *In groups of eight, each person chooses one of these moments from the story (A–H). Your group then lines up in the order you think they happened. Then compare with other groups. If there are differences, explain what's right and wrong.*

A. Jim opened his eyes in hospital.
B. Everyone arrived.
C. Holly broke her arm.
D. Jim went to his car.
E. The nurse called Claire.
F. Claire took the Tudor photo.
G. The girl crashed into Jim.
H. Jim took the Victorian photo.

c) *Your turn: What books, films or TV shows do you know which use flashbacks? In a few sentences, describe a key scene.*

Reading skills

A **flashback** is a part of a story when a character remembers things that had happened before another point in the story.

Example:
Part A: Jim was trying to remember what had happened earlier in the day. → His first flashback to some of the events at the photo shoot is described in Parts B–D.

Flashbacks are often used to make a story more interesting, like a puzzle for the reader.

SPEAKING

4 Key moments from the story: Freeze frames → WB 58/24

Your group chooses one of these three scenes from the story. Discuss how you can present your scene as a freeze frame. Talk about what each of the characters is thinking / feeling / doing?

A. Holly arrives with her arm in plaster.
B. Jay has fun in front of the camera for his Victorian photo.
C. Claire tries to organise the friends for the Tudor photo.

The girl from the past
→ S22–23

SPEAKING

1 School or work?

Many years ago, children from poorer families in Britain and Europe often had to work to earn money for their family. Lots of parents couldn't afford to send their children to school.

In the film you're going to watch, Marley says "I'd rather work than go to school and do this history homework." Can you identify with Marley's statement? Explain why or why not.

VIEWING

2 This is the year 1888?
→ WB 59/25

5

a) *Watch the film. What happens? Think of Violet, her problem and how Marley can help her.*

Word bank

pawn shop | school fees | to travel through time | tea bag | pineapple | vitamins

b) *Read the skills box and look at the stills. How is the dream sequence shown in the film? And how does Marley travel through time? What other details in the film make you think of time travel?*

Film skills

A **dream sequence** is often used to show **time travel** in films. **Audio-visual effects** like music or blurred pictures mark the start and end of the sequence. The viewer (and the film character too) usually only realises at the end of the sequence that it's been a dream – when the character wakes up.

A

B

c) *Your turn: Talk about another film that you've seen with a dream sequence and/or time travel. Tell your partner how it's done in that film.*

WRITING

3 Violet's diary

→ S12

Write a diary entry from Violet's point of view. How did she experience her trip to the 21st century? Remember to write about feelings too.

LISTENING

1 At the museum → WB 61/1

L 2/47–48

a) *Listen to the conversation between a teacher and a group of students at the British Museum. There are ten things the teacher tells the students to do. Make a list.*

Start like this: 1. pick up audio guide 2. …

b) *Which group at the museum would you choose? Explain why.*

c) *Which kinds of museums are near where you live? In small groups, discuss which kinds of displays you'd like to add to them. Then present your ideas to the class.*

LANGUAGE

2 What's new? → WB 61/2

a) *Olivia has to do a presentation for school. She's found this article about the history of different foods. Complete the text with the verbs in the* ***past perfect****.*

There's a saying in English that goes like this: 'as American as apple pie'. But before 1625, people **1** (not grow) apples in America. Asians **2** (bring) them to Europe before they were taken to America. Did you know that the same thing happened with oranges and bananas? The people of South America **3** (never see) these fruits before the Spanish and Portuguese[1] explorers brought them along on their ships. And what about coffee? The people of South and North America didn't like coffee at first because they **4** (never taste) it before. Before it arrived in the Americas, coffee **5** (travel) from Yemen to Europe; the French brought it to South America and the British to North America.

Things travelled in the other direction too. Until the 1500s people in Europe **6** (never hear) of the drink that was so popular in South America – chocolate. After the Spanish **7** (defeat) the Aztecs[2], they started bringing chocolate as a drink to Spain with them. They made it sweeter with sugar and honey. By 1847 a British company **8** (produce) the first chocolate bar. Other food travelled too. Before the American turkey[3] arrived in Britain, Spanish explorers **9** (already take) it to the country of Turkey. After the Spanish **10** (see) the beautiful tomatoes in South America, they brought them to Europe. But even as late as 1800 most Europeans **11** (never taste) a tomato. They were only grown as decorations because for a long time people **12** (think) you could die if you ate them.

b) *Find out about five other foods and drinks that you can buy in Germany. Where do they come from originally? How did they come here? Make notes and present your results to the class.*

1 **Portuguese** [ˌpɔːtʃəˈgiːz] portugiesisch | 2 **the Aztecs** [ˈæzteks] die Azteken | 3 **turkey** [ˈtɜːki] Truthahn

LANGUAGE

3 TTS Visitor's Day

In June, students at TTS had to prepare for their Visitor's Day for family and friends. Read what happened before the event. Complete the sentences with the correct tense: ***past perfect*** *or* ***simple past****.*

Example: At the start of Visitor's Day, the students **were** very nervous because of all the things that **had gone** wrong before.

1. After Mr Johnson ___ (ask) Julie to do a presentation on North America, she ___ (decide) to grow some tobacco in her garden. But then her cat ___ (find) it. Luckily, she ___ (buy) some extra seeds[1]!
2. When Mr Johnson ___ (tell) Tom and Rakesh about the noisy workshop in Room 103, they ___ (be) upset at first because they ___ (plan) to stage their play in Room 102. But after he ___ (find) a new room for them, they ___ (be) happy again.
3. Ayesha and Max ___ (just finish) their model of the Globe Theatre when they ___ (smell) something funny. Luke ___ (leave[2]) a candle on and part of the model ___ (catch) fire. But after they ___ (put out) the fire, they ___ (realise) that it ___ (look) even better because it ___ (show) the fire at the original Globe.
4. The students ___ (just put up[3]) the last posters when the first visitors ___ (invade) the school.
5. They ___ (not know) if it would go well because they ___ (never do) a Visitor's day like this before.
6. After the last visitors ___ (leave), they finally ___ (relax). And then they ___ (realise) that everything ___ (go) well!

CABULARY

4 Which one doesn't belong?

a) *Find the word in each group that doesn't belong. Match each of these words to one of the other five groups. Write down the six new groups.*

1
Roman
bath
emperor
French

2
lady-in-waiting
play
Globe Theatre
writer

3
to attack
Spanish Armada
battle
Industrial Revolution

4
to defeat
factory
British Empire
steam train

5
heating
dress
to take care of
queen

6
Norman
William the Conqueror
belt
entertainment

b) *For each group of words, write 1–3 sentences. Use all four words.*

c) *Give your sentences to a partner. Add one of these words to each of your partner's five sentences or write a new sentence with the word.*

everyday | mystery | lifestyle | back then | noisy | weapon

1 seed [si:d] Samen | **2 to leave on** ['li:v‿ɒn] anlassen | **3 to put up** [pʊt‿'ʌp] aufstellen; aufhängen; errichten

LANGUAGE

5 At Balmoral Castle

a) *First change the **adjectives** into **adverbs**. Then make as many pairs with the verbs as possible.*

awful | happy | good | perfect | safe | thankful | cheap | fast

sing | run | act | smile | speak | arrive | answer | eat

b) *Adjective or adverb? Complete the text with the right forms.*

I just had to see William and Kate! I thought it would be very **1** (easy). In the news it said they'd be at Balmoral Castle at the weekend. I packed my backpack with **2** (warm) clothes, food and drinks. At 2:00 I arrived **3** (safe) at Balmoral Castle and **4** (confident) sat down in front of it. You can stay in **5** (little) houses at the castle, but it's very **6** (expensive), so I decided **7** (brave) to camp until the Royal Family arrived.
I took everything out of my backpack. I had planned everything **8** (perfect).
But then a guard came from behind and said to me **9** (rude), "What are you doing? You can't just sit here!" I answered very **10** (sweet), "I'm waiting for the Royal Family. I'd like to meet them **11** (personal)." He grabbed my arm **12** (rough[1]) and then **13** (quick) threw everything into my backpack. He walked me back to the road and that's when it happened. A car drove **14** (slow) towards the castle and then stopped **15** (quick). The guard greeted William and Kate and I could **16** (easy) see them through the open car windows. And they gave me a **17** (friendly) smile.
So I was **18** (successful) after all!

LANGUAGE

6 Scotland is the country which ...

*Match the sentence parts and make sentences about Scotland **with or without a relative pronoun**.*

1. The Fringe is one of the many festivals	a) the Scots fought long and hard for in the 14th century.
2. Ewan McGregor is the Scottish actor	b) history goes back thousands of years.
3. Many people	c) discovery changed the world.
4. Independence from England is something	d) many people outside of Scotland have never played.
5. Shinty is a typical Scottish game	e) English and Scottish soldiers fought in 1314 was won by the Scots.
6. Haggis is a Scottish meal	f) they do at a ceilidh is easy to learn.
7. Glasgow is a very old city	g) not everybody likes to eat.
8. The dancing	h) is best known for his role in *Star Wars*.
9. The battle[2]	i) are held in Edinburgh each year.
10. Alexander Fleming was a Scottish scientist	j) are looking for an adventure go to Loch Ness.

Example: 1. The Fringe ist one of the many festivals which / that are held in Edinburgh each year.

1 rough [rʌf] grob | **2 battle** ['bætl] Schlacht; Kampf

LANGUAGE

7 History – right or wrong? → WB 62/3–4

*Are the verbs in the sentences right or wrong? Write down the correct verb form. Use the **simple past** or the **present perfect**.*

Example: Who has written the play *Romeo and Juliet*? – wrong, correct verb form: wrote

1. Henry VIII founded the Church of England. Has he founded the Navy too?
2. Has England ever defeated Spain?
3. The Industrial Revolution started in England. Since then people invented many more things.
4. Which British colonies have become independent so far?
5. India has become independent in 1947.
6. The British have made a lot of great music.
7. Air travel became more important than sea travel today.

MEDIATION

8 Who said it and why?

a) *While you were on a class trip to England, you read these quotes in the brochure of a museum you visited. Back home, your grandparents have a look at the brochure and ask you about the quotes. Explain their meaning in German. Why did the people say it? What did they mean?*

1. "All the world's a stage."
   William Shakespeare, 1599, from the play *As You Like It*

2. "I came. I saw. I conquered."
   Julius Caesar, 46 BC

3. "Rome wasn't built in a day."
   Queen Elizabeth, 1563, in a speech in Cambridge

4. "The important thing is not what they think of me, but what I think of them."
   Queen Victoria

5. "History is written by the winners."
   Napoleon Bonaparte or Winston Churchill

6. "History is herstory too."
   Unknown

b) *Your exchange partner asks you about famous German quotes. Find quotes on the internet. Then explain their meaning in English.*

Find more online: 63vs2a

Text smart 3
Fictional texts

What are fictional texts? Why do people read them? In Text smart 3, you're going to read the opening lines of two different books which show you how fictional texts create suspense for the reader.

SPEAKING

1 Why you like to read

Read the statements about why teens read fiction. Which ones can you relate to? Why?

A: I want action and a great plot when I read, right away on the first page!
B: I love characters whose lives are really different to my own. Reading is my escape.
C: I don't like a good book to end, so I love books in a series.
D: I love scary stories – but only when they're fiction. Then I can tell myself, "It didn't really happen!"
E: I want to read about people just like me so I can identify with the characters.

VOCABULARY

2 Crime, horror, romance or ...?

a) *The box on the right lists several genres of fiction. In groups of 3–4, talk about which features are typical of* ***two*** *of the genres. Make a grid and fill it in; the word bank can help you. Then share your results with the other groups. (And if your favourite genre is missing, add it! That can be one of the two genres for your grid.)*

→ △ 136/1

b) *Your turn: Think about your favourite genre. Tell your group why yours is 'the best'! Try to really 'sell' it to the others, with good reasons.*

crime | romance | mystery / detective | horror | science fiction | travel adventure | disaster | animal stories | teen comedy | teen drama | fantasy | comics / graphic novels

Word bank

happy ending | adventure | death | murder | violence | puzzle / problem to solve | action | surviving (against all odds) | friendship | enemies | technology / gadgets | humour

LISTENING

3 What are you reading?

L 3/1–2

→ S19–21

a) *Read what Tina and Rick say and then listen to the first part of their conversation. Then: 1. Say why each of them thinks that their book is the 'best ever'. 2. Whose arguments do you agree with? Say why.*

b) *Listen to the second part of their conversation. Who do you agree with now: Tina or Rick? Explain why.*

Opening lines of a fictional text: Text 1

Among the Hidden: Chapter One

by Margaret Peterson Haddix (b. 1964)

He saw the first tree shudder and fall, far off in the distance. Then he heard his mother call out the kitchen window: "Luke! Inside. Now."

He had never disobeyed the order to hide. Even as a toddler, barely able to walk in the backyard's tall grass, he had somehow understood the fear in his mother's voice. But on this day, the day they began taking the woods away, he hesitated. He took one extra breath of the fresh air, scented with clover and honeysuckle and – coming from far away – pine smoke. He laid his hoe down gently, and enjoyed one last moment of feeling warm soil beneath his bare feet. He reminded himself, "I will never be allowed outside again. Maybe never again as long as I live."

He turned and walked into the house, as silently as a shadow.

SPEAKING

4 Your reaction

The novel Among the Hidden *opens with the lines above. Read them and then answer these questions:*

1. Does the text make you want to read more? Or in other words: Does it 'hook' you? Explain why or why not.
2. The photos can help you to feel the atmosphere and understand more about the setting. Describe how.

Tip

Some words in the text are new and perhaps difficult for you. But they can often be important for atmosphere, e.g. 'shudder'. Don't worry: You already know ways to deal with new words! →S10

READING

5 Understanding the text → WB 63/1

→ △ 136/2
→ S5–6

Read the opening lines again and answer these questions:

1. What exactly do you learn about Luke? Work with a partner and note down what the text tells you.
2. What do you **want** to learn about Luke?

READING

6 Key lines from the text

→ △ 136/3

Below you see key lines from the text. Explain what they mean, and what they tell you about Luke's life.

- He had never disobeyed the order to hide.
- He had somehow understood the fear in his mother's voice.
- But on this day, he hesitated.
- I will never be allowed outside again. Maybe never again as long as I live.
- He turned and walked into the house, as silently as a shadow.

Useful phrases

- It feels like something scary / dangerous / … is happening. Words like … or … in line … tell me so.
- The lines … and … are both key lines because …

READING

7 The five senses

→ S7

First, read the skills box. Then go back to the text and say how the author uses the five senses there. What can Luke see, hear, feel? What do you think it feels like to be in his shoes?

Example:
A: Luke loves the way things smell outside.
B: Yes, everything outside seems better for him than what's inside. That's my feeling.

Reading skills

Every writer wants to **draw the reader into the story** with a great plot and interesting characters in a special setting. Many writers work with **the five senses** to do this. When you understand what the characters **see, hear, smell, taste** and **feel**, it's easier for you to understand what they do because you're 'in their shoes'.

READING

8 Suspense in fictional texts → WB 63/2

→ S7

a) *Think – pair – share: Read the skills box on your own. Then go back to the text and note down words or lines that create suspense and reader interest. Share your ideas with each other and then with the class.*

Example:
Why was the mother so sharp with Luke? Why was there fear in her voice? For me, that's suspense!

Reading skills

An exciting book creates **suspense** and **reader interest**. This can happen in the first lines to draw the reader into the action. Or, the writer might build the suspense slowly.

Also, **strong** or **dramatic language** can draw the reader into the plot.

b) *Choose the line or lines in the text with the most suspense. Which words and ideas make you think so? Group your words / ideas around your line like a mind map.*

Example:

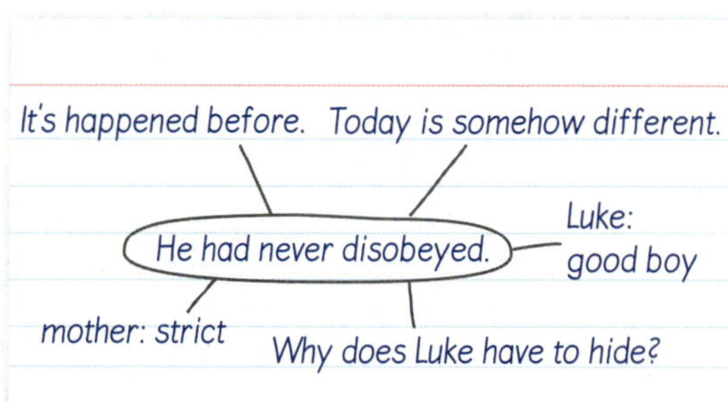

c) *How could Luke's story go on?*

Opening lines of a fictional text: Text 2

S 2/16
L 3/3

Pig-Heart Boy by Malorie Blackman (b. 1962)

Chapter 1 – Dying

I am drowning in this roaring silence. I am drowning. I'm going to die.

I look up through the grey-white shimmer of the swimming pool water. High, high above I can see where the quality of the light changes. The surface. But it is metres above me. It might as well be kilometres. The chlorine stings my eyes. My lungs are on fire. Just one breath. Just one.

I have to take a breath, even though I know that I'll be breathing in water. But my lungs are burning and my blood is roaring and my whole body is screaming out for air. If I don't take a breath, I'll burst. If I do take a breath, I'll drown. Some choice. No choice.

I close my eyes, praying hard. And kick, kick, kick. I open my eyes. The surface of the water seems even further away. I'm going to drown. A fact. A fact as clear, as real as the silence around me. Part of me – a tiny, tiny part of me – laughs. I am going to drown. After everything I've been through in the last few months, this is how I'm going to bow out. One thought rises up in my mind. One thought.

Alex …

I stop kicking. I have no energy left.

I stop fighting. I'm so tired. I can feel my body begin to sink.

SPEAKING

9 Your reaction

→ △ 137/4

a) *What adjectives would you use to describe the situation and atmosphere above?*

b) *Is this the kind of book you'd like to read more of? Explain why or why not.*

READING

10 Key lines from the text → WB 64/3–4

→ △ 137/5
→ S5–7

In Ex. 6, you saw a collection of key lines from Text 1 to discuss. For Text 2, find the key lines yourself. Then explain why they're important. Think of ***suspense*****,** ***characters*** *and* ***atmosphere****. Work with a partner.*

READING

11 The five senses → WB 64/5

a) *How are the five senses featured in Text 2? Note down examples.*

b) *Now compare Texts 1 and 2. Describe in 5–6 sentences how the senses are featured similarly or differently. Is there is a bigger focus on some senses? Describe that too when you compare the texts.*

Examples:
- In Text 2, the focus is more on what the character in the water can feel. He's feeling pain, so that sense plays the biggest role here.
- In Text 1, the focus is more on …
- What the texts have in common is that the characters both feel / smell / …

READING

12 Another look at suspense

a) *In Text 2, what ways does the writer use to draw the reader into the story? (Look back at Ex. 8 for help and ideas, e.g. in the skills box.)*

b) *Now compare the suspense in Text 2 with Text 1. Which text 'hooks' you more?*

READING

13 Narrative perspectives

→ S7 **a)** *First, read the skills box. Then go back and reread the opening of Text 2.*

Reading skills

The writer of a fictional text has a choice: "Who tells my story?" Or in other words:

"Who is my narrator?"
- **First-person narrator** (e.g. in *Pig-Heart Boy*): This kind of narrator tells the story from his / her own perspective. This person is often (but not always) the main character. The reader and a first-person narrator experience the story together, 'live'.
- **Third-person narrator** (e.g. in *Among the Hidden*): This kind of narrator tells the story from the outside. The perspective is *not* the main character's perspective.

b) *Now go back and re-read the opening of Text 1. Then answer these questions:*

1. When you compare Text 1 and Text 2, think of which features could be typical of a first-person narrator, a third-person narrator – or maybe both. Make a grid. Start with the ideas on the right.
2. How do you think Text 1 and Text 2 would feel differently if they were written from the **other** perspective?

The writer gives you time to think.

You jump into the action right away.

It's always clear what the main character is thinking.

You get close to the main character.

The writer gives you time to get to know the atmosphere, setting, characters.

MEDIATION

14 ‹ Finding out more about the books ›

a) *Think: Which genre is each of these books? Find out more and see if you were right!*

→ S18

b) *Students at your school have been asked to send 'summer reading tips' to the school's website. Each tip should feature a short summary of the storyline, and each tip should be in German so that everyone can understand it. Find out more about one of the books and then write your tip.*

WRITING

15 Writing options

→ △ 137/6
→ S11–14

Now that you know more about suspense, atmosphere and other ingredients of fictional texts, try out your new skills with one or more of the writing options below.

Option A: *Look at the pictures. They both show the opening scene of two different fictional texts. What could each book be about exactly? Decide for yourself and write 8–10 opening lines. Think of the points below:*

- How could the opening lines really draw the reader into the story?
- Who is telling the story: a first- or third-person narrator?
- Think of how you can include the different senses.

Option B: *If you have time, you can do both parts of Option B. Or, you can do just one:*
- *Rewrite Text 1 from Luke's perspective, as a* ***first-person narrator****.*
- *Rewrite Text 2 from a* ***third-person narrator's*** *perspective. For this you need to think of who could tell the story:*

  Could it be a character who is looking back after days / months / years?
  Could it be a character who is watching what is happening?

Option C: *Write your own opening lines (8–10) or opening page to a fictional text. Try to include* ***all five senses****, if you can. Be as creative as you want to be. Think of these points as you plan your text:*

- What genre of fiction would you like to write in?
- Do you want a first- or a third-person narrator? Why?
- Do you want to 'jump' into the story with your characters, as in *Pig-Heart Boy*? Or do you want to 'step' into the story more slowly, as in *Among the Hidden*?

Find more online: 89d4ps

Dos and don'ts

SPEAKING

1 Good or bad behaviour? → WB 67/1

→ S16–17

a) *Work with a partner. Look at the situations in the pictures. Then look at the dos and don'ts below which are typical for English-speaking countries (and for others too). Which ones can you use to describe each situation? Explain why.*

Say thank you. | Don't stare. | Don't point. | Be polite. | Don't stand in the way. | Hold the door open for others. | Don't jump the queue. | Don't talk with your mouth full. | Smile. | Say hello back. | Don't litter. | Don't stand too close to others.

b) *What counts as good or bad behaviour in your family / your school / among your friends? You can look at the dos and don'ts in a) for help.*

SPEAKING

2 Your turn: Your experiences → WB 67/2

Can you remember a situation in which someone behaved differently to what you'd normally expect (in Germany or in another country)? Tell your partner about what happened. How did you feel about it? How did you react?

Useful phrases

Just imagine what happened to me when … | I saw something really funny / strange / odd when … | I was really surprised. | I couldn't believe my eyes / ears. | I didn't understand what was going on. | Well, I guess every country has its own customs. | For me, it looked like good / bad behaviour, but then I realised …

VIEWING

3 Aliens in London!

6

Just imagine: Aliens have landed in central London. It's a strange experience for everyone. Find out more!

→ S22–23

a) *Watch the film. What did the aliens do wrong from a British point of view? Take notes.*

b) *Look at the stills. What's the situation and what goes wrong? Work with your notes from a).*

WRITING

4 Role play: Breaking the ice

→ S17

a) *You're at a train station and your train is late. Another person is waiting for the train too. The person looks friendly and smiles at you. Write down a conversation you could have with him / her. Look at the icebreakers in the box for ideas.*

b) *Act out your conversation in class.*

Useful phrases

Icebreakers

I hope the train will arrive soon. | How long do you think we'll have to wait for …?! | How long have you been …? | I'm glad it isn't so crowded / busy / hot / cold here today. Yesterday it was so … | Cool T-shirt! You must be a … fan. | I've heard the film / show / band / … is really good. | Have you seen the latest film with …?

WRITING

5 Tips for aliens → WB 67/3

→ S11–14

Work in groups of 3–4. Write a leaflet for aliens who have come to visit earth. Give them tips about how to behave.

Tips for aliens

It's good / bad manners to …
You should always …
You shouldn't ever …
People here (don't) usually … when …
It's a good / bad idea to … because …
People (don't) like it when you …

Find more online: 58c3ir

Unit 4
On the move

A

SPEAKING

1 Reasons for travelling → WB 68/1

a) *Look at the photos above. What are the people doing? What might they be thinking?*

b) *Why do you think these people are travelling? Share your ideas in class. The words and phrases in the box can help you.*

c) *Collect more reasons for travelling.*

Word bank

class trip | family holiday | have fun | escape from hard life | get to know other cultures | hope for a better future | visit family | learn a foreign language | have a break | meet exchange partners

LISTENING

2 Travel situations

a) *What can happen when you're travelling to another country? Share your ideas in class.*

L 3/5–9

b) *Listen to different travel situations. Match the speakers with the problems they're talking about. You don't need all the ideas.*

→ S19–21

feel seasick | get lost | have too much luggage | have communication problems | be afraid of flying | lose money | forget tickets | miss train / plane

D

In Unit 4 you learn

… how to talk about travel experiences and reasons for travelling. You learn:

- how to report what people have said
- how to report questions, commands and requests
- words and phrases for talking about travel

CABULARY

3 Travel words → WB 68/2–3

→ S4

a) *Make a grid and sort the words into the following categories:*

transport | places | people | things you need

b) *Can you think of more travel words? Add them to the grid.*

departure lounge | by bike / car / bus | passport | boarding card | check-in desk | on foot | visa | passenger | flight attendant | train station | by train / plane | customs | suitcase | public transport | tickets | guide | airport | by boat / ferry / ship | tourist | passport control | arrivals hall | luggage | foreign currency | duty-free shop

c) *Your turn: Choose five of the words from your grid and use them to write a short text about your last holiday or trip.*

Example: Sometimes we go by car to another town to visit my grandparents. During our last holiday we went by plane to … We left for the airport very early in the morning …

SPEAKING

4 Your turn: Your travel plan

→ △ 138/1

What type of travelling would you like to do when you're older? Where would you like to go? Get into groups of three and share your ideas. Then tell the class how your plans are similar or different.

L 3/10

You told us there was free wifi!

My first trip away from home was really exciting, and I tried to enjoy every minute of it. But my best friend Steve is completely different. I'll tell you why.

On the way to France with our athletics team, Steve and I were out on the top deck of the ferry. It was a nice, quiet moment. Then Steve's phone rang.

"YEAH?" he said, in his big loud special telephone voice. "No, sorry, I didn't have time. Uh huh … Uh huh … WHAAAT?! Ha ha ha! OK, see you!"

"Who was that?" I asked.

"It was my friend Eddie," Steve answered. "He said he was at the leisure centre with Amarjit. He told me they were having crisps and drinks from the vending machine."

"Wow," I said. "That's so much more interesting than a ferry trip to another country. Why did you go 'WHAAAT'?"

"Er … oh yeah. Eddie said Amarjit had just spilt his drink over his crisps."

"Amarjit's crisps or Eddie's crisps?"

"Oh, I've forgotten. Hang on, I'll send them a message to ask."

It's only an hour from Dover to the French coast, and we could already see the houses of Calais. French houses often have shutters at the windows. British houses never have shutters. I love things that remind me I'm in a different country.

Ms Woodruff, the coach, came out of a door and onto the deck.

"It's time to get back on the coach," she said. Then she saw that Steve was still busy with his phone.

"I promised your parents I wouldn't let you use your phone in France!" she said. "You know it's really expensive to use it abroad!"

"But we aren't in France yet," said Steve. "We're still on the ferry."

"Where do you think the signal is coming from?" she said.

With a big groan Steve gave her his phone.

"Can I have it back when we arrive? You told us there was free wifi at the hostel. My parents said I could use my phone over wifi. They did. Honest!"

"Really? They told *me* you were an addict, and they thought you needed a break from your smartphone. You can have your phone for half an hour in the evenings, OK?"

"This is going to be an awful trip," muttered Steve.

"This is going to be a great trip," I thought.

READING

1 Understanding the text → WB 69/4

→ S5–6

a) *What do the narrator and Steve like / not like about the trip? Make a grid and write down what the text tells you about the two characters.*

b) *What does the coach decide about Steve's smartphone? Do you agree with her decision? Explain why or why not.*

c) *Your turn: Can you identify more with Steve or with the narrator? Say what's important for you when you travel.*

LANGUAGE

2 From direct to indirect speech → WB 69/5 → G12

→ △ 138/2
→ ▲ 138/3

a) *The following sentences are in the text, but in indirect speech. Copy the grid. Write down the sentences in direct speech. Then add the sentences in indirect speech from the text. Underline the words that change from direct to indirect speech.*

Direct speech	Indirect speech
1. Eddie: **I'm** at the leisure centre with Amarjit.	Eddie said **he was** at the leisure centre with Amarjit.

2. "We're having crisps and drinks from the vending machine." 3. "Amarjit has just spilled his drink over my crisps." 4. "I won't let Steve use his phone in France." 5. "There's free wifi at the hostel." 6. "You can use your phone over wifi." 7. "Steve is an addict. He needs a break from his smartphone."

b) *How do tenses change when you report what someone has said? Look at the sentences from a) and write down the verb forms.*

Example: I'm → he was **simple present → simple past**

c) *Read these sentences from the text. Report what the people say. Use* ***indirect speech****.*

1. Steve: I didn't have time. 2. Steve: I've forgotten. I'll send them a message to ask. 3. Ms Woodruff: It's time to get back on the coach. 4. Steve: We aren't in France yet. We're still on the ferry. 5. Coach: You can have your phone for half an hour in the evenings.

d) *Which verbs are used to introduce indirect speech in the text? Can you think of more verbs? Make a list.*

Example: He **told** me they were …

LANGUAGE

3 Steve's latest post → WB 69/6, 70/7–8 → G13

You're a friend of Steve's. While he was in France with his athletics team, he wrote this post. A few days later, you tell a friend about it. Look at the sentences with the words in green. Report them to your friend. Change the words in green to the words below. Then explain why you need to do this.

Start like this: Steve wrote a post a few days ago. He said that **he was having** a really good time **there**. …

that | there (2x) | that day | the next day | the day before

Just a quick post. (I'm only allowed half an hour on my phone!) 😜 You won't believe it. I'm having a really good time here. Today we went into a cute little town. I thought it was a holiday because all the shops were closed. Then I found out that French shops close for lunch! I think lunch is a big deal in France. Anyway, it's all been *fantastique* here. Well, apart from the food! Yesterday we had a kind of soup with lots of herbs and garlic in it. Ugh! But I guess that's typical of French cooking. This evening we had 'burger au cheval'. I thought that meant 'burger in the style of a town called Cheval' but then I realised that it was MADE OF HORSE! Some people just ate the chips and salad, but I thought, "Well, why not finish it?" To be fair, it tasted OK. Got to go and get some sleep now. The event starts tomorrow. *A bientôt!*

4 Role play: Around the world

SPEAKING → △ 139/4 → S17

a) A: *You're a film star. For your latest film, you act in some amazing places around the world. First make notes about where you are now, what you did last week, and what you're going to do next.*

B: *You're a magazine reporter who wants to interview the film star. You're going to call him/her and ask about his/her journey. First make notes about the questions you're going to ask. After the role play, report to the class what A told you. Just report the most important information!*

Start like this: I interviewed … He/she said he/she was …

b) *Now change roles: B is the film star and A is the reporter.*

5 What happened? → WB 71/9–10, 72/11

WRITING → △ 139/5

a) *The Jones family had some problems during their holiday. Now their friends want to know about everything that went wrong. Look at the pictures and write down what they tell their friends.*

→ △ 139/6

b) *Your turn: Think of a funny, scary or embarrassing situation which you experienced during your last holiday or on a trip. Tell your partner about it. Try to make it as interesting as possible.*

6 ‹A song: Island in the sun› Weezer

LISTENING L3/12 → S19–21

When you're on a holiday
You can't find the words to say
All the things that come to you
And I wanna feel it too

On an island in the sun
We'll be playing and having fun
And it makes me feel so fine
I can't control my brain

When you're on a golden sea
You don't need no memory
Just a place to call your own
As we drift into the zone

On an island in the sun
…

We'll run away together
We'll spend some time forever
We'll never feel bad any more

a) *Listen to the song. Which words/phrases tell you how the main character feels?*

b) *Write an extra verse for the song. Think of words that rhyme first.*

Start like this: When you're on a lonely beach …/When you're feeling really cool …

L3/13 ⊙

Idiot nephew?

Rafiq: Did I tell you about my trip to Bangladesh last month?
Anya: No, you didn't. How was it?
Rafiq: Not bad, thanks, although it didn't start very well.
Anya: What happened?
Rafiq: At passport control, the man asked me what the purpose of my visit was. I was really surprised, and I just couldn't think of an answer. So I said I didn't know.
Anya: Ha! That wasn't very clever.
Rafiq: I know. I think he thought I was some kind of idiot. But it was my parents' idea for me to visit my family in Bangladesh. Next the man asked me if I was travelling with my parents.
Anya: What did you say?
Rafiq: I told him I was travelling alone. So then he asked me how old I was.
Anya: And you said you were fourteen, right?
Rafiq: I was really tired. I forgot about my last birthday, and I said I was thirteen. Then he looked at the date of birth on my passport, and it didn't match. I think that's when he started to get suspicious. He told me not to lie to him.
Anya: Oh dear. What happened then?
Rafiq: He told me to go into a side room to answer some more questions. I was lucky I had the address and phone number of my uncle and aunt with me. The airport security people called them, and asked if they knew who I was.

Anya: And they said, "No, we don't have an idiot nephew who can't even remember how old he is."
Rafiq: Very funny. Anyway, my uncle said my aunt was waiting for me at the airport, and gave them her mobile number. They called her, and asked her to come to the immigration office in the arrivals hall. Then a security guard took me there to meet her. When we got there, he asked her if I really was her nephew.
Anya: Did the security guy believe her?
Rafiq: Yeah. I think he knew she was telling the truth because she didn't seem worried.

READING

7 At passport control → WB 72/12

→ S5–6

a) *Explain Rafiq's problem when he arrives in Bangladesh.*

b) *How do you think Rafiq felt during his conversation with the man at passport control? And how do you think he felt when he left the airport?*

Start like this: Rafiq feels **embarrassed** because the man at passport control thinks that he's lying to him. He's **worried** …

→ S17

c) *Role play: Act out the scene between Rafiq and the man at passport control.*

LANGUAGE

8 Find the rule: Indirect questions → G14

a) *Look at the following sentences. What do you need to make indirect questions? Write down the rules for questions with and without question words.*

"What's the purpose of your visit?" → The man **asked me what** the purpose of my visit **was**.
"Are you travelling with your parents?" → He **asked me if** I **was travelling** with my parents.

b) *Find more examples of indirect questions in the text on p. 97. Write them down in your grid from Station 1, Ex. 2, and add the direct questions that go with them.*

LANGUAGE

9 Rafiq's questions → WB 72/13

→ △ 139/7
→ ▲ 140/8

Before the trip to Bangladesh, Rafiq had a lot of questions for his parents. Turn them into ***indirect questions****.*

Start like this: Rafiq asked his parents if they …

1. "Did you give Aunt Sadia my flight details?"
2. "Do I need a large suitcase for the trip?"
3. "Does the flight take long?"
4. "Don't you want to come too?"
5. "What can I bring them as a present?"
6. "Where will I meet them at the airport?"
7. "Where have you put my passport?"
8. "Why do I have to go at all?"

LANGUAGE

10 Getting around in Dhaka and London → WB 73/14 → G15

→ △ 140/9
→ ▲ 140/10

a) *Find the sentences that report these commands and requests in the text on p. 97. Write them down in your grid. What do you need to make indirect commands and requests?*

1. Man at passport control: Don't lie to me!
2. Man at passport control: Go into this side room to answer some more questions.
3. Airport security people: Please come to the immigration office in the arrivals hall.

b) *Rafiq is talking to Masud, his cousin from Dhaka, the capital of Bangladesh. What do they tell each other to do? Use* ***indirect commands and requests****.*

Start like this: Masud tells Rafiq to visit …

Masud: You must visit the old centre of Dhaka. It's quite small, but it's very interesting.
Rafiq: OK, I will. What's the best way to get there?
Masud: Walk. The traffic here is *very* slow. It's usually quicker to walk.
Rafiq: But it's so hot! I don't want to walk.
Masud: Then take a taxi. They're very cheap, but only if you agree on the price first.
Rafiq: OK, I'll remember that. When you go to London next month, use buses or the Tube. They're *much* cheaper than taxis.
Masud: Thanks for telling me. Send me a transport map when you are back in London. I want to study it before I travel.
Rafiq: You can download one from the internet. Just search for 'Transport for London'. Their website has all the information you need.
Masud: Yes, OK. I'll do that.

LANGUAGE **11**

A travel joke → WB 73/15

a) *Read what happened to Jenny, a young business traveller, while she was waiting for her flight to Seattle.*

In the departure lounge, Jenny sat down next to an old man who was looking very nervous.

"Sorry to bother you," he said. "Could I ask your advice about something?"

Jenny took off her headphones. "I'm sorry," she said. "Could you repeat that?"

"I'm going to meet my daughter in Seattle," the old man told her. "I'm worried about the flight because air travel always makes my ears hurt. Can you suggest anything to help?"

"Don't worry. Use chewing gum during take-off and landing. It always helps me."

Seven hours later, the plane landed in Seattle. When Jenny was waiting for her luggage, she saw the old man.

"How was your flight? Did my advice help?"

"Sorry, I didn't catch that," he said.

Jenny repeated her question.

"The chewing gum worked very well, thank you," replied the old man, "but … can you tell me how to get it out of my ears?"

b) *At the airport in Seattle, Jenny tells a friend what happened between her and the old man. Write down what she says.*

c) *Make a grid with the following headings:* ***asking for information*****,** ***asking for advice*****,** ***asking for clarification / repetition*** *and* ***apologising****. Find examples for these categories in the text. Can you think of more examples? Write them down in the grid.*

MEDIATION **12**

Airport announcements → WB 74/16

L3/15

→ S18, 19–21

a) *After a holiday in Great Britain, you're waiting with your family at London Heathrow for your flight back to Berlin. You're taking British Airways flight BA 0982 at 9:15. While you're waiting, you hear several announcements. First read the skills box. Then listen to the announcements. Which of them are important for you? Take notes. The key words in the box can help you.*

b) *Your parents were busy when the announcements were made. Report the most important points to them in German.*

Mediation skills

Announcements at airports or train stations often contain new words, and background sounds make them difficult to understand. It can help you to focus on important words, e.g. names of people or places, numbers or times, nouns and verbs as key words.

flight number | boarding time | gate | delay / why? | luggage

SPEAKING **13**

Your turn: Travel plans → WB 74/17–18

→ 141/11

Choose a foreign capital you'd like to visit. Use websites in English to find out how to get there by plane. Which airport will you use? How long will the flight take? What would you like to do there? Take turns to tell each other about your plans. Then report to the class what your partner told you.

How to tell a travel story

1 Listening: One travel story – two versions

L 3/17–18 → S19–21

a) *Listen to a young man's travel story and say if you find it interesting or not. Give reasons for your opinion.*

b) *Listen to another version of the same travel story. Compare the two versions.*

c) *Note down which phrases from the box you can hear in the story.*

Useful phrases

Did I tell you about …? | As I've already told you, … | … and then I realised / remembered that … | The next thing I knew … | A few seconds later … | The weirdest / funniest / scariest thing happened to me the other day. | After a while … | Anyway, it turned out that … | In the end, I decided to …

2 What makes a good travel story? → WB 75/19

→ S7

a) *Talk about what makes a travel story a* ***good*** *travel story. List your points. The ideas on the skills page in Unit 2 (p. 46) can help you.*

b) *Read this travel story. Find examples of the points you listed in a).*

The weirdest thing happened to me last year. I was on holiday in Italy. We visited a really nice little hill town, and then we decided to have a picnic. We walked out of the town into a small forest. It seemed like the perfect place to stop for a picnic. The next thing I knew, I started to have a really strange feeling. There was something about the place I just didn't like, and I *really* wanted to leave. I told my parents. At first they thought I was joking, but after a while they realised I was serious. I think they were disappointed I didn't want to stay, but they're cool (well, when it isn't about the music I like!) and they agreed. We left the forest area and found another place to have a picnic. Anyway, a few days later, I looked up the town on the internet. I found that a lot of people had died there in a war in the 16th century. Some soldiers had killed almost all the people in the town – women, children, old men. And guess where it had happened? In that forest! I don't believe in ghosts, but something weird definitely happened to me while I was there!

3 Write a travel story

→ S11–14

a) *This travel story is very short and it wouldn't be very interesting to listen to. Rewrite it as you'd tell it to a friend. Use the phrases from Ex. 1 and your ideas from Ex. 2 for help.*

I was on holiday in Egypt. I made a mistake when I ate with my left hand. My brother and I met some Egyptian guys about our age in a café. They invited us to play dominoes with them. Then they ordered some food to share with us. My brother and I started eating with our left hands. Then we realised that was a mistake. In Egypt and other Arab countries you should only eat with your right hand because people think the left hand isn't clean.

b) *Take turns to tell your travel story and give each other feedback.*

True or not true?

You're going to have a storytelling competition in two teams! Your task is to think of travel stories which you must present to the other team. The other team then has to guess if your team's stories are true or not.

Step 1

Plan your travel story → WB 76/21

Divide your class up into two teams. In each team there are five groups of 2–3 students. Each group thinks of two travel stories – one true and one not. In your groups, first collect ideas for your travel stories. These questions can help you:

- Where did you go?
- Why did you go there?
- What happened?
- What was funny / scary / embarrassing about it?

If your story isn't true, try to make it sound as convincing as possible. If it's true, it's important to make the other team believe that you've invented it. So be creative!

Step 2

Write a prompt card → WB 76/22

Write a prompt card for each travel story. Remember not to write whole sentences, but just key words with the most important points. Don't forget to include useful phrases that will make your story more interesting or exciting. → indirect speech (pp. 94–96, pp. 97–99) → How to tell a travel story (p. 100)

Step 3

Practise telling your stories → WB 77/23

Decide who will present your group's travel stories to the other team. Then practise your presentation. The other group member(s) should make suggestions about how you could improve each story. → How to tell a travel story (p. 100)

Step 4

Start your competition

Get into the two teams and take turns to tell the different groups' stories. When the other team guesses correctly, they get a point. The team with the most points wins.

Step 5

Give your feedback → WB 77/24

After the competition, think of the travel stories you've heard. What did you find good / not so good about them? Explain why.

S 2/21–24
L 3/19–22

Where I belong

SPEAKING

1 Before you read

With your partner, talk about reasons why people might want to leave their country.

A My father grabbed my arms and looked down at me. "Listen," he said. "You can't do anything here. It's getting harder and harder for people like us who travel around with our animals. Soon we'll have nothing left. If you go to England, you'll be able to help the whole family. And maybe, one day, you can come back and help Somalia too."

A week ago, I'd been nothing but a girl who would lead the same kind of life as her mother. I thought I would have a husband one day, and children to look after and teach. But now, suddenly, I was responsible for my whole family – and the future of my country too.

For a moment I was too scared to answer my father. But I knew he wouldn't change his mind. He had chosen me for this task and I had to accept it. "Yes," I said. "Yes, I will."

There was no time for anything else. My father jumped back into his car, turned round quickly and drove off, his face like a mask. I walked down the road to join the man who was taking me away.

Stop and think:
What do you think the narrator's journey will be like?

B The smuggler first took me to Kenya in a boat. Those journeys are very dangerous because the boats are always overloaded and the sea is full of sharks. Many people have died while they were trying to do what I was doing. But I didn't know that until much later. While we were at sea, I had other things to worry about.

It was a little boat, and I was crushed between men I had never seen before. It was the first time I had ever been in a boat, and Uncle didn't tell me that it would rock so badly as the waves smashed against it. I was scared, and I thought every moment that I was going to be sick.

I closed my eyes and repeated the things that Uncle had told me to learn.

My name is Khadija Ahmed Mussa. I'm thirteen years old. I'm going to England to join my mother and my brother and sisters. My sisters' names are Fowsia, Maryan and Sabra. Fowsia is eleven, Maryan is seven and Sabra is four. And my brother Abdi is fourteen.

I didn't try to imagine their faces or what they were like. They weren't people at all, just words that I had to learn. *My name is Khadija …*

Those hours in the boat were the worst hours of my life. I survived by closing myself away from what was happening, and when we landed in Kenya, I felt like a different person.

C What happened to me is called piggyback. Uncle was giving me a 'piggyback' to England. That was his business, and he did exactly what my father had paid for. Nothing else.

After we had left the boat, we travelled by road and then by plane, and every time we went through a checkpoint Uncle smiled at me. That was part of his routine. When we were through, the smile was put away together with my passport and he ignored me again, even when we were sitting next to each other.

I could have run away when we changed planes in Dubai. He showed me a seat in the airport and told me to sit there until he came back. But where would I have run to? I didn't know anything about that place and I had no passport except the one in Uncle's pocket. My father had paid for me to go to England and that was where I had to go.

I felt cold in the air-conditioning, and I concentrated on repeating the same words inside my head. *My name is Khadija …*

Stop and think:

How do you think Britain will be different for the narrator?

D When we landed in England, the sky was grey, and it was raining. Not clean, heavy rain, like the *gu*, but a steady, depressing drizzle. I didn't see how it was going to make anything grow because everywhere I looked the ground was covered with concrete. I felt hard and cold, like that concrete ground. If I hadn't, maybe everything would have happened differently and the officials would have sent me home. But they didn't. They looked at my face and then at my passport and let me into the country.

On the train, there were people from all over the world – they were all taking care not to look at each other. Was the whole city like that? Thousands of people who were all pretending that nobody else was there?

We travelled through streets of tall, yellow-grey buildings, and all the time the useless rain went on falling. When I looked up at the sky, I couldn't see any sign of the sun. Was it always invisible here?

I thought Uncle would take me to my new family's house. But when we got off the train, he took some coins out of his pocket and gave them to me. "Can you use a telephone?" he said.

I looked at him. "Of course I can!"

"You see the phone there?" He pointed down the road. "Call the number I give you. Then stay in the phone box. The person who answers the phone will come and fetch you."

I was too surprised to do anything except stare at him. "Don't waste time," he said. "People will notice you. Go!" The piggyback was over and suddenly I was on my own, walking down this strange road.

The phone was different from the phones I had used before, but it was easy to see how to use it. I pressed the buttons very carefully: I had no more money to put in if I made a mistake the first time.

"Hello," said a boy's voice. He spoke Somali, but his accent was very strange. "Are you in the phone box?"

"Yes," I said. "But I don't know where –"

"Just wait," he said. "I'm coming."

I knew it was him as soon as he came round the corner. A tall Somali boy who came straight towards me. He opened the door and stared at me.

"I'm Abdi," he said. When I hesitated, he said his full name this time. "I'm Abdirahman Ahmed Mussa."

He was much older than my brother Mahmoud, and tall too, but he was – more of a boy. That was when I really understood how far I had travelled. I was far away from Somalia, and far from myself, in a place where the people were going to be different. And I had to learn how to live there.

I stared straight back at Abdi. "And I'm Khadija Ahmed Mussa," I said.

From: *Where I belong* by Gillian Cross

SPEAKING

2 Your reaction

a) *Do you like the story? Explain why or why not.*

b) *Have you heard or read about people who try to come to Europe as refugees? How are these stories similar to the narrator's experience? The ideas from the introduction pages can help you.*

READING

3 Understanding the story → WB 78/25–26

→ S5–7

a) *Explain why the narrator must leave her country.*

b) *Look at the map on p. 102 and the text again. How does the narrator get from Somalia to England? Copy the grid and fill in the first line.*

	Part A	Part B	Part C	Part D
How?	by boat, overloaded			
Feelings?	I was scared … (l. 35)			

c) *How does the narrator feel during her journey? Find lines in the text that tell you about her feelings. Add them to your grid from b).*

d) *Imagine you'd have to go on a journey like the narrator in the story. What would be the scariest part for you? Share your ideas with a partner.*

READING

4 Reading between the lines

→ △ 141/12

First read the skills box. Then find information in the text that answers these questions.

1. What's the situation of the narrator's family?
2. What do you think the relationship is between the narrator and her father?
3. What kind of person is Uncle, the smuggler who takes the narrator to England?

Reading skills

Sometimes important information is not mentioned directly in a text. You need to **read between the lines** to get ideas about the characters and their relationships.

Example: When the narrator's father drives away, his face is like a mask. (l. 21) That might tell us that he tries to hide his feelings.

WRITING

5 More thoughts about the story → WB 78/27

a) *After she was picked up by Abdi at the phone box, the narrator meets her 'new' family. What do you think will happen? What might be new for the narrator compared with her old life? Make notes. The ideas in the box can help you.*

Word bank

different culture | new gadgets | modern house | different climate | no friends | be homesick | go to school | new rules

b) *Get into groups of 3–4. Together write a plan of how you think the story might continue. Present your ideas to the class.*

The guitar lesson → S22–24

SPEAKING

1 Warm-up

What do you think of when you hear the words "I go wherever the wind takes me"?

VIEWING

2 Ciara and Hayley → WB 79/28

7

a) *Watch the film and collect information about Ciara and Hayley. Think of the topics below. Then compare the two women.*

future plans / dreams

origin | work

travel destinations (past and future)

b) *What do you think of Ciara and Hayley? Would you like to meet them? Say why / why not.*

Word bank

friendly | outgoing | interesting | nice | boring | cool | sad | easy-going | strange | silly | rude | funny | happy | quiet | clever | crazy | odd

VIEWING

3 Film genres

a) *Read the skills box. What elements match the film 'The guitar lesson'?*

b) *Make a list with the genres from the box and add two films you've already seen (or heard of) for each genre.*

Film skills

There are many different **kinds of films**, or 'film genres'. Films from one genre usually have similar **main elements**. Here are some examples:

Science fiction: inventions in science / technology; often set in the future; time travel; aliens; unreal atmosphere

Romance: relationship between two characters; love; adventure; happy ending

Historical: set in specific historical era; often about real historical person / event; often lavish costumes / props

Fantasy: story about magic or supernatural forces; set in mythical time; often tells the story of a hero / heroine

WRITING

4 A film poster

Design a film poster for your favourite film from Ex. 3b).

Text smart 4
Drama

Find more online: 2b59em

What does it feel like to be an actor on stage? What is special about plays?
In Text smart 4 you're going to get to know different scenes from one play. Have fun!

LISTENING

1 Warm-up: Thinking about the theatre

a) *Is there a drama group at your school / in your town? Tell the class about plays or shows you've seen.*

L 3/23 → S19–21

b) *Listen to three friends (Laura, Jack and Simon) as they talk about plays.*

1. What do the friends like about plays?
2. What do they find difficult?
3. What do you think about their comments?

VOCABULARY

2 Theatre collocations

→ 142/1 → S3

a) *Match the verbs with the nouns to make useful collocations about the theatre.*

entertain | stage | act in | learn | forget | follow | use | get into | play | wear | stay | mess up | give | go to | identify with

a great performance | a role | stage directions | the director's instructions | character | props | your lines | in character | the audience | a costume | a scene | the theatre | the protagonist | a part | a play

b) *Now start a glossary of theatre terms with 2–3 entries. You can add on to your glossary over the next pages. Try to use your collocations.*

Example: **in character:** When an actor is 'in character', it means that he / she is acting and thinking like the character. It's important to stay in character too.

SPEAKING

3 Warm-up: Getting into character → WB 81/1

As a warm-up for some of the activities on the next pages, look at the photo and think about what the characters could say. Then say / shout / whisper / … the lines out loud. Be creative and play with your voice!

Example:
A: You look so silly!
B: Well, have *you* looked in the mirror today?

A British production of *The Wind in the Willows*

Claire's Devil by Dave Draper

You're going to read different scenes from a play about a teenage girl and a dilemma she's facing.

The characters are:

- Claire, the story's protagonist
- Rob, a friend
- Claire's mum
- Claire's dad
- Claire's devil
- Claire's angel

READING **4**

Scene 1: Rob and Claire

→ WB 81/2

S 2/25 L 3/24

→ S7

Before you read: Talk about what role you think 'Claire's devil' could be. And what about 'Claire's angel'? Then read the scene.

(Rob and Claire are walking home from school.)

Rob: Listen, there's a party in West Street tomorrow night. It'll be fantastic: Do you fancy coming with us?

Claire: In West Street? Isn't that on the other side of town? It's a pretty rough area, isn't it?

Rob: We'll be okay! The station is only a few minutes away. Nearly everyone we know will be there. What do you say?

Claire: I'll phone you tonight. At about six, OK?

Rob: If you're worried about what your parents will say, then there's a simple solution – don't tell them. Say you're staying over at my house with my sister. My mum will cover up for us – she does what I tell her!

Claire: I'll phone you.

(Rob goes off. Claire is alone with her conscience.)

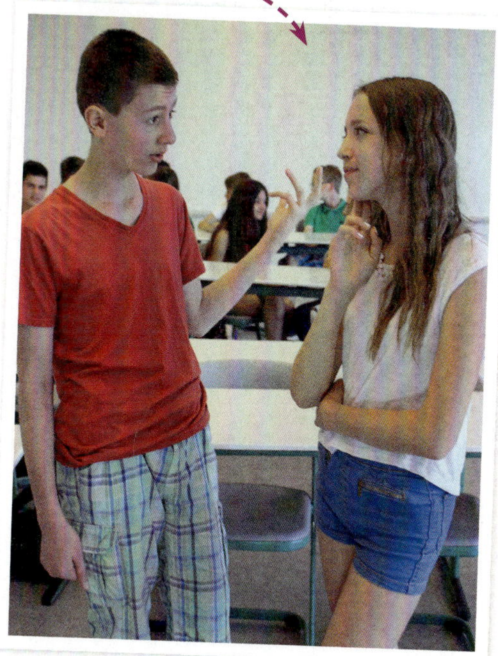

READING **5**

The main characters

a) *In your own words, sum up what happens in this first scene.*

→ △ 142/2

b) *What can you say about Rob and Claire's motivations and feelings?*

Example:
On the one hand, Claire wants to …, but on the other hand, she …

Useful phrases

- Rob tries to convince her …
- The dilemma starts when …
- Claire seems / feels confused / unsure / convinced …
- Claire has doubts about …
- I think Claire feels tempted …
- Rob tempts Claire when he …

READING

S 2/26–27
L 3/25–26

6 Scene 2: The angel and the devil → WB 81/3

a) *In Scene 2, Claire's 'angel' and 'devil' speak for the first time. Before you read the scene, read the skills box.*

b) *Now read how the angel and the devil try to tell Claire what to do.*

Drama skills

Most stories feature characters in **typical roles.** There might be a hero / heroine on the one side and a villain on the other ('good guy' / 'bad guy'). These characters have good or bad motives. What characters from plays / films / books do you know in typical 'good' or 'bad' roles?

Devil:

The trouble with you is that you never take risks. You always worry about what your parents tell you. What's the matter with you? Just have a little fun!

How boring can you get?! Do you want to lose *all* your friends? They'll all be there, and you'll be at home in front of the TV, like a good little girl.

Let's face it – you're scared! You always back down from things.

All kids lie to their parents. And it would only be a small lie, a white lie. Say you're going to stay with Rob's sister; that's partly true: You can sleep at their house after the party.

Angel:

What if something bad happened? What if there's a fight? And you're not old enough to go. They'll see that you're not old enough; you'll end up embarrassed and miserable in front of Rob. Tell him you're sorry but you can't go.

Rob is exaggerating as usual. Most of your school friends won't be allowed to go because their parents are as sensible as yours.

It wouldn't be right to lie to your parents. You know they love you, and only want what's best for you. If they found out you had lied they'd never trust you again.

READING

7 Understanding Scene 2

→ S5–6

a) *What makes the devil and angel 'typical roles'? Read what these three students say about it. Say why you agree or disagree. (You can also look back at the skills box on p. 108.)*

Example:
A: That's easy! The devil is mean. He's a bad guy.
B: I agree that he's a typical bad guy, but I don't agree that a bad guy is always mean. This devil is pushy, but not mean. But what about the angel?
C: The angel sounds so scared. Is that typical for an angel? Maybe it is …

b) *Sum up the arguments of the devil and angel. Say which arguments you find the most convincing, and why.*

Example:
The devil says, "Just have a little fun!" Well, I think he's right.
How can you beat *that* argument?

c) *How would you decide if you were Claire?*

SPEAKING

8 White lies

→ △ 142/3

a) *Go back to Scene 2 and read the devil's suggestion for a 'white lie' in lines 11–14. Explain what a white lie is, and if there's a difference between a white lie and a normal one.*

b) *Your turn: Have you ever told a white lie? What was it, and why did you tell it? Tell a partner.*

SPEAKING

9 Getting into character: Reading a scene out loud → WB 82/4

→ S15–17

a) *Think – pair – share: Read the skills box. Then look at the words below the box. Which ones describe how a 'devil' voice or an 'angel' voice should sound? Which words match* ***both*** *voices? Write down your ideas and exchange them with your partner. Then tell the class what you've both agreed on.*

Drama skills

When you read the lines of a play, think about how they'll sound on stage. **Play with your voice** so you can get into character.
A voice on stage can be many things: angry, happy, loud, quiet, …

helpful | sweet | nice | quiet | fearful | loud | tempting | angry | scary | fast | pushy | friendly

b) *Warm-up: Take turns with your partner to read lines 1–14 in a devil voice and lines 15–26 in an angel voice.*

c) *Reading in chorus: Half your class reads the devil's lines out loud together, the other half reads the angel's lines together. Think about which key lines need more 'angel' or 'devil' feeling than the others.*

→ △ 142/4

d) *In groups of four, practise* ***the whole scene****.*
The angel and devil use their voices, but Claire never speaks: She only uses her face and gestures to show her dilemma. And one of you is the director; you give the others feedback. Then swap roles and find out which part each of you can read best. When you're ready, read your version of the scene to the class.

READING **10**

S 2/29–31
L 3/28–30

Scene 3: Claire and her parents

Before you read: In the next scene, Claire makes her decision. How do you think she'll decide: Has she listened to her angel or her devil? Explain why you think so.

(Later at Claire's house. Claire is talking to her mum and dad.)

Claire: Mum, is it okay if I stay over at Jenny's house on Saturday night?

Mum: I didn't know you two were friendly.

Claire: Well, I like her a lot.

Mum: I hope you're not getting involved with that brother of hers. Rob isn't the sort of boy you should be mixing with.

Claire: Rob isn't as bad as people think.

Mum: From what I've heard, he's heading for trouble. So be warned!

Claire: Rob has his own circle of friends – we hardly ever speak to each other. Is it okay then, Mum?

Mum: All right. But check with your dad first.

(Claire's mother goes out. Claire is alone with her conscience.)

Angel: See! So many lies already. She'll be terribly hurt if she finds out you've been so dishonest. She trusts you, Claire!

Devil: She'll sleep easy and you can have a great time. Now, you need a good story to convince your dad.

(Later, Claire is with her dad.)

Claire: Dad, Mum says it's okay for me to stay at Jenny Costello's on Saturday, as long as you agree too.

Dad: As long as her parents don't mind, then, that's fine! Have I met her?

Claire: No, she's new in my class. We're working on a design project and I need money for materials.

Dad: What sort of design work is it?

Claire: Er … it's a dress design project. Could I have £25?

Dad: That's a lot! What's this dress going to be made out of? Silk?

Claire: Of course not. But we'd like to do really well on the project so we're buying a couple of books to help us.

Dad: Well, I don't mind paying out if it's to help with schoolwork. Here you are.

(He gives Claire £25 and leaves.)

READING

11 Understanding Scene 3

a) *Compare your answer from Ex. 10 with Claire's decision. Explain why Claire makes this decision.*

b) *Now answer these questions:*

1. Are Claire's parents worried about her? If yes, what do they say to express it?

   Example: Well, when the mother says, "I didn't know you two were friendly," that shows that she is surprised and unsure about who her daughter's friends are.

2. What lies does Claire tell in Scene 3?

c) *Discuss with your partner why you think Claire's decision was right or wrong.*

SPEAKING

12 Acting out Scene 3 → WB 82/5–6

In Ex. 9, you had the chance to practise 'getting into character' with different roles, and how it feels to read them out loud. Here, you'll take a step further: It's your turn to act out a whole scene.

→ △ 143/5
→ S15–17

a) *First, read the skills box. Then read out and **act** out Scene 3. Focus on your voice, your face and your gestures. (Decide if the five roles are enough, or if you need a director again too.)*

b) *Do you think it helps to understand the characters more when you act out a scene like this?*

Example:
A: When I was playing the angel, I almost felt like I needed to help Claire. I think I was 'in character' as an angel, as someone who helps.
B: Yeah, when I played Claire, I really had to fake an 'extra friendly' face when I was lying to my parents. I felt a bit fake myself!

Drama skills

Think about these ideas before you act out a scene:

- Decide **who is going to play which role**.
- First **read out your role**, but look up from the page again and again to learn your part, bit by bit.
- Try out **different voices**.
- **Get into character**: Sometimes it helps to think of a person you know who is similar to the person you're playing.
- On stage, your **face** and **gestures** are almost as important as your lines. Make sure your face matches your lines, and make sure that you sit, stand or move in the right way too.

READING **13** S 2/32 L 3/31

Scene 4: Farewell

Before you read: Look at these lines from the next scene. Which characters from the play do you think will say each line? Explain why.

You've got to make the most of your youth while you still have it!

You'll have to live with that on your conscience.

You've been dishonest.

One lie nearly always leads to another.

Stop preaching!

Devil: Easy, wasn't it? Now everyone's happy: Your parents think you're a really keen student and that they're supporting you. What could be better?

Angel: But you've been dishonest and you'll have to live with that on your conscience. Once you start being dishonest it is hard to stop. One lie nearly always leads to another.

Devil: It's their own fault. If they were a bit more tolerant and easy-going then there'd be no need to lie to them.

Angel: Wouldn't you feel safer if your parents knew where you were and what time to expect you?

Devil: Safer? Where's the danger? A lively night out with a group of friends: Sounds safe enough to me. You've got to make the most of your youth while you still have it! Enjoy yourself while you've got the chance.

Claire: Yes! It's time I started living.

(On Saturday evening at Claire's house, with her dad and mum.)

Claire: Bye, then. I'll see you tomorrow lunchtime.

Mum: Have a good time. Why not bring Jenny round here next weekend? It would be nice to meet your new friend. Perhaps I should ring Jenny's mother later this evening. Just to check it's still okay for you to stop the night. It'll give me the chance to thank her.

Claire: There's no need. Anyway, you can't. Their phone is out of order.

Mum: But I thought Jenny rang you a little while ago. You did say it was Jenny, didn't you?

Claire: Er … Yes, it was. She had to ring from somewhere else. Bye, now.

Angel: See? What did I tell you? Lies lead to more lies. It never stops.

Devil: Stop preaching! It was an excellent piece of quick thinking. Well done, Claire! Now for a night out on the town! Let's go!

READING

14 Understanding Scene 4

a) *Were you right about who said the different key lines in Ex. 13? Were there any surprises at all? Tell the class.*

b) *Explain Claire's sentence "It's time I started living". Why is it a key line in the play?*

→ △ 143/6

c) *Imagine you're acting the play for your school's Drama Club and you're practising the scene when Claire leaves the house for her night out ("Bye, now", line 40). In groups of six, show the **freeze frame** of **Claire**, **her parents** – and her **angel** and **devil** too! One of you is the **director**: He / She takes a photo and makes sure you're all in character. Before you do your freeze frame, make a grid with important words to help you to get into character for this scene. The word bank can help you. (Some words fit more than one role.)*

Word bank

shocked | happy | confused | fearful | guilty | angry | fantastic | worried

Claire	Mum	Dad	Devil	Angel
…	confused …	…	…	fearful …

LISTENING

15 A happy ending? → WB 83/7

a) *Now think about the whole story. For each of the four scenes, write a short summary of 2–3 lines.*

b) *With a partner, think about an ending for the play: a happy / sad / surprising / strange ending? Then present your ideas to the class.*

L 3/32

c) *Listen to the original ending of the play* Claire's Devil. *What happens?*

d) *Now that you know the whole story, do you feel the story has a message? If yes, a message for whom? Write about it in 5–6 lines.*

16 Options: Bring the story to life → WB 83/8

Choose one of these options and bring Claire's Devil *to life!*

→ △ 143/7

Option A: Stage the play

You've practised reading and acting different roles and one scene. Now you can stage the whole play. Look back at the tips on these pages for help, and you'll find helpful tips in your Workbook too. Think about:

- casting
- costumes and props
- where to stage your play
- learning your lines by heart
- playing with your voice

Option B: Write a photo story

In different groups, take photos of the key parts of each scene with yourselves as the actors. Your 'freeze frame' skills can help you. When you have the photos you need, do the following:

- Write speech bubbles for the characters.
- Write short texts to explain more background information from the plot / action that isn't in the bubbles.

Legende

Diese Symbole und Erklärungen zeigen dir, wie du mit den Hilfen, Aufgaben und Aktivitäten auf den *Diff pool*-Seiten arbeiten kannst.

△ Hilfe zur Unit-Aufgabe | oder eine leichtere Variante der Unit-Aufgabe | oder eine zusätzliche Aufgabe

▲ eine zusätzliche Herausforderung

Unit 1

△ 1 Your turn: Your kind of 'smart' → Help with Introduction, p. 9/3

Read what Julie says. Maybe some of her words can help you when you talk to your partner.

I think I'm body smart because I'm very good at sports. I like running, cycling and playing volleyball. And I never have problems when I learn new sports. Also, I'm self smart: I know what I'm good at, and I often think about what I want to do *before* I start something. When you are self smart you often learn from your mistakes. That's what I do too.

△ 2 Maybe in the next show ... → After Station 1, p. 11/3

Find the right verb forms. In most of the sentences you have ***conditional clauses type 1****.*

Right now, Jay **1** (be) sad because he **2** (not get) the lead part in the show. If he **3** (practise) hard enough, maybe he **4** (get) the lead part in the next show. But if his parents **5** (make sure) that he works harder for school, he **6** (not have) enough time to practise. "Don't be upset," Shahid tells Jay. "If you **7** (not get) good marks, you **8** (not find) a job later." "That's easy for you to say," Jay answers. "But if I **9** (work) hard *and* **10** (practise), I **11** (not have) time for my friends!"

▲ 3 Go on with the story → After Station 1, p. 11/3

Play a game in class: One student starts with an if-sentence. The next student uses the main clause as an if-clause and makes a new sentence, and so on.

Example: If I go on holiday, I'll take my dog. → If I take my dog, he'll be happy. → If my dog is happy, he'll ... → ...

△ 4 Another chat comment for Jay → After Station 1, p. 12/4a)

Read this advice for Jay. Put the verbs in the right form.

mr_know_it_all_14 September 5, 19:27

If I **1** (be) you, I **2** (not worry) about dancing[1] and singing[2].
I **3** (worry) about SCHOOL! I mean, if your brother **4** (be) smarter, he **5** (not earn) his money as a model – what kind of a career is THAT?! No magazine **6** (put) his photo on the cover if he **7** (not look) good and young, but you can't stay young FOREVER. If I **8** (be) your father, I **9** (make sure) that you worked harder. And I **10** (stop) paying for your dancing lessons!

▲ 5 What would an adult say? → After Station 1, p. 12/4a)

Read the chat room comments on p. 12 again. How do you think advice from an adult would be different? Write comments from the point of view of an adult, e.g. a sports star, a famous singer, a teacher, an uncle / aunt. Use ***conditional clauses type 2****.*

△ 6 Your friends need you! → Help with Station 1, p. 12/4b)

Here are some problems to start with, and some ideas for advice. Use ***conditional clauses type 2****.*

Start like this: If I **were** you, I **would / wouldn't** …

My friend always wants to copy my homework!	My parents don't let me go out with my friends!	Everyone has a smartphone – but not me! It isn't fair.
tell him / her to do it himself / herself | ask to copy his / her homework next time | look for new friends	promise to take your phone and not turn it off | try to find a compromise | explain that friends are important	explain that smartphones are important to stay in touch | do jobs at home for extra money | babysit for friends

△ 7 Ivy's model → After Station 1, p. 12/5

Read what one of Ivy's models tells a fashion magazine. Complete his sentences with ***conditional clauses type 2****.*

"If I **1** (not love) fashion so much, I **2** (not be) a model. I'm lucky that there aren't so many boys and young men in the modelling business. I **3** (find) it a lot harder to get a job if I **4** (be) a girl! It's also great that I can choose who I work for. If I **5** (not like) Ivy's clothes, I **6** (not work) for her. We all love Ivy. If we **7** (not be) such a great team, we **8** (have) less success, I'm sure!"

1 dancing ['dɑːnsɪŋ] Tanzen | **2 singing** [sɪŋɪŋ] Singen

▲ 8 What would you do if … → After Station 1, p. 12/5

What could happen to you and your classmates? Think of a situation.

Examples: you forgot about the Maths test | you miss the bus after school | your dad / mum cooks the worst dinner ever | you see a famous person

Write down your situation on a piece of paper. Take turns to show each other what you wrote. Ask the others what they would do in this situation. Find at least three different ideas for each situation. Use ***conditional clauses type 2****.*

▲ 9 The outfit → After Station 1, p. 12/5

Complete the dialogue with the correct verb forms for ***conditional clauses type 1 or 2****. Then practise the dialogue with your partner.*

Lisa: Listen, if I go to the audition, I **1** (have to) find a really cool outfit.
Dylan: But you look good in everything. Even if you **2** (wear) really ugly[1] clothes, you'd look great.
Lisa: Well, thanks, but I won't wear ugly clothes. If you were in my shoes, what **3** (you choose)?
Dylan: It's your first audition, so if I **4** (be) you, I'd wear something comfortable[2].
Lisa: Oh, but everyone will do that, so if all of us wear jeans, I **5** (feel) stupid. I need something better!
Dylan: OK, but even if you have a really original outfit, it doesn't mean you **6** (win) the audition.
Lisa: Great help, thanks. I **7** (not go) to the audition if I can't find anything to wear.
Dylan: Hmmm. Skirt, overall, dress, leggings and trainers … If I say something that[3] you like, you **8** (tell) me, right? Can I stop?
Lisa: Leggings and trainers … I like that one. Here's my idea: If I **9** (wear) leggings and trainers, I'll feel more comfortable. And if I feel more comfortable, I **10** (perform[4]) better, right?
Dylan: Aarrgghh! You do this every time. If you just listened to me sooner, we **11** (save) a lot of time!

△ 10 A German talent show → Help with Station 1, p. 13/6

Look at this list of things to do and ***not*** *to do at an audition.*
The words can help you with your message.

✔
- *prepare well*
- *practise a lot*
- *make sure you look great*
- *make a good impression*[5]

✘
- *choose a popular song*
- *come without an adult*
- *do embarrassing things on stage*[6]

1 ugly ['ʌgli] hässlich | **2 comfortable** ['kʌmftəbl] bequem | **3 something that** [ˌsʌmθɪŋ 'ðæt] etwas, das | **4 to perform** [pə'fɔ:m] auftreten; aufführen | **5 impression** [ɪm'preʃn] Eindruck | **6 stage** [steɪdʒ] Bühne

▲ 11 More helpful tips for your English friend → After Station 1, p. 13/6

*Write some more helpful tips about what to do or **not** to do at an audition.*

△ 12 The Azads and the Frasers → Help with Station 2, p. 14/9a)

Copy the grid and complete it. Here are some ideas to help you:

Personality:	bossy | strong | serious | messy | clever | creative | is good at … | likes to get organised | likes to dream[1] (about the future) | likes to play … | likes to have fun
Opinions:	school is important | hobbies are good for you | find time to enjoy yourself | you must work hard and get good marks | no good job without good marks at school | you should teach yourself new things | you're too laid-back
Problems:	can't agree with parents | room is messy | gets bad marks | can't focus on important things | can only focus on important things like school

	Personality	Opinions	Problems
Olivia			
Claire			
…			

△ 13 If I were Olivia, I'd … → Help with Station 2, p. 14/9b)

You can use these phrases to talk about Olivia's reaction.

Useful phrases

She could also try to … | It would be a good idea if she … | It would be great for her if … | If that doesn't work, she can … | I'm sure her parents will … if …

△ 14 What Olivia told Holly → Help with Station 2, p. 15/10b)

*Use the words below to do Ex. 10b). Be careful: You need **four** of the words **twice**!*

him | yourself | her | me | you | ourselves | himself | herself

1 **to dream** [dri:m] träumen

△ 15 Help! I can't do it myself! → After Station 2, p. 15/10b)

Lucy is tidying up her room – but not alone. Complete the dialogue with the right forms.

Lucy: I'm going to tidy up my room. Can you help [1], Olivia?
Olivia: No, I can't. Do it [2], Lucy.
Claire: Why can't you help [3]?
Olivia: Why should I? When I was a little girl, I always had to tidy up my room [4].
Claire: Well, not exactly: I often helped [5], remember? I tidied up your wardrobe for [6]!
Olivia: Well, maybe you're right. But it wasn't very often, believe me! And …
Lucy: Can you two please stop fighting now and show [7] where I can put my old clothes? I've already tidied up my wardrobe [8]!

△ 16 *Themselves* or *each other*? → After Station 2, p. 15/11

Sometimes people do things ***themselves****, sometimes with* ***each other****. Read the situations A–D and decide if you need 'themselves' or 'each other'. The pictures can help you.*

A. There are lots of things that[1] very small children can't do [1] because they need their parents' help. These children are playing with [2]. That's easy!
B. Friends like to talk to [3]. But lonely people often talk to [4].
C. Some people like to take photos with no people in them. Other people like to take photos of [5].
D. Some people like the sound of their own voice. They like listening to [6].

A

B

C

D

1 **things that** [θɪŋz 'ðæt] Dinge, die

▲ 17 Each other? Themselves? There's a difference! → After Station 2, p. 15/11

a) *Complete these sentence pairs with **each other** and **themselves** so that they make sense[1].*

1. The children hurt themselves when … / The children hurt each other when …
2. Claire told the girls to look after themselves … / Claire told the girls to look at each other …
3. Some students teach themselves to … / Some students help each other to …

b) *Write more sentences like these and test your partner.*

△ 18 Questions and answers → Help with Station 3, p. 17/14

Here are some ideas for your questions and answers.

Activities:
watch a … / join a … win an important match / race play tennis / rugby / handball run for charity / run for fun have an accident / a serious injury finish first / last in a race enjoy a Sports lesson

When (simple past):
last year / week / month when I was smaller / a baby / younger yesterday in May / January / October / …
When (present perfect):
never / before / yet / ever

△ 19 Boys' day! → After Station 3, p. 17/15

Dave and Jay are on the phone. They're planning Dave's visit to Greenwich at the weekend. They want to have a picnic in the park with Luke, and then go to the match between Greenwich RFC and Sidcup RFC.

Complete their phone call with the right verb form in the simple past or present perfect. Sometimes you just need a short answer.

Dave: So what's the plan for Saturday, Jay? You **1** (tell) me yet!
Jay: Oh yes, I **2** ! Luke and I **3** (talk) about it yesterday in the Maths lesson and I **4** (send) you a text afterwards. I have tickets for the rugby match between Greenwich and Sidcup! My dad **5** (buy) them as a present for me and two friends!
Dave: Hey, you've got a cool dad. – So what *is* the plan?
Jay: Well, I **6** (think) it would be a good idea to have a picnic in the park first.
Dave: Cool. And what **7** (Luke say) when you **8** (tell) him?
Jay: He thinks it sounds great too. He **9** (already ask) his dad for help with the food.
Dave: Great, and I can buy drinks for us at the kiosk. My mum **10** (just give) me some extra pocket money because I **11** (do) well in the Maths test last week. By the way, **12** (you ask) the girls if they want to come, Jay?
Jay: The girls?! No, I **13** . It's a *boys'* day, remember? And they **14** (not ask) *us* to come to their sleepover party last weekend.
Dave: Well, who would *want* to be at their sleepover anyway?!

1 **to make sense** [meɪk 'sens] einen Sinn ergeben

▲ 20 A game: Who is it? → After Station 3, p. 17/15

1. *Choose a famous star, a person in the class or somebody else.* ***Everybody*** *should know the person!*
2. *On a card, write what that person has already / never done, or did at some time (five activities). But don't write his / her name!*
3. *Then collect and shuffle[1] all the cards.*
4. *Take turns to read out the information. The others must guess who it is.*

Example:
- started to play football when he was five
- has played for Schalke and Bayern
- has been a member of the German national football team since[2] 2009
- became the world's best goalkeeper[3] in January 2014
- won the World Cup in 2014

Answer: Manuel Neuer

△ 21 Act it out! → Help with Skills, p. 18/3

a) *Look at the words for feelings and match them with the photos, if possible. Then try to make the same face. Work with a partner. Can he / she guess which feeling you're acting?*

disappointed | angry | sad | not sure what to do | happy / excited | shocked[4]

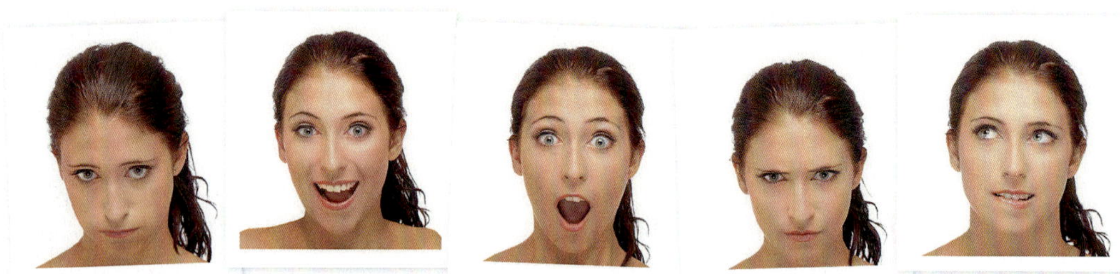

b) *Which words can you use in your dialogue on p. 18? Can you think of more?*

△ 22 What happens next: Ideas for the ending → Help with Story, p. 22/4

First choose an idea for the story's ending. Then follow the instructions.

1. Jay decides to get help from his friends. → Go to **A**!
2. Jay tells his parents. → Go to **B**!
3. Jay tells nobody – he helps himself. → Go to **C**!

A. Dave – can ask his new friends in Cornwall
OR Gwen – she's good with computers / she's clever and knows what to do

B. they tell Shahid
OR they're upset, but they promise to help

C. Jay finds help on the internet
OR Jay takes Shahid's laptop to an IT expert

Word bank

at first | then | suddenly | finally | feel awful / bad / sorry / scared / guilty[5] | be shocked / horrified | shout angrily / loudly | quickly need a lot of money / more information / a really good IT expert | explain / fix carefully | be thankful | relax

1 to shuffle [ʃʌfl] mischen | **2 since** [sɪns] seit | **3 goalkeeper** [ˈɡəʊlˌkiːpə] Torwart | **4 shocked** [ʃɒkt] geschockt | **5 guilty** [ˈɡɪlti] schuldig

Text smart 1

△ 1 Your turn: Poems and songs in your life → Help with Introduction, p. 28/2b)

Here are some ideas to help you with your own lines:

Verbs from the photo:
live | love | laugh | sing | dance | dream | play | give | smile

Example: Smile
Till someone smiles back

Ideas for extra lines:
Like you had pockets full of money | As if you had no limits | As if you couldn't lose | As if you were a star | Until you cry | Until someone laughs with you | As if this was your last day | As if you had nothing to lose | Like you've found the greatest person in the world | As if you had the stage[1] to yourself

△ 2 Your turn: What makes you happy? → Help with Station 1, p. 29/5c) + d)

The rhyme words in the word bank can help you to write your own poem. Then you can use the phrases to talk about your changes.

Word bank

sun / fun / run | child / wild | day / play / way | tree / free / sea | pool / cool / rule | cake / break / make / take | grow / go / slow | hour / flower / power

Useful phrases

I changed the poem because for me, happiness is when … | … makes me happy because … | I feel good when … | I think … is great / wonderful / really cool.

Example: Happy as a child / Looking at the sun / Happy as friends / When they're having fun

△ 3 Taking a second look → Instead of Station 1, p. 30/7a)

Read the lines from the poem and the simpler, more direct versions[2] of them. Which of the two versions do you like best?

Line 2:
It fell to earth, I knew not where
1. I never found it.
2. I couldn't see where it landed.

Lines 3–4:
For, so swiftly it flew, the sight
Could not follow it in its flight.
1. I couldn't follow the flight of the arrow with my eyes.
2. I couldn't see where the arrow was going to land.

Lines 7–8:
For who has sight so keen and strong,
That it can follow the flight of song?
1. Who has eyes good enough to see where a song goes?
2. Who has eyes to see how people react to a song?

Lines 11–12:
And the song, from beginning to end,
I found again in the heart of a friend.
1. For me, finding a good friend was like singing that song again.
2. My friend liked the same song and sang it for me.

1 **stage** [steɪdʒ] Bühne | 2 **version** ['vɜːʃn] Version; Fassung

△ 4 Trouble usually finds me … → After Station 2, p. 32/10d)

*First, match the situations below with the expressions in the box. Sometimes more than one expression can be right. Which one do you think is best? Then use the situations and expressions to write **if-clauses**.*

be stuck in the middle of the sea | be the light to guide your friend | need a shoulder to cry on | be there for your friends | know what you are made of | be lost in the dark | count on me

1. A bully at school is making trouble for a classmate. You want to stop this and help.
2. You're on the bus to meet a friend. You fall asleep and when you wake up, you're in a part of the city you don't know at all. The neighbourhood doesn't look very nice, it's early evening, and now you're scared.
3. You're really trying to do better at History, but when you get your test back, you see that you got a really bad mark. The worst mark in the class!
4. A friend is going to have a big party for his birthday and needs a lot of help.
5. You go to an audition for a singing competition, but the people there tell you that you have no talent at all: "You'll *never* be a singer!"
6. Your best friend would like to become a member of the school's Drama Club, like you, but he / she doesn't know anything about acting.

Example: If I help my classmate with that bully, the bully will know what I'm made of!

△ 5 Poem and song options → Help with Options, p. 33/12

Here are some ideas and tips to help you with the option you choose on p. 33:

Option A:

Word bank

We were very close friends / always played together / often met at the weekends / … | One day something terrible / bad / strange happened … | We were at school / at my friend's house / at a party when I decided to … / when suddenly my friend … | I didn't mean to / didn't want to, but my friend … | When he left, I felt terrible, but I tried to call him / went to his house / talked to his parents / …

Option B:

Useful phrases

I think the photo goes well with the song / poem / topic because … | The song / poem is about …, and the photo shows … | The song / poem matches the atmosphere in the photo because … | The music of the song is … | In the photo you can see … | I often listen to songs like this when I'm …

Option C:

Useful phrases

The lyrics are about … / are interesting because … | The lines are catchy / easy / difficult to understand / … | The music is happy / sad / slow / fast / makes you want to dance / to tap your feet / to sing along. | The main instrument[1] is … | The atmosphere is … because of the music / the lyrics / …

Option D:

Tip

Practise your poem in front of a mirror[2] / to a friend or family. Write difficult parts on a piece of paper and put it where you can often see it.
Try to match gestures with lines – this will help you remember more easily!

1 **instrument** ['ɪnstrəmənt] Instrument | 2 **mirror** ['mɪrə] Spiegel

Unit 2

△ 1 Typically German? → Help with Introduction, p. 37/3d)

The picture and phrases can help you to talk about typical ideas people have about Germany.

Start like this: People from other countries believe / think that most / many Germans …

Word bank

good / great at football | like beer | love fast / good / expensive cars | drive fast | work hard / a lot | wear lederhosen and dirndl | never late | make high quality products[1]

△ 2 Talking about Holly and Amber → Help with Station 1, p. 39/1

Complete these mind maps on Holly and Amber. Then use them to talk about the two girls.

doesn't want to do what Amber says

worried about the trip

…

…

always tells Holly what to do

likes to play older sister

…

…

△ 3 He has been doing that since … → After Station 1, p. 39/2

Here are some famous people from Scotland and information on what they've been doing since they were very young – but everything is mixed up. Work with a partner. Ask each other questions and find the right answers. One person is not from Scotland – who is it?

Example: 1. Has Ewan McGregor been playing tennis since he was very young? –
No, he hasn't been playing tennis. He's been acting in plays[2] and in films. /
He's been working hard to become an actor.

1. Ewan McGregor – make music, play in a band 2. Andy Murray – sing, write her own songs 3. KT Tunstall – play football, train hard 4. David Beckham – act in plays and in films, work hard to become an actor 5. Simple Minds – play tennis, do sports

1 **product** ['prɒdʌkt] Produkt | 2 **play** [pleɪ] Theaterstück

▲ 4 Scots and kilts → After Station 1, p. 39/2

Read the text and complete it with the ***present perfect simple*** *or the* ***present perfect progressive****.*

1. The kilt ___ (be) a traditional piece of Scottish clothing[1] for hundreds of years, but it was only in the 19th century that kilts became part of the national costume. 2. Since then people ___ (joke) about Scots in skirts. 3. For some years now, tourists ___ (wear) kilts wherever they go in Scotland, but true Scotsmen only wear kilts to Scottish dances or weddings. 4. Ethan ___ (wear) a kilt at gigs since he started to play in a traditional Scottish band. 5. He ___ (have) his old kilt for some years, but the other band members ___ (tell) him for months that he should get a new one. All the others ___ (buy) new kilts with the same tartan pattern.

△ 5 Point in time or period of time? → After Station 1, p. 39/3

Copy the grid and fill in the phrases. Remember: a point in time can be long too!

Point in time: *since*	Period of time: *for*
he was a small boy …	many years …

half past ten | ages | the 16th century | some months | September 7th, 1565 | last July | a few days | November last year | last week | he was a small boy ✔ | a second | as long as she can remember | she was in kindergarten | centuries | he was ten | yesterday | his birthday last year | many years ✔ | the break

▲ 6 Scary castles → After Station 1, p. 39/3

a) *Write a short text about old Scottish castles. Use the correct tenses:* ***simple past****,* ***present perfect simple*** *and* ***present perfect progressive****.*

Start like this: Scottish clans[2] have been living in castles for centuries. Awful things …

Scottish clans | live in castles | for centuries. Awful things | happen there. In Ethie Castle | some men | kill[3] Cardinal Beaton | in 1546. Mysterious sounds | scare[4] visitors | since then. In Duntrune Castle | people | hear sounds of bagpipes | since death[5] of bagpiper | in 17th century. In Meggernie Castle | white lady | kiss[6] men in their sleep | for hundreds of years. Her husband[7] | kill her and cut her in half | centuries ago. The upper part of body | walk upstairs | while lower part | walk downstairs | since that time.

b) *Find more Scottish ghost castles on the internet. Make notes about the stories and legends people tell about them. Present your castles in class.*

1 **piece of clothing** [ˌpiːs_ɒv ˈkləʊðɪŋ] Kleidungsstück | 2 **clan** [klæn] Clan; Sippe | 3 **to kill** [kɪl] töten | 4 **to scare** [skeə] erschrecken | 5 **death** [deθ] Tod | 6 **to kiss** [kɪs] küssen | 7 **husband** [ˈhʌzbənd] Ehemann

△ 7 Let's dance! → After Station 1, p. 39/4

*Angus and Ian are talking about their plans for the weekend. Read their conversation and fill in **for** or **since**.*

Angus: Hey, Ian. Do you want to come to the ceilidh[1] with us on Saturday? I haven't been to one **1** ages[2]!

Ian: Well, I haven't been to one **2** last year, and I'm not even sure if I still know what to do!

Angus: I'm sure you'll remember. Just come with us on Saturday.

Ian: OK, but let's ask Fiona too.

Angus: Fiona? I haven't seen her **3** she moved to Glasgow last year.

Ian: She's staying in Edinburgh with her aunt and uncle for the summer holidays. She's loved Scottish music and ceilidhs **4** she was in kindergarten, and I guess she still knows the right steps. She's been dancing at festivals with a group of dancers **5** she went to Glasgow.

Angus: Oh, I didn't know that. I haven't heard from her **6** a very long time. How long has she been back?

Ian: She's been back **7** last Saturday. I'll text her – it'll be great to see her again!

▲ 8 A strange country → After Station 1, p. 39/4

In this unit you've learned that in Scotland some men wear kilts, that even young people like traditional Scottish music, and that lots of people enjoy a strange meal called haggis. Write a short text about a country that[3] you've made up[4] and think of things that[5] people have been doing there for a very long time. Present your text to the class.

Start like this: In the strange country of Galumphia, men have been …
All the people there have …

△ 9 Famous Scots → Help with Station 2, p. 42/10b)

Here are some ideas to help you with the exercise:

- radar[6] – invent – Robert Wattson-Watt
- tunnels, canals[7] and roads – build – Thomas Telford
- Scottish castles – design – Robert Adams
- James Bond – play – Sean Connery
- lots of money – give to charity – Andrew Carnegie
- *Treasure Island* – write – Robert Louis Stevenson

1 **ceilidh** ['keɪli] *schottisches Fest* | 2 **ages** [eɪdʒɪz] eine Ewigkeit | 3 **a country that** [ə ˌkʌntri 'ðæt] ein Land, das | 4 **to make up** [ˌmeik‿'ʌp] sich ausdenken | 5 **things that …** [ˌθɪŋz 'ðæt] Dinge, die… | 6 **radar** ['reɪdɑ:] Radar | 7 **canal** [kə'næl] Kanal

△ 10 Scottish heroes and heroines → After Station 2, p. 42/11

Complete the text with passive forms: ***simple present, simple past*** *or* ***present perfect simple.***

Stories about heroes and heroines **1** (tell) in Scotland for centuries. There is even a story about a dog. In 1872, a statue[1] of Greyfriar's Bobby **2** (put up[2]) in a park in Edinburgh. Bobby, a Skye terrier, was so sad about his owner's[3] death that he sat on his grave[4] for fourteen years. Another Scottish heroine is Flora Macdonald. Her father died when she was a child, and her mother **3** (kidnap[5]) – so Flora **4** (bring) to her father's cousin, the chief[6] of the Macdonald clan. Later, Flora **5** (tell) to move to the island of Benbecula. Today Flora **6** (always describe) in stories as a very brave young woman. And so she was! Bonnie Prince Charlie wanted to become King of Scotland, but he **7** (defeat) by British soldiers. He then escaped[7] to Benbecula and **8** (hide) by Flora.

▲ 11 The story of Greyfriar's Bobby → After Station 2, p. 42/11

Read the text and present it in your own words. Explain why you think the dog was a hero or not.

John Gray worked for the City Police in Edinburgh more than a hundred years ago. He had a small dog: a Skye terrier called Bobby. When John Gray died, Bobby was so sad that he didn't want to leave John's grave. He sat there for fourteen years, and the people of Edinburgh brought him food and drink. He became one of the most famous dogs in the world. His story has been told in a number of books and films. When you go to Edinburgh, you can see his statue in the Old Town or have a drink in the bar "Greyfriar's Bobby".

△ 12 Glasgow is amazing! → Help with Station 2, p. 43/14b)

Here are some notes on famous Glasgow sights. They can help you with your answer:

The Tall Ship | built in 1896 | explore every corner | sit in captain's chair | read the log book | learn about ship's history	The Willow[8] Tearooms | order a traditional afternoon tea | enjoy Scottish cakes and scones[9] | relax in rooms designed over 100 years ago	Escape Glasgow | play team game for groups of 2–6 | work together as a team | find clues | solve problems | escape the room | have fun

△ 13 What were Olivia and her family doing? → After Station 3, p. 45/17a)

Put in the correct verb forms.

It's Saturday, 10:00
1. *Olivia: I* ***am*** *play****ing*** *the saxophone.*
2. *Lucy* ***is*** *tidy****ing*** *her room.*
3. *Hey Lucy, you ___ my mp3 player!*
4. *Claire and Desmond* ***are*** *prepar****ing*** *lunch.*
5. *We ___ for tips for the weekend on the internet.*

Last Saturday, 10:00
1. *Olivia: I* ***was*** *play****ing*** *the saxophone.*
2. *Lucy ___ her room.*
3. *Hey Lucy, you* ***were*** *us****ing*** *my mp3 player!*
4. *Claire and Desmond ___ lunch.*
5. *We* ***were*** *look****ing*** *for tips for the weekend on the internet.*

1 statue [ˈstætʃuː] Statue | **2 to put up** [pʊt ˈʌp] aufstellen; aufhängen; errichten | **3 owner** [ˈəʊnə] Besitzer/-in | **4 grave** [ɡreɪv] Grab | **5 to kidnap** [ˈkɪdnæp] entführen | **6 chief** [tʃiːf] Anführer; Oberhaupt | **7 to escape** [ɪˈskeɪp] fliehen; flüchten | **8 willow** [ˈwɪləʊ] Weide | **9 scone** [skɒn] *brötchenartiges Gebäck*

▲ 14 Act it out and guess! → After Station 3, p. 45/17a)

One student leaves the classroom. 3–4 other students act an activity ***without*** *words. When the teacher shouts "Stop!", everyone stops. Now the student comes back in and sees the 'frozen'[1] students. With yes / no questions, he / she must guess what the others were doing.*

△ 15 When or while? → After Station 3, p. 45/17b)

Fill the gaps with ***when*** *or* ***while****.*

1. We were watching a film ___ Mum came home.
2. ___ I saw my brother, he was buying lots of sweets.
3. I read a whole magazine ___ I was waiting for the bus.
4. ___ my dog was sleeping, my cat stole his dinner!
5. My sister was preparing a presentation ___ her phone rang.
6. ___ the friends were walking home from school, they discovered a new shop.

▲ 16 A crazy day at home → After Station 3, p. 45/17b)

Use these photos and write a short story about a crazy day at home. Think of your own crazy ideas too. Use the simple past and the past progressive.

Start like this:
First, breakfast was crazy. While Mum was…, our dog … her breakfast! Then, while Mum and Dad were …, we … in the kitchen. But when …

△ 17 An interview with Holly and Amber → Help with Story, p. 50/5

Reporters are interested in the main facts of a story, but also in feelings and thoughts, because these make their reports more interesting. Here are some useful phrases for your interview.

Useful phrases

What happened? | When / Where did it happen? | Who was there? | Why did it happen? | What did you feel when … | Were you scared / upset / worried / …? | Did you think about … / think of … | What did you think when … | What has changed for you?

1 **frozen** ['frəʊzn] *hier:* erstarrt

Text smart 2

△ 1 What's that in English? → Help with Station 1, p. 58/4a)

Match the German words on the left with the English words on the right. Then find sentences with the English words in the hedgehog text.

Winterschlaf | überleben | vermeiden | Dosenfutter | Schicht aus Zeitungspapier | zunehmen | menschenscheu | aufsaugen | Auslauf | aktiv halten

layer of newspaper | fearful of humans | gain weight | tinned food | hibernation | run area | avoid | survive | soak up | keep active

△ 2 Writing instructions → Help with Station 1, p. 58/5

These words and phrases can help you to start your grid:

Steps:
1. The right time to help
2. A warm area for your hedgehog
3. Your hedgehog's bed
4. …

Phrases:
- Take care …
- Keep it …
- It is essential to …
- Give the hedgehog …
- …

△ 3 FAQs: Only important questions, please! → After Station 1, p. 58/6

Which of the questions below are important enough to show in an FAQ about a new smartphone model[1]? Choose the important questions and write answers for them.

1. Are there lots of new apps for the new model?
2. Does its screen[2] break easily?
3. Why is the new model better than the old one?
4. Has the design changed a lot?
5. Is the new phone waterproof[3]?
6. Are there new games on it now?
7. Does the new model have a better camera?

▲ 4 Time traveller with a smartphone → After Station 1, p. 58/6

You've travelled back in time to 1960. The people you meet see your smartphone and have lots of questions: How do you answer them? Use strong adjectives!

1 **model** ['mɒdl] Modell | 2 **screen** [skri:n] Bildschirm | 3 **waterproof** ['wɔ:təpru:f] wasserdicht

△ 5 From blog to news report → Help with Station 2, p. 59/8d)

Look at the expressions in the box – they can help you to write down facts. Don't forget to read the tip too!

Many animals are burnt / killed / saved / rescued / … | When the animals are found, they are often confused / helpless / thirsty / … | Photos of koalas with burns / with injuries make people think about …

Tip

In the blog post, expressions like "It breaks my heart" or "I'm not sure …" are part of the writer's **opinion**, not the facts. So don't use sentences with '**I**' or '**me**' for your facts.

△ 6 Understanding the text → Instead of Station 2, p. 61/11b)

Match the parts to make sentences.

- Elephants and rhinos in Africa are …
- There is a danger that soon …
- Those in power …
- We must do something about poaching …
- An elephant is … / A rhino is …

… killed for its tusk. / for its horn.
… on the brink of extinction.
… nobody will care about elephants any more.
… must learn about the situation in Africa.
… before it's too late.

△ 7 Is that a text about elephants? → Help with Station 2, p. 61/11c)

These words and phrases can help you to explain the main ideas of the text in German:

Stoßzähne | auf die Straße gehen | Klaviertasten und Dekoartikel aus Elfenbein | verbotene Wilderei | vom Aussterben bedroht | weltweite Protestmärsche

△ 8 Writing your own texts → Help with Options, p. 61/13

Here are some ideas to help you with your options:

Option A:
*Start with very **basic** information / tips first before you write about lots of details.*

Your family will *really* like the breakfast you make if you make their favourite things. So always think about what each person likes first. Then, follow these steps …

Option B:
*If your introduction is interesting, your reader will want to read the **whole** report!*

Beautiful actor Jennifer Ashton was seen … She came to present her wonderful new …, but the people were much more interested in …

Before you start writing, go through your text in your head and make notes. What do you want to focus on? Sometimes pictures give you ideas. Find some on the internet!

Unit 3

△ 1 Look what I found in the attic! → Help with Introduction, p. 64/1b)

The pictures and the list below can give you ideas for your text.

Word bank

baking moulds[1] / pots[2] / pans[3] | old toys (china doll[4] / soft toy[5]) | a pair of snowshoes[6] | old photos / letters / postcards | a telescope | keys | jewellery | chair / table / wardrobe / …

Useful phrases

I found this in … | It belonged to my grandad / grandma / … | He / She used it to … | It was very important to my …, so he / she didn't throw it away. | Today we use … instead.

△ 2 The past perfect → Instead of Station 1, p. 69/3

a) *Read these sentences. Find the* ***simple past*** *and* ***past perfect*** *forms. Make a list.*

1. Before the Romans came, the Celts had already been in Britain for a long time.
2. Elizabeth's mother, Anne, had lived in France, so she spoke very good French.
3. After William of Normandy had become king of England in 1066, more and more people learned French.
4. People in Victorian Britain were able to see more and more of their own country after the steam trains had made it quicker and easier to travel.

b) *Make a diagram to show which actions in each sentence happend* ***before*** *and which happened* ***after****.*

1 **baking mould** [ˈbeɪkɪŋ ˌməʊld] Backform | 2 **pot** [pɒt] Topf | 3 **pan** [pæn] Pfanne | 4 **china doll** [ˌtʃaɪnə ˈdɒl] Porzellanpuppe | 5 **soft toy** [ˌsɒft‿ˈtɔɪ] Plüsch- / Stofftier | 6 **snowshoes** [ˈsnəʊʃuːz] Schneeschuhe

△ 3 Shakespeare's school days → After Station 1, p. 69/4

Read the text below and complete it with the correct forms of the ***past perfect****.*

Before William Shakespeare moved to London, he **1** (live) in the small town of Stratford-upon-Avon. His father John Shakespeare **2** (not learn) to read and write himself, but he **3** (understand) how important a good education was, so he sent his son to the local grammar school. Back then, the school days were very long – the students could only go home after they **4** (sit) at their desks from 6 a.m. to 5 p.m.! When Shakespeare finally left school, he **5** (learn) enough Latin to read any Latin book.

▲ 4 Where was he? → After Station 1, p. 69/4

Shakespeare had left Stratford-upon-Avon some years before he became a famous writer in London – but nobody knows where he was or what he did exactly. Look at the three ideas below and decide which one you'd like to write about. Then add some more details and explain why you think it's right. Use a dictionary if you need more words.

Start like this: I think that before Shakespeare came to London, he had …

a) join a group of actors and travel across England | act in lots of different plays | see many different cities
b) work as a teacher for a rich man and read a lot of books | meet a lot of famous and important people | become a friend to some of them
c) travel to Italy and get the idea for his play *Romeo and Juliet* there | learn more about Roman history | visit a lot of Italian cities

△ 5 An Elizabethan actor → After Station 1, p. 70/5

Complete the text about a young actor. Use the correct tenses: ***simple past*** *or* ***past perfect****.*

When Nathan Field **1** (be) born in 1587, there **2** (be) only a few theatres. Most actors **3** (travel) around the country and **4** (perform[1]) their plays outside pubs. Back then, actors **5** (have) a bad reputation[2] and people **6** (not trust) them. Nathan's own father, a priest[3], **7** (often talk) angrily about them too before he **8** (die) in 1588. So, for Nathan, a career in acting **9** (not seem) possible at first. But later in the 16th century, after the Elizabethans **10** (build) a lot of theatres, opinions about actors finally **11** (begin) to change. And in 1600, after he **12** (just turn) 13, Nathan **13** (join) a group of boy actors. Soon he **14** (be) one of their best players and **15** (become) very famous. By the age of 26, he **16** (already act) in front of the Queen and **17** (become) one of the superstars of his time.

1 **to perform** [pəˈfɔːm] auftreten; aufführen | 2 **reputation** [ˌrepjəˈteɪʃn] Ruf | 3 **priest** [priːst] Priester

▲ 6 A superstar of the stage → After Station 1, p. 70/5

*Use the key words below to write a text about Nathan Field, an actor from the time of Queen Elizabeth and a superstar of the stage. Use the **simple past** and the **past perfect**. (Look at the bottom of p. 131 for the meaning of the new words here.)*

When Nathan Field | born in 1587 | only a few theatres. Most actors | travel around country | perform[1] plays outside pubs. Back then | actors | have bad reputation | people | not trust them. | Nathan's own father | a priest | talk angrily about them too | before | die | in 1588. So, for Nathan, | career in acting | not seem possible | at first. But | later years of 16th century | after | Elizabethans | build | a lot of theatres | opinions about acting and actors | finally | begin to change. And in 1600 | after just turn 13 | Nathan | join | group of boy actors. Soon | be | one of their best players | become very famous. By the age of 26 | already act | in front of Queen | become one of the superstars | of his time.

△ 7 Tell the story → Help with Station 1, p. 70/6

These phrases can help you to write your story:

Then, on his first big adventure, he went to America to … | When he was in America … | This made him angry … | He never forgot … | In 1577, Drake sailed … | After he had stolen … the Spanish really hated … | As soon as Drake had returned to … he wasted … | He gave the queen … | She was … and couldn't believe her … | After Drake had defeated the …, England felt … | Drake was now a …

△ 8 Your turn: Funny or interesting things in your life → Help with Station 1, p. 70/7

Here are some ideas for Ex. 7. Maybe things like this have happened to you?

Before: take wrong bag | hurry to meet friends | ask mum for money | **At pool:** people having fun | open bag | find tennis clothes | wrong bag! | **After:** go home | get right bag

Before: go to first concert[2] | take phone | tell parents not to worry | **At concert:** enjoy the show | loud music | not hear phone | **After:** lots of calls | angry texts from parents

Before: excited about party | not sure what to wear | not read the whole invitation | **At party:** only one in colourful clothes | feel stupid | **After:** look at invitation again | see 'dress code'[3]

1 **to perform** [pəˈfɔːm] auftreten; aufführen | 2 **concert** [ˈkɒnsət] Konzert | 3 **dress code** [ˈdres kəʊd] Kleiderordnung (z. B. für Mottoparty)

△ 9 Useful phrases for presenting facts → Instead of Skills, p. 71/1b)

Copy the grid and complete it with the list of phrases under the grid. The tip box on the right can help you to remember what kind of words you need.

Tip

- **Prepositions** are words like 'for', 'from' or 'at'.
- **Common history verbs** often tell us what people did, e.g. 'travel' or 'fight'.
- **Biographical information** tells you about important events in a person's life, e.g. when he / she was born or died.

Prepositions with times and dates	Descriptions of places / objects	Biographical information	Typical history verbs
in 1564	*... was used for ...*	*was born **in** 1878*	*reigned*
		*was born **on** 15th April 1878*	

for 200 years · at the beginning of · was worn by · it has · invented · was given to · moved to · from 1066 to 1154 · it looks · you can see a / an · at the end of · was brought from

△ 10 A class trip which was really cool → After Station 2, p. 73/11

*Do you need **who / that**, **which / that** or **whose**? Put in the right relative pronoun.*

The teacher 1 lessons we like the most is Mrs Jordan. Last year, she took us on a class trip and the coolest place 2 we visited was the Tower of London. Two men 3 costumes were black and red and very funny asked us about our visit. They were 'Beefeaters'[1]. They're the men 4 show the Tower to all the visitors 5 come specially to see the Crown Jewels. One of the Beefeaters was the Raven Master too. His job is to look after the ravens 6 live in the Tower. Did you know that in the past, the Tower was a castle, a prison and even a royal zoo with lions and bears?! The Beefeaters also told us about the ghosts 7 voices you can hear if you're quiet enough. They're the ghosts of all the people 8 lost their heads in the Tower many, many years ago!

1 **Beefeater** ['bi:f‚i:tə] königlicher Leibgardist

△ 11 Contact clauses → After Station 2, p. 73/12

*Read the sentence pairs. Which sentence in each pair **doesn't** need a relative pronoun?*

1. a) Lots of children that are interested in history go to the museum.
   b) Lots of children that I know go to the museum.
2. a) I'm friends with lots of the students who go to Drama class.
   b) I'm friends with lots of the students who I see at Drama class.
3. a) This is a website which I use a lot for my homework.
   b) This is a website which helps me a lot with my homework.
4. a) I think the guided tours that we go on are fun.
   b) I think the guided tours that help us to understand history are fun.

△ 12 Make one sentence from two → After Station 2, p. 73/13

Replace[1] the words in blue with a relative pronoun and make a new sentence.

Examples: Last lesson we talked about a famous person. We all know him.
→ Last lesson we talked about a famous person **who / that** we all know.
The History Club organises guided tours. They're really exciting.
→ The History Club organises guided tours **which / that** are really exciting.

1. Yesterday, we watched a film about Shakespeare. It was really interesting.
2. In Drama classes we learn about different actors. I like them very much.
3. I can show you a cool dance. We learned it last week.
4. Do you know the new girl? She's talking to Luke.

▲ 13 Puzzles → After Station 2, p. 73/13

a) *Complete the sentences with **who / that**, **which / that** or **whose**.*

1. It's something ___ has four legs but can't walk.
2. It's something ___ you must break before you can eat it!
3. I'm someone ___ is always cold but I must never feel warm!
4. It's something ___ is yours but your friends use it more than you do!
5. I'm a person ___ chair is a throne[2].
6. It's something ___ is tall when it's new and not so tall when it's old!

b) *Can you guess the answers?*

Answers: a table | an egg | a snowman[3] | your name | a king / a queen | a candle

1 Replace [rɪˈpleɪs] Ersetze … | **2 throne** [θrəʊn] Thron | **3 snowman** [ˈsnəʊmæn] Schneemann

△ 14 Adverbs → After Station 2, p. 74/15

Here are some tips for people who visit London. Find the right adverb for each sentence.

Always cross[1] the street 1 (careful). Remember: In England cars drive[2] on the left! Sometimes people in England speak very 2 (fast). You can always ask people to talk 3 (slow) and 4 (clear). They're usually friendly when you ask them 5 (polite). You should try 6 (hard) to understand, but if you have problems, don't react[3] 7 (nervous). When you get back home, you can talk 8 (happy) about the great things you did in London!

△ 15 Act it out! → After Station 2 p. 74/15

Write these activities on cards. One of you chooses an activity and acts it without words. The others guess what you're doing, and how.

sing loudly | jump quickly
dance slowly | look around nervously
talk excitedly | walk carefully
write fast | smile happily

△ 16 Adjective or adverb? → After Station 2, p. 74/16

Decide if you need the adjective or the adverb in these sentences.

1. When Jamal came to London, he was ___ because he travelled alone. At Victoria Station he looked around ___ to find his cousin and his aunt and uncle. (nervous)
2. But he was also ___: his cousin always talked so ___ about all the things you can do in London! (excited)
3. Jamal, his cousin and his aunt and uncle went home by bus. The old London buses are very ___. They travel around the city very ___ so tourists can have a ___ look at all the sights. You can see them very ___ from the top of a real London bus. (slow, good)
4. On the bus, Jamal smiled ___. A whole week in London! And he was ___ to see his cousin and his family. (happy)

▲ 17 Adjective or adverb? → After Station 2, p. 74/16

From the two boxes, choose an activity and an adjective. Then write sentences about yourself – and use the adverb form too!

Example: I'm good at sports, but I don't play football very well. I'm nervous before a test, but I don't …

walk to school | do my homework | talk to teachers | dance | sing pop songs | go cycling | …	good | nervous | excited | happy | angry | crazy | loud | slow | fast | …

1 **to cross** [krɒs] überqueren | 2 **to drive** [draɪv] fahren | 3 **to react** [ri'ækt] reagieren

Text smart 3

△ 1 Your turn: Your favourite genre → Help with Introduction, p. 84/2b)

These phrases can help you to talk about your favourite genre:

I think the best books are … | I love … / really enjoy …

I can never put[1] … books down. They're real page-turners[2].

My absolutely favourite genre is … | I only read …

… are fantastic because … | You must read … because …

… books open up[3] new worlds to you / allow you to travel in your mind[4].

△ 2 Who is Luke? → Help with Station 1, p. 85/5

a) *Read the text on p. 85 again. Decide which parts of the sentences below make the most sense[5].*

1. Luke and his family live in the woods | in a city | near the sea.
2. Luke is a toddler | a teenager | old enough to work in the garden.
3. Luke's mother likes Luke to be outside | is afraid when he's outside | is always scared.
4. Luke often works in the garden | is often told to go inside | often plays outside.
5. Luke might not be allowed to go barefoot | go outside | go into the woods again.
6. This has something to do with the people who are working on the farm | are taking down the trees | are living nearby[6].

b) *These categories can help you to find questions to ask about Luke:*

Luke: Age? Activities? Link to the title of the book?

Family: Brothers / sisters? Parents? Parents' jobs?

Home: Farm? Flat? Big house? Neighbours?

Friends: School? Neighbourhood? Internet? Lonely?

△ 3 Key lines from the text → Instead of Station 1, p. 86/6

Match these key lines from the text with the explanations on the right.

1. He had never disobeyed the order to hide.
2. He had somehow understood the fear in his mother's voice.
3. But on this day, he hesitated.
4. I will never be allowed outside again. Maybe never again as long as I live.
5. He turned and walked into the house, as silently as a shadow.

a) This day is different from all the other days, so Luke doesn't obey immediately.
b) Something has changed in Luke's life that will stop him from going outside.
c) Nobody should see or hear Luke.
d) His mother is afraid of something outside that might hurt Luke.
e) It's extremely important that Luke hides when he's told to do so.

1 **to put down** [ˌpʊt ˈdaʊn] weglegen | 2 **page-turner** [ˈpeɪdʒˌtɜːnə] fesselndes Buch | 3 **to open up** [ˌəʊpn ˈʌp] eröffnen | 4 **mind** [maɪnd] Geist; Verstand | 5 **to make sense** [meɪk ˈsens] Sinn ergeben | 6 **nearby** [ˌnɪəˈbaɪ] in der Nähe

△ 4 Your reaction → Help with Station 2, p. 87/9a)

Choose five adjectives that you think best describe the atmosphere and situation. Then discuss your words with a partner. Together, decide on the three best adjectives.

scary | challenging | calm | strange | bad | relaxed | sunny | cheerful[1] | terrible
depressing[2] | frightening[3] | exciting | dark | confusing | sad | fantastic | friendly

△ 5 Key lines from the text → Instead of Station 2, p. 87/10

*Which of these lines are key lines from the text, which ones are **not**? Why? Discuss with a partner. The useful phrases on p. 86, Ex. 6 can help you.*

1. I'm going to die.
2. I look up through the grey-white shimmer of the swimming pool water.
3. My lungs are on fire.
4. Just one breath. Just one.
5. I have to take a breath, even though I know that I'll be breathing in water.
6. I close my eyes, praying hard.
7. Part of me – a tiny, tiny part of me – laughs.
8. After everything I've been through in the last few months, this is how I'm going to bow out.
9. Alex …
10. I stop fighting. I'm so tired. I can feel my body begin to sink.

△ 6 Writing options → Help with Options, p. 89/15

Here are some ideas to help you with your options:

Option A:
Choose from one of these first lines. Then take your story from there.

"Run!" Mike shouted, but Laura … | I had never wanted to go on a camping trip – it was … | Sam entered his office on the 25th floor with a smile. How could he know what … | I could hear their footsteps. They were coming closer …

Option B:
Choose one of these two perspectives for Text 2. (Cameron is the main character in Pig-Heart-Boy*). Use the key phrases below to start your story.*

Marlon, Cameron's friend
often go to the pool together | parents don't know | Cameron too sick | always look out for Cameron | can't see him | panic | …

Cathy, Cameron's mum
always worried about Cameron | thinks he is at Marlon's home, doing homework | at the pool instead | call from the hospital | …

1 cheerful [ˈtʃɪəfl] fröhlich | **2 depressing** [dɪˈpresɪŋ] deprimierend | **3 frightening** [ˈfraɪtnɪŋ] Furcht erregend; beängstigend

Unit 4

△ 1 Your turn: Your travel plans → Instead of Introduction, p. 93/4

Where would you like to spend your holiday? Choose one of these places. Find two other people who have chosen a different place. Use the phrases below to tell each other about your holiday plans.

enjoy nature | see wild animals / flowers | breathe fresh air | go for long walks / climbing | good food | …

go swimming / on a sailing trip / surfing | relax in the sun | build a sand castle | eat seafood[1] | …

go sightseeing / shopping | visit museums | travel on hop-on hop-off bus | eat international food | …

△ 2 Eating on board the ferry → After Station 1, p. 95/2

*Some friends from the athletics team are talking about the different breakfasts on board the ferry. Read their conversation and answer the questions. Use **indirect speech**.*

Fiona: I don't want to eat a French breakfast here. I've heard it's terrible.
Andrew: I tried it on my trip to France last year and it was really good.
Sally: Kevin and I are having the full English breakfast. We're really hungry because we didn't have breakfast this morning.
Andrew: Oh, I think that's too expensive. My parents only gave me €150 for the whole trip.

1. Why didn't Fiona want to have a French breakfast? **2.** Why did Andrew want to eat the French breakfast? **3.** Why were Kevin and Sally hungry? **4.** Why couldn't Andrew afford the full Englisch breakfast?

Start like this: **1.** Fiona said she … That's why she didn't want to have a French breakfast.

▲ 3 Trips without parents → After Station 1, p. 95/2

Most parents are very worried when their children travel alone. Would you tell your parents about everything that went wrong? Look at these problems Steve had on the trip and think of more. Then say what he told his parents and what he didn't.

1. was ten minutes late for the coach **2.** paid too much for the breakfast and didn't ask for the change **3.** had to borrow some money from other team members **4.** had trouble with his host family because he took photos of the food **5.** …

1 **seafood** ['si:fu:d] Meeresfrüchte

△ 4 What did she say? → Instead of Station 1, p. 96/4

Before their trip to France, Ms Woodruff told the team everything about the trip. Here's what she said – but what did the narrator tell his parents?

"I have some important information about our trip to France for you. Our coach will leave at 5 a.m., and it can't wait for people who are late – we need to catch the ferry in Dover at 8:40 a.m. We'll arrive in Calais at 9:10 a.m. There's a food court[1] on board the ferry where we can enjoy our first French breakfast. The last time I was on board a P&O ferry they also had free wifi. Some people spent most of the trip playing video games. But I hope nobody on our team wants to stare at a video screen[2] when they can enjoy the sea instead. Oh, I forgot to give you this form. All parents must sign it before we leave."

Start like this: "Ms Woodruff said she had … She told us our coach …"

△ 5 What happened? → Help with Station 1, p. 96/5a)

These words and phrases can help you to talk about the experiences of the Jones family:

Picture 1:
in Italy – go swimming – leave everything on the beach – come back – all things gone – see thief – can't catch – too far away

Picture 2:
very hot – wear shorts and tops – visit old city – go into church – want to take photos – priest[3] – tell us to leave – no shorts / tops and camera

Picture 3:
camp – long day – tired – sleep in tent[4] – suddenly hear noise – tent start to shake[5] – open – cow looking at us

△ 6 Travel situations → Help with Station 1, p. 96/5b)

These phrases can help you to talk about your travel experiences:

When I was in … last year … | During the holidays, I … | I felt very stupid / embarrassed / terrible / scared when … | Everyone / Someone was staring / looking at me / trying to explain something to me. | I was confused / upset / angry because … | I wanted to …, but I couldn't … | Next time, I'll use my mobile / ask someone about … / remember to …

△ 7 A curious[6] aunt → After Station 2, p. 98/9

*At the airport, Rafiq's aunt wants to know exactly what happened. Turn her questions into **indirect speech**.*

1. "What happened at passport control?" **2.** "Why did the man become suspicious?" **3.** "Who told you to go to the side room?" **4.** "What did the security people say?" **5.** "Did they scare you?" **6.** "Have you really forgotten your birthday?" **7.** "Where's your luggage?" **8.** "Do you need help with the suitcase?" **9.** "Will you tell your parents about this?"

1 food court [fu:d kɔ:t] Gastronomiebereich | **2 screen** [skri:n] Bildschirm | **3 priest** [pri:st] Priester | **4 tent** [tent] Zelt | **5 to shake** [ʃeɪk] wackeln | **6 curious** ['kjʊəriəs] neugierig

▲ 8 What did he ask? → After Station 2, p. 98/9

*Write down **five questions** you could ask your classmates. Then get into groups of three (Student A, B and C). Student A whispers the first question on his list into the ear of Student B. Student C asks Student B: "What did he / she ask?" and Student B reports the question in **indirect speech**. Student C gives an answer, then Student B whispers a question into his ear – and Student A asks: "What did he / she say?" Take turns until you've answered all the questions on your lists.*

△ 9 I told you to call! → After Station 2, p. 98/10

When Rafiq comes back from Bangladesh, his mother is happy to see him again – but she's angry too. What did she tell him to do before he left? Complete her sentences.

Example: Did you take photos out of the plane? – I **asked you to take** photos out of the plane.

1. You didn't call when you arrived. Why not? I told you …
2. I don't think you said 'hello' to your aunt and uncle from us. But I …
3. Masud didn't take you to the old centre, did he? I know I …
4. Did you go there all alone? That's so dangerous! I …
5. I hope your aunt and uncle showed you my village. I …
6. Did Aunt Sadia cook black rice[1] for you? I …
7. I haven't got a postcard yet – did you write one? I …
8. Where is the saree[2] for me? Did you buy one? I …
9. Someone stole your money? You didn't take it to the old centre, did you? I …
10. I hope your aunt and uncle will visit us next year. Did you invite them? I …

▲ 10 Everyone orders me about[3] … → After Station 2, p. 98/10

*Young people hear commands from lots of different people in their lives. What commands do you get from these people? Complete the list. Then tell the class what they tell you to do. Use **indirect speech**.*

Teachers	Parents	Coach
Do your homework! …	Tidy up your room! …	Don't be late for training! …

1 rice [raɪs] Reis | **2 saree** ['sɑːri] Sari | **3 to order sb about** ['ɔːdə ə'baʊt] jmdn. herumkommandieren

△ 11 Your turn: Travel plans → Help with Station 2, p. 99/13

You can choose from these European cities to find ideas for your plans:

	Barcelona	Dublin	Vienna
Flights from Frankfurt / Munich	1 h 55 / 2 h 5	2 h 5 / 2 h 35	1 h 20 / 1 h 5
Places of interest / Things to do	La Sagrada Familia church | Las Ramblas street | Magic Fountain[1] show | Camp Nou football stadium | beach	Ha'penny Bridge | O'Connell Street | The Book of Kells | Dublin Ghost Bus Tour | National Aquatic Centre	opera[2] house | Schönbrunn Zoo | Imperial Palace | National History Museum | Prater fun park

△ 12 Reading between the lines → After Story, p. 104/4

Read these short texts. Then decide which important information can be found between the lines.

1. It was wet outside. Very wet. Ryan looked at the kitchen clock: football training was at 4 p.m., and now it was already 3:50. He picked up his shoes and jacket, and with a sigh[3] walked out into the rain.
   a) Ryan lives close to the football stadium.
   b) Ryan hates playing football in the rain.
   c) The kitchen clock doesn't show the right time.

2. Kimberly ran all the way home, her Maths test still in her hand and a big smile on her face. "Mum!" she shouted. "You won't believe this!"
   a) Kimberly hurries home to help her mum in the kitchen.
   b) Kimberly is a very good student, especially[4] in Maths.
   c) She has a good mark in a Maths test, which is a surprise for her.

3. Mrs Lynch looked at the students who were playing outside the school building. Laura was standing all by herself under what looked like 'her' tree now. She was staring down at her feet, as usual.
   a) Laura is unhappy because the other students don't talk to her.
   b) Mrs Lynch likes trees and students.
   c) The weather is great, so everyone can play outside.

4. Ethan checked his mobile for the tenth time – still no message. He played with the empty glass in front of him and asked himself if he should ask for another drink or give up and go home.
   a) Ethan likes drinks in restaurants and cafés.
   b) Ethan doesn't know what to do when he is alone in a restaurant.
   c) Ethan is waiting for someone, but that person doesn't come.

1 fountain ['faʊntɪn] Brunnen | **2 opera** ['ɒprə] Oper | **3 sigh** [saɪ] Seufzer | **4 especially** [ɪ'speʃli] besonders

Text smart 4

△ 1 Theatre collocations → Instead of Introduction, p. 106/2a)

Read the following conversation between two actors and note down the theatre collocations they use.

Alex: Ian! You've forgotten your lines again! We can't give a great performance if you don't learn the lines! If you go on like that, you'll mess up the whole play.
Ian: Sorry, I just can't get into my character today. He's such a sad guy, and I'm just too happy right now.
Alex: Well, if you can't identify with your character, just try following the director's instructions, OK? They help you to understand your role. We've staged the play before – if you don't feel you can do it, Sam can play your part.
Ian: Sam? You can't be serious. He never stays in character – one moment he's a super hero, and the next a sad old man.
Alex: At least he knows how to follow the stage directions and play the scene right.
Ian: Are you sure? Remember how he forgets to use the props – he was supposed to give me the magic book in our last play but he forgot it backstage! I looked like a fool!
Alex: I don't think the audience noticed. Now just learn your role well and let's get on with our rehearsal.

△ 2 The main characters → Instead of Station 1, p. 107/5b)

Try to get into Claire's head and say what might happen.

Start like this: If I ask my parents, they'll say no. If they say no, I can't … If I can't …, Rob will …
If I tell my parents that I want to spend the night at Rob's house, …

△ 3 Telling lies → Help with Station 2, p. 109/8

*In which of the following situations are people telling a white lie? Discuss if it's OK to tell these white lies, or if it's **never** OK!*

1. Your friend has bought a new dress and looks terrible in it. She asks you if you like it and you say "It's just great!"
2. You forgot to do your homework yesterday, so you tell the teacher that you didn't understand it.
3. A friend calls, but you don't feel like talking to him and don't answer. When he asks you later why you didn't answer the phone, you say you didn't hear it.
4. You lost your mum's sunglasses, and you hadn't asked her if you could borrow them before. She asks you if you know where they are – you just tell her to take better care of her things.

△ 4 Getting into character → Help with Station 2, p. 109/9d)

Get into groups of three. One student stands in the middle. Now one of you doesn't want this student to do something, but he/she can only say "Don't!" Your partner wants the student to do it, but he/she can only say "Come on!" Keep repeating your words in as many different ways as possible to convince the student in the middle. Who is more convincing? How does the student in the middle show that?

△ 5 Acting out a scene → Help with Station 3, p. 111/12

Work together with another group of five. Decide who is going to play which role. Now go through the following steps together:

1. Work together with the person in the second group who has the same role as you.
2. One of you reads out the lines (reader), the other acts them (actor). If you're the reader, make sure that you read slowly and pay a lot of attention to your voice; if you're the actor, make sure that you listen carefully to the lines and pay a lot of attention to facial expressions and gestures[1].
3. Change roles and practise again.
4. Now one group acts out the scene while the other watches. Take turns. What ideas do you have to improve the scene? Try them out.

△ 6 Staying in character → Help with Station 4, p. 113/14c)

Copy these adjectives onto little pieces of paper and put them face down on the desk. Take turns to pick up a piece of paper, and use facial expressions and gestures to demonstrate[2] the feeling on your piece of paper. Don't speak! Your partner must guess which feeling you're trying to express.

angry | worried | afraid | scared | nervous | guilty | ashamed[3] | sad | shocked

disappointed | happy | confused | like an idiot | tired | fantastic

△ 7 Bringing the story to life → Help with Options, p. 113/16

These ideas can help you with your options:

Option A:
When you act each scene, ask the students who aren't playing in that scene to watch. Pay attention to these points:

Where does each of you stand? | When do you move, and where do you go? | Who do you look at when you speak? | Make sure you don't turn your back on the audience!

Take notes for each scene and repeat the scenes with these notes in mind.

Option B:
This is what you should think about before you start:

What scenes do you want to take a photo of? | What effects can the camera angle and field size have? | What lighting do you want? | Do you need props?

When you edit the photos, these tips can be helpful:

Add the text which is necessary to understand what the scene is about (key information, dialogue, thoughts, and exclamations). | Write short texts that link the photos so that someone who doesn't know the play can understand it too.

1 **gesture** ['dʒestʃə] Geste; Handbewegung | 2 **to demonstrate** ['demənstreɪt] zeigen | 3 **ashamed** [ə'ʃeɪmd] beschämt

Vocabulary

S1 Vokabelheft

Lege ein dreispaltiges Vokabelheft an, in dem du auch neue Vokabeln notierst, die nicht in der Wortliste stehen (1. Spalte: englische Vokabel; 2. Spalte: Übersetzung; 3. Spalte: Beispielsätze oder alles, was dir hilft, dir die Bedeutung zu merken, z. B. *mind maps*).

S2 Vokabelkartei

Lerne neue Vokabeln mit einer Vokabelkartei. Sie besteht aus Karteikarten für die Vokabeln und einem Karton mit fünf Fächern für die Karten. (Vorderseite: englische Vokabel, Rückseite: Übersetzung sowie weitere Merkhilfen)
Stelle alle Karten ins erste Fach. Übe jeden Tag fünf bis zehn Minuten. Wenn du die Übersetzung weißt, stellst du die Karten ins zweite Fach. Mache weiter, bis das erste Fach leer ist. Das zweite Fach bearbeitest du dann einmal in der Woche, das dritte Fach alle zwei Wochen, usw.

S3 Wörter im Zusammenhang

Wörter sind die Bausteine der Sprache. Du musst sie natürlich lernen und jedes für sich verstehen. Zur Beherrschung einer Sprache gehört aber auch zu wissen, welche Kombinationen dieser Bausteine möglich sind. Deshalb ist es wichtig, mit den Wörtern die richtigen Kombinationen mitzulernen. Schreibe deshalb Wörter möglichst immer in typischen Zusammenhängen auf.

Lerne bei Verben passende Ergänzungen mit, z. B.:

*to **read** a book, a magazine, a comic, a manga*
*to **write** a letter, an e-mail, an invitation, a blog*
*to **go** swimming, shopping, home, away, to the cinema*

Schreibe auf, welche bestimmten grammatischen Formen auf bestimmte Wörter folgen, z. B.:

*I **would like** **to** swim, **to** read, **to** go shopping*
*I **like** swimm**ing**, read**ing**, go**ing** shopping*

Notiere dir Beispiele bei Wörtern mit Präpositionen:

*The party is **on** **Friday**, **at** **seven**, **at** **the weekend**.*
*My house is **in** **Dover Street**. We're **on** **the road to London**.*
*London is **on** **the Thames**.*

Achte beim Lesen unterschiedlicher Textsorten auf hilfreiche Formulierungen (*useful phrases*). Diese kannst du später in eigenen Texten immer wieder verwenden.

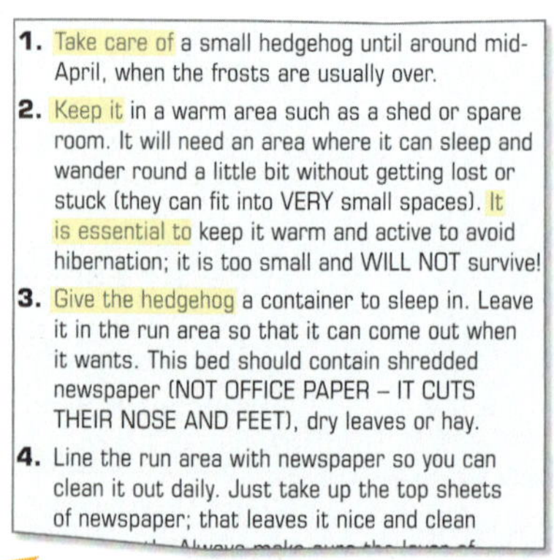

1. Take care of a small hedgehog until around mid-April, when the frosts are usually over.
2. Keep it in a warm area such as a shed or spare room. It will need an area where it can sleep and wander round a little bit without getting lost or stuck (they can fit into VERY small spaces). It is essential to keep it warm and active to avoid hibernation; it is too small and WILL NOT survive!
3. Give the hedgehog a container to sleep in. Leave it in the run area so that it can come out when it wants. This bed should contain shredded newspaper (NOT OFFICE PAPER – IT CUTS THEIR NOSE AND FEET), dry leaves or hay.
4. Line the run area with newspaper so you can clean it out daily. Just take up the top sheets of newspaper; that leaves it nice and clean

S4 Methoden

Du hast schon mehrere Methoden gelernt, wie du dir Vokabeln besser einprägen kannst:

- Klebezettel mit englischen Wörtern an die entsprechenden Gegenstände in deinem Zimmer kleben
- Wörter als Bildwörter oder mit passenden Bildern aufmalen
- Wörter mit anderen Begriffen, die zu einem Thema gehören, anhand von Überbegriffen in *mind maps* oder Tabellen strukturieren
- Wörter pantomimisch darstellen und gegenseitig erraten lassen
- Wörter aussprechen, zusammen mit ihrer Übersetzung und vielleicht einem Beispielsatz aufnehmen und immer wieder anhören
- Wörter mit ähnlichen Wörtern in anderen Sprachen notieren
- Wörter, die miteinander in Beziehung stehen, zusammen notieren, z. B. verwandte Wörter, Gegensatzpaare, zusammengehörige Paare

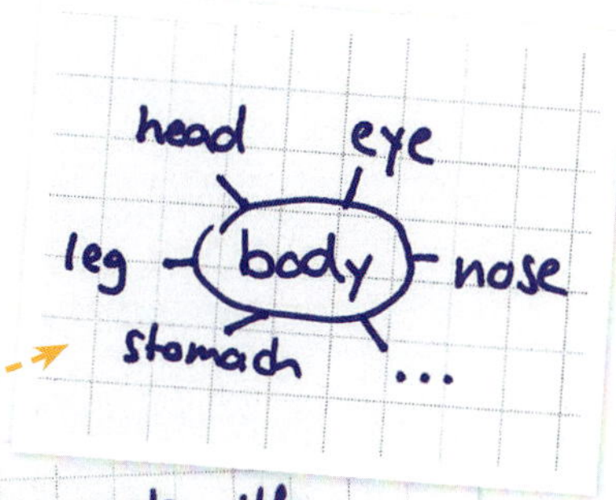

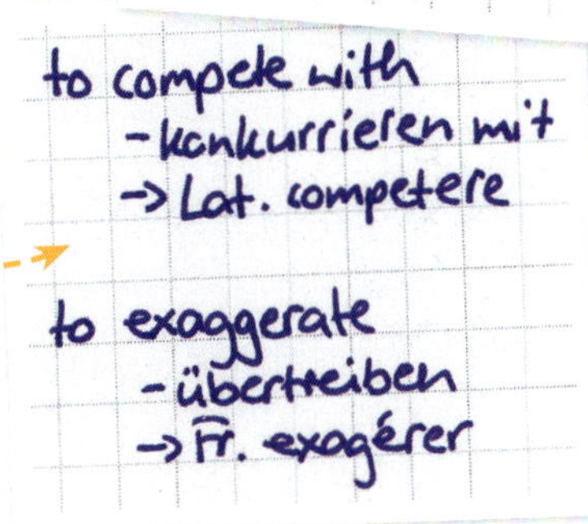

Reading

S5 Schnelllesetechniken

Wenn du eine Aufgabe zu einem Text bekommst oder eine bestimmte Information suchst, liest du den Text ganz gezielt. Diese Techniken helfen dir, wenn die Zeit begrenzt ist.

Skimming („den Rahm abschöpfen“)	**Scanning („maschinell durchsuchen“)**
Wenn du danach gefragt wirst, worum es in einem Text geht, sollst du ihn nicht einfach nacherzählen, sondern nur das Wichtigste *(gist)* zusammenfassen. Dazu kannst du den ganzen Text überfliegen und darauf achten, ob bestimmte Wörter *(key words)* oder Personen häufiger vorkommen. Auch die Überschrift oder Bilder können dir helfen einzuschätzen, was wichtig ist und was nicht. Diese Art des Schnelllesens nennt man *skimming*.	Wenn du nach bestimmten Einzelheiten *(details)* in einem Text gefragt wirst, musst du ihn überfliegen und die Stellen mit der wichtigen Information finden. Dazu suchst du gezielt nach passenden Stichwörtern *(key words)*. Sie zeigen an, welche Teile du genauer lesen solltest, um die gesuchte Information zu bekommen. Diese Art des Überfliegens nennt man auch *scanning*.

S6 Wichtige Inhalte von Texten herausfinden

Wenn du einen Text liest, solltest du danach immer folgende Fragen beantworten können:

Who ...? *Wer ist beteiligt?*	*What ...?* *Was geschieht?*	*When ...?* *Wann?*	*Where ...?* *Wo?*

Wende hierzu Schnelllesetechniken an, markiere Textstellen und notiere Fragen und Anmerkungen (→ S9). Wenn du Informationen aus einer bestimmten Textstelle entnimmst, notiere die Quelle (Seitenzahl, Zeilennummer). So kannst du deine Ergebnisse anhand des Texts belegen und findest die Textstelle später leicht wieder. Wenn du den Text noch genauer liest, kannst du weitere Fragen beantworten, z. B. Für wen wurde der Text geschrieben? Wer erzählt die Geschichte? Warum geschieht etwas? (→ S7)

S7 Wichtige Merkmale von Erzähltexten, Gedichten und Theaterstücken erkennen

1. Story

Wenn du eine Geschichte genauer liest oder analysierst, solltest du nicht nur über die Handlung (*plot*) selbst nachdenken, sondern auch darüber, wie die Geschichte erzählt wird. Zu den wichtigsten Erzähltechniken (*narrative techniques*) gehören:

Atmosphere / Mood	Bestimmte Wörter und Beschreibungen schaffen in einer Geschichte eine gewisse Stimmung (*atmosphere* oder *mood*). Stimmung entsteht z. B. dadurch, dass die fünf Sinne (*five senses*) angesprochen werden: Wenn man liest, was die Figuren sehen, hören, riechen, schmecken und fühlen, ist es leichter, sich in sie hineinzuversetzen.
Climax	Der Höhepunkt (*climax*) ist der Hauptwendepunkt in einer Geschichte. Die Spannung ist hier am höchsten. Die Hauptfigur befindet sich oft in einer schwierigen Situation und macht Veränderungen durch, sie wird z. B. stärker oder selbstbewusster. (Siehe auch *turning point*.)
Flashback	Eine Rückblende (*flashback*) erzählt Ereignisse, die vor einem bestimmten Zeitpunkt in der Geschichte stattgefunden haben, z. B. wird die Erinnerung einer Figur an etwas Vergangenes beschrieben.
Narrative perspective	Die Wirkung, die eine Geschichte auf den Leser hat, wird stark von der Erzählperspektive (*narrative perspective*) beeinflusst. Wer ist der Erzähler und wie ist seine Einstellung zu den Figuren der Geschichte? Was erzählt er und wann? Die häufigsten Erzählperspektiven sind: **1. Ich-Erzähler *(first-person narrator)*** Der Ich-Erzähler erzählt die Geschichte aus seiner Perspektive. Oft (aber nicht immer) ist der Ich-Erzähler die Hauptfigur der Geschichte. Der Leser und der Ich-Erzähler erleben die Geschichte sozusagen „gemeinsam". **2. Er- / Sie-Erzähler *(third-person narrator)*** Dieser Erzähler erzählt die Geschichte „von außen". Die Perspektive ist nicht die der Hauptfigur.

Suspense	Spannung (*suspense*) ist eine wichtige Erzähltechnik, um den Leser in die Geschichte hineinzuziehen. Spannung kann direkt in den ersten Zeilen der Geschichte aufgebaut werden oder aber langsam im Verlauf der Geschichte. Sie wird z. B. durch starke, dramatische Sprache erzeugt oder durch das Zurückhalten von Informationen.
Turning point	Ein Wendepunkt ist der Teil einer Geschichte, in dem eine Figur eine wichtige Entscheidung treffen muss. Diese Entscheidung beeinflusst den weiteren Verlauf der Geschichte. Sie kann für die Hauptfigur und die anderen Figuren gut oder schlecht sein. (Siehe auch *climax*.)

2. Poetry

Ein Gedicht ist wie eine Zeichnung oder ein Gemälde, das mit Wörtern „gemalt" wurde. In einem Gedicht ist jedes einzelne Wort wichtig. Denke daran: Beim Verständnis von Gedichten geht es nicht darum, die „richtige" Bedeutung zu finden – das gleiche Gedicht kann von verschiedenen Menschen ganz unterschiedlich verstanden werden. Wichtig ist aber, dass du deine Deutung am Text belegen kannst. Dazu ist es hilfreich, auch formale Merkmale zu untersuchen und mit dem Inhalt in Verbindung zu bringen. Zu den wichtigsten Merkmalen von Gedichten gehören:

Rhyme scheme	Gedichte, die sich reimen, folgen immer einem bestimmten Reimschema (*rhyme scheme*). Typische Reimschemata sind: **AABB** und **ABAB** sowie **ABCB**. Es gibt aber auch Gedichte, die sich nicht reimen, sogenannte *free verse poems*.
Rhythm / Stress	Ein Gedicht funktioniert nur mit dem richtigen Rhythmus (*rhythm*). Er bestimmt, welche Stelle in jeder Zeile betont wird. Die Betonung (*stress*) liegt dann immer an der gleichen Stelle. Bei Gedichten, die sich nicht reimen (*free verse poems*), ist es wichtig, dass du selbst entscheidest, wo die Betonung liegt oder wo eine Pause gemacht werden sollte.
Symbol / Simile / Metaphor	In Gedichten spielen Symbole eine wichtige Rolle. Ein **Symbol** (*symbol*) steht stellvertretend für etwas anderes, z. B. für ein Gefühl, eine Idee oder eine Handlung. So ist das Herz ein Symbol für die Liebe. Bei einem **Vergleich** (*simile*) werden Dinge oder Personen mit etwas anderem verglichen, um auszudrücken, dass sie die gleichen Eigenschaften besitzen. Dabei wird *like* oder *as* verwendet: *Happy as a rainbow.* Eine **Metapher** (*metaphor*) ist ein verkürzter Vergleich ohne *like* oder *as*: *I'll be the light to guide you.*

3. Drama

Theaterstücke sind in Akte (*act*) und Szenen (*scene*) unterteilt. Sie sind dafür vorgesehen, von Schauspielerinnen und Schauspielern auf der Bühne aufgeführt zu werden. Es gibt in der Regel keinen Erzähler, der die Figuren genauer beschreibt. Stattdessen wird die Handlung direkt durch die gesprochene Sprache und durch die Darstellung der Figuren vermittelt. Deshalb ist es bei der Interpretation von Theaterstücken besonders wichtig, neben dem Text auch auf die Sprechweise, Gestik und Mimik zu achten. So kannst du Rückschlüsse auf Charaktereigenschaften, Gedanken und Gefühle der Figuren ziehen.

Characters	Die Figuren (*characters*) stellen oft klassische Typen (oder Rollen) dar. Auf der einen Seite gibt es einen Helden / eine Heldin (*good guy*), auf der anderen Seite einen Bösewicht (*bad guy*). Das Handeln dieser Figuren wird von guten oder bösen Motiven angetrieben.
Language	In Theaterstücken wird die Handlung durch gesprochene Sprache vermittelt. Die Figuren sprechen in Dialogen miteinander.
Stage directions	Alles, was nicht durch gesprochene Sprache vermittelt werden kann, wird in Regieanweisungen (*stage directions*) vorgegeben. Sie beschreiben, wie die Schauspieler ihre Figur spielen sollen und wie sie sprechen. Sie machen auch Angaben zu Requisiten (*props*), Bühnenbild, Licht, usw. Wenn man ein Theaterstück liest, können die Regieanweisungen wichtige Hinweise auf z. B. die Stimmung der Szene und die Gefühle der Figuren geben. Sieht man das Theaterstück auf der Bühne, wird die Handlung und Stimmung des Stückes auch von Körpersprache, Bewegungen, Bühnenbild, Licht, usw. getragen.

S8 Gliederung als Hilfe

Um einen Text besser zu verstehen, kann es dir helfen, ihn in mehrere Abschnitte zu gliedern. Orientiere dich dabei z. B. an Absätzen und inhaltlichen Punkten, die du dir markiert hast. Überlege anschließend, was in den einzelnen Teilen jeweils das Wichtigste ist und formuliere passende Überschriften. Dies erleichtert es dir, Texte zusammenzufassen oder *Mediation*-Aufgaben zu lösen.

A Lonely Jay
B Meeting in the park
C Hanging out with the cool boys

S9 Textbearbeitung mit Markierungen und Notizen

Im geliehenen Buch darfst du das zwar nicht, aber auf Kopien oder in Arbeitsheften solltest du dir angewöhnen, wichtige Stellen in Texten zu markieren und Randnotizen zu machen (z. B. Fragen oder Anmerkungen). Verwende am besten verschiedene Farben:

Markiere z. B. wichtige inhaltliche Punkte grün und Informationen zu den Figuren / Charakteren blau. Wörter, die du nachschlagen musst, solltest du auch hervorheben. Unterstreiche sie beispielsweise und notiere die richtige Übersetzung am Rand. So fällt dir das erneute Lesen leichter.

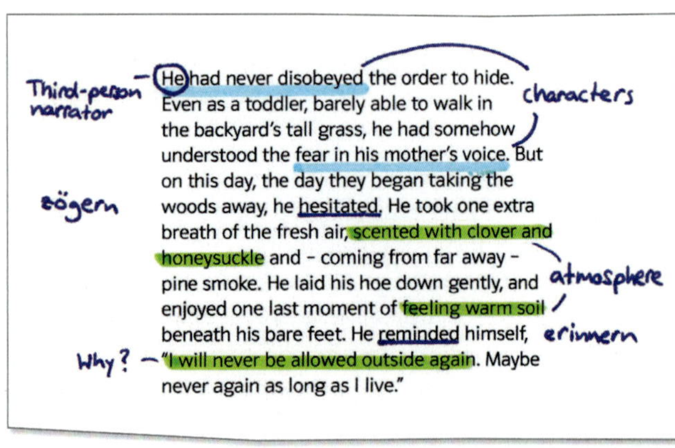
He had never disobeyed the order to hide. Even as a toddler, barely able to walk in the backyard's tall grass, he had somehow understood the fear in his mother's voice. But on this day, the day they began taking the woods away, he hesitated. He took one extra breath of the fresh air, scented with clover and honeysuckle and – coming from far away – pine smoke. He laid his hoe down gently, and enjoyed one last moment of feeling warm soil beneath his bare feet. He reminded himself, "I will never be allowed outside again. Maybe never again as long as I live."

S10 Umgang mit neuen Wörtern

Viele Wörter kannst du schon verstehen, obwohl du sie noch nicht gelernt hast.

1. **Ähnlichkeit mit Wörtern, die du schon kennst**
   Oft haben verwandte Wörter den gleichen Stamm, aber andere Präfixe oder Suffixe. Wenn du z. B. *usual* schon kennst, wirst du *unusual* sicher verstehen. Englische Wörter haben oft keine Suffixe, aber es gibt sie in verschiedenen Wortarten. Wenn du also das Wort *guide* als Nomen kennst, kannst du dir bestimmt denken, was das Verb *to guide* oder die Zusammensetzung *travel guide bedeutet*.

2. **Ähnlichkeit mit Wörtern, die du aus einer anderen Sprache kennst**
   Viele englische Wörter gibt es genauso oder ähnlich auch im Deutschen, z. B. *computer* oder *hobby*. Manchmal hilft dir auch ein Wort, das du aus einer anderen Sprache kennst (Französisch, Latein, …) ein englisches Wort zu verstehen, z. B. weil es ähnlich geschrieben wird oder ähnlich klingt.

3. **Verstehen der Wörter im Zusammenhang**
   Manchmal kannst du dir anhand eines Bildes oder einer Überschrift denken, was ein Wort in einem Text bedeutet. Und wenn du alle Wörter in einem Satz verstehst außer einem, kann dieses oft nur eine bestimmte Bedeutung haben. Was bedeutet z. B. *ridiculous* in folgendem Satz: *That's the silliest thing I've ever heard. It's **ridiculous**!*

Writing

S11 Arbeit mit dem zweisprachigen Wörterbuch

> **Kette** <-, -n> ['kɛtə] *f* ① (*Gliederkette*) chain; (*Fahrradkette*) [bicycle] chain; (*Schmuckkette*) necklace ② (*Serie*) line; **eine ~ von Ereignissen** a chain of events; **eine ~ von Unglücksfällen** a series of accidents

Ein zweisprachiges Wörterbuch – English-Deutsch / Deutsch-Englisch – enthält meistens folgende Informationen:

1. Aussprache
2. Wortart (Nomen, Adjektiv, Verb (regelmäßig/unregelmäßig) etc.)
3. weitere hilfreiche Informationen wie z. B., ob das Wort formal, Umgangssprache, Amerikanisches Englisch etc. ist
4. Beispielsätze sowie Wörter oder besondere Ausdrücke, mit denen das Wort oft verwendet wird (Präpositionen, Kollokationen etc.)
5. unterschiedliche Bedeutungen des Wortes
6. andere Wörter aus der gleichen Wortfamilie

Beachte bei der Arbeit mit einem Wörterbuch folgende Punkte:

- Du findest meist mehrere Bedeutungen für ein Wort. Achte also auf den Zusammenhang, wenn du ein Wort nachschlägst:
  Take the second street on the right. That's the right way for the station.
- Achte darauf, welche Wortart du suchst – Nomen, Verb, Adjektiv, …?
- Lies auch immer die besonderen Ausdrücke, denn das Wort könnte Teil einer Redewendung sein: *to take place* bedeutet nicht 'Platz nehmen'; es bedeutet 'stattfinden'!

S12 Textsorten und ihre Besonderheiten

Du kennst schon einige wichtige Textsorten und ihre Haupteigenschaften:

Blog	Ein Blog ist eine Art Online-Tagebuch, in dem regelmäßig Beiträge veröffentlicht werden. Es gibt unterschiedliche Arten von Blogs, z. B. Reiseblogs, Nachrichtenblogs oder Musikblogs. Meist sind Blog-Posts in der Ich-Perspektive geschrieben und sind von dem persönlichen Standpunkt des Bloggers / der Bloggerin geprägt.
Dialogue / Film script	Wenn du einen Dialog, z. B. für eine Filmszene, schreibst, denke daran, dass du ihn kurz hältst und echte mündliche Sprache verwendest, also z. B. *short forms*, *question tags*, verstärkende Ausdrücke usw. Beachte bei den *stage directions* für ein Filmskript, dass du nur das angibst, was man auch sehen oder darstellen kann. Gedanken kann man nicht sehen. Aber du kannst in den *stage directions* Hinweise auf die Gefühle einer Person geben, z. B. durch Anweisungen für Gesichtsausdrücke.
Diary entry	Ein Tagebucheintrag erzählt und kommentiert vergangene und erwartete Ereignisse aus der ganz persönlichen Sicht einer Person und ist normalerweise nicht für andere Leser bestimmt. Verwende ausdrucksstarke Adjektive und Adverbien, um Gedanken und Gefühle zu beschreiben.
E-mail / Letter Postcard / Invitation	Achte auf die richtige Anrede für den Adressaten, z. B. *Dear …*, Grußformeln am Schluss, z. B. *Yours / Love / Best wishes*, und beachte die Höflichkeitsregeln. Bei formellen E-Mails oder Briefen verwendet man eher die Langformen, z. B. *I am* statt *I'm*. Denke bei einem Brief an die Angabe der Empfänger- und Absenderadresse und an das Datum.
Flyer	Ein Flyer sollte gut lesbar sein (Schriftart- und größe) und alle wichtigen Informationen enthalten: *Who? What? When? Where? Why?* Formuliere außerdem einen ansprechenden Slogan.
Instructions	Anweisungen sind meist in mehrere, klare Schritte gegliedert. Diese Schritte können von Überschriften eingeleitet werden. Sprachlich werden vor allem Imperative und *phrases* wie *Make sure …*, *You / It must …* oder *Never …* verwendet.
News report	Konzentriere dich bei einem Tatsachenbericht auf die Fakten und spare deine persönliche Meinung aus. Achte außerdem auf eine sachliche Sprache und vermeide emotionale Ausdrücke. Die Schlagzeile sollte direkt auf das Thema des Artikels hinweisen und außerdem das Interesse des Lesers wecken. In Zeitungsberichten werden häufig Passivformen verwendet.
Persuasive text	Ein Werbetext soll den Leser direkt ansprechen und überzeugen. Dies gelingt z. B. mit rhetorischen Fragen, persönlichen Formulierungen und etwas Humor. Verbinde deine Sätze mit Konjunktionen und mache sie mit ausdrucksstarken Adjektiven interessant. Überlege dir für den Schluss einen besonders überzeugenden Satz, der dem Leser im Gedächtnis bleibt.

Prompt cards	Wenn du dich auf eine Präsentation vorbereitest, notiere auf Karteikarten nur Stichwörter, die dich an die einzelnen Punkte des Vortrags erinnern. Schreibe z. B. wichtige Namen, Ereignisse, Orte und Daten unter die Überschriften *Who? What? Where? When?*
Report	Bei einem Bericht ist die Vollständigkeit und Verständlichkeit der sachlichen Informationen das Wichtigste. Er wird im *simple past* geschrieben.
Review	Eine Rezension bzw. Kritik bietet dem Leser eine Entscheidungshilfe, ob es sich lohnt, z. B. eine bestimmte Veranstaltung zu besuchen oder ein Buch zu lesen. Zuerst werden kurz die wichtigsten Details beschrieben, dann wird eine mit Argumenten belegte Bewertung abgegeben.
Story	Wenn du Geschichten oder Bildergeschichten schreibst, schmücke sie aus und gestalte sie sprachlich abwechslungsreich. Meistens sind Geschichten im *simple past* geschrieben. Wenn du eine Geschichte vervollständigen sollst, muss dein Teil zum vorgegebenen Text passen. Vermeide also inhaltliche Widersprüche. Außerdem sollten die Erzählperspektive und die Erzählzeit nicht wechseln.

S13 Planung und Überarbeitung deines Textes

Überlege, für wen dein Text bestimmt ist (Adressat) und welchen Zweck er erfüllen soll. Mach dir vor dem Schreiben einen Plan, in dem du Stichpunkte zu Einleitung, Hauptteil und Schluss deines Textes notierst.
Wenn du einen ersten Entwurf deines Textes erstellt hast, liest du ihn am besten noch einmal gründlich durch. So kannst du Fehler entdecken und holprige Formulierungen verbessern. Nimm dabei eine Checkliste zu Hilfe (siehe rechts). Es ist auch hilfreich, die Texte mit einem Partner zu tauschen.

Checkliste

Rechtschreibung:
- Wörter richtig geschrieben?
- Am Satzanfang groß?
- Getrennt oder zusammen?

Grammatik:
- Richtige Zeitformen?
- Richtige Formenbildung?

Inhalt:
- Alle wesentlichen Punkte enthalten?
- Keine inhaltlichen Fehler?
- Zusammenhänge erkennbar und logisch?

S14 Sprachliche Verbesserungen

Je größer dein Wortschatz wird, desto mehr Möglichkeiten eröffnen sich dir beim Schreiben von Texten.
Gestalte Sätze interessanter, indem du z. B. Nomen durch Adjektive oder durch weitere Nomen näher beschreibst. Verben kannst du durch adverbiale Bestimmungen ergänzen. Vergleiche die folgenden beiden Sätze:

A *I went to the shop.*

B *I went to the big pet shop in Greenwich with my sister last Saturday.*

Ein Text liest sich leichter, wenn die Sätze darin miteinander verknüpft sind. Mit Hilfe von Konjunktionen (*linking words*) werden logische Zusammenhänge hergestellt.
Vergleiche die beiden folgenden Textausschnitte. Der erste wirkt durch die unverbundenen Hauptsätze abgehackt. Der zweite liest sich durch Satzgefüge aus Haupt- und Nebensätzen und durch Konjunktionen flüssiger. Außerdem geben die vielen Adjektive und Adverbien genauere Informationen und machen den Text interessanter.

A *I went to the shop. I wanted a guinea pig. We looked at all the guinea pigs. I didn't like them. We wanted to leave. A girl came in with a box. She brought back a guinea pig. It was cute! I bought it. I'm happy.*

B *I went to the big pet shop in Greenwich with my sister last Saturday **because** I wanted to buy a nice guinea pig. We looked at all the guinea pigs, **but** I didn't like them. **Just when** I wanted to leave, a girl came in with a box. She brought back a guinea pig **which** was really cute. **So** I bought it **and** I'm very happy now.*

Speaking

S15 Sprechen üben

Sprechen lernt man nur durch Sprechen. Du solltest dir angewöhnen, im Englischunterricht immer Englisch zu sprechen, ob mit deiner Lehrerin / deinem Lehrer oder in der Partner- und Gruppenarbeit. Auch zu Hause kannst du Englisch sprechen – vielleicht üben deine Freunde, Eltern oder Geschwister mit dir?

Wichtig ist, dass du englische Wörter richtig aussprichst. Im Buch kann dir die Lautschrift dabei helfen. Sage sie dir immer wieder laut vor. Einfacher und einprägsamer ist es, die Vokabeln anzuhören und nachzusprechen. Hilfsmittel dafür sind Audio-CDs mit den Schülerbuchtexten, Lernsoftware, Online-Wörterbücher oder Vokabel-Apps, in denen du jedes Wort anklicken und anhören kannst.

Übe Laute, die anders sind als im Deutschen, z. B. das stimmhafte oder stimmlose *th*, das *w* im Kontrast zum *v* oder ein stimmhaftes *d* oder *g* am Wortende. Dazu kannst du (lustige) Sätze erfinden, sie dir immer wieder vorsprechen und dabei das Tempo steigern, bis die Aussprache zuverlässig klappt.

Wenn du ganze Texte hörst, bekommst du ein Gefühl dafür, wie die Wörter im Textzusammenhang ausgesprochen werden. Die Aussprache unterscheidet sich manchmal stark von der Aussprache der Einzelwörter. Aufeinander treffende Laute werden z. B. häufig miteinander verbunden.

They **th**ought of **th**e **th**ree **th**ousand **th**ankful **th**ieves.

Why **w**ork **w**ith **v**ocabulary **w**hen you can **v**isit a **w**onderful **v**illage **w**orld?

She wante**d** her ba**g** back and sai**d** what a nice hat she ha**d**.

This is the end of the story. They know over a hundred different stories.

Du kannst auch üben, wie die Betonung die Aussprache beeinflusst, wenn jemand besonders starke Gefühle ausdrücken will.

It's **so** unfair! Why doesn't anyone **ever** ask **me** what I'm feeling?

S16 Gesprochene Sprache

Beim Sprechen kommt es auf die Situation und deinen Gesprächspartner an, wie du dich ausdrückst. Denke z. B. auch an Höflichkeitsregeln (siehe Beispiele rechts).
In der gesprochenen Sprache ist es normal, dass Pausen, unvollständige Sätze, Wiederholungen oder Füllwörter vorkommen:

***Well, I – I** really don't know. It's – **er**, maybe you want to …?*

- Während bei Gleichaltrigen ein *Hi!* als Begrüßung ausreicht, ist Lehrpersonen oder fremden Erwachsenen gegenüber ein *Good morning!* / *Good afternoon!* / … eher angemessen.
- Statt *I want …* sagst du höflicher *I would like …* oder *Could I please have …?*
- Entscheidungsfragen beantwortest du mit Kurzantworten, nicht einfach mit *Yes* oder *No: Yes, I do.* / *No, I'm not.*

Es ist wichtig, einem Dialogpartner immer das Gefühl zu geben, dass er einbezogen wird. Dazu dienen *feedback phrases*, Nachfragen und *question tags*.

*Then we went to the new shoe shop in the city centre, **you know**. And there were these amazing trainers – **I showed you a photo, didn't I? Guess what Linda said when she saw them!***

S17 Mündliche Aufgaben und ihre Besonderheiten

Beim Sprechen gibt es ganz unterschiedliche Situationen. Wenn du dich mit einem Gesprächspartner abwechselst, nennt man das dialogisches Sprechen. Beim monologischen Sprechen hingegen sprichst du längere Zeit am Stück allein. Hier sind einige Beispiele:

1. Dialogisches Sprechen

Dialogue / Discussion / Role play	Gib deinem **Gesprächspartner** immer das Gefühl, dass er einbezogen wird. Dazu dienen *feedback phrases* und Nachfragen *(… you know./ Guess what …!)*. Wenn du ***Small talk*** führst, vermeide sehr persönliche Themen und achte darauf, dass die Konversation nicht abrupt abbricht. Bei **Rollenspielen** musst du versuchen nachzufühlen, was die Person weiß, denkt und fühlt. Unterstütze deine Worte mit Mimik und Gestik.

Interview	Sei höflich, aber scheue dich nicht nachzufragen, wenn du etwas nicht sofort verstehst. Achte bei den Fragen und Antworten auf die richtige Zeitform und das richtige Hilfsverb.
Asking / Showing the way	Auch hier ist Höflichkeit wichtig, ebenso wie bestimmte *phrases*, z. B. *go down X Street, go straight on, go past / turn left / right into Y Lane, it's on the left / right / opposite Z.*

2. Monologisches Sprechen

Presentation	Bereite deine Präsentation gut vor. Recherchiere die Fakten gründlich und konzentriere dich auf das Wichtige. Besorge Material, das du zeigen willst, und bereite es so auf, dass es gut aussieht und verständlich ist. Mache dir einen Ablaufplan. Schreibe dir Notizen auf *prompt cards*. Sprich langsam und deutlich und möglichst ohne abzulesen. Übe deine Präsentation vorher und stoppe die Zeit, die du brauchst.

Mediation

S18 Bearbeitung von Mediation-Aufgaben

Mediation ist die Übertragung wichtiger Informationen aus einem gesprochenen oder geschriebenen Text in eine andere Sprache, z. B. aus dem Englischen ins Deutsche oder umgekehrt. Das machst du, wenn du einen Text für jemanden zusammenfassen sollst, der die Sprache des Ausgangstexts nicht versteht. Gelegentlich kann es auch sein, dass du dolmetschen musst, also zwischen Gesprächspartnern vermittelst, die nicht dieselbe Sprache sprechen. Ganz wichtig: Es geht bei der *Mediation* niemals um eine wörtliche Übersetzung *(translation)*!

Lies dir die *Mediation*-Aufgabe gut durch und beachte besonders folgende Dinge:

Adressat:
Für wen ist die Information bestimmt?
--> Je nachdem, wer die Person ist und wie viel sie schon weiß, sprichst du sie unterschiedlich an.

Zweck:
Wozu benötigt die Person die Information?
--> Du musst nur die Informationen wiedergeben, die für den Adressaten in der jeweiligen Situation wichtig sind. Alles andere kannst du weglassen. Es kann aber auch vorkommen, dass du Dinge zusätzlich erklären musst.

Beispiel: Dein Ausgangstext ist die Infobroschüre eines Museums, die alle Öffnungszeiten und Eintrittspreise enthält. Wenn dein Gegenüber dich fragt, ob das Museum heute geöffnet ist, musst du nicht unbedingt alle anderen Öffnungszeiten nennen. Will die Person den Eintrittspreis wissen, kommt es auf ihr Alter an und darauf, ob sie allein oder mit einer Gruppe unterwegs ist.

Einen schriftlichen Ausgangstext kannst du in Ruhe durchlesen und die wichtigen Informationen auswählen. Dabei helfen dir alle Techniken, die unter *Reading* (→ S5–S10) beschrieben sind. Formuliere die entsprechenden Inhalte so, dass der Adressat sie gut verstehen kann.
Bei einer Dolmetschaufgabe wird eine echte mündliche Gesprächssituation simuliert. Deshalb musst du schneller reagieren, um möglichst viel von dem sinngemäß wiederzugeben, was die Gesprächspartner zueinander sagen.

Wenn dir ein Wort in der Zielsprache nicht einfällt, umschreibe es mit anderen Worten *(paraphrasing)*. Beachte bei der schriftlichen und mündlichen Bearbeitung von *Mediation*-Aufgaben außerdem die Tipps unter *Writing* (→ S11–S14) und *Speaking* (→ S15–S17).

Auch bei einer *Translation* geht es nicht darum, wortwörtlich, sondern sinngemäß zu übersetzen. Im Unterschied zur *Mediation* musst du aber alle Informationen wiedergeben und darfst Wörter nur dann umschreiben, wenn du keine geeignete Übersetzung findest. Halte dich also so genau wie möglich an den Ausgangstext und schreibe im gleichen Stil.

Listening

S19 Hörverstehen üben

Es ist immer sinnvoll, viele echte englische Texte anzuhören, z. B. Nachrichten in Radio und Fernsehen oder Hörbücher. Dabei ist es nicht schlimm, wenn du nicht jedes Wort verstehst. Dir wird außerdem auffallen, wie unterschiedlich die Aussprache des Englischen je nach Herkunft des Sprechers sein kann. So gibt es neben Unterschieden zwischen britischem und amerikanischem Englisch auch innerhalb Großbritanniens verschiedene Dialekte oder regionale Akzente. Auch dann ist es nicht schlimm, wenn du nicht alles verstehst. Selbst ein Engländer aus London könnte Schwierigkeiten haben, einen Schotten aus Glasgow auf Anhieb zu verstehen.

S20 Techniken des Hörverstehens

Analog zum Lesen helfen dir auch beim Hörverstehen unterschiedliche Techniken.

Listening for gist	**Listening for detail**
Versuche, das Wichtigste in einem Hörtext zu erkennen und zusammenzufassen. Achte dabei besonders auf Wörter und Themen, die mehrmals vorkommen und vermutlich eine wichtige Rolle spielen.	Versuche gezielt, dem Text bestimmte Einzelinformationen zu entnehmen. Achte dabei besonders auf Wörter, die du in der Antwort erwartest, und die Informationen dazu.

Auch beim Hörverstehen kann dir wie beim Leseverstehen eine Tabelle mit den nachfolgenden Fragen helfen. In der Tabelle kannst du dir während des Hörens Notizen machen.

Who ...?	What ...?	When ...?	Where ...?

S21 Typische Hörverstehenssituationen

Manchmal hilft dir beim Hörverstehen auch die Kenntnis von typischen Textsorten und Situationen. Wenn du die Textsorte des Hörtextes kennst, überlege dir, worauf es beim Telefonieren, beim Dolmetschen, bei Präsentationen, Durchsagen, Radio- oder Fernsehsendungen ankommt und welche Themen jeweils zu erwarten sind. Gelegentlich geben dir auch Bilder Hinweise zur entsprechenden Situation: Wenn z. B. bestimmte Personen oder Orte dargestellt sind, kannst du leichter einschätzen, worum es in dem Hörtext geht. Achte beim Hören auf Geräusche sowie Stimme und Tonfall des Sprechers. In echten Gesprächssituationen oder Filmen können dir auch Gestik und Mimik das Verständnis erleichtern.

Film skills / Viewing

S22 Inhalt und Gliederung

Ein Film ist auch eine Art Text. Deshalb lassen sich viele ähnliche Fragen dazu stellen:

- Worum geht es?
- Wird eine Geschichte erzählt?
- Welche Personen spielen mit?
- Welches sind die Hauptpersonen?
- Was passiert in welcher Reihenfolge?
- Wann und wo passiert es?
- Welche Gliederung und welche Themen sind zu erkennen?
- Aus wessen Sicht wird die Geschichte erzählt?
- Wer hat den Film gemacht, für welches Publikum und wozu?

Das Anschauen und Verstehen eines Films verlangt dir jedoch nicht nur das Verständnis der Sprache ab, sondern du musst auch auf viele weitere Dinge achten.

S23 Wichtige filmische Mittel

Wie stellen die Schauspieler den Charakter der Personen dar, die sie verkörpern? Wie drücken sie Gefühle aus?

--➤ Achte vor allem auf Sprache, Mimik und Gestik. Aber auch Kleidung oder Frisuren können eine Rolle spielen.

Wie werden Handlungsort und -zeit dargestellt *(setting)*?
--➤ Achte auf Landschaften, Gebäude und Innenräume, Kleidung und Gegenstände.

Wie wird eine bestimmte Atmosphäre geschaffen *(atmosphere)*?
--➤ Achte auf Bilder, Licht, Farben, Musik, Geräusche.

Wie unterstützt die Musik den Inhalt des Films?
--➤ Achte darauf, wann welche Musik ertönt und wann sie wechselt.

Wie helfen bestimmte Kameraeinstellungen den Inhalt deutlicher darzustellen *(shot)*?
--➤ Achte z. B. auf Nahaufnahmen *(close-ups)*.

Wie wird Spannung erzeugt *(suspense)*?
--➤ Achte auf Vorandeutungen, Musik, Licht, Geräusche und natürlich die Gestik und Mimik der Schauspieler.

Mit der Zeit wirst du weitere filmische Mittel kennen lernen, die bestimmte Wirkungen auf den Zuschauer erzeugen.

S24 Filmgenres

Es gibt viele unterschiedliche Arten von Filmen, man nennt sie auch Genres. Du erkennst Filme eines Genres normalerweise daran, dass sie ähnliche Hauptmerkmale aufweisen.

Hier sind einige Beispiele:

Action	In Actionfilmen geht es meist um einen Helden oder eine Heldin im Kampf gegen das Böse. Dabei kommen häufig spektakuläre Stunts, Verfolgungsjagden und Gewaltszenen vor.
Crime	Im Mittelpunkt eines Kriminalfilms steht ein Verbrechen, das häufig im Laufe des Films aufgeklärt wird. Dabei gibt es viele spannende Szenen und überraschende Wendungen.

Action

Crime

Comedy	Komödien haben eine humorvolle Handlung, die zum Lachen anregt. Häufig werden die Charaktere übertrieben dargestellt und Sprachwitz spielt eine wichtige Rolle.
Fantasy	Fantasyfilme handeln von magischen oder übernatürlichen Kräften. Häufig steht ein Held oder eine Heldin im Mittelpunkt der Handlung.
Historical	Historienfilme spielen in einer bestimmten geschichtlichen Epoche. Häufig basieren sie auf wahren Begebenheiten. Die Kostüme und Requisiten sind meist aufwändig gestaltet.
Romance	In Liebesfilmen steht die Beziehung zwischen zwei Figuren im Mittelpunkt. Das Ende dieser Filme fällt meist positiv aus.
Science Fiction	Science-Fiction-Filme handeln z.B. von Erfindungen in Wissenschaft und Technik, von Zeitreisen oder Außerirdischen. Sie spielen häufig in der Zukunft und wirken unrealistisch.

Fantasy

Historical

Science Fiction

Kooperative Lernformen

Hier findest du die Erklärung für einige ausgewählte Methoden der kooperativen Arbeit.

S25 Think – Pair – Share

1. *Think:* Du sammelst still mögliche Lösungen zu der Aufgabe. Du kannst deine Ideen in Stichpunkten notieren.
2. *Pair:* Zusammen mit deinem Partner besprichst du leise deine gesammelten Ideen.
3. *Share:* Im Klassengespräch meldet ihr euch und teilt euren Mitschülern die Ergebnisse eurer Partnergespräche mit.

Variante: *Placemat* in Vierergruppen

S26 Milling around (Marktplatz)

Du gehst durch das Klassenzimmer, erfragst von deinen Mitschülern bestimmte Informationen und gibst auch selbst Auskunft. Versuche mit möglichst vielen Mitschülern zu sprechen und verschiedene Informationen zu sammeln. Ihr könnt auch ein Signal vereinbaren, zu dem ihr eure Gesprächspartner wechselt.

S27 Inside outside circle (Kugellager)

1. Bildet zwei Stuhlkreise, einen inneren und einen äußeren.
2. Setzt euch in den Stuhlkreisen so hin, dass immer ein Schüler des äußeren und des inneren Stuhlkreises sich gegenüber sitzen.
3. Stellt euch gegenseitig eure Fragen und beantwortet diese.
4. Rutscht im inneren oder äußeren Kreis nach dem Ende der Gesprächsrunde einen Platz weiter und beginnt ein Gespräch mit einem neuen Mitschüler.

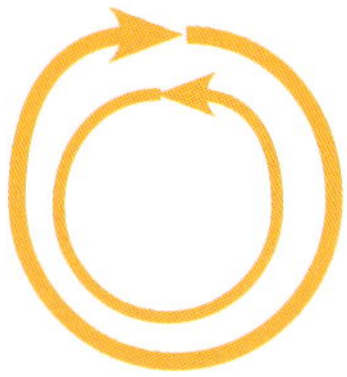

S28 Bus stop (Lerntempoduett)

Sobald du deine Aufgabe fertig bearbeitet hast, gehst du zu einem vereinbarten Treffpunkt, dem *bus stop*. Dort wartest du auf den nächsten Mitschüler, der fertig ist, und zusammen besprecht und vergleicht ihr eure Lösungen. Anschließend verlasst ihr den *bus stop* und bearbeitet die nächste Aufgabe.

S29 Gallery walk (Museumsgang)

1. *Group work:* In der Gruppe erarbeitet ihr ein Thema und haltet euer Ergebnis, z.B. auf einem Poster, fest.
2. *Gallery walk:* Es werden neue Gruppen gebildet. In jeder Gruppe ist ein Schüler jeder Ausgangsgruppe. Jede Gruppe betrachtet die verschiedenen Ergebnisse der Gruppenarbeiten. Jeder präsentiert nun in der neuen Gruppe das Ergebnis seiner Ausgangsgruppe.

Grammar

Liebe Schülerin, lieber Schüler,
in dieser *Grammar* findest du ausführliche Erklärungen zu allen grammatischen Themen in Green Line 3. Die Grammatikkapitel (**G**) helfen dir, die Grammatik zu verstehen, einzelne Punkte nachzuholen, wenn du im Unterricht gefehlt hast, oder bestimmte Regeln für Hausaufgaben und die Vorbereitung von Tests und Klassenarbeiten nachzuschlagen. Regeln sind mit einem blauen Punkt (●) gekennzeichnet. Ein Ausrufezeichen (❗) bedeutet, dass du hier besonders aufpassen musst. Die **English summary** fasst die wichtigsten Regeln auf Englisch zusammen. Am Ende jedes Kapitels überprüfst du mit **Test yourself**, ob du alles verstanden hast. Die Lösungen findest du ab Seite 286.

Grammatical terms

English term		Example	*Deutsche Bezeichnung*
adverb of manner; adverb of degree comparison of adverbs	G10 G11	They could see the blood **very clearly** on the wall. Our guide knows London's history **better** than anyone.	*Adverb der Art und Weise; Gradadverbien* *Steigerung der Adverbien*
conditional clause type 1	G1	**If** I **become** a famous dancer, I'**ll earn** a lot of money.	*Bedingungssatz Typ 1*
conditional clause type 2	G2	**If** I **had** the choice, I **would drop out of** school.	*Bedingungssatz Typ 2*
defining relative clause contact clause	G9 G9b	The Globe is a theatre **that** was popular in Shakespeare's days. **The man Jay** saw was a ghost.	*notwendiger Relativsatz* *– mit Relativpronomen* *– ohne Relativpronomen*
indirect speech statements expressions of time and place questions commands/requests	G12–G15 G12 G13 G14 G15	 They **said** (that) there **was** free wifi! He told me (that) they had been to Paris **the day before**. Grandma **asked** me when my flight **was**. She **told** him **to call** her back.	*Indirekte Rede* *Aussagen* *Zeit- und Ortsangaben* *Fragen* *Befehle/Aufforderungen/Bitten*
passive	G6	Haggis **is made** with meat.	*Passiv*
past perfect simple	G8	In 43 AD the Romans arrived in Britain. But, of course, they **had been** here before.	*Plusquamperfekt*
past progressive	G7	Holly **was looking** for souvenirs when she found the Loch Ness monsters.	*Verlaufsform der Vergangenheit*
present perfect vs. simple past	G4	**Have** you ever **run** in a real marathon? – No, but I **ran** in a half marathon last year.	*Gegenüberstellung von* present perfect *und* simple past
present perfect progressive	G5	Tell us what you'**ve been doing**.	*Verlaufsform des Perfekts*
reflexive pronouns and *each other*	G3	Come to northwest Scotland – and enjoy **yourself**!	*Reflexivpronomen*

Unit 1

G1 If I become a famous dancer, I'll earn a lot of money.

→ Seiten 10–12

Bedingungssätze Typ 1
Conditional clauses type 1

Mit dem Bedingungssatz Typ 1 drückst du aus, was unter einer bestimmten Bedingung passieren wird. Der Sprecher hält die Bedingung für erfüllbar. Es ist also wahrscheinlich, dass die Folge eintritt.

- *Der Bedingungssatz Typ 1 besteht aus einem* **if-*Satz*** *(Nebensatz) und einem* ***Hauptsatz***. *Im* **if-*Satz*** *drückst du die Bedingung aus, im* ***Hauptsatz*** *sagst du, was passiert oder passieren kann, falls diese Bedingung erfüllt wird.*
- *Im* **if-*Satz*** *verwendest du das* **simple present**, *im* ***Hauptsatz*** *das* **will future**.

Bedingung im if-*Satz:* simple present	*Folge im Hauptsatz:* will future
If Jay **becomes** a famous dancer,	he'**ll earn** a lot of money.
But **if** he **drops out** of school now,	he **won't have** many choices later.

- *Neben dem* **will future** *kannst du im* ***Hauptsatz*** *häufig auch die* ***Modalverben*** (can, must, should + infinitive) *oder den* ***Imperativ*** *verwenden.*

if-*Satz:* simple present	*Hauptsatz:* *Modalverb* + infinitive *oder Imperativ*
If you **want** to be a pop star,	you **must be able to** sing and dance. (*Notwendigkeit*)
If Jay **wants** to be the lead dancer,	he **should practise** more often. (*Ratschlag*)
If he **needs** advice,	he **can ask** Shahid. (*Möglichkeit*)
If you **need** advice,	**have** a look on the internet. There are lots of good websites. (*Aufforderung*)

❗ *Bedingungssätze können entweder mit dem* **if-*Satz*** *oder mit dem* ***Hauptsatz*** *beginnen:*
If Jay **leaves** school before he's 18, his parents **won't be** happy.
Jay's parents **won't be** happy **if** he **leaves** school before he's 18. *(Kein Komma vor* **if***!)*

❗ *Verwechsle nicht* **if** *(wenn / falls = Bedingung) mit* **when** *(wenn = zeitlicher Zusammenhang)!*
If Jay's parents tell him to focus on school again, he'll go crazy.
Wenn / Falls Jays Eltern ihm noch einmal sagen, dass er sich auf die Schule konzentrieren soll, wird er durchdrehen.
He hates it **when** they do that.
Er hasst es, wenn sie das tun.

Test yourself *Shahid and Jay want to go to the cinema together. They want to catch the train at 6:30, but Shahid isn't ready. This is what Jay says. Complete his sentences.*

1. If we (not leave) now, we (miss) our train.
2. If we (miss) our train, we (be late) for the film.
3. If we (be late) for the film, they probably (not let) us in.
4. And I (be) really upset if that (happen), Shahid. So, please hurry up!

G2 They wouldn't worry if they didn't care.

→ Seiten 10–12

Bedingungssätze Typ 2
Conditional clauses type 2

Mit dem Bedingungssatz Typ 2 drückst du aus, was unter einer bestimmten Bedingung passieren könnte. Der Sprecher hält diese Bedingung für nicht oder nicht so einfach erfüllbar. Es ist also (zur Zeit) eher unwahrscheinlich, dass die Folge eintritt.

- *Für die Bedingung im* **if-*Satz*** *verwendest du das* **simple past**, *für die Folge im* ***Hauptsatz*** **would(n't) / could(n't) + infinitive**.
Die entsprechende Kurzform von would *lautet* **'d** (I'd, you'd, he'd …).

Bedingung im if-*Satz:* simple past	*Folge im Hauptsatz:* conditional (would / could + infinitive)
If I **had** the choice,	I **would** / I'**d drop out of** school.
Wenn ich die Wahl hätte, würde ich die Schule abbrechen.	
If I **didn't have to** go to school,	I **could dance** all day.
Wenn ich nicht zur Schule gehen müsste, könnte ich den ganzen Tag tanzen.	
If Jay **looked** as good as Shahid,	he'**d work** as a model too.
Wenn Jay so gut aussehen würde wie Shahid, würde er auch als Model arbeiten.	
If I **were** Jay,	I'**d take** Shahid's advice.
Wenn ich Jay wäre, würde ich Shahids Rat annehmen.	

- *Nach* I / he / she / it *kannst du* **was** *oder* **were** *verwenden.*
  If I **were / was** rich, I'**d** …
  If he / she / it **were / was** famous, he'**d** …

! *Achte darauf, dass du* **would** *nur für die* ***Folge im Hauptsatz*** *verwendest! Die* **Bedingung** *im* **if-*Satz*** *steht immer im* **simple past**.
If Shahid **didn't work** as a model, he **wouldn't** have so much money.
Wenn Shahid ***nicht*** *als Model* ***arbeiten würde***, ***hätte*** *er nicht so viel Geld.*

English summary

A conditional sentence has two parts: an **if-clause** and a **main clause**.

- You use **type 1** for actions that are **probable / possible**.
  The verb in the **if-clause** is in the **simple present**; the verb in the **main clause** is in the **will future**. *If you make the right decisions now, you'll have more choices later.*
- You use **type 2** for actions that are **not probable** or **not possible**.
  The verb in the **if-clause** is in the **simple past**; the verb in the **main clause** is in the **conditional** tense. *If I had a million pounds, I'd travel the world.*

Test yourself *Jay has had another fight with his parents. He's talking to Shahid about his problems with them now. Complete this part of their conversation.*

Jay: If Mum and Dad (try) to understand me, we (not fight) so often.
Shahid: They're just worried about you, Jay. You (not have) so many fights if you (work) harder for school and (get) better marks.
Jay: The problem is that they don't believe in me, Shahid. If they (believe) in me, they (not worry) about my marks.
Shahid: They only worry because they care about you, Jay. Maybe if you (not be) so laid-back, they (not have to) worry so much.

G3 You have to push yourself.

→ Seiten 14–15

Reflexivpronomen
Reflexive pronouns and each other

Im Englischen verwendest du die Reflexivpronomen (Pronomen auf -self / -selves*), wenn das* ***Objekt*** *sich auf das* ***Subjekt*** *im Satz zurückbezieht. Subjekt und Objekt sind dabei* ***dieselbe Person.***
Du verwendest die Reflexivpronomen auch, wenn du eine Person oder Sache im Satz hervorheben willst.

- *Die Singularformen der Reflexivpronomen enden auf* -self (herself); *die Pluralformen auf* -selves (themselves).

	1. Person	*2. Person*	*3. Person*
Singular:	(I) … myself	(you) … yourself	(he, she, it) … himself, herself, itself
Plural:	(we) … ourselves	(you) … yourselves	(they) … themselves

- *Die* -self*-Pronomen kommen im Englischen als Reflexivpronomen (rückbezügliche Pronomen) und als verstärkende Pronomen vor.*

a) ***Reflexiver Gebrauch***

- *Im Englischen verwendest du die Pronomen auf* -self / -selves, *wenn das* ***Objekt*** ***dieselbe Person*** *bezeichnet wie das* ***Subjekt****. In diesem Fall entsprechen sie den deutschen Pronomen mich / mir, dich / dir, sich (selbst), usw. Vergleiche:*

Did **you** teach **her**?	her = *andere Person (Objektpronomen)*
She taught **herself**.	herself = *dieselbe Person (Reflexivpronomen)*

	Subjekt	*Verb*	*Objekt / Reflexivpronomen*	*Deutsch*
I'm so angry	**I**	could hit	**myself**.	ich – mich
Did	**you**	hurt	**yourself**?	du – dich / du – dir
Jay wants to become a famous singer.	**He**	really pushes	**himself** with singing and dancing.	er – sich
Claire often feels like	**she**'s	talking to	**herself**.	sie – (mit) sich (selbst)
	We	always enjoy	**ourselves**.	wir – uns
Why can't	**you**	behave	**yourselves**?	ihr – euch
Don't worry about the boys.	**They**	can look after	**themselves**.	sie – sich

❗ *Die Reflexivpronomen werden im Englischen wesentlich seltener gebraucht als im Deutschen. Viele Verben, die* ***im Deutschen reflexiv*** *sind, werden* ***im Englischen ohne*** **-self** *oder* **-selves** *gebildet.*
How do you feel today? – *Wie fühlst du* ***dich*** *heute?*
I'm looking forward to the weekend. – *Ich freue* ***mich*** *auf das Wochenende.*

change	*sich (ver)ändern*	look forward to	*sich freuen auf*
decide	*sich entscheiden*	meet	*sich treffen*
feel	*sich fühlen*	relax	*sich entspannen*
hide	*sich verstecken*	remember	*sich erinnern*
hurry	*sich beeilen*	sit down	*sich hinsetzen*
imagine	*sich vorstellen*	worry	*sich Sorgen machen*

b) ***Verstärkender Gebrauch***

- *Mit den Reflexivpronomen kannst du auch eine Person oder eine Sache im Satz besonders hervorheben. In diesem Fall entspricht* myself, yourself, himself … *dem deutschen* ***selbst / allein****:*
  Wow, that's a cool song. – Thanks, **I** wrote it **myself**. *(selbst)*
  You don't have to help us. **We** can do it **ourselves**. *(allein, ohne fremde Hilfe)*

c) Themselves *oder* each other?

- *Wenn du ausdrücken möchtest, dass zwischen Personen etwas wechselseitig geschieht oder es um Gegenseitigkeit geht, verwendest du* **each other**. *Im Deutschen wird* each other *meist mit* ***sich***, ***einander*** *oder* ***gegenseitig*** *wiedergegeben.*

They're looking at **themselves**.

They're looking at **each other**.

❗ *Achte darauf, dass du die Reflexivpronomen nicht mit* each other *verwechselst.*

English summary

- The singular forms of the reflexive pronouns end in -**self** (myself); the plural forms end in -**selves** (ourselves).
- You use the reflexive pronoun
  a) when subject and object of the sentence are the same person: *He hurt himself.*
  b) as an emphasizing (*hervorhebendes*) pronoun: *Nobody helped me. I did it myself.*
- You use **each other** to talk about an interaction between people: *We talk to each other every day.*

Test yourself *Olivia and Lucy are fighting again. Complete these sentences. Decide whether you need an object pronoun, a reflexive pronoun or each other.*

Olivia: Claire, I'm hungry. Can I make … a sandwich?
Lucy: That's a good idea, Olivia. Can you make … one too?
Olivia: No, I can't. You can do that …
Claire: Hey you two, please behave … You know I hate it when you fight with …

G4 An interview with Ayla

→ Seiten 16–17

Gegenüberstellung von present perfect *und* simple past
Comparing the present perfect and the simple past

Mit dem present perfect simple *und dem* simple past *berichtest du über Handlungen, die bereits geschehen sind. Anders als im Deutschen kannst du diese beiden Zeitformen im Englischen jedoch nicht beliebig verwenden.*

- *Das* **present perfect simple** (have / has + past participle) *verwendest du für*

Handlungen, die sich zwar in der Vergangenheit abgespielt haben, deren Ergebnis jedoch in der Gegenwart noch sichtbar oder spürbar ist.	Holly and Olivia **have interviewed** Ayla Bayram for the school magazine. They're sure that lots of students will be interested to read about her success.
Handlungen, die gerade erst (just) *oder bereits* (already) *abgeschlossen wurden.*	She **has just run** in her first half marathon. She **has already won** lots of competitions.
Handlungen, die in einem Zeitraum liegen, der von der Vergangenheit bis in die Gegenwart (und vielleicht auch darüber hinaus) andauert. Häufige Signalwörter hierfür sind: ever, never, yet, so far.	But she **has never run** in a real marathon. She **hasn't done** that **yet**.

- *Das* **simple past** (2. Verbform) *verwendest du für*

Handlungen, die in einem Zeitraum liegen, der bereits abgeschlossen ist, z. B. gestern oder letztes Jahr. Häufige Signalwörter hierfür sind: yesterday, last (week), (2 days) ago, when.	Two months ago Ayla **ran** in her first half marathon. Last year Olivia **twisted** her ankle.

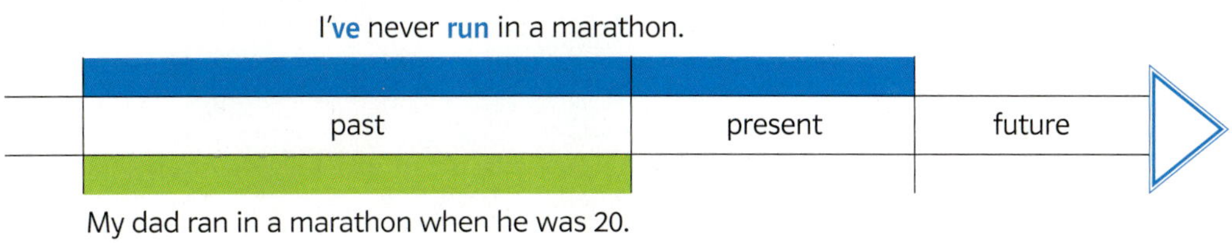

English summary

You use the present perfect simple and the simple past for actions that have already happened.

You use the present perfect simple for past actions that have a strong connection to the present. — *Ayla has had lots of accidents but she has never broken anything so far.*

You use the simple past for actions that happened at a time in the past which is now finished. — *Last year she twisted her ankle.*

Test yourself a) *You and your classmates are talking about Sports Day. Make questions and write them down.*

Have you …	(prepare) (buy) already (start) ever (hurt) (find)	eating healthy food? a name for your team yet? your foot? for Sports Day yet? new sports shoes yet?

b) *Work in small groups. Ask and answer the questions from exercise a).*

Example:
Sabrina: Have you prepared for Sports Day yet?
Martin: Yes, I have. I've already run around the park three times.
Ella: Yes, I have. I went jogging yesterday.

Unit 2

G5 How long have they been chatting?

→ Seiten 38–40

Die Verlaufsform des Perfekts
The present perfect progressive

Das **present perfect progressive** *ist die Verlaufsform des* present perfect. *Mit dieser Zeitform drückst du aus, dass eine Handlung in der Vergangenheit begann, bis zum Zeitpunkt des Sprechens (also in die Gegenwart) hineinreicht und möglicherweise auch in der Zukunft noch andauern wird.*

- *Das* **present perfect progressive** *bildest du aus* **have / has + been + present participle** (verb + -ing).

Aussage:	Amber **has been chatting** with Ethan online.
Verneinung:	She **hasn't been doing** her homework.
Ergänzungsfrage:	How long **has** she **been doing** that?
Entscheidungsfrage mit Kurzantwort:	**Have** they **been talking** to each other on the phone too? Yes, they **have**. / No, they **haven't**.

- *Mit dem* **present perfect** *verbindest du die Vergangenheit mit der Gegenwart.*
  Wie du schon weißt, verwendest du das **present perfect simple** (I have done), *um das* ***Ergebnis*** *einer vergangenen Handlung zu betonen.*
  Das **present perfect progressive** (I have been doing) *verwendest du hingegen, um den* ***Verlauf*** *oder die* ***Dauer*** *der Handlung in den Vordergrund zu stellen.*

  Vergleiche:

Gwen **has invited** Holly and Amber to Scotland.	*Diese Handlung ist beendet; das Ergebnis steht im Vordergrund.*
Gwen and her family **have been planning** things they can do together.	*Diese Handlung dauert bis zum Zeitpunkt des Sprechens und möglicherweise darüber hinaus an; im Vordergrund steht die Handlung selbst.*

- *Oft verwendest du mit dem* present perfect progressive *eine Zeitangabe, die angibt, seit wann* **(since)** *oder wie lange* **(for)** *die Handlung schon andauert.*

Mit **since** *(seit, seitdem) gibst du den* ***Zeitpunkt*** *an, an dem eine Handlung begann.*	*z. B.* since 1996; since 10 o'clock; since Monday; since last week; since August; since he moved to Scotland
Mit **for** *(seit) gibst du den* ***Zeitraum*** *an, den eine Handlung bereits andauert.*	*z. B.* for hours; for days; for weeks; for months; for years; for a long time

I have been . . .ing since . . .	
Gwen's uncle and aunt **have been living** in Scotland **since 1996**.	
	. . . wohnen schon seit 1996 in Schottland.
Amber **has been talking about** their trip to Scotland **since Gwen invited them**.	
	spricht schon davon, seitdem Gwen sie eingeladen hat.

I have been . . .ing for . . .	
Amber and Ethan **have been chatting** online **for a few days now**.	
	. . . unterhalten sich (jetzt schon) seit ein paar Tagen.
Amber **has been telling** Holly what to do **for years**.	
	. . . erzählt . . . schon seit Jahren / jahrelang . . .

! *Denke daran, dass es diese Zeitform im Deutschen nicht gibt. Wir benutzen stattdessen das* ***Präsens*** *und betonen die Dauer des Vorgangs mit* ***schon****.*

- *Weitere Signalwörter für das* present perfect progressive *sind:* how long; recently *(in letzter Zeit)*; all day / week / year *(den ganzen Tag . . .) sowie* all the time *(die ganze Zeit).*

! *Beachte, dass du das* present perfect progressive *wie alle Verlaufsformen* ***nur bei Tätigkeitsverben*** *verwenden kannst (z. B.* work, play, live*). Bei Verben, die keine Tätigkeit, sondern einen Zustand bezeichnen (z. B.* be, know, believe, see*) benutzt du das* present perfect simple, *z. B.* Gwen and Holly **have known** each other for a long time now.

Beachte, dass die unterschiedlichen progressive-*Formen auch unterschiedlich verwendet werden.*

Present progressive:	Gwen is running.	*Dies tut sie gerade.*
Past progressive:	Gwen was running when …	*Dies tat sie gerade, als …*
Present perfect progressive:	Gwen has been running since / for …	*Dies tut sie seit …*

English summary

You use the present perfect progressive **(have / has + been + present participle)**

1. for an activity which began in the past, is still happening in the present and may still go on in the future. — *Amber and Holly have been fighting with each other again.*
2. to say how long an action has been happening. — *Ethan has been sending Amber messages since the weekend / for a few days now.*
   You use **since** with a **point in time** (since 1996; since yesterday) and **for** with a **period of time** (for years; for a long time).

Test yourself *Read this information about the Wilsons. Then ask a question and give an answer for each situation. Start your question with 'how long' and use 'since' or 'for' in your answer.*

Example:
The Wilsons live in Aberdeen.
→ They moved there in 2008.
How long **have** the Wilsons **been living** in Aberdeen?
→ They **have been living** there **since** 2008.

1. Mr Wilson works in a hotel. He started his job there in 2012.
2. Mrs Wilson teaches English. She started five years ago.
3. Their children Sam and Jack both go to school. Sam started three years ago and Jack started last year.

G6 Is Haggis made with meat?

→ Seiten 41–43

Das Passiv
The passive

Active:
They build ships in Scotland.

Passive:
Ships **are built** in Scotland.

Du benutzt das Passiv, wenn der Ausführende einer Handlung unwichtig oder nicht bekannt ist. Damit rückt die Handlung selbst in den Vordergrund. Das Passiv wird häufig in Zeitungsberichten, Sachtexten und technischen Beschreibungen verwendet.

- *Das Passiv bildest du mit einer Form von* **be** *in der jeweiligen Zeitform und dem* **past participle** *des Vollverbs* (infinitive + -ed *oder unregelmäßige Form).*

Zeitform	*Form von* **be + past participle**	*Beispiel*
simple present	am / is / are + past participle	Haggis **is made** with meat. *… wird … gemacht.*
simple past	was / were + past participle	The house **was built** 20 years ago. *… wurde vor … gebaut.*
present perfect simple	have / has been + past participle	Whisky **has been produced** in Scotland for 500 years. *… wird seit … hergestellt.*

❗ *Im Deutschen verwendest du für das Passiv eine Form von „werden".*

- *Wenn du in einem Passivsatz sagen möchtest, von wem die Handlung ausgeführt wird, verwendest du die Präposition* **by** *(auf Deutsch: von). Du entscheidest im Einzelfall, ob diese Zusatzinformation wichtig ist oder nicht:*
  Gaelic **is only spoken by** a few people today.
  Gälisch ***wird*** *heute nur* ***von*** *wenigen Menschen* ***gesprochen****.*
  Der Ausführende der Handlung wird **by-agent** *genannt.*

- *Wenn du einen Aktivsatz in einen Passivsatz umwandelst, musst du Folgendes beachten:*
  1. *Das Objekt des Aktivsatzes wird zum Subjekt im Passivsatz. Aus* ***Objektpronomen*** *werden* ***Subjektpronomen:*** me, you, him, her, it, us, you, them → I, you, he, she, it, we, you, they.
  2. *Die Aktivform des Verbs wird zur Passivform, indem du die passende Form von* **be** *mit dem* **past participle** *des Aktivverbs verbindest* (take → are taken).
  3. *Das Subjekt des Aktivsatzes wird nicht genannt. Ist der Ausführende der Handlung jedoch für den Kontext wichtig, wird das Subjekt mit dem* **by-agent** *angefügt.*

Aktiv:	Passiv:
People all over the world **have read** the Sherlock Holmes' stories.	The Sherlock Holmes' stories **have been read by** people all over the world.
The Scottish author Sir Arthur Conan Doyle **wrote** them.	They **were written by** the Scottish author Sir Arthur Conan Doyle.
Every year thousands of fans **visit** his famous home in Baker Street.	Every year his famous home in Baker Street **is visited by** thousands of fans.

! *Die Zeitform im Aktivsatz und im Passivsatz bleibt gleich.*

English summary

You form the passive voice with a form of **be** and the **past participle**.

1. You use the active to stress what the subject does.
2. You use the passive to stress what is done. Often you don't know who has done the action, or you think this is not important.
3. If it's important to say who does the action, you use the **by-agent**.

The electric clock ***was invented by*** *the Scotsman Alexander Bain.*

Test yourself *Complete this short text about the Scottish game of shinty. Use passive forms of the verbs in brackets and be careful with the tenses.*

Shinty is one of the oldest games in the world. Some people think that it (invent) in Ireland 2000 years ago and that it (bring) to Scotland by the Irish in the 6th century. Others say that it (play) in Scotland since Celtic times. Shinty is similar to field hockey but faster and more dangerous. In the past, whole villages played against each other. Today, shinty is a club sport which (play) between two teams of 12 players.

G7 What were they doing when Holly took the picture?

→ Seiten 44–45

Die Verlaufsform der Vergangenheit
The past progressive

Das **past progressive** *ist die Verlaufsform der Vergangenheit. Mit dieser Zeitform drückst du aus, dass* ***eine Handlung zu einem bestimmten Zeitpunkt in der Vergangenheit gerade ablief*** *und* ***noch nicht zu Ende*** *war. Häufige Signalwörter hierfür sind* while *und* still.

- *Du bildest das* **past progressive** *aus der Vergangenheitsform von* **be (was/were)** *und dem* **present participle** *(= Verb + -ing).*

Aussage:	The two men in Holly's picture **were wearing** kilts.
Verneinung:	They **weren't wearing** skirts.
Ergänzungsfrage:	What **was** the guy on the right **doing**?
Entscheidungsfrage mit Kurzantwort:	**Was** he **dancing** too? – No, he **wasn't**.

- *Mit dem* **past progressive** *betonst du den Verlauf einer Handlung, die zu einem bestimmten Zeitpunkt in der Vergangenheit bereits angefangen hatte und noch nicht zu Ende war.*

9 p.m. → → 7 a.m.	At 6 a.m. Holly **was** still **sleeping**.
6 a.m.	Um 6 Uhr schlief Holly noch.

- *Du verwendest es auch, wenn sich in der Vergangenheit eine Handlung noch im Verlauf befand, als etwas Neues einsetzte. Diese neu eintretende Handlung steht dann im* **simple past**.

Past progressive: gerade ablaufende Handlung	*Simple past:* neu eintretende Handlung
Holly **was looking for** souvenirs	when she **found** the Loch Ness monsters.
While Holly **was looking for** souvenirs,	she **found** the Loch Ness monsters.

! *Das past progressive gibt es im Deutschen nicht. Du kannst es mit „gerade dabei sein, etwas zu tun" oder mit „während" wiedergeben.*

English summary

You use the past progressive

1. to describe an action that was still happening at a certain time in the past. — *At 4 p.m. yesterday afternoon Gwen and Holly were walking around Glasgow.*
2. to describe an action that was going on at a time when something else happened. — *They were walking around Glasgow when it started to rain.*

Test yourself *Write dialogues. Use the past progressive and the simple past.*

Example:
1. Holly sleep / Gwen take photo? – No / write blog.
   A: Was Holly sleeping when Gwen took a photo?
   B: No, she wasn't. She was writing her blog.
2. Will and Kate visit Edinburgh / Holly and Gwen see them? – No / visit Glasgow.
3. Gwen run in park / fall over? – No / run down the road.
4. Holly and Gwen walk through field / cows start to follow them? – No / walk past it.

Unit 3

G8 He hadn't finished his game

→ Seiten 68–70

Das Plusquamperfekt
The past perfect simple

Mit dem past perfect simple *betonst du, dass etwas* ***vor einem Zeitpunkt in der Vergangenheit*** *stattgefunden hat und abgeschlossen ist.*

Drake **wasn't** worried when he **heard** about the Spanish Armada …	because he **had fought** a lot of battles before.
Drake war nicht beunruhigt, als er von der spanischen Armada erfuhr,	*weil er (zuvor) schon viele Schlachten geschlagen hatte.*

- *Das* **past perfect simple** *bildest du aus* **had + past participle** *(3. Verbform).*

Aussage:	Drake **had seen** the Spanish Armada.
Verneinung:	But he **hadn't finished** his game of bowls.
Ergänzungsfrage:	Why **had** they **come**?
Entscheidungsfrage mit Kurzantwort:	**Had** they **come** to destroy his ships? Yes, they **had**.

- *Das* **past perfect simple** *spielt vor allem in literarischen Texten, Erzählungen und Berichten eine Rolle. Es steht meist in Verbindung mit dem* **simple past**.
  Mit dem **simple past** *drückst du aus, was sich in der* ***Vergangenheit*** *ereignet hat. Für Handlungen oder Zustände, die noch* ***vor diesem Zeitpunkt der Vergangenheit*** *stattgefunden haben, verwendest du das* **past perfect simple**.

simple past *(Vergangenheit)*	past perfect simple *(Vorvergangenheit)*
Before Elizabeth I **became** queen,	she **had said**: "I'll never marry."
When she **died** in 1603,	she **had been** queen for 45 years.

❗ *Das Ereignis / die Handlung im* **past perfect simple** *kann auch am* ***Satzanfang*** *stehen.*

past perfect simple *(Vorvergangenheit)*	simple past *(Vergangenheit)*
People in England **had** never **tasted** potatoes	before Walter Raleigh **brought** them back from America.
After Drake **had defeated** the Spanish,	he **became** a national hero.

❗ *Wenn du in einer Erzählung oder in einem Bericht die Ereignisse der Reihe nach erzählst, benutzt du das* **simple past***:*
Elizabeth I **was** born in 1533 and **became** Queen of England in 1588 when she **was** 25 years old.
Blickst du bei deiner Erzählung jedoch auf ein Ereignis zurück, das zuvor stattgefunden hat und abgeschlossen ist, verwendest du das **past perfect simple***:*
She **was** the daughter of Henry VIII and his second wife Anne Boleyn. But Elizabeth I never really **knew** her mother because she **had died** in 1536.

English summary

You use the **past perfect simple (had + past participle)** to show that one event happened before another in the past.

Shakespeare took many of the ideas for his plays from stories which he ***had read*** *at school.*

Test yourself

Henry VIII and the Church of England

Read the text and put the verbs into the correct form of the simple past or past perfect simple.

In 1509, seven weeks after Henry VIII (become) the new king of England, he (marry) Catherine of Aragon. She had been the wife of his older brother Arthur, who (die) in 1502. Together, Henry and Catherine (have) a daughter, Mary. But Henry (need) a boy who could become the next king.
So, in 1533, after Catherine (become) too old to have any more children, Henry (decide) to marry Anne Boleyn, who he (meet) and (fall in love) with in about 1525. When the Pope (say) "no", Henry (break) with Rome and (found) his own Church – the Church of England.

G9 The people who really knew how to have fun

→ Seiten 72–73

Notwendige Relativsätze
Defining relative clauses

Defining relative clauses *sind Nebensätze, die ihr Bezugswort (Person oder Sache) im Hauptsatz näher beschreiben oder definieren. Sie sind notwendig, um zu verstehen, wer oder was genau gemeint ist: Welche Menschen? Welche Gebäude?*

- *Relativsätze leitest du durch ein* **Relativpronomen** *ein, das meist direkt nach dem* **Bezugswort** *steht. Du verwendest …*

who *für Personen*

which *für Sachen*

that *für Personen oder Sachen*

- *Das Relativpronomen* **whose** *(deren, dessen) benutzt du, um Besitz oder Zugehörigkeit auszudrücken. Es kann für Personen oder Sachen verwendet werden:*
  How could Jay find people **whose mobile phones were all turned off** for the tour?

! *Im Gegensatz zum Deutschen trennst du solche notwendigen Relativsätze nicht durch Kommas vom Hauptsatz ab.*

- *Die Relativpronomen* **who / which / that** *können Subjekt oder Objekt im notwendigen Relativsatz sein:*

a) ***Das Relativpronomen als Subjekt***

Subjekt + Verb			
Jay is a boy	who / that	**talks** a lot.	… ein Junge, **der** …
The Globe is a theatre	which / that	**was** popular in Shakespeare's day.	… ein Theater, **das** …

- *Ist* **who / which / that** ***Subjekt*** *im Relativsatz, darfst du es* ***nie weglassen****. Das erkennst du daran, dass auf das Relativpronomen ein Verb folgt (hier:* talks; was*)*

b) ***Das Relativpronomen als Objekt***

Objekt + Subjekt + Verb			
The man	(who / that)	**Jay** saw was a ghost.	… der Mann, **den Jay** …
The Globe is a theatre	(which / that)	**Shakespeare** built.	… ein Theater, **das Shakespeare** …

- *Ist* **who / which / that** ***Objekt*** *im Relativsatz, kannst du es* ***weglassen****.*
  Das erkennst du am ***neuen Subjekt****, das nach dem Relativpronomen steht (hier:* Jay; Shakespeare*). Solche Relativsätze nennt man* **contact clauses**. *Sie stehen ohne Relativsatz in direktem Kontakt zum Bezugswort im Hauptsatz.*

Relative clause	The man **who**	**Jay** saw was a ghost.
Contact clause	The man	**Jay** saw was a ghost.

English summary

Defining relative clauses tell you which person or thing the speaker is talking about.

Defining relative clauses begin with a relative pronoun. You use 'who / that' for people, 'which / that' for things and 'whose' for people or things. You do not use a comma between the noun and the relative clause.

*Jay saw **a man who** was wearing Victorian clothes.*
*He heard a scary story about **a murder which** had happened in the street.*
*How can you call **people whose mobiles** are turned off?*

If the relative pronoun 'who / which / that' is the object of the relative clause, you can leave it out.

*Jay thought that the Victorian pipe **(which)** he found in the street would be perfect for the calendar photo.*

Test yourself **Elizabethan England**

Complete these sentences with a relative pronoun. Use 'who', 'which' or 'whose'. If you can leave them out, put them in brackets ().

1. Anyone … is interested in Shakespeare should visit the Globe.
2. The Globe is the name of the theatre … he built in London.
3. The Elizabethans were people … loved all kinds of entertainment.
4. Elizabeth I was the queen … reign became a golden age for literature, music and arts.
5. At the Globe, you'll find many activities … you can do to learn more about Elizabethan England.

G10 All's well that ends well.

→ Seiten 72, 74

Adverbien der Art und Weise; Gradadverbien
Adverbs of manner; adverbs of degree

*Mit Adjektiven beschreibst du ein Nomen. Mit **Adverbien der Art und Weise** bestimmst du ein **Verb** näher. Du beschreibst also, **wie** jemand etwas tut.*

"It was right here in this street that on the night of the 31st October 1889 a terrible murder took place," the guide said **quietly** but **very dramatically**.

*Die meisten Adverbien bildest du aus dem **Adjektiv** und der Endung -ly.*

Adjektiv + -ly:	The guide took the tourists **slowly** past the scene of the murder.
	They could see the blood **clearly** on the wall.

! *Beachte folgende Rechtschreibregeln:*
Endet das Adjektiv auf -y, *wird* y *zu* i: angry → angr**i**ly, happy → happ**i**ly;
außer: shy → shyly.
Endet das Adjektiv auf -ic, *wird meist* ally *angehängt:* dramatic → dramatic**ally**
Endet das Adjektiv auf -le, *fällt* e *weg:* terrible → terribl**y**

! *Merke dir folgende Ausnahmen:*

good → well	The guide told the scary story **well**.
fast → fast	The friends walked **fast** through the dark narrow streets.
hard → hard	Jay thought **hard**.

! *Wenn eine Form von* **be** *das einzige Verb im Satz ist, benutzt du kein Adverb, sondern ein* ***Adjektiv,*** *z. B.:* The road was **dark** and **narrow**.

- *Mit einem* **Gradadverb** *kannst du eine Aussage verstärken oder abschwächen. Gradadverbien können vor einem Verb, vor einem Adjektiv oder vor einem zweiten Adverb stehen.*

! enough *bildet eine Ausnahme und steht immer hinter dem Wort, auf das es sich bezieht.*

Gradadverbien: very, terribly, really, extremely, completely, quite, too, almost, *und* enough	Jay's friends **completely** ignored him. (adverb + verb) The story was **quite** dramatic. (adverb + adjective) The woman screamed **very** loudly. (adverb + adverb) But it wasn't loud **enough**. (adjective + adverb)

English summary

For most adverbs you use the adjective + -ly.

Adverbs of manner tell you **how** people do things. — *The woman screamed **loudly**. The boy shouted **angrily**.*

Adverbs of degree modify the meaning of the verb, adjective or adverb which follow them. — *Jay's friends **clearly** ignored him. She was **terribly** scared. Jay picked up the pipe **very** carefully.*

Test yourself *Read the tips and complete the sentences. Do you need an adjective or an adverb?*

Tips for London visitors

1. Buy an Oyster Card and travel through London (cheap).
2. Stand on Westminster Bridge and take (fantastic) photos of Big Ben.
3. On a (nice) day, take a picnic with you and have lunch in one of London's (great) parks.
4. Take the ghost tour of London. It's really (scary)!
5. Don't miss Madame Tussauds. The museum shows famous people very (realistic).
6. If you are in London for a day or two only, take a sightseeing bus. Most guides know London and its history (extreme / good).

G11 You can see London faster and more easily with a guide.

→ Seiten 72, 74

Steigerung der Adverbien
The comparison of adverbs

EXPLORE LONDON BY BUS

Only £16

Buy a ticket for one of our sightseeing buses and you can see London **faster** and **more easily** than if you explore alone. Our guides know London's history **better** than anyone.

Mit den Steigerungsformen der Adverbien kannst du Vorgänge vergleichen.

- ***Einsilbige Adverbien** steigerst du auf **-er** (1. Steigerung / Komparativ) bzw. **-est** (2. Steigerung / Superlativ).*

	Grundform	*1. Steigerung*	*2. Steigerung*
	einsilbige Adverbien		
Endungen **-er**, **-est**	(run) fast	fast**er**	fast**est**
	(try) hard	hard**er**	hard**est**
	(jump) high	high**er**	high**est**
	(go) near	near**er**	near**est**

- *Alle **Adverbien**, die auf **-ly** enden oder **mehrsilbig** sind, steigerst du mit **more** (1. Steigerung / Komparativ) bzw. **most** (2. Steigerung / Superlativ).*

	Grundform	*1. Steigerung*	*2. Steigerung*
	Adverbien auf -ly sowie mehrsilbige Adverbien		
more, **most**	(finish) easily	**more** easily	**most** easily
	(see) clearly	**more** clearly	**most** clearly
	(sing) beautifully	**more** beautifully	**most** beautifully
	(eat) cheaply	**more** cheaply	**most** cheaply

! *Beachte, dass die Formen von* **early earlier** *und* **earliest** *lauten, obwohl* early *auf* -ly *endet.*

! *Merke dir folgende Ausnahmen:*

badly – worse – worst
much – more – most

well – better – best
little – less – least

Test yourself *Peter, David and Jamal are all good at something. Look at the table and make comparisons.*

	Peter	**David**	**Jamal**
works hard	✓	✓✓✓	✓✓
paints beautifully	✓✓✓	✓✓	✓
dances well	✓	✓✓	✓✓✓
jumps high	✓✓	✓	✓✓✓

Example:
Peter works hard, Jamal works harder, but David works hardest of all.

Unit 4

G12 You told us there was free wifi!

→ Seiten 94–96

Aussagen in der indirekten Rede
Statements in indirect speech

Direct speech:	**Indirect speech:**
Steve's parents: We'**re** worried about Steve, Ms Woodruff. He **can't** live without **his** phone. He'**s** addicted to it.	Your parents told me (that) they **were** worried about you. They said (that) you **couldn't** live without **your** phone and they thought (that) you **were** addicted to it.

Wenn du wiedergeben möchtest, was ein anderer dir mitgeteilt hat, verwendest du gewöhnlich nicht die direkte, sondern die indirekte Rede.

- *Wie du schon weißt, besteht die indirekte Rede aus einem* ***Einführungssatz*** *(Hauptsatz)* (They told me … / They said …), *und einem* ***Nebensatz****, der mit oder ohne* that *eingeleitet werden kann* (… that they were worried about you).
- Anders *als im Deutschen steht zwischen dem Einführungssatz und dem Nebensatz* **kein** *Komma.*
- *Wenn du eine Aussage in der indirekten Rede wiedergibst, musst du Personalpronomen und Possessivbegleiter anpassen* (**we** → **they**; **his** → **your**).
- *Steht das Verb im Einleitungssatz im* **simple present***, wird die Zeitform aus der direkten Rede in den Nebensatz der indirekten Rede übernommen.*

- *Steht das Verb im Einleitungssatz jedoch im* **simple past**, *ändert sich die Zeitform im Nebensatz folgendermaßen:*

Direkte Rede Direct speech	*Indirekte Rede* Indirect speech
simple present → Steve's parents: We **are** worried about Steve.	**simple past** Steve's parents told Ms Woodruff that they **were** worried about Steve.
present progressive → We think he **is spending** too much time on his phone.	**past progressive** They thought he **was spending** too much time on his phone.
present perfect → I **have tried** to take his phone away, …	**past perfect** His mum explained that she **had tried** to take his phone away, …
simple past → … but that **didn't work**.	**past perfect** … but that **hadn't worked**.
can → We **can't** help him.	**could** They said they **couldn't** help him.
will → Ms Woodruff: OK, I'**ll** talk to him.	**would** Ms Woodruff promised that she **would** talk to him.

English summary

You use indirect speech when you want to report what somebody has said.

When the reporting verb is in the simple past (He said that … / They told her that … / She thought …), the verbs used in the original speech usually move one tense further back **(present → past; past → past perfect simple; will → would; can → could)**.

Steve: *I'm on the ferry to Calais. I'll call you back later.*

Steve told Eddie that he was on the ferry to Calais and that he'd call him back later.

Test yourself **A message from Jack**

When Jack (the narrator of the story) arrived in France, he sent this message to his mother. What did she tell Jack's father when he came home?

Start like this: Jack sent me a message this afternoon. He said that …

> I had a good trip and arrived safely. I haven't had time to look around yet, so I can't tell you much, but the hostel is clean and the people are very friendly. I'll call again later, but I don't know when because we're going into town for dinner and I'm not sure when we'll be back.

G13 Steve's blog

→ Seiten 94–96

Zeit- und Ortsangaben in der indirekten Rede
Expressions of time and place in indirect speech

Friday morning:	Friday afternoon:	A few days later:
Steve: We **had** horsemeat for dinner **yesterday**.	Steve told me that they **had had** horsemeat for dinner **yesterday**.	Last Friday Steve told me that they **had had** horsemeat for dinner **the day before**.

Wenn die indirekte Rede sich auf eine Aussage aus der Vergangenheit bezieht, musst du auch die Zeit- und Ortsangaben im Satz verändern.

- *Die Zeitangaben ändern sich folgendermaßen:*

today → that day	this evening → that evening
tomorrow → the next day	three days ago → three days before
yesterday → the day before	last week / year → the week / year before
next year → the following year	now → then

- *Auch Ortsangaben ändern sich, wenn die Aussage später an einem anderen Ort wiedergegeben wird:* here → there.
- *Weitere Wörter, die meist in der indirekten Rede verändert werden, um sie dem Standpunkt des Berichtenden anzupassen, sind:* this → that; these → those; come → go *und* bring → take.

It's quite cold over **here**.
This is unusual for the time of year. So when you **come**, you shouldn't forget to **bring** some warm clothes,
Michel Lebrun

Listen boys and girls,
I've had an e-mail from Monsieur Lebrun.
He said that it was quite cold over **there**.
That was unusual for the time of year.
So when we **go**, we shouldn't forget to **take** some warm clothes.

English summary

In indirect speech, adverbs of time often change too, e.g. **today** → **that day**, **yesterday** → **the day before** etc.
But if you report something **on the same day** as it was said, the adverbs of time **don't** change.
Other words that you may need to change are:
this → that; here → there; come → go; bring → take.

Steve: *I'm going to France tomorrow.*

(the same day)
Steve said he was going to France tomorrow.

(a week later):
Steve said he was going to France the next day.

Test yourself *While Steve was in France last week, he sent this text message to his friend Eddie. A week later Eddie met Amarjit. What did he tell him?*

Start like this: Steve sent me a message from France last week. He said that …

The athletics event started yesterday and our team is doing well. But it's very cold here. If I ever come back to this place, I'll bring warmer clothes. I wish I had listened to Ms W.

G14 He asked me what the purpose of my visit was

→ Seiten 97–99

Fragen in der indirekten Rede
Questions in indirect speech

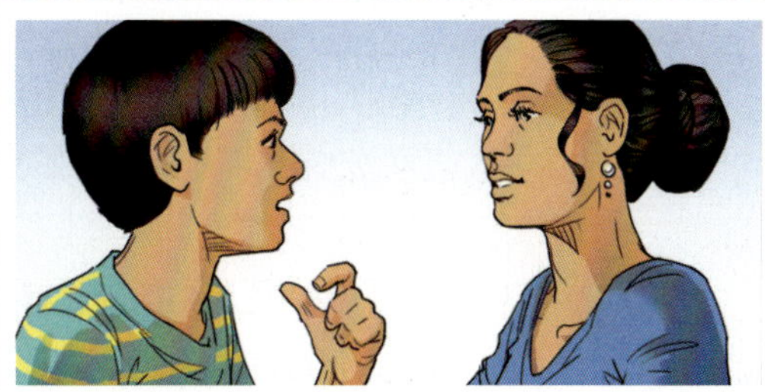

Direct question:	Indirect speech:
Steve's grandma: When **is** your flight, Rafiq?	Grandma **asked** me when my flight **was**.
How **are** you **getting** to the airport?	She **asked** me how I **was getting** to the airport.
Have you **weighed** your suitcase?	She **asked** me **if** I **had weighed** my suitcase.
Are you nervous about the trip?	She **asked** me **if** I **was** nervous about the trip.
Did you **find** a nice present for Aunt Sadia?	She **wanted to know if** I **had found** a nice present for Aunt Sadia.
When **will** you be back?	She **wanted to know** when I **would** be back.

Fragen werden in der indirekten Rede als Aussagesätze wiedergegeben.

- *Das Verb im* ***Einführungssatz*** *(Hauptsatz) muss deutlich machen, dass es sich um eine indirekte Frage handelt* (Grandma **asked** me … / She **wanted to know** …).
- *Das Fragewort* (what, when, where, why …) *wird in der indirekten Frage als Bindewort zwischen Haupt- und Nebensatz übernommen. Steht* ***kein*** *Fragewort, leitest du den Nebensatz mit* **if** *ein.*
- *Die Wortstellung im Nebensatz ist die gleiche wie in einem Aussagesatz: Das* ***Subjekt*** *steht immer* ***vor*** *dem* ***Verb****. Umschreibungen mit* do / does / did *fallen weg.*
- *Wie bei indirekten Aussagesätzen (→ G12) werden bei indirekten Fragen die Zeitformen meist um eine Zeitstufe zurückverschoben, wenn das Einleitungsverb im* simple past *steht.*

English summary

1. If you report questions that begin with a question word (what, when, how …), you use **asked / wanted to know + question word**.
2. If there is no question word, you use **if**.
3. The word order in indirect questions is the same as in statements: Subject – Verb.
4. The verb in the direct question moves one tense further back.

Steve's grandma: *How long is the flight to Dhaka?*
Grandma ***wanted to know how long*** *the flight to Dhaka* ***was****.*

Steve's grandma: *Will you be able to sleep on the plane?*
She asked Rafiq if *he* ***would*** *be able to sleep on the plane.*

Test yourself *When Rafiq arrives at Dhaka airport, the man at passport control asks him a lot of questions. What does Rafiq tell his uncle and aunt later?*

Start like this: The man at passport control asked me …

1. Why are you travelling alone?
2. Where are you from?
3. How long do you plan to stay?
4. Do you have family in Bangladesh?
5. Can you speak Bengali?
6. Is anybody meeting you at the airport?

G15 He told me to go into a side room

→ Seiten 97–99

Befehle, Aufforderungen und Bitten in der indirekten Rede
Commands and requests in indirect speech

Direct command / request:	Indirect command / request:
Steve's grandma: Don't spend all your money in the first week. Please send me some photos from Bangladesh.	She **told** him (Rafiq) **not to spend** all his money in the first week. Grandma **asked** him (Rafiq) **to send** her some photos from Bangladesh.

Befehle, Aufforderungen und Bitten werden in der indirekten Rede als Infinitivkonstruktion mit **to** *oder* **not to** *wiedergegeben.*

- *In der indirekten Rede verwendest du meist* **tell somebody to do something** *für Befehle und Aufforderungen und* **ask somebody to do something** *für Bitten.*
- *Enthält der Befehlssatz ein Verbot (also eine Verneinung), wird* **don't** *zu* **not to** (Don't shout → … not to shout).
- *Dem Einleitungsverb* (told, asked) ***folgt*** *kein Nebensatz, sondern ein* ***Personenobjekt*** **+ to-*Infinitiv*** (She asked **Rafiq to send** …).
- *Wird* ***kein*** *Eigenname genannt, verwendest du ein* ***Pronomen*** *in der* ***Objektform*** (me, you, him, her, us, them) (She asked **him** …).

! *Beachte, dass es hier keine Zeitverschiebung gibt, da der Befehl selbst durch einen Infinitiv wiedergegeben wird.*
Für weitere Verben im Satz gelten jedoch die Regeln für indirekte Aussagesätze (→ G12).
Grandma: **Don't spend** all your money on things you **don't** need.
Grandma told Rafiq **not to spend** all his money on things he **didn't** need.

English summary

In indirect speech, you use **to tell somebody (not) to do something** for indirect commands and **to ask somebody (not) to do something** for indirect requests.

Flight attendant: *Fasten your seatbelt, please, and don't use your phone during take-off and landing.*
The flight attendant ***asked*** *Rafiq* ***to fasten*** *his seatbelt and* ***told*** *him* ***not to use*** *his phone during take-off and landing.*

Test yourself *What did Rafiq's mum say to him at the airport? Put her words into indirect speech.*

Start like this: Rafiq's mum asked …

1. Please say hello to everyone from us.
2. Be careful with your passport. Don't lose it.
3. Please call me as soon as you get to Dhaka.
4. Have fun while you're there and take lots of photos.

Vocabulary

Im ***Vocabulary*** findest du alle wichtigen englischen Wörter und Redewendungen aus *Green Line* 3. Sie stehen in der Reihenfolge, in der sie im Buch vorkommen. Diese Wörter solltest du lernen und anwenden können. Mager gedruckte Einträge musst du **nicht** auswendig lernen. Sie helfen dir, Texte zu verstehen. Weitere nützliche Wörter und Begriffe (z. B. Arbeitsanweisungen), die du **nicht** auswendig lernen musst, findest du ab S. 281. Auf das *Vocabulary* folgt das ***Dictionary (English - German, German - English)***. Falls du ein Wort vergessen hast, kannst du in diesen alphabetischen Wortlisten nachsehen.

Englische Begriffe wie *e-mail*, *cool* oder *cornflakes*, die du auch im Deutschen verwendest, stehen nicht im *Vocabulary*. Du kannst ihre Aussprache und Übersetzung aber im *Dictionary* nachschlagen. Das gleiche gilt für Wörter, die auf Englisch und Deutsch fast gleich geschrieben und ausgesprochen werden, wie z. B. *park* oder *partner*.

In den vier Teilen von ***Text smart*** musst du nicht alle neuen Vokabeln auswendig lernen. Die Wörter und Ausdrücke, die im *Vocabulary* aufgelistet sind, sind die wichtigsten und sie solltest du lernen und anwenden können. Alle anderen neuen Wörter aus *Text smart* kannst du ebenfalls hinten im *Dictionary* ab S. 227 nachschlagen.

Abkürzungen und Zeichen

pl	Mehrzahl (Plural)	↔	ist das Gegenteil von
sg	Einzahl (Singular)	→	ist verwandt mit
coll/ugs	umgangssprachlich	=	entspricht
5	In dieser Übung kommen die Wörter vor.	≠	entspricht nicht
!	Achtung!	*Fr./Lat.*	verwandte Wörter in anderen Fremdsprachen

Englische Laute

Konsonanten

[b]	**b**ed	[p]	**p**icture
[d]	**d**ay	[r]	**r**ed
[ð]	**th**e	[s]	**s**ix
[f]	**f**amily	[ʃ]	**sh**e
[g]	**g**o	[t]	**t**en
[ŋ]	morni**ng**	[tʃ]	**ch**air
[h]	**h**ouse	[v]	**v**ideo
[j]	**y**ou	[w]	**w**e, **o**ne
[k]	**c**an, mil**k**	[z]	ea**s**y
[l]	**l**etter	[ʒ]	revi**si**on
[m]	**m**an	[dʒ]	pa**ge**
[n]	**n**o	[θ]	**th**ank you

Vokale

[ɑː]	c**ar**	[i]	happ**y**
[æ]	**a**pple	[iː]	t**ea**cher
[e]	p**e**n	[ɒ]	d**o**g
[ə]	**a**gain	[ɔː]	b**a**ll
[ɜː]	g**ir**l	[ʊ]	b**oo**k
[ʌ]	b**u**t	[u]	Jan**u**ary
[ɪ]	**i**t	[uː]	t**oo**, tw**o**

Doppellaute

[aɪ]	**I**, m**y**
[aʊ]	n**ow**, m**ou**se
[eɪ]	n**a**me, th**ey**
[eə]	th**ere**, p**air**
[ɪə]	h**ere**, id**ea**
[əʊ]	hell**o**
[ɔɪ]	b**oy**
[ʊə]	s**ure**

[ː] der vorangehende Laut ist lang, z. B. *you* [juː]
[‿] der Bindebogen zeigt, dass zwei Wörter in der Aussprache verbunden werden
[ˈ] die folgende Silbe trägt den Hauptakzent
[ˌ] die folgende Silbe trägt den Nebenakzent

Unit 1 Find your place

Introduction

	would [wʊd]	würde/-st/-n/-t	What *would* you do in this situation?
	personality [ˌpɜ:sn'æləti]	Persönlichkeit	*personality* → person
	to **disagree** [ˌdɪsə'gri:]	anderer Meinung sein; nicht einverstanden sein	*to disagree* ↔ to agree
	to **compromise** ['kɒmprəmaɪz]	Kompromisse eingehen	It isn't always easy to *compromise*.
	smart [smɑ:t]	schlau; klug; intelligent	*smart* ↔ stupid
	logic ['lɒdʒɪk]	Logik	
	self [self], **selves** [selvz] *(pl)*	das Selbst	
	body ['bɒdi]	Körper	Are you logic smart, self smart or *body* smart? Or anything else?
1	**saying** ['seɪɪŋ]	Redensart; Sprichwort	"When the cat's away, the mice will play" is an English *saying*.
	to **judge** [dʒʌdʒ]	beurteilen; bewerten	Never *judge* people by their clothes.
	cover ['kʌvə]	Cover; Titelblatt	I like the *cover* of this book – it's crazy!
	practice ['præktɪs]	Training; Übung	*practice* = training *practice* → to practise
	It doesn't matter. [ɪt ˌdʌznt 'mætə]	Es ist egal.	*It doesn't matter* if you win or lose!
2	**call-in** ['kɔ:lɪn]	*Sendung, bei der sich das Publikum telefonisch beteiligen kann*	
	imagination [ɪˌmædʒɪ'neɪʃn]	Fantasie; Vorstellungskraft	*Fr.* imagination *(f)*
	to **compete (with)** [kəm'pi:t]	konkurrieren (mit); sich messen (mit); in Wettbewerb treten (mit)	*to compete with* → competition *Lat.* competere
	imaginative [ɪ'mædʒɪnətɪv]	einfallsreich; fantasievoll	*imaginative* → imagination → to imagine
	subject ['sʌbdʒɪkt]	Thema	What are you talking about? What's the *subject* of the conversation?
	doubt [daʊt]	Zweifel	Claire isn't sure if she's made the right decision. She has *doubts*.
	to **learn about** ['lɜ:n‿əˌbaʊt]	erfahren über	What did they *learn about* themselves?

Station 1: I want to be the lead dancer!

condition [kən'dɪʃn]	Kondition; Bedingung	
lead dancer ['li:d ˌdɑ:nsə]	Vortänzer/-in	
millionaire [ˌmɪljə'neə]	Millionär/-in	*millionaire* → million
rich [rɪtʃ]	reich	= to have lots of money *Fr.* riche

	success [sək'ses]	Erfolg	If you work hard for school, you'll probably have *success*.
	to **be stressed out** [bi ˌstrest‿'aʊt]	völlig gestresst sein	Why are you so *stressed out*? Just relax.
	lead part [ˌliːd 'pɑːt]	Hauptrolle	My favourite actor has had the *lead part* in lots of films.
	dance [dɑːns]	Tanz; Tanzveranstaltung	*dance* → to dance *Fr.* danse *(f)*
	backing dancer ['bækɪŋ ˌdɑːnsə]	Backgroundtänzer/-in	*backing dancer* ↔ lead dancer
	to **want sb to do sth** [ˌwɒnt tə 'duː]	wollen, dass jmd. etwas tut	My parents always *want me to study* for school.
	to **focus (on)** ['fəʊkəs‿ɒn]	sich konzentrieren (auf)	My parents want me to *focus on* school.
	to **support** [sə'pɔːt]	unterstützen	Do your parents *support* you in what you do?
	mark [mɑːk]	Note	What was your worst *mark* in English?
	laid-back [leɪd'bæk]	entspannt; locker	= very relaxed
	to **drop out (of)** [ˌdrɒp 'aʊt‿əv]	abbrechen	She *dropped out of* school when she was 14. = She didn't finish school.
	modelling ['mɒdəlɪŋ]	Modeln	Shahid does *modelling* just for fun. *Fr.* modèle *(m)*
	to **rely (on)** [rɪ'laɪ‿ɒn]	sich verlassen (auf); vertrauen (auf)	Can I *rely on* you?
	looks *(pl)* [lʊks]	Aussehen	If you want to be a model, you need good *looks*.
	to **study** ['stʌdi]	studieren; lernen	If you *study* a subject, you learn a lot about it.
	career [kə'rɪə]	Beruf; Laufbahn; Karriere	*Fr.* carrière *(f)*
	IT *(= Information Technology)* [ˌaɪ'tiː]	Informatik; Informations-technik	In *IT* you work a lot with computers.
3	**business** ['bɪznɪs]	Geschäft; Business	My mum has got her own *business*.
	billion ['bɪliən]	Milliarde	*billion* = 1,000,000,000
	age [eɪdʒ]	Alter	at the *age* of 15 = when he was 15
	company ['kʌmpəni]	Gesellschaft; Firma; Unternehmen	My dad works for an American *company*.
	to **succeed (in)** [sək'siːd‿ɪn]	Erfolg haben (in/bei/mit)	*to succeed* → success
	to **save** [seɪv]	sparen	! to *save* time or money = sparen to *save* a person's life = retten
4	**in Jay's shoes** [ɪn dʒeɪz 'ʃuːz]	an Jays Stelle	What would you do *in Jay's shoes*?
	to **give up** [ˌgɪv‿'ʌp]	aufgeben	I can't play this game. I *give up*.
5	**successful** [sək'sesfl]	erfolgreich	*successful* → to succeed → success
	to **get to know** [ˌget tə 'nəʊ]	kennen lernen	I would like to *get to know* your friends.
6	**audition** [ɔː'dɪʃn]	Vorsprechen; Vorsingen; Vortanzen	He didn't get the lead part in the dance show because his *audition* didn't go well.

Station 2: You have to push yourself!

to **push oneself** ['pʊʃ wʌnˌself]	sich alles abverlangen; sich Mühe geben	Olivia's parents don't push her. She *pushes herself*.
messy ['mesi]	unordentlich	Lucy must tidy up her room because it's *messy*.
bossy ['bɒsi]	herrisch; rechthaberisch	*bossy* → boss
recorder [rɪ'kɔ:də]	Flöte	
to **enjoy oneself** [ɪn'dʒɔɪ]	Spaß haben; sich amüsieren	= to have a good time
doorbell ['dɔ:bel]	Türklingel	I rang the *doorbell* three times but nobody heard me.
saved by the bell [ˌseɪvd baɪ ðə 'bel]	noch mal Glück gehabt	
funny ['fʌni]	merkwürdig; komisch	*funny* = strange
to **give sb funny looks** [ˌgɪv fʌni 'lʊks]	jmdn. schief/komisch anschauen	Olivia and Lucy are *giving* each other *funny looks*.
to **behave** [bɪ'heɪv]	sich benehmen; sich verhalten	You're silly! You *behave* like a little child.
pause [pɔ:z]	Pause	
What's up? [ˌwɒts‿'ʌp]	Was ist los?	Why are you shouting at each other? *What's up?*
I was just telling [ˌaɪ wəz dʒʌst 'telɪŋ]	ich habe gerade gesagt	
to **be in charge (of)** [bi‿ɪn 'tʃɑ:dʒ‿əv]	die Verantwortung tragen (für); zuständig sein (für)	Who *is in charge of* the food for the party?

Reflexive pronouns

Many words are used with a reflexive pronoun in German, but not in English.

to **change**	sich (ver)ändern	to **meet**	sich treffen
to **decide**	sich entscheiden	to **move**	sich bewegen
to **feel**	sich fühlen	to **relax**	sich entspannen
to **hide**	sich verstecken	to **remember**	sich erinnern
to **hurry**	sich beeilen	to **sit down**	sich hinsetzen
to **imagine**	sich vorstellen	to **worry**	sich Sorgen machen
to **look forward to**	sich freuen auf		

Write sentences with five of these verbs and translate them.

to **be hard on sb** [bi 'hɑ:d‿ɒn]	streng mit jmdm. sein	Don't *be* so *hard on* him.
such [sʌtʃ]	solch; solche/-r/-s	It was *such* a good film! I really liked it.
Stay the way you are. [ˌsteɪ ðə weɪ ju 'ɑ:]	Bleib wie du bist.	
Miss [mɪs]	Fräulein *(Anrede)*	*Miss* Perfect – Mr Perfect

Station 3: An interview with Ayla

	award [ə'wɔ:d]	Auszeichnung; Preis	Have you won any competitions or *awards*?
	not … either [nɒt … 'aɪðə; nɒt … 'i:ðə]	auch nicht	He doesn't like her. She does*n't* like him *either*.
15	to **be sick** [bi 'sɪk]	sich übergeben	I *was sick* in the car.
16	**show-off** ['ʃəʊ‿ɒf]	Angeber/-in	*show-off* → to show off
	to **be fed up (with)** [bi fed‿'ʌp wɪð]	sauer sein (auf); die Nase voll haben (von)	Jay *was fed up* with his friends.
	to **enter** ['entə]	hineingehen; betreten; eintreten; *hier:* mitmachen	He *entered* the competition. The teacher *entered* the room.
	offer ['ɒfə]	Angebot	*offer* → to offer

Skills: How to compromise

How to compromise

Asking for/Giving an opinion:	**Nach einer Meinung fragen/seine Meinung sagen:**
What do you think about …?	Was denkst du über …?
How do you feel about …?	Was hältst du von …?
What's your opinion about …?	Wie ist deine Meinung zu …?
I think …	Ich glaube/denke …
In my opinion …	Meiner Meinung nach …
Making a suggestion:	**Einen Vorschlag machen:**
Why don't we …?	Warum machen/… wir nicht …?
If we did it this way, we could …	Wenn wir es so machen würden, dann könnten wir …
I've got an idea. Can we …?	Ich habe eine Idee. Können wir …?
It would be better to …	Es wäre besser, wenn wir …
Agreeing:	**Zustimmen:**
Yes, we should do that.	Ja, das sollten wir tun.
No, I don't mind doing that.	Nein, es macht mir nichts aus, das zu tun.
I agree with you.	Ich stimme dir zu.
Yes, you're right.	Ja, du hast recht.
Disagreeing:	**Nicht zustimmen:**
I don't think that's a good idea.	Ich halte das für keine gute Idee.
You've got a point but …	Da hast du recht, aber …
I don't think we can do that.	Ich glaube nicht, dass wir das machen können.
I disagree.	Da bin ich anderer Meinung.
I think you're wrong here.	Ich glaube, du liegst hier falsch.
I don't think you're right.	Ich glaube nicht, dass du recht hast.
Finding a compromise:	**Einen Kompromiss finden:**
Can we meet halfway?	Können wir uns in der Mitte treffen?
The compromise (between the two suggestions) is …	Der Kompromiss (zwischen den beiden Vorschlägen) lautet …

You want to go to the cinema and the film ends at nine in the evening. Your parents think that's too late. Discuss and find a compromise.

	to **have a point** [ˌhæv‿ə 'pɔɪnt]	nicht ganz Unrecht haben	Yes, you*'ve got a point*. I've never thought about it like that.
1	to **meet halfway** [ˌmi:t hɑ:f'weɪ]	sich auf halbem Weg treffen	I don't agree! But I don't want to fight, so let's *meet halfway*.
	I don't mind … [ˌaɪ dəʊnt 'maɪnd]	Ich habe nichts dagegen (zu) …; Mir macht es nichts aus (zu) …	*I don't mind* doing that.
2	**misunderstood** [ˌmɪsʌndə'stʊd]	missverstanden	Every time I talk to my parents I feel *misunderstood*.
3	**guest** [gest]	Gast	a person you invite to your house or to a party, or who stays at your house for a time

Unit task: Make a personality test!

competitive [kəm'petɪtɪv]	leistungsorientiert; konkurrierend	*competitive* → competition → to compete
to **seem** [si:m]	scheinen	The dog *seemed* friendly at first, but then he suddenly became aggressive.
else [els]	andere/-r/-s; sonst noch	We've got everything on Mum's list now. I don't think we need anything *else*.
limit ['lɪmɪt]	Limit; Grenze	Find out what your talents and *limits* are. *Fr.* limite *(f)*
gadget ['gædʒɪt]	Gerät; technische Spielerei	Smartphones and play stations are *gadgets*.

Story: Hang out with us instead!

to **hang out (with)** [ˌhæŋ‿'aʊt wɪð], **hung out (with)** [ˌhʌŋ‿'aʊt wɪð], **hung out (with)** [ˌhʌŋ‿'aʊt wɪð] *(infml)*	sich herumtreiben (mit); rumhängen (mit); sich treffen (mit)	When you *hang out* with friends, you meet them and spend time with them.
instead [ɪn'sted]	stattdessen	If the weather is too cold for swimming, we could go for a walk *instead*.
the only person who … [ði‿əʊnli ˌpɜ:sn 'hu:]	der einzige Mensch, der …	
argument ['ɑ:gjəmənt]	Auseinandersetzung; Streit	The boys didn't agree with each other. They had a big *argument*.
could [kʊd]	konnte/-n	My best friend *couldn't* come to my party because she was on holiday.
these days [ˌði:z 'deɪz]	zurzeit	*these days* ↔ in the past
to be able to (do sth) [bi‿'eɪbl tə]	fähig sein zu; können; dürfen	
to be allowed to (do sth) [bi‿ə'laʊd tə]	dürfen	
to **be grounded** [bi 'graʊndɪd]	Hausarrest haben	Jay *was grounded* for five days.
to **trust** [trʌst]	vertrauen	I know what I'm doing. Please *trust* me.
to **put on** [ˌpʊt‿'ɒn]	anziehen	We're going out now. *Put* your shoes *on*, please.

	trainer ['treɪnə]	Turnschuh	*Trainers* are special shoes that people wear for running. 
	freedom *(no pl)* ['fri:dəm]	Freiheit; Unabhängigkeit	*freedom* → free
	in-crowd ['ɪnkraʊd]	Szene; die Angesagten; die Beliebten	Finn and Max are part of the *in-crowd*.
	they were laughing [ˌðeɪ wə 'lɑ:fɪŋ]	sie lachten gerade	
	blond [blɒnd]	blond	
	the high street [ðə 'haɪ ˌstri:t]	die Haupteinkaufsstraße	Let's go to *the high street* for some burgers. ! In größeren Städten wie London gibt es in jedem Viertel eine *high street*.
	bloke *(fam)* [bləʊk]	Typ *(ugs.)*	
	to **lend** [lend], **lent** [lent], **lent** [lent] **(to)**	leihen; verleihen	Can you borrow Shahid's laptop? – He'll never *lend* it to me!
	overnight [ˌəʊvə'naɪt]	über Nacht	Shahid won't be back until tomorrow. He's got an *overnight* modelling job.
	usual ['ju:ʒl]	üblich	*usual* → usually
	to **treat** [tri:t]	behandeln	If you don't *treat* your dog right, you'll have trouble with it.
	everyone was dancing [ˌevriwʌn wəz 'dɑ:nsɪŋ]	alle tanzten	
	to **ignore** [ɪg'nɔ:]	ignorieren; außer Acht lassen	If you don't look at sth and don't listen to it, even if you know it's there, you *ignore* it.
	pretty ['prɪti]	hübsch	*pretty* eyes 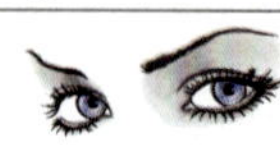
	to come up to sb [kʌm‿'ʌp tə]	auf jmdn. zukommen	The girls *came up to* Jay. = The girls walked towards Jay.
	poor [pɔ:; pʊə]	arm	*poor* ↔ rich
	mummy ['mʌmi]	Mama; Mami; Mutti	
	piece of junk [ˌpi:s‿əv 'dʒʌŋk]	Stück Schrott	After the party Shahid's laptop was a *piece of junk*.
	anger *(no pl)* ['æŋgə]	Zorn; Wut	Jay was white with *anger*! *anger* → angry
1	**lie** [laɪ]	Lüge	*lie* → to lie
	somebody who … [ˌsʌmbədi 'hu:]	jemand, der …	
	to **tease sb** [ti:z]	jmdn. aufziehen; jmdn. hänseln; jmdn. ärgern	Olivia sometimes *teases* Lucy.
2	**peer pressure** ['pɪə ˌpreʃə]	Gruppenzwang	
	excitement *(no pl)* [ɪk'saɪtmənt]	Aufregung	*excitement* → excited → exciting
	confused [kən'fju:zd]	verwirrt; wirr; konfus	What happened? Why is Jay so *confused*?
	honest ['ɒnɪst]	ehrlich	Don't lie. Be *honest*! ***Lat.*** honestus

Action UK! When Sean came to visit

1	to **react** [ri'ækt]	reagieren	*to react* → reaction
	singing ['sɪŋɪŋ]	Singen; Gesang	*singing* → to sing
2	**sense of humour** *(no pl)* [ˌsens‿əv 'hju:mə]	Sinn für Humor	Do your teachers have a *sense of humour*?
	to **feel sorry for** [ˌfi:l 'sɒri fɔ:]	Mitleid haben mit; bedauern	I *felt sorry for* him. = Er hat mir leid getan.
	optimistic [ˌɒptɪ'mɪstɪk]	optimistisch	Everything will be fine, let's be *optimistic*!
	to **cheer sb up** [ˌtʃɪər‿'ʌp]	jmdn. aufheitern	Are you sad? What can I do to *cheer you up*?
	to **apologise** [ə'pɒlədʒaɪz]	sich entschuldigen	= to say sorry
	to **delete** [dɪ'li:t]	löschen	They *deleted* all the music on Shahid's laptop.
	wall [wɔ:l]	Online-Pinnwand	
	account settings [ə'kaʊnt ˌsetɪŋz]	Profileinstellungen	Check your *account settings* for your social network carefully.
	bench [benʃ]	Bank; Sitzbank	Let's sit down on this *bench*. 
	to **work out** [ˌwɜ:k‿'aʊt]	funktionieren; klappen	How did things *work out* in the end?

Describing different personalities

to **have a sense of humour**	(einen Sinn für) Humor haben
to **be a show-off**	angeberisch sein
to **be creative/confident/ competitive/honest/funny/ bossy/messy/laid-back/ optimistic/smart**	kreativ/selbstsicher/selbstbewusst/ konkurrierend/ehrlich/lustig/ rechthaberisch/unordentlich/ locker/optimistisch/klug sein
to **never give up**	nie aufgeben
to **always get into trouble**	immer in Schwierigkeiten geraten
to **start fights**	Streit anfangen
to **push oneself to**	sich zwingen zu
to **follow the crowd**	der Masse folgen
to **compare oneself with**	sich vergleichen mit
to **be good with/at**	gut sein bei/in
...	...

Describe your friend's personality.

Text smart 1 Poems and songs

Introduction

1	**board** [bɔ:d]	Brett; Tafel	You can make a box with *boards*. 
	fair play [feə 'pleɪ]	Fairplay	*Fair play* in sports is very important.
	generous ['dʒenrəs]	großzügig	A *generous* person likes to give things to others. *Fr.* généreux
2	**(song) lyrics** *(pl)* [sɒŋ 'lɪrɪks]	Liedtext	Are the *lyrics* of songs important to you, or just the music?
	to **sing along** [ˌsɪŋ‿ə'lɒŋ]	mitsingen	
	to **rhyme** [raɪm]	(sich) reimen	'Bee' *rhymes* with 'sea'.
	advert ['ædvɜ:t]	Anzeige; Werbespot	I saw a really funny *advert* for dog food on TV yesterday.

Station 1: Say it with a poem!

3	**rainbow** ['reɪnbəʊ]	Regenbogen	
	bee [bi:]	Biene	
	dolphin ['dɒlfɪn]	Delfin	
	bare [beə]	nackt; bloß	His legs/arms/feet/hands were *bare*.
	sunflower ['sʌnflaʊə]	Sonnenblume	
	peach [pi:tʃ]	Pfirsich	*Fr.* pêche *(f)*
	spoon [spu:n]	Löffel	I like eating pasta with a *spoon*.
	honey ['hʌni]	Honig	We get *honey* from bees.
	tune [tju:n]	Melodie	I don't like the lyrics of that song, but I like the *tune*.
	lazy ['leɪzi]	faul	*lazy* ↔ busy
4	to **read/sing out loud** [ˌri:d/sɪŋ‿aʊt 'laʊd]	laut vorlesen/vorsingen	*Read* the poem *out loud*.
	a poem which … [ə ˌpəʊɪm 'wɪtʃ]	ein Gedicht, das …	
6	**arrow** ['ærəʊ]	Pfeil	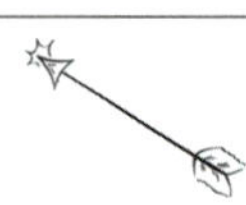
	to **shoot** [ʃu:t], **shot** [ʃɒt], **shot** [ʃɒt] **(at)**	schießen (auf)	He *shot* an arrow into the air.

	air [eə]	Luft	Let's go for a walk and get some fresh *air*.
	to **fly** [flaɪ], **flew** [flu:], **flown** [fləʊn]	fliegen	The bird *flew* up to the top of the church.
	sight [saɪt]	*hier:* Blick	*sight* → to see
	flight [flaɪt]	Flug	*flight* → to fly
	oak [əʊk]	Eiche	= a tree that you find in the forest
7	**direct** [dɪ'rekt]	direkt	Being too *direct* in conversations is not always a good thing.
	simple ['sɪmpl]	einfach; simpel	*simple* ↔ difficult *Fr.* simple

Station 2: Say it with a song!

9	**stuck in the middle of …** [ˌstʌk ɪn ðə 'mɪdl‿əv]	mitten in … stecken; feststecken in …	Whenever I'm *stuck in the middle of* my homework, the phone rings.
	to **sail** [seɪl]	segeln; umsegeln	*to sail* → sailor
	to **guide** [gaɪd]	führen; leiten	*to guide* → guide *Fr.* guider
	to **be made of** [bi 'meɪd‿əv]	bestehen aus	Windows *are made of* glass.
	to **be called to do sth** [bi 'kɔ:ld tə du:]	auserwählt sein, etw. zu tun	
	to **remind (sb of sth/sb)** [rɪ'maɪnd əv]	(jmdn. an etw./jmdn.) erinnern	! I didn't *remember* Dad's birthday. Mum had to *remind* me.
	to **repeat** [rɪ'pi:t]	wiederholen	Can you *repeat* that, please. – Can you say that again, please.
	to **cry** [kraɪ]	weinen	*to cry* ↔ to laugh
10	**play on words** [ˌpleɪ‿ɒn 'wɜ:dz]	Wortspiel	
11	**catchy** ['kætʃi]	eingängig; einprägsam	If a song has a *catchy* tune, it's easy to remember.
	to **dance to** ['dɑ:ns tə]	tanzen zu	The song is great – let's *dance to* it. *Fr.* danser
	to **keep one's feet or hands still** [ˌki:p wʌnz 'fi:t‿ɔ: 'hændz stɪl]	die Beine und Hände ruhig halten	My brother can't *keep his feet and hands still*!
	over and over again [ˌəʊvər‿ən‿ˌəʊvər‿ə'gen]	immer wieder	I could watch that film *over and over again*.
	to **get sth out of one's head** [get ˌaʊt‿əv wʌnz 'hed]	etw. aus dem Kopf bekommen	They can't *get the pictures* of the accident *out of their heads*.
	melody ['melədi]	Melodie	*Fr.* mélodie *(f)*
	You can do it! [ˌju: kən 'du: ɪt]	Du schaffst es!	It's not difficult. I'm sure *you can do it*!
	to **survive** [sə'vaɪv]	überleben	
	to **fall down** [ˌfɔ:l‿'daʊn]	stürzen; hinunterfallen	I *fell down* the wall and hurt my leg.
	to **die** [daɪ]	sterben	Robert has only got one grandma. His other grandma *died* four years ago.
	champion ['tʃæmpiən]	Gewinner/-in; Sieger/-in; Champion	We are the *champions*!

Across cultures 1 Reacting to a new situation

1	**plate** [pleɪt]	Teller	There's too much food on the *plate*.
	mug [mʌg]	Becher	
	cup [kʌp]	Tasse	Put the *cups* into the cupboard please.
	knife [naɪf], **knives** [naɪvz] *(pl)*	Messer	! Achtung Aussprache: Das ***k*** wird nicht gesprochen.
	fork [fɔ:k]	Gabel	*fork* and knife 
	bread roll ['bred rəʊl]	Brötchen	
	butter ['bʌtə]	Butter	
	jam [dʒæm]	Marmelade; Konfitüre	I love my bread rolls with butter and *jam*.
	marmalade ['mɑ:məleɪd]	Marmelade aus Zitrusfrüchten	! Achte auf die Schreibung: *marm**a**lade*
	muesli ['mju:zli]	Müsli	
	ham [hæm]	Schinken	I'd like a sandwich. – With cheese and tomato? Or *ham*?
	sausage ['sɒsɪdʒ]	Wurst; Bratwurst	
	sugar ['ʃʊgə]	Zucker	Do you like your tea with *sugar* or honey?
3	**host family** ['həʊst ˌfæmli]	Gastfamilie	While I'm in Greenwich, I'll be at the Jacksons' house. The Jacksons are my *host family*.
	exchange student [ɪks'tʃeɪndʒ ˌstju:dnt]	Austauschschüler/-in	Our *exchange student* comes from England and wants to learn German.
	unfamiliar [ˌʌnfə'mɪliə]	nicht vertraut; unbekannt	Staying with a host family is an *unfamiliar* situation for Brad.
4	to **make sb angry** [meɪk 'æŋgri]	jmdn. wütend machen; jmdn. verärgern	Don't *make* me *angry*!
	to **upset** [ʌp'set], **upset** [ʌp'set], **upset** [ʌp'set]	aus der Fassung bringen	The fights between Jay and Luke *upset* Olivia.
	gratitude ['grætɪtju:d]	Dankbarkeit	If you want to say thank you to somebody, you can show your *gratitude* in different ways.
	impolite [ˌɪmp'laɪt]	unhöflich	*impolite* ↔ polite *Fr.* impoli/e
	this early ['ðɪs ˌɜ:li]	so früh	Do you really have to go home *this early*?
	that much [ðæt 'mʌtʃ]	so viel	Sorry, I can't eat *that much* in the morning.
	to **be used to** [bi 'ju:s‿tə]	gewöhnt sein an; gewohnt sein	I'm not *used to* drinking coffee.

I'm (not) sure ... [ˌaɪm nɒt ˈʃʊə]	Ich bin mir (nicht) sicher ...	*I'm not sure* if I can help you with your homework, but I'll try.

Unit 2 Let's go to Scotland!

Introduction

	actions which ... [ˌækʃnz ˈwɪtʃ]	Handlungen, die ...	
	fringe [frɪndʒ]	Rand-; Alternativ-	The Edinburgh *Fringe* Festival takes place every year.
1	**historic** [hɪˈstɒrɪk]	historisch	*historic* → history
	traditional [trəˈdɪʃnl]	traditionell	*traditional* → tradition *Fr.* traditionnel/le
2	to **be like** [bi ˈlaɪk]	sein	Please tell me more about your school. What *is* it *like*?
3	**typically** [ˈtɪpɪkli]	typisch	What's *typically* German?
	haggis [ˈhægɪs]	Haggis *(schottisches Gericht aus in einem Schafsmagen gekochten Schafsinnereien und Haferschrot)*	
	tartan [ˈtɑːtn]	Schottenkaro *(bestimmtes Muster eines Clans);* karierter Schottenstoff	Different families have *tartans* of different colours, e. g. with a red, blue or green background.
	kilt [kɪlt]	Kilt; Schottenrock	

Typically Scottish

the **Scottish flag**

bagpipes

a **thistle**

a **kilt**

tartan

haggis

	bagpipes *(pl)* ['bægpaɪps]	Dudelsack	
	independence *(no pl)* [ˌɪndɪ'pendəns]	Unabhängigkeit	*Fr.* indépendance *(f)*; ***Lat.*** de + pendere
	loch [lɒx; lɒk]	See *(in Schottland)*	! Achtung Aussprache: In Schottland wird das „ch“ in *loch* wie ein deutsches „ch“ ausgesprochen.
	referendum [ˌrefr'endəm]	Referendum; Volksentscheid	In 2014, the Scottish people voted in a *referendum* on independence.
	independent [ˌɪndɪ'pendənt]	unabhängig	*independent* → independence *Fr.* indépendant/e
	flag [flæg]	Flagge; Fahne	The colours of the German *flag* are black, red and gold.
	thistle ['θɪsl]	Distel	A *thistle* is a plant with beautiful pink flowers.

Station 1: A new Holly?

	son [sʌn]	Sohn	Ethan is the *son* of Gwen's uncle and aunt.
	backpack ['bækpæk]	Rucksack	a bag that you carry on your back 
	since *(+ Zeitpunkt)* [sɪns]	seit; seitdem	They have been living in Scotland *since* 1996.
	for *(+ Zeitraum)* [fɔː; fə]	seit	We've been learning English *for* three years. = We started to learn English three years ago.
3	to **look forward to** [ˌlʊk 'fɔːwəd tə]	sich freuen auf	I'*m looking forward to* my grandma's visit next week.
	period ['pɪəriəd]	Periode; Zeitspanne	An hour is a short *period* of time. ! Achtung Aussprache.
4	to **produce** [prə'djuːs]	herstellen; produzieren	What does your company *produce*?
	litre (l) ['liːtə]	Liter	***Fr.*** litre *(m)*
	party ['pɑːti]	Partei	Which *party* does Mrs Merkel belong to?
	to **campaign (for)** [kæm'peɪn fɔː]	demonstrieren (für); aufmerksam machen (auf); sich engagieren (für)	The Scottish National Party *campaigns for* Scotland's independence.
	shinty ['ʃɪnti]	Shinty *(eine Art Hockey)*	= a popular sport in Scotland
5	**gig** [gɪg]	Auftritt; Gig	Ethan and his band play *gigs* every weekend.
	drums *(pl)* [drʌmz]	Schlagzeug	
6	**official** [ə'fɪʃl]	offiziell	
	anthem ['ænθəm]	Hymne	Can you sing Germany's national *anthem*?
	several ['sevrl]	einige; mehrere; verschiedene	*several* = three or more, but not many

	unofficial [ˌʌnəˈfɪʃl]	inoffiziell	*unofficial* ↔ official
	to **defeat** [dɪˈfiːt]	besiegen	*to defeat* = to beat
	soldier [ˈsəʊldʒə]	Soldat/-in	

Station 2: Is that made with meat?

	meat *(no pl)* [miːt]	Fleisch	
	object [ˈɒbdʒɪkt]	Objekt; Gegenstand	Describe a historical *object*.
	vegetable [ˈvedʒtəbl]	Gemüse	Carrots are *vegetables*.
	vegetarian [ˌvedʒɪˈteəriən]	Vegetarier/-in	*Vegetarians* don't eat meat.
	jacket [ˈdʒækɪt]	Jacke	In summer you don't need a *jacket*.
	to **pull down** [ˌpʊl‿ˈdaʊn]	abreißen	They *pulled down* the house to build a new one.
	musical [ˈmjuːzɪkl]	musikalisch; Musik-	*musical* → music
	shipbuilding [ˈʃɪpbɪldɪŋ]	Schiffsbau	
	industry [ˈɪndəstri]	Industrie; Branche; Gewerbe	Scotland still has a shipbuilding *industry*.
9	**midnight** [ˈmɪdnaɪt]	Mitternacht	= twelve o'clock at night
	to **set off** [ˌset‿ˈɒf], **set off** [ˌset‿ˈɒf], **set off** [ˌset‿ˈɒf]	*hier:* ein Feuerwerk zünden	
10	**Scot** [skɒt]	Schotte/Schottin	*Scot* → Scotland, Scottish
	invention [ɪnˈvenʃn]	Erfindung	***Fr.*** invention *(f)*; ***Lat.*** inventio *(f)*
	discovery [dɪˈskʌvri]	Entdeckung	*discovery* → to discover
	by [baɪ]	von	a CD *by* Beyoncé
	to **clone** [kləʊn]	klonen	It's possible to *clone* animals.
	scientist [ˈsaɪəntɪst]	Wissenschaftler/-in	*scientist* → science
	raincoat [ˈreɪnkəʊt]	Regenmantel	
	to **invent** [ɪnˈvent]	erfinden	*to invent* → invention ***Fr.*** inventer
	penicillin [ˌpenɪˈsɪlɪn]	Penicillin	
	steam engine [ˈstiːm‿ˌendʒɪn]	Dampfmaschine	The *steam engine* was the most important invention of the 18th century.
	to **start** [stɑːt]	*hier:* gründen	John Logie Baird *started* the first television station.
11	to **fill** [fɪl]	(sich) füllen	She *filled* her glass with water.
	vegetarian [ˌvedʒɪˈteəriən]	vegetarisch	Today you can even buy *vegetarian* sausages.
	mashed potatoes *(pl)* [ˌmæʃt pəˈteɪtəʊz]	Kartoffelpüree	Haggis is often eaten with *mashed potatoes*.
	sauce [sɔːs]	Soße	I love ice cream with chocolate *sauce*.
	to **ban** [bæn]	bannen; verbieten; sperren	If sth has been banned, you mustn't do or use it.
13	**close** [kləʊs]	schmaler Durchgang	The people in Edinburgh call the narrow streets '*closes*'.
	hundreds of [ˈhʌndrədz‿əv]	Hunderte (von)	*Hundreds of* people listened to Ethan's band last weekend.
	narrow [ˈnærəʊ]	eng; schmal	a *narrow* street, a *narrow* bridge

	closes which … [ˌkləʊsɪz ˈwɪtʃ]	Durchgänge, die …	
	to **lead off** [liːd‿ˈɒf]	wegführen	Closes *lead off* from the main streets.
	to **lead** [liːd], **led** [led], **led** [led]	führen; anführen	Where does this way *lead*?
	a person who … [ə ˌpɜːsn ˈhuː]	eine Person, die …	
	to **leave behind** [ˌliːv‿ bɪˈhaɪnd]	zurücklassen	Never *leave* your rubbish *behind* after a picnic.
14	**crane** [kreɪn]	Kran	If you want to fix the roof of a tall building, you'll need a *crane*. 

Station 3: Holly's blog

	update [ˈʌpdeɪt]	Aktualisierung; Update	
	latest [ˈleɪtɪst]	neueste/-r/-s	What's the *latest* news from your brother in Australia?
	pic (= picture) [pɪk]	Foto	*pic* = picture
	actually [ˈæktʃuəli]	tatsächlich; wirklich; eigentlich	! *Actually* heißt nicht ‚aktuell'!
	in fact [ɪn ˈfækt]	tatsächlich; eigentlich; genau genommen	*in fact* → fact
	south [saʊθ]	südlich; im Süden	We don't have cows like this down *south*.
	to **hold** [həʊld], **held** [held], **held** [held]	abhalten	The Highland Games are *held* in September.
	dancing [ˈdɑːnsɪŋ]	Tanzen	*dancing* → to dance → dancer
	gentleman [ˈdʒentlmən], **gentlemen** [ˈdʒentlmen] *(pl)*	Gentleman; feiner Herr	
	clan [klæn]	Clan; Sippe; Stamm	
17	**ceilidh** [ˈkeɪli]	*schottisches Fest, bei dem getanzt und musiziert wird*	

Skills: How to write a persuasive text

1	**humour** *(no pl)* [ˈhjuːmə]	Humor; Stimmung	My grandad's sense of *humour* is very special.
	final [ˈfaɪnl]	letzte/-r/-s	*final* = last
	further [ˈfɜːðə]	weiter (weg)	*further* → far
	north [nɔːθ]	nördlich; im Norden	Which is further *north*: Scotland or Ireland?
	fascinating [ˈfæsɪneɪtɪŋ]	faszinierend	= very, very interesting
	museums which … [mjuːˌzɪəmz ˈwɪtʃ]	Museen, die …	
	present [ˈpreznt]	heutig; Gegenwarts-	The museum shows the life on the islands from Roman times to the *present* day.

spectacular [spek'tækjələ]	spektakulär	*Fr.* spectaculaire
cliff [klɪf]	Klippe; Kliff	The views from the *cliffs* are spectacular.
tiny ['taɪni]	klein; winzig	A mouse looks *tiny* next to a horse.
3 an event which … [ən‿ɪˌvent 'wɪtʃ]	eine Veranstaltung, die …	

Describing nature and buildings

nature	cliff, mountain, hill, park, island, coastline, …	beautiful, amazing, fascinating, wonderful, fantastic, spectacular, …	
buildings	castle, museum, church, tower, …	old, modern, big, huge, nice, tiny, interesting, fascinating, made of stone/wood, stairs, wall, …	

Describe your school building. Write 3–5 sentences.

Unit task: Visit Scotland!

to **rent (out)** [ˌrent‿'aʊt]	(ver)mieten	Last year our friends *rented* their house in England *out* to us.
travel agency ['trævl‿ˌeɪdʒnsi]	Reisebüro	You can book a holiday at the *travel agency*.

Story: I don't believe in ghosts!

sky [skaɪ]	Himmel	At the end of the festival the *sky* was getting dark.
entrance ['entrəns]	Eingang; Eintritt	Where is the *entrance* to the castle? *entrance* → to enter
ticket office ['tɪkɪt ˌɒfɪs]	Kartenschalter	The *ticket office* is at the entrance.
empty ['emti]	leer	*empty* ↔ full
stone [stəʊn]	Stein; Stein-	The castle has a *stone* floor and *stone* walls.
pocket ['pɒkɪt]	Tasche; Hosentasche	He put his smartphone into his trouser *pocket*.
signal ['sɪgnl]	Signal; Empfang	I can't use my phone because there's no *signal*.
thick [θɪk]	dick *(nicht für Personen)*	The stone walls of the castle are very *thick*.
perhaps [pə'hæps]	vielleicht	*perhaps* = maybe
to **go round in circles** [gəʊ ˌraʊnd ɪn 'sɜːklz]	sich im Kreis drehen	

	wounded ['wu:ndɪd]	verwundet; verletzt	We found a small bird in the garden. It was *wounded*, so we took it to the vet.
	tower [taʊə]	Turm	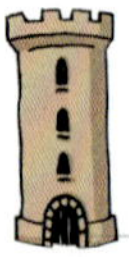
	moonlight ['mu:nlaɪt]	Mondlicht	There's no *moonlight* tonight because the sky is cloudy.
	stairs *(pl)* [steəz]	Treppe	! The stair**s** go up. = Die Treppe führ**t** nach oben. *stairs* → downstairs → upstairs
	wooden ['wʊdn]	hölzern; aus Holz	Our house has *wooden* stairs.
	danger ['deɪndʒə]	Gefahr	*danger* → dangerous *Fr.* danger *(m)*
	to **keep out (of)** [ˌki:p‿'aʊt əv]	draußen bleiben; draußen halten	Parents must *keep out* of my room!
	cracking ['krækɪŋ]	knackend; brechend	
	to **realise** ['rɪəlaɪz]	erkennen; realisieren	Holly *realised* they didn't have much time.
	key ring ['ki: ˌrɪŋ]	Schlüsselbund; Schlüsselanhänger	
	to **tie (to)** ['taɪ tə]	binden (an); fesseln (an)	If you *tie* a dog to something, it can't run away.
	rope [rəʊp]	Seil	
	to **hold onto** [ˌhəʊld‿'ɒntə]	(sich) festhalten an	Amber caught the rope and *held onto* it.
	crack [kræk]	Knacken; Krachen	*crack* → cracking
	wood [wʊd]	Holz	*wood* → wooden
	heavy ['hevi]	schwer; stark	I can't carry this box – it's too *heavy*.
	a sign that … [ə ˌsaɪn 'ðæt]	ein Schild, das …	
	definitely ['defɪnətli]	bestimmt; definitiv; eindeutig	Do you want a pink backpack? – No, *definitely* not.
7	**spider** ['spaɪdə]	Spinne	
	to **convince** [kən'vɪns]	überzeugen	*Fr.* convaincre; *Lat.* convincere
	web [web]	Netz; Spinnennetz	Spiders make *webs*.

Action UK! How times change

1	to **help out** [ˌhelp‿'aʊt]	aushelfen	Our neighbour couldn't go shopping, so I *helped* her *out*.
	neighbourhood ['neɪbəhʊd]	Nachbarschaft	*neighbourhood* → neighbour

to **do the shopping** [ˌduː ðə ˈʃɒpɪŋ]	Einkäufe machen; Besorgungen machen	
elderly [ˈeldəli]	älter	= a more polite word for 'old' (when you speak about people)
2 **inventor** [ɪnˈventə]	Erfinder/-in	*inventor* → to invent → invention
tin can [ˈtɪn kæn]	Blechdose	You can buy most drinks in *tin cans*.
switch [swɪtʃ]	Schalter	I can't see anything. Where's the light *switch*?
3 **versus (vs.)** [ˈvɜːsəs]	gegen	old *vs.* new old *vs.* young
rotary phone [ˈrəʊtri fəʊn]	Telefon mit Wählscheibe	

Nouns and adjectives

adjectives with -y	
anger	angry
cloud	cloudy
day	daily
friend	friendly
fun	funny
health	healthy
mud	muddy
adjectives with -al	
centre	central
history	historical
music	musical
person	personal
tradition	traditional
adjectives with -ing	
excitement	exciting
interest	interesting
surprise	surprising

adjectives with -ful/-less	
colour	colourful
help	helpful, helpless
hope	hopeful, hopeless
power	powerful
success	successful
other adjectives	
competition	competitive
crowd	crowded
danger	dangerous
difference	different
freedom	free
independence	independent
possibility	possible
vegetarian	vegetarian
wood	wooden

Text smart 2 Factual texts

Introduction

1	**library** ['laɪbri]	Bibliothek; Bücherei	You can borrow books from the *library*.
2	**news report** ['nju:z rɪˌpɔ:t]	Tatsachenbericht; Nachrichtenbeitrag; Meldung	What did the *news report* say about the car accident?
	entry ['entri]	Eintrag	a diary *entry*, a dictionary *entry*
	recipe ['resɪpi]	Rezept	! Achtung Aussprache.
	questions that … [ˌkwestʃənz 'ðæt]	Fragen, die …	
	reference article ['refrns ˌɑ:tɪkl]	Referenzartikel	If you need basic information about something, look for a *reference article*.
3	**headline** ['hedlaɪn]	Schlagzeile	= the title of a news report
	hedgehog ['hedʒhɒg]	Igel	

Station 1: What do the instructions say?

winter ['wɪntə]	Winter	= the months of December, January and February
hibernation [ˌhaɪbə'neɪʃn]	Winterschlaf	During *hibernation* the animals sleep and don't eat.
food [fu:d]	Futter	Hedgehogs eat cat and dog *food*.
ill [ɪl]	krank	If you're *ill*, it's best to go to bed.
weight [weɪt]	Gewicht	You should only feed small hedgehogs that don't have enough *weight* to survive the winter.
ready ['redi]	fertig; bereit	I'm *ready*. Let's go.
spring [sprɪŋ]	Frühling	= the months of March, April and May
warm [wɔ:m]	warm	*warm* ↔ cold
to **avoid** [ə'vɔɪd]	vermeiden; meiden; aus dem Weg gehen	Try to *avoid* spelling mistakes in your texts.
run area ['rʌn ˌeəriə]	Gehege; Auslauf	My rabbits live in a *run area* in our garden. *run* → to run → runner
newspaper ['nju:sˌpeɪpə]	Zeitung	My dad reads the *newspaper* every morning while he's having breakfast. *newspaper* → news
dry [draɪ]	trocken	*dry* ↔ wet
clean [kli:n]	sauber	If you clean something, it becomes *clean*.
layer (of) ['leɪər‿əv]	Schicht (aus); Lage (aus)	On the floor of the run area is a *layer* of newspaper.
to **soak up** [səʊk‿'ʌp]	aufsaugen	The layer of newspaper *soaks up* water.
to **weigh** [weɪ]	wiegen	*to weigh* → weight
animals which … [ˌænɪmlz 'wɪtʃ]	Tiere, die …	

	fearful ['fɪəfl]	ängstlich	*fearful* → fear
5	steps which … [steps 'wɪtʃ]	Schritte, denen …	
6	people who … [ˌpi:pl 'hu:]	Menschen, die …	
	treat [tri:t]	*hier:* Leckerli; Belohnung	A *treat* is often something good to eat.

Station 2: Didn't you hear? It was in the news!

7	**celebrity** [sə'lebrəti]	Prominente/-r; berühmte Person	*Celebrities* are famous people you often see on TV or read about in magazines.
8	koalas who … [kəʊˌɑ:ləz 'hu:]	Koalas, die…	
	Australian [ɒs'treɪliən]	australisch; Australier/-in	
	bush [bʊʃ]	Busch *(Buschlandschaft)*; Wildnis	*Bush* is the word you use to describe open country, e. g. in Australia or Africa.
	fire [faɪə]	Feuer	Did you hear about the bush *fire* in Australia?
	extremely [ɪk'stri:mli]	äußerst; sehr	*extremely* = very much
	hot [hɒt]	heiß	The sun is *hot*.
	to **rescue** ['reskju:]	retten	*to rescue* → rescue
	flame [fleɪm]	Flamme	
	thirsty ['θɜ:sti]	durstig	I'm *thirsty*. Can I have a glass of water, please?
	animal shelter ['ænɪml ˌʃeltə]	Tierheim	I sometimes walk the dogs from the *animal shelter*.
9	**rhino** ['raɪnəʊ]	Rhinozeros; Nashorn	
	to **kill** [kɪl]	töten; umbringen	People *kill* rhinos for their horns.
	elephant ['elɪfənt]	Elefant	
	on the brink of [ˌɒn ðə 'brɪŋk‿əv]	am Rande von; kurz vor	
	extinction *(no pl)* [ɪks'tɪŋkʃn]	Aussterben	A lot of animals are on the brink of *extinction*.
	protest ['prəʊtest]	Protest	! Achtung Aussprache.
	illegal [ɪ'li:gl]	illegal; unrechtmäßig; rechtswidrig	
	poaching *(no pl)* ['pəʊtʃɪŋ]	Wilderei	*Poaching* is illegal.
	rhinos that … [ˌraɪnəʊz 'ðæt]	Nashörner, die …	
	tusk [tʌsk]	Stoßzahn	People kill elephants for their *tusks*.
	ivory *(no pl)* ['aɪvri]	Elfenbein	Elephant tusks are made of *ivory*.
	to **march** [mɑ:tʃ]	marschieren	The people *marched* together in a protest against illegal poaching. *Fr.* marcher

medicine *(no pl)* ['medsn]	Medizin; Medikamente	If you don't feel well, you should ask the doctor for some *medicine*.
to **become extinct** [bɪˌkʌm‿ɪk'stɪŋkt]	aussterben	There is a danger that elephants and rhinos will *become extinct*. *to become extinct* → extinction
violent ['vaɪəlnt]	gewaltsam; gewalttätig; brutal	*Violent* criminals often carry knives.
those in power [ˌðəʊz ɪn 'paʊə]	die Regierenden; die Herrschenden	

Across cultures 2 Making small talk

1	**light** [laɪt]	leicht	Small talk is *light* conversation.
	pattern ['pætn]	Muster	= how sth is done or repeated
	talker ['tɔ:kə]	Sprecher/-in	*talker* → to talk
	to **hog a conversation** [ˌhɒg‿ə kɒnvə'seɪʃn]	ein Gespräch für sich in Beschlag nehmen; ein Gespräch dominieren	You shouldn't *hog a conversation*, you should also listen to your partner.
2	to **keep the ball bouncing** [ˌki:p ðə bɔ:l 'baʊntsɪŋ]	*hier:* das Gespräch am Laufen halten	= to keep the conversation going
	to **bounce** [baʊnts]	springen; hüpfen	The ball *bounced* away and broke the window.
	next door [ˌnekst 'dɔ:]	(von) nebenan	Your neighbours live *next door*.
	to **check out** *(coll)* [ˌtʃek‿'aʊt]	prüfen; abchecken; auschecken	I've got a great tip: *Check out* the new swimming pool in Greenwich.
	worried ['wʌrid]	beunruhigt; besorgt	I feel a bit *worried* about the Maths test next week.
	Cheers! [tʃɪəz]	Danke!	Young people in Britain often say "*Cheers!*" when they want to say "Thanks!".
	to **catch** [kætʃ], **caught** [kɔ:t], **caught** [kɔ:t]	mitbekommen *(ugs.)*; mitkriegen *(ugs.)*	*to catch* = to understand
3	**student exchange** ['stju:dnt ɪksˌtʃeɪndʒ]	Schüleraustausch	
4	**script** [skrɪpt]	Drehbuch; Skript	The actor didn't want to act in the film because he didn't like the *script*.
	stage direction ['steɪdʒ dɪˌrekʃn]	Regieanweisung	A *stage direction* is an instruction in the script of a play that tells the actors what to do.
	hint [hɪnt]	Hinweis; Andeutung; Tipp	Can't you give me just a little *hint* about my birthday present? Please!
	facial expression [ˌfeɪʃl ɪk'spreʃn]	Gesichtsausdruck	The *facial expression* of people sometimes tells you more than what they say. *Lat.* expressio *(f)*
	to the point [tə ðə 'pɔɪnt]	prägnant; treffend	Keep your dialogues short and *to the point*.

Unit 3 What was it like?

Introduction

What was it like? [ˌwɒt wɒz‿ɪt ˈlaɪk]	Wie war es?	*What was life like* in the 18th century?
tribe [traɪb]	Stamm; Volksstamm	2,000 years ago, people lived in *tribes*. *Fr.* tribu *(f)*
smoky [ˈsməʊki]	verraucht	This room is very *smoky*. Let's open the window.
BC (= before Christ) [ˌbiːˈsiː]	vor Christus	
empire [ˈempaɪə]	Reich; Kaiserreich	the Roman *Empire*, the British *Empire*
emperor [ˈemprə]	Kaiser	*Fr.* empereur *(m)*
underfloor heating *(no pl)* [ˌʌndəflɔː ˈhiːtɪŋ]	Fußbodenheizung	The Romans used *underfloor heating* to keep their houses warm.
baths *(pl)* [bɑːθs]	Badehaus; Therme	
AD (= Anno Domini) [ˌeɪˈdiː]	nach Christus	*AD* ↔ BC
belt [belt]	Gürtel	
Norman [ˈnɔːmən]	Normanne/Normannin; normannisch	The *Normans* came to Britain in the 11th century.
lord [lɔːd]	Lord; Herr	
husband [ˈhʌzbənd]	Ehemann	My dad is my mum's *husband*.
to **grow** [grəʊ], **grew** [gruː], **grown** [grəʊn]	anbauen; züchten	We *grow* vegetables in our garden.
Tudor [ˈtjuːdə]	Tudor-	
monarch [ˈmɒnək]	Monarch/-in	*monarchs* = kings and queens
to **found** [faʊnd]	gründen	! to find, found, found (finden) *to found, founded, founded* (gründen)
to **marry** [ˈmæri]	heiraten	Henry VIII *married* six times.
daughter [ˈdɔːtə]	Tochter	How many *daughters* did Henry VIII have? – Two: Mary I and Elizabeth I.
Spanish [ˈspænɪʃ]	spanisch; Spanisch; die Spanier	During Elizabeth's time as queen, the English defeated the *Spanish* Armada.
golden age [ˌgəʊldn ˈeɪdʒ]	goldenes Zeitalter	Queen Elizabeth's time was a *golden age* for art, music and drama.
play [pleɪ]	Theaterstück	William Shakespeare wrote lots of *plays*.
Victorian [vɪkˈtɔːriən]	viktorianisch; Viktorianer/-in	The *Victorian* period was in the 19th century.
noisy [ˈnɔɪzi]	laut	*noisy* → noise
factory [ˈfæktri]	Fabrik; Werk	Cars, washing machines and cookers are all made in *factories*.

less [les]	weniger	*less* ↔ more
music that … [ˌmjuːzɪk ˈðæt]	Musik, die …	
to **experience** [ɪkˈspɪəriəns]	erfahren; erleben	*to experience* → experience

History words

Celts	Kelten	people who had come to the British Isles from Europe a long time before the Romans arrived
Roman Empire	Römisches Reich	Rome and the area the Romans had invaded from the 8th century BC to the 7th century AD
Romans	Römer	people who were born in the Roman Empire
Normans	Normannen	people who lived in France and fought against the English in 1066
Church of England		official Christian church in England – its head is the British king or queen
Spanish Armada	spanische Armada	the Spanish navy that attacked England in the 16th century
Henry VIII	(1491–1547)	King of England from 1509 to 1547, King of Ireland from 1541 to 1547
Anne Boleyn	(1501/1507–1536)	second wife of Henry VIII, mother of Elizabeth I
Elizabeth I	(1533–1603)	Queen of England from 1558 to 1603
Elizabethan	elisabethanisch	the time when Elizabeth I ruled
Tudors		family of kings and queens that ruled England and Wales
William Shakespeare	(1564–1616)	famous English writer
Anne Hathaway	(1556–1623)	wife of William Shakespeare
Robert Dudley	(1532–1588)	favourite of Queen Elizabeth I.
Walter Raleigh	(1552/1554–1618)	favourite of Queen Elizabeth I.
Francis Drake	(1540–1596)	English sailor who fought against the Spanish Armada
Queen Victoria	(1819–1901)	Queen of Great Britain from 1837 to 1901
Victorian Age	viktorianisches Zeitalter	the time when Queen Victoria reigned
Industrial Revolution	Industrielle Revolution	the period between 1750 and 1914 when important inventions (e.g. the steam engine) were made

1	**back then** [bæk ˈðen]	damals	My grandparents didn't have smartphones *back then*.
2	to **smell** [smel], **smelt** [smelt], **smelt** [smelt]	riechen; duften	The flowers *smell* beautiful. 
	comfortable [ˈkʌmftəbl]	bequem; komfortabel	This sofa is really *comfortable*.
3	**calendar** [ˈkæləndə]	Kalender	You can find all the dates in a *calendar*.
	boot [buːt]	Stiefel	You wear *boots* in winter because they're warmer than shoes.
	axe [æks]	Axt	

	mirror ['mɪrə]	Spiegel	If you look in a *mirror*, you see yourself.
	necklace ['nekləs]	Halskette	A *necklace* is a piece of jewellery.
	sandal ['sændl]	Sandale	*Sandals* are shoes that you wear when it's hot.
	hairbrush ['heəbrʌʃ]	Haarbürste	
4	objects which … [ˌɒbdʒɪkts 'wɪtʃ]	Gegenstände, die …	
	generation [ˌdʒenə'reɪʃn]	Generation	Your parents come from a different *generation*.
	lifestyle ['laɪfstaɪl]	Lebensstil; Lifestyle	

Station 1: He hadn't finished his game

	favourite ['feɪvrɪt]	Favorit/-in; Günstling	Robert Dudley was the queen's *favourite*.
	to **change one's mind** [ˌtʃeɪndʒ wʌnz 'maɪnd]	seine Meinung ändern	I hated the film at first, but now I like it. I've *changed my mind* about it.
	tobacco *(no pl)* [tə'bækəʊ]	Tabak	
	to **taste** [teɪst]	schmecken; probieren	Mmm! This cake *tastes* fantastic!
	stage [steɪdʒ]	Bühne	In Shakespeare's time, only men and boys could act on *stage*.
	writer ['raɪtə]	Autor/-in; Verfasser/-in	William Shakespeare was a very famous *writer*.
	to **invade** [ɪn'veɪd]	einmarschieren (in); eindringen (in); überfallen	The Spanish tried to *invade* England.
	to **play bowls** [ˌpleɪ 'bəʊlz]	Bowling spielen	
	battle ['bætl]	Schlacht; Kampf	Armies fight in *battles*.
	dress [dres]	Kleid	My sister hates *dresses*. She only wears jeans.
	crown [kraʊn]	Krone	
3	**Celt** [kelt]	Kelte/Keltin	*Celt* → Celtic
4	**everyday** ['evrideɪ]	alltäglich	An *everyday* situation is the kind of thing that happens every day.
	to **grow up** [ˌgrəʊ_'ʌp]	aufwachsen; erwachsen werden	Shakespeare *grew up* in Stratford-upon-Avon and later moved to London.
	education *(no pl)* [ˌedʒʊ'keɪʃn]	Erziehung; Bildung	It's important to go to school and get a good *education*. ! *Education* steht immer im Singular.
5	**reign** [reɪn]	Herrschaft; Regierungszeit	Queen Elizabeth I's *reign* was from 1558 to 1603.
6	to **attack** [ə'tæk]	angreifen	Yesterday a cat *attacked* my dog but he wasn't hurt badly.
	slave [sleɪv]	Sklave/Sklavin	
	to **capture** ['kæptʃə]	ergreifen; einfangen	Drake *captured* people in Africa and sold them in America as slaves.

7	**snow** [snəʊ]	Schnee	

Skills: How to talk about history

1	**entertainment** *(no pl)* [ˌentəˈteɪnmənt]	Unterhaltung	The Globe Theatre was used for all kinds of *entertainment*.
	to **reign** [reɪn]	herrschen; regieren	*to reign* → reign
	to **be born** [bi ˈbɔːn]	geboren werden	*to be born* ↔ to die
	to **burn down** [ˌbɜːn ˈdaʊn]	abbrennen; niederbrennen	The first Globe Theatre *burnt down* in 1613.
	to **burn** [bɜːn], **burnt** [bɜːnt], **burnt** [bɜːnt]	brennen; verbrennen	Dry wood *burns* very well.
	to **rebuild** [ˌriːˈbɪld], **rebuilt** [ˌriːˈbɪlt], **rebuilt** [ˌriːˈbɪlt]	wieder aufbauen	The Globe Theatre was *rebuilt* in the 20th century. *to rebuild* → building → to build
	biographical [ˌbaɪəʊˈɡræfɪkl]	biografisch	What do we know about his life? How much *biographical* information do we have?
2	**quill** [kwɪl]	Federkiel	In Victorian times people wrote with *quills*.
	feather [ˈfeðə]	Feder	

Describing objects

It's **(very) old/big/small/expensive** …	Es ist (sehr) alt/groß/klein/teuer/…
It **has** …	Es hat …
It's **made of gold/wood** …	Es ist aus Gold/Holz/… (gemacht).
It **looks like** …	Es sieht aus wie …
It **dates back to the year/period** …	Es stammt aus dem Jahr/der Zeit …
People **used it for** …	Man verwendete es für …
We got it from …	Wir haben es von/vom … (bekommen).

Describe a family object you like.

Station 2: All's well that ends well

	All's well that ends well. [ˌɔːlz wel ðət ˈendz wel]	Ende gut, alles gut.	
8	**audience** [ˈɔːdiəns]	Publikum	Make eye contact with your *audience* during a presentation.
	start [stɑːt]	Anfang; Start	*start* → to start

	Elizabethan [ɪˌlɪzəˈbiːθn]	Elisabethaner/-in; elisabethanisch	
	who [huː]	der; die; das; dem; den *(Relativpronomen)*	This is the girl *who* comes from Germany.
	right [raɪt]	direkt	Jay turned *right* into a dark, narrow road.
	to **turn back** [tɜːn ˈbæk]	umkehren; zurückgehen	*to turn back* → to turn (a)round
	to **pass** [pɑːs]	durchgehen; vorbeigehen (an)	He was *passing* buildings he had never seen before.
	which [wɪtʃ]	der; die; das; dem; den *(Relativpronomen)*	The subject *which* I like most is English.
	quite [kwaɪt]	ziemlich; ganz; völlig	This road is *quite* narrow.
	whose [huːz]	dessen; deren *(Relativpronomen)*	Sally has a brother *whose* name is Mark.
	murder [ˈmɜːdə]	Mord	The guide told a scary story about a *murder*.
	What luck! [wɒt ˈlʌk]	Was für ein Glück!	I lost my mobile but my brother found it. *What luck*!
	blood [blʌd]	Blut	There's *blood* on your T-shirt. Did you hurt yourself?
	dirt [dɜːt]	Schmutz; Dreck	*dirt* → dirty
	that [ðæt]	der; die; das; dem; den *(Relativpronomen)*	They all saw the man *that* had just entered the street.
	silent [ˈsaɪlənt]	still; ruhig; schweigsam; stumm	If you say nothing, you stay *silent*.
	terrible [ˈterəbl]	schrecklich; schlimm; furchtbar	*terrible* = awful
	forward [ˈfɔːwəd]	vorwärts; nach vorn(e)	Don't turn around. Move *forward*.
	to **pick up** [ˌpɪk ˈʌp]	aufheben; mitnehmen; abholen	There's a pen on the floor, please *pick* it *up*.
11	**bloody** [ˈblʌdi]	blutig	*bloody* → blood
	murderer [ˈmɜːdrə]	Mörder/-in	! murder ≠ Mörder
12	**kid** [kɪd]	Jugendliche/-r; Kind	*kid* = child
	detective [dɪˈtektɪv]	Detektiv/-in	! Achtung Betonung.
13	**seat** [siːt]	Sitz; Sitzplatz	the place where you sit (in a train, plane, theatre, etc.)
15	**obvious** [ˈɒbviəs]	offensichtlich	= easy to see or understand
	otherwise [ˈʌðəwaɪz]	sonst	
	to **display** [dɪˈspleɪ]	anzeigen	to show sth *to display* → display *(n)*
	photo shoot [ˈfəʊtəʊ ˌʃuːt]	Fotoshooting; Fotoaufnahmen	

Unit task: Our historical gallery walk

jewel [ˈdʒuːəl]	Juwel; Edelstein	*jewel* → jewellery
secret [ˈsiːkrət]	geheim	It's *secret*. = It's a secret.
weapon [ˈwepən]	Waffe	What kind of *weapons* did the Romans fight with?

Story: It's a mystery!

	mystery ['mɪstri]	Mysterium; Rätsel; Geheimnis	
1	**photographer** [fə'tɒgrəfə]	Fotograf/-in	! Achtung Betonung.
	set [set]	Aufnahmeort; Drehort	The *set* is the place where a photo shoot takes place.
	chaos ['keɪɒs]	Chaos; Durcheinander	When everything goes wrong at the same time, there's *chaos*.
	to **mix (up)** [mɪks‿'ʌp]	mischen; vermischen	Don't *mix up* the historical periods.
	lady-in-waiting [ˌleɪdiɪn'weɪtɪŋ]	Hofdame	Queens usually have *ladies-in-waiting*.

Monarchy words

empire	(Kaiser-)Reich
emperor	Kaiser
lord	Adeliger
monarch	Monarch/Monarchin
king/queen	König/Königin
crown	Krone
to reign	regieren; herrschen
lady-in-waiting	Hofdame

Write five sentences about Queen Elizabeth I of England.

1	to **take care of sb/sth** [ˌteɪk‿'keər‿əv]	sich um jmdn./etw. kümmern; für jmdn. sorgen	While my neighbours were on holiday, I *took care* of their cats.
	plaster cast ['plɑːstə kɑːst]	Gipsverband	If you break your leg or arm, it has to be put in a *plaster cast*. 
	to **zoom in (on)** [ˌzuːm‿'ɪn ɒn]	heranzoomen (auf)	If the camera *zooms in on* somebody, you get a close-up picture of that person.
	to **roll one's eyes** [ˌrəʊl wʌnz‿'aɪz]	die Augen verdrehen	
	shot [ʃɒt]	Aufnahme	*shot* → photo shoot
	nurse [nɜːs]	Krankenschwester; Kranken-pfleger	
	boot [buːt]	Kofferraum	I've put all the bags into the *boot* of the car. We're ready to leave now.
	to **drive off** [draɪv‿'ɒf]	wegfahren	She jumped into the car and *drove off*.

	to **drive** [draɪv], **drove** [drəʊv], **driven** ['drɪvn]	fahren	Who usually *drives* the family car?
	half an hour [ˌhɑːf‿ən‿'aʊər]	eine halbe Stunde	*half an hour* = 30 minutes
	out of focus [ˌaʊt‿əv 'fəʊkəs]	unscharf	The photo was *out of focus* because Gwen didn't stand still.
	to **photobomb** ['fəʊtəʊbɒm]	ins Foto laufen	No *photobombing*!
	flash [flæʃ]	Blitz; Lichtblitz	
	to **edit out** [ˌedɪt‿'aʊt]	herausschneiden	Jim could *edit out* the mistakes in the photo.
	to **crop (a photo)** [krɒp]	(ein Foto) zurechtschneiden	The photo doesn't fit, we'll have to *crop* it.
	to **crash** [kræʃ]	zusammenstoßen	
	ambulance ['æmbjələns]	Krankenwagen	! Achtung Betonung.
2	to **lighten** ['laɪtn]	aufhellen	*to lighten* → light
3	**flashback** ['flæʃbæk]	Rückblende; Flashback	*Flashbacks* are often used in films and books to show an event that happened in the past.

Action UK! The girl from the past

1	to **afford** [ə'fɔːd]	sich leisten	My grandparents didn't have much money so they could never *afford* to go on holiday.
	I'd rather [aɪd 'rɑːðə]	ich würde lieber	I don't want to watch the film on TV. *I'd rather* watch it at the cinema.
2	**pawn shop** ['pɔːn ʃɒp]	Pfandhaus; Pfandleihe	People who need money sometimes take their jewellery or other expensive things to the *pawn shop*.
	school fees *(pl)* ['skuːl fiːz]	Schulgeld; Schulgebühren	In the past, parents had to pay *school fees* to send their children to school. Today most schools are free.
	tea bag ['tiː bæg]	Teebeutel	 *Fr.* thé *(m)*
	pineapple ['paɪnæpl]	Ananas	
	vitamin ['vɪtəmɪn]	Vitamin	
	blurred [blɜːd]	verschwommen; verwischt	In dream sequences, the pictures are often *blurred*.
	to **wake up** [ˌweɪk‿'ʌp], **woke up** [ˌwəʊk‿'ʌp], **woken up** [ˌwəʊkn‿'ʌp]	aufwachen; aufwecken	It's 7:30 and he has just *woken up*.

Text smart 3 Fictional texts

Introduction

1	**teen** [ti:n]	Teenager; Jugendliche/-r	*teen* = teenager
	fiction *(no pl)* ['fɪkʃn]	Erzählliteratur; Prosa	I'd rather read *fiction* than stories about real people.
	plot [plɒt]	Handlung	What happens in the film? What is the *plot*?
	escape [ɪ'skeɪp]	Flucht	Reading is my *escape*.
	series ['sɪəri:z], **series** ['sɪəri:z] *(pl)*	Serie	"Harry Potter" is a *series* of seven books.
	fiction *(no pl)* ['fɪkʃn]	Erfindung; Fiktion	I don't like real stories. I only read *fiction*.
	to **identify with** [aɪ'dentɪfaɪ wɪð]	sich identifizieren mit	I love the book because it's easy to *identify with* the characters.
2	**horror** ['hɒrə]	Horrorgeschichte; Horrorfilm; Horror	
	romance [rə'mæns]	Liebesgeschichte; Liebesfilm	
	genre ['ʒɑ̃:nrə]	Gattung	This film belongs to the horror *genre*.
	detective [dɪ'tektɪv]	Detektivgeschichte; Kriminalroman; Kriminalfilm; Krimi	! Achtung Betonung.
	comedy ['kɒmədi]	Komödie	= a play or film that is written to make the audience laugh
	graphic novel [ˌgræfɪk 'nɒvl]	Bildergeschichte; Comic	
	happy ending [ˌhæpi 'endɪŋ]	Happy End	My sister only watches films with *happy endings*.
	death [deθ]	Tod	*death* → dead
	violence *(no pl)* ['vaɪəlns]	Gewalt	*violence* → violent *Fr.* violence *(f)*
	against all odds [əˌgenst_ɔ:l_'ɒdz]	entgegen allen Erwartungen	The main character survived *against all odds*.
	enemy ['enəmi]	Feind/-in	*enemy* ↔ friend
3	**the best … ever** ['best ˌevə]	der/die/das beste … überhaupt	It's a fantastic film. For me, it's *the best* film *ever*.

Station 1: Opening lines of a fictional text: Text 1

among [ə'mʌŋ]	unter; inmitten	! *among ≠ under* He stood *among* his friends. He stood under a tree.
to **disobey** [ˌdɪsə'beɪ]	nicht gehorchen; ungehorsam sein	
order ['ɔ:də]	Befehl	I've never disobeyed my parents' *orders*.
backyard [ˌbæk'jɑ:d]	Garten; Hinterhof	My friend's parents have a beautiful *backyard* with lots of flowers and plants.
wood [wʊd]	Wald; Wäldchen	= a small forest
to **hesitate** ['hezɪteɪt]	zögern	She *hesitated* for a few seconds, then she entered the room.

	smoke [sməʊk]	Rauch	*smoke* → smoky
	to **turn** [tɜːn]	drehen; (sich) umdrehen	I *turned* to look for my dog.
	shadow ['ʃædəʊ]	Schatten	
4	to **hook** [hʊk]	*hier:* fesseln	Did the story *hook* you?
7	**sense** [sens]	Sinn	With your five *senses* you see, hear, smell, taste and feel.
	to **be in sb's shoes** [ˌbiː ɪn sʌmbɒdɪz 'ʃuːz]	an jmds. Stelle sein; in jmds. Haut stecken	If I *were in your shoes*, I wouldn't do it. = If I were you, I wouldn't do it.
8	**sharp** [ʃɑːp]	scharf; schneidend	Be careful. This knife is very *sharp*.
	strict [strɪkt]	streng; strikt	The rules at our school are very *strict*.

Station 2: Opening lines of a fictional text: Text 2

	to **drown** [draʊn]	ertrinken; ertränken	Children should learn how to swim so that they don't *drown*.
	roaring ['rɔːrɪŋ]	dröhnend; tosend; donnernd	There was a *roaring* sound in the air.
	silence *(no pl)* ['saɪləns]	Stille; Schweigen; Ruhe	*silence* → silent *Fr.* silence *(f)*
	It might as well be … [ˌɪt maɪt əs 'wel biː]	Es könnte/-n auch … sein.	It's only a few metres away but *it might as well be* kilometres.
	to **sting** [stɪŋ], **stung** [stʌŋ], **stung** [stʌŋ]	stechen; brennen	Bees can *sting*.
	the lungs *(pl)* [ðə 'lʌŋz]	die Lunge	If there's water in your *lungs*, you can't breathe.
	to **be on fire** [ˌbiː‿ɒn 'faɪə]	brennen	*to be on fire* = to burn
	to **take a breath** [ˌteɪk‿ə 'breθ]	Luft holen; Atem holen	*Take a* deep *breath* and relax.
	to **roar** [rɔː]	dröhnen; brüllen; rauschen	A lion *roars*. *to roar* → roaring
	to **pray** [preɪ]	beten	A lot of people *pray* before they go to bed.
	to **rise up in one's mind** [raɪz‿ˌʌp ɪn wʌnz 'maɪnd]	jmdm. in den Sinn kommen	The thought of my next exam suddenly *rose up in my mind*.
	to **rise** [raɪz], **rose** [rəʊz], **risen** ['rɪzn]	steigen; sich erheben	*to rise* = to go up
	mind [maɪnd]	Geist; Verstand; Kopf	I don't know what he's thinking. I don't know what's going on in his *mind*.
	energy ['enədʒi]	Energie; Kraft	*Fr.* énergie *(f)*
	to **sink** [sɪŋk], **sank** [sæŋk], **sunk** [sʌŋk]	untergehen; sinken	
11	**focus** ['fəʊkəs]	Blickpunkt; Schwerpunkt; Fokus	*focus* → to focus (on)
	to **have in common** [ˌhæv‿ɪn 'kɒmən]	gemeinsam haben	Friends usually *have* a lot *in common*.

Options

15	to **step into a story slowly** [step‿ɪntʊ ə ˌstɔːri ˈsləʊli]	eine Geschichte langsam entwickeln	I'd rather *step into a story slowly* than jump into it.

Across cultures 3 Dos and don'ts

	dos and don'ts [ˌduːz‿ənd ˈdəʊnts]	Ge- und Verbote; was man tun und was man nicht tun sollte	The *dos and don'ts* are the things you should and shouldn't do.
1	**behaviour** *(no pl)* [bɪˈheɪvjə]	Verhalten; Benehmen; Betragen	*behaviour* → to behave
	to **point at sb/sth** [ˈpɔɪnt æt]	mit dem Finger auf jmdn./etw. zeigen	Don't *point at* people. It's rude.
	to **stand in the way of sb/sth** [ˌstænd ɪn ðə ˈweɪ‿əv]	jmdm./etw. im Weg stehen	Excuse me, you*'re standing in my way*.
	to **hold open** [ˌhəʊld‿ˈəʊpn]	aufhalten	You should always *hold* the door *open* for others.
	to **talk with your mouth full** [ˌtɔːk wɪð jɔː ˈmaʊθ fʊl]	mit vollem Mund sprechen	Never *talk with your mouth full*.
	to **litter** [ˈlɪtə]	verschmutzen; verunreinigen; Müll herumliegen lassen	Don't *litter* the playground. Take your rubbish home with you.
2	**odd** [ɒd]	seltsam; komisch	*odd* = strange
	ear [ɪə]	Ohr	
	to **guess** [ges]	annehmen	You look tired. I *guess* you want to go home.
	custom [ˈkʌstəm]	Gewohnheit; Brauch; Sitte	People often wear funny costumes at Halloween. It's a *custom*.
4	**icebreaker** [ˈaɪsˌbreɪkə]	Eisbrecher *(Sätze, um mit jmdm. ins Gespräch zu kommen)*	*Icebreakers* are phrases which people use to start a conversation.
	glad [glæd]	froh	I'm *glad* you aren't angry with me.
	crowded [ˈkraʊdɪd]	überfüllt	= full of people
5	**leaflet** [ˈliːflət]	Broschüre; Informationsblatt; Prospekt	
	manners *(pl)* [ˈmænəz]	Manieren; Benehmen	It's good *manners* to say hello.

Unit 4 On the move

Introduction

	on the move [ˌɒn‿ðə ˈmuːv]	unterwegs	He has to travel a lot in his job. He is always *on the move*.
	travelling *(no pl)* [ˈtrævlɪŋ]	(das) Reisen	*travelling* → to travel
1	**foreign language** [ˌfɒrɪn ˈlæŋgwɪdʒ]	Fremdsprache	A lot of British schools teach French as the first *foreign language*.

2	**seasick** ['si:sɪk]	seekrank	People sometimes feel *seasick* when they're travelling on boats or ships in bad weather.
	luggage *(no pl)* ['lʌgɪdʒ]	Gepäck	
	to **be afraid (of)** [bi‿ə'freɪd‿əv]	(sich) fürchten; Angst haben (vor)	He's *afraid of* dogs.
	plane [pleɪn]	Flugzeug	We're on our way to the airport. Our *plane* leaves in two hours.
3	**departure lounge** [dɪ'pɑ:tʃə ˌlaʊndʒ]	Abflughalle	
	passport ['pɑ:spɔ:t]	Pass; Reisepass	If you want to travel from Germany to New York, you'll need a *passport*.
	boarding card ['bɔ:dɪŋ ˌkɑ:d]	Bordkarte	A *boarding card* is the ticket you need before you get onto the plane.
	desk [desk]	Schalter	
	visa ['vi:zə], **visas** ['vi:zəz] *(pl)*	Visum, Visa *(Pl.)*; Einreisebewilligung	You can't enter the USA without a *visa*.
	passenger ['pæsndʒə]	Passagier/-in; Fahrgast	a person who is travelling by plane, train, bus, etc.
	flight attendant ['flaɪt‿əˌtendnt]	Flugbegleiter/-in	The *flight attendant* looks after the passengers on a plane.
	customs *(sg)* ['kʌstəmz]	Zoll	! *Customs* steht immer ohne Artikel und hat keine Pluralform: *Customs* **is** on your right.
	suitcase ['su:tkeɪs]	Koffer	Have you packed your *suitcase* yet? 
	ferry ['feri]	Fähre	= a boat that takes passengers and cars across a river or a narrow part of sea
	control [kən'trəʊl]	Kontrolle	If you want to travel by plane, you have to go through passport *control*.
	arrivals hall [ə'raɪvlz ˌhɔ:l]	Ankunftshalle	*arrivals hall* → arrival → to arrive
	foreign ['fɒrɪn]	ausländisch; fremd	
	currency ['kʌrnsi]	Währung	The *currency* in the UK is the British Pound.
	duty-free [ˌdju:ti'fri:]	zollfrei	Every airport has *duty-free* shops.

Station 1: You told us there was free wifi!

athletics *(no pl)* [æθ'letɪks]	Leichtathletik	! *Athletics* **is** an important part of PE in British schools.
vending machine ['vendɪŋ məˌʃi:n]	Automat	Let's get some drinks from the *vending machine*.
to **spill** [spɪl], **spilt** [spɪlt], **spilt** [spɪlt]	verschütten; auslaufen	Don't put too much water in the glass or you'll *spill* it.
to **hang on** [ˌhæŋ‿'ɒn]	(einen Augenblick) warten	*Hang on*. I'll ask them.
coast [kəʊst]	Küste	= where the land meets the sea *coast* → coastal path

	shutter [ˈʃʌtə]	Fensterladen	If it's hot outside, you should keep the *shutters* closed.
	abroad [əˈbrɔːd]	im Ausland; ins Ausland	! They live *abroad*. (= im Ausland) They went *abroad*. (= ins Ausland)
	groan [grəʊn]	Stöhnen	= a 'slow' sound that shows you are hurt, unhappy or disappointed
	hostel [ˈhɒstl]	Herberge	A *hostel* is cheaper than a hotel.
	addict [ˈædɪkt]	Süchtige/-r; Abhängige/-r	Steve is a phone *addict*.
	to **mutter** [ˈmʌtə]	murmeln	to speak – to talk – to shout – *to mutter*
3	**closed** [kləʊzd]	geschlossen; zu	*closed* ↔ open *closed* → to close
	big deal [bɪg ˈdiːl]	große Sache	That's no *big deal*. = It's not a problem.
	apart from [əˈpɑːt frəm]	abgesehen von; außer	I'm going to the supermarket later. What else do we need *apart from* bread, milk and sugar?
	soup [suːp]	Suppe	A bowl of hot *soup* does you good on a cold day. 
	herb [hɜːb]	Kraut	*Herbs* are plants that people add to food to make it taste good.
	garlic [ˈgɑːlɪk]	Knoblauch	The soup had too much *garlic* in it.
	style [staɪl]	Stil	She always wears her own *style* of clothes.
	to **be called** [bi ˈkɔːld]	heißen; genannt werden	What's your sister *called*?
	sleep [sliːp]	Schlaf	*sleep* → to sleep

Station 2: Idiot nephew?

	nephew [ˈnefjuː]	Neffe	= the son of your sister or your brother
	although [ɔːlˈðəʊ]	obwohl	Jenny's father speaks very good English *although* he's German.
	purpose [ˈpɜːpəs]	Ziel; Absicht; Zweck	If you have a *purpose*, you have a reason to do something.
	date of birth [ˌdeɪt‿əv ˈbɜːθ]	Geburtsdatum	*date of birth* → birthday
	suspicious [səˈspɪʃəs]	misstrauisch; argwöhnisch	When Rafiq told the man he was only 13, he started to get *suspicious*.
	side room [ˈsaɪd ˌrʊm]	Nebenraum	We celebrated my birthday in a *side room* of the restaurant.
	security [sɪˈkjʊərəti]	Sicherheit; Schutz; Wachdienst	The *security* people at the airport are very strict.
	immigration office [ˌɪmɪˈgreɪʃn ˌɒfɪs]	Einwanderungsbehörde	The officials asked Rafiq's aunt to come to the *immigration office*.
	immigration [ˌɪmɪˈgreɪʃn]	Immigration; Einwanderung; Einreise	The USA is a popular country for *immigration*.
	truth [truːθ]	Wahrheit	*truth* ↔ lie *truth* → true
10	**traffic** [ˈtræfɪk]	Verkehr	= all the cars, buses, etc. that are moving on a road

	to **search for** ['sɜːtʃ fə]	suchen (nach)	*to search for* = to look for
11	**traveller** ['trævlə]	Reisende/-r	*traveller* → to travel
	to **bother** ['bɒðə]	stören; belästigen	Sorry to *bother* you, but I need your help.
	to **suggest** [sə'dʒest]	vorschlagen	*to suggest* → suggestion
	chewing gum ['tʃuːɪŋ ˌgʌm]	Kaugummi	*Chewing gum* has been banned at our school.
	take-off ['teɪk‿ɒf]	Start; Abheben	
	landing ['lændɪŋ]	Landung	*landing* ↔ take-off
	out of ['aʊt‿əv]	aus … heraus	Take a pencil *out of* your pencil case, please.
12	to **contain** [kən'teɪn]	enthalten	What does this box *contain*? = What's in the box?
	gate [geɪt]	Gate; Flugsteig; Ausgang	Our plane leaves from *Gate* 9.
	delay [dɪ'leɪ]	Verzögerung; Verspätung	The train will be half an hour late. We apologise for the *delay*.

At the airport

arrival(s hall)	Ankunft(shalle)
boarding (card)	Boarding/Bordkarte
customs	Zoll
delay	Verspätung
departure (lounge)	Abflug(halle)
desk	Schalter
duty free	Duty Free
flight	Flug
flight attendant	Flugbegleiter/-in
gate	Gate
immigration office	Einwanderungsbehörde
landing	Landung
passenger	Passagier/-in
passport	Pass/Ausweis
plane	Flugzeug
security control	Sicherheitskontrolle
suitcase	Koffer
take-off	Start
visa	Visum

Have you ever travelled by plane? Write 4–5 sentences.

Skills: How to tell a travel story

1	**the other day** [ði‿ʌðə 'deɪ]	neulich	! False friend: *the other day* ≠ *am anderen Tag*
	It turned out that … [ɪt ˌtɜːnd‿'aʊt ðæt]	Es stellte sich heraus, dass …	
2	**war** [wɔː]	Krieg	World *War* II

3	**Egyptian** [ɪ'dʒɪpʃn]	Ägypter/-in; ägyptisch	= from Egypt
	dominoes ['dɒmɪnəʊz]	Domino	
	to **order** ['ɔ:də]	bestellen	At the restaurant, I *ordered* a burger and a glass of water.
	Arab ['ærəb]	arabisch	Egypt is an *Arab* country.

Nouns and verbs with the same form

answer	to answer	hope	to hope	reply	to reply
change	to change	interest	to interest	rescue	to rescue
chat	to chat	interview	to interview	run	to run
compromise	to compromise	joke	to joke	search	to search
dance	to dance	land	to land	show	to show
design	to design	lie	to lie	smile	to smile
dream	to dream	link	to link	surprise	to surprise
drink	to drink	look	to look	talk	to talk
e-mail	to e-mail	love	to love	test	to test
end	to end	name	to name	travel	to travel
exchange	to exchange	order	to order	use	to use
film	to film	plan	to plan	visit	to visit
fight	to fight	plant	to plant	walk	to walk
guide	to guide	post	to post	work	to work
help	to help	rain	to rain		

Unit task: True or not true?

convincing [kən'vɪnsɪŋ]	überzeugend	The story doesn't sound *convincing*. ***Lat.*** convincere

Story: Where I belong

where I belong [ˌweər‿aɪ bɪ'lɒŋ]	wo ich hingehöre	
responsible [rɪs'pɒnsəbl]	verantwortlich; verantwortungsvoll	Who is *responsible* for the pets?
to **accept** [ək'sept]	akzeptieren; hinnehmen; annehmen	I had to *accept* my father's decision.
mask [mɑ:sk]	Maske	He showed no feelings. His face looked like a *mask*.
smuggler ['smʌglə]	Schmuggler/-in	I'm reading an exciting adventure story about *smugglers*.
overloaded [ˌəʊvə'ləʊdɪd]	überladen	The bus was completely *overloaded*.
shark [ʃɑ:k]	Hai	

crushed [krʌʃt]	eingequetscht; eingeklemmt	The girl was *crushed* between two men and couldn't move.
to **rock** [rɒk]	schaukeln	The wind was very strong and the boat *rocked* badly.
to **smash** [smæʃ]	zerschlagen; zerschmettern	The waves *smashed* against the boat.
to **close oneself away from** [ˌkləʊz əˈweɪ frəm]	sich abschotten von	I *closed myself away from* what was happening around me.
to **give sb a piggyback** [gɪv‿ə ˈpɪgibæk]	jmdn. Huckepack nehmen	
checkpoint [ˈtʃekpɔɪnt]	Kontrollpunkt	*checkpoint* → to check
except [ɪkˈsept]	außer; bis auf	Everybody's here, *except* Jenny.
air-conditioning [ˌeəkənˈdɪʃnɪŋ]	Klimaanlage	I'm cold. Please turn off the *air-conditioning*.
to **concentrate** [ˈkɒnsntreɪt]	(sich) konzentrieren	Khadija *concentrated* on what Uncle had told her.
rain [reɪn]	Regen	*rain* → to rain
steady [ˈstedi]	kontinuierlich; unaufhörlich	
depressing [dɪˈpresɪŋ]	deprimierend; bedrückend	It rained for more than a week, which was very *depressing* for everyone.
drizzle [ˈdrɪzl]	Nieselregen	
ground [graʊnd]	Boden; Erdboden	My phone fell onto the *ground* and broke.
to **cover** [ˈkʌvə]	abdecken; bedecken; zudecken	
concrete [ˈkɒŋkriːt]	Beton	The streets in a city are *covered* with concrete.
would have happened [ˌwʊd həv ˈhæpnd]	wäre passiert	
official [əˈfɪʃl]	Beamter/Beamtin	The *officials* just looked at her passport and then let her into the country.
would have sent [ˌwʊd həv ˈsent]	hätten geschickt	
to **pretend** [prɪˈtend]	vortäuschen; tun als ob	Let's *pretend* to be on holiday.
useless [ˈjuːsləs]	nutzlos	*useless* ↔ useful
invisible [ɪnˈvɪzəbl]	unsichtbar	If something becomes *invisible*, you can't see it any more.
phone box [ˈfəʊn ˌbɒks]	Telefonzelle	
to **fetch** [fetʃ]	holen; abholen	Wait at the station. I'm going to *fetch* you.
on my own [ˌɒn maɪ‿ˈəʊn]	allein; für mich	If you're *on your own*, you're alone.
button [ˈbʌtn]	Knopf	
Somali [səˈmɑːli]	Somali; somalisch	In Somalia people speak *Somali*.
straight [streɪt]	gerade; direkt; geradewegs	Go *straight* to school, you're late.

2	**refugee** [ˌrefjʊ'dʒi:]	Flüchtling	A lot of *refugees* have come to live in our town.
5	**climate** ['klaɪmət]	Klima	= the kind of weather that is typical of a country or area
	to **be homesick** [bi 'həʊmsɪk]	Heimweh haben	*Are* you *homesick* when you're away from home?

Action UK! The guitar lesson

	guitar [gɪ'tɑ:]	Gitarre	
1	**I go wherever the wind takes me.** [aɪ ˌgəʊ weəˌrevə ðə wɪnd 'teɪks mi:]	Ich lasse mich treiben.	Let's *go wherever the wind takes us*.
2	**future** ['fju:tʃə]	zukünftig	Talk about your *future* plans.
	origin ['ɒrɪdʒɪn]	Ursprung; Herkunft; Abstammung	The girl is of African *origin*.
	destination [ˌdestɪ'neɪʃn]	Ziel; Reiseziel	Where are you travelling to? What's your *destination*?
	outgoing [aʊt'gəʊɪŋ]	kontaktfreudig	*outgoing* ↔ shy
	easy-going [ˌi:zi'gəʊɪŋ]	locker; unkompliziert	Who is more *easy-going* – your dad or your mum?
3	to **be set (in)** [bi 'set ɪn]	spielen (in); seinen Schauplatz haben (in)	"Star-Trek" *is set in* the future.
	unreal [ˌʌn'rɪəl]	irreal	*unreal* ↔ real
	specific [spə'sɪfɪk]	spezifisch; speziell	
	era ['ɪərə]	Ära; Zeitalter	The Industrial Revolution was an exciting *era* in British history.
	lavish ['lævɪʃ]	üppig; verschwenderisch	Only rich people can afford *lavish* lifestyles.
	magic ['mædʒɪk]	Magie; Zauberei	*magic* → magical
	supernatural ['su:pəˌnætʃrl]	übernatürlich	Fantasy stories are usually about people with magical or *supernatural* powers.
	force [fɔ:s]	Kraft; Macht	The hero couldn't defeat the supernatural *forces*.
	mythical ['mɪθɪkl]	sagenhaft; sagenumwoben	

Text smart 4 Drama

Introduction

2	to **entertain** [ˌentə'teɪn]	unterhalten	Theatre plays *entertain* the audience. *to entertain* → entertainment
	to **stage** [steɪdʒ]	aufführen	This year our tutor group is going to *stage* a play by Shakespeare.
	to **mess sth up** [ˌmes‿'ʌp]	etw. durcheinanderbringen; etw. vergeigen	= to do sth badly or wrong
	performance [pə'fɔ:məns]	Aufführung; Vorstellung	All the actors gave great *performances* in the school play.
	director [dɪ'rektə]	Regisseur/-in	When a film is made, the *director* tells everyone what to do.

lines *(pl)* [laɪnz]	Text	They've learnt their *lines* by heart.
protagonist [prəʊ'tægnɪst]	Protagonist/-in; Hauptfigur	The *protagonist* is the main character in a play or story.

Station 1

devil ['devl]	Teufel	
teenage ['tiːneɪdʒ]	jugendlich; Jugend-	Your *teenage* years are the time from age 13 to age 19.
dilemma [daɪ'lemə]	Dilemma; Zwickmühle	Claire is in a *dilemma*: should she go to the party or not?
to **face** [feɪs]	gegenüber stehen; konfrontiert werden mit	This is a problem we have to *face*.
angel ['eɪndʒl]	Engel	
4 to **phone** [fəʊn]	anrufen; telefonieren	*to phone* = to call *to phone* → (tele)phone
tonight [tə'naɪt]	heute Abend; heute Nacht	*tonight* = this evening
conscience ['kɒnʃns]	Gewissen	Does Claire have a bad *conscience* when she lies to her parents?
5 **motivation** [ˌməʊtɪ'veɪʃn]	Motivation; Beweggründe	
unsure [ʌn'ʃʊə]	unsicher	I'm *unsure* about what to do. = I'm not sure about what I should do.
convinced [kən'vɪnst]	überzeugt	*convinced* → to convince
tempted ['temptɪd]	in Versuchung gebracht	She feels *tempted* to lie to her parents.
to **tempt** [tempt]	in Versuchung führen; reizen	Rob *tempts* Claire to break the rules.

Station 2

6 **motive** ['məʊtɪv]	Motiv; Beweggrund	
to **take a risk** [ˌteɪk‿ə 'rɪsk]	ein Risiko eingehen	If you *take a risk*, you do something that could be dangerous.
to **exaggerate** [ɪg'zædʒəreɪt]	übertreiben	If you *exaggerate* something, you make it sound better or worse than it really is. *Fr.* exagérer
sensible ['sensɪbl]	vernünftig	! engl. *sensible* ≠ *dt. sensibel* *sensible* ↔ stupid
Let's face it. [lets 'feɪs‿ɪt]	Machen wir uns doch nichts vor.	*Let's face it*: nobody likes this situation.
white lie [ˌwaɪt 'laɪ]	Notlüge	= a small lie that you use when you don't want to hurt somebody's feelings

7	**mean** [miːn]	gemein	*mean* = nasty
	pushy ['pʊʃi]	aufdringlich; penetrant; aggressiv	Try to get what you want – but don't be too *pushy*!
	argument ['ɑːgjəmənt]	Argument	You use *arguments* to explain the reasons for your opinion.
9	**tempting** ['temptɪŋ]	verführerisch	*tempting* → tempted → to tempt

Station 3

10	to **warn** [wɔːn]	warnen	They *warned* me of the dangers. 
	hardly ['hɑːdli]	kaum	I can *hardly* believe it.
	dishonest [dɪ'sɒnɪst]	unehrlich	*dishonest* ↔ honest
	to **do well** [ˌduː 'wel]	gute Leistungen erbringen	They would like to *do* really *well* on the project.
	schoolwork ['skuːlwɜːk]	Schularbeiten	
12	**bit by bit** [ˌbɪt baɪ 'bɪt]	Stück für Stück	They've learnt their lines *bit by bit*.
	fake [feɪk]	falsch; gefälscht	A *fake* person pretends to be somebody that he or she isn't. *fake* → to fake

Station 4

13	**youth** [juːθ]	Jugend	= the period in your life before you become an adult
	tolerant ['tɒlrnt]	tolerant	! Achtung Betonung.
	to **expect** [ɪk'spekt]	erwarten	What you *expect* is what you think will happen.
	lively ['laɪvli]	lebendig	Their presentation was really convincing – very interesting and *lively*.
	to **ring** [rɪŋ], **rang** [ræŋ], **rung** [rʌŋ]	anrufen	= to call sb on the phone
	There's no need to … [ˌðeəz nəʊ 'niːd tə]	Es gibt keinen Grund zu …	*There's no need to* shout. I'm listening to you.
	out of order [ˌaʊt‿əv 'ɔːdə]	kaputt; außer Betrieb	The vending machine is *out of order*. It isn't working.
14	**shocked** [ʃɒkt]	schockiert; geschockt	
	guilty ['gɪlti]	schuldig	I didn't feel *guilty* because I hadn't done anything wrong.

Options

16	**casting** ['kɑːstɪŋ]	Casting; Rollenbesetzung	= the job of choosing actors to play particular roles

Dictionary

In dieser alphabetischen Wortliste findest du das gesamte Vokabular von *Green Line* 1, 2 und 3.
Namen stehen in einer extra Liste am Ende des *Dictionary*.
Einträge, die aus mehreren Wörtern bestehen, kannst du meist unter verschiedenen Stichwörtern nachschlagen. So ist z.B. *after all* unter *after* und unter *all* eingetragen.
Die Fundstellen stehen immer hinter dem jeweiligen Wort und zeigen dir an, wo es zum ersten Mal vorkommt, z.B.:
anger ['æŋgə] Zorn; Wut **III U1**, 21 kommt zum ersten Mal vor in Band 3, Unit 1, Seite 21
angel ['eɪndʒl] Engel **III TS4**, 107 kommt zum ersten Mal vor in Band 3, Text smart 4, Seite 107
U = Unit, AC = Across cultures, TS = Text smart
Die mit * gekennzeichneten Verben sind unregelmäßig.
Die mit ° gekennzeichneten Vokabeln sind rezeptiv.
Die mit ⟨ ⟩ gekennzeichneten Vokabeln sind fakultativ.

A

a [ə] ein/-e **I**
 a bit [ə 'bɪt] ein bisschen; ein wenig **II**
 a couple of [ə 'kʌpl‿əv] ein paar **I**
 a few [ə 'fju:] ein paar; wenige; einige **I**
 a little [ə 'lɪtl] ein wenig; etwas **I**
 a lot [ə 'lɒt] viel **I**
 a lot of [ə 'lɒt‿əv] viel/-e; eine Menge **I**
 a lot to learn [ə ˌlɒt tə 'lɜ:n] viel zu lernen **I**
a.m. [ˌeɪ'em] vormittags *(Uhrzeit)* **I**
*to be **able to** (do sth) [bi‿'əbl tə] fähig sein zu; können; dürfen °**III U1**, 20
aboard [ə'bɔ:d] an Bord **I**
about [ə'baʊt] ungefähr; circa; etwa **I**
about [ə'baʊt] über; von **I**
 out and **about** [ˌaʊt‿ən‿ə'baʊt] unterwegs **II**
 What **about** …? ['wɒt‿əbaʊt] Wie wär's mit …?; Was ist mit …? **I**
 What is … **about**? [ˌwɒt‿ɪz …‿ə'baʊt] Worum geht es in/im …? **I**
above [ə'bʌv] oben **II**
abroad [ə'brɔ:d] im Ausland; ins Ausland **III U4**, 94
accent ['æksnt] Akzent **II**
to **accept** [ək'sept] akzeptieren; hinnehmen; annehmen **III U4**, 102
accident ['æksɪdnt] Unfall **II**
account settings [ə'kaʊnt ˌsetɪŋz] Profileinstellungen **III U1**, 23
across [ə'krɒs] auf der anderen Seite von; über; hinüber; herüber; quer durch **I**
 Across cultures [əˌkrɒs 'kʌltʃəz] Interkulturelles **I**
to **act** [ækt] spielen *(Theater)* **I**
 to **act** like ['ækt laɪk] tun als ob **II**
 to **act** out [ækt 'aʊt] nachspielen **II**
 acting a scene [ˌæktɪŋ‿ə 'si:n] eine Theaterszene spielen **I**
acting ['æktɪŋ] Schauspielen **II**
action ['ækʃn] Handlung; Action; Aktion **I**
 actions which … [ˌækʃnz 'wɪtʃ] Handlungen, die … °**III U2**, 37
active ['æktɪv] aktiv °**III U2**, 43
activity [æk'tɪvəti] Aktivität **I**
actor ['æktə] Schauspieler **II**
actually ['æktʃuəli] tatsächlich; wirklich; eigentlich **III U2**, 44
AD (= Anno Domini) [ˌeɪ'di:] nach Christus **III U3**, 64
to **add** [æd] hinzufügen; ergänzen **I**
addict ['ædɪkt] Süchtige/-r; Abhängige/-r **III U4**, 94
additional [ə'dɪʃnl] zusätzlich **II**
address [ə'dres] Adresse **I**
adjective ['ædʒɪktɪv] Adjektiv; Eigenschaftswort **II**
adult ['ædʌlt] Erwachsene/-r **II**
adventure [əd'ventʃə] Abenteuer **II**
adverb ['ædvɜ:b] Adverb °**III U3**, 74
 adverb of manner [ˌædvɜ:b‿əv 'mænə] Adverb der Art und Weise °**III U3**, 74
advert ['ædvɜ:t] Anzeige; Werbespot **III TS1**, 28
advice [əd'vaɪs] Rat; Ratschlag **II**
to **afford** [ə'fɔ:d] sich leisten **III U3**, 79
*to be **afraid** (of) [bi‿ə'freɪd‿əv] (sich) fürchten; Angst haben (vor) **III U4**, 92
after ['ɑ:ftə] nach *(zeitlich)* **I**
 after all [ˌɑ:ftər‿'ɔ:l] doch; schließlich; immerhin **I**
 after that [ˌɑ:ftə 'ðæt] danach **I**
afternoon [ˌɑ:ftə'nu:n] Nachmittag **I**
 this **afternoon** [ðɪs 'ɑ:ftənu:n] heute Nachmittag **II**
afterward ['ɑ:ftəwəd] danach; hinterher ⟨**III TS1**, 30⟩
again [ə'gen] wieder; noch einmal; noch mal **I**
 over and over **again** [ˌəʊvər‿ən‿əʊvər‿ə'gen] immer wieder **III TS1**, 32
against [ə'genst] gegen **II**
 against all odds [əˌgenst‿ɔ:l‿'ɒdz] entgegen allen Erwartungen **III TS3**, 84
age [eɪdʒ] Alter **III U1**, 11
 golden **age** [ˌgəʊldn 'eɪdʒ] goldenes Zeitalter **III U3**, 66
travel **agency** ['trævl‿eɪdʒnsi] Reisebüro **III U2**, 47
travel **agent's** ['trævl‿eɪdʒnts] Reisebüro **II**
aggressive [ə'gresɪv] aggressiv **II**
ago [ə'gəʊ] vor *(zeitlich)* **II**
agony aunt ['ægəni‿ɑ:nt] Kummerkastentante **II**
to **agree** (on) [ə'gri:] sich einigen (auf) **II**
to **agree** (with) [ə'gri:] einer Meinung sein (mit); zustimmen **II**
to **aim** [eɪm] anstreben; abzielen auf ⟨**III TS2**, 60⟩
air [eə] Luft **III TS1**, 30
air-conditioning [ˌeəkən'dɪʃnɪŋ] Klimaanlage **III U4**, 103
airport ['eəpɔ:t] Flughafen **II**
alien ['eɪliən] Außerirdische/-r; außerirdisches Wesen **I**
alive [ə'laɪv] lebend; am Leben; lebendig ⟨**III TS2**, 60⟩
all [ɔ:l] alle/-s; ganz **I**
 after **all** [ˌɑ:ftər‿'ɔ:l] doch; schließlich; immerhin **I**
 all day [ˌɔ:l 'deɪ] den ganzen Tag **II**
 all night [ˌɔ:l 'naɪt] die ganze Nacht **I**
 all over [ˌɔ:l‿'əʊvə] überall (in) **I**
 all the time [ˌɔ:l ðə 'taɪm] die ganze Zeit **II**
 all of them ['ɔ:l‿əv ˌðem] alle **I**
 all of us ['ɔ:l‿əv ˌʌs] wir alle **II**
 at **all** [ət‿'ɔ:l] überhaupt **I**
 All's well that ends well. [ˌɔ:lz wel ðət 'endz wel] Ende gut, alles gut. **III U3**, 72
bowling **alley** ['bəʊlɪŋ‿æli] Bowlingbahn **I**
*to be **allowed to** (do sth) [bi‿ə'laʊd tə] dürfen °**III U1**, 20
almost ['ɔ:lməʊst] fast; beinahe **II**
alone [ə'ləʊn] allein; ohne fremde Hilfe **I**
along [ə'lɒŋ] entlang **I**
 *to sing **along** [ˌsɪŋ‿ə'lɒŋ] mitsingen **III TS1**, 28
alphabet ['ælfəbet] Alphabet **I**
alphabetical [ˌælfə'betɪkl] alphabetisch **II**
already [ɔ:l'redi] schon; bereits **I**
also ['ɔ:lsəʊ] auch **II**
although [ɔ:l'ðəʊ] obwohl **III U4**, 97
always ['ɔ:lweɪz] immer; ständig **I**

amazing [ə'meɪzɪŋ] unglaublich; toll; erstaunlich **II**
ambulance ['æmbjələns] Krankenwagen **III U3**, 77
American [ə'merɪkən] Amerikanisch; amerikanisch; aus Amerika; Amerikaner/-in **II**
among [ə'mʌŋ] unter; inmitten **III TS3**, 85
an [ən] ein/-e **I**
ancient history [ˌeɪnʃnt 'hɪstri] antike Geschichte; Frühgeschichte **II**
and [ænd; ənd] und **I**
angel ['eɪndʒl] Engel **III TS4**, 107
anger *(no pl)* ['æŋgə] Zorn; Wut **III U1**, 21
angry ['æŋgri] wütend; zornig; verärgert; böse **I**
*to make sb **angry** [meɪk 'æŋgri] jmdn. wütend machen; jmdn. verärgern **III AC1**, 35
animal ['ænɪməl] Tier **I**
animal shelter ['ænɪml ˌʃeltə] Tierheim **III TS2**, 59
animals which … [ˌænɪmlz 'wɪtʃ] Tiere, die … °**III TS2**, 57
ankle ['æŋkl] Fußgelenk; Fußknöchel **II**
to twist your **ankle** [ˌtwɪst jɔ:r‿'æŋkl] sich den Knöchel verrenken **II**
announcement [ə'naʊnsmənt] Ankündigung; Durchsage **II**
anonymous [ən'ɒnɪməs] anonym **II**
another [ə'nʌðə] ein/-e andere/-r/-s; noch ein/-e; ein/-e andere/-r/-s **I**
answer ['ɑ:nsə] Antwort **I**
short **answer** [ˌʃɔ:t‿'ɑ:nsə] Kurzantwort **I**
to answer ['ɑ:nsə] antworten; beantworten **I**
to **answer** the phone [ˌɑ:nsə ðə 'fəʊn] einen Anruf entgegennehmen **I**
answering machine ['ɑ:nsrɪŋ məˌʃi:n] Anrufbeantworter **I**
anthem ['ænθəm] Hymne **III U2**, 40
any ['eni] irgendein/-e/-er; irgendwelche **I**
not **any** more [ˌnɒt‿eni 'mɔ:] nicht mehr **I**
not … **any** [nɒt … eni] kein/-e/-en **I**
anyone else [ˌeniwʌn 'els] irgendjemand; jemand anderes **II**
Anything else? [ˌeniθɪŋ‿'els] Sonst noch etwas? **I**
not … anything [ˌnɒt 'eniθɪŋ] nichts **I**
anyway ['eniweɪ] trotzdem; jedenfalls; sowieso **II**
anywhere ['eniweə] irgendwo; überall (egal, wo) **II**
apart from [ə'pɑ:t frəm] abgesehen von; außer **III U4**, 95
to apologise [ə'pɒlədʒaɪz] sich entschuldigen **III U1**, 23
app [æp] App **II**
apple ['æpl] Apfel **I**
appropriate [ə'prəʊpriət] angemessen °**III AC1**, 35
April ['eɪprəl] April **I**
Arab ['ærəb] arabisch **III U4**, 100
area ['eəriə] Areal; Gebiet; Fläche **II**
run **area** ['rʌn ˌeəriə] Gehege; Auslauf **III TS2**, 57
argument ['ɑ:gjəmənt] Auseinandersetzung; Streit **III U1**, 20; Argument **III TS4**, 109
arm [ɑ:m] Arm **II**
army ['ɑ:mi] Armee ⟨**III U2**, 40⟩
around [ə'raʊnd] um … herum; umher **I**
to turn **around** [ˌtɜ:n‿(ə)'raʊnd] (sich) umdrehen; wenden **II**
around [ə'raʊnd] ungefähr; gegen ⟨**III TS2**, 60⟩
to arrange [ə'reɪndʒ] arrangieren; anordnen °**III U2**, 47
to arrest [ə'rest] festnehmen; verhaften **II**
arrival [ə'raɪvl] Ankunft **III U4**, 93
arrivals hall [ə'raɪvlz ˌhɔ:l] Ankunftshalle **III U4**, 93
to arrive [ə'raɪv] ankommen **II**
arrow ['ærəʊ] Pfeil **III TS1**, 30
Art [ɑ:t] Kunstunterricht **I**
art [ɑ:t] Kunst **II**
reference article ['refrns ˌɑ:tɪkl] Referenzartikel **III TS2**, 56
as [æz; əz] als **II**
as if [əz‿'ɪf] als ob ⟨**III TS1**, 28⟩
as … **as** [əz … əz] so … wie **I**
as [æz; əz] wie **II**
as long **as** [əz 'lɒŋ‿əz] solange ⟨**III TS4**, 110⟩
as soon **as** [əz 'su:n‿əz] sobald **II**
as [æz] während; indem **I**
Asian ['eɪʒn] asiatisch ⟨**III TS2**, 60⟩
to ask [ɑ:sk] fragen; bitten **I**
Ask about … ['ɑ:sk‿əˌbaʊt] Frage/Fragt nach … **I**
to **ask** for ['ɑ:sk fə] fragen nach; bitten um **I**
***to be asleep** [ˌbi ə'sli:p] schlafen **II**
***to fall asleep** [ˌfɔ:l‿ə'sli:p] einschlafen **I**
assembly [ə'sembli] Versammlung; Morgenappell **II**
assistant [ə'sɪstnt] Assistent/-in; Verkäufer/-in **II**
at [æt; ət] in; auf; bei; an; um *(bei Uhrzeitangaben)* **I**
at 7:30 [ət ˌsevn‿'θɜ:ti] um halb acht **I**
at all [ət‿'ɔ:l] überhaupt **I**
at first [ət 'fɜ:st] zuerst; zunächst **II**
at home [ət 'həʊm] zu Hause **I**
at last [ət 'lɑ:st] endlich; schließlich **I**
at least [ət 'li:st] mindestens; wenigstens **II**
at the back of [ət ðə 'bæk‿əv] hinten; am Ende; im hinteren Teil **II**
at the moment [ət ðə 'məʊmənt] im Moment; gerade **I**
at the same time [ət ðə ˌseɪm 'taɪm] zur selben Zeit; gleichzeitig **I**
at the weekend [ət ðə ˌwi:k'end] am Wochenende **I**
athletics *(no pl)* [æθ'letɪks] Leichtathletik **III U4**, 94
atlas ['ætləs] Atlas **II**
atmosphere ['ætməsfɪə] Atmosphäre; Stimmung **II**
to attack [ə'tæk] angreifen **III U3**, 70
flight attendant ['flaɪt‿əˌtendnt] Flugbegleiter/-in **III U4**, 93
attention [ə'tenʃn] Aufmerksamkeit; Beachtung **II**
attic ['ætɪk] Dachboden **II**
attraction [ə'trækʃn] Attraktion; Sehenswürdigkeit **II**
audience ['ɔ:diəns] Publikum **III U3**, 72
audio ['ɔ:diəʊ] Audio-; Hör- **I**
audio tour ['ɔ:diəʊ ˌtʊə] Audioführung **II**
audio-visual effect [ˌɔ:diəʊvɪʒuəl ɪ'fekt] audiovisueller Effekt **II**
audition [ɔ:'dɪʃn] Vorsprechen; Vorsingen; Vortanzen **III U1**, 13
August ['ɔ:gəst] August **I**
aunt [ɑ:nt] Tante **I**
agony **aunt** ['ægəni‿ˌɑ:nt] Kummerkastentante **II**
Australian [ɒs'treɪliən] australisch; Australier/-in **III TS2**, 59
author ['ɔ:θə] Autor/-in °**III TS1**, 33
autumn ['ɔ:təm] Herbst ⟨**III U2**, 40⟩
to avoid [ə'vɔɪd] vermeiden; meiden; aus dem Weg gehen **III TS2**, 57
award [ə'wɔ:d] Auszeichnung; Preis **III U1**, 16
away [ə'weɪ] weg **I**
right **away** [ˌraɪt‿ə'weɪ] sofort; gleich **I**
*to run **away** [ˌrʌn‿ə'weɪ] wegrennen **I**
straight **away** [ˌstreɪt‿ə'weɪ] sofort; gleich °**III TS2**, 59
*to throw **away** [ˌθrəʊ‿ə'weɪ] wegwerfen **I**
awful ['ɔ:fl] schrecklich; furchtbar **I**
axe [æks] Axt **III U3**, 66

B

baby ['beɪbi] Baby; Säugling **I**
back [bæk] Rückseite; Rücken **II**
at the **back** of [ət ðə 'bæk‿əv] hinten; am Ende; im hinteren Teil **II**
back to **back** [ˌbæk tʊ 'bæk] Rücken an Rücken **I**
to back down [ˌbæk 'daʊn] einen Rückzieher machen ⟨**III TS4**, 108⟩
back [bæk] zurück **I**
back then [bæk 'ðen] damals **III U3**, 64
*to go right **back** to [ˌgəʊ raɪt 'bæk tə] zurückgehen auf **II**
to turn **back** [tɜ:n 'bæk] umkehren; zurückgehen **III U3**, 72
backache ['bækeɪk] Rückenschmerzen; Rückenweh **II**
background ['bækgraʊnd] Hintergrund **I**
backing ['bækɪŋ] Hintergrund-; Background- **III U1**, 10

backing dancer ['bækɪŋ ˌdɑ:nsə] Backgroundtänzer/-in **III U1**, 10
backpack ['bækpæk] Rucksack **III U2**, 38
backyard [ˌbæk'jɑ:d] Garten; Hinterhof **III TS3**, 85
bacon ['beɪkn] Schinkenspeck; Speck **I**
bad [bæd] schlecht; böse; schlimm *(ugs.)* **I**
Too **bad**! [ˌtu: 'bæd] Zu dumm!; Schade! **I**
badminton ['bædmɪntən] Badminton **I**
bag [bæg] Tasche; Tüte **I**
tea **bag** ['ti: bæg] Teebeutel **III U3**, 79
bagpipes *(pl)* ['bægpaɪps] Dudelsack **III U2**, 37
baked **beans** *(pl)* [ˌbeɪkt 'bi:nz] weiße Bohnen in Tomatensoße **I**
ball [bɔ:l] Ball **I**
*to keep the **ball** bouncing [ˌki:p ðə bɔ:l 'baʊntsɪŋ] *hier:* das Gespräch am Laufen halten **III AC2**, 62
to **ban** [bæn] bannen; verbieten; sperren **III U2**, 42
banana [bə'nɑ:nə] Banane **I**
band [bænd] Band; Musikgruppe **III U2**, 38
Bang! [bæŋ] Peng! **II**
banjo ['bændʒəʊ] Banjo ⟨**III TS1**, 29⟩
bank [bæŋk] Ufer **II**
word **bank** ['wɜ:d ˌbæŋk] Wortsammlung °**III TS1**, 32
snack **bar** ['snæk ˌbɑ:] Café; Imbissstube **I**
bare [beə] nackt; bloß **III TS1**, 29
barely ['beəli] kaum ⟨**III TS3**, 85⟩
bargain ['bɑ:gɪn] Schnäppchen **I**
to **bark** [bɑ:k] bellen **I**
basic ['beɪsɪk] grundlegend; Grund- **II**
basics *(pl)* ['beɪsɪks] Grundlagen °**III TS1**, 29
basketball ['bɑ:skɪtbɔ:l] Basketball **I**
bath [bɑ:θ] Bad; Badewanne **I**
baths *(pl)* [bɑ:θs] Badehaus; Therme **III U3**, 64
bathroom ['bɑ:θrʊm] Bad; Badezimmer **I**
battery ['bætri] Batterie; Akku **II**
battle ['bætl] Schlacht; Kampf **III U3**, 68
BC (= before Christ) [ˌbi:'si:] vor Christus **III U3**, 64
*to **be** [bi:] sein **I**
*to be **able to** (do sth) [bi‿'əbl tə] fähig sein zu; können; dürfen °**III U1**, 20
*to **be** about [bi:‿ə'baʊt] sich handeln um **I**
*to **be** afraid (of) [bi‿ə'freɪd‿əv] (sich) fürchten; Angst haben (vor) **III U4**, 92
*to be **allowed to** (do sth) [bi‿ə'laʊd tə] dürfen °**III U1**, 20
*to **be** asleep [ˌbi ə'sli:p] schlafen **II**
*to **be** born [bi 'bɔ:n] geboren werden **III U3**, 71
*to **be** called [bi 'kɔ:ld] heißen; genannt werden **III U4**, 95
*to **be** called to do sth [bi 'kɔ:ld tə du:] auserwählt sein, etw. zu tun **III TS1**, 31
*to **be** fed up (with) [bi fed‿'ʌp wɪð] sauer sein (auf); die Nase voll haben (von) **III U1**, 17
*to **be** gone [bi: 'gɒn] verschwunden sein; weg sein **II**
*to **be** good at [bi: 'gʊd‿ət] gut sein in **I**
*to **be** grounded [bi 'graʊndɪd] Hausarrest haben **III U1**, 20
*to **be** hard on sb [bi 'hɑ:d‿ɒn] streng mit jmdm. sein **III U1**, 15
*to **be** homesick [bi 'həʊmsɪk] Heimweh haben **III U4**, 104
*to **be** impressed [bi ɪm'prest] beeindruckt sein **II**
*to **be** in [bi‿'ɪn] dabei sein; mitmachen **II**
*to **be** in charge (of) [bi‿ɪn 'tʃɑ:dʒ‿əv] die Verantwortung tragen (für); zuständig sein (für) **III U1**, 14
*to **be** in sb's shoes [ˌbi: ɪn sʌmbɒdɪz 'ʃu:z] an jmds. Stelle sein; in jmds. Haut stecken **III TS3**, 86
*to **be** in the way [bi:‿ɪn ðə 'weɪ] im Weg sein/stehen **I**
*to **be** interested in [bi‿'ɪntrəstɪd‿ɪn] interessiert sein an; sich interessieren für **II**
*to **be** into [bi:‿'ɪntə] mögen; stehen auf **I**
*to **be** jealous (of) [bi: 'dʒeləs] eifersüchtig sein (auf); neidisch sein (auf) **I**
*to **be** late [bi: 'leɪt] zu spät dran sein; zu spät kommen **I**
*to **be** like [bi 'laɪk] sein **III U2**, 36
*to **be** lucky [bi‿'lʌki] Glück haben **II**
*to **be** made of [bi 'meɪd‿əv] bestehen aus **III TS1**, 31
*to **be** on [bi‿'ɒn] an sein; laufen **II**
*to **be** on fire [ˌbi:‿ɒn 'faɪə] brennen **III TS3**, 87
*to **be** right [bi 'raɪt] recht haben **I**
*to **be** scared (of) [bi: 'skeəd‿əv] Angst haben (vor) **I**
*to **be** set (in) [bi 'set ɪn] spielen (in); seinen Schauplatz haben (in) **III U4**, 105
*to **be** sick [bi 'sɪk] sich übergeben **III U1**, 17
*to **be** sorry [bi: 'sɒri] leid tun **I**
*to **be** stressed out [bi ˌstrest‿'aʊt] völlig gestresst sein **III U1**, 10
*to **be** supposed to (do) [bi sə'pəʊzd tə] (tun) sollen ⟨**III TS1**, 31⟩
*to **be** sure [bi 'ʃʊə] sicher sein **II**
*to **be** surprised [bi sə'praɪzd] überrascht sein **II**
*to **be** trapped [bi 'træpt] eingeschlossen sein; in der Falle sitzen °**III U2**, 50
*to **be** unlucky [bi:‿ʌn'lʌki] Pech haben **I**
*to **be** up to [bi‿'ʌp tə] vorhaben **II**
*to **be** used to [bi 'ju:s‿tə] gewöhnt sein an; gewohnt sein **III AC1**, 35
*to **be** worried [bi 'wʌrid] beunruhigt sein; besorgt sein **II**
*to **be** worth [bi: 'wɜ:θ] wert sein **I**
*to **be** wrong [bi: 'rɒŋ] unrecht haben; sich irren **I**
Be careful! [bi: 'keəfl] Vorsicht!; Pass/Passt auf! **I**
beach [bi:tʃ] Strand **II**
baked **beans** *(pl)* [ˌbeɪkt 'bi:nz] weiße Bohnen in Tomatensoße **I**
bear [beə] Bär **II**
*to **beat** [bi:t] schlagen; besiegen **II**
beautiful ['bju:tɪfl] schön; hübsch; wunderbar **II**
because [bɪ'kɒz] weil; da **I**
because of [bɪ'kɒz‿əv] wegen **II**
*to **become** [bɪ'kʌm] werden **II**
*to **become** extinct [bɪˌkʌm‿ɪk'stɪŋkt] aussterben **III TS2**, 60
bed [bed] Bett **I**
*to go to **bed** [ˌgəʊ tə 'bed] ins Bett gehen **I**
bedroom ['bedrʊm] Schlafzimmer **I**
bee [bi:] Biene **III TS1**, 29
Beefeater ['bi:fˌi:tə] königlicher Leibgardist **II**
before [bɪ'fɔ:] schon einmal; vorher; zuvor **II**
before [bɪ'fɔ:] vor *(zeitlich)*; bevor **I**
*to **begin** [bɪ'gɪn] beginnen; anfangen **II**
beginning [bɪ'gɪnɪŋ] Anfang; Beginn **II**
to **behave** [bɪ'heɪv] sich benehmen; sich verhalten **III U1**, 14
behaviour *(no pl)* [bɪ'heɪvjə] Verhalten; Benehmen; Betragen **III AC3**, 90
behind [bɪ'haɪnd] hinter **I**
*to leave **behind** [ˌli:v‿bɪ'haɪnd] zurücklassen **III U2**, 43
to **believe** [bɪ'li:v] glauben **I**
I couldn't **believe** my eyes. [ai ˌkʊdnt bɪˌli:v maɪ‿'aɪz] Ich traute meinen Augen nicht. **II**
bell [bel] Glocke **II**
saved by the **bell** [ˌseɪvd baɪ ðə 'bel] noch mal Glück gehabt **III U1**, 14
to **belong** (to) [bɪ'lɒŋ (tə)] gehören (zu) **II**
where I **belong** [ˌweər‿aɪ bɪ'lɒŋ] wo ich hingehöre **III U4**, 102
below [bɪ'ləʊ] unterhalb; unten **I**
belt [belt] Gürtel **III U3**, 65
bench [benʃ] Bank; Sitzbank **III U1**, 23
beneath [bɪ'ni:θ] unter; unterhalb ⟨**III TS3**, 85⟩
beside [bɪ'saɪd] neben ⟨**III TS1**, 31⟩
besides [bɪ'saɪdz] neben **II**
(the) **best** [best] (der/die/das) Beste **II**
best [best] beste/-r/-s; am besten **I**
Best wishes [ˌbest 'wɪʃɪz] Viele Grüße; Herzliche Grüße **II**
the **best** … ever ['best … ˌevə] der/die/das beste … überhaupt **III TS3**, 84
I **bet** [aɪ 'bet] ich wette **II**
better ['betə] besser; lieber **I**
between [bɪ'twi:n] zwischen **I**
in **between** [ˌɪn bɪ'twi:n] dazwischen °**III TS1**, 33

big [bɪɡ] groß **I**
big deal [bɪɡ 'diːl] große Sache **III U4**, 95
bike [baɪk] Fahrrad **I**
mountain **biking** ['maʊntɪn ˌbaɪkɪŋ] Mountainbikefahren **II**
bilingual [baɪ'lɪŋɡwl] zweisprachig **II**
billion ['bɪliən] Milliarde **III U1**, 11
biographical [ˌbaɪəʊ'ɡræfɪkl] biografisch **III U3**, 71
bird [bɜːd] Vogel **II**
birdwatching ['bɜːdˌwɒtʃɪŋ] Vogelbeobachtung **II**
date of **birth** [ˌdeɪt‿əv 'bɜːθ] Geburtsdatum **III U4**, 97
birthday ['bɜːθdeɪ] Geburtstag **I**
Happy **Birthday**! [ˌhæpi 'bɜːθdeɪ] Alles Gute zum Geburtstag!; Herzlichen Glückwunsch zum Geburtstag! **I**
biscuit ['bɪskɪt] Keks **I**
a **bit** [ə 'bɪt] ein bisschen; ein wenig **II**
bit by **bit** [ˌbɪt baɪ 'bɪt] Stück für Stück **III TS4**, 111
wee **bit** ['wiː bɪt] klitzeklein ⟨**III U2**, 40⟩
*to **bite** [baɪt] beißen **II**
black [blæk] schwarz **I**
*to go **black** [ˌɡəʊ 'blæk] schwarz werden **II**
building **block** ['bɪldɪŋ blɒk] Baustein **II**
to **block** [blɒk] blockieren; abblocken **II**
blog [blɒɡ] Blog; Internettagebuch **III U2**, 44
bloke *(fam)* [bləʊk] Typ *(ugs.)* **III U1**, 20
blond [blɒnd] blond **III U1**, 20
blood [blʌd] Blut **III U3**, 72
bloody ['blʌdi] blutig **III U3**, 73
*to **blow** out [ˌbləʊ‿'aʊt] ausblasen; auspusten **I**
blue [bluː] blau **I**
blurred [blɜːd] verschwommen; verwischt **III U3**, 79
BMX [ˌbiːem'eks] BMX **II**
board [bɔːd] Brett; Tafel **III TS1**, 28
tourist **board** ['tʊərɪst bɔːd] Touristeninformation **II**
boarding ['bɔːdɪŋ] Boarding **III U4**, 93
boarding card ['bɔːdɪŋ ˌkɑːd] Bordkarte **III U4**, 93
boat [bəʊt] Boot **I**
boating lake ['bəʊtɪŋ ˌleɪk] See zum Rudern **I**
body ['bɒdi] Körper **III U1**, 9
human **body** [ˌhjuːmən 'bɒdi] menschlicher Körper **II**
bold [bəʊld] fett gedruckt °**III U3**, 71
bonfire ['bɒnfaɪə] Lagerfeuer; Freudenfeuer **I**
book [bʊk] Buch **I**
exercise **book** ['eksəsaɪz ˌbʊk] Übungsheft **I**
to **book** [bʊk] buchen; reservieren **II**
to **boom** [buːm] dröhnen **II**
boot [buːt] Stiefel **III U3**, 66; Kofferraum **III U3**, 77
bored [bɔːd] gelangweilt **I**
*to get **bored** [ɡet‿'bɔːd] sich langweilen **II**
boring ['bɔːrɪŋ] langweilig **I**
*to be **born** [bi 'bɔːn] geboren werden **III U3**, 71
to **borrow** ['bɒrəʊ] (sich) ausleihen **II**
boss [bɒs] Boss; Chef **III U1**, 20
bossy ['bɒsi] herrisch; rechthaberisch **III U1**, 14
both [bəʊθ] beide **II**
to **bother** ['bɒðə] stören; belästigen **III U4**, 99
bottle ['bɒtl] Flasche **I**
to **bounce** [baʊnts] springen; hüpfen **III AC2**, 62
*to keep the ball **bouncing** [ˌkiːp ðə bɔːl 'baʊntsɪŋ] *hier:* das Gespräch am Laufen halten **III AC2**, 62
to **bow** out [baʊ‿'aʊt] sich verabschieden ⟨**III TS3**, 87⟩
bowl [bəʊl] Schale; Schälchen; Schüssel **I**
to play **bowls** [ˌpleɪ 'bəʊlz] Bowling spielen **III U3**, 68
bowling alley ['bəʊlɪŋ‿æli] Bowlingbahn **I**
box [bɒks] Box; Kasten; Schachtel; Kiste **I**
phone **box** ['fəʊn ˌbɒks] Telefonzelle **III U4**, 103
boxing ['bɒksɪŋ] Boxen **II**
round of **boxing** [ˌraʊnd‿əv 'bɒksɪŋ] Boxrunde **II**
boy [bɔɪ] Junge **I**
cabin **boy** ['kæbɪn ˌbɔɪ] Schiffsjunge **I**
bracelet ['breɪslət] Armband **I**
brain(s) [breɪn] Gehirn; Verstand ⟨**III U4**, 96⟩
brave [breɪv] mutig; tapfer **I**
bread [bred] Brot **I**
bread roll ['bred rəʊl] Brötchen **III AC1**, 34
break [breɪk] Pause **II**
half-term **break** [ˌhɑːftɜːm 'breɪk] Halbjahresferien **I**
lunch **break** ['lʌnʃbreɪk] Mittagspause **I**
*to **break** [breɪk] brechen; zerbrechen **I**
broken ['brəʊkn] gebrochen; kaputt **I**
breakfast ['brekfəst] Frühstück **I**
*to have **breakfast** [ˌhæv 'brekfəst] frühstücken **I**
breath [breθ] Atem; Atemzug **III TS3**, 87
*to take a **breath** [ˌteɪk‿ə 'breθ] Luft holen; Atem holen **III TS3**, 87
to **breathe** [briːð] atmen **II**
bridge [brɪdʒ] Brücke **II**
*to **bring** [brɪŋ] bringen; mitbringen **I**
*to **bring** round [ˌbrɪŋ‿'raʊnd] mitbringen ⟨**III TS4**, 112⟩
on the **brink** of [ˌɒn ðə 'brɪŋk‿əv] am Rande von; kurz vor **III TS2**, 60
British ['brɪtɪʃ] britisch; Brite/Britin **I**
brochure ['brəʊʃə] Broschüre; Prospekt **I**
broken ['brəʊkn] gebrochen; kaputt **I**
brother ['brʌðə] Bruder **I**
brown [braʊn] braun **I**
bucket ['bʌkɪt] Eimer **II**
*to **build** [bɪld] bauen **II**; aufbauen °**III TS3**, 86
*to **build** up [ˌbɪld‿'ʌp] aufbauen; *hier:* zunehmen ⟨**III TS2**, 57⟩
building ['bɪldɪŋ] Gebäude **I**
building block ['bɪldɪŋ blɒk] Baustein **II**
cyber **bully** [ˌsaɪbə 'bʊli] *jemand, der andere in sozialen Netzwerken belästigt oder mobbed* **II**
*to give the **bumps** [ˌɡɪv ðə 'bʌmps] hochleben lassen **I**
burger ['bɜːɡə] Hamburger **I**
*to **burn** [bɜːn] brennen; verbrennen **III U3**, 71
*to **burn** down [ˌbɜːn 'daʊn] abbrennen; niederbrennen **III U3**, 71
burnt [bɜːnt] verbrannt ⟨**III TS2**, 59⟩
*to **burst** [bɜːst] bersten; platzen ⟨**III TS3**, 87⟩
bus [bʌs] Bus **I**
bus station ['bʌs ˌsteɪʃn] Busbahnhof **I**
bush [bʊʃ] Busch *(Buschlandschaft)*; Wildnis **III TS2**, 59
business ['bɪznɪs] Geschäft; Business **III U1**, 11
busy ['bɪzi] belebt; beschäftigt **I**
but [bʌt] aber **I**
butter ['bʌtə] Butter **III AC1**, 34
button ['bʌtn] Knopf **III U4**, 103
*to **buy** [baɪ] kaufen **I**
buyer ['baɪə] Käufer/-in **I**
by [baɪ] bei; neben; an **II**; von **III U2**, 42
by (bike) [baɪ] mit *(dem Fahrrad)* **I**
Bye! [baɪ] Tschüss! **II**

C

cabin boy ['kæbɪn ˌbɔɪ] Schiffsjunge **I**
cache [kæʃ] Cache **II**
café ['kæfeɪ] Café **I**
cafeteria [ˌkæfə'tɪəriə] Cafeteria **I**
cake [keɪk] Kuchen; Torte **I**
calendar ['kæləndə] Kalender **III U3**, 66
(phone) **call** ['fəʊn ˌkɔːl] Anruf; Telefonanruf **I**
to **call** [kɔːl] nennen; anrufen; rufen **I**
*to be **called** [bi 'kɔːld] heißen; genannt werden **III U4**, 95
*to be **called** to do sth [bi 'kɔːld tə duː] auserwählt sein, etw. zu tun **III TS1**, 31
caller ['kɔːlə] Anrufer/-in **I**
call-in ['kɔːlɪn] *Sendung, bei der sich das Publikum telefonisch beteiligen kann* **III U1**, 9
to **calm** down [ˌkɑːm 'daʊn] sich beruhigen **II**
camel racing ['kæml ˌreɪsɪŋ] Kamelrennen **II**
camera ['kæmrə] Fotoapparat; Kamera **II**
caught on **camera** [ˌkɔːt‿ɒn 'kæmrə] ertappt; mit der Kamera festgehalten **II**
summer **camp** ['sʌmə kæmp] Sommerferienlager **II**
to **camp** [kæmp] campen; zelten **II**

to **campaign** (for) [kæm'peɪn fɔ:] demonstrieren (für); aufmerksam machen (auf); sich engagieren (für) **III U2**, 39
camping ['kæmpɪŋ] Camping; Zelten **II**
can [kæn] Dose; Büchse **I**
tin **can** ['tɪn kæn] Blechdose **III U2**, 51
can [kæn; kən] können; dürfen **I**
can't [kɑ:nt] kann nicht; können nicht **I**
candle ['kændl] Kerze **I**
candlelight *(no pl)* ['kændlaɪt] Kerzenlicht **II**
cannot ['kænɒt] kann nicht; können nicht **II**
capital ['kæpɪtl] Hauptstadt **II**
capital letter [ˌkæpɪtl 'letə] Großbuchstabe **I**
captain ['kæptɪn] Kapitän/-in; Mannschaftsführer/-in **I**
caption ['kæpʃn] Bildunterschrift; Untertitel °**III U3**, 65
to **capture** ['kæptʃə] ergreifen; einfangen **III U3**, 70
car [kɑ:] Auto **I**
card [kɑ:d] Karte; Spielkarte **I**
boarding **card** ['bɔ:dɪŋ ˌkɑ:d] Bordkarte **III U4**, 93
*to take **care** of sb [ˌteɪk‿'keər‿əv] sich um jmdn. kümmern; für jmdn. sorgen ⟨**III TS2**, 57⟩
*to take **care** of sb/sth [ˌteɪk‿'keər‿əv] sich um jmdn./etw. kümmern; für jmdn. sorgen **III U3**, 76
to **care** (about) ['keər‿əˌbaʊt] wichtig nehmen; sich kümmern (um); sich interessieren (für) **II**
career [kə'rɪə] Beruf; Laufbahn; Karriere **III U1**, 10
careful ['keəfl] vorsichtig; sorgfältig **II**
Be **careful**! [bi: 'keəfl] Vorsicht!; Pass/Passt auf! **I**
carnival ['kɑ:nɪvl] Karneval **II**
carrot ['kærət] Karotte; Möhre **I**
to **carry** ['kæri] tragen **II**
cartoon [kɑ:'tu:n] Cartoon; Zeichentrickfilm **III AC2**, 62
plaster **cast** ['plɑ:stə kɑ:st] Gipsverband **III U3**, 76
casting ['kɑ:stɪŋ] Casting; Rollenbesetzung **III TS4**, 113
castle ['kɑ:sl] Schloss; Burg **II**
cat [kæt] Katze **I**
*to **catch** [kætʃ] fangen **II**; mitbekommen *(ugs.)*; mitkriegen *(ugs.)* **III AC2**, 62
catchy ['kætʃi] eingängig; einprägsam **III TS1**, 32
category ['kætəgri] Kategorie; Klasse **II**
caught on camera [ˌkɔ:t‿ɒn 'kæmrə] ertappt; mit der Kamera festgehalten **II**
to **cause** [kɔ:z] verursachen **II**
'cause [kɒz] weil; da ⟨**III TS1**, 31⟩
cave [keɪv] Höhle **II**
ceilidh ['keɪli] *schottisches Fest, bei dem getanzt und musiziert wird* **III U2**, 45
to **celebrate** ['seləbreɪt] feiern **I**
celebration [ˌselə'breɪʃn] Feier ⟨**III U1**, 13⟩
celebrity [sə'lebrəti] Prominente/-r; berühmte Person **III TS2**, 59
Celt [kelt] Kelte/Keltin **III U3**, 69
Celtic ['keltɪk; 'seltɪk] keltisch **II**
cent [sent] Cent *(Währung)* **I**
central ['sentrl] zentral; Zentral- **II**
centre ['sentə] Zentrum; Center **I**
community **centre** [kə'mju:nəti ˌsentə] Gemeindezentrum **I**
leisure **centre** ['leʒə ˌsentə] Freizeitzentrum **I**
tourist information **centre** [ˌtʊərɪst ɪnfə'meɪʃn ˌsentə] Touristeninformation **I**
century ['senʃri] Jahrhundert **II**
cereal *(no pl)* ['sɪəriəl] Frühstückszerealie; Getreideprodukt *(z. B. Cornflakes oder Müsli)* **I**
chair [tʃeə] Stuhl; Sessel **I**
challenge ['tʃælɪndʒ] Herausforderung **II**
champion ['tʃæmpiən] Gewinner/-in; Sieger/-in; Champion **III TS1**, 32
chance [tʃɑ:ns] Chance; Gelegenheit; Möglichkeit **II**
change [tʃeɪndʒ] Änderung; Veränderung; Wechsel **II**
to **change** [tʃeɪndʒ] wechseln; (sich) ändern **II**
to **change** (onto) [tʃeɪndʒ ('ɒntʊ)] umsteigen (in) **II**
to **change** one's mind [ˌtʃeɪndʒ wʌnz 'maɪnd] seine Meinung ändern **III U3**, 68
chant [tʃɑ:nt] Sprechgesang **II**
chaos ['keɪɒs] Chaos; Durcheinander **III U3**, 76
chapter ['tʃæptə] Kapitel °**III TS3**, 85
character ['kærəktə] Charakter; Figur **I**
*to be in **charge** (of) [bi‿ɪn 'tʃɑ:dʒ‿əv] die Verantwortung tragen (für); zuständig sein (für) **III U1**, 14
charity ['tʃærɪti] Wohltätigkeitsverein; wohltätige Zwecke; Wohlfahrt **I**
charity shop ['tʃærɪti ʃɒp] Second-Hand-Laden **I**
lucky **charm** [ˌlʌki 'tʃɑ:m] Glücksbringer; Talisman **I**
chart [tʃɑ:t] Tabelle ⟨**III TS2**, 57⟩
to **chase** [tʃeɪs] jagen; nachjagen **I**
chat [ˌtʃæt] Chat **III U2**, 40
chat room ['tʃæt rʊm] Chatroom **II**
video **chat** ['vɪdiəʊ ˌtʃæt] Videochat **II**
to **chat** [tʃæt] plaudern; chatten *(sich online unterhalten)* **I**
chatroom ['tʃætrʊm] Chatroom **III U1**, 12
cheap [tʃi:p] billig; preiswert **I**
to **check** [tʃek] überprüfen; prüfen; kontrollieren **I**
to **check** out *(coll)* [ˌtʃek‿'aʊt] prüfen; abchecken; auschecken **III AC2**, 62
to **check** with ['tʃek wɪð] nachfragen bei ⟨**III TS4**, 110⟩
Check-in ['tʃekɪn] Einchecken **I**
checklist ['tʃeklɪst] Checkliste **II**
Check-out ['tʃekaʊt] Auschecken **I**
checkpoint ['tʃekpɔɪnt] Kontrollpunkt **III U4**, 102
to **cheer** [tʃɪə] anfeuern; jubeln; zujubeln **II**
to **cheer** sb up [ˌtʃɪər‿'ʌp] jmdn. aufheitern **III U1**, 23
Cheers! [tʃɪəz] Danke! **III AC2**, 62
cheese [tʃi:z] Käse **I**
to **cherish** ['tʃerɪʃ] schätzen ⟨**III TS1**, 28⟩
chess [tʃes] Schach **II**
chewing gum ['tʃu:ɪŋ ˌgʌm] Kaugummi **III U4**, 99
chicken ['tʃɪkɪn] Huhn; Hähnchen **I**
child [tʃaɪld], **children** ['tʃɪldrən] *(pl)* Kind **I**
only **child** ['əʊnli ˌtʃaɪld] Einzelkind **I**
chimney ['tʃɪmni] Kamin; Schornstein **II**
chips *(pl) (BE)* [tʃɪps] Pommes frites **I**
chlorine *(no pl)* ['klɔ:ri:n] Chlor ⟨**III TS3**, 87⟩
chocolate ['tʃɒklət] Schokolade **I**
choice [tʃɔɪs] Wahl; Auswahl **II**
***choose** [tʃu:z] auswählen; wählen **I**
chorus ['kɔ:rəs] Refrain °**III TS1**, 31
in **chorus** [ɪn 'kɔ:rəs] im Chor °**III TS4**, 109
Christmas ['krɪsməs] Weihnachten **I**
church [tʃɜ:tʃ] Kirche **I**
cinema ['sɪnəmə] Kino **I**
circle ['sɜ:kl] Kreis; Ring **I**
*to go round in **circles** [gəʊ ˌraʊnd ɪn 'sɜ:klz] sich im Kreis drehen **III U2**, 48
city ['sɪti] Stadt; Großstadt **I**
clan [klæn] Clan; Sippe; Stamm **III U2**, 44
to **clap** [klæp] klatschen **I**
Clap your hands. [ˌklæp jɔ: 'hændz] Klatsch/Klatscht in die Hände. **I**
clarification [ˌklærɪfɪ'keɪʃn] Klärung; Klarstellung °**III U4**, 99
class [klɑ:s] Klasse; Schulklasse **I**; *hier:* Unterricht **II**
class display ['klɑ:s dɪˌspleɪ] Ausstellung in der Klasse **I**
class poster ['klɑ:s ˌpəʊstə] Klassenposter **I**
classmate ['klɑ:smeɪt] Klassenkamerad/-in; Mitschüler/-in **I**
classroom ['klɑ:srʊm] Klassenzimmer **I**
clause [klɔ:z] Satz *(Teil eines Satzgefüges)* °**III U1**, 11
conditional **clause** [kənˌdɪʃnl 'klɔ:z] Bedingungssatz °**III U1**, 9
contact **clause** ['kɒntækt ˌklɔ:z] *Relativsatz ohne Relativpronomen* °**III U3**, 73
defining relative **clause** [dɪˌfaɪnɪŋ 'relətɪv ˌklɔ:z] notwendiger Relativsatz °**III U3**, 72
if-**clause** ['ɪfˌklɔ:z] if-Satz °**III U1**, 11
main **clause** ['meɪn ˌklɔ:z] Hauptsatz °**III U1**, 11
clay pipe ['kleɪ paɪp] Tonpfeife **II**
to **clean** [kli:n] säubern; reinigen **I**
clean [kli:n] sauber **III TS2**, 57
to **clear** out [ˌklɪər‿'aʊt] ausräumen; entrümpeln **I**
clear [klɪə] klar; deutlich **I**

clever ['klevə] schlau; klug **II**
click [klɪk] Klicken; Klick **II**
to **click** on ['klɪk‿ɒn] anklicken **II**
cliff [klɪf] Klippe; Kliff **III U2**, 46
climate ['klaɪmət] Klima **III U4**, 104
climax ['klaɪmæks] Höhepunkt °**III U2**, 50
to **climb** [klaɪm] klettern; besteigen; steigen **I**
climbing ['klaɪmɪŋ] Klettern **II**
clock [klɒk] Uhr **I**
o'**clock** [ə'klɒk] Uhr *(Zeitangabe bei vollen Stunden)* **I**
to **clone** [kləʊn] klonen **III U2**, 42
close [kləʊs] schmaler Durchgang **III U2**, 43
closes which … [ˌkləʊsɪz 'wɪtʃ] Durchgänge, die … °**III U2**, 43
to **close** [kləʊz] schließen; zumachen **I**
to **close** oneself away from [ˌkləʊz ə'weɪ frəm] sich abschotten von **III U4**, 102
close [kləʊs] eng; knapp **I**; nahe **II**
Look **closely** … [ˌlʊk 'kləʊsli] Schau(t) genau … **II**
That was **close**! [ˌðæt wəz 'kləʊs] Das war knapp! **I**
closed [kləʊzd] geschlossen; zu **III U4**, 95
close-up ['kləʊsʌp] Nahaufnahme **II**
clothes *(pl)* [kləʊðz] Kleider; Kleidung **I**
cloud [klaʊd] Wolke **II**
word **cloud** ['wɜːd ˌklaʊd] Wörterwolke **II**
cloudy ['klaʊdi] bedeckt; bewölkt **II**
clover *(no pl)* ['kləʊvə] Klee ⟨**III TS3**, 85⟩
clown [klaʊn] Clown **II**
club [klʌb] Klub; Verein; AG **I**
Cooking **Club** ['kʊkɪŋ ˌklʌb] Koch-AG **I**
clue [kluː] Hinweis; Spur **II**
coach [kəʊtʃ] Trainer/-in **I**; Reisebus **II**
coast [kəʊst] Küste **III U4**, 94
coastal path [ˌkəʊstl 'pɑːθ] Küstenweg **II**
coastline ['kəʊstlaɪn] Küste; Küstenverlauf **II**
coconut ['kəʊkənʌt] Kokosnuss **II**
coffee ['kɒfi] Kaffee **I**
coin [kɔɪn] Münze **I**
coke ['kəʊk] Cola **I**
cold [kəʊld] Erkältung **II**
cold [kəʊld] kalt **II**
to **collect** [kə'lekt] sammeln **I**
collection [kə'lekʃn] Kollektion; Sammlung **II**
collocation [ˌkɒlə'keɪʃn] Wortverbindung **II**
colony ['kɒləni] Kolonie **II**
colour ['kʌlə] Farbe **I**
What **colour** is …? [ˌwɒt 'kʌlər‿ɪz] Welche Farbe hat …? **I**
colourful ['kʌləfl] farbenfroh; bunt **I**
column ['kɒləm] Spalte °**III U1**, 14
*to **come** [kʌm] kommen **I**
*to **come** down [ˌkʌm 'daʊn] herunterkommen **I**
*to **come** in [ˌkʌm‿'ɪn] hereinkommen **II**
*to **come** up [ˌkʌm‿'ʌp] vorkommen °**III U3**, 78
*to **come** up to sb [kʌm‿'ʌp tə] auf jmdn. zukommen **III U1**, 21
Come on! [ˌkʌm‿'ɒn] Komm schon!; Komm jetzt! **I**
comedian [kə'miːdiən] Komiker/-in; Comedian **II**
comedy ['kɒmədi] Komödie **III TS3**, 84
comedy show ['kɒmədi ˌʃəʊ] Comedy Show **II**
comic ['kɒmɪk] Comicheft **II**
comfortable ['kʌmftəbl] bequem; komfortabel **III U3**, 65
command [kə'mɑːnd] Befehl °**III U4**, 93
comment ['kɒment] Kommentar **II**
to **comment** (on) ['kɒment‿(ɒn)] kommentieren **II**
*to have in **common** [ˌhæv‿ɪn 'kɒmən] gemeinsam haben **III TS3**, 88
to **communicate** [kə'mjuːnɪkeɪt] kommunizieren; sich verständigen **II**
communication [kəˌmjuːnɪ'keɪʃn] Kommunikation **II**
community centre [kə'mjuːnəti ˌsentə] Gemeindezentrum **I**
company ['kʌmpəni] Gesellschaft; Firma; Unternehmen **III U1**, 11
comparative [kəm'pærətɪv] Komparativ **II**
to **compare** (with/to) [kəm'peə] vergleichen (mit) **I**
comparison [kəm'pærɪsn] Vergleich **II**
to **compete** (with) [kəm'piːt] konkurrieren (mit); sich messen (mit); in Wettbewerb treten (mit) **III U1**, 9
competition [ˌkɒmpə'tɪʃn] Wettbewerb; Turnier **II**
competitive [kəm'petɪtɪv] leistungsorientiert; konkurrierend **III U1**, 19
Complete … [kəm'pliːt] Vervollständige/Vervollständigt … **I**
completely [kəm'pliːtli] völlig **II**
compound word ['kɒmpaʊnd wɜːd] Kompositum *(zusammengesetztes Wort)* **II**
compromise ['kɒmprəmaɪz] Kompromiss **II**
to **compromise** ['kɒmprəmaɪz] Kompromisse eingehen **III U1**, 9
computer [ˌkəm'pjuːtə] Computer **I**
con [kɒn] Argument dagegen **II**
to **concentrate** ['kɒnsntreɪt] (sich) konzentrieren **III U4**, 103
concrete ['kɒŋkriːt] Beton **III U4**, 103
condition [kən'dɪʃn] Kondition; Bedingung **III U1**, 10
conditional clause [kənˌdɪʃnl 'klɔːz] Bedingungssatz °**III U1**, 9
confident ['kɒnfɪdnt] selbstsicher; selbstbewusst **II**
confused [kən'fjuːzd] verwirrt; wirr; konfus **III U1**, 22
connection [kə'nekʃn] Verbindung **II**
conscience ['kɒnʃns] Gewissen **III TS4**, 107
contact ['kɒntækt] Kontakt **II**
contact clause ['kɒntækt ˌklɔːz] *Relativsatz ohne Relativpronomen* °**III U3**, 73
to **contact** ['kɒntækt] sich in Verbindung setzen; kontaktieren ⟨**III TS2**, 57⟩
to **contain** [kən'teɪn] enthalten **III U4**, 99
container [kən'teɪnə] Container; Behälter; Behältnis ⟨**III TS2**, 57⟩
contest ['kɒntest] Wettkampf; Wettbewerb **I**
to **continue** [kən'tɪnjuː] fortfahren; andauern; weitermachen °**III U2**, 37; weitergehen °**III U4**, 104
control [kən'trəʊl] Kontrolle **III U4**, 93
to **control** [kən'trəʊl] kontrollieren; beherrschen; steuern ⟨**III U4**, 96⟩
conversation [ˌkɒnvə'seɪʃn] Konversation; Gespräch; Unterhaltung **I**
to hog a **conversation** [ˌhɒg‿ə kɒnvə'seɪʃn] ein Gespräch für sich in Beschlag nehmen; ein Gespräch dominieren **III AC2**, 62
command [kə'mɑːnd] Befehl °**III U4**, 93
to **convince** [kən'vɪns] überzeugen **III U2**, 50
convinced [kən'vɪnst] überzeugt **III TS4**, 107
convincing [kən'vɪnsɪŋ] überzeugend **III U4**, 101
to **cook** [kʊk] kochen **II**
cooker ['kʊkə] Herd **I**
cooking ['kʊkɪŋ] Kochen **I**
Cooking Club ['kʊkɪŋ ˌklʌb] Koch-AG **I**
*to leave it to **cool** [ˌliːv‿ɪt tə 'kuːl] kalt stellen **I**
cool [kuːl] cool; super **I**
to **copy** ['kɒpi] abschreiben; kopieren **I**
corner ['kɔːnə] Ecke **II**
Cornish ['kɔːnɪʃ] in Cornwall; kornisch; Kornisch **II**
Correct … [kə'rekt] Korrigiere/Korrigiert … **I**
correct [kə'rekt] richtig; korrekt **I**
*to **cost** [kɒst] kosten **I**
costume ['kɒstjuːm] Kostüm **I**
cough [kɒf] Husten **II**
could [kʊd] könnte/-n **II**; konnte/-n **III U1**, 20
to **count** (on) ['kaʊnt‿ɒn] zählen (auf) **I**
country ['kʌntri], **countries** ['kʌntriz] *(pl)* Land **I**
countryside ['kʌntrisaɪd] Land **II**
couple ['kʌpl] Paar **II**
a **couple** of [ə 'kʌpl‿əv] ein paar **I**
course [kɔːs] Kurs **II**
of **course** [əv 'kɔːs] natürlich; selbstverständlich **I**
court [kɔːt] Spielfeld **II**
cousin ['kʌzn] Cousin/Cousine **I**
cover ['kʌvə] Cover; Titelblatt **III U1**, 8
cover version ['kʌvə ˌvɜːʃn] Coverversion °**III TS1**, 33
to **cover** ['kʌvə] abdecken; bedecken; zudecken **III U4**, 103
to **cover** up for sb [ˌkʌvər‿'ʌp fə] jmdn. decken °**III U2**, 47; ⟨**III TS4**, 107⟩
cow [kaʊ] Kuh **II**
crack [kræk] Knacken; Krachen **III U2**, 49
cracking ['krækɪŋ] knackend; brechend **III U2**, 48
cramp [kræmp] Krampf **II**

crane [kreɪn] Kran **III U2**, 43
to **crash** [kræʃ] abstürzen **II**; zusammenstoßen **III U3**, 77
crazy ['kreɪzi] verrückt **I**
*to go **crazy** [ˌgəʊ 'kreɪzi] ausflippen; durchdrehen; verrückt werden **II**
cream [kri:m] Creme; Sahne **I**
ice **cream** [ˌaɪs 'kri:m] Eis; Eiscreme **I**
to **create** [kri'eɪt] schaffen; erschaffen; erfinden **I**
creative [kri'eɪtɪv] kreativ **I**
credit ['kredɪt] Guthaben **II**
cricket ['krɪkɪt] Cricket **II**
crime [kraɪm] Verbrechen; Kriminalität **II**
criminal ['krɪmɪnəl] Kriminelle/-r; Verbrecher/-in **II**
crisp [krɪsp] Kartoffelchip **I**
criterion [kraɪ'tɪəriən], **criteria** [kraɪ'tɪəriə] *(pl)* Kriterium; Argument °**III U2**, 46
to **crop** (a photo) [krɒp] (ein Foto) zurechtschneiden **III U3**, 77
to **cross** [krɒs] überqueren; kreuzen **II**
*to keep your fingers **crossed** [ˌki:p jɔ: ˌfɪŋgəz 'krɒst] die Daumen drücken **I**
crowd [kraʊd] Menschenmenge **II**
crowded ['kraʊdɪd] überfüllt **III AC3**, 91
crown [kraʊn] Krone **III U3**, 68
crown jewels [ˌkraʊn 'dʒu:əlz] Kronjuwelen **II**
cruel ['kru:əl] grausam **II**
crushed [krʌʃt] eingequetscht; eingeklemmt **III U4**, 102
to **cry** [kraɪ] schreien; rufen **II**; weinen **III TS1**, 31
CU *(= See you)* ['si: ju] Bis dann!; Bis ... **I**
culture ['kʌltʃə] Kultur **I**
Across **cultures** [əˌkrɒs 'kʌltʃəz] Interkulturelles **I**
cup [kʌp] Tasse **III AC1**, 34
cupboard ['kʌbəd] Küchenschrank; Schrank **I**
currency ['kʌrnsi] Währung **III U4**, 93
curry ['kʌri] Curry *(Gewürz oder Gericht)* **I**
custard ['kʌstəd] Vanillesoße; Vanillepudding **I**
custom ['kʌstəm] Gewohnheit; Brauch; Sitte **III AC3**, 90
customer ['kʌstəmə] Kunde/Kundin **II**
customs *(sg)* ['kʌstəmz] Zoll **III U4**, 93
*to **cut** (off) [kʌt (ɒf)] schneiden; abschneiden **II**
cute [kju:t] niedlich; süß **I**
cyber bully [ˌsaɪbə 'bʊli] *jemand, der andere in sozialen Netzwerken belästigt oder mobbed* **II**
cycling ['saɪklɪŋ] Radfahren **I**

D

dad [dæd] Papa **I**
daily ['deɪli] täglich ⟨**III TS2**, 57⟩
dance [dɑ:ns] Tanz; Tanzveranstaltung **III U1**, 10
dance *(no pl)* [dɑ:ns] Tanz; Tanzveranstaltung **II**
to **dance** [dɑ:ns] tanzen **I**
to **dance** to ['dɑ:ns tə] tanzen zu **III TS1**, 32
everyone was **dancing** [ˌevriwʌn wəz 'dɑ:nsɪŋ] alle tanzten °**III U1**, 21
dancer ['dɑ:nsə] Tänzer/-in **III U1**, 10
backing **dancer** ['bækɪŋ ˌdɑ:nsə] Backgroundtänzer/-in **III U1**, 10
lead **dancer** ['li:d ˌdɑ:nsə] Vortänzer/-in **III U1**, 10
dancing ['dɑ:nsɪŋ] Tanzen **III U2**, 44
danger ['deɪndʒə] Gefahr **III U2**, 48
dangerous ['deɪndʒrəs] gefährlich **I**
the **dark** [ðə 'dɑ:k] Dunkelheit **II**
dark [dɑ:k] dunkel **II**
darkness ['dɑ:knəs] Dunkelheit **II**
date [deɪt] Datum **I**
date of birth [ˌdeɪt‿əv 'bɜ:θ] Geburtsdatum **III U4**, 97
daughter ['dɔ:tə] Tochter **III U3**, 66
day [deɪ] Tag **I**
all **day** [ˌɔ:l 'deɪ] den ganzen Tag **II**
one **day** [wʌn 'deɪ] eines Tages **II**
the other **day** [ði‿ˌʌðə 'deɪ] neulich **III U4**, 100
these **days** [ˌði:z 'deɪz] zurzeit **III U1**, 20
a **day** out in ... [ə ˌdeɪ‿'aʊt ɪn] ein Tag in ... **II**
the next **day** [ðə ˌnekst 'deɪ] am nächsten Tag **II**
dead [ded] tot **II**
deadly ['dedli] tödlich ⟨**III TS2**, 59⟩
big **deal** [bɪg 'di:l] große Sache **III U4**, 95
*to **deal** (with) [di:l] sich befassen mit; umgehen mit **II**
Oh **dear**! [ˌəʊ 'dɪə] Oje! **II**
Dear ... [dɪə] Lieber ...; Liebe ... *(Anrede in Briefen)* **I**
Dear Sir or Madam [dɪə ˌsɜ:r‿ɔ: 'mædəm] Sehr geehrte Dame, sehr geehrter Herr **II**
dearly ['dɪəli] lieb ⟨**III U2**, 40⟩
death [deθ] Tod **III TS3**, 84
December [dɪ'sembə] Dezember **I**
to **decide** [dɪ'saɪd] (sich) entscheiden **I**
decision [dɪ'sɪʒn] Entscheidung **II**
*to make a **decision** [ˌmeɪk‿ə dɪ'sɪʒn] eine Entscheidung treffen **II**
deck [dek] Deck **I**
to **decorate** ['dekəreɪt] dekorieren; verzieren; schmücken **I**
decorations *(pl)* [ˌdekə'reɪʃnz] Dekoration; Schmuck **I**
deep [di:p] tief **II**
to **defeat** [dɪ'fi:t] besiegen **III U2**, 40
defining relative clause [dɪˌfaɪnɪŋ 'relətɪv ˌklɔ:z] notwendiger Relativsatz °**III U3**, 72
definitely ['defɪnətli] bestimmt; definitiv; eindeutig **II**
definition [ˌdefɪ'nɪʃn] Definition **II**
delay [dɪ'leɪ] Verzögerung; Verspätung **III U4**, 99
to **delete** [dɪ'li:t] löschen **III U1**, 23
to **depart** [dɪ'pɑ:t] abfahren **II**
departure [dɪ'pɑ:tʃə] Abflug; Abreise **III U4**, 93
departure lounge [dɪ'pɑ:tʃə ˌlaʊndʒ] Abflughalle **III U4**, 93
to **depend** (on) [dɪ'pend‿(ɒn)] abhängen von **II**
depressing [dɪ'presɪŋ] deprimierend; bedrückend **III U4**, 103
to **describe** [dɪ'skraɪb] beschreiben **I**
description [dɪ'skrɪpʃn] Beschreibung **II**
to **deserve** [dɪ'zɜ:v] verdienen **II**
to **design** [dɪ'zaɪn] entwerfen; gestalten **II**
design [dɪ'zaɪn] Design; Gestaltung; Entwurf **III U3**, 64
designer [dɪ'zaɪnə] Designer/-in **III U1**, 12
web **designer** ['web dɪˌzaɪnə] Webdesigner **III U1**, 14
desk [desk] Schalter **III U4**, 93
destination [ˌdestɪ'neɪʃn] Ziel; Reiseziel **III U4**, 105
detail ['di:teɪl] Detail; Einzelheit **II**
detective [dɪ'tektɪv] Detektiv/-in **III U3**, 73; Detektivgeschichte; Kriminalroman; Kriminalfilm; Krimi **III TS3**, 84
private **detective** [ˌpraɪvət dɪ'tektɪv] Privatdetektiv/-in **II**
to **develop** [dɪ'veləp] (sich) entwickeln ⟨**III U1**, 11⟩
devil ['devl] Teufel **III TS4**, 107
diagram ['daɪəgræm] Diagramm **I**
dialect ['daɪəlekt] Dialekt **II**
dialogue ['daɪəlɒg] Dialog; Gespräch **I**
diary ['daɪəri] Tagebuch **II**
diary entry ['daɪəri entri] Tagebucheintrag **II**
dice [daɪs] Würfel **II**
Roll two **dice**. [ˌrəʊl ˌtu: 'daɪs] Würfle/Würfelt mit zwei Würfeln. **I**
dictionary ['dɪkʃnri] Wörterbuch **I**
to **die** [daɪ] sterben **III TS1**, 32
difference ['dɪfrəns] Unterschied **I**
*to make a **difference** [ˌmeɪk‿ə‿'dɪfrns] etw. verändern **II**
different ['dɪfrnt] anders; unterschiedlich; verschieden **I**
It feels so **different** from ... [ˌɪt‿fi:lz səʊ 'dɪfrnt frɒm] Es ist so anders hier im Vergleich zu ... **II**
difficult ['dɪfɪklt] schwierig **II**
dilemma [daɪ'lemə] Dilemma; Zwickmühle **III TS4**, 107
dinner ['dɪnə] Abendessen **I**
dinosaur ['daɪnəsɔ:] Dinosaurier **II**
direct [dɪ'rekt] direkt **III TS1**, 30
direct speech [dɪˌrekt 'spi:tʃ] direkte Rede °**III U4**, 95
direction [dɪ'rekʃn] Richtung **I**
stage **direction** ['steɪdʒ dɪˌrekʃn] Regieanweisung **III AC2**, 63
director [dɪ'rektə] Regisseur/-in **III TS4**, 106

dirt [dɜːt] Schmutz; Dreck **III U3**, 72
dirty ['dɜːti] dreckig; schmutzig **II**
to **disagree** [ˌdɪsə'griː] anderer Meinung sein; nicht einverstanden sein **III U1**, 9
disappointed [ˌdɪsə'pɔɪntɪd] enttäuscht **I**
disaster [dɪ'zɑːstə] Desaster; Katastrophe; Unglück **II**
to **discover** [dɪ'skʌvə] entdecken **II**
discovery [dɪ'skʌvri] Entdeckung **III U2**, 42
to **discuss** [dɪ'skʌs] diskutieren **I**
discussion [dɪ'skʌʃn] Diskussion **II**
dishonest [dɪ'sɒnɪst] unehrlich **III TS4**, 110
to **disobey** [ˌdɪsə'beɪ] nicht gehorchen; ungehorsam sein **III TS3**, 85
display [dɪ'spleɪ] Ausstellung **II**
class **display** ['klɑːs dɪˌspleɪ] Ausstellung in der Klasse **I**
to **display** [dɪ'spleɪ] anzeigen **III U3**, 74
distance ['dɪstns] Distanz; Entfernung **II**
to **divide** (up) [dɪ'vaɪd] aufteilen °**III TS1**, 30
DJ [ˌdiː'dʒeɪ] DJ; Discjockey **III U1**, 21
*to **do** [duː] machen; tun **I**
*to **do** about ['duː‿əˌbaʊt] unternehmen wegen **II**
*to **do** our hair [ˌduː‿aʊə 'heə] uns frisieren; unsere Haare machen **I**
*to **do** the shopping [ˌduː ðə 'ʃɒpɪŋ] Einkäufe machen; Besorgungen machen **III U2**, 51
*to **do** well [ˌduː 'wel] gute Leistungen erbringen **III TS4**, 110
Don't worry! [ˌdəʊnt 'wʌri] Keine Sorge! **I**
dos and **don'ts** [ˌduːz‿ənd 'dəʊnts] Gebote und Verbote; was man tun und was man nicht tun sollte **III AC3**, 90
We **did** it! [ˌwiː 'dɪd‿ɪt] Wir haben es geschafft! **II**
You can **do** it! [ˌjuː kən 'duː ɪt] Du schaffst es! **III TS1**, 32
doctor ['dɒktə] Arzt/Ärztin **II**
dog [dɒg] Hund **I**
to walk the **dog** [ˌwɔːk ðə 'dɒg] den Hund ausführen; mit dem Hund spazieren gehen **I**
I'm **dog-tired**. [ˌaɪm ˌdɒg'taɪəd] Ich bin hundemüde. **I**
dollar ['dɒlə] Dollar *(Währung)* **III U1**, 11
dolphin ['dɒlfɪn] Delfin **III TS1**, 29
dominoes ['dɒmɪnəʊz] Domino **III U4**, 100
door [dɔː] Tür **I**
front **door** [ˌfrʌnt 'dɔː] Haustür **II**
next **door** [ˌnekst 'dɔː] (von) nebenan **III AC2**, 62
doorbell ['dɔːbel] Türklingel **III U1**, 14
doubt [daʊt] Zweifel **III U1**, 9
down [daʊn] nach unten; herunter; hinunter **II**
*to come **down** [ˌkʌm 'daʊn] herunterkommen **I**
*to go **down** [ˌgəʊ 'daʊn] hinuntergehen; nach unten gehen; entlanggehen **I**
to note **down** [ˌnəʊt 'daʊn] notieren; aufschreiben **II**
to pull **down** [ˌpʊl‿'daʊn] abreißen **III U2**, 41
*to sit **down** [ˌsɪt 'daʊn] sich hinsetzen; sich setzen **I**
*to write **down** [ˌraɪt 'daʊn] aufschreiben **I**
to **download** [ˌdaʊn'ləʊd] herunterladen *(aus dem Internet)* **II**
downstairs [ˌdaʊn'steəz] nach unten; im Untergeschoss; unten **II**
draft [drɑːft] Entwurf; Konzept **I**
drama ['drɑːmə] Theater; Drama **II**
dramatic [drə'mætɪk] dramatisch **II**
*to **draw** [drɔː] zeichnen **I**; ziehen **II**
*to **draw** the reader into the story/action [ˌdrɔː ðə ˌriːdə ɪntə ðə 'stɔːri/'ækʃn] den Leser/die Leserin in die Geschichte/Handlung hineinziehen °**III TS3**, 86
drawing ['drɔːɪŋ] Zeichnung **I**
dream [driːm] Traum **II**
*to **dream** [driːm; dremt; dremt] träumen ⟨**III TS1**, 28⟩
dress [dres] Kleid **III U3**, 68
fancy **dress** ['fænsi dres] Verkleidung; Kostüm **II**
to **drift** [drɪft] schweben; treiben ⟨**III U4**, 96⟩
drink [drɪŋk] Getränk **I**
*to **drink** [drɪŋk] trinken **I**
to **drip** [drɪp] tropfen ⟨**III TS1**, 29⟩
*to **drive** [draɪv] fahren **III U3**, 77
*to **drive** off [draɪv‿'ɒf] wegfahren **III U3**, 77
driver ['draɪvə] Fahrer/-in **II**
drizzle ['drɪzl] Nieselregen **III U4**, 103
to **drop** [drɒp] fallen (lassen) **II**
to **drop** out (of) [ˌdrɒp 'aʊt‿əv] abbrechen **III U1**, 10
to **drown** [draʊn] ertrinken; ertränken **III TS3**, 87
drums *(pl)* [drʌmz] Schlagzeug **III U2**, 40
dry [draɪ] trocken **III TS2**, 57
during *(+ noun)* ['djʊərɪŋ] während *(+ Nomen)* **II**
duty-free [ˌdjuːti'friː] zollfrei **III U4**, 93
DVD [ˌdiːviː'diː] DVD **I**

E

e.g. *(= for example)* [ˌiː'dʒiː] z.B. *(= zum Beispiel)* **I**
each [iːtʃ] jede/-r/-s **I**
each other [ˌiːtʃ‿'ʌðə] einander; sich; sich gegenseitig **I**
each [iːtʃ] pro Person; pro Stück **I**
ear [ɪə] Ohr **III AC3**, 90
early ['ɜːli] früh **I**
this **early** ['ðɪs ˌɜːli] so früh **III AC1**, 35
to **earn** [ɜːn] verdienen **I**
earth [ɜːθ] Erdboden; Erde; die Erde **II**
What on **earth** …? [ˌwɒt‿ɒn‿'ɜːθ] Was um alles in der Welt …? **II**
east [iːst] Osten; Ost- **I**
Easter ['iːstə] Ostern **I**
easy ['iːzi] einfach; leicht **I**
easy-going [ˌiːzi'gəʊɪŋ] locker; unkompliziert **III U4**, 105
*to **eat** [iːt] essen; fressen **I**
Eco ['iːkəʊ] Öko- **II**
to **edit** out [ˌedɪt‿'aʊt] herausschneiden **III U3**, 77
education *(no pl)* [ˌedʒʊ'keɪʃn] Erziehung; Bildung **III U3**, 69
audio-visual **effect** [ˌɔːdiəʊvɪʒuəl ɪ'fekt] audiovisueller Effekt **II**
egg [eg] Ei **I**
Egyptian [ɪ'dʒɪpʃn] Ägypter/-in; ägyptisch **III U4**, 100
eight [eɪt] acht **I**
not … **either** [nɒt … 'aɪðə; nɒt … 'iːðə] auch nicht **III U1**, 16
elderly ['eldəli] älter **III U2**, 51
electrician [ˌelɪk'trɪʃn] Elektriker/-in **II**
electricity [ˌelɪk'trɪsəti] Elektrizität; Strom **II**
electrics [ɪ'lektrɪks] Elektrik **II**
electronic [ˌelek'trɒnɪk] elektronisch **II**
element ['elɪmənt] Element **II**
elephant ['elɪfənt] Elefant **III TS2**, 60
eleven [ɪ'levn] elf **I**
Elizabethan [ɪˌlɪzə'biːθn] Elisabethaner/-in; elisabethanisch **III U3**, 72
else [els] andere/-r/-s; sonst noch **III U1**, 19
nobody **else** ['nəʊbədi els] niemand anderes **II**
what **else** [ˌwɒt‿'els] was sonst; was noch **I**
e-mail ['iːmeɪl] E-Mail **I**
to **e-mail** ['iːmeɪl] mailen; per E-Mail schicken **II**
embarrassed [ɪm'bærəst] verlegen **II**
embarrassing [ɪm'bærəsɪŋ] peinlich **II**
emotional [ɪ'məʊʃnl] emotional; Gefühls- °**III TS2**, 59
emperor ['emprə] Kaiser **III U3**, 64
empire ['empaɪə] Reich; Kaiserreich **III U3**, 64
empty ['emti] leer **III U2**, 48
end [end] Ende; Schluss **I**
in the **end** [ˌɪn ðiˌ'end] schließlich; zum Schluss **II**
to **end** [end] enden; beenden **II**
to **end** up [ˌend‿'ʌp] enden; landen **II**
All's well that **ends** well. [ˌɔːlz wel ðət 'endz wel] Ende gut, alles gut. **III U3**, 72
ending ['endɪŋ] Ende; Schluss *(einer Geschichte)* **I**
happy **ending** [ˌhæpi 'endɪŋ] Happy End **III TS3**, 84
enemy ['enəmi] Feind/-in **III TS3**, 84
energy ['enədʒi] Energie; Kraft **II**
steam **engine** ['stiːm‿endʒɪn] Dampfmaschine **III U2**, 42
English ['ɪŋglɪʃ] englisch; Englisch; aus England; Engländer/-in **I**

English-speaking ['ɪŋglɪʃ,spi:kɪŋ] englischsprachig **I**
I'm **English**. [aɪm‿'ɪŋglɪʃ] Ich bin Engländer/-in. **I**
to **enjoy** [ɪn'dʒɔɪ] genießen; sich freuen an **II**
to **enjoy** oneself [ɪn'dʒɔɪ] Spaß haben; sich amüsieren **III U1**, 14
enough [ɪ'nʌf] genug; genügend **I**
to **enter** ['entə] hineingehen; betreten; eintreten; *hier:* mitmachen **III U1**, 17
to **entertain** [,entə'teɪn] unterhalten **III TS4**, 106
entertainment *(no pl)* [,entə'teɪnmənt] Unterhaltung **III U3**, 71
entrance ['entrəns] Eingang; Eintritt **III U2**, 48
entrepreneur [,ɒntrəprə'nɜ:] Unternehmer/-in ⟨**III U1**, 11⟩
entry ['entri] Eintrag **III TS2**, 56
diary **entry** ['daɪəri entri] Tagebucheintrag **II**
equipment [ɪ'kwɪpmənt] Ausstattung; Ausrüstung **II**
er [ɜ:] äh **I**
era ['ɪərə] Ära; Zeitalter **III U4**, 105
escalator ['eskəleɪtə] Rolltreppe **I**
escape [ɪ'skeɪp] Flucht **III TS3**, 84
essential [ɪ'senʃl] essenziell; entscheidend ⟨**III TS2**, 57⟩
etc. *(= et cetera)* [ɪt'setrə] usw. *(= und so weiter)* **II**
euro ['jʊərəʊ] Euro *(Währung)* **I**
even ['i:vn] sogar; selbst **I**
even though [,i:vn 'ðəʊ] auch wenn; obwohl ⟨**III TS3**, 87⟩
evening ['i:vnɪŋ] Abend **I**
in the **evenings** [ɪn ði‿'i:vnɪŋz] abends **I**
event [ɪ'vent] Ereignis; Veranstaltung **I**
an **event** which ... [ən ɪ,vent 'wɪtʃ] eine Veranstaltung, die ... °**III U2**, 46
ever ['evə] jemals **II**
the best ... **ever** ['best ,evə] der/die/das beste ... überhaupt **III TS3**, 84
every ['evri] jede/-r/-s **I**
everybody ['evribɒdi] jeder; alle **II**
everyday ['evrideɪ] alltäglich **III U3**, 69
everyone ['evriwʌn] jeder; alle **I**
everyone was dancing [,evriwʌn wəz 'dɑ:nsɪŋ] alle tanzten °**III U1**, 21
everything ['evriθɪŋ] alles **I**
everywhere ['evriweə] überall **I**
exactly [ɪg'zæktli] genau **II**
to **exaggerate** [ɪg'zædʒreɪt] übertreiben **III TS4**, 108
exam [ɪg'zæm] Examen; Prüfung **II**
examination [ɪg,zæmɪ'neɪʃn] Untersuchung; Prüfung ⟨**III TS2**, 57⟩
example [ɪg'zɑ:mpl] Beispiel **I**
for **example** [fər‿ɪg'zɑ:mpl] zum Beispiel **II**

excellent piece of quick thinking [,ekslnt pi:s‿əv kwɪk 'θɪŋkɪŋ] ausgezeichnete Reaktionsschnelligkeit ⟨**III TS4**, 112⟩
except [ɪk'sept] außer; bis auf **III U4**, 103
exchange [ɪks'tʃeɪndʒ] Austausch; Austausch- **III AC1**, 34
exchange student [ɪks'tʃeɪndʒ ,stju:dnt] Austauschschüler/-in **III AC1**, 34
student **exchange** ['stju:dnt ɪks,tʃeɪndʒ] Schüleraustausch **III AC2**, 63
excited [ɪk'saɪtɪd] aufgeregt; begeistert **I**
excitement *(no pl)* [ɪk'saɪtmənt] Aufregung **III U1**, 22
exciting [ɪk'saɪtɪŋ] spannend; aufregend **I**
Excuse me ... [ɪk'skju:z mi] Entschuldigung!; Entschuldigen Sie! **I**
exercise ['eksəsaɪz] Übung; Aufgabe **I**
exercise book ['eksəsaɪz ,bʊk] Übungsheft **I**
to **expect** [ɪk'spekt] erwarten **III TS4**, 112
expensive [ɪk'spensɪv] teuer **I**
experience [ɪk'spɪəriəns] Erfahrung **II**
to **experience** [ɪk'spɪəriəns] erfahren; erleben **III U3**, 67
expert ['ekspɜ:t] Experte/Expertin **II**
to **explain** [ɪk'spleɪn] erklären **I**
to **explore** [ɪk'splɔ:] auf Entdeckungsreise gehen; sich umschauen; erkunden; erforschen **I**
to **express** [ɪk'spres] ausdrücken **II**
expression [ɪk'spreʃn] Ausdruck; Wendung; Äußerung **II**
facial **expression** [,feɪʃl ɪk'spreʃn] Gesichtsausdruck **III AC2**, 63
*to become **extinct** [bɪ,kʌm‿ɪk'stɪŋkt] aussterben **III TS2**, 60
extinction *(no pl)* [ɪks'tɪŋkʃn] Aussterben **III TS2**, 60
extra ['ekstrə] extra; zusätzlich **I**
extremely [ɪk'stri:mli] äußerst; sehr **III TS2**, 59
eye [aɪ] Auge **II**
to roll one's **eyes** [,rəʊl wʌnz‿'aɪz] die Augen verdrehen **III U3**, 76
I couldn't believe my **eyes**. [ai ,kʊdnt bɪ,li:v maɪ‿'aɪz] Ich traute meinen Augen nicht. **II**
eyewitness ['aɪwɪtnəs] Augenzeuge/Augenzeugin **II**

F

face [feɪs] Gesicht **I**
Put ... **face** down. [pʊt ,feɪs 'daʊn] Lege/Legt ... umgedreht hin. **I**
to **face** [feɪs] gegenüber stehen; konfrontiert werden mit **III TS4**, 107
Let's **face** it. [lets 'feɪs‿ɪt] Machen wir uns doch nichts vor. **III TS4**, 108
face-to-face [,feɪstə'feɪs] *hier:* persönlich; von Angesicht zu Angesicht **II**

facial expression [,feɪʃl ɪk'spreʃn] Gesichtsausdruck **III AC2**, 63
fact [fækt] Fakt; Tatsache **II**
in **fact** [ɪn 'fækt] tatsächlich; eigentlich; genau genommen **III U2**, 44
factory ['fæktri] Fabrik; Werk **III U3**, 67
factual ['fæktʃʊəl] sachlich °**III TS2**, 56
factual text [,fæktʃʊəl 'tekst] Sachtext °**III TS2**, 56
fair [feə] gerecht; fair **I**
fair play [feə 'pleɪ] Fairplay **III TS1**, 28
to **fake** [feɪk] vortäuschen; fälschen **II**
fake [feɪk] falsch; gefälscht **III TS4**, 111
*to **fall** [fɔ:l] fallen; hinfallen **I**
*to **fall** asleep [,fɔ:l‿ə'sli:p] einschlafen **I**
*to **fall** down [,fɔ:l‿'daʊn] stürzen; hinunterfallen **III TS1**, 32
*to **fall** off [,fɔ:l‿'ɒf] herunterfallen; hinunterfallen **II**
*to **fall** over [,fɔ:l‿'əʊvə] hinfallen; umkippen **I**
family ['fæmli] Familie **I**
family tree ['fæmli ,tri:] Stammbaum **I**
host **family** ['həʊst ,fæmli] Gastfamilie **III AC1**, 34
famous ['feɪməs] berühmt **I**
fan [fæn] Fan; Anhänger/-in **III AC3**, 91
to **fancy** *(+ ing) (infml) (BE)* ['fænsi] Lust haben zu ⟨**III TS4**, 107⟩
fancy dress ['fænsi dres] Verkleidung; Kostüm **II**
fantastic [fæn'tæstɪk] fantastisch; großartig **II**
fantasy ['fæntəsi] Fantasie; Traum- **I**; Fantasy **III TS3**, 84
FAQ [,efeɪ'kju:] Liste mit häufig gestellten Fragen °**III TS2**, 56
far [fɑ:] weit **II**
far more ['fɑ: mɔ:] weitaus ⟨**III TS1**, 33⟩
so **far** [,səʊ 'fɑ:] bis jetzt **II**
fare [feə] Fahrpreis **II**
farewell [,feə'wel] Lebewohl; Abschied ⟨**III TS4**, 112⟩
farm [fɑ:m] Farm; Bauernhof **I**
farmer ['fɑ:mə] Farmer/-in; Landwirt/-in **II**
fascinating ['fæsɪneɪtɪŋ] faszinierend **III U2**, 46
fashion ['fæʃn] Mode **II**
fast [fɑ:st] schnell **I**
father ['fɑ:ðə] Vater **I**
their **fault** [,deə 'fɔ:lt] ihre Schuld ⟨**III TS4**, 112⟩
favourite ['feɪvrɪt] Favorit/-in; Günstling **III U3**, 68
favourite ['feɪvrɪt] Lieblings- **I**
My **favourite** ... [maɪ 'feɪvrɪt] Mein/e Lieblings ... **I**
What's your **favourite** ...? ['wɒts jə ,feɪvrɪt] Was ist dein/-e Lieblings...? **I**
fear [fɪə] Angst; Furcht; Befürchtung **II**
fearful ['fɪəfl] ängstlich **III TS2**, 57
feather ['feðə] Feder **III U3**, 71

feature ['fi:tʃə] Eigenschaft; Merkmal °**III TS2**, 56
to **feature** ['fi:tʃə] zeigen; aufweisen °**III TS3**, 84
February ['februri] Februar **I**
*to be **fed** up (with) [bi fed͜ˈʌp wɪð] sauer sein (auf); die Nase voll haben (von) **III U1**, 17
fee [fi:] Gebühr **II**
school **fees** *(pl)* ['sku:l fi:z] Schulgeld; Schulgebühren **III U3**, 79
*to **feed** [fi:d] füttern; ernähren **II**
feedback ['fi:dbæk] Feedback; Rückmeldung °**III U1**, 22
*to **feel** [fi:l] fühlen; sich fühlen **I**
*to **feel** left out [ˌfi:l left͜ˈaʊt] sich ausgeschlossen fühlen **II**
*to **feel** sick [ˌfi:l ˈsɪk] Übelkeit verspüren; sich schlecht fühlen **II**
*to **feel** sorry for [ˌfi:l ˈsɒri fɔ:] Mitleid haben mit; bedauern **III U1**, 23
It **feels** so different from … [ˌɪt͜ fi:lz səʊ ˈdɪfrnt frɒm] Es ist so anders hier im Vergleich zu … **II**
feeling ['fi:lɪŋ] Gefühl **II**
ferry ['feri] Fähre **III U4**, 93
festival ['festɪvl] Festival; Fest **I**
to **fetch** [fetʃ] holen; abholen **III U4**, 103
fever ['fi:və] Fieber **II**
few [fju:] wenige **II**
a **few** [ə ˈfju:] ein paar; wenige; einige **I**
fiction *(no pl)* ['fɪkʃn] Erzählliteratur; Erfindung; Prosa; Fiktion **III TS3**, 84
science **fiction** [ˌsaɪəns ˈfɪkʃn] Science-Fiction *(Zukunftsdichtung)* **II**
fictional ['fɪkʃnl] fiktional; fiktiv; erdichtet °**III TS3**, 84
field [fi:ld] Feld; Spielfeld; Wiese; Weide; Acker **II**
fifteen [ˌfɪfˈti:n] fünfzehn **I**
fight [faɪt] Kampf; Streit **II**
*to **fight** [faɪt] kämpfen; (sich) streiten **II**
figure ['fɪgə] Figur; Gestalt **II**; Ziffer; Zahl °**III U3**, 71
wax **figure** ['wæks ˌfɪgə] Wachsfigur **II**
to **fill** [fɪl] (sich) füllen **III U2**, 42
to **fill** in [ˌfɪl͜ˈɪn] ausfüllen **II**
film [fɪlm] Film **I**
to **film** [fɪlm] filmen; drehen **II**
filmmaker ['fɪlmˌmeɪkə] Filmemacher/-in **II**
final ['faɪnl] endgültig **II**; letzte/-r/-s **III U2**, 46
finally ['faɪnli] schließlich; endlich; zum Schluss; letztlich **II**
*to **find** [faɪnd] finden; herausfinden **I**
*to **find** out [ˌfaɪnd͜ˈaʊt] herausfinden **I**
fine [faɪn] gut; in Ordnung; schön **I**
I'm **fine**. [ˌaɪm ˈfaɪn] Mir geht's gut. **I**
finger ['fɪŋgə] Finger **I**
*to keep your **fingers** crossed [ˌki:p jɔ: ˌfɪŋgəz ˈkrɒst] die Daumen drücken **I**
finish line ['fɪnɪʃ ˌlaɪn] Ziellinie **II**
to **finish** ['fɪnɪʃ] beenden; enden; fertigstellen; aufhören **I**
finished ['fɪnɪʃt] fertig **II**
fire [faɪə] Feuer **III TS2**, 59
*to be on **fire** [ˌbi:͜ɒn ˈfaɪə] brennen **III TS3**, 87
firefighter ['faɪəˌfaɪtə] Feuerwehrmann/-frau ⟨**III TS2**, 59⟩
fireworks *(pl)* ['faɪəwɜ:ks] Feuerwerk **I**
first [fɜ:st] zuerst; als Erstes; erste/-r/-s **I**
at **first** [ət ˈfɜ:st] zuerst; zunächst **II**
first language [ˌfɜ:st ˈlæŋgwɪdʒ] Muttersprache **II**
first person narrator [ˌfɜ:st ˌpɜ:sn nəˈreɪtə] Ich-Erzähler/-in °**III TS3**, 87
fish [fɪʃ], **fish** [fɪʃ] *(pl)* Fisch **I**
to **fit** [fɪt] passen **II**
*to get **fit** [ˌget ˈfɪt] in Form kommen; fit werden **I**
five [faɪv] fünf **I**
to **fix** [fɪks] reparieren; befestigen **II**
flag [flæg] Flagge; Fahne **III U2**, 37
flair [fleə] Flair; Atmosphäre **II**
flame [fleɪm] Flamme **III TS2**, 59
flash [flæʃ] Blitz; Lichtblitz **III U3**, 77
flashback ['flæʃbæk] Rückblende; Flashback **III U3**, 78
flat [flæt] Wohnung **I**
flea market ['fli: ˌmɑ:kɪt] Flohmarkt **I**
flight [flaɪt] Flug **III TS1**, 30
flight attendant ['flaɪt͜əˌtendnt] Flugbegleiter/-in **III U4**, 93
floor [flɔ:] Fußboden **I**
to **flow** out [fləʊ͜ˈaʊt] hinausfließen **II**
flower ['flaʊə] Blume **II**
*to **fly** [flaɪ] fliegen **III TS1**, 30
flyer ['flaɪə] Flyer **I**
focus ['fəʊkəs] Blickpunkt; Schwerpunkt; Fokus **III TS3**, 88
out of **focus** [ˌaʊt͜əv ˈfəʊkəs] unscharf **III U3**, 77
to **focus** (on) ['fəʊkəs͜ɒn] sich konzentrieren (auf) **III U1**, 10
folder ['fəʊldə] Ordner; Mappe **I**
to **follow** ['fɒləʊ] folgen; hinterhergehen; befolgen **II**
the **following** [ðə ˈfɒləʊɪŋ] folgende/-r/-s **II**
food [fu:d] Essen; Lebensmittel **I**; Futter **III TS2**, 57
foot [fʊt], **feet** [fi:t] *(pl)* Fuß **I**
*to keep one's **feet** or hands still [ˌki:p wʌnz: ˈfi:t͜ɔ: ˈhændz stɪl] die Beine und Hände ruhig halten **III TS1**, 32
on **foot** [ɒn ˈfʊt] zu Fuß **II**
football ['fʊtbɔ:l] Fußball **I**
for [fɔ:; fə] wegen **II**
for example [fər͜ɪgˈzɑ:mpl] zum Beispiel **II**
for *(+ Zeitraum)* [fɔ:; fə] seit **III U2**, 38
for … [fɔ:; fə] … lang **II**
for [fɔ:; fə] denn ⟨**III TS1**, 30⟩
force [fɔ:s] Kraft; Macht **III U4**, 105
weather **forecast** ['weðə ˌfɔ:kɑ:st] Wettervorhersage **II**
foreign ['fɒrɪn] ausländisch; fremd **III U4**, 93
foreign language [ˌfɒrɪn ˈlæŋgwɪdʒ] Fremdsprache **III U4**, 92
forest ['fɒrɪst] Wald **II**
forever [fəˈrevə] für immer; ewig **II**
*to **forget** [fəˈget] vergessen **I**
*to **forgive** [fəˈgɪv] vergeben; verzeihen **II**
fork [fɔ:k] Gabel **III AC1**, 34
form [fɔ:m] Form **I**; Formular **II**
negative **form** ['negətɪv ˌfɔ:m] verneinte Form **I**
past **form** ['pɑ:st fɔ:m] Vergangenheitsform **II**
possessive **form** [pəˌsesɪv ˈfɔ:m] Possessivform **I**
short **form** ['ʃɔ:t fɔ:m] Kurzform **I**
to **form** [fɔ:m] formen; bilden **II**
formal ['fɔ:ml] formal; formell; förmlich **II**
forum ['fɔ:rəm] Forum **II**
forward ['fɔ:wəd] vorwärts **III U3**, 72
to look **forward** to [ˌlʊk ˈfɔ:wəd tə] sich freuen auf **III U2**, 39
to **found** [faʊnd] gründen **III U3**, 66
founder ['faʊndə] Gründer/-in ⟨**III U1**, 11⟩
four [fɔ:] vier **I**
freeze **frame** ['fri:z ˌfreɪm] Standbild °**III U3**, 78
free [fri:] frei; kostenlos **I**
free time [ˌfri: ˈtaɪm] Freizeit **I**
freedom *(no pl)* ['fri:dəm] Freiheit; Unabhängigkeit **III U1**, 20
freeze frame ['fri:z ˌfreɪm] Standbild °**III U3**, 78
French [frenʃ] französisch; Französisch **II**
frequently asked [ˌfri:kwəntli͜ˈɑ:skt] häufig gefragt **I**
fresh [freʃ] frisch **I**
Friday ['fraɪdeɪ] Freitag **I**
fridge [frɪdʒ] Kühlschrank **I**
friend [frend] Freund/-in **I**
*to make **friends** [ˌmeɪk ˈfrendz] Freundschaft schließen **II**
That's what **friends** are for. [ˌðæts wɒt ˈfrendz͜ɑ: ˌfɔ:] Dafür sind Freunde da. **I**
friendly ['frendli] freundlich; nett **II**
friendship ['frendʃɪp] Freundschaft **II**
fringe [frɪndʒ] Rand-; Alternativ- **III U2**, 37
from [frɒm; frəm] aus; von **I**
from … to [frəm tə] von … bis **I**
Where … **from**? [ˌweə ˈfrɒm] Woher …? **I**
front [frʌnt] Vorderseite; Front-; Vorder- **II**
front door [ˌfrʌnt ˈdɔ:] Haustür **II**
in **front** of [ɪn ˈfrʌnt͜əv] vor **I**
frost [frɒst] Frost ⟨**III TS2**, 57⟩
fruit [fru:t] Frucht; Obst **I**
full (of) [fʊl͜əv] voll (von) **I**
to talk with your mouth **full** [ˌtɔ:k wɪð jɔ: ˈmaʊθ fʊl] mit vollem Mund sprechen **III AC3**, 90
fun [fʌn] Freude; Spaß **I**

*to have **fun** [ˌhæv ˈfʌn] Spaß haben; sich amüsieren **I**
It's **fun**. [ɪts ˈfʌn] Es macht Spaß. **I**
fun [fʌn] lustig; witzig; fröhlich **I**
funny [ˈfʌni] lustig; witzig **I**; merkwürdig; komisch **III U1**, 14
further [ˈfɜːðə] weiter (weg) **III U2**, 46
future [ˈfjuːtʃə] Zukunft **II**
future [ˈfjuːtʃə] zukünftig **III U4**, 105

G

gadget [ˈɡædʒɪt] Gerät; technische Spielerei **III U1**, 19
to **gain** weight [ˌɡeɪn ˈweɪt] zunehmen ⟨**III TS2**, 57⟩
gallery walk [ˈɡælri ˌwɔːk] Museumsrundgang; Vernissage **I**
game [ɡeɪm] Spiel **I**
guessing **game** [ˈɡesɪŋ ˌɡeɪm] Ratespiel **II**
gap [ɡæp] Lücke; Spalt; Abstand **I**
garage [ˈɡærɑːʒ] Garage **I**
garden [ˈɡɑːdn] Garten **I**
garlic [ˈɡɑːlɪk] Knoblauch **III U4**, 95
gate [ɡeɪt] Gate; Flugsteig; Ausgang **III U4**, 99
generation [ˌdʒenəˈreɪʃn] Generation **III U3**, 67
generous [ˈdʒenrəs] großzügig **III TS1**, 28
genius [ˈdʒiːniəs] Genie **II**
genre [ˈʒɑ̃ːnrə] Gattung **III TS3**, 84
gentle [ˈdʒentl] behutsam; sanft ⟨**III TS3**, 85⟩
gentleman [ˈdʒentlmən], **gentlemen** [ˈdʒentlmen] *(pl)* Gentleman; feiner Herr **III U2**, 44
geocaching [ˈdʒiːəʊkæʃɪŋ] Geocaching **II**
Geography [dʒiˈɒɡrəfi] Geografie; Erdkunde **II**
German [ˈdʒɜːmən] deutsch; Deutsch; aus Deutschland; Deutsche/-r **I**
gesture [ˈdʒestʃə] Geste; Gebärde °**III TS4**, 109
*to **get** [ɡet] holen; bringen; bekommen; besorgen; kaufen **I**; werden **II**
*to **get** around [ˌɡet‿əˈraʊnd] *hier:* sich fortbewegen **II**
*to **get** away with [ˌɡet‿əˈweɪ wɪð] davonkommen mit **II**
*to **get** bored [get‿ˈbɔːd] sich langweilen **II**
*to **get** fit [ˌɡet ˈfɪt] in Form kommen; fit werden **I**
*to **get** in the way [ˌɡet‿ɪn ðə ˈweɪ] stören; im Weg stehen **II**
*to **get** into [ˌɡet‿ˈɪntə] einsteigen; hineingelangen **I**
*to **get** involved with sb [ˌɡet‿ɪnˈvɒlvd wɪð] sich einlassen mit jmdm. ⟨**III TS4**, 110⟩
*to **get** lost [ˌɡet ˈlɒst] verloren gehen; sich verirren **II**
*to **get** off (a bus/train) [ˌɡet‿ˈɒf] aussteigen (aus einem Bus/Zug) **II**
*to **get** on (the bus) [ˌɡet‿ˈɒn] einsteigen (in den Bus) **II**
*to **get** on somebody's nerves [ˌɡet‿ɒn sʌmbɒdiz ˈnɜːvz] jemandem auf die Nerven gehen **I**
*to **get** organised [ɡet ˈɔːɡənaɪzd] sich organisieren **II**
*to **get** out of [ɡet ˌaʊt‿əv] aussteigen; herauskommen aus **II**
*to **get** right [ɡet ˈraɪt] richtig beantworten **II**
*to **get** sth out of one's head [ɡet ˌaʊt‿əv wʌnz ˈhed] etw. aus dem Kopf bekommen **III TS1**, 32
*to **get** stuck [ˌɡet ˈstʌk] stecken bleiben ⟨**III TS2**, 57⟩
*to **get** there [ˈɡet ðeə] hinkommen **I**
*to **get** to [ˈɡet tə] kommen zu; kommen nach; erreichen **I**
to **get** to know [ˌɡet tə ˈnəʊ] kennen lernen **III U1**, 12
*to **get** up [ˌɡet‿ˈʌp] aufstehen *(aus dem Bett)* **I**
ghost [ɡəʊst] Geist; Gespenst **II**
giant [dʒaɪənt] Riese; Gigant ⟨**III TS2**, 56⟩
gig [ɡɪɡ] Auftritt; Gig **III U2**, 40
girl [ɡɜːl] Mädchen **I**
girlfriend [ˈɡɜːlfrend] Freundin *(in einer Paarbeziehung)* **II**
gist [dʒɪst] das Wesentliche **II**
*to **give** [ɡɪv] geben; schenken **I**
*to **give** sb a piggyback [ɡɪv‿ə ˈpɪɡibæk] jmdn. Huckepack nehmen **III U4**, 102
*to **give** sb funny looks [ˌɡɪv fʌni ˈlʊks] jmdn. schief anschauen **III U1**, 14
*to **give** the bumps [ˌɡɪv ðə ˈbʌmps] hochleben lassen **I**
*to **give** up [ˌɡɪv‿ˈʌp] aufgeben **III U1**, 12
glad [ɡlæd] froh **III AC3**, 91
glass [ɡlɑːs] Glas **I**
glasses *(pl)* [ˈɡlɑːsɪz] Brille **II**
glen [ɡlen] Schlucht ⟨**III U2**, 40⟩
global [ˈɡləʊbl] global; weltweit ⟨**III TS2**, 60⟩
glossary [ˈɡlɒsri] Glossar; Stichwortverzeichnis °**III TS4**, 106
glove [ɡlʌv] Handschuh **I**
*to **go** [ɡəʊ] gehen; fahren **I**
*to **go** black [ˌɡəʊ ˈblæk] schwarz werden **II**
*to **go** crazy [ˌɡəʊ ˈkreɪzi] ausflippen; durchdrehen; verrückt werden **II**
*to **go** down [ˌɡəʊ ˈdaʊn] hinuntergehen; nach unten gehen; entlanggehen **I**
*to **go** for a walk [ˌɡəʊ fər‿ə ˈwɔːk] spazieren gehen **II**
*to **go** on [ˌɡəʊ‿ˈɒn] weitergehen; weitermachen; weiterführen; fortfahren **I**
*to **go** out [ˌɡəʊ‿ˈaʊt] ausgehen; hinausgehen **II**
*to **go** over to [ˌɡəʊ ˈəʊvə tə] hinübergehen zu; zu jmdm. nach Hause gehen **II**
*to **go** right back to [ˌɡəʊ raɪt ˈbæk tə] zurückgehen auf **II**
*to **go** round in circles [ɡəʊ ˌraʊnd ɪn ˈsɜːklz] sich im Kreis drehen **III U2**, 48
*to **go** shopping [ˌɡəʊ ˈʃɒpɪŋ] einkaufen gehen **I**
*to **go** swimming [ˌɡəʊ ˈswɪmɪŋ] Schwimmen gehen **I**
*to **go** to bed [ˌɡəʊ tə ˈbed] ins Bett gehen **I**
*to **go** together [ˌɡəʊ təˈɡeðə] zueinander passen; zueinander gehören **I**
*to **go** with [ˈɡəʊ wɪð] passen zu; gehören zu **I**
*to **go** wrong [ˌɡəʊ ˈrɒŋ] schiefgehen **I**
*to let **go** (of) [ˌlet ˈɡəʊ (əv)] loslassen **II**
It's **gone**. [ɪts ˈɡɒn] Es ist weg. **II**
goal [ɡəʊl] Tor; Ziel **I**
gold [ɡəʊld] Gold **III U3**, 70
golden [ˈɡəʊldn] golden; Gold- ⟨**III U4**, 96⟩
golden age [ˌɡəʊldn ˈeɪdʒ] goldenes Zeitalter **III U3**, 66
*to be **gone** [biː ˈɡɒn] verschwunden sein; weg sein **II**
gonna (= going to) *(coll)* [ˈɡɒnə] wird/werden ⟨**III U1**, 13⟩
good [ɡʊd] gut **I**
*to be **good** at [biː ˈɡʊd‿ət] gut sein in **I**
Good morning. [ˌɡʊd ˈmɔːnɪŋ] Guten Morgen. **I**
goodbye [ɡʊdˈbaɪ] auf Wiedersehen **I**
gorge scrambling [ˈɡɔːdʒ ˌskræmblɪŋ] Schluchtenklettern **II**
to **grab** [ɡræb] greifen; ergreifen; schnappen **II**
grammar school [ˈɡræmə ˌskuːl] Gymnasium **II**
grandad [ˈɡrændæd] Opa **I**
grandma [ˈɡrænmɑː] Oma **I**
grandparents *(pl)* [ˈɡrænˌpeərənts] Großeltern **I**
granny [ˈɡræni] Oma **I**
graphic novel [ˌɡræfɪk ˈnɒvl] Bildergeschichte; Comic **III TS3**, 84
grass [ɡrɑːs] Gras ⟨**III TS3**, 85⟩
gratitude [ˈɡrætɪtjuːd] Dankbarkeit **III AC1**, 35
great [ɡreɪt] großartig; toll; super **I**
It's **great** for … [ɪts ˈɡreɪt fə] Es ist super zum/für … **I**
green [ɡriːn] grün **I**
Greenwich Mean Time *(= GMT)* [ˌɡrenɪdʒ ˈmiːn ˌtaɪm] westeuropäische Zeit **I**
greeting [ˈɡriːtɪŋ] Gruß **I**
grey [ɡreɪ] grau **I**
grid [ɡrɪd] Gitter; Tabelle; Raster **I**
groan [ɡrəʊn] Stöhnen **III U4**, 94
ground [ɡraʊnd] Boden; Erdboden **III U4**, 103
*to be **grounded** [bi ˈɡraʊndɪd] Hausarrest haben **III U1**, 20

group [gru:p] Gruppe; Klasse **I**
tutor **group** ['tju:tə ˌgru:p] Klasse *(in einer englischen Schule)* **I**
to **group** (around) [gru:p (ə'raʊnd)] gruppieren (um) °**III TS3**, 86
*to **grow** [grəʊ] wachsen **II**; anbauen; züchten **III U3**, 65
*to **grow** up [ˌgrəʊ‿'ʌp] aufwachsen; erwachsen werden **III U3**, 69
guard [gɑ:d] Wache; Wächter/-in **II**
to **guess** [ges] raten; erraten; vermuten **I**; annehmen **III AC3**, 90
guessing game ['gesɪŋ ˌgeɪm] Ratespiel **II**
guest [gest] Gast **III U1**, 18
guide [gaɪd] Führer/-in; Reiseführer **II**
to **guide** [gaɪd] führen; leiten **III TS1**, 31
guilty ['gɪlti] schuldig **III TS4**, 113
guinea pig ['gɪni: ˌpɪg] Meerschweinchen **I**
guitar [gɪ'tɑ:] Gitarre **III U4**, 105
chewing **gum** ['tʃu:ɪŋ ˌgʌm] Kaugummi **III U4**, 99
guy [gaɪ] Typ; Kerl; *(Pl.)* Leute **II**

H

haggis ['hægɪs] Haggis *(schottisches Gericht aus in einem Schafsmagen gekochten Schafsinnereien und Haferschrot)* **III U2**, 37
*to do our **hair** [ˌdu:‿aʊə 'heə] uns frisieren; unsere Haare machen **I**
hairbrush ['heəbrʌʃ] Haarbürste **III U3**, 66
half [hɑ:f], **halves** [hɑ:vz] *(pl)* (of) die Hälfte **I**
half an hour [ˌhɑ:f‿ən‿'aʊər] eine halbe Stunde **III U3**, 77
half [hɑ:f] halb **I**
half past [ˌhɑ:f 'pɑ:st] halb *(bei Uhrzeitangaben)* **I**
half-sister ['hɑ:fˌsɪstə] Halbschwester **I**
half-term break [ˌhɑ:ftɜ:m 'breɪk] Halbjahresferien **I**
*to meet **halfway** [ˌmi:t hɑ:f'weɪ] sich auf halbem Weg treffen **III U1**, 18
hall [hɔ:l] Halle; Saal; Flur; Diele; Korridor **II**
arrivals **hall** [ə'raɪvlz ˌhɔ:l] Ankunftshalle **III U4**, 93
ham [hæm] Schinken **III AC1**, 34
hand [hænd] Hand **I**
Clap your **hands**. [ˌklæp jɔ: 'hændz] Klatsch/Klatscht in die Hände. **I**
On the one **hand** …, (but) on the other **hand** … [ɒn ðə‿'wʌn ˌhænd … (bʌt) ɒn ði‿'ʌðə ˌhænd …] Einerseits …, (aber) andererseits … **II**
to **handle** ['hændl] umgehen mit; *hier:* anfassen ⟨**III TS2**, 57⟩
*to **hang** on [ˌhæŋ‿'ɒn] (einen Augenblick) warten **III U4**, 94
*to **hang** out (with) *(infml)* [ˌhæŋ‿'aʊt wɪð] sich herumtreiben (mit); rumhängen (mit); sich treffen (mit) **III U1**, 20

to **happen** ['hæpn] geschehen; passieren **I**
happiness ['hæpɪnəs] Glück; Zufriedenheit; Fröhlichkeit ⟨**III TS1**, 29⟩
happy ['hæpi] glücklich; froh; fröhlich **I**
happy ending [ˌhæpi 'endɪŋ] Happy End **III TS3**, 84
Happy Birthday! [ˌhæpi 'bɜ:θdeɪ] Alles Gute zum Geburtstag!; Herzlichen Glückwunsch zum Geburtstag! **I**
harbour ['hɑ:bə] Hafen **II**
hard [hɑ:d] hart; schwer; schwierig **II**
*to be **hard** on sb [bi 'hɑ:d‿ɒn] streng mit jmdm. sein **III U1**, 15
hardly ['hɑ:dli] kaum **III TS4**, 110
hat [hæt] Hut **I**
to **hate** [heɪt] hassen; nicht mögen **II**
*to **have** [hæv] haben **I**
*to **have** *(a sweet)* [hæv] *(ein Bonbon)* nehmen; *(ein Bonbon)* essen **I**
*to **have** a look (at) [ˌhæv‿ə 'lʊk] anschauen **II**
*to **have** a point [ˌhæv‿ə 'pɔɪnt] nicht ganz Unrecht haben **III U1**, 18
*to **have** breakfast [ˌhæv 'brekfəst] frühstücken **I**
*to **have** fun [ˌhæv 'fʌn] Spaß haben; sich amüsieren **I**
*to **have** got [hæv 'gɒt] besitzen; haben **I**
*to **have** in common [ˌhæv‿ɪn 'kɒmən] gemeinsam haben **III TS3**, 88
*to **have** to ['hæv tə] müssen **II**
Have a good time. [ˌhæv‿ə gʊd 'taɪm] Viel Spaß. ⟨**III TS4**, 112⟩
hay [heɪ] Heu ⟨**III TS2**, 57⟩
he [hi:] er **I**
head [hed] Kopf **I**
*to get sth out of one's **head** [get ˌaʊt‿əv wʌnz 'hed] etw. aus dem Kopf bekommen **III TS1**, 32
head of state [ˌhed‿əv 'steɪt] Staatsoberhaupt **II**
With a very big **head**! [ˌwɪð ə ˌveri bɪg 'hed] Und ein Angeber! **II**
to **head** for ['hed fə] zusteuern auf ⟨**III TS4**, 110⟩
headache *(no pl)* ['hedeɪk] Kopfschmerzen; Kopfweh **II**
heading ['hedɪŋ] Überschrift; Titel **I**
headline ['hedlaɪn] Schlagzeile **III TS2**, 56
headphones *(pl)* ['hedfəʊnz] Kopfhörer **II**
health [helθ] Gesundheit **II**
healthy ['helθi] gesund **I**
*to **hear** [hɪə] hören **I**
I **hear** … [aɪ 'hɪə] Ich habe gehört, dass … **I**
heart [hɑ:t] Herz; *hier:* Zentrum **II**
*to learn … by **heart** [ˌlɜ:n baɪ 'hɑ:t] auswendig lernen **I**
heating ['hi:tɪŋ] Heizung **III U3**, 64
underfloor **heating** *(no pl)* [ˌʌndəflɔ:'hi:tɪŋ] Fußbodenheizung **III U3**, 64
heaven ['hevn] Himmel ⟨**III TS1**, 28⟩

heavy ['hevi] schwer; stark **III U2**, 49
hedgehog ['hedʒhɒg] Igel **III TS2**, 56
Hello. [hel'əʊ] Hallo. **I**
*to say **hello** (to) [ˌseɪ hel'əʊ tə] grüßen; Grüße ausrichten (an) **I**
help [help] Hilfe **I**
to **help** [help] helfen **I**
to **help** out [ˌhelp‿'aʊt] aushelfen **III U2**, 51
helpful ['helpfl] hilfsbereit; hilfreich **I**
helpless ['helpləs] hilflos **I**
her [hɜ:] ihr/-e; sie **I**
herb [hɜ:b] Kraut **III U4**, 95
here [hɪə] hier **I**
right **here** [ˌraɪt 'hɪə] genau hier **II**
Here you are. [ˌhɪə ju‿'ɑ:] Bitte schön. **I**
hero ['hɪərəʊ], **heroes** ['hɪərəʊz] *(pl)* Held **II**
heroine ['herəʊɪn] Heldin **II**
to **hesitate** ['hezɪteɪt] zögern **III TS3**, 85
Hey! [heɪ] Hi.; He!; Hallo. **I**
Hi. [haɪ] Hi.; Hallo. **I**
hibernation [ˌhaɪbə'neɪʃn] Winterschlaf **III TS2**, 57
hidden ['hɪdn] versteckt ⟨**III TS3**, 85⟩
*to **hide** [haɪd] (sich) verstecken **II**
hiding place ['haɪdɪŋ ˌpleɪs] Versteck ⟨**III TS1**, 33⟩
high [haɪ] hoch; groß **II**
high tide ['haɪ ˌtaɪd] Flut **II**
the **high** street [ðə 'haɪ ˌstri:t] die Haupteinkaufsstraße **III U1**, 20
highlight ['haɪlaɪt] Highlight; Höhepunkt **II**
hiking ['haɪkɪŋ] Wandern **II**
hill [hɪl] Berg; Hügel **II**
him [hɪm] ihn; ihm **I**
himself [hɪm'self] er/sich (selbst); selber **II**
hint [hɪnt] Hinweis; Andeutung; Tipp **III AC2**, 63
his [hɪz] sein/-e **I**
historic [hɪ'stɒrɪk] historisch **III U2**, 36
historical [hɪ'stɒrɪkl] historisch; geschichtlich **I**
History ['hɪstri] Geschichte **II**
ancient **history** [ˌeɪnʃnt 'hɪstri] antike Geschichte; Frühgeschichte **II**
living **history** show [ˌlɪvɪŋ 'hɪstəri ˌʃəʊ] *Show, in der historischer Alltag nachgespielt wird* **II**
*to **hit** [hɪt] schlagen; treffen **I**
hobby ['hɒbi], **hobbies** ['hɒbiz] *(pl)* Hobby **I**
hockey [hɒki] Hockey **II**
hoe [həʊ] Hacke ⟨**III TS3**, 85⟩
to **hog** a conversation [ˌhɒg‿ə kɒnvə'seɪʃn] ein Gespräch für sich in Beschlag nehmen; ein Gespräch dominieren **III AC2**, 62
*to **hold** [həʊld] halten; festhalten **I**
*to **hold** [həʊld] abhalten **III U2**, 44
*to **hold** onto [ˌhəʊld‿'ɒntə] (sich) festhalten an **III U2**, 49
*to **hold** open [ˌhəʊld‿'əʊpn] aufhalten **III AC3**, 90
holiday ['hɒlədeɪ] Urlaub; Feiertag **I**
holidays *(pl)* ['hɒlədeɪz] Ferien **I**

home [həʊm] Zuhause; Heim **I**
at **home** [ət 'həʊm] zu Hause **I**
home [həʊm] nach Hause **I**
homepage ['həʊmpeɪdʒ] Homepage **I**
*to be **homesick** [bi 'həʊmsɪk] Heimweh haben **III U4**, 104
homeward ['həʊmwəd] heimwärts ⟨**III U2**, 40⟩
homework ['həʊmwɜːk] Hausaufgabe(n) **I**
honest ['ɒnɪst] ehrlich **III U1**, 22
honey ['hʌni] Honig **III TS1**, 29
honeysuckle ['hʌnisʌkl] Geißblatt ⟨**III TS3**, 85⟩
to **hook** [hʊk] *hier:* fesseln **III TS3**, 85
hope [həʊp] Hoffnung **II**
to **hope** [həʊp] hoffen **I**
hopeful ['həʊpfl] hoffnungsvoll **I**
horn [hɔːn] Horn **III TS2**, 60
horrified ['hɒrɪfaɪd] entsetzt **I**
horror ['hɒrə] Horrorgeschichte; Horrorfilm; Horror **III TS3**, 84
horse [hɔːs] Pferd **I**
hospital ['hɒspɪtl] Krankenhaus; Hospital **II**
host family ['həʊst ˌfæmli] Gastfamilie **III AC1**, 34
hostel ['hɒstl] Herberge **III U4**, 94
hot [hɒt] heiß **II**
hour [aʊə] Stunde **II**
half an **hour** [ˌhɑːf‿ən‿'aʊər] eine halbe Stunde **III U3**, 77
house [haʊs] Haus **I**
to move (**house**) [muːv (haʊs)] umziehen **II**
how [haʊ] wie **I**
How many …? [ˌhaʊ 'meni] Wie viele …? **I**
How are you? [ˌhaʊ‿'ɑː jə] Wie geht es dir/euch/Ihnen?; Wie geht es euch?; Wie geht es Ihnen? **I**
How much (is/are) …? [ˌhaʊ 'mʌtʃ‿ɪz/ɑː] Wie viel (kostet/kosten) …? **I**
How old are you? [haʊ‿'əʊld‿ə juː] Wie alt bist du?; Wie alt sind Sie? **I**
How to … ['haʊ tə] Wie man … **I**
that's **how** [ðæts 'haʊ] so **II**
to **hug** [hʌg] umarmen **I**
huge [hjuːdʒ] riesig; riesengroß; gewaltig **II**
human ['hjuːmən] Mensch ⟨**III TS2**, 57⟩
human ['hjuːmən] menschlich; Menschen- ⟨**III TS2**, 59⟩
human body [ˌhjuːmən 'bɒdi] menschlicher Körper **II**
Humanities *(pl)* [hjuː'mænətiz] Sozialwissenschaften **II**
humour *(no pl)* ['hjuːmə] Humor; Stimmung **III U2**, 46
sense of **humour** *(no pl)* [ˌsens‿əv 'hjuːmə] Sinn für Humor **III U1**, 23
hundreds of ['hʌndrədz‿əv] Hunderte (von) **III U2**, 43
hungry ['hʌŋgri] hungrig **I**
to **hurry** ['hʌri] eilen; sich beeilen **I**
*to **hurt** [hɜːt] verletzen; weh tun **II**
you have never been **hurt** [ˌju hæv ˌnevə biːn 'hɜːt] du bist noch nie verletzt worden ⟨**III TS1**, 28⟩
hurt [hɜːt] verletzt **II**
husband ['hʌzbənd] Ehemann **III U3**, 65

I

I [aɪ] ich **I**
I don't know! [ˌaɪ ˌdəʊnt 'nəʊ] Ich weiß (es) nicht! **I**
I don't like … [aɪ 'dəʊnt laɪk] Ich mag … nicht.; Ich mache … nicht gern. **I**
I hear … [aɪ 'hɪə] Ich habe gehört, dass … **I**
I like … [aɪ 'laɪk] Mir gefällt …; Ich mag … **I**
I love you. [aɪ 'lʌv ju] Ich liebe dich.; Ich mag dich. **I**
I love … [aɪ 'lʌv] Ich liebe …; Ich mag … total gern. **I**
I'd like to … *(= I would like to)* [aɪd 'laɪk tə] Ich möchte …; Ich würde gern … **I**
I'd rather [aɪd 'rɑːðə] ich würde lieber **III U3**, 79
I'm (not) scared of … [ˌaɪm (nɒt) 'skeəd‿əv] Ich habe (keine) Angst vor … **I**
I'm dog-tired. [ˌaɪm ˌdɒg'taɪəd] Ich bin hundemüde. **I**
I'm English. [aɪm‿'ɪŋglɪʃ] Ich bin Engländer/-in. **I**
I'm fine. [ˌaɪm 'faɪn] Mir geht's gut. **I**
I'm from … [ˌaɪm frɒm] Ich bin aus … **I**
I'm sorry! [ˌaɪm 'sɒri] Tut mir leid! **I**
ice [aɪs] Eis **I**
ice cream [ˌaɪs 'kriːm] Eis; Eiscreme **I**
ice rink ['aɪs ˌrɪŋk] Eisbahn; Schlittschuhbahn **I**
icebreaker ['aɪsˌbreɪkə] Eisbrecher *(Sätze, um mit jmdm. ins Gespräch zu kommen)* **III AC3**, 91
idea [aɪ'dɪə] Idee; Einfall **I**
no **idea** [ˌnəʊ‿aɪ'dɪə] keine Ahnung **II**
to **identify** with [aɪ'dentɪfaɪ wɪð] sich identifizieren mit **III TS3**, 84
identity [aɪ'dentəti] Identität **II**
idiot ['ɪdiət] Idiot/-in **II**
if [ɪf] wenn; falls; ob **I**
as **if** [əz‿'ɪf] als ob ⟨**III TS1**, 28⟩
if-clause ['ɪfˌklɔːz] if-Satz °**III U1**, 11
to **ignore** [ɪg'nɔː] ignorieren; außer Acht lassen **III U1**, 21
ill [ɪl] krank **III TS2**, 57
illegal [ɪ'liːgl] illegal; unrechtmäßig; rechtswidrig **III TS2**, 60
imagination [ɪˌmædʒɪ'neɪʃn] Fantasie; Vorstellungskraft **III U1**, 9
imaginative [ɪ'mædʒɪnətɪv] einfallsreich; fantasievoll **III U1**, 9
to **imagine** [ɪ'mædʒɪn] sich (etwas) vorstellen **I**
immigration [ˌɪmɪ'greɪʃn] Immigration; Einwanderung; Einreise **III U4**, 97
immigration office [ˌɪmɪ'greɪʃn ˌɒfɪs] Einwanderungsbehörde **III U4**, 97
imperative [ɪm'perətɪv] Imperativ; Befehlsform °**III TS2**, 58
impolite [ˌɪmp'laɪt] unhöflich **III AC1**, 34
important [ɪm'pɔːtnt] wichtig **I**
impossibility [ɪmˌpɒsə'bɪləti] (Ding der) Unmöglichkeit ⟨**III TS1**, 28⟩
*to be **impressed** [bi ɪm'prest] beeindruckt sein **II**
impressive [ɪm'presɪv] beeindruckend ⟨**III TS2**, 60⟩
to **improve** [ɪm'pruːv] sich verbessern; verbessern **I**
in [ɪn] in; im; rein; herein **I**
in between [ˌɪn bɪ'twiːn] dazwischen °**III TS1**, 33
in chorus [ɪn 'kɔːrəs] im Chor °**III TS4**, 109
in fact [ɪn 'fækt] tatsächlich; eigentlich; genau genommen **III U2**, 44
in front of [ɪn 'frʌnt‿əv] vor **I**
in need [ɪn 'niːd] bedürftig; in Not **II**
in secret [ɪn 'siːkrət] heimlich **II**
in the end [ˌɪn ði‿'end] schließlich; zum Schluss **II**
in the evenings [ɪn ði‿'iːvnɪŋz] abends **I**
in the mornings [ˌɪn ðə 'mɔːnɪŋz] morgens; vormittags **I**
in the photo(s) [ˌɪn ðə 'fəʊtəʊ(z)] auf dem Foto/den Fotos **I**
in the street [ˌɪn ðə 'striːt] in der Straße; auf der Straße **I**
in progress [ɪn 'prəʊgres] im Verlauf °**III U2**, 44
to **include** [ɪn'kluːd] einschließen; beinhalten **II**; aufnehmen; einbeziehen °**III U2**, 47
in-crowd ['ɪnkraʊd] Szene; die Angesagten; die Beliebten **III U1**, 20
independence *(no pl)* [ˌɪndɪ'pendəns] Unabhängigkeit **III U2**, 37
independent [ˌɪndɪ'pendənt] unabhängig **III U2**, 37
Indian ['ɪndiən] Inder/-in; indisch **I**
indirect ['ɪndɪrekt] indirekt °**III U4**, 95
indirect speech [ˌɪndɪrekt 'spiːtʃ] indirekte Rede °**III U4**, 95
individual [ˌɪndɪ'vɪdʒuəl] individuell; einzeln **II**
industry ['ɪndəstri] Industrie; Branche; Gewerbe **III U2**, 41
infinitive [ɪn'fɪnətɪv] Infinitiv **I**
to **influence** ['ɪnfluəns] beeinflussen **II**
information *(no pl)* [ˌɪnfə'meɪʃn] Information; Informationen **I**
ingredient [ɪn'griːdiənt] Zutat **II**
injury ['ɪndʒəri] Verletzung **II**
inline skating ['ɪnlaɪn ˌskeɪtɪŋ] Inlineskatefahren **I**
inside [ˌɪn'saɪd] innen; im Innern; hinein; nach drinnen; in; drin **I**

instead [ɪn'sted] stattdessen **III U1**, 20
instruction [ɪn'strʌkʃn] Instruktion; Anweisung **I**
instructor [ɪn'strʌktə] Lehrer/-in; Betreuer/-in **II**
interest ['ɪntrəst] Interesse **II**
to **interest** ['ɪntrəst] (sich) interessieren °**III TS2**, 60
*to be **interested** in [bi‿'ɪntrəstɪd‿ɪn] interessiert sein an; sich interessieren für **II**
interesting ['ɪntrəstɪŋ] interessant **I**
international [ˌɪntə'næʃnl] international **I**
internet ['ɪntənet] Internet **I**
interview ['ɪntəvju:] Interview; Befragung **I**
to **interview** ['ɪntəvju:] interviewen; befragen **I**
into ['ɪntə] in; in … hinein **I**
*to be **into** [bi:‿'ɪntə] mögen; stehen auf **I**
You're **into** … ['jɔ:r‿ˌɪntə] Du magst …; Du stehst auf … **I**
to **introduce** [ˌɪntrə'dju:s] einführen; einleiten °**III U4**, 95
Introduce … [ˌɪntrə'dju:s] Stelle/Stellt … vor. **I**
introduction [ˌɪntrə'dʌkʃn] Einführung; Einleitung; Vorstellung **II**
to **invade** [ɪn'veɪd] einmarschieren (in); eindringen (in); überfallen **III U3**, 68
to **invent** [ɪn'vent] erfinden **III U2**, 42
invention [ɪn'venʃn] Erfindung **III U2**, 42
inventor [ɪn'ventə] Erfinder/-in **III U2**, 51
invisible [ɪn'vɪzəbl] unsichtbar **III U4**, 103
invitation [ˌɪnvɪ'teɪʃn] Einladung **I**
to **invite** [ɪn'vaɪt] einladen **I**
*to get **involved** with sb [ˌget‿ɪn'vɒlvd wɪð] sich einlassen mit jmdm. ⟨**III TS4**, 110⟩
inward ['ɪnwəd] ankommend **II**
irregular [ɪ'regjələ] unregelmäßig **I**
island ['aɪlənd] Insel **II**
it [ɪt] es **I**
*to make **it** ['meɪk‿ɪt] es schaffen ⟨**III TS2**, 57⟩
It's fun. [ɪts 'fʌn] Es macht Spaß. **I**
It's great for … [ɪts 'greɪt fə] Es ist super zum/für … **I**
It's your turn. [ˌɪts 'jɔ: tɜ:n] Du bist dran. **I**
It's …/They're … [ɪts/ðeə] Es kostet …/ Sie kosten … **I**
IT *(= Information Technology)* [ˌaɪ'ti:] Informatik; Informationstechnik **III U1**, 10
its [ɪts] sein/-e; ihr/-e **I**
ivory *(no pl)* ['aɪvri] Elfenbein **III TS2**, 60

J

jacket ['dʒækɪt] Jacke **III U2**, 41
jam [dʒæm] Marmelade; Konfitüre **III AC1**, 34
January ['dʒænjuri] Januar **I**
*to be **jealous** (of) [bi: 'dʒeləs] eifersüchtig sein (auf); neidisch sein (auf) **I**
jewel ['dʒu:əl] Juwel; Edelstein **III U3**, 75
crown **jewels** [ˌkraʊn 'dʒu:əlz] Kronjuwelen **II**
jewellery ['dʒu:əlri] Schmuck **I**
job [dʒɒb] Arbeit; Aufgabe; Job **I**
to **join** [dʒɔɪn] beitreten; sich anschließen; verbinden **II**
joke [dʒəʊk] Witz **I**
to **joke** [dʒəʊk] scherzen **II**
journey ['dʒɜ:ni] Reise; Fahrt **II**
to **judge** [dʒʌdʒ] beurteilen; bewerten **III U1**, 8
juice [dʒu:s] Saft **I**
July [dʒʊ'laɪ] Juli **I**
to **jump** [dʒʌmp] springen **I**
to **jump** back [ˌdʒʌmp‿'bæk] zurückspringen; *hier:* zurückschrecken **II**
to **jump** the queue [ˌdʒʌmp ðə 'kju:] sich vordrängeln **I**
June [dʒu:n] Juni **I**
piece of **junk** [ˌpi:s‿əv 'dʒʌŋk] Stück Schrott **III U1**, 21
just [dʒʌst] gerade; nur; einfach **I**

K

keen [ki:n] scharf; fein ⟨**III TS1**, 30⟩; begeistert; leidenschaftlich ⟨**III TS4**, 112⟩
*to **keep** [ki:p] behalten; aufbewahren; halten **I**
*to **keep** away from [ˌki:p‿ə'weɪ frəm] (sich) fernhalten von **II**
*to **keep** going [ˌki:p 'gəʊɪŋ] aufrechterhalten **II**
*to **keep** one's feet or hands still [ˌki:p wʌnz: 'fi:t‿ɔ: 'hændz stɪl] die Beine und Hände ruhig halten **III TS1**, 32
*to **keep** out (of) [ˌki:p‿'aʊt əv] draußen bleiben; draußen halten **III U2**, 48
*to **keep** the ball bouncing [ˌki:p ðə bɔ:l 'baʊntsɪŋ] *hier:* das Gespräch am Laufen halten **III AC2**, 62
*to **keep** up (with) [ˌki:p‿'ʌp (wɪð)] mithalten (mit); Schritt halten (mit) **II**
*to **keep** your fingers crossed [ˌki:p jɔ: ˌfɪŋgəz 'krɒst] die Daumen drücken **I**
key [ki:] Schlüssel **II**
key ring ['ki: ˌrɪŋ] Schlüsselbund; Schlüsselanhänger **III U2**, 49
key word ['ki: wɜ:d] Stichwort; Schlüsselbegriff **I**
piano **key** [pi'ænəʊ ˌki:] Klaviertaste ⟨**III TS2**, 60⟩
to **kick** [kɪk] schießen; treten **II**
kid [kɪd] Jugendliche/-r; Kind **III U3**, 73
to **kill** [kɪl] töten; umbringen **III TS2**, 60
killing ['kɪlɪŋ] Töten ⟨**III TS2**, 60⟩
kilometre (km) ['kɪləˌmi:tə; kɪ'lɒmɪtə] Kilometer **III TS3**, 87
kilt [kɪlt] Kilt; Schottenrock **III U2**, 37
kind [kaɪnd] Art; Sorte **I**
king [kɪŋ] König **I**
kitchen ['kɪtʃɪn] Küche **I**
knife [naɪf], **knives** [naɪvz] *(pl)* Messer **III AC1**, 34
knight [naɪt] Ritter **II**
knob [nɒb] Griff **II**
*to **know** [nəʊ] kennen; wissen **I**
to get to **know** [ˌget tə 'nəʊ] kennen lernen **III U1**, 12
I don't **know**! [ˌaɪ ˌdəʊnt 'nəʊ] Ich weiß (es) nicht! **I**
You **know** how to … [ju: 'nəʊ ˌhaʊ tə] Du weißt, wie man …; Ihr wisst, wie man … **I**
koala [kəʊ'ɑ:lə] Koala **III TS2**, 59
koalas who … [kəʊˌɑ:ləz 'hu:] Koalas, die … °**III TS2**, 59
Korean [kə'ri:ən] koreanisch; Koreanisch; Koreaner/-in **II**
South **Korean** [ˌsaʊθ kə'ri:ən] Südkoreaner/-in; südkoreanisch; Südkoreanisch **II**

L

lady ['leɪdi] Lady; Dame **III U3**, 76
lady-in-waiting [ˌleɪdiɪn'weɪtɪŋ] Hofdame **III U3**, 76
laid-back [leɪd'bæk] entspannt; locker **III U1**, 10
lake [leɪk] See **I**
boating **lake** ['bəʊtɪŋ ˌleɪk] See zum Rudern **I**
lamb [læm] Lamm; Lämmchen **I**
land [lænd] Land **I**
to **land** [lænd] landen **II**
landing ['lændɪŋ] Landung **III U4**, 99
landscape ['lændskeɪp] Landschaft **II**
language ['læŋgwɪdʒ] Sprache **I**
first **language** [ˌfɜ:st 'læŋgwɪdʒ] Muttersprache **II**
foreign **language** [ˌfɒrɪn 'læŋgwɪdʒ] Fremdsprache **III U4**, 92
official **language** [əˌfɪʃl 'læŋgwɪdʒ] Amtssprache **II**
laptop ['læptɒp] Laptop **II**
large [lɑ:dʒ] groß; riesig **II**
lassi ['lʌsi] Lassi **I**
last [lɑ:st] letzte/-r/-s **I**
at **last** [ət 'lɑ:st] endlich; schließlich **I**
late [leɪt] spät; zu spät **I**
*to be **late** [bi: 'leɪt] zu spät dran sein; zu spät kommen **I**
later ['leɪtə] später **I**
latest ['leɪtɪst] neueste/-r/-s **III U2**, 44
to **laugh** [lɑ:f] lachen **I**
they were **laughing** [ˌðeɪ wər 'lɑ:fɪŋ] sie lachten gerade °**III U1**, 20
lavish ['lævɪʃ] üppig; verschwenderisch **III U4**, 105
*to **lay** down [ˌleɪ 'daʊn] hinlegen ⟨**III TS3**, 85⟩
layer (of) ['leɪər‿əv] Schicht (aus); Lage (aus) **III TS2**, 57
layout ['leɪaʊt] Layout; Anordnung **III U1**, 19
lazy ['leɪzi] faul **III TS1**, 29

lead part [ˌli:d 'pɑ:t] Hauptrolle **III U1**, 10
*to **lead** [li:d] führen; anführen **III U2**, 43
*to **lead** off [li:dˬ'ɒf] wegführen **III U2**, 43
lead [li:d] Haupt- **III U1**, 10
lead dancer ['li:d ˌdɑ:nsə] Vortänzer/-in **III U1**, 10
leaf [li:f], **leaves** [li:vz] *(pl)* Blatt ⟨**III U2**, 40⟩
leaflet ['li:flət] Broschüre; Informationsblatt; Prospekt **III AC3**, 91
*to **learn** [lɜ:n] lernen **I**
*to **learn** about ['lɜ:nˬəˌbaʊt] erfahren über **III U1**, 9
*to **learn** … by heart [ˌlɜ:n baɪ 'hɑ:t] auswendig lernen **I**
at **least** [ət 'li:st] mindestens; wenigstens **II**
*to **leave** [li:v] losgehen; abfahren; verlassen **II**
*to **leave** a message [ˌli:vˬə 'mesɪdʒ] eine Nachricht hinterlassen **I**
*to **leave** behind [ˌli:vˬbɪ'haɪnd] zurücklassen **III U2**, 43
*to **leave** it to cool [ˌli:vˬɪt tə 'ku:l] kalt stellen **I**
*to **leave** space [li:v 'speɪs] Platz lassen **I**
left [left] linke/-r/-s; links **I**
on the **left** [ɒn ðə 'left] auf der linken Seite; links **I**
left [left] übrig **I**
leg [leg] Bein **II**
legend ['ledʒənd] Legende; Sage **II**
leisure ['leʒə] Freizeit; Freizeit- **I**
leisure centre ['leʒə ˌsentə] Freizeitzentrum **I**
lemon ['lemən] Zitrone **II**
lemonade [ˌlemə'neɪd] Limonade **I**
*to **lend** ['lend tə] leihen; verleihen **III U1**, 21
less [les] weniger **III U3**, 67
lesson ['lesn] Unterrichtsstunde; Schulstunde; Unterricht **I**
*to **let** [let] lassen **I**
*to **let** go (of) [ˌlet 'gəʊ (əv)] loslassen **II**
Let's face it. [lets 'feɪsˬɪt] Machen wir uns doch nichts vor. **III TS4**, 108
Let's … [lets] Lass/Lasst uns … **I**
letter ['letə] Buchstabe **I**; Brief **II**
capital **letter** [ˌkæpɪtl 'letə] Großbuchstabe **I**
library ['laɪbri] Bibliothek; Bücherei **III TS2**, 56
lie [laɪ] Lüge **III U1**, 22
white **lie** [ˌwaɪt 'laɪ] Notlüge **III TS4**, 108
to **lie** [laɪ] lügen **II**
life [laɪf], **lives** [laɪvz] *(pl)* Leben **II**
lifeboat ['laɪfbəʊt] Rettungsboot **I**
lifestyle ['laɪfstaɪl] Lebensstil; Lifestyle **III U3**, 67
light [laɪt] Licht; Lampe **II**
light [laɪt] leicht **III AC2**, 62
to **lighten** ['laɪtn] aufhellen **III U3**, 78
lightning *(no pl)* ['laɪtnɪŋ] Blitz **II**
your **like** [jɔ: 'laɪk] jemanden wie dich ⟨**III U2**, 40⟩

to **like** [laɪk] mögen; gern haben **I**
I don't **like** … [aɪ 'dəʊnt laɪk] Ich mag … nicht.; Ich mache … nicht gern. **I**
I **like** singing and dancing. [ˌaɪ laɪk ˌsɪŋɪŋˬənd 'dɑ:nsɪŋ] Ich singe und tanze gern. **I**
I **like** … [aɪ 'laɪk] Mir gefällt …; Ich mag … **I**
I'd **like** to … *(= I would like to)* [aɪd 'laɪk tə] Ich möchte …; Ich würde gern … **I**
Would you **like** …? [ˌwʊd jʊ 'laɪk] Möchtest du …?; Möchten Sie …?; Möchtet ihr …? **II**
like [laɪk] wie; als ob **I**
*to be **like** [bi 'laɪk] sein **III U2**, 36
like that [laɪk 'ðæt] so **I**
like this [laɪk 'ðɪs] so **I**
What was it **like**? [ˌwɒt wɒzˬɪt 'laɪk] Wie war es? **III U3**, 64
limit ['lɪmɪt] Limit; Grenze **III U1**, 19
line [laɪn] Zeile; Linie **I**
finish **line** ['fɪnɪʃˌlaɪn] Ziellinie **II**
opening **line** ['əʊpnɪŋˬˌlaɪn] der erste Satz °**III TS3**, 84
time **line** ['taɪm ˌlaɪn] Zeitstrahl **I**
lines *(pl)* [laɪnz] Text **III TS4**, 106
to **line** [laɪn] auslegen ⟨**III TS2**, 57⟩
to **line** up [laɪnˬ'ʌp] (sich) aufstellen °**III U3**, 78
link [lɪŋk] Link; Verbindung **II**
to **link** [lɪŋk] verbinden **II**
linking word ['lɪŋkɪŋ ˌwɜ:d] Bindewort **I**
lion [laɪən] Löwe **II**
list [lɪst] Liste **I**
to **listen** (to) ['lɪsn] zuhören; anhören **I**
to **listen** for ['lɪsn fə] horchen auf **I**
listener ['lɪsənə] Zuhörer/-in **II**
listening ['lɪsnɪŋ] Hören **I**
litre (l) ['li:tə] Liter **III U2**, 39
to **litter** ['lɪtə] verschmutzen; verunreinigen; Müll herumliegen lassen **III AC3**, 90
little ['lɪtl] klein **I**
a **little** [ə 'lɪtl] ein wenig; etwas **I**
to **live** [lɪv] wohnen; leben **I**
live [laɪv] live **III TS3**, 88
lively ['laɪvli] lebendig **III TS4**, 112
living room ['lɪvɪŋ rʊm] Wohnzimmer **I**
local ['ləʊkl] örtlich; lokal **II**
location [ləʊ'keɪʃn] Handlungsort; Lage; Standort **II**
loch [lɒx; lɒk] See *(in Schottland)* **III U2**, 37
locked [lɒkt] abgeschlossen **II**
locker ['lɒkə] Schließfach; Spind **I**
loft [lɒft] Dachboden **I**
logic ['lɒdʒɪk] Logik **III U1**, 9
LOL (= laughing out loud) [lɒl] LOL **II**
Londoner ['lʌndənə] Londoner/-in **I**
lonely ['ləʊnli] einsam **I**
long [lɒŋ] lang **I**
as **long** as [əz 'lɒŋˬəz] solange ⟨**III TS4**, 110⟩
(not) any **longer** [nɒtˬˌeni 'lɒŋgə] (nicht) mehr; (nicht) länger **II**

look [lʊk] Blick **I**
*to give sb funny **looks** [ˌgɪv fʌni 'lʊks] jmdn. schief anschauen **III U1**, 14
*to have a **look** (at) [ˌhævˬə 'lʊk] anschauen **II**
to **look** [lʊk] schauen; sehen; aussehen **I**
Look! [lʊk] Schau/Schaut mal! **I**
to **look** after [ˌlʊkˬ'ɑ:ftə] aufpassen auf; hüten; sich kümmern um **I**
to **look** at ['lʊkˬət] anschauen; ansehen **I**
to **look** for ['lʊk fɔ:] suchen nach **I**
to **look** forward to [ˌlʊk 'fɔ:wəd tə] sich freuen auf **III U2**, 39
to **look** out [ˌlʊkˬ'aʊt] aufpassen **II**
to **look** up [ˌlʊkˬ'ʌp] nachschlagen; nachschauen **I**
Look closely … [ˌlʊk 'kləʊsli] Schau(t) genau … **II**
looks *(pl)* [lʊks] Aussehen **III U1**, 10
lord [lɔ:d] Lord; Herr **III U3**, 65
*to **lose** [lu:z] verlieren **II**
loss [lɒs] Verlust ⟨**III TS2**, 59⟩
*to get **lost** [ˌget 'lɒst] verloren gehen; sich verirren **II**
a **lot** [ə 'lɒt] viel **I**
a **lot** of [ə 'lɒtˬəv] viel/-e; eine Menge **I**
lots (of) ['lɒtsˬəv] viel/-e; jede Menge **I**
loud [laʊd] laut **I**
*to read/sing out **loud** [ˌri:d/sɪŋˬaʊt 'laʊd] laut vorsingen **III TS1**, 29
departure **lounge** [dɪ'pɑ:tʃə ˌlaʊndʒ] Abflughalle **III U4**, 93
love [lʌv] Liebe **II**
Love … [lʌv] Liebe Grüße *(am Briefende)*; Herzliche Grüße *(am Briefende)* **I**
to **love** [lʌv] lieben; gern mögen **I**
I **love** you. [aɪ 'lʌv ju] Ich liebe dich.; Ich mag dich. **I**
I **love** … [aɪ 'lʌv] Ich liebe …; Ich mag … total gern. **I**
lovebirds *(pl)* ['lʌvˌbɜ:dz] Turteltauben **II**
low [ləʊ] niedrig **II**
low tide ['ləʊ ˌtaɪd] Ebbe **II**
What **luck**! [wɒt 'lʌk] Was für ein Glück! **III U3**, 72
lucky … ['lʌki] … der/die Glückliche **I**
*to be **lucky** [biˬ'lʌki] Glück haben **II**
lucky charm [ˌlʌki 'tʃɑ:m] Glücksbringer; Talisman **I**
luggage *(no pl)* ['lʌgɪdʒ] Gepäck **III U4**, 92
lunch [lʌnʃ] Mittagessen **I**
lunch break ['lʌnʃbreɪk] Mittagspause **I**
lunchtime ['lʌnʃtaɪm] Mittagszeit; Mittagspause ⟨**III TS4**, 112⟩
the **lungs** *(pl)* [ðə 'lʌŋz] die Lunge **III TS3**, 87
(song) **lyrics** *(pl)* [sɒŋ 'lɪrɪks] Liedtext **III TS1**, 28

M

machine [mə'ʃi:n] Automat; Maschine; Apparat; Gerät **I**
answering **machine** ['ɑ:nsrɪŋ mə‚ʃi:n] Anrufbeantworter **I**
vending **machine** ['vendɪŋ mə‚ʃi:n] Automat **III U4**, 94
washing **machine** ['wɒʃɪŋ mə‚ʃi:n] Waschmaschine **II**
mad [mæd] verrückt **II**
Dear Sir or **Madam** [dɪə ‚sɜ:r‿ɔ: 'mædəm] Sehr geehrte Dame, sehr geehrter Herr **II**
magazine [‚mægə'zi:n] Zeitschrift **I**
magic ['mædʒɪk] Magie; Zauberei **III U4**, 105
magical ['mædʒɪkəl] magisch; Zauber- **II**
to **mail** ['i:meɪl] mailen; per E-Mail schicken **II**
main [meɪn] Haupt- **I**
main clause ['meɪn ‚klɔ:z] Hauptsatz °**III U1**, 11
*to **make** [meɪk] machen; tun; bilden; *hier:* ergeben **I**
*to be **made** of [bi 'meɪd‿əv] bestehen aus **III TS1**, 31
*to **make** a decision [‚meɪk‿ə dɪ'sɪʒn] eine Entscheidung treffen **II**
*to **make** a difference [‚meɪk‿ə 'dɪfrns] etw. verändern **II**
*to **make** a wish [‚meɪk‿ə 'wɪʃ] sich etwas wünschen **I**
*to **make** friends [‚meɪk 'frendz] Freundschaft schließen **II**
*to **make** it ['meɪk‿ɪt] es schaffen ⟨**III TS2**, 57⟩
*to **make** money [‚meɪk 'mʌni] Geld verdienen **I**
*to **make** notes [‚meɪk 'nəʊts] Notizen machen **I**
*to **make** sb angry [meɪk 'æŋgri] jmdn. wütend machen; jmdn. verärgern **III AC1**, 35
*to **make** somebody do something [meɪk] jmdn. dazu bringen, etw. zu tun **II**
*to **make** sure [‚meɪk 'ʃɔ:] sich versichern **I**
*to **make** trouble [‚meɪk 'trʌbl] Ärger machen; in Schwierigkeiten bringen **I**
man [mæn], **men** [men] *(pl)* Mann **I**
mango ['mæŋgəʊ] Mango **I**
manners *(pl)* ['mænəz] Manieren; Benehmen **III AC3**, 91
adverb of **manner** [‚ædvɜ:b‿əv 'mænə] Adverb der Art und Weise °**III U3**, 74
software **manual** ['sɒftweə ‚mænjuəl] Softwarehandbuch °**III TS2**, 61
many ['meni] viele **I**
How **many** …? [‚haʊ 'meni] Wie viele …? **I**
map [mæp] Stadtplan; Landkarte **I**
marathon ['mærəθn] Marathon **II**
March [mɑ:tʃ] März **I**
march [mɑ:tʃ] Marsch; Kundgebung ⟨**III TS2**, 60⟩
to **march** [mɑ:tʃ] marschieren **III TS2**, 60
mark [mɑ:k] Note **III U1**, 10
to **mark** [mɑ:k] markieren; kennzeichnen **II**
market ['mɑ:kɪt] Markt **I**
flea **market** ['fli: ‚mɑ:kɪt] Flohmarkt **I**
marmalade ['mɑ:məleɪd] Marmelade aus Zitrusfrüchten **III AC1**, 34
to **marry** ['mæri] heiraten **III U3**, 66
mashed potatoes *(pl)* [‚mæʃt pə'teɪtəʊz] Kartoffelpüree **III U2**, 42
mask [mɑ:sk] Maske **III U4**, 102
match [mætʃ] Spiel; Match **II**
to **match** [mætʃ] zuordnen; passen zu; entsprechen **I**
mate [meɪt] Schiffsoffizier; Maat **I**
material [mə'tɪəriəl] Material **II**
Maths [mæθs] Mathematik; Mathe **II**
What's the **matter?** [‚wɒts ðə 'mætə] Was ist los?; Was hast du? **II**
It doesn't **matter.** [ɪt ‚dʌznt 'mætə] Es ist egal. **III U1**, 8
May [meɪ] Mai **I**
may [meɪ] (vielleicht) können; dürfen **II**
maybe ['meɪbi] vielleicht **I**
me [mi:] ich; mich; mir **I**
meal [mi:l] Mahlzeit; Essen **II**
ready **meal** [‚redi 'mi:l] Fertiggericht **I**
*to **mean** [mi:n] bedeuten; meinen **II**
mean [mi:n] gemein **III TS4**, 109
meaning ['mi:nɪŋ] Bedeutung; Sinn **II**
meat *(no pl)* [mi:t] Fleisch **III U2**, 41
mechanic [mə'kænɪk] Mechaniker/-in; Kfz-Mechaniker/-in **II**
media ['mi:diə] Medien **II**
mediation [‚mi:di'eɪʃn] Sprachmittlung **I**
medicine *(no pl)* ['medsn] Medizin; Medikamente **III TS2**, 60
medieval [‚medi'i:vl] mittelalterlich **II**
*to **meet** [mi:t] treffen; sich treffen **I**
*to **meet** halfway [‚mi:t hɑ:f'weɪ] sich auf halbem Weg treffen **III U1**, 18
melody ['melədi] Melodie **III TS1**, 32
member ['membə] Mitglied **II**
memory ['memri] Erinnerung; Gedächtnis **II**
to **mention** ['menʃn] erwähnen **II**
merchant ['mɜ:tʃənt] Kaufmann; Händler **II**
mess [mes] Unordnung; Durcheinander **II**
to **mess** sth up [‚mes‿'ʌp] etw. durcheinanderbringen; etw. vergeigen **III TS4**, 106
message ['mesɪdʒ] Botschaft; Nachricht **I**
*to leave a **message** [‚li:v‿ə 'mesɪdʒ] eine Nachricht hinterlassen **I**
*to take a **message** [‚teɪk‿ə 'mesɪdʒ] eine Nachricht entgegennehmen; jmdm. etw. ausrichten **I**
text (**message**) ['tekst ‚mesɪdʒ] SMS; Kurznachricht **I**
messy ['mesi] unordentlich **III U1**, 14
metre ['mi:tə] Meter **II**
mid- [mɪd] Mitte ⟨**III TS2**, 57⟩
middle ['mɪdl] Mitte **I**
midnight ['mɪdnaɪt] Mitternacht **III U2**, 41
It **might** as well be … [‚ɪt maɪt əs 'wel bi: …] Es könnte/-n auch … sein. **III TS3**, 87
mile [maɪl] Meile *(brit. Längenmaß)* **II**
milk [mɪlk] Milch **I**
to **milk** [mɪlk] melken **II**
million ['mɪljən] Million **II**
I've done this a **million** times before. [‚aɪv dʌn ðɪs ə ‚mɪljən taɪmz bɪ'fɔ:] Ich habe das schon eine Million Mal gemacht. **II**
millionaire [‚mɪljə'neə] Millionär/-in **III U1**, 10
mind [maɪnd] Geist; Verstand; Kopf **III TS3**, 87
to change one's **mind** [‚tʃeɪndʒ wʌnz 'maɪnd] seine Meinung ändern **III U3**, 68
*to rise up in one's **mind** [raɪz‿ʌp ɪn wʌnz 'maɪnd] jmdm. in den Sinn kommen **III TS3**, 87
to **mind** [maɪnd] etwas dagegen haben; einem etwas ausmachen ⟨**III TS4**, 110⟩
I don't **mind** … [‚aɪ dəʊnt 'maɪnd] Ich habe nichts dagegen (zu) …; Mir macht es nichts aus (zu) … **III U1**, 18
mine [maɪn] Mine **II**
mine [maɪn] mein/-er/-e/-es **II**
mini [mɪni] Mini- **II**
minute ['mɪnɪt] Minute **I**
mirror ['mɪrə] Spiegel **III U3**, 66
miserable ['mɪzrəbl] elend; armselig; jämmerlich ⟨**III TS4**, 108⟩
Miss [mɪs] Fräulein *(Anrede)* **III U1**, 15
to **miss** [mɪs] verpassen; versäumen; vermissen **II**
missing ['mɪsɪŋ] fehlend; verschwunden **II**
What is **missing**? [‚wɒt‿ɪz 'mɪsɪŋ] Was fehlt? **I**
mistake [mɪ'steɪk] Fehler **I**
misunderstood [‚mɪsʌndə'stʊd] missverstanden **III U1**, 18
mix [mɪks] Mix **III U1**, 21
to **mix** [mɪks] Umgang haben ⟨**III TS4**, 110⟩
to **mix** (up) [mɪks‿'ʌp] mischen; vermischen **III U3**, 76
mobile ['məʊbaɪl] Handy; Mobiltelefon **II**
modal ['məʊdl] Modalverb **II**
model ['mɒdl] Modell; Tonmodell; Model **I**
modelling ['mɒdəlɪŋ] Modeln **III U1**, 10
modern ['mɒdn] modern **II**
moment ['məʊmənt] Moment; Augenblick **II**
at the **moment** [ət ðə 'məʊmənt] im Moment; gerade **I**
monarch ['mɒnək] Monarch/-in **III U3**, 66
Monday ['mʌndeɪ] Montag **I**
on **Mondays** [ɒn 'mʌndeɪz] montags **I**
money ['mʌni] Geld **I**
*to make **money** [‚meɪk 'mʌni] Geld verdienen **I**
pocket **money** ['pɒkɪt ‚mʌni] Taschengeld **I**
to raise **money** [‚reɪz 'mʌni] Geld sammeln **II**

monster ['mɒnstə] Monster; Ungeheuer **I**
month [mʌnθ] Monat **II**
monument ['mɒnjəmənt] Monument; Denkmal **II**
mood [mu:d] Stimmung; Laune **II**
moonlight ['mu:nlaɪt] Mondlicht **III U2**, 48
more [mɔ:] mehr; weitere **I**
not any **more** [ˌnɒt‿eni 'mɔ:] nicht mehr **I**
more … than ['mɔ: ðən] mehr … als **I**
morning ['mɔ:nɪŋ] Morgen; Vormittag **I**
in the **mornings** [ˌɪn ðə 'mɔ:nɪŋz] morgens; vormittags **I**
Good **morning**. [ˌgʊd 'mɔ:nɪŋ] Guten Morgen. **I**
(the) **most** [ðə 'məʊst] der/die/das meiste; die meisten **I**
mother ['mʌðə] Mutter **I**
to **motivate** ['məʊtɪveɪt] motivieren **I**
motivation [ˌməʊtɪ'veɪʃn] Motivation; Beweggründe **III TS4**, 107
motive ['məʊtɪv] Motiv; Beweggrund **III TS4**, 108
mountain ['maʊntɪn] Berg **II**
mountain biking ['maʊntɪn ˌbaɪkɪŋ] Mountainbikefahren **II**
mouse [maʊs], **mice** [maɪs] *(pl)* Maus/Mäuse **I**
mouth [maʊθ] Mund **I**
to talk with your **mouth** full [ˌtɔ:k wɪð jɔ: 'maʊθ fʊl] mit vollem Mund sprechen **III AC3**, 90
move [mu:v] Bewegung **I**
on the **move** [ˌɒn‿ðə 'mu:v] unterwegs **III U4**, 92
to **move** [mu:v] (sich) bewegen **I**
to **move** (house) [mu:v (haʊs)] umziehen **II**
to **move** in/into [ˌmu:v‿'ɪn/'ɪntə] einziehen in **II**
Mr ['mɪstə] Herr *(Anrede)* **I**
Mrs ['mɪsɪz] Frau *(Anrede)* **I**
much [mʌtʃ] viel **I**
that **much** [ðæt 'mʌtʃ] so viel **III AC1**, 35
mud [mʌd] Schlamm **II**
muddy ['mʌdi] schlammig **II**
muesli ['mju:zli] Müsli **III AC1**, 34
mug [mʌg] Becher **III AC1**, 34
multi-ethnic [ˌmʌlti'eθnɪk] Vielvölker-; international **II**
mum [mʌm] Mama **I**
mummy ['mʌmi] Mama; Mami; Mutti **III U1**, 21
murder ['mɜ:də] Mord **III U3**, 72
murderer ['mɜ:drə] Mörder/-in **III U3**, 73
museum [mju:'zi:əm] Museum **I**
museums which … [mju:ˌzɪəmz 'wɪtʃ] Museen, die … °**III U2**, 46
music ['mju:zɪk] Musik **I**
music that … [ˌmju:zɪk 'ðæt] Musik, die … °**III U3**, 67
musical ['mju:zɪkl] musikalisch; Musik- **III U2**, 41
musician [mju:'zɪʃn] Musiker/-in **II**
must [mʌst] müssen **I**
mustn't ['mʌsnt] nicht dürfen **I**
to **mutter** ['mʌtə] murmeln **III U4**, 94
my [maɪ] mein/-e **I**
My favourite … [maɪ 'feɪvrɪt] Mein/e Lieblings … **I**
My name is … [maɪ 'neɪm‿ɪz] Ich heiße … **I**
myself [maɪ'self] ich/mir/mich (selbst); selber **II**
mysterious [mɪ'stɪəriəs] mysteriös; geheimnisvoll **II**
mystery ['mɪstri] Mysterium; Rätsel; Geheimnis **III U3**, 76
mythical [mɪθɪkl] sagenhaft; sagenumwoben **III U4**, 105

N

name [neɪm] Name **I**
name day ['neɪm ˌdeɪ] Namenstag **I**
My **name** is … [maɪ 'neɪm‿ɪz] Ich heiße … **I**
What's your **name**? [ˌwɒts jə 'neɪm] Wie heißt du?; Wie heißen Sie? **I**
to **name** [neɪm] nennen; benennen **I**
narrative perspective [ˌnærətɪv pə'spektɪv] Erzählperspektive °**III TS3**, 88
narrator [nə'reɪtə] Erzähler/-in °**III TS3**, 85
first person **narrator** [ˌfɜ:st ˌpɜ:sn nə'reɪtə] Ich-Erzähler/-in °**III TS3**, 87
third person **narrator** [ˌθɜ:d ˌpɜ:sn nə'reɪtə] Er/Sie-Erzähler/-in °**III TS3**, 85
narrow ['nærəʊ] eng; schmal **III U2**, 43
nasty ['nɑ:sti] garstig; gemein **II**
nation ['neɪʃn] Nation ⟨**III U1**, 13⟩
national ['næʃnl] national; landesweit **I**
nature ['neɪtʃə] Natur **II**
near [nɪə] nahe; in der Nähe von **I**
nearly ['nɪəli] fast; annähernd **II**
necessary ['nesəsri] nötig; notwendig; erforderlich ⟨**III TS2**, 57⟩
necklace ['nekləs] Halskette **III U3**, 66
in **need** [ɪn 'ni:d] bedürftig; in Not **II**
There's no **need** to … [ˌðeəz nəʊ 'ni:d tə] Es gibt keinen Grund zu … **III TS4**, 112
with special **needs** [wɪð ˌspeʃl 'ni:dz] behindert **II**
to **need** (to) [ni:d] brauchen; benötigen **I**
to **need** (to do) [ni:d] (tun) müssen **I**
needn't ['ni:dnt] nicht brauchen; nicht müssen **I**
negative ['negətɪv] negativ; verneint **II**
negative form ['negətɪv ˌfɔ:m] verneinte Form **I**
neighbour *(BE)* ['neɪbə] Nachbar/-in **I**
neighbourhood ['neɪbəhʊd] Nachbarschaft **III U2**, 51
Me **neither**. [mi: 'naɪðə] Ich auch nicht. **II**
nephew ['nefju:] Neffe **III U4**, 97
*to get on somebody's **nerves** [ˌget‿ɒn sʌmbɒdiz 'nɜ:vz] jemandem auf die Nerven gehen **I**
nervous ['nɜ:vəs] nervös; aufgeregt **II**
net [net] Netz **II**
netball ['netbɔ:l] Korbball **I**
social **network** [ˌsəʊʃl 'netwɜ:k] soziales Netzwerk **II**
never ['nevə] nie; niemals **I**
new [nju:] neu **I**
news *(sg)* [nju:z] Nachrichten; Neuigkeiten **II**
news report ['nju:z rɪˌpɔ:t] Tatsachenbericht; Nachrichtenbeitrag; Meldung **III TS2**, 56
newspaper ['nju:sˌpeɪpə] Zeitung **III TS2**, 57
next [nekst] nächste/-r/-s; der/die Nächste(n) **I**
next door [ˌnekst 'dɔ:] (von) nebenan **III AC2**, 62
next to ['nekst tə] neben **I**
the **next** day [ðə ˌnekst 'deɪ] am nächsten Tag **II**
next [nekst] als Nächstes **I**
nice [naɪs] nett; schön; lieb **I**
night [naɪt] Nacht **I**
all **night** [ˌɔ:l 'naɪt] die ganze Nacht **I**
night walk ['naɪt wɔ:k] Nachtwanderung **II**
nine [naɪn] neun **I**
2nite *(= tonight)* [tə'naɪt] heute Abend **I**
no [nəʊ] kein/-e **I**
no idea [ˌnəʊ‿aɪ'dɪə] keine Ahnung **II**
no such thing as [ˌnəʊ sʌtʃ θɪŋ‿'æz] nicht so etwas wie **II**
no [nəʊ] nein **I**
nobody ['nəʊbədi] niemand **II**
nobody else ['nəʊbədi els] niemand anderes **II**
noise [nɔɪz] Lärm; Geräusch **II**
noisy ['nɔɪzi] laut **III U3**, 67
non- [nɒn] nicht- **II**
normal ['nɔ:ml] normal **II**
normally ['nɔ:mli] normalerweise °**III AC3**, 90
Norman ['nɔ:mən] Normanne/Normannin; normannisch **III U3**, 65
north [nɔ:θ] Norden; Nord- **II**
north [nɔ:θ] nördlich; im Norden **III U2**, 46
nose [nəʊz] Nase **II**
not [nɒt] nicht **I**
not any more [ˌnɒt‿eni 'mɔ:] nicht mehr **I**
not … any [nɒt … eni] kein/-e/-en **I**
not … anything [ˌnɒt 'eniθɪŋ] nichts **I**
not … either [nɒt … 'aɪðə; nɒt … 'i:ðə] auch nicht **III U1**, 16
not … yet [nɒt 'jet] noch nicht **II**
note [nəʊt] Notiz; Anmerkung **I**
*to make **notes** [ˌmeɪk 'nəʊts] Notizen machen **I**
*to take **notes** [ˌteɪk 'nəʊts] sich Notizen machen **I**

to note down [ˌnəʊt ˈdaʊn] notieren; aufschreiben **II**
nothing [ˈnʌθɪŋ] nichts **I**
to notice [ˈnəʊtɪs] bemerken; wahrnehmen **II**
noticeboard [ˈnəʊtɪsbɔːd] schwarzes Brett **II**
noun [naʊn] Nomen; Hauptwort **I**
novel [ˈnɒvl] Roman °**III TS3**, 85
graphic **novel** [ˌgræfɪk ˈnɒvl] Bildergeschichte; Comic **III TS3**, 84
November [nəˈvembə] November **I**
now [naʊ] jetzt; nun **I**
right **now** [ˌraɪt ˈnaʊ] jetzt gleich; sofort; gerade **II**
nowhere [ˈnəʊweə] nirgendwo; nirgendwohin **II**
number [ˈnʌmbə] Zahl; Nummer **I**
nurse [nɜːs] Krankenschwester; Krankenpfleger **III U3**, 77
nut [nʌt] Nuss **I**

O

o'clock [əˈklɒk] Uhr *(Zeitangabe bei vollen Stunden)* **I**
o'er [ˈəʊə] über ⟨**III U2**, 40⟩
oak [əʊk] Eiche **III TS1**, 30
object [ˈɒbdʒɪkt] Objekt; Gegenstand **III U2**, 41
object pronoun [ˌɒbdʒɪkt ˈprəʊnaʊn] Objektpronomen °**III U1**, 15
objects which … [ˌɒbdʒɪkts ˈwɪtʃ] Gegenstände, die … °**III U3**, 67
obvious [ˈɒbviəs] offensichtlich **III U3**, 74
October [ɒkˈtəʊbə] Oktober **I**
against all odds [əˌgenst ˌɔːl ˈɒdz] entgegen allen Erwartungen **III TS3**, 84
odd [ɒd] seltsam; komisch **III AC3**, 90
of [ɒv; əv] von **I**
of course [əv ˈkɔːs] natürlich; selbstverständlich **I**
of one's own [ˌəv wʌnz ˈəʊn] eigen °**III TS1**, 28
off [ɒf] von … weg/ab/herunter ⟨**III TS3**, 85⟩
*to take **off** [ˌteɪk ˈɒf] abnehmen; herunternehmen; ausziehen **I**
to turn **off** [ˌtɜːn ˈɒf] abschalten; ausschalten **II**
offer [ˈɒfə] Angebot **III U1**, 17
special **offer** [ˌspeʃl ˈɒfə] Sonderangebot **I**
to offer [ˈɒfə] anbieten **II**
office [ˈɒfɪs] Büro **I**
immigration **office** [ˌɪmɪˈgreɪʃn ˌɒfɪs] Einwanderungsbehörde **III U4**, 97
ticket **office** [ˈtɪkɪt ˌɒfɪs] Kartenschalter **III U2**, 48
official [əˈfɪʃl] Schiedsrichter/-in **II**; Beamter/Beamtin **III U4**, 103
official [əˈfɪʃl] offiziell **III U2**, 40
official language [əˌfɪʃl ˈlæŋgwɪdʒ] Amtssprache **II**
offline [ˈɒflaɪn] offline **II**
often [ˈɒfn] oft; häufig **I**
oh [əʊ] null *(bei Telefonnummern und Uhrzeitangaben)* **I**
Oh! [əʊ] O! **I**
Oh dear! [ˌəʊ ˈdɪə] Oje! **II**
ointment [ˈɔɪntmənt] Salbe **II**
OK [əʊˈkeɪ] o.k.; in Ordnung **I**
okay [əˈkeɪ] okay **III TS4**, 107
old [əʊld] alt **I**
How **old** are you? [haʊ ˈəʊld ə ˌjuː] Wie alt bist du?; Wie alt sind Sie? **I**
11-year-old [ɪˌlevnˈjɪərəʊld] 11-Jährige/-r **II**
OMG! (Oh my god!) [ˌəʊ maɪ ˈgɒd] OMG! (Oh mein Gott!) ⟨**III TS2**, 59⟩
on [ɒn] auf; an; am; in; im **I**
*to be **on** [bi ˈɒn] an sein; laufen **II**
on Mondays [ɒn ˈmʌndeɪz] montags **I**
on my own [ˌɒn maɪ ˈəʊn] allein; für mich **III U4**, 103
on the brink of [ˌɒn ðə ˈbrɪŋk əv] am Rande von; kurz vor **III TS2**, 60
on the left [ɒn ðə ˈleft] auf der linken Seite; links **I**
on the right [ɒn ðə ˈraɪt] auf der rechten Seite; rechts **I**
on top [ɒn ˈtɒp] oben; obendrauf **I**
Come **on**! [ˌkʌm ˈɒn] Komm schon!; Komm jetzt! **I**
on the move [ˌɒn ðə ˈmuːv] unterwegs **III U4**, 92
once [wʌns] einmal; einst **I**
one [wʌn] eins **I**
one day [wʌn ˈdeɪ] eines Tages **II**
one-way ticket [ˈwʌnweɪ ˌtɪkɪt] einfache Fahrkarte **II**
one [wʌn], **ones** [wʌnz] *(pl)* eine/-r/-s **II**
online [ɒnˈlaɪn] online **II**
only [ˈəʊnli] einzige/-r/-s **II**
only [ˈəʊnli] erst; bloß; nur **I**
only child [ˈəʊnli ˌtʃaɪld] Einzelkind **I**
Oops! [uːps] Hoppla!; Huch! **I**
to open [ˈəʊpn] öffnen; aufmachen **I**; *hier:* beginnen °**III TS3**, 85
open [ˈəʊpn] offen; geöffnet; aufgeschlagen **I**
*to hold **open** [ˌhəʊld ˈəʊpn] aufhalten **III AC3**, 90
opening [ˈəʊpnɪŋ] Öffnung; Beginn °**III TS3**, 88
opening line [ˈəʊpnɪŋ ˌlaɪn] der erste Satz °**III TS3**, 84
opinion [əˈpɪnjən] Meinung **II**
opposite [ˈɒpəzɪt] gegenüber; auf der anderen Seite von **I**
optimistic [ˌɒptɪˈmɪstɪk] optimistisch **III U1**, 23
option [ˈɒpʃn] Möglichkeit; Wahl; Option °**III TS1**, 33
or [ɔː] oder **I**
orange [ˈɒrɪndʒ] Orange **I**
orange [ˈɒrɪndʒ] orange **I**
order [ˈɔːdə] Reihenfolge; Ordnung **I**; Befehl **III TS3**, 85
out of **order** [ˌaʊt əv ˈɔːdə] kaputt; außer Betrieb **III TS4**, 112
word **order** [ˈwɜːd ˌɔːdə] Wortstellung; Satzstellung **I**
to order [ˈɔːdə] bestellen **III U4**, 100
organisation [ˌɔːgnaɪˈzeɪʃn] Organisation **II**
to organise [ˈɔːgənaɪz] organisieren **I**
*to get **organised** [get ˈɔːgənaɪzd] sich organisieren **II**
organiser [ˈɔːgənaɪzə] Organisator/-in ⟨**III TS2**, 60⟩
origin [ˈɒrɪdʒɪn] Ursprung; Herkunft; Abstammung **III U4**, 105
original [əˈrɪdʒnl] Original °**III TS1**, 33
original [əˈrɪdʒnl] original; ursprünglich °**III TS1**, 30
originally [əˈrɪdʒnli] ursprünglich **II**
ornament [ˈɔːnəmənt] Schmuckstück ⟨**III TS2**, 60⟩
other [ˈʌðə] anders; andere/-r/-s; weitere **I**
each **other** [ˌiːtʃ ˈʌðə] einander; sich; sich gegenseitig **I**
the **others** [ði ˈʌðəz] die anderen **I**
otherwise [ˈʌðəwaɪz] sonst **III U3**, 74
Ouch! [aʊtʃ] Aua! **II**
our [aʊə; ɑː] unser/-e **I**
out [aʊt] außerhalb; heraus; hinaus; nach draußen **I**
to clear **out** [ˌklɪər ˈaʊt] ausräumen; entrümpeln **I**
to drop **out** (of) [ˌdrɒp ˈaʊt əv] abbrechen **III U1**, 10
*to hang **out** (with) *(infml)* [ˌhæŋ ˈaʊt wɪð] sich herumtreiben (mit); rumhängen (mit); sich treffen (mit) **III U1**, 20
out of [ˈaʊt əv] aus … heraus **III U4**, 99
out of focus [ˌaʊt əv ˈfəʊkəs] unscharf **III U3**, 77
out of order [ˌaʊt əv ˈɔːdə] kaputt; außer Betrieb **III TS4**, 112
a day **out** in … [ə ˌdeɪ ˈaʊt ɪn] ein Tag in … **II**
out and about [ˌaʊt ən əˈbaʊt] unterwegs **II**
outdoor [ˌaʊtˈdɔː] Freiluft-; Outdoor- **II**
outfit [ˈaʊtfɪt] Outfit; Kleidung **II**
outgoing [aʊtˈgəʊɪŋ] kontaktfreudig **III U4**, 105
outlaw [ˈaʊtlɔː] Geächtete/-r; Gesetzlose/-r **II**
outline [ˈaʊtlaɪn] Skizze; Umriss **II**
outside [aʊtˈsaɪd] nach draußen; draußen; außerhalb **I**
outward [ˈaʊtwəd] abfahrend **II**
over [ˈəʊvə] hinüber; über **I**; vorüber; vorbei **II**
*to go **over** to [ˌgəʊ ˈəʊvə tə] hinübergehen zu; zu jmdm. nach Hause gehen **II**
over and **over** again [ˌəʊvər ən ˌəʊvər əˈgen] immer wieder **III TS1**, 32

overloaded [ˌəʊvəˈləʊdɪd] überladen **III U4**, 102
overnight [ˌəʊvəˈnaɪt] über Nacht **III U1**, 21
to **overreact** [ˌəʊvəriˈækt] überreagieren **II**
over-wintering [ˌəʊvəˈwɪntrɪŋ] Überwintern ⟨**III TS2**, 57⟩
own [əʊn] eigene/-r/-s **I**
of one's **own** [ˌəv wʌnz‿ˈəʊn] eigen °**III TS1**, 28
on my **own** [ˌɒn maɪ‿ˈəʊn] allein; für mich **III U4**, 103

P

p.m. [ˌpiːˈem] nachmittags *(Uhrzeit)*; abends *(Uhrzeit)* **I**
packet [ˈpækɪt] Päckchen; Paket; Packung **I**
page [peɪdʒ] Seite **I**
pain [peɪn] Schmerz **II**
to **paint** [peɪnt] anmalen; malen **I**
painting [ˈpeɪntɪŋ] Malerei; Gemälde **II**
pair [peə] Paar **I**
pair work [ˈpeə wɜːk] Partnerarbeit **II**
to **pair** [peə] Paare bilden °**III TS3**, 86
palm tree [ˈpɑːm ˌtriː] Palme **II**
to **panic** [ˈpænɪk] panisch werden **II**
paper [ˈpeɪpə] Papier **I**
piece of **paper** [ˌpiːs‿əv ˈpeɪpə] Stück Papier **I**
paradise [ˈpærədaɪs] Paradies **II**
parcel [ˈpɑːsl] Paket; Päckchen **I**
parents *(pl)* [ˈpeərənts] Eltern **I**
park [pɑːk] Park **I**
part [pɑːt] Teil; Stadtteil **I**; Rolle **III U1**, 10
lead **part** [ˌliːd ˈpɑːt] Hauptrolle **III U1**, 10
*to take **part** (in) [ˌteɪk ˈpɑːt (ɪn)] teilnehmen (an) **II**
partially sighted [ˌpɑːʃəli ˈsaɪtɪd] sehbehindert **II**
past **participle** [ˌpɑːst pɑːˈtɪsɪpl] Partizip **II**
particular [pəˈtɪkjələ] bestimmte/-r/-s °**III U2**, 46
partly [ˈpɑːtli] teilweise ⟨**III TS4**, 108⟩
partner [ˈpɑːtnə] Partner/-in **I**
party [ˈpɑːti] Party; Feier **I**; Partei **III U2**, 39
to **pass** [pɑːs] zupassen; zuspielen **II**; durchgehen; vorbeigehen (an) **III U3**, 72
to **pass** (on) [ˌpɑːs‿ˈɒn] weitergeben **I**
passed [pɑːst] vorüber ⟨**III U2**, 40⟩
passenger [ˈpæsndʒə] Passagier/-in; Fahrgast **III U4**, 93
passive [ˈpæsɪv] Passiv °**III U2**, 37
passive [ˈpæsɪv] passiv °**III U2**, 41
passport [ˈpɑːspɔːt] Pass; Reisepass **III U4**, 93
past [pɑːst] Vergangenheit **II**
past form [ˈpɑːst fɔːm] Vergangenheitsform **II**
past participle [ˌpɑːst pɑːˈtɪsɪpl] Partizip **II**
past perfect [ˌpɑːst ˈpɜːfɪkt] Plusquamperfekt °**III U3**, 65
past progressive [ˌpɑːst prəˈgresɪv] Verlaufsform der Vergangenheit °**III U2**, 45
simple **past** [ˌsɪmpl ˈpɑːst] Vergangenheitsform **II**
past [pɑːst] nach *(bei Uhrzeitangaben)*; vorbei (an); vorüber (an) **I**
half **past** [ˌhɑːf ˈpɑːst] halb *(bei Uhrzeitangaben)* **I**
quarter **past**/to [ˈkwɔːtə pɑːst/tə] Viertel nach/vor **I**
pasta [ˈpæstə] Pasta; Nudeln **I**
pattern [ˈpætn] Muster **III AC2**, 62
coastal **path** [ˌkəʊstl ˈpɑːθ] Küstenweg **II**
pause [pɔːz] Pause **III U1**, 14
paw [pɔː] Pfote ⟨**III TS2**, 59⟩
pawn shop [ˈpɔːn ʃɒp] Pfandhaus; Pfandleihe **III U3**, 79
*to **pay (for)** [peɪ] bezahlen **I**
*to **pay** out [peɪ‿ˈaʊt] ausgeben ⟨**III TS4**, 110⟩
PC *(= Personal Computer)* [piːˈsiː] PC **II**
PE *(= Physical Education)* [ˌpiːˈiː; ˌfɪzɪkl‿edʒʊˈkeɪʃn] Sportunterricht **II**
peach [piːtʃ] Pfirsich **III TS1**, 29
peer pressure [ˈpɪə ˌpreʃə] Gruppenzwang **III U1**, 22
pen [pen] Füller **I**
penny [ˈpeni], **pence** [pens] *(pl)* Penny *(brit. Währungseinheit)*; Pence *(brit. Währungseinheit)* **I**
pencil [ˈpensl] Bleistift; Buntstift **I**
pencil-case [ˈpensl ˌkeɪs] Federmäppchen; Mäppchen **I**
penicillin [ˌpenɪˈsɪlɪn] Penicillin **III U2**, 42
penny [ˈpeni], **pence** [pens] *(pl)* Penny *(brit. Währungseinheit)*; Pence *(brit. Währungseinheit)* **I**
people *(pl)* [ˈpiːpl] Leute; Menschen **I**
people who … [ˌpiːpl ˈhuː] Menschen, die … °**III TS2**, 58
per [pɜː; pə] pro **II**
past **perfect** [ˌpɑːst ˈpɜːfɪkt] Plusquamperfekt °**III U3**, 65
present **perfect** [ˌpreznt ˈpɜːfɪkt] das Perfekt **II**
present **perfect** progressive [ˌpreznt ˌpɜːfɪkt prəˈgresɪv] Verlaufsform des Perfekts °**III U2**, 39
perfect [ˈpɜːfɪkt] perfekt; vollkommen **I**
performance [pəˈfɔːməns] Aufführung; Vorstellung **III TS4**, 106
perhaps [pəˈhæps] vielleicht **III U2**, 48
period [ˈpɪəriəd] Periode; Zeitspanne **III U2**, 39
person [ˈpɜːsn], **people** [ˈpiːpl] *(pl)* Person; Mensch **I**
first **person** narrator [ˌfɜːst ˌpɜːsn nəˈreɪtə] Ich-Erzähler/-in °**III TS3**, 87
third **person** narrator [ˌθɜːd ˌpɜːsn nəˈreɪtə] Er/Sie-Erzähler/-in °**III TS3**, 85
a **person** who … [ə ˌpɜːsn ˈhuː] eine Person, die … °**III U2**, 43
personal [ˈpɜːsnl] persönlich **I**
personality [ˌpɜːsnˈæləti] Persönlichkeit **III U1**, 9
perspective [pəˈspektɪv] Perspektive; Blickwinkel **II**
narrative **perspective** [ˌnærətɪv pəˈspektɪv] Erzählperspektive °**III TS3**, 88
to **persuade** [pəˈsweɪd] überreden **II**
persuasive [pəˈsweɪsɪv] überzeugend °**III U2**, 46
pet [pet] Haustier **I**
phone [fəʊn] Telefon; Handy **I**
to answer the **phone** [ˌɑːnsə ðə ˈfəʊn] einen Anruf entgegennehmen **I**
phone box [ˈfəʊn ˌbɒks] Telefonzelle **III U4**, 103
phone call [ˈfəʊn ˌkɔːl] Anruf; Telefonanruf **I**
rotary **phone** [ˈrəʊtri fəʊn] Telefon mit Wählscheibe **III U2**, 51
to **phone** [fəʊn] anrufen; telefonieren **III TS4**, 107
photo [ˈfəʊtəʊ] Foto; Fotografie **I**
in the **photo**(s) [ˌɪn ðə ˈfəʊtəʊ(z)] auf dem Foto/den Fotos **I**
photo shoot [ˈfəʊtəʊ ˌʃuːt] Fotoshooting; Fotoaufnahmen **III U3**, 74
photo story [ˈfəʊtəʊ ˌstɔːri] Fotostory; Bildgeschichte **I**
*to take **photos** [ˌteɪk ˈfəʊtəʊz] fotografieren; Fotos machen **I**
to **photobomb** [ˈfəʊtəʊbɒm] ins Foto laufen **III U3**, 77
photographer [fəˈtɒgrəfə] Fotograf/-in **III U3**, 76
phrase [freɪz] Redewendung; Ausdruck; Satz **I**
Useful **phrases** [ˌjuːsfl ˈfreɪsɪz] nützliche Ausdrücke **I**
piano key [piˈænəʊ ˌkiː] Klaviertaste ⟨**III TS2**, 60⟩
pic (= picture) [pɪk] Foto **III U2**, 44
to **pick** [pɪk] auswählen; aussuchen **II**
to **pick** up [ˌpɪk‿ˈʌp] aufheben; mitnehmen; abholen **III U3**, 72
pick-up [ˈpɪkʌp] Pick-up; Wiederaufnehmen **I**
picnic [ˈpɪknɪk] Picknick **I**
picture [ˈpɪktʃə] Bild; Foto **I**
pie [paɪ] Kuchen; Pastete **I**
piece [piːs] Stück **I**
excellent **piece** of quick thinking [ˌekslnt piːs‿əv kwɪk ˈθɪŋkɪŋ] ausgezeichnete Reaktionsschnelligkeit ⟨**III TS4**, 112⟩
piece of junk [ˌpiːs‿əv ˈdʒʌŋk] Stück Schrott **III U1**, 21
piece of paper [ˌpiːs‿əv ˈpeɪpə] Stück Papier **I**
pier [pɪə] Pier; Hafendamm **I**
pig [pɪg] Schwein **I**
guinea **pig** [ˈgɪniː ˌpɪg] Meerschweinchen **I**

*to give sb a **piggyback** [gɪv‿ə 'pɪgibæk] jmdn. Huckepack nehmen **III U4**, 102
pill [pɪl] Pille; Tablette **II**
pine [paɪn] Kiefer ⟨**III TS3**, 85⟩
pineapple ['paɪnæpl] Ananas **III U3**, 79
pink [pɪŋk] pink; rosa **I**
pipe [paɪp] Pfeife; Rohr; Rohrleitung **II**
clay **pipe** ['kleɪ paɪp] Tonpfeife **II**
pitch [pɪtʃ] Spielfeld; Platz **II**
pizza ['pi:tsə] Pizza **I**
place [pleɪs] Ort; Stelle; Platz **I**
hiding **place** ['haɪdɪŋ ˌpleɪs] Versteck ⟨**III TS1**, 33⟩
starting **place** ['stɑ:tɪŋ pleɪs] Startpunkt **II**
*to take **place** [ˌteɪk 'pleɪs] stattfinden **I**
to **place** [pleɪs] legen **II**
placemat ['pleɪsmæt] Placemat; Platzdeckchen **I**
plan [plæn] Plan; Entwurf **I**
to **plan** [plæn] planen **I**
plane [pleɪn] Flugzeug **III U4**, 92
planet ['plænɪt] Planet **II**
planner ['plænə] Handbuch; Kalender **I**
plaster cast ['plɑ:stə kɑ:st] Gipsverband **III U3**, 76
plate [pleɪt] Teller **III AC1**, 34
platform ['plætfɔ:m] Plattform; Bahnsteig **II**
play [pleɪ] Theaterstück **III U3**, 66
fair **play** [feə 'pleɪ] Fairplay **III TS1**, 28
play on words [ˌpleɪ‿ɒn 'wɜ:dz] Wortspiel **III TS1**, 32
role **play** ['rəʊl ˌpleɪ] Rollenspiel **I**
to **play** [pleɪ] spielen **I**
to **play** a trick (on) [ˌpleɪ‿ə 'trɪk‿ɒn] einen Streich spielen **I**
to **play** bowls [ˌpleɪ 'bəʊlz] Bowling spielen **III U3**, 68
player ['pleɪə] Spieler/-in; Mitspieler/-in **II**
Please. [pli:z] Bitte. **I**
plot [plɒt] Handlung **III TS3**, 84
to **pluck** [plʌk] zupfen ⟨**III TS1**, 29⟩
plumber ['plʌmə] Installateur/-in; Klempner/-in **II**
plumbing ['plʌmɪŋ] Sanitärarbeit **II**
plural ['plʊərəl] Plural; Mehrzahl **I**
poacher ['pəʊtʃə] Wilderer ⟨**III TS2**, 60⟩
poaching *(no pl)* ['pəʊtʃɪŋ] Wilderei **III TS2**, 60
pocket ['pɒkɪt] Tasche; Hosentasche **III U2**, 48
pocket money ['pɒkɪt ˌmʌni] Taschengeld **I**
poem ['pəʊɪm] Gedicht **I**
a **poem** which … [ə ˌpəʊɪm 'wɪtʃ] ein Gedicht, das … °**III TS1**, 29
point [pɔɪnt] Punkt; Zeitpunkt **II**
*to have a **point** [ˌhæv‿ə 'pɔɪnt] nicht ganz Unrecht haben **III U1**, 18
point of view [ˌpɔɪnt‿əv 'vju:] Standpunkt; Ansicht; Perspektive **II**
to the **point** [tə ðə 'pɔɪnt] prägnant; treffend **III AC2**, 63
turning **point** ['tɜ:nɪŋ ˌpɔɪnt] Wendepunkt °**III U1**, 22
to **point** at sb/sth ['pɔɪnt æt] mit dem Finger auf jmdn./etw. zeigen **III AC3**, 90
police [pə'li:s] Polizei **II**
polite [pə'laɪt] höflich **I**
Be **polite**. [bi: pə'laɪt] Sei/Seid höflich. **I**
pollution [pə'lu:ʃn] Verschmutzung **II**
pony ['pəʊni] Pony **I**
pony trekking ['pəʊni ˌtrekɪŋ] Ponyreiten im Gelände **II**
swimming **pool** ['swɪmɪŋ ˌpu:l] Swimmingpool; Schwimmbecken **III TS3**, 87
the **poor** [ðə pʊə] die Armen **II**
poor [pɔ:; pʊə] arm **III U1**, 21
pop star ['pɒp ˌstɑ:] Popstar **III U1**, 17
poppy ['pɒpi] Mohnblume ⟨**III TS1**, 29⟩
popular ['pɒpjələ] beliebt; populär **I**
positive ['pɒzətɪv] positiv **II**
possessive form [pəˌsesɪv 'fɔ:m] Possessivform **I**
possible ['pɒsəbl] möglich **I**
post [pəʊst] Post *(Eintrag im Internet)* **I**
to **post** [pəʊst] online stellen; posten **II**
postcard ['pəʊstkɑ:d] Postkarte **II**
poster ['pəʊstə] Poster **I**
postman ['pəʊstmən] Briefträger **II**
potato [pə'teɪtəʊ], **potatoes** [pə'teɪtəʊz] *(pl)* Kartoffel **III U2**, 42
mashed **potatoes** *(pl)* [ˌmæʃt pə'teɪtəʊz] Kartoffelpüree **III U2**, 42
pound (£) [paʊnd] Pfund *(brit. Währungseinheit)* **I**
to **pour** [pɔ:] einschenken; eingießen; schütten **I**
power [paʊə] Kraft; Macht; Stärke **II**
power cut ['paʊə ˌkʌt] Stromausfall **II**
those in **power** [ˌðəʊz ɪn 'paʊə] die Regierenden; die Herrschenden **III TS2**, 60
powerful ['paʊəfl] stark; mächtig **II**
practical ['præktɪkl] praktisch **II**
practice ['præktɪs] Training; Übung **III U1**, 8
to **practise** ['præktɪs] üben; trainieren **I**
practising ['præktɪsɪŋ] Üben **I**
to **pray** [preɪ] beten **III TS3**, 87
to **preach** [pri:tʃ] predigen ⟨**III TS4**, 112⟩
prediction [prɪ'dɪkʃn] Vorhersage; Voraussage **II**
prehistoric [ˌpri:hɪ'stɒrɪk] vorgeschichtlich **II**
to **prepare** [prɪ'peə] vorbereiten; zubereiten **I**
preposition [ˌprepə'zɪʃn] Präposition **I**
pre-reading [ˌpri:'ri:dɪŋ] vor dem Lesen **I**
prescription [prɪ'skrɪpʃn] Rezept *(für Arzneimittel)* **II**
present ['preznt] Geschenk **I**
present ['preznt] Gegenwart; Präsens **II**
present perfect [ˌpreznt 'pɜ:fɪkt] das Perfekt **II**
present perfect progressive [ˌpreznt ˌpɜ:fɪkt prə'gresɪv] Verlaufsform des Perfekts °**III U2**, 39
present progressive [ˌpreznt prə'gresɪv] Verlaufsform des Präsens/der Gegenwart **I**
simple **present** [ˌsɪmpl 'preznt] Gegenwart; Präsens **I**
to **present** [prɪ'zent] präsentieren; vorstellen **I**
present ['preznt] heutig; Gegenwarts- **III U2**, 46
presentation [ˌprezn'teɪʃn] Präsentation; Vortrag **I**
presenter [prɪ'zentə] Moderator/-in **I**
to **press** [pres] drücken; pressen **II**
pressure ['preʃə] Druck ⟨**III U1**, 13⟩
peer **pressure** ['pɪə ˌpreʃə] Gruppenzwang **III U1**, 22
to **pretend** [prɪ'tend] vortäuschen; tun als ob **III U4**, 103
pretty ['prɪti] hübsch **III U1**, 21
price [praɪs] Preis **I**
primary school ['praɪmri ˌsku:l] Grundschule **I**
print [prɪnt] gedruckt; Druck- **II**
prison ['prɪzn] Gefängnis **II**
private detective [ˌpraɪvət dɪ'tektɪv] Privatdetektiv/-in **II**
prize [praɪz] Preis; Gewinn **I**
pro [prəʊ] Argument dafür **II**
probably ['prɒbəbli] möglicherweise; wahrscheinlich **II**
problem ['prɒbləm] Problem; Schwierigkeit **I**
to **produce** [prə'dju:s] herstellen; produzieren **III U2**, 39
production [prə'dʌkʃn] Produktion; Inszenierung °**III TS4**, 106
profile ['prəʊfaɪl] Profil; Porträt **I**
programme ['prəʊgræm] Programm; Sendung **II**
in **progress** [ɪn 'prəʊgres] im Verlauf °**III U2**, 44
past **progressive** [ˌpɑ:st prə'gresɪv] Verlaufsform der Vergangenheit °**III U2**, 45
present perfect **progressive** [ˌpreznt ˌpɜ:fɪkt prə'gresɪv] Verlaufsform des Perfekts °**III U2**, 39
present **progressive** [ˌpreznt prə'gresɪv] Verlaufsform des Präsens/der Gegenwart **I**
project ['prɒdʒekt] Projekt **I**
to **promise** ['prɒmɪs] versprechen **II**
prompt [prɒmpt] Stichwort °**III U3**, 71
object **pronoun** [ˌɒbdʒɪkt 'prəʊnaʊn] Objektpronomen °**III U1**, 15
reflexive **pronoun** [rɪˌfleksɪv 'prəʊnaʊn] Reflexivpronomen °**III U1**, 14
relative **pronoun** [ˌrelətɪv 'prəʊnaʊn] Relativpronomen °**III U3**, 73
pronunciation [prəˌnʌnsi'eɪʃn] Aussprache **I**
prop [prɒp] Requisite **II**
protagonist [prəʊ'tægənɪst] Protagonist/-in; Hauptfigur **III TS4**, 106

to **protect** [prə'tekt] schützen **II**
protest ['prəʊtest] Protest **III TS2**, 60
proud (of) ['praʊd‿əv] stolz (auf) **II**
public ['pʌblɪk] öffentlich **II**
public transport *(no pl)* [ˌpʌblɪk 'trænspɔ:t] öffentliche Verkehrsmittel **II**
pudding ['pʊdɪŋ] Pudding; Nachtisch **I**
to **pull** [pʊl] ziehen **I**
to **pull** down [ˌpʊl‿'daʊn] abreißen **III U2**, 41
purple ['pɜ:pl] violett; lila **I**
purpose ['pɜ:pəs] Ziel; Absicht; Zweck **III U4**, 97
to **push** [pʊʃ] stoßen; schieben; schubsen **II**
to **push** oneself ['pʊʃ wʌnˌself] sich alles abverlangen; sich Mühe geben **III U1**, 14
pushy ['pʊʃi] aufdringlich; penetrant; aggressiv **III TS4**, 109
*to **put** [pʊt] setzen; stellen; legen **I**
Put in … [ˌpʊt‿'ɪn] Setze/Setzt ein … **I**
Put it in … [ˌpʊt‿ɪt‿'ɪn] Lege/Legt es in …; Stelle/Stellt es in … **I**
*to **put** on [ˌpʊt‿'ɒn] anziehen **III U1**, 20
*to **put** through [ˌpʊt‿'θru:] verbinden **I**
Put … face down. [pʊt ˌfeɪs 'daʊn] Lege/Legt … umgedreht hin. **I**
puzzle ['pʌzl] Rätsel; Puzzle **I**
pyjamas *(pl)* [pɪ'dʒɑ:məz] Schlafanzug; Pyjama **II**

Q

quality ['kwɒləti] Qualität **I**
quarter past/to ['kwɔ:tə pɑ:st/tə] Viertel nach/vor **I**
queen [kwi:n] Königin **II**
question ['kwestʃən] Frage **I**
questions that … [ˌkwestʃənz 'ðæt] Fragen, die … °**III TS2**, 56
questionnaire [ˌkwestʃə'neə] Fragebogen °**III U1**, 19
queue [kju:] Schlange; Warteschlange **I**
to jump the **queue** [ˌdʒʌmp ðə 'kju:] sich vordrängeln **I**
quick [kwɪk] schnell **I**
quiet [kwaɪət] still; ruhig; leise **I**
quill [kwɪl] Federkiel **III U3**, 71
quite [kwaɪt] ziemlich; ganz; völlig **III U3**, 72
quite a ['kwaɪt‿ə] ein/-e wirkliche/-r/-s; ein/-e ziemliche/-r/-s ⟨**III TS1**, 33⟩
quiz [kwɪz] Quiz; Rätsel **I**
quote [kwəʊt] Zitat **II**

R

rabbit ['ræbɪt] Kaninchen **I**
race [reɪs] Wettlauf; Rennen **II**
camel **racing** ['kæml ˌreɪsɪŋ] Kamelrennen **II**
racquet ['rækɪt] Schläger **II**
radio ['reɪdiəʊ] Radio **II**
rain [reɪn] Regen **III U4**, 103
to **rain** [reɪn] regnen **II**
rainbow ['reɪnbəʊ] Regenbogen **III TS1**, 29
raincoat ['reɪnkəʊt] Regenmantel **III U2**, 42
to **raise** money [ˌreɪz 'mʌni] Geld sammeln **II**
rap [ræp] Rap **I**
to **rap** [ræp] rappen **I**
rat [ræt] Ratte **I**
I'd **rather** [aɪd 'rɑ:ðə] ich würde lieber **III U3**, 79
raven ['reɪvn] Rabe **II**
RE *(= Religious Education)* [ˌɑ:r'i:; rɪˌlɪdʒəs‿edʒʊ'keɪʃn] Religion *(Schulfach)* **II**
to **reach** [ri:tʃ] erreichen; dran kommen **II**
to **react** [ri'ækt] reagieren **III U1**, 23
reaction [ri'ækʃn] Reaktion **II**
*to **read** [ri:d] lesen **I**
*to **read** out loud [ˌri:d/sɪŋ‿aʊt 'laʊd] laut vorsingen **III TS1**, 29
reader ['ri:də] Leser/-in **I**
*to draw the **reader** into the story/action [ˌdrɔ: ðə ˌri:də ɪntə ðə 'stɔ:ri/'ækʃn] den Leser/die Leserin in die Geschichte/ Handlung hineinziehen °**III TS3**, 86
reading ['ri:dɪŋ] Lesen **I**
ready ['redi] fertig; bereit **III TS2**, 57
ready meal [ˌredi 'mi:l] Fertiggericht **I**
real [rɪəl] echt; richtig; wirklich **II**
to **realise** ['rɪəlaɪz] erkennen; realisieren **III U2**, 48
realistic [ˌrɪə'lɪstɪk] realistisch **II**
really ['rɪəli] wirklich **I**
reason ['ri:zn] Grund **II**
*to **rebuild** [ˌri:'bɪld] wieder aufbauen **III U3**, 71
to **receive** [rɪ'si:v] empfangen; erhalten; bekommen **II**
recipe ['resɪpi] Rezept **III TS2**, 56
to **recite** [rɪ'saɪt] vortragen; rezitieren °**III TS1**, 29
to **record** [rɪ'kɔ:d] aufnehmen; aufzeichnen **II**
recorder [rɪ'kɔ:də] Flöte **III U1**, 14
recording [rɪ'kɔ:dɪŋ] Aufnahme; Aufzeichnung **I**
recording studio [rɪ'kɔ:dɪŋ ˌstju:diəʊ] Aufnahmestudio; Tonstudio **I**
to **recycle** [ˌri:'saɪkl] recyceln; wiederverwerten **II**
red [red] rot **I**
reference article ['refrns ˌɑ:tɪkl] Referenzartikel **III TS2**, 56
referendum [ˌrefr'endəm] Referendum; Volksentscheid **III U2**, 37
reflexive [rɪ'fleksɪv] reflexiv; Reflexiv- °**III U1**, 15
reflexive pronoun [rɪˌfleksɪv 'prəʊnaʊn] Reflexivpronomen °**III U1**, 14
refugee [ˌrefjʊ'dʒi:] Flüchtling **III U4**, 104
region ['ri:dʒn] Region; Gegend **II**
registration [ˌredʒɪs'treɪʃn] Anwesenheitskontrolle **II**
regular ['regjələ] regelmäßig; gleichmäßig **I**
to **rehearse** [rɪ'hɜ:s] proben °**III AC1**, 35
reign [reɪn] Herrschaft; Regierungszeit **III U3**, 70
to **reign** [reɪn] herrschen; regieren **III U3**, 71
to **relate** to [rɪ'leɪt tə] Zugang finden zu °**III TS3**, 84
relationship [rɪ'leɪʃnʃɪp] Beziehung **II**
defining **relative** clause [dɪˌfaɪnɪŋ 'relətɪv ˌklɔ:z] notwendiger Relativsatz °**III U3**, 72
relative pronoun [ˌrelətɪv 'prəʊnaʊn] Relativpronomen °**III U3**, 73
to **relax** [rɪ'læks] sich entspannen; sich ausruhen; sich beruhigen **II**
release [rɪ'li:s] Freigabe; Freisetzung; *hier:* Aussetzen ⟨**III TS2**, 57⟩
to **release** [rɪ'li:s] loslassen ⟨**III U1**, 13⟩; *hier:* freilassen ⟨**III TS2**, 57⟩
religious [rɪ'lɪdʒəs] religiös; gläubig **I**
to **rely** (on) [rɪ'laɪ‿ɒn] sich verlassen (auf); vertrauen (auf) **III U1**, 10
to **remain** [rɪ'meɪn] bleiben ⟨**III U2**, 40⟩
to **remember** [rɪ'membə] sich erinnern (an); sich merken; denken an **I**
to **remind** (sb of sth/sb) [rɪ'maɪnd əv] (jmdn. an etw./jmdn.) erinnern **III TS1**, 31
to **remove** [rɪ'mu:v] entfernen ⟨**III TS2**, 60⟩
to **rent** (out) [ˌrent‿'aʊt] mieten **III U2**, 47
to **repeat** [rɪ'pi:t] wiederholen **III TS1**, 31
repetition [ˌrepɪ'tɪʃn] Wiederholung °**III U4**, 99
reply [rɪ'plaɪ] Antwort; Erwiderung; Entgegnung **I**
to **reply** [rɪ'plaɪ] antworten; erwidern; entgegnen **I**
report [rɪ'pɔ:t] Bericht; Meldung **II**
news **report** ['nju:z rɪˌpɔ:t] Tatsachenbericht; Nachrichtenbeitrag; Meldung **III TS2**, 56
travel **report** [ˌtrævl rɪ'pɔ:t] Reisebericht **II**
to **report** [rɪ'pɔ:t] berichten; melden **II**; wiedergeben °**III U4**, 93
reporter [rɪ'pɔ:tə] Reporter/-in **II**
request [rɪ'kwest] Bitte °**III U4**, 93
*to **reread** ['ri:ri:d] noch einmal lesen °**III TS3**, 88
rescue ['reskju:] Rettung **II**
to **rescue** ['reskju:] retten **III TS2**, 59
research *(no pl)* [rɪ'sɜ:tʃ] Recherche; Forschung; Untersuchung °**III U2**, 47
responsible [rɪs'pɒnsəbl] verantwortlich; verantwortungsvoll **III U4**, 102
the **rest** [rest] der Rest **I**
restaurant ['restrɒnt] Restaurant; Gaststätte **I**
result [rɪ'zʌlt] Ergebnis; Resultat **II**
*to **retell** [ˌri:'tel] nacherzählen; nochmals erzählen **I**
return ticket [rɪ'tɜ:n ˌtɪkɪt] Hin- und Rückfahrkarte **II**
to **return** [rɪ'tɜ:n] zurückkehren; zurückfahren **II**
revision [rɪ'vɪʒn] Wiederholung **II**

*to **rewrite** [ˌriː'raɪt] umschreiben; neu schreiben °**III TS1**, 30
rhino ['raɪnəʊ] Rhinozeros; Nashorn **III TS2**, 60
rhinos that ... [ˌraɪnəʊz 'ðæt] Nashörner, die ... °**III TS2**, 60
rhyme [raɪm] Reim **I**
rhyme scheme ['raɪm skiːm] Reimschema °**III TS1**, 29
to **rhyme** [raɪm] (sich) reimen **III TS1**, 28
rhyming ['raɪmɪŋ] sich reimend °**III TS1**, 29
rhythm ['rɪðm] Rhythmus **I**
the **rich** [ðə rɪtʃ] die Reichen **II**
rich [rɪtʃ] reich **III U1**, 10
right [raɪt] richtig; korrekt; rechts; rechte/-r/-s **I**
*to be **right** [bi 'raɪt] recht haben **I**
*to get **right** [get 'raɪt] richtig beantworten **II**
on the **right** [ɒn ðə 'raɪt] auf der rechten Seite; rechts **I**
right away [ˌraɪt‿ə'weɪ] sofort; gleich **I**
right here [ˌraɪt 'hɪə] genau hier **II**
right now [ˌraɪt 'naʊ] jetzt gleich; sofort; gerade **II**
right [raɪt] direkt **III U3**, 72
ring [rɪŋ] Ring **III U3**, 64
key **ring** ['kiː ˌrɪŋ] Schlüsselbund; Schlüsselanhänger **III U2**, 49
*to **ring** [rɪŋ] klingeln; läuten **I**; anrufen **III TS4**, 112
ice **rink** ['aɪs ˌrɪŋk] Eisbahn; Schlittschuhbahn **I**
*to **rise** [raɪz] sich erheben; aufstehen ⟨**III U2**, 40⟩; steigen **III TS3**, 87
*to **rise** up in one's mind [raɪz‿ʌp ɪn wʌnz 'maɪnd] jmdm. in den Sinn kommen **III TS3**, 87
*to take a **risk** [ˌteɪk‿ə 'rɪsk] ein Risiko eingehen **III TS4**, 108
river ['rɪvə] Fluss **I**
road [rəʊd] Straße **II**
on the **roadside** [ˌɒn ðə 'rəʊdsaɪd] am Straßenrand ⟨**III TS2**, 59⟩
to **roar** [rɔː] dröhnen; brüllen; rauschen **III TS3**, 87
roaring ['rɔːrɪŋ] dröhnend; tosend; donnernd **III TS3**, 87
robber ['rɒbə] Räuber/-in **II**
rock [rɒk] Rock *(Musik)* **III U2**, 48
to **rock** [rɒk] schaukeln **III U4**, 102
rock 'n' roll [ˌrɒk‿ən 'rəʊl] Rock 'n' Roll **II**
rocky ['rɒki] felsig; steinig **II**
role [rəʊl] Rolle **I**
role play ['rəʊl ˌpleɪ] Rollenspiel **I**
to swap **roles** [ˌswɒp 'rəʊlz] Rollen tauschen **I**
bread **roll** ['bred rəʊl] Brötchen **III AC1**, 34
rock 'n' **roll** [ˌrɒk‿ən 'rəʊl] Rock 'n' Roll **II**
to **roll** off [rəʊl] hinunterrollen; herunterrollen **II**
to **roll** one's eyes [ˌrəʊl wʌnz‿'aɪz] die Augen verdrehen **III U3**, 76
Roll two dice. [ˌrəʊl ˌtuː 'daɪs] Würfle/Würfelt mit zwei Würfeln. **I**
Roman ['rəʊmən] Römer/-in; römisch **II**
romance [rə'mæns] Liebesgeschichte; Liebesfilm **III TS3**, 84
Romanian [rʊ'meɪniən] Rumäne/Rumänin; rumänisch; Rumänisch **II**
roof [ruːf] Dach **II**
room [ruːm; rʊm] Zimmer; Raum **I**
chat **room** ['tʃæt rʊm] Chatroom **II**
living **room** ['lɪvɪŋ rʊm] Wohnzimmer **I**
side **room** ['saɪd ˌrʊm] Nebenraum **III U4**, 97
spare **room** [ˌspeə 'rʊm] Gästezimmer ⟨**III TS2**, 57⟩
roommate ['ruːmmeɪt] Zimmergenosse/Zimmergenossin **I**
rope [rəʊp] Seil **III U2**, 49
rose [rəʊz] Rose ⟨**III TS1**, 29⟩
rotary phone ['rəʊtri fəʊn] Telefon mit Wählscheibe **III U2**, 51
rough [rʌf] rau; derb; grob ⟨**III TS4**, 107⟩
round [raʊnd] Runde **II**
round of boxing [ˌraʊnd‿əv 'bɒksɪŋ] Boxrunde **II**
the **Round** Table [ðə ˌraʊnd 'teɪbl] die Tafelrunde **II**
round [raʊnd] um ... herum **II**
*to bring **round** [ˌbrɪŋ‿'raʊnd] mitbringen ⟨**III TS4**, 112⟩
*to go **round** in circles [gəʊ ˌraʊnd ɪn 'sɜːklz] sich im Kreis drehen **III U2**, 48
to turn **round** [ˌtɜːn‿(ə)'raʊnd] (sich) umdrehen; wenden **II**
route [ruːt] Strecke; Route **II**
routine [ruː'tiːn] Routine **III U4**, 102
royal ['rɔɪəl] königlich **I**
rubber ['rʌbə] Radiergummi **I**
rubbish ['rʌbɪʃ] Müll; Gerümpel **I**
rude [ruːd] unhöflich; unverschämt **I**
rugby ['rʌgbi] Rugby **II**
to **ruin** ['ruːɪn] ruinieren; zerstören **II**
rule [ruːl] Regel **I**
to **rule** [ruːl] herrschen; regieren **II**
ruler ['ruːlə] Lineal **I**
run [rʌn] Rennen; Lauf **II**
run area ['rʌn ˌeəriə] Gehege; Auslauf **III TS2**, 57
*to **run** [rʌn] rennen; laufen **I**
*to **run** away [ˌrʌn‿ə'weɪ] wegrennen **I**
runner ['rʌnə] Läufer/-in **II**
running ['rʌnɪŋ] Laufen; Rennen **II**

S

sad [sæd] traurig **I**
safe [seɪf] sicher; ungefährlich **II**
to **sail** [seɪl] segeln; umsegeln **III TS1**, 31
sailboat ['seɪlbəʊt] Segelboot **II**
sailor ['seɪlə] Seemann; Matrose **I**
salad ['sæləd] Salat **I**
sale [seɪl] Verkauf **II**
the **same** [ðə 'seɪm] der-/die-/dasselbe; der/die/das gleiche **I**
the **same** way as [ˌðə seɪm 'weɪ æz] genauso wie **II**
sandal ['sændl] Sandale **III U3**, 66
sandwich ['sænwɪdʒ] Sandwich; belegtes Brot **I**
sandy ['sændi] sandig; Sand- **II**
Saturday ['sætədeɪ] Samstag **I**
sauce [sɔːs] Soße **III U2**, 42
sausage ['sɒsɪdʒ] Wurst; Bratwurst **III AC1**, 34
to **save** [seɪv] retten; bergen **I**; sparen **II**
saved by the bell [ˌseɪvd baɪ ðə 'bel] noch mal Glück gehabt **III U1**, 14
sax ['sæks] Saxofon **I**
saxophone ['sæksəfəʊn] Saxofon **I**
*to **say** [seɪ] sagen; aufsagen; sprechen **I**
*to **say** hello (to) [ˌseɪ hel'əʊ tə] grüßen; Grüße ausrichten (an) **I**
saying ['seɪɪŋ] Redensart; Sprichwort **III U1**, 8
to **scan** [skæn] scannen; nach Details durchsuchen **II**
*to be **scared** (of) [biː 'skeəd‿əv] Angst haben (vor) **I**
scary ['skeəri] unheimlich; gruselig; beängstigend **II**
scene [siːn] Szene **I**; Schauplatz **II**
acting a **scene** [ˌæktɪŋ‿ə 'siːn] eine Theaterszene spielen **I**
scented ['sentɪd] duftend; parfümiert ⟨**III TS3**, 85⟩
rhyme **scheme** ['raɪm skiːm] Reimschema °**III TS1**, 29
school [skuːl] Schule **I**
grammar **school** ['græmə ˌskuːl] Gymnasium **II**
primary **school** ['praɪmri ˌskuːl] Grundschule **I**
school fees *(pl)* ['skuːl fiːz] Schulgeld; Schulgebühren **III U3**, 79
schoolbag ['skuːlbæg] Schultasche **I**
schoolwork ['skuːlwɜːk] Schularbeiten **III TS4**, 110
Science [saɪəns] Naturwissenschaften **II**
science fiction [ˌsaɪəns 'fɪkʃn] Science-Fiction *(Zukunftsdichtung)* **II**
scientist ['saɪəntɪst] Wissenschaftler/-in **III U2**, 42
score [skɔː] Punktestand; Spielstand **II**
Scot [skɒt] Schotte/Schottin **III U2**, 42
Scottish ['skɒtɪʃ] schottisch **II**
gorge **scrambling** ['gɔːdʒ ˌskræmblɪŋ] Schluchtenklettern **II**
to **scream** [skriːm] schreien; kreischen **II**
script [skrɪpt] Drehbuch; Skript **III AC2**, 63
sea [siː] Meer **I**
search [sɜːtʃ] Suche; Such- **II**

to search for ['sɜ:tʃ fə] suchen (nach) **III U4**, 98
seasick ['si:sɪk] seekrank **III U4**, 92
seat [si:t] Sitz; Sitzplatz **III U3**, 73
second ['seknd] zweite/-r/-s **I**
secret ['si:krət] Geheimnis **II**
in **secret** [ɪn 'si:krət] heimlich **II**
secret ['si:krət] geheim **III U3**, 75
section ['sekʃn] Abschnitt; Paragraf **II**
security [sɪ'kjʊərəti] Sicherheit; Schutz; Wachdienst **III U4**, 97
*to **see** [si:] sehen **I**
See you! ['si: jə] Bis dann!; Bis ... **I**
Wait and **see**! [ˌweɪt‿ənd 'si:] Warte ab! **I**
to **seem** [si:m] scheinen **III U1**, 19
self [self], **selves** [selvz] *(pl)* das Selbst **III U1**, 9
self-critical ['selfˌkrɪtɪkl] selbstkritisch **II**
self-evaluation [ˌselfɪˌvælju'eɪʃn] Selbsteinschätzung **I**
selfie ['selfi] Selfie **II**
*to **sell** [sel] verkaufen **I**
seller ['selə] Verkäufer/-in *(auf einem Flohmarkt)* **I**
*to **send** [send] schicken; senden **I**
*to **send** off [send‿'ɒf] abschicken **II**
sense [sens] Sinn **III TS3**, 86
sense of humour *(no pl)* [ˌsens‿əv 'hju:mə] Sinn für Humor **III U1**, 23
sensible ['sensɪbl] vernünftig **III TS4**, 108
sentence ['sentəns] Satz **I**
separate ['seprət] separat; getrennt; verschieden **II**
September [sep'tembə] September **I**
sequel ['si:kwl] Fortsetzung; Folge **II**
sequence ['si:kwəns] Sequenz; Szene °**III U3**, 79
series ['sɪəri:z], **series** ['sɪəri:z] *(pl)* Serie **III TS3**, 84
serious ['sɪəriəs] ernsthaft; ernst **I**
*to take sth **seriously** [ˌteɪk 'sɪəriəsli] etw. ernst nehmen **II**
set [set] Umgebung; Rahmen **II**; Aufnahmeort; Drehort **III U3**, 76
a **set** of [ə 'set‿əv] eine Liste von °**III TS2**, 61
*to be **set** (in) [bi 'set ɪn] spielen (in); seinen Schauplatz haben (in) **III U4**, 105
*to **set** off [ˌset'ɒf] *hier:* ein Feuerwerk zünden **III U2**, 41
*to **set** up [ˌset‿'ʌp] einrichten; aufbauen **I**
setting ['setɪŋ] Schauplatz; Rahmen **II**
account **settings** [ə'kaʊnt ˌsetɪŋz] Profileinstellungen **III U1**, 23
seven ['sevn] sieben **I**
several ['sevrl] einige; mehrere; verschiedene **III U2**, 40
shadow ['ʃædəʊ] Schatten **III TS3**, 85
to **share** [ʃeə] teilen **II**
shark [ʃɑ:k] Hai **III U4**, 102
sharp [ʃɑ:p] scharf; schneidend **III TS3**, 86
she [ʃi:] sie **I**
shed [ʃed] Schuppen; Stall; Gartenhäuschen ⟨**III TS2**, 57⟩
sheep [ʃi:p], **sheep** [ʃi:p] *(pl)* Schaf **II**
sheet [ʃi:t] Blatt ⟨**III TS2**, 57⟩
animal **shelter** ['ænɪml ˌʃeltə] Tierheim **III TS2**, 59
shimmer ['ʃɪmə] Schimmer; Schimmern ⟨**III TS3**, 87⟩
shinty ['ʃɪnti] Shinty *(eine Art Hockey)* **III U2**, 39
ship [ʃɪp] Schiff **I**
shipbuilding ['ʃɪpbɪldɪŋ] Schiffsbau **III U2**, 41
shock [ʃɒk] Schock **II**
shocked [ʃɒkt] schockiert; geschockt **III TS4**, 113
shoe [ʃu:] Schuh **I**
*to be in sb's **shoes** [ˌbi: ɪn sʌmbɒdɪz 'ʃu:z] an jmds. Stelle sein; in jmds. Haut stecken **III TS3**, 86
in Jay's **shoes** [ɪn dʒeɪz 'ʃu:z] an Jays Stelle **III U1**, 12
photo **shoot** ['fəʊtəʊ ˌʃu:t] Fotoshooting; Fotoaufnahmen **III U3**, 74
*to **shoot** [ʃu:t‿(ət)] schießen (auf) **III TS1**, 30
shop [ʃɒp] Geschäft; Laden **I**
charity **shop** ['tʃærɪti ʃɒp] Second-Hand-Laden **I**
pawn **shop** ['pɔ:n ʃɒp] Pfandhaus; Pfandleihe **III U3**, 79
shopping ['ʃɒpɪŋ] Einkaufen; Einkäufe **I**
*to do the **shopping** [ˌdu: ðə 'ʃɒpɪŋ] Einkäufe machen; Besorgungen machen **III U2**, 51
*to go **shopping** [ˌgəʊ 'ʃɒpɪŋ] einkaufen gehen **I**
shore [ʃɔ:] Ufer; Küste **II**
short [ʃɔ:t] kurz **I**
short answer [ˌʃɔ:t‿'ɑ:nsə] Kurzantwort **I**
short form ['ʃɔ:t fɔ:m] Kurzform **I**
shorts *(pl)* [ʃɔ:ts] Shorts; kurze Hose **III U1**, 17
shot [ʃɒt] Einstellung; Kameraeinstellung **II**; Aufnahme **III U3**, 76
should [ʃʊd] sollte; solltest; sollten; solltet **II**
shouldn't ['ʃʊdnt] sollte(n) nicht **II**
shoulder ['ʃəʊldə] Schulter **II**
to **shout** [ʃaʊt] schreien; rufen **I**
show [ʃəʊ] Show; Schau; Aufführung **II**
comedy **show** ['kɒmədi ˌʃəʊ] Comedy Show **II**
living history **show** [ˌlɪvɪŋ 'hɪstəri ˌʃəʊ] *Show, in der historischer Alltag nachgespielt wird* **II**
talent **show** ['tælənt ˌʃəʊ] Talentwettbewerb **I**
to **show** [ʃəʊ] zeigen **I**
to **show** off [ʃəʊ‿'ɒf] angeben **II**
shower ['ʃaʊə] Dusche **I**
show-off ['ʃəʊ‿ɒf] Angeber/-in **III U1**, 17
shredded ['ʃredɪd] zerrissen ⟨**III TS2**, 57⟩
to **shudder** ['ʃʌdə] zittern; beben ⟨**III TS3**, 85⟩
to **shuffle** ['ʃʌfl] mischen **II**
shutter ['ʃʌtə] Fensterladen **III U4**, 94
shy [ʃaɪ] schüchtern **II**
sick [sɪk] krank; unwohl **II**
*to be **sick** [bi 'sɪk] sich übergeben **III U1**, 17
*to feel **sick** [ˌfi:l 'sɪk] Übelkeit verspüren; sich schlecht fühlen **II**
side [saɪd] Seite **II**
side room ['saɪd ˌrʊm] Nebenraum **III U4**, 97
sight [saɪt] Sehenswürdigkeit; Anblick **II**; *hier:* Blick **III TS1**, 30
sightseeing ['saɪtsi:ɪŋ] Sightseeing-; Besichtigungs- **II**
sign [saɪn] Zeichen; Schild **II**
a **sign** that ... [ə ˌsaɪn 'ðæt] ein Schild, das ... °**III U2**, 49
signal ['sɪgnl] Signal; Empfang **III U2**, 48
signal word ['sɪgnəl ˌwɜ:d] Signalwort **I**
silence *(no pl)* ['saɪləns] Stille; Schweigen; Ruhe **III TS3**, 87
silent ['saɪlənt] still; ruhig; schweigsam; stumm **III U3**, 72
silk [sɪlk] Seide ⟨**III TS4**, 110⟩
silly ['sɪli] Dummkopf **II**
silly ['sɪli] dumm; doof; albern **I**
silver ['sɪlvə] Silber **II**
similar ['sɪmɪlə] ähnlich **II**
simple ['sɪmpl] einfach; simpel **III TS1**, 30
simple past [ˌsɪmpl 'pɑ:st] Vergangenheitsform **II**
simple present [ˌsɪmpl 'preznt] Gegenwart; Präsens **I**
since *(+ Zeitpunkt)* [sɪns] seit; seitdem **III U2**, 38
*to **sing** [sɪŋ] singen **I**
*to **sing** along [ˌsɪŋ‿ə'lɒŋ] mitsingen **III TS1**, 28
*to **sing** out loud [ˌri:d/sɪŋ‿aʊt 'laʊd] laut vorsingen **III TS1**, 29
singer ['sɪŋə] Sänger/-in **II**
singing [sɪŋɪŋ] Singen; Gesang **III U1**, 23
single ticket ['sɪŋgl ˌtɪkɪt] einfache Fahrkarte **II**
*to **sink** [sɪŋk] untergehen; sinken **III TS3**, 87
Dear **Sir** or Madam [dɪə ˌsɜ:r‿ɔ: 'mædəm] Sehr geehrte Dame, sehr geehrter Herr **II**
sister ['sɪstə] Schwester **I**
half-**sister** ['hɑ:fˌsɪstə] Halbschwester **I**
*to **sit** [sɪt] sitzen **I**
Sit! [sɪt] Sitz! *(Befehl für Hunde)*; Platz! *(Befehl für Hunde)* **I**
*to **sit** down [ˌsɪt 'daʊn] sich hinsetzen; sich setzen **I**
*to **sit** face to face [ˌsɪt feɪs tə ˌfeɪs] sich gegenüber sitzen **I**
site [saɪt] Webseite **II**
situation [ˌsɪtju'eɪʃn] Situation **I**
six [sɪks] sechs **I**
size [saɪz] Größe; Kleidergröße **I**
to **skate** [skeɪt] Inlineskates fahren; Schlittschuh laufen **I**
skateboard ['skeɪtbɔ:d] Skateboard **II**

skateboarding ['skeɪtbɔ:dɪŋ] Skateboardfahren I
skates *(pl)* [skeɪts] Inlineskates; Rollschuhe; Schlittschuhe I
(inline) **skating** ['ɪnlaɪn ˌskeɪtɪŋ] Inlineskatefahren I
skill [skɪl] Fertigkeit; Geschick I
to **skim** [skɪm] überfliegen II
skirt [skɜ:t] Rock II
sky [skaɪ] Himmel III U2, 48
slave [sleɪv] Sklave/Sklavin III U3, 70
sleep [sli:p] Schlaf III U4, 95
*to **sleep** [sli:p] schlafen I
sleepover ['sli:pˌəʊvə] Übernachtung I
to **slice** [slaɪs] in Scheiben schneiden I
slide [slaɪd] Rutschbahn I
water **slide** ['wɔ:tə ˌslaɪd] Wasserrutsche I
slogan ['sləʊgən] Slogan; Werbespruch II
slow [sləʊ] langsam I
to step into a story **slowly** [step‿ˌɪntʊ ə ˌstɔ:ri 'sləʊli] eine Geschichte langsam entwickeln III TS3, 89
small [smɔ:l] klein I
small talk ['smɔ:l ˌtɔ:k] Smalltalk III AC2, 62
smart [smɑ:t] schlau; klug; intelligent III U1, 9
smartcard ['smɑ:tkɑ:d] Chipkarte II
smartphone ['smɑ:tfəʊn] Smartphone II
to **smash** [smæʃ] zerschlagen; zerschmettern III U4, 102
*to **smell** [smel] riechen; duften III U3, 65
smile [smaɪl] Lächeln I
to **smile** [smaɪl] lächeln I
smoke [sməʊk] Rauch III TS3, 85
smoky ['sməʊki] verraucht III U3, 64
smuggler ['smʌglə] Schmuggler/-in III U4, 102
snack [snæk] Snack; Imbiss I
snack bar ['snæk ˌbɑ:] Café; Imbissstube I
word **snake** ['wɜ:d ˌsneɪk] Wortschlange I
to **sneak** around [ˌsni:k‿ə'raʊnd] herumschleichen II
to **snore** [snɔ:] schnarchen I
snow [snəʊ] Schnee III U3, 70
so [səʊ] so; also I
so far [ˌsəʊ 'fɑ:] bis jetzt II
so is ['səʊ ɪz] ebenso wie °III TS1, 29
to **soak** up [səʊk‿'ʌp] aufsaugen III TS2, 57
social network [ˌsəʊʃl 'netwɜ:k] soziales Netzwerk II
society [sə'saɪəti] Verein; Gesellschaft II
sofa ['səʊfə] Sofa; Couch I
soft [sɒft] weich; sanft ⟨III TS1, 33⟩
software manual ['sɒftweə ˌmænjuəl] Softwarehandbuch °III TS2, 61
soil [sɔɪl] Erde; Boden ⟨III TS3, 85⟩
soldier ['səʊldʒə] Soldat/-in III U2, 40
solution [sə'lu:ʃn] Lösung II
to **solve** [sɒlv] lösen II
Somali [sə'mɑ:li] Somali III U4, 103
some [sʌm; səm] einige; ein paar; etwas I
somebody ['sʌmbədi] jemand I
somebody who … [ˌsʌmbədi 'hu:] jemand, der … °III U1, 22
somehow ['sʌmhaʊ] irgendwie ⟨III TS3, 85⟩
someone ['sʌmwʌn] jemand II
something ['sʌmθɪŋ] etwas I
sometimes ['sʌmtaɪmz] manchmal I
somewhere ['sʌmweə] irgendwo II
son [sʌn] Sohn III U2, 38
song [sɒŋ] Song; Lied I
soon [su:n] bald II
as **soon** as [əz 'su:n‿əz] sobald II
Sorry! ['sɒri] Entschuldigung!; Tut mir leid! I
*to be **sorry** [bi: 'sɒri] leid tun I
*to feel **sorry** for [ˌfi:l 'sɒri fɔ:] Mitleid haben mit; bedauern III U1, 23
I'm **sorry**! [ˌaɪm 'sɒri] Tut mir leid! I
sort [sɔ:t] Sorte; Art ⟨III TS4, 110⟩
to **sort** into [sɔ:t 'ɪntʊ] einsortieren; sortieren nach °III AC1, 35
sound [saʊnd] Ton; Geräusch; Klang I
to **sound** [saʊnd] klingen I
soup [su:p] Suppe III U4, 95
source [sɔ:s] Quelle II
south [saʊθ] Süden; Süd- II
South Korean [ˌsaʊθ kə'ri:ən] Südkoreaner/-in; südkoreanisch; Südkoreanisch II
south [saʊθ] südlich; im Süden III U2, 44
south-eastern [ˌsaʊθ'i:stn] südöstlich ⟨III TS2, 59⟩
souvenir [ˌsu:vn'ɪə] Souvenir; Andenken II
space [speɪs] Raum; Fläche; Platz; Ort II
*to leave **space** [li:v 'speɪs] Platz lassen I
spaceship ['speɪsʃɪp] Raumschiff II
Spanish ['spænɪʃ] spanisch; Spanisch; die Spanier III U3, 66
spare room [ˌspeə 'rʊm] Gästezimmer ⟨III TS2, 57⟩
*to **speak** [spi:k] sprechen I
speaker ['spi:kə] Redner/-in; Sprecher/-in I
speaking ['spi:kɪŋ] Sprechen I
spear [spɪə] Speer II
special ['speʃl] besonders; speziell I
special offer [ˌspeʃl‿'ɒfə] Sonderangebot I
with **special** needs [wɪð ˌspeʃl 'ni:dz] behindert II
species ['spi:ʃi:z], **species** ['spi:ʃi:z] *(pl)* Art; Spezies ⟨III TS2, 60⟩
specific [spə'sɪfɪk] spezifisch; speziell III U4, 105
spectacular [spek'tækjələ] spektakulär III U2, 46
speech [spi:tʃ] Rede °III U3, 71
direct **speech** [dɪˌrekt 'spi:tʃ] direkte Rede °III U4, 95
indirect **speech** [ˌɪndɪrekt 'spi:tʃ] indirekte Rede °III U4, 95
speech bubble ['spi:tʃ ˌbʌbl] Sprechblase I
*to **spell** [spel] buchstabieren I
spelling ['spelɪŋ] Rechtschreibung I
*to **spend** [spend] ausgeben *(Geld)* I; verbringen *(Zeit)* II
spider ['spaɪdə] Spinne III U2, 50
*to **spill** [spɪl] verschütten; auslaufen III U4, 94
to **splash** [splæʃ] spritzen; planschen ⟨III TS1, 29⟩
spoken ['spəʊkn] gesprochen II
sponge [spʌndʒ] Rühr-; Biskuit- I
spontaneous [spɒn'teɪniəs] spontan II
spoon [spu:n] Löffel III TS1, 29
sport [spɔ:t] Sport; Sportart I
*to **spread** [spred] (sich) verbreiten ⟨III U1, 13⟩
spring [sprɪŋ] Frühling III TS2, 57
squirrel ['skwɪrəl] Eichhörnchen I
stadium ['steɪdiəm] Stadion II
stage [steɪdʒ] Bühne III U3, 68
stage direction ['steɪdʒ dɪˌrekʃn] Regieanweisung III AC2, 63
to **stage** [steɪdʒ] aufführen III TS4, 106
stairs *(pl)* [steəz] Treppe III U2, 48
*to **stand** [stænd] stehen I
*to **stand** in the way of sb/sth [ˌstænd ɪn ðə 'weɪ‿əv] jmdm./etw. im Weg stehen III AC3, 90
*to **stand** up [ˌstænd‿'ʌp] aufstehen *(von einer Sitzgelegenheit)* I
star [stɑ:] Star; Stern I
pop **star** ['pɒp ˌstɑ:] Popstar III U1, 17
to **stare** [steə] starren; anstarren I
start [stɑ:t] Anfang; Start III U3, 72
to **start** [stɑ:t] anfangen; beginnen; starten I; *hier:* gründen III U2, 42
starting place ['stɑ:tɪŋ pleɪs] Startpunkt II
head of **state** [ˌhed‿əv 'steɪt] Staatsoberhaupt II
statement ['steɪtmənt] Aussage; Behauptung; Erklärung II
station ['steɪʃn] Haltestelle; Bahnhof; Station I; Sender II
bus **station** ['bʌs ˌsteɪʃn] Busbahnhof I
to **stay** [steɪ] bleiben I; übernachten II
to **stay** away from [ˌsteɪ‿ə'weɪ frəm] fernbleiben von; meiden II
to **stay** in touch (with) [ˌsteɪ ɪn 'tʌtʃ wɪð] in Kontakt bleiben (mit) II
to **stay** with ['steɪ wɪð] wohnen bei II
Stay the way you are. [ˌsteɪ ðə weɪ ju 'ɑ:] Bleib wie du bist. III U1, 15
steady ['stedi] kontinuierlich; unaufhörlich III U4, 103
steak [steɪk] Steak I
*to **steal** [sti:l] stehlen II
steam [sti:m] Dampf III U2, 42
steam engine ['sti:m‿endʒɪn] Dampfmaschine III U2, 42
step [step] Stufe; Schritt I
step-by-**step** [ˌstepbaɪ'step] Schritt-für-Schritt- II
steps which … [steps 'wɪtʃ] Schritte, die … °III TS2, 58

to **step** into a story slowly [stepˌɪntʊ ə ˌstɔːri 'sləʊli] eine Geschichte langsam entwickeln **III TS3**, 89
stepmum ['stepmʌm] Stiefmutter **I**
still [stɪl] Standbild **II**
still [stɪl] still **I**
*to keep one's feet or hands **still** [ˌkiːp wʌnz: 'fiːtˌɔː 'hændz stɪl] die Beine und Hände ruhig halten **III TS1**, 32
still [stɪl] noch; immer noch **I**; dennoch **II**
*to **sting** [stɪŋ] stechen **III TS3**, 87
stomach ['stʌmək] Magen; Bauch **II**
stomachache ['stʌməkeɪk] Bauchschmerzen; Bauchweh **II**
stone [stəʊn] Stein; Stein- **III U2**, 48
stop [stɒp] Haltestelle; Halt **II**
to **stop** [stɒp] aufhören (mit); anhalten; stoppen **I**
Stop it! ['stɒpˌɪt] Mach/Macht das aus!; Hör/Hört auf! **I**
storm [stɔːm] Sturm **I**
story ['stɔːri], **stories** ['stɔːriz] *(pl)* Story; Geschichte; Erzählung **I**
photo **story** ['fəʊtəʊ ˌstɔːri] Fotostory; Bildgeschichte **I**
to step into a **story** slowly [stepˌɪntʊ ə ˌstɔːri 'sləʊli] eine Geschichte langsam entwickeln **III TS3**, 89
storyline ['stɔːrilaɪn] Handlung ⟨**III TS3**, 89⟩
straight [streɪt] gerade; direkt; geradewegs **III U4**, 103
straight away [ˌstreɪtˌə'weɪ] sofort; gleich °**III TS2**, 59
straight on [streɪtˌ'ɒn] geradeaus **I**
strange [streɪndʒ] fremd; seltsam; merkwürdig **I**
street [striːt] Straße *(in der Stadt)* **I**
in the **street** [ˌɪn ðə 'striːt] in der Straße; auf der Straße **I**
*to take to the **streets** [ˌteɪk tu ðə 'striːts] auf die Straße gehen ⟨**III TS2**, 60⟩
the high **street** [ðə 'haɪ ˌstriːt] die Haupteinkaufsstraße **III U1**, 20
stress [stres] Betonung °**III TS1**, 29
to **stress** [stres] betonen; hervorheben °**III TS1**, 29
*to be **stressed** out [bi ˌstrestˌ'aʊt] völlig gestresst sein **III U1**, 10
strict [strɪkt] streng; strikt **III TS3**, 86
strong [strɒŋ] stark **II**
structure ['strʌktʃə] Struktur; Aufbau; Gliederung °**III TS1**, 29
*to get **stuck** [ˌget 'stʌk] stecken bleiben ⟨**III TS2**, 57⟩
stuck in the middle of … [ˌstʌk ɪn ðə 'mɪdlˌ əv] mitten in … stecken; feststecken in … **III TS1**, 31
student ['stjuːdnt] Schüler/-in; Student/-in **I**
exchange **student** [ɪks'tʃeɪndʒ ˌstjuːdnt] Austauschschüler/-in **III AC1**, 34
student exchange ['stjuːdnt ɪksˌtʃeɪndʒ] Schüleraustausch **III AC2**, 63

studies *(pl)* ['stʌdiz] Studium; Lernen; Arbeit für die Schule **II**
recording **studio** [rɪ'kɔːdɪŋ ˌstjuːdiəʊ] Aufnahmestudio; Tonstudio **I**
to **study** ['stʌdi] studieren; lernen **III U1**, 10
stuff [stʌf] Zeug **I**
stupid ['stjuːpɪd] dumm; blöd **II**
style [staɪl] Stil **III U4**, 95
subject ['sʌbdʒɪkt] Schulfach **II**; Thema **III U1**, 9; Subjekt; Satzgegenstand °**III U3**, 73
to **succeed** (in) [sək'siːdˌɪn] Erfolg haben (in/bei/mit) **III U1**, 11
success [sək'ses] Erfolg **III U1**, 10
successful [sək'sesfl] erfolgreich **III U1**, 12
such [sʌtʃ] solch; solche/-r/-s **III U1**, 15
such as ['sʌtʃˌəz] (solche) wie; wie (zum Beispiel) ⟨**III TS2**, 57⟩
suddenly ['sʌdnli] plötzlich; auf einmal **I**
sugar ['ʃʊgə] Zucker **III AC1**, 34
to **suggest** [sə'dʒest] vorschlagen **III U4**, 99
suggestion [sə'dʒestʃn] Vorschlag; Anregung **I**
suitcase ['suːtkeɪs] Koffer **III U4**, 93
summary ['sʌmri] Zusammenfassung ⟨**III TS3**, 89⟩; °**III TS4**, 113
summer ['sʌmə] Sommer **II**
summer camp ['sʌmə kæmp] Sommerferienlager **II**
sun [sʌn] Sonne **II**
Sunday ['sʌndeɪ] Sonntag **I**
sunflower ['sʌnflaʊə] Sonnenblume **III TS1**, 29
sunny ['sʌni] sonnig **II**
superlative [suː'pɜːlətɪv] Superlativ **II**
supermarket ['suːpəˌmɑːkɪt] Supermarkt **I**
supernatural ['suːpəˌnætʃrl] übernatürlich **III U4**, 105
superpower ['suːpəˌpaʊə] Supermacht **II**
to **supply** [sə'plaɪ] versorgen **II**
to **support** [sə'pɔːt] unterstützen **III U1**, 10
*to be **supposed** to (do) [bi sə'pəʊzd tə] (tun) sollen ⟨**III TS1**, 31⟩
sure [ʃʊə; ʃɔː] sicher **I**
*to be **sure** [bi 'ʃʊə] sicher sein **II**
*to make **sure** [ˌmeɪk 'ʃɔː] sich versichern **I**
I'm (not) **sure** … [ˌaɪm nɒt 'ʃʊə] Ich bin mir (nicht) sicher … **III AC1**, 35
surface ['sɜːfɪs] Oberfläche ⟨**III TS3**, 87⟩
surfing ['sɜːfɪŋ] Surfen **II**
surgery ['sɜːdʒəri] Arztpraxis; Praxis; Praxisräume **I**
surprise [sə'praɪz] Überraschung **I**
to **surprise** [sə'praɪz] überraschen **II**
*to be **surprised** [bi sə'praɪzd] überrascht sein **II**
surprising [sə'praɪzɪŋ] überraschend **II**
survey ['sɜːveɪ] Umfrage; Studie **I**
to **survive** [sə'vaɪv] überleben **III TS1**, 32
suspense [sə'spens] Spannung **II**
suspicious [sə'spɪʃəs] misstrauisch; argwöhnisch **III U4**, 97

to **swap** roles [ˌswɒp 'rəʊlz] Rollen tauschen **I**
sweet [swiːt] süß **I**
sweets *(pl)* [swiːts] Süßigkeiten; Bonbons **I**
swift [swɪft] schnell ⟨**III TS1**, 30⟩
*to **swim** [swɪm] schwimmen **I**
swimming ['swɪmɪŋ] Schwimmen **I**
*to go **swimming** [ˌgəʊ 'swɪmɪŋ] Schwimmen gehen **I**
swimming pool ['swɪmɪŋ ˌpuːl] Swimmingpool; Schwimmbecken **III TS3**, 87
switch [swɪtʃ] Schalter **III U2**, 51
syllable ['sɪləbl] Silbe °**III TS1**, 29
symbol ['sɪmbl] Symbol **II**

T

table ['teɪbl] Tisch **I**
tablet ['tæblət] Tablet **II**
tae [tə] um zu ⟨**III U2**, 40⟩
tail [teɪl] Schwanz; Schweif **I**
*to **take** [teɪk] nehmen; mitnehmen; wegnehmen; bringen; mitbringen **I**; dauern; (Zeit) brauchen **II**
*to **take** a breath [ˌteɪkˌə 'breθ] Luft holen; Atem holen **III TS3**, 87
*to **take** a message [ˌteɪkˌə 'mesɪdʒ] eine Nachricht entgegennehmen; jmdm. etw. ausrichten **I**
*to **take** a risk [ˌteɪkˌə 'rɪsk] ein Risiko eingehen **III TS4**, 108
*to **take** a test [ˌteɪkˌə 'test] einen Test machen **II**
*to **take** a vote [ˌteɪkˌə 'vəʊt] abstimmen **I**
*to **take** care of sb [ˌteɪkˌ'keərˌəv] sich um jmdn. kümmern; für jmdn. sorgen ⟨**III TS2**, 57⟩
*to **take** care of sb/sth [ˌteɪkˌ'keərˌəv] sich um jmdn./etw. kümmern; für jmdn. sorgen **III U3**, 76
*to **take** notes [ˌteɪk 'nəʊts] sich Notizen machen **I**
*to **take** off [ˌteɪkˌ'ɒf] abnehmen; herunternehmen; ausziehen **I**
*to **take** part (in) [ˌteɪk 'pɑːt ɪn] teilnehmen (an) **II**
*to **take** photos [ˌteɪk 'fəʊtəʊz] fotografieren; Fotos machen **I**
*to **take** place [ˌteɪk 'pleɪs] stattfinden **I**
*to **take** sth seriously [ˌteɪk 'sɪəriəsli] etw. ernst nehmen **II**
*to **take** to the streets [ˌteɪk tu ðə 'striːts] auf die Straße gehen ⟨**III TS2**, 60⟩
*to **take** up [ˌteɪkˌ'ʌp] beanspruchen ⟨**III TS2**, 57⟩
Take turns. [ˌteɪk 'tɜːnz] Wechselt euch ab. **I**
take-off ['teɪkˌɒf] Start; Abheben **III U4**, 99
talent ['tælənt] Talent **I**
talent show ['tælənt ˌʃəʊ] Talentwettbewerb **I**
small **talk** ['smɔːl ˌtɔːk] Smalltalk **III AC2**, 62

to talk [tɔ:k] sprechen; reden **I**
to **talk** about … ['tɔ:k‿əbaʊt] sprechen über; erzählen von **I**
to **talk** to ['tɔ:k tə] reden mit **I**
to **talk** with your mouth full [ˌtɔ:k wɪð jɔ: 'maʊθ fʊl] mit vollem Mund sprechen **III AC3**, 90
talker ['tɔ:kə] Sprecher/-in **III AC2**, 62
talking ['tɔ:kɪŋ] Sprechen **I**
tall [tɔ:l] groß; hoch **II**
to tap [tæp] antippen **II**
target ['tɑ:gɪt] Ziel; Ziel- ⟨**III TS2**, 57⟩
tartan ['tɑ:tn] Schottenkaro *(bestimmtes Muster eines Clans)*; karierter Schottenstoff **III U2**, 37
task [tɑ:sk] Aufgabe; Auftrag **I**
to taste [teɪst] schmecken; probieren **III U3**, 68
tattoo [tæt'u:] Tattoo; Tätowierung **III U1**, 18
taxi ['tæksi] Taxi **II**
tea [ti:] Tee **I**
tea bag ['ti: bæg] Teebeutel **III U3**, 79
*__to teach__ [ti:tʃ] unterrichten; lehren; beibringen **II**
*to **teach** somebody a lesson [ˌti:tʃ‿ə 'lesn] jmdm. eine Lehre/Lektion erteilen **II**
teacher ['ti:tʃə] Lehrer/-in **I**
team [ti:m] Team; Gruppe **II**
to tease sb [ti:z] jmdn. aufziehen; jmdn. hänseln; jmdn. ärgern **III U1**, 22
Technology [tek'nɒlədʒi] Technik; Computerunterricht **II**
technology [tek'nɒlədʒi] Technologie **II**
teen [ti:n] Jugend- **II**; Teenager; Jugendliche/-r **III TS3**, 84
teenage ['ti:neɪdʒ] jugendlich; Jugend- **III TS4**, 107
teenager ['ti:nˌeɪdʒə] Teenager; Jugendliche/-r **I**
telephone ['telɪfəʊn] Telefon **I**
*__to tell__ [tel] erzählen; sagen; mitteilen **I**
I was just **telling** [ˌaɪ wəz dʒʌst 'telɪŋ] ich habe gerade gesagt °**III U1**, 14
to tempt [tempt] in Versuchung führen; reizen **III TS4**, 107
tempted ['temptɪd] in Versuchung gebracht **III TS4**, 107
tempting ['temptɪŋ] verführerisch **III TS4**, 109
ten [ten] zehn **I**
ten times [ten 'taɪmz] zehnmal **I**
tennis ['tenɪs] Tennis **I**
tense [tens] Zeit; Zeitform *(grammatisch)* **II**
term [tɜ:m] Begriff °**III TS4**, 106
terrible ['terəbl] schrecklich; schlimm; furchtbar **III U3**, 72
test [test] Test; Klassenarbeit; Prüfung **I**
*to take a **test** [ˌteɪk‿ə 'test] einen Test machen **II**
to test [test] testen; prüfen **II**
text [tekst] Text **I**
factual **text** [ˌfæktʃʊəl 'tekst] Sachtext °**III TS2**, 56
text (message) ['tekst ˌmesɪdʒ] SMS; Kurznachricht **I**
to text [tekst] eine SMS schicken **II**
than [ðæn] als *(bei Vergleichen)* **II**
more … **than** ['mɔ: ðən] mehr … als **I**
to thank [θæŋk] danken **II**
Thank you. ['θæŋk ju] Danke. **I**
thankful ['θæŋkfl] dankbar **I**
Thanks. [θæŋks] Danke. **I**
that [ðæt] so *(Betonung)* **III AC1**, 35
that much [ðæt 'mʌtʃ] so viel **III AC1**, 35
that [ðæt; ðət] dass **I**
that [ðæt] das; jenes **I**
after **that** [ˌɑ:ftə 'ðæt] danach **I**
like **that** [laɪk 'ðæt] so **I**
That was close! [ˌðæt wəz 'kləʊs] Das war knapp! **I**
that's how [ðæts 'haʊ] so **II**
That's what friends are for. [ˌðæts wɒt 'frendz‿ɑ: ˌfɔ:] Dafür sind Freunde da. **I**
that's why [ðæts 'waɪ] deshalb **II**
That's … [ðæts] Das macht … **I**
that [ðæt] der; die; das; den *(Relativpronomen)* **III U3**, 72
a sign **that** … [ə ˌsaɪn 'ðæt] ein Schild, das … °**III U2**, 49
music **that** … [ˌmju:zɪk 'ðæt] Musik, die … °**III U3**, 67
questions **that** … [ˌkwestʃənz 'ðæt] Fragen, die … °**III TS2**, 56
rhinos **that** … [ˌraɪnəʊz 'ðæt] Nashörner, die … °**III TS2**, 60
the [ðə; ði] der; die *(auch Pl.)*; das **I**
the others [ði‿'ʌðəz] die anderen **I**
the same [ðə 'seɪm] der-/die-/dasselbe; der/die/das gleiche **I**
the … **the** [ðə … ðə] je … desto **II**
theatre ['θɪətə] Theater **I**
their [ðeə] ihr/-e *(Pl.)* **I**
their fault [ˌdeə 'fɔ:lt] ihre Schuld ⟨**III TS4**, 112⟩
them [ðem] sie *(Pl.)*; ihnen **I**
theme [θi:m] Thema; Motto **I**
then [ðen] dann; danach **I**
back **then** [bæk 'ðen] damals **III U3**, 64
there [ðeə] da; dort; dahin; dorthin **I**
there is/are [ðər‿'ɪz/'ɑ:] da ist/sind; es gibt **I**
There's no need to … [ˌðeəz nəʊ 'ni:d tə] Es gibt keinen Grund zu … **III TS4**, 112
these [ði:z] diese (hier) **I**
these days [ˌði:z 'deɪz] zurzeit **III U1**, 20
they [ðeɪ] sie *(Pl.)* **I**
It's …/**They**'re … [ɪts/ðeə] Es kostet …/ Sie kosten … **I**
thick [θɪk] dick *(nicht für Personen)* **III U2**, 48
thing [θɪŋ] Ding; Sache **I**
*__to think__ [θɪŋk] denken; nachdenken; glauben **I**
*to **think** of ['θɪŋk‿əv] halten von; denken über **I**; (sich) ausdenken; sich etwas einfallen lassen **II**
Think of … ['θɪŋk‿əv] Denke/Denkt an … **I**
excellent piece of quick thinking [ˌekslnt pi:s‿əv kwɪk 'θɪŋkɪŋ] ausgezeichnete Reaktionsschnelligkeit ⟨**III TS4**, 112⟩
third [θɜ:d] dritte/-r/-s **I**
third person narrator [ˌθɜ:d ˌpɜ:sn nə'reɪtə] Er/Sie-Erzähler/-in °**III TS3**, 85
thirsty ['θɜ:sti] durstig **III TS2**, 59
thirteen [ˌθɜ:'ti:n] dreizehn **I**
this [ðɪs] dies; diese/-r/-s **I**
this afternoon [ðɪs 'ɑ:ftənu:n] heute Nachmittag **II**
this early ['ðɪs ˌɜ:li] so früh **III AC1**, 35
This is … ['ðɪs‿ɪz] Das (hier) ist … **I**
thistle ['θɪsl] Distel **III U2**, 37
those [ðəʊz] diese dort; jene **I**
those in power [ˌðəʊz ɪn 'paʊə] die Regierenden; die Herrschenden **III TS2**, 60
even though [ˌi:vn 'ðəʊ] auch wenn; obwohl ⟨**III TS3**, 87⟩
thought [θɔ:t] Gedanke **II**
thousands of ['θaʊzndz‿əv] tausende (von) **I**
three [θri:] drei **I**
through [θru:] durch **I**
*__to throw (at)__ [θrəʊ] werfen (nach) **I**
*to **throw** away [ˌθrəʊ‿ə'weɪ] wegwerfen **I**
thunder *(no pl)* ['θʌndə] Donner **II**
Thursday ['θɜ:zdeɪ] Donnerstag **I**
to tick [tɪk] abhaken **II**
ticket ['tɪkɪt] Los; Ticket; Eintrittskarte **I**; Fahrschein **II**
one-way **ticket** ['wʌnweɪ ˌtɪkɪt] einfache Fahrkarte **II**
return **ticket** [rɪ'tɜ:n ˌtɪkɪt] Hin- und Rückfahrkarte **II**
single **ticket** ['sɪŋgl ˌtɪkɪt] einfache Fahrkarte **II**
ticket office ['tɪkɪt ˌɒfɪs] Kartenschalter **III U2**, 48
high tide ['haɪ ˌtaɪd] Flut **II**
low tide ['ləʊ ˌtaɪd] Ebbe **II**
to tidy *(a room)* ['taɪdi] aufräumen; in Ordnung bringen **I**
to tie (to) ['taɪ tə] binden (an); fesseln (an) **III U2**, 49
till [tɪl] bis **I**
time [taɪm] Zeit **I**; Mal **II**
all the **time** [ˌɔ:l ðə 'taɪm] die ganze Zeit **II**
at the same **time** [ət ðə ˌseɪm 'taɪm] zur selben Zeit; gleichzeitig **I**
free **time** [ˌfri: 'taɪm] Freizeit **I**
ten **times** [ten 'taɪmz] zehnmal **I**
time line ['taɪm ˌlaɪn] Zeitstrahl **I**
Have a good **time**. [ˌhæv‿ə gʊd 'taɪm] Viel Spaß. ⟨**III TS4**, 112⟩

I can't wait till next **time**. [aɪ kɑ:nt ˌweɪt tɪl nekst 'taɪm] Ich kann es bis zum nächsten Mal kaum erwarten. **II**
Time to get up! [ˌtaɪm tə ˌget‿'ʌp] Es ist Zeit aufzustehen! **I**
What **time**? [ˌwɒt 'taɪm] Um wie viel Uhr? **I**
What's the **time**? [ˌwɒts ðə 'taɪm] Wie spät ist es?; Wie viel Uhr ist es? **I**
timetable ['taɪmˌteɪbl] Stundenplan; Fahrplan **I**
tin [tɪn] Zinn **II**
tin can ['tɪn kæn] Blechdose **III U2**, 51
tinned [tɪnd] Dosen-; aus der Dose **I**
tiny ['taɪni] klein; winzig **III U2**, 46
tip [tɪp] Tipp; Ratschlag **I**
to **tiptoe** ['tɪptəʊ] auf Zehenspitzen gehen **II**
tired [taɪəd] müde **I**
Get your **tissues** out! [ˌget jɔ: 'tɪsju:z aʊt] Das ist so unglaublich traurig! ⟨**III TS2**, 59⟩
title ['taɪtl] Titel; Überschrift **II**
to [tʊ; tə] zu; nach; auf; in; vor *(bei Uhrzeitangaben)* **I**
from … **to** [frəm tə] von … bis **I**
quarter past/**to** ['kwɔ:tə pɑ:st/tə] Viertel nach/vor **I**
to the point [tə ðə 'pɔɪnt] prägnant; treffend **III AC2**, 63
toast [təʊst] Toast **I**
tobacco *(no pl)* [tə'bækəʊ] Tabak **III U3**, 68
today [tə'deɪ] heute **I**
toddler ['tɒdlə] Kleinkind ⟨**III TS3**, 85⟩
together [tə'geðə] zusammen; miteinander; gemeinsam **I**
toilet ['tɔɪlət] Toilette **I**
tolerant ['tɒlrnt] tolerant **III TS4**, 112
tomato [tə'mɑ:təʊ], **tomatoes** [tə'mɑ:təʊz] *(pl)* Tomate **I**
tomorrow [tə'mɒrəʊ] morgen **I**
tonight [tə'naɪt] heute Abend; heute Nacht **III TS4**, 107
too [tu:] auch; zu **I**
Too bad! [ˌtu: 'bæd] Zu dumm!; Schade! **I**
You **too**? [ju: 'tu:] Du auch? **I**
tool [tu:l] Werkzeug; Gerät **II**
top [tɒp] Spitze; oberer Teil; oberes Ende **I**
on **top** [ɒn 'tɒp] oben; obendrauf **I**
to **top** up [tɒp‿'ʌp] aufladen **II**
topic ['tɒpɪk] Thema **II**
torch [tɔ:tʃ] Fackel; Taschenlampe **II**
to **toss** and **turn** (in bed) ['tɒs ənd ˌtɜ:n] sich (im Bett) hin und her wälzen ⟨**III TS1**, 31⟩
to stay in **touch** (with) [ˌsteɪ ɪn 'tʌtʃ wɪð] in Kontakt bleiben (mit) **II**
tour [tʊə] Tour; Fahrt; Rundgang **II**
audio **tour** ['ɔ:diəʊ ˌtʊə] Audioführung **II**
tourist ['tʊərɪst] Tourist/-in **I**
tourist board ['tʊərɪst bɔ:d] Touristeninformation **II**
tourist information centre [ˌtʊərɪst ɪnfə'meɪʃn ˌsentə] Touristeninformation **I**
towards [tə'wɔ:dz] in Richtung; auf … zu; darauf zu **II**

tower [taʊə] Turm **III U2**, 48
town [taʊn] Stadt **I**
toy [tɔɪ] Spielzeug **I**
to **trace** [treɪs] verfolgen; nachspüren **I**
trade [treɪd] Handel ⟨**III TS2**, 60⟩
to **trade** [treɪd] austauschen **II**
tradition [trə'dɪʃn] Tradition **I**
traditional [trə'dɪʃnl] traditionell **III U2**, 36
traffic ['træfɪk] Verkehr **III U4**, 98
train [treɪn] Zug **I**
to **train** [treɪn] trainieren **II**
trainer ['treɪnə] Turnschuh **III U1**, 20
training ['treɪnɪŋ] Training **II**
to **translate** [trænz'leɪt] übersetzen **I**
translation [trænz'leɪʃn] Übersetzung **I**
transport ['trænspɔ:t] Verkehrsmittel; Transport **II**
public **transport** *(no pl)* [ˌpʌblɪk 'trænspɔ:t] öffentliche Verkehrsmittel **II**
*to be **trapped** [bi 'træpt] eingeschlossen sein; in der Falle sitzen °**III U2**, 50
travel ['trævl] (das) Reisen; Reise **II**
travel agency ['trævl‿ˌeɪdʒnsi] Reisebüro **III U2**, 47
travel agent's ['trævl‿ˌeɪdʒnts] Reisebüro **II**
travel report [ˌtrævl rɪ'pɔ:t] Reisebericht **II**
to **travel** ['trævl] fahren; reisen **II**
traveller ['trævlə] Reisende/-r **III U4**, 99
travelling *(no pl)* ['trævlɪŋ] (das) Reisen **III U4**, 93
treasure ['treʒə] Schatz **II**
treat [tri:t] *hier:* Leckerli; Belohnung **III TS2**, 58
to **treat** [tri:t] behandeln **III U1**, 21
tree [tri:] Baum **I**
family **tree** ['fæmli ˌtri:] Stammbaum **I**
palm **tree** ['pɑ:m ˌtri:] Palme **II**
pony **trekking** ['pəʊni ˌtrekɪŋ] Ponyreiten im Gelände **II**
trial [traɪəl] Qualifikation **II**
tribe [traɪb] Stamm; Volksstamm **III U3**, 64
trick [trɪk] Trick; Streich **I**
to play a **trick** (on) [ˌpleɪ‿ə 'trɪk‿ɒn] einen Streich spielen **I**
trip [trɪp] Trip; Reise; Ausflug; Fahrt **II**
trouble ['trʌbl] Ärger; Probleme; Schwierigkeiten **II**
*to make **trouble** [ˌmeɪk 'trʌbl] Ärger machen; in Schwierigkeiten bringen **I**
trousers *(pl)* ['traʊzəz] Hose **II**
trowel ['traʊəl] kleiner Spaten **II**
true [tru:] wahr **II**
to **trust** [trʌst] vertrauen **III U1**, 20
truth [tru:θ] Wahrheit **III U4**, 97
to **try** [traɪ] versuchen; probieren **I**
to **try** on [ˌtraɪ‿'ɒn] anprobieren **II**
to **try** out [ˌtraɪ‿'aʊt] ausprobieren °**III TS3**, 89
T-shirt ['ti:ʃɜ:t] T-Shirt **I**
the **Tube** [ðə 'tju:b] die Londoner U-Bahn **II**
Tudor ['tju:də] Tudor- **III U3**, 66
Tuesday ['tju:zdeɪ] Dienstag **I**

tune [tju:n] Melodie **III TS1**, 29
tunnel ['tʌnl] Tunnel **I**
It's your **turn**. [ˌɪts 'jɔ: tɜ:n] Du bist dran. **I**
Take **turns**. [ˌteɪk 'tɜ:nz] Wechselt euch ab. **I**
Your **turn**. ['jɔ: tɜ:n] Du bist dran. **I**
to **turn** [tɜ:n] einbiegen; abbiegen **I**; drehen; (sich) umdrehen **III TS3**, 85
to toss and **turn** (in bed) ['tɒs ənd ˌtɜ:n] sich (im Bett) hin und her wälzen ⟨**III TS1**, 31⟩
to **turn** (a)round [ˌtɜ:n‿(ə)'raʊnd] (sich) umdrehen; wenden **II**
to **turn** back [ˌtɜ:n 'bæk] umkehren; zurückgehen **III U3**, 72
to **turn** into [ˌtɜ:n‿'ɪntə] ändern in; umwandeln in °**III U4**, 98
to **turn** off [ˌtɜ:n‿'ɒf] abschalten; ausschalten **II**
to **turn** to ['tɜ:n tə] sich wenden an; sich zuwenden **II**
It **turned** out that … [ɪt ˌtɜ:nd‿'aʊt ðæt] Es stellte sich heraus, dass … **III U4**, 100
turning point ['tɜ:nɪŋ ˌpɔɪnt] Wendepunkt °**III U1**, 22
tusk [tʌsk] Stoßzahn **III TS2**, 60
tutor ['tju:tə] Klassenlehrer/-in **I**
tutor group ['tju:tə ˌgru:p] Klasse *(in einer englischen Schule)* **I**
TV (= television) [ˌti:'vi: ('telɪvɪʒn)] Fernsehen; Fernseher **I**
to watch **TV** [ˌwɒtʃ ti:'vi:] fernsehen **I**
twelve [twelv] zwölf **I**
twin [twɪn] Zwilling; Zwillings- **II**
to **twist** your ankle [ˌtwɪst jɔ:r‿'æŋkl] sich den Knöchel verrenken **II**
two [tu:] zwei **I**
the **two** of them [ðə 'tu:‿əv ðəm] beide **II**
type [taɪp] Typ; Art; Sorte °**III U1**, 9
typical ['tɪpɪkl] typisch **I**
typically ['tɪpɪkli] typisch **III U2**, 37

U

u *(= you)* [ju:; jə] du; Sie; ihr **I**
UFO [ˌju:ef'əʊ] UFO **II**
unbroke [ʌn'brəʊk] unbeschädigt ⟨**III TS1**, 30⟩
uncle ['ʌŋkl] Onkel **I**
under ['ʌndə] unter **I**
underfloor heating *(no pl)* [ˌʌndəflɔ: 'hi:tɪŋ] Fußbodenheizung **III U3**, 64
underground ['ʌndəgraʊnd] U-Bahn **II**
to **underline** [ˌʌndə'laɪn] unterstreichen °**III U2**, 39
underneath [ˌʌndə'ni:θ] unterhalb; unten ⟨**III TS2**, 57⟩
*to **understand** [ˌʌndə'stænd] verstehen **I**
understanding [ˌʌndə'stændɪŋ] Verständnis **II**
unfair [ʌn'feə] unfair **II**

unfamiliar [ˌʌnfəˈmɪliə] nicht vertraut; unbekannt **III AC1**, 34
unfriendly [ʌnˈfrendli] unfreundlich **II**
uniform [ˈjuːnɪfɔːm] Uniform **I**
unit [ˈjuːnɪt] Lektion; Kapitel; Einheit **I**
unknown [ˌʌnˈnəʊn] unbekannt ⟨**III TS1**, 33⟩
*to be **unlucky** [biːˌʌnˈlʌki] Pech haben **I**
unofficial [ˌʌnəˈfɪʃl] inoffiziell **III U2**, 40
unreal [ˌʌnˈrɪəl] irreal **III U4**, 105
unsure [ʌnˈʃʊə] unsicher **III TS4**, 107
until [ʌnˈtɪl] bis; erst wenn **II**
untitled [ʌnˈtaɪtld] ohne Titel ⟨**III TS1**, 33⟩
to **unwrap** [ʌnˈræp] auswickeln; auspacken **I**
up [ʌp] hinauf; (nach) oben **II**
to end **up** [ˌendˈʌp] enden; landen **II**
*to get **up** [ˌgetˈʌp] aufstehen *(aus dem Bett)* **I**
*to give **up** [ˌgɪvˈʌp] aufgeben **III U1**, 12
to look **up** [ˌlʊkˈʌp] nachschlagen; nachschauen **I**
What's **up**? [ˌwɒtsˈʌp] Was ist los? **III U1**, 14
update [ˈʌpdeɪt] Aktualisierung; Update **III U2**, 44
*to **upset** [ʌpˈset] aus der Fassung bringen **III AC1**, 35
upset [ʌpˈset] aufgebracht; bestürzt **II**
upstairs [ʌpˈsteəz] nach oben; im Obergeschoss; oben **II**
urine [ˈjʊərɪn] Urin ⟨**III TS2**, 57⟩
us [ʌs] uns **I**
to **use** [juːz] benutzen; verwenden; gebrauchen **I**
*to be **used** to [bi ˈjuːsˌtə] gewöhnt sein an; gewohnt sein **III AC1**, 35
useful [ˈjuːsfl] nützlich; hilfreich **I**
Useful phrases [ˌjuːsfl ˈfreɪsɪz] nützliche Ausdrücke **I**
useless [ˈjuːsləs] nutzlos **III U4**, 103
usual [ˈjuːʒl] üblich **III U1**, 21
usually [ˈjuːʒli] normalerweise; gewöhnlich; meistens **I**

V

valuable [ˈvæljuəbl] wertvoll ⟨**III TS2**, 57⟩
vegetable [ˈvedʒtəbl] Gemüse **III U2**, 41
vegetarian [ˌvedʒɪˈteəriən] Vegetarier/-in **III U2**, 41
vegetarian [ˌvedʒɪˈteəriən] vegetarisch **III U2**, 42
vending machine [ˈvendɪŋ məˌʃiːn] Automat **III U4**, 94
verb [vɜːb] Verb **I**
verse [vɜːs] Vers; Strophe °**III TS1**, 29
version [ˈvɜːʃn] Version °**III TS1**, 29
cover **version** [ˈkʌvə ˌvɜːʃn] Coverversion °**III TS1**, 33
versus (vs.) [ˈvɜːsəs] gegen **III U2**, 51
very [ˈveri] sehr **I**
very much [ˌveri ˈmʌtʃ] sehr **I**
vet [vet] Tierarzt/Tierärztin **I**
Victorian [vɪkˈtɔːriən] viktorianisch; Viktorianer/-in **III U3**, 67
video [ˈvɪdiəʊ] Video **II**
video chat [ˈvɪdiəʊ ˌtʃæt] Videochat **II**
view [vjuː] Aussicht; Sicht; Ausblick; Blick **II**
point of **view** [ˌpɔɪntˌəv ˈvjuː] Standpunkt; Ansicht; Perspektive **II**
viewer [ˈvjuːə] Zuschauer/-in **II**
viewing [ˈvjuːɪŋ] Hör-/Sehverstehen **I**
village [ˈvɪlɪdʒ] Dorf **I**
villain [ˈvɪlən] Bösewicht **II**
violence *(no pl)* [ˈvaɪəlns] Gewalt **III TS3**, 84
violent [ˈvaɪəlnt] gewaltsam; gewalttätig; brutal **III TS2**, 60
violet [ˈvaɪələt] Veilchen ⟨**III TS1**, 29⟩
visa [ˈviːzə], **visas** [ˈviːzəz] *(pl)* Visum, Visa *(Pl.)*; Einreisebewilligung **III U4**, 93
visit [ˈvɪzɪt] Besuch **I**
to **visit** [ˈvɪzɪt] besichtigen; besuchen **I**
visitor [ˈvɪzɪtə] Besucher/-in **I**
vitamin [ˈvɪtəmɪn] Vitamin **III U3**, 79
vocabulary [vəˈkæbjələri] Vokabular; Wortschatz **I**
voice [vɔɪs] Stimme **I**
volleyball [ˈvɒlibɔːl] Volleyball **I**
volunteer [ˌvɒlənˈtɪə] freiwillig; ehrenamtlich ⟨**III TS2**, 59⟩
*to take a **vote** [ˌteɪkˌə ˈvəʊt] abstimmen **I**
to **vote** [vəʊt] abstimmen; wählen **I**

W

to **wait** (for) [weɪt] warten (auf) **I**
I can't **wait** till next time. [aɪ kɑːnt ˌweɪt tɪl nekst ˈtaɪm] Ich kann es bis zum nächsten Mal kaum erwarten. **II**
Wait and see! [ˌweɪtˌənd ˈsiː] Warte ab! **I**
*to **wake** up [weɪkˈʌp] aufwachen; aufwecken **III U3**, 79
gallery **walk** [ˈgæləri ˌwɔːk] Museumsrundgang; Vernissage **I**
*to go for a **walk** [ˌgəʊ fərˌə ˈwɔːk] spazieren gehen **II**
night **walk** [ˈnaɪt wɔːk] Nachtwanderung **II**
to **walk** [wɔːk] gehen; laufen **I**
to **walk** the dog [ˌwɔːk ðə ˈdɒg] den Hund ausführen; mit dem Hund spazieren gehen **I**
walking [ˈwɔːkɪŋ] Wandern **II**
wall [wɔːl] Wand; Mauer **I**; Online-Pinnwand **III U1**, 23
to **wander** round [ˌwɒndə ˈraʊnd] herumlaufen ⟨**III TS2**, 57⟩
wanna *(= want to) (infml)* [ˈwɒnə] will/wollen ⟨**III U4**, 96⟩
to **want** (to) [ˈwɒnt tə] wollen; mögen **I**
to **want** sb to do sth [ˌwɒnt təˈ duː] wollen, dass jmd. etwas tut **III U1**, 10
war [wɔː] Krieg **III U4**, 100
wardrobe [ˈwɔːdrəʊb] Kleiderschrank **I**
to **warm** up [ˌwɔːmˈʌp] aufwärmen; sich aufwärmen **I**
warm [wɔːm] warm **III TS2**, 57
warm-up [ˈwɔːmˌʌp] Aufwärmübung **I**
to **warn** [wɔːn] warnen **III TS4**, 110
warrior [ˈwɒriə] Krieger **II**
to **wash** [wɒʃ] waschen; sich waschen **I**
to **wash** up [ˌwɒʃˈʌp] angespült werden **II**
washing machine [ˈwɒʃɪŋ məˌʃiːn] Waschmaschine **II**
to **waste** [weɪst] verschwenden **II**
to **watch** [wɒtʃ] beobachten; (sich) ansehen; zuschauen **I**
to **watch** TV [ˌwɒtʃ tiːˈviː] fernsehen **I**
water [ˈwɔːtə] Wasser **I**
water slide [ˈwɔːtə ˌslaɪd] Wasserrutsche **I**
wave [weɪv] Welle **I**
wax [wæks] Wachs **II**
wax figure [ˈwæks ˌfɪgə] Wachsfigur **II**
way [weɪ] Weg; Art und Weise **I**
*to be in the **way** [biːˌɪn ðə ˈweɪ] im Weg sein/stehen **I**
*to get in the **way** [ˌgetˌɪn ðə ˈweɪ] stören; im Weg stehen **II**
in other **ways** [ɪnˈʌðə weɪz] auf andere Weise **II**
the same **way** as [ˌðə seɪm ˈweɪ æz] genauso wie **II**
we [wiː; wi] wir **I**
weapon [ˈwepən] Waffe **III U3**, 75
*to **wear** [weə] anhaben; tragen *(Kleidung)* **I**
weather [ˈweðə] Wetter **I**
weather forecast [ˈweðə ˌfɔːkɑːst] Wettervorhersage **II**
web [web] Netz; Spinnennetz **III U2**, 50
web designer [ˈweb dɪˌzaɪnə] Webdesigner **III U1**, 14
website [ˈwebsaɪt] Website; Internetauftritt **I**
wedding [ˈwedɪŋ] Hochzeit **I**
Wednesday [ˈwenzdeɪ] Mittwoch **I**
wee bit [ˈwiː bɪt] klitzeklein ⟨**III U2**, 40⟩
week [wiːk] Woche **I**
weekday [ˈwiːkdeɪ] Wochentag **II**
weekend [ˌwiːkˈend] Wochenende **I**
at the **weekend** [ət ðə ˌwiːkˈend] am Wochenende **I**
to **weigh** [weɪ] wiegen **III TS2**, 57
weight [weɪt] Gewicht **III TS2**, 57
to gain **weight** [ˌgeɪn ˈweɪt] zunehmen ⟨**III TS2**, 57⟩
weird [wɪəd] merkwürdig; seltsam; sonderbar **II**
Welcome! [ˈwelkəm] Willkommen! **II**
to **welcome** [ˈwelkəm] willkommen heißen **II**
You're **welcome**. [jɔː ˈwelkəm] Bitte schön.; Nichts zu danken.; Gern geschehen. **I**
All's **well** that ends **well**. [ˌɔːlz wel ðət ˈendz wel] Ende gut, alles gut. **III U3**, 72
*to do **well** [ˌduː ˈwel] gute Leistungen erbringen **III TS4**, 110

well [wel] tja; nun **I**
Welsh [welʃ] walisisch; Walisisch; Waliser/-in **II**
west [west] Westen; West- **I**
wet [wet] nass **II**
what [wɒt] was; welche/-r/-s; was für ein **I**
What about ... ? ['wɒt‿əbaʊt] Wie wär's mit ...?; Was ist mit ...? **I**
What are ...? ['wɒt‿ɑ:] Welche ... sind es? **I**
What colour is ...? [ˌwɒt 'kʌlər‿ɪz] Welche Farbe hat ...? **I**
what else [ˌwɒt‿'els] was sonst; was noch **I**
What is missing? [ˌwɒt‿ɪz 'mɪsɪŋ] Was fehlt? **I**
What is ... about? [ˌwɒt‿ɪz ...‿ə'baʊt] Worum geht es in/im ...? **I**
What luck! [wɒt 'lʌk] Was für ein Glück! **III U3**, 72
What on earth ...? [ˌwɒt:‿ɒn‿'ɜ:θ] Was um alles in der Welt ...? **II**
What time? [ˌwɒt 'taɪm] Um wie viel Uhr? **I**
what to ... ['wɒt tə] was man ... **I**
What was it like? [ˌwɒt wɒz‿ɪt 'laɪk] Wie war es? **III U3**, 64
What's that? [wɒts 'ðæt] Was ist das? **I**
What's the rule for ...? [ˌwɒts ðə 'ru:l fə] Was ist die Regel für ...? **I**
What's up? [ˌwɒts‿'ʌp] Was ist los? **III U1**, 14
What's your favourite ...? ['wɒts jə ˌfeɪvrɪt] Was ist dein/-e Lieblings...? **I**
What's your name? [ˌwɒts jə 'neɪm] Wie heißt du?; Wie heißen Sie? **I**
What's the matter? [ˌwɒts ðə 'mætə] Was ist los?; Was hast du? **II**
What's the time? [ˌwɒts ðə 'taɪm] Wie spät ist es?; Wie viel Uhr ist es? **I**
wheel [wi:l] Rad; Steuerrad; Steuer **I**
wheelchair ['wi:ltʃeə] Rollstuhl **II**
when [wen] wenn; wann; als **I**
whenever [wen'evə] wann immer; jedes Mal, wenn; so oft **II**
where [weə] wo; wohin **I**
Where ... from? [ˌweə 'frɒm] Woher ...? **I**
where I belong [ˌweər‿aɪ bɪ'lɒŋ] wo ich hingehöre **III U4**, 102
I go **wherever** the wind takes me. [aɪ ˌgəʊ weəˌrevə ðə wɪnd 'teɪks mi:] Ich lasse mich treiben. **III U4**, 105
which [wɪtʃ] welche/-r/-s **I**
which [wɪtʃ] der; die; das; dem; den *(Relativpronomen)* **III U3**, 72
a poem **which** ... [ə ˌpəʊɪm 'wɪtʃ] ein Gedicht, das ... °**III TS1**, 29
actions **which** ... [ˌækʃnz 'wɪtʃ] Handlungen, die ... °**III U2**, 37
an event **which** ... [ən ɪˌvent 'wɪtʃ] eine Veranstaltung, die ... °**III U2**, 46
animals **which** ... [ˌænɪmlz 'wɪtʃ] Tiere, die ... °**III TS2**, 57
closes **which** ... [ˌkləʊsɪz 'wɪtʃ] Durchgänge, die ... °**III U2**, 43
museums **which** ... [mju:ˌzɪəmz 'wɪtʃ] Museen, die ... °**III U2**, 46
objects **which** ... [ˌɒbdʒɪkts 'wɪtʃ] Gegenstände, die ... °**III U3**, 67
steps **which** ... [steps 'wɪtʃ] Schritte, die ... °**III TS2**, 58
a **while** [ə 'waɪl] eine Weile **II**
while [waɪl] während **I**
to **whip** [wɪp] schlagen **I**
whisky ['wɪski] Whisky **III U2**, 39
to **whisper** ['wɪspə] flüstern **I**
white [waɪt] weiß **I**
white lie [ˌwaɪt 'laɪ] Notlüge **III TS4**, 108
who [hu:] wer; wem; wen **I**
Who ... for? [ˌhu: 'fɔ:] Für wen ...? **I**
Who is it? [ˌhu:‿'ɪz‿ɪt] Wer ist es? **I**
Who's in? [hu:z‿'ɪn] Wer macht mit?; Wer ist dabei? **II**
who ... [hu:] der; die; das; dem; den (Relativpronomen) **III U3**, 72
a person **who** [ə ˌpɜ:sn 'hu:] eine Person, die ... °**III U2**, 43
koalas **who** ... [kəʊˌɑ:ləz 'hu:] Koalas, die ... °**III TS2**, 59
people **who** ... [ˌpi:pl 'hu:] Menschen, die ... °**III TS2**, 58
somebody **who** ... [ˌsʌmbədi 'hu:] jemand, der ... °**III U1**, 22
the only person **who** ... [ði‿əʊnli ˌpɜ:sn 'hu:] der einzige Mensch, der ... °**III U1**, 20; °**III U2**, 43
whole [həʊl] ganz **I**
whom [hu:m] wem; wen °**III TS4**, 113
whose [hu:z] dessen *(Relativpronomen)*; deren *(Relativpronomen)* **III U3**, 72
why [waɪ] warum **I**
that's **why** [ðæts 'waɪ] deshalb **II**
wide [waɪd] breit; weit; ausgedehnt **II**
wife [waɪf], **wives** [waɪvz] *(pl)* Ehefrau **II**
wifi ['waɪfaɪ] WLAN **III U4**, 94
the **wild** [ðə 'waɪld] Wildnis; freie Wildbahn ⟨**III TS2**, 57⟩
wild [waɪld] wild **II**
wildlife ['waɪldlaɪf] Tierwelt *(in freier Wildbahn)* **II**
*to **win** [wɪn] gewinnen; siegen **I**
wind [wɪnd] Wind **II**
I go wherever the **wind** takes me. [aɪ ˌgəʊ weəˌrevə ðə wɪnd 'teɪks mi:] Ich lasse mich treiben. **III U4**, 105
window ['wɪndəʊ] Fenster **I**
windsurfing ['wɪndsɜ:fɪŋ] Windsurfen **II**
wine [waɪn] Wein **I**
winner ['wɪnə] Gewinner/-in; Sieger/-in **I**
winter ['wɪntə] Winter **III TS2**, 57
wish [wɪʃ] Wunsch **I**
*to make a **wish** [ˌmeɪk‿ə 'wɪʃ] sich etwas wünschen **I**
Best **wishes** [ˌbest 'wɪʃɪz] Viele Grüße; Herzliche Grüße **II**
with [wɪð] mit; bei **I**
within [wɪ'ðɪn] innerhalb ⟨**III TS2**, 60⟩
without [wɪ'ðaʊt] ohne **I**
witness ['wɪtnəs] Zeuge/Zeugin **II**
wizard ['wɪzəd] Zauberer **II**
wobbly ['wɒbli] wackelig **II**
woman ['wʊmən], **women** ['wɪmɪn] *(pl)* Frau **I**
wonderful ['wʌndəfl] wunderbar **II**
wood [wʊd] Holz **III U2**, 49; Wald; Wäldchen **III TS3**, 85
wooden ['wʊdn] hölzern; aus Holz **III U2**, 48
word [wɜ:d] Wort **I**
compound **word** ['kɒmpaʊnd wɜ:d] Kompositum *(zusammengesetztes Wort)* **II**
key **word** ['ki: wɜ:d] Stichwort; Schlüsselbegriff **I**
linking **word** ['lɪŋkɪŋ ˌwɜ:d] Bindewort **I**
play on **words** [ˌpleɪ‿ɒn 'wɜ:dz] Wortspiel **III TS1**, 32
signal **word** ['sɪgnəl ˌwɜ:d] Signalwort **I**
word bank ['wɜ:d ˌbæŋk] Wortsammlung °**III TS1**, 32
word cloud ['wɜ:d ˌklaʊd] Wörterwolke **II**
word order ['wɜ:d‿ˌɔ:də] Wortstellung; Satzstellung **I**
word snake ['wɜ:d ˌsneɪk] Wortschlange **I**
work [wɜ:k] Arbeit **I**
pair **work** ['peə wɜ:k] Partnerarbeit **II**
to **work** [wɜ:k] arbeiten **I**; funktionieren **II**
to **work** out [ˌwɜ:k‿'aʊt] herausfinden; ausarbeiten **II**; funktionieren; klappen **III U1**, 23
workbook ['wɜ:kbʊk] Arbeitsheft; Übungsheft °**III TS4**, 113
worker ['wɜ:kə] *hier:* Mitarbeiter/-in ⟨**III TS2**, 59⟩
workshop ['wɜ:kʃɒp] Workshop **I**
world [wɜ:ld] Erde; Welt **I**
worm [wɜ:m] Wurm **I**
worried ['wʌrid] beunruhigt; besorgt **III AC2**, 62
*to be **worried** [bi 'wʌrid] beunruhigt sein; besorgt sein **II**
to **worry** ['wʌri] sich Sorgen machen **II**
Don't **worry**! [ˌdəʊnt 'wʌri] Keine Sorge! **I**
the **worst** [ðə 'wɜ:st] der/die/das schlimmste; der/die/das schlechteste **II**
*to be **worth** [bi: 'wɜ:θ] wert sein **I**
would [wʊd] würde/-st/-n/-t **III U1**, 9
Would you like ...? [ˌwʊd jʊ 'laɪk] Möchtest du ...?; Möchten Sie ...?; Möchtet ihr ...? **II**
would have happened [ˌwʊd həv 'hæpnd] wäre passiert °**III U4**, 103
would have sent [ˌwʊd həv 'sent] hätten geschickt °**III U4**, 103
wounded ['wu:ndɪd] verwundet; verletzt **III U2**, 48
to **wrap** [ræp] einwickeln; einpacken **I**
wrapping ['ræpɪŋ] Verpackung; Hülle **I**
to **wrinkle** ['rɪŋkl] zerknittern ⟨**III TS1**, 33⟩
wrist [rɪst] Handgelenk **II**
*to **write** [raɪt] schreiben **I**

*to **write** down [ˌraɪt ˈdaʊn] aufschreiben **I**
writer [ˈraɪtə] Autor/-in; Verfasser/-in **III U3**, 68
writing [ˈraɪtɪŋ] Schreiben **I**
wrong [rɒŋ] falsch **I**
*to be **wrong** [biː ˈrɒŋ] unrecht haben; sich irren **I**
*to go **wrong** [ˌɡəʊ ˈrɒŋ] schiefgehen **I**

X

XOXO [ˌhʌɡzˌən ˈkɪsɪz] Umarmungen und Küsse *(am Ende von E-Mails und SMS)* **I**

Y

yeah *(infml)* [jeə] ja **I**
year [jɪə] Jahr; Schuljahr **I**
11-year-old [ɪˌlevnˈjɪərəʊld] 11-Jährige/-r **II**
18-year-old [ˌeɪtiːn ˈjɪərˌəʊld] 18-jährig **II**
yearbook [ˈjɪəbʊk] Jahrbuch **II**
yellow [ˈjeləʊ] gelb **I**
yes [jes] ja **I**
yesterday [ˈjestədeɪ] gestern **II**
yet [jet] schon; noch **II**
not … **yet** [nɒt ˈjet] noch nicht **II**
yoghurt [ˈjɒɡət] Joghurt **I**
you [juː; jə] du; ihr; Sie **I**
You too? [juː ˈtuː] Du auch? **I**
You're welcome. [jɔː ˈwelkəm] Bitte schön.; Nichts zu danken.; Gern geschehen. **I**
young [jʌŋ] jung **I**
your [jɔː; jə] dein/-e; euer/eure; Ihr/-e **I**
What's **your** name? [ˌwɒts jə ˈneɪm] Wie heißt du?; Wie heißen Sie? **I**
Your turn. [ˈjɔː tɜːn] Du bist dran. **I**
yours [jɔːz] dein/-er/-e/-es; eure/-r/-s; Ihr/-e **II**
Yours … [jɔːz] Viele Grüße … *(am Ende von Briefen und Mails)* **II**
yourself [jɔːˈself] du/dir/dich/Sie/sich (selbst); selber **I**
yourselves [jɔːˈselvz] ihr/euch/Sie/sich (selbst); selber **II**
youth [juːθ] Jugend **III TS4**, 112

Z

zero [ˈzɪərəʊ] null **I**
zone [zəʊn] Zone (**III U4**, 96)
zoo [zuː] Zoo; Tierpark **II**
to zoom in (on) [zuːmˈɪn ɒn] heranzoomen (auf) **III U3**, 76

Boys' names

Abdi [ˈæbdi] **III U4**, 102
Abdirahman [ˌæbdirəˈmɑːn] **III U4**, 103
Ahmed [ˈæmed] **III U4**, 102
Amarjit [əˈmɑːdʒɪt] **III U4**, 94
Amir [ɑːˈmiːr] **II**
Brad [bræd] **III AC1**, 34
Dave [deɪv] **I**
Desmond [ˈdezmənd] **I**
Eddie [ˈedi] **III U4**, 94
Ethan [ˈiːθn] **III U2**, 38
Finn [fɪn] **III U1**, 20
Frank [fræŋk] **II**
Ian [ˈiːən] **III U1**, 17
Jack [dʒæk] **I**
Jahangir [dʒəˈhʌŋɡɪə] **I**
Jamie [ˈdʒeɪmi] **I**
Jay [dʒeɪ] **I**
Jim [dʒɪm] **III U3**, 76
Jinsoo [ˈdʒɪnzuː] **II**
John [dʒɒn] **II**
Luke [luːk] **I**
Mario [ˈmæriəʊ] **III TS1**, 28
Marley [ˈmɑːli] **II**
Masud [məˈsuːd] **III U4**, 98
Matt [mæt] **III U1**, 18
Max [mæks] **III U1**, 20
Nathan [ˈneɪθn] **II**
Peter [ˈpiːtə] **II**
Rafiq [ræˈfɪk] **III U4**, 97
Rick [rɪk] **III TS3**, 84
Rob [rɒb] **III TS4**, 107
Sean [ʃɔːn] **III U1**, 23
Shahid [ʃɑːˈhiːd] **I**
Simon [ˈsaɪmən] **III TS4**, 106
Steve [stiːv] **I**
Stuart [ˈstuːət] **III U2**, 37
Thomas [ˈtɒməs] **III U3**, 69
Tony [ˈtəʊni] **I**
Tyler [ˈtaɪlə] **I**

Girls' names

Alicia [əˈlɪsiə; əˈlɪʃə] **I**
Alva [ˈælvə] **III U2**, 51
Amber [ˈæmbə] **I**
Anna [ˈænə] **I**
Anne [æn] **I**
Annie [ˈæni] **III U2**, 43
Anya [ˈænjə] **III U4**, 97
Ayla [ˈeɪlə] **III U1**, 16
Carol [ˈkærəl] **I**
Ciara [sˈjærə] **III U4**, 105
Claire [ˈkleə] **I**
Fowsia [faʊˈziːə] **III U4**, 102
Frances [ˈfrɑːnsɪs] **I**
Gwen [ɡwen] **II**
Hayley [ˈheɪli] **III U4**, 105
Holly [ˈhɒli] **I**
Irina [ɪˈriːnə] **I**
Ivy [ˈaɪvi] **III U1**, 12
Jean [dʒiːn] **III U2**, 37
Jenny [ˈdʒeni] **III U4**, 99
Judith [ˈdʒuːdɪθ] **II**
Julie [ˈdʒuːli] **I**
Khadija [kəˈdiːdʒə] **III U4**, 102
Kirsty [ˈkɜːsti] **III U2**, 41
Laura [ˈlɔːrə] **I**
Lauren [ˈlɔːrən] **II**
Lucy [ˈluːsi] **I**
Maisie [ˈmeɪzi] **II**
Margaret [ˈmɑːɡrət] **III U3**, 69
Maryan [ˈmærjən] **III U4**, 102
Megan [ˈmeɡən] **II**
Olivia [ɒlˈɪviə] **I**
Rose [rəʊz] **I**
Ruby [ˈruːbi] **II**
Sabra [ˈsæbrə] **III U4**, 102
Sadia [ˈseɪdjə] **III U4**, 98
Sally [ˈsæli] **I**
Tamara [təˈmɑːrə] **II**
Tina [ˈtiːnə] **III TS3**, 84
Violet [ˈvaɪələt] **III U3**, 79
Vivien [ˈvɪvjən] **II**

Surnames

Azad [əˈzɑːd] **I**
Bayram [ˈbeɪrəm] **III U1**, 16
Costello [kəˈsteləʊ] **III TS4**, 110
Elliot [ˈeliət] **I**
Francis [ˈfrɑːnsɪs] **III U1**, 12
Fraser [ˈfreɪzə] **I**
Jones [dʒəʊnz] **III U4**, 96
Karp [kɑːp] **III U1**, 11
King [kɪŋ] **III U2**, 43
Mahmoud [mæˈmuːd] **III U4**, 103
Miller [ˈmɪlə] **III U3**, 69
Mussa [ˈmuːsə] **III U4**, 102
Preston [ˈprestən] **I**
Pulsford [ˈpʌlsfɔːd] **III TS2**, 60
Swindon [ˈswɪndən] **I**
Woodruff [ˈwʊdrʌf] **III U4**, 94

Place names

Aberdeen [ˌæbəˈdiːn] **III U2**, 36
Bankside [ˈbæŋksaɪd] *Stadtteil von London* **III U3**, 71
Birmingham [ˈbɜːmɪŋəm] **III TS2**, 60
Bristol [ˈbrɪstl] **III TS2**, 60
Calais [ˈkæleɪ] **III U4**, 94
Camden Market [ˈkæmdən ˌmɑːkɪt] **II**
Cologne [kəˈləʊn] Köln **I**
Covent Garden [ˌkɒvnt ˈɡɑːdn] **II**
Dhaka [ˈdɑːkə] **III U4**, 98
Dover [ˈdəʊvə] *englische Küstenstadt am Ärmelkanal* **III U4**, 94
Dubai [duːˈbaɪ] **III U4**, 102
Dunrossness [dʌnrɒsˈnes] **III U2**, 46
Edinburgh [ˈedɪnbrə] **II**
Glasgow [ˈɡlɑːzɡəʊ] **III U2**, 37
Heathrow [ˌhiːθˈrəʊ] **III U4**, 99
Hollywood [ˈhɒliwʊd] **II**
Hyde Park [ˌhaɪd ˈpɑːk] **II**
Isle of Man [ˌaɪlˌəv ˈmæn] **II**
Liverpool [ˈlɪvəpuːl] **III TS2**, 60
London [ˈlʌndən] **I**
Moondarra [ˈmuːndrə] *Ort in Australien* **III TS2**, 59

New York [ˌnjuː ˈjɔːk] **III U1**, 11
Seattle [siˈætl] **III U4**, 99
Stratford-upon-Avon [ˌstrætfədəpɒnˈeɪvn] *Geburtsort Shakespeares* **III U3**, 71
Tatley [ˈtætli] **III U3**, 69
Wimbledon [ˈwɪmbldən] **I**

Geographical names

Africa [ˈæfrɪkə] Afrika **III U3**, 70
America [əˈmerɪkə] **II**
Australia [ɒsˈtreɪliə] Australien **II**
Austria [ˈɔːstrɪə] Österreich **II**
Bangladesh [ˌbæŋgləˈdeʃ] Bangladesch **III U4**, 97
Ben Nevis [ben ˈnevɪs] *Berg in Schottland* **III U2**, 37
Britain [ˈbrɪtn] Großbritannien **I**
British Empire [ˌbrɪtɪʃ‿ˈempaɪə] britisches Königreich **II**
British Isles [ˌbrɪtɪʃ‿ˈaɪlz] Britische Inseln **II**
Canada [ˈkænədə] Kanada **I**
China [ˈtʃaɪnə] China **I**
Cornwall [ˈkɔːnwɔːl] **II**
Egypt [ˈiːdʒɪpt] Ägypten **III U4**, 100
England [ˈɪŋglənd] England **I**
European Union (EU) [ˌjʊərəpiən ˈjuːnjən; iːˈjuː] Europäische Union **II**
France [frɑːns] Frankreich **II**
Germany [ˈdʒɜːməni] Deutschland **I**
Great Britain (GB) [ˌgreɪt ˈbrɪtn] Großbritannien **II**
India [ˈɪndiə] Indien **II**
Kenya [ˈkenjə] Kenia **III U4**, 102
Loch Lomond [ˌlɒx ˈləʊmənd] *See in Schottland* **III U2**, 44
Loch Ness [ˌlɒx ˈnes; ˌlɒk ˈnes] *See in Schottland* **III U2**, 37
the **Lowlands** [ðə ˈləʊləndz] *schottische Region* **III U2**, 44
North Sea [ˌnɔːθ ˈsiː] Nordsee **II**
Northern Ireland [ˌnɔːðn‿ˈaɪələnd] Nordirland **II**
Pakistan [ˌpɑːkɪˈstɑːn] **I**
Poland [ˈpəʊlənd] Polen **I**
Republic of Ireland [rɪˌpʌblɪk‿əv‿ˈaɪələnd] Republik Irland **II**
Scandinavia [ˌskændɪˈneɪviə] Skandinavien **III U2**, 42
Scotland [ˈskɒtlənd] Schottland **II**
the **Shetland Islands** [ðə ˈʃetlənd ˌaɪləndz] die Shetlandinseln **III U2**, 46
Somalia [səˈmɑːliə] Somalia **III U4**, 102
South Africa [ˌsaʊθ‿ˈæfrɪkə] Südafrika **II**
Spain [speɪn] Spanien **II**
Thames [temz] **I**
United Kingdom (UK) [juːˌnaɪtɪd ˈkɪŋdəm; juːˈkeɪ] Vereinigtes Königreich von Großbritannien und Nordirland **I**
USA (United States of America) [ˌjuːesˈeɪ; juːˌnaɪtɪd ˌsteɪts‿əv‿əˈmerɪkə] USA (Vereinigte Staaten von Amerika) **II**
Wales [weɪlz] **II**

Other names

Auld Lang Syne [ˌɔːld læŋ ˈsaɪn] *schottisches Volkslied* **III U2**, 41
Balmoral Castle [bælˌmɒrəl ˈkɑːsl] *schottische Residenz der britischen Königsfamilie* **III U2**, 44
Best Young Tech Entrepreneur [ˌbest jʌŋ ˌtek ɒntrəprəˈnɜː] **III U1**, 11
Big Ben [ˌbɪg ˈben] **II**
British Airways [ˌbrɪtɪʃ‿ˈeəweɪz] *Fluggesellschaft* **III U4**, 99
Buckingham Palace [ˌbʌkɪŋəm ˈpælɪs] **II**
Business Week [ˈbɪznɪs wiːk] *Wirtschaftszeitung* **III U1**, 11
Church of England [ˌtʃɜːtʃ‿əv ˈɪŋglənd] **III U3**, 66
Cutty Sark [ˌkʌti ˈsɑːk] **I**
Docklands Light Railway *(DLR)* [ˌdɒklændz ˌlaɪt ˈreɪlweɪ] *Regionalbahn im Osten Londons* **I**
Dunnottar Castle [dʌnˌɒtə ˈkɑːsl] **III U2**, 36
Edinburgh Fringe Festival [ˌedɪnbrə ˈfrɪndʒ ˌfestɪvl] **III U2**, 37
the **Globe Theatre** [ðə ˌgləʊb ˈθɪətə] **III U3**, 71
God Save the Queen [ˈgɒd seɪv ðə ˌkwiːn] Gott schütze die Königin *(britische Nationalhymne)* **III U2**, 40
Halloween [ˌhæləʊˈiːn] *Tag vor Allerheiligen* **I**
the **Highland Games** [ˈhaɪlənd geɪmz] **III U2**, 44
Hogmanay [ˈhɒgməneɪ] *traditionelles schottisches Neujahrsfest* **III U2**, 41
the **Houses of Parliament** [ðə ˌhaʊzɪz‿əv ˈpɑːləmənt] *britisches Parlamentsgebäude* **II**
HTML [ˌeɪdʒtiːemˈel] **III U1**, 10
Industrial Revolution [ɪnˌdʌstriəl revlˈuːʃn] die industrielle Revolution **III U3**, 67
Navy [ˈneɪvi] Marine **III U3**, 66
Regina [rɪˈdʒaɪnə] **III U3**, 75
Roman Empire [ˌrəʊmən ˈempaɪə] Römisches Reich **III U3**, 64
Shetland Crofthouse Museum [ˌʃetlənd ˈkrɒfthaʊs mjuːˌziːəm] **III U2**, 46
Spanish Armada [ˌspænɪʃ ɑːˈmɑːdə] *Spanische Flotte* **III U3**, 66
The Wind in the Willows [ðə ˌwɪnd ɪn ðə ˈwɪləʊz] *engl. Kinderbuchklassiker* **III TS4**, 106
Titan Clydebank [ˌtaɪtən ˈklaɪdbæŋk] **III U2**, 43
the **Tower of London** [ðə ˌtaʊər‿əv ˈlʌndən] **II**
Tumblr [ˈtʌmblə] **III U1**, 11
Weezer [ˈwiːzə] **III U4**, 96
World War II [ˌwɜːld ˌwɔː ˈtuː] Zweiter Weltkrieg **II**
Yahoo [jəˈhuː] **III U1**, 11

Famous names

Alexander Fleming [ˌælɪgzɑːndə ˈflemɪŋ] **III U2**, 42
Alexander Graham Bell [ˌælɪgzɑːndə ˌgreɪəm ˈbel] **III U2**, 51
Andy Murray [ˌændi ˈmʌri] *schottischer Tennisspieler* **III U2**, 43
Anne Boleyn [ˌæn ˈbɒlɪn] *Mutter von Elizabeth I.* **III U3**, 75
Anne Hathaway [ˌæn ˈhæðəweɪ] *Shakespeares Frau* **III U3**, 71
Bruno Mars [ˌbruːnəʊ ˈmɑːz] **III TS1**, 31
Charles Macintosh [tʃɑːlz ˈmækɪntɒʃ] **III U2**, 42
Dave Draper [ˌdeɪv ˈdreɪpə] **III TS4**, 107
Elizabeth I [ɪˌlɪzəbəθ ðə ˈfɜːst] **III U3**, 66
Francis Drake [ˌfrɑːnsɪs ˈdreɪk] **III U3**, 68
Henry VIII [ˌhenri ði ˈeɪtθ] Heinrich VIII. **III U3**, 66
Henry Wadsworth Longfellow [ˌhenri ˌwɒdzwəθ ˈlɒŋfeləʊ] **III TS1**, 30
James Carter [ˌdʒeɪmz ˈkɑːtə] **III TS1**, 29
James Watt [ˌdʒeɪmz ˈwɒt] **III U2**, 42
John Henry Holmes [ˌdʒɒn ˌhenri ˈhəʊmz] **III U2**, 51
John Logie Baird [ˌdʒɒn ˌləʊgi ˈbeəd] **III U2**, 42
King Edward [kɪŋ ˈedwəd] **III U2**, 40
Langston Hughes [ˌlæŋstən ˈhjuːs] **III TS1**, 33
Malorie Blackman [ˌmælri ˈblækmən] **III TS3**, 87
Margaret Peterson Haddix [ˌmɑːgrət ˌpiːtəsən ˈhædɪks] **III TS3**, 85
Queen Victoria [ˌkwiːn vɪkˈtɔːriə] **II**
Robert Dudley [ˌrɒbət ˈdʌdli] **III U3**, 68
Robert Hooke [ˌrɒbət ˈhʊk] **III U2**, 51
Robert the Bruce [ˌrɒbət ðə ˈbruːs] **III U2**, 40
Walter Raleigh [ˌwɔːltə ˈrɔːli] **III U3**, 68
William Shakespeare [ˌwɪljəm ˈʃeɪkspɪə] *englischer Dramatiker (1564–1616)* **III U3**, 66
William the Conqueror [ˌwɪljəm ðə ˈkɒŋkrə] **II**

A

abbiegen to turn **I**
abblocken to block **II**
abbrechen to drop out (of) **III U1**, 10
abbrennen *to burn down **III U3**, 71
abchecken to check out *(coll)* **III AC2**, 62
abdecken to cover **III U4**, 103
Abend evening **I**
heute **Abend** 2nite *(= tonight)* **I**; tonight **III TS4**, 107
Abendessen dinner **I**
abends in the evenings **I**
abends *(Uhrzeit)* p.m. **I**
Abenteuer adventure **II**
aber but **I**
abfahren *to leave; to depart **II**
Abflug departure **III U4**, 93
Abflughalle departure lounge **III U4**, 93
abgeschlossen locked **II**
abgesehen von apart from **III U4**, 95
abhaken to tick **II**
abhalten *to hold **III U2**, 44
abhängen von to depend (on) **II**
Abhängige/-r addict **III U4**, 94
Abheben take-off **III U4**, 99
abholen to pick up **III U3**, 72; to fetch **III U4**, 103
Abreise departure **III U4**, 93
abreißen to pull down **III U2**, 41
abschalten to turn off **I**
Schalt/Schaltet es ab! Turn it off! **I**
abschicken *to send off **II**
abschneiden *to cut (off) **II**
Abschnitt section **II**
sich abschotten von to close oneself away from **III U4**, 102
abschreiben to copy **I**
Absicht purpose **III U4**, 97
Abstammung origin **III U4**, 105
Abstand gap **I**
abstimmen *to take a vote; to vote **I**
abstürzen to crash **II**
sich alles abverlangen to push oneself **III U1**, 14
außer Acht lassen to ignore **III U1**, 21
acht eight **I**
Acker field **II**
Action action **I**
Adjektiv adjective **II**
Adresse address **I**
AG club **I**
aggressiv aggressive **II**; pushy **III TS4**, 109
Ägypter/-in Egyptian **III U4**, 100
ägyptisch Egyptian **III U4**, 100
ähnlich similar **II**
keine Ahnung no idea **II**
Akku battery **II**
Aktion action **I**
Aktivität activity **I**
Aktualisierung update **III U2**, 44
Akzent accent **II**
akzeptieren to accept **III U4**, 102
albern silly **I**
alle all of them; everyone **I**; everybody **II**
alle/-s all **I**
wir **alle** all of us **II**
allein alone **I**; on my own **III U4**, 103
alles everything **I**
alltäglich everyday **III U3**, 69
Alphabet alphabet **I**
alphabetisch alphabetical **II**
als as **II**
als *(bei Vergleichen)* than **II**
als when **I**
also so **I**
alt old **I**
Wie **alt** bist du? How old are you? **I**
Wie **alt** sind Sie? How old are you? **I**
Alter age **III U1**, 11
älter elderly **III U2**, 51
am on **I**
am besten best **I**
am Wochenende at the weekend **I**
aus Amerika American **II**
Amerikaner/-in American **II**
amerikanisch American **II**
Amtssprache official language **II**
sich amüsieren *to have fun **I**; to enjoy oneself **III U1**, 14
an on; at **I**; by **II**
an Bord aboard **I**
an sein *to be on **II**
Ananas pineapple **III U3**, 79
anbauen *to grow **III U3**, 65
anbieten to offer **II**
Anblick sight **II**
die anderen the others **I**
andere/-r/-s other **I**; else **III U1**, 19
ein/-e **andere**/-r/-s another **I**
Einerseits …, (aber) andererseits … On the one hand …, (but) on the other hand … **II**
seine Meinung ändern to change one's mind **III U3**, 68
(sich) ändern to change **II**
anders different; other **I**
Änderung change **II**
Andeutung hint **III AC2**, 63
Anfang beginning **II**; start **III U3**, 72
anfangen to start **I**; *to begin **II**
anfeuern to cheer **II**
anführen *to lead **III U2**, 43
angeben to show off **II**
Angeber/-in show-off **III U1**, 17
Angebot offer **III U1**, 17
die Angesagten in-crowd **III U1**, 20
von Angesicht zu Angesicht face-to-face **II**
angreifen to attack **III U3**, 70
Angst fear **II**
Angst haben (vor) *to be scared (of) **I**; *to be afraid (of) **III U4**, 92
Ich habe (keine) **Angst** vor … I'm (not) scared of … **I**
ängstlich fearful **III TS2**, 57
anhaben *to wear **I**
anhalten to stop **I**
Anhänger/-in fan **III AC3**, 91
anhören to listen (to) **I**
anklicken to click on **II**
ankommen to arrive **II**
ankommend inward **II**
Ankündigung announcement **II**
Ankunft arrival **III U4**, 93
Ankunftshalle arrivals hall **III U4**, 93
anmalen to paint **I**
Anmerkung note **I**
annähernd nearly **II**
annehmen to guess **III AC3**, 90; to accept **III U4**, 102
anonym anonymous **II**
Anordnung layout **III U1**, 19
anprobieren to try on **II**
Anregung suggestion **I**
Anruf phone call **I**
einen **Anruf** entgegennehmen to answer the phone **I**
Anrufbeantworter answering machine **I**
anrufen to call **I**; to phone **III TS4**, 107; *to ring **III TS4**, 112
Anrufer/-in caller **I**
anschauen to look at **I**; *to have a look (at) **II**
jmdn. schief/komisch **anschauen** *to give sb funny looks **III U1**, 14
sich anschließen to join **II**
ansehen to look at **I**
(sich) ansehen to watch **I**
Ansicht point of view **II**
anstarren to stare **I**
antike Geschichte ancient history **II**
antippen to tap **II**
Antwort answer; reply **I**
antworten to answer; to reply **I**
Anweisung instruction **I**
Anwesenheitskontrolle registration **II**
Anzeige advert **III TS1**, 28
anzeigen to display **III U3**, 74
anziehen *to put on **III U1**, 20
Apfel apple **I**
Apparat machine **I**
April April **I**
Ära era **III U4**, 105
arabisch Arab **III U4**, 100
Arbeit job; work **I**
Arbeit für die Schule studies *(pl)* **II**
arbeiten to work **I**
Areal area **II**
Ärger trouble **II**
Ärger machen *to make trouble **I**
jmdn. ärgern to tease sb **III U1**, 22
Argument argument **III TS4**, 109
Argument dafür pro **II**
Argument dagegen con **II**
argwöhnisch suspicious **III U4**, 97
Arm arm **II**
arm poor **III U1**, 21

die **Armen** the poor **II**
Art kind **I**
  Art und Weise way **I**
Arzt/**Ärztin** doctor **II**
Arztpraxis surgery **I**
Assistent/-in assistant **II**
Atem breath **III TS3**, 87
  Atem holen *to take a breath **III TS3**, 87
Atemzug breath **III TS3**, 87
Atlas atlas **II**
atmen to breathe **II**
  Atme(t) tief ein. Take a deep breath. **II**
Atmosphäre flair; atmosphere **II**
Attraktion attraction **II**
Aua! Ouch! **II**
auch too **I**; also **II**
  auch nicht not … either **III U1**, 16
  Du **auch**? You too? **I**
Audio- audio **I**
Audioführung audio tour **II**
audiovisueller Effekt audio-visual effect **II**
auf on; at; to **I**
  auf dem Foto/den Fotos in the photo(s) **I**
  auf der anderen Seite von across; opposite **I**
  auf der Straße in the street **I**
  auf einmal suddenly **I**
  auf Wiedersehen goodbye **I**
  auf … zu towards **II**
aufbauen *to set up **I**
  wieder **aufbauen** *to rebuild **III U3**, 71
aufbewahren *to keep **I**
aufdringlich pushy **III TS4**, 109
aufführen to stage **III TS4**, 106
Aufführung show **II**; performance **III TS4**, 106
Aufgabe task; exercise; job **I**
aufgeben *to give up **III U1**, 12
aufgebracht upset **II**
aufgeregt excited **I**; nervous **II**
aufgeschlagen open **I**
aufhalten *to hold open **III AC3**, 90
aufheben to pick up **III U3**, 72
jmdn. **aufheitern** to cheer sb up **III U1**, 23
aufhellen to lighten **III U3**, 78
aufhören to finish **I**
  Hör/Hört auf! Stop it! **I**
aufhören (mit) to stop **I**
aufladen to top up **II**
aufmachen to open **I**
aufmerksam machen (auf) to campaign (for) **III U2**, 39
Aufmerksamkeit attention **II**
Aufnahme recording **I**; shot **III U3**, 76
Aufnahmeort set **III U3**, 76
Aufnahmestudio recording studio **I**
aufnehmen to record **II**
aufpassen to look out **II**
  aufpassen auf to look after **I**
  Pass/Passt auf! Be careful! **I**
aufräumen to tidy *(a room)* **I**
aufrechterhalten *to keep going **II**
aufregend exciting **I**
Aufregung excitement *(no pl)* **III U1**, 22
aufsagen *to say **I**
aufsaugen to soak up **III TS2**, 57
aufschreiben *to write down **I**; to note down **II**
Es ist Zeit **aufzustehen**! Time to get up! **I**
aufstehen *(aus dem Bett)* *to get up **I**
aufstehen *(von einer Sitzgelegenheit)* *to stand up **I**
Auftrag task **I**
Auftritt gig **III U2**, 40
aufwachen *to wake up **III U3**, 79
aufwachsen *to grow up **III U3**, 69
aufwärmen to warm up **I**
  sich **aufwärmen** to warm up **I**
Aufwärmübung warm-up **I**
aufwecken *to wake up **III U3**, 79
aufzeichnen to record **II**
Aufzeichnung recording **I**
jmdn. **aufziehen** to tease sb **III U1**, 22
Auge eye **II**
  die **Augen** verdrehen to roll one's eyes **III U3**, 76
  Ich traute meinen **Augen** nicht. I couldn't believe my eyes. **II**
Augenblick moment **II**
Augenzeuge/**Augenzeugin** eyewitness **II**
August August **I**
aus from **I**
  aus Cornwall Cornish **II**
  aus … heraus out of **III U4**, 99
ausarbeiten to work out **II**
ausblasen *to blow out **I**
Ausblick view **II**
Auschecken Check-out **I**
auschecken to check out *(coll)* **III AC2**, 62
(sich) **ausdenken** *to think of **II**
Ausdruck phrase **I**; expression **II**
  nützliche **Ausdrücke** Useful phrases **I**
ausdrücken to express **II**
Auseinandersetzung argument **III U1**, 20
auserwählt sein, etw. zu tun *to be called to do sth **III TS1**, 31
ausflippen *to go crazy **II**
Ausflug trip **II**
den Hund **ausführen** to walk the dog **I**
ausfüllen to fill in **II**
Ausgang gate **III U4**, 99
ausgeben *(Geld)* *to spend **I**
ausgedehnt wide **II**
ausgehen *to go out **II**
sich **ausgeschlossen** fühlen *to feel left out **II**
aushelfen to help out **III U2**, 51
im **Ausland** abroad **III U4**, 94
ins **Ausland** abroad **III U4**, 94
ausländisch foreign **III U4**, 93
Auslauf run area **III TS2**, 57
auslaufen *to spill **III U4**, 94
(sich) **ausleihen** to borrow **II**
Mach/Macht das aus! Stop it! **I**
auspacken to unwrap **I**
auspusten *to blow out **I**
ausräumen to clear out **I**
jmdm. etw. **ausrichten** *to take a message **I**
sich **ausruhen** to relax **II**
Ausrüstung equipment **II**
Aussage statement **II**
ausschalten to turn off **I**
  Schalt/Schaltet es aus! Turn it off! **I**
aussehen to look **I**
Aussehen looks *(pl)* **III U1**, 10
außer Acht lassen to ignore **III U1**, 21
außer apart from **III U4**, 95; except **III U4**, 103
  außer Betrieb out of order **III TS4**, 112
außerhalb outside; out **I**
Außerirdische/-r alien **I**
äußerst extremely **III TS2**, 59
Äußerung expression **II**
Aussicht view **II**
Aussprache pronunciation **I**
Ausstattung equipment **II**
aussteigen *to get out of **II**
aussteigen (aus einem Bus/Zug) *to get off (a bus/train) **II**
Ausstellung display **II**
  Ausstellung in der Klasse class display **I**
Aussterben extinction *(no pl)* **III TS2**, 60
aussterben *to become extinct **III TS2**, 60
aussuchen to pick **II**
Austausch exchange **III AC1**, 34
Austausch- exchange **III AC1**, 34
austauschen to trade **II**
Austauschschüler/-in exchange student **III AC1**, 34
Australier/-in Australian **III TS2**, 59
australisch Australian **III TS2**, 59
Auswahl choice **II**
auswählen choose **I**; to pick **II**
auswendig lernen *to learn … by heart **I**
auswickeln to unwrap **I**
Auszeichnung award **III U1**, 16
ausziehen *to take off **I**
Auto car **I**
Automat machine **I**; vending machine **III U4**, 94
Autor/-in writer **III U3**, 68
Axt axe **III U3**, 66

B

Baby baby **I**
Background- backing **III U1**, 10
Backgroundtänzer/-in backing dancer **III U1**, 10
Bad bath **I**
Badehaus baths *(pl)* **III U3**, 64
Badewanne bath **I**
Badezimmer bathroom **I**
Badminton badminton **I**
Bahnhof station **I**
Bahnsteig platform **II**
bald soon **II**

Ball ball I
Banane banana I
Band band III U2, 38
Bank bench III U1, 23
bannen to ban III U2, 42
Bär bear II
Basketball basketball I
Batterie battery II
Bauch stomach II
Bauchschmerzen stomachache II
Bauchweh stomachache II
bauen *to build II
Bauernhof farm I
Baum tree I
Baustein building block II
Beachtung attention II
Beamter/Beamtin official III U4, 103
beängstigend scary II
beantworten to answer I
richtig **beantworten** *to get right II
Becher mug III AC1, 34
bedauern *to feel sorry for III U1, 23
bedecken to cover III U4, 103
bedeckt cloudy II
bedeuten *to mean II
Bedeutung meaning II
Bedingung condition III U1, 10
bedrückend depressing III U4, 103
bedürftig in need II
sich beeilen to hurry I
beeindruckt sein *to be impressed II
beeinflussen to influence II
beenden to finish I; to end II
sich befassen mit *to deal (with) II
Befehl order III TS3, 85
befestigen to fix II
befolgen to follow II
befragen to interview I
Befragung interview I
Befürchtung fear II
begeistert excited I
Beginn beginning II
beginnen to start I; *to begin II
behalten *to keep I
behandeln to treat III U1, 21
Behauptung statement II
behindert with special needs II
bei with; at I; by II
beibringen *to teach II
beide both II
beide the two of them II
Bein leg II
die **Beine** und Hände ruhig halten *to keep one's feet or hands still III TS1, 32
beinahe almost II
beinhalten to include II
Beispiel example I
zum **Beispiel** for example II
beißen *to bite II
beitreten to join II
bekommen *to get I; to receive II
etw. aus dem Kopf **bekommen** *to get sth out of one's head III TS1, 32
belästigen to bother III U4, 99
belebt busy I
beliebt popular I
die Beliebten in-crowd III U1, 20
bellen to bark I
Belohnung treat III TS2, 58
bemerken to notice II
Benehmen behaviour *(no pl)* III AC3, 90; manners *(pl)* III AC3, 91
sich benehmen to behave III U1, 14
benötigen to need (to) I
benutzen to use I
beobachten to watch I
bequem comfortable III U3, 65
bereit ready III TS2, 57
bereits already I
Berg mountain; hill II
bergen to save I
Bericht report II
berichten to report II
Beruf career III U1, 10
sich beruhigen to relax; to calm down II
berühmt famous I
berühmte Person celebrity III TS2, 59
beschäftigt busy I
beschreiben to describe I
Beschreibung description II
besichtigen to visit I
Besichtigungs- sightseeing II
besiegen *to beat II; to defeat III U2, 40
besitzen *to have got I
besonders special I
besorgen *to get I
besorgt worried III AC2, 62
besorgt sein *to be worried II
Besorgungen machen *to do the shopping III U2, 51
besser better I
(der/die/das) Beste (the) best II
bestehen aus *to be made of III TS1, 31
besteigen to climb I
bestellen to order III U4, 100
beste/-r/-s best I
am **besten** best I
der/die/das **beste** … überhaupt the best … ever III TS3, 84
bestimmt definitely II
bestürzt upset II
Besuch visit I
besuchen to visit I
Besucher/-in visitor I
beten to pray III TS3, 87
Beton concrete III U4, 103
Betragen behaviour *(no pl)* III AC3, 90
betreten to enter III U1, 17
Betreuer/-in instructor II
außer Betrieb out of order III TS4, 112
Bett bed I
ins **Bett** gehen *to go to bed I
beunruhigt worried III AC2, 62
beunruhigt sein *to be worried II
beurteilen to judge III U1, 8
bevor before I
(sich) bewegen to move I
Beweggrund motive III TS4, 108
Beweggründe motivation III TS4, 107
Bewegung move I
bewerten to judge III U1, 8
bewölkt cloudy II
bezahlen *to pay (for) I
Beziehung relationship II
Bibliothek library III TS2, 56
Biene bee III TS1, 29
bieten to offer II
Bild picture I
bilden *to make I; to form II
Bildergeschichte graphic novel III TS3, 84
Bildgeschichte photo story I
Bildung education *(no pl)* III U3, 69
billig cheap I
binden (an) to tie (to) III U2, 49
Bindewort linking word I
biografisch biographical III U3, 71
Bis … CU *(= See you)*; See you! I
Bis dann! CU *(= See you)*; See you! I
bis jetzt so far II
von … **bis** from … to I
bis auf except III U4, 103
bis till I; until II
Biskuit- sponge I
ein bisschen a bit II
Bitte. Please. I
Bitte schön. Here you are.; You're welcome. I
bitten to ask I
bitten um to ask for I
blau blue I
Blechdose tin can III U2, 51
bleiben to stay I
draußen **bleiben** *to keep out (of) III U2, 48
Bleib wie du bist. Stay the way you are. III U1, 15
Bleistift pencil I
Blick look I; view II
Blick sight III TS1, 30
Blickpunkt focus III TS3, 88
Blickwinkel perspective II
Blitz lightning *(no pl)* II; flash III U3, 77
blockieren to block II
blöd stupid II
blond blond III U1, 20
bloß bare III TS1, 29
bloß only I
Blume flower II
Blut blood III U3, 72
blutig bloody III U3, 73
Boarding boarding III U4, 93
Boden ground III U4, 103
Bonbons sweets *(pl)* I
Boot boat I
an Bord aboard I

Bordkarte boarding card III U4, 93
böse angry; bad I
Bösewicht villain II
Boss boss III U1, 20
Botschaft message I
Bowling spielen to play bowls III U3, 68
Bowlingbahn bowling alley I
Boxen boxing II
Boxrunde round of boxing II
Branche industry III U2, 41
Bratwurst sausage III AC1, 34
Brauch custom III AC3, 90
brauchen to need (to) I
  nicht **brauchen** needn't I
  (Zeit) **brauchen** *to take II
braun brown I
brechen *to break I
brechend cracking III U2, 48
breit wide II
brennen *to burn III U3, 71; *to be on fire III TS3, 87
Brett board III TS1, 28
  schwarzes **Brett** noticeboard II
Brief letter II
Briefträger postman II
Brille glasses *(pl)* II
bringen *to bring; *to get; *to take I
  in Schwierigkeiten **bringen** *to make trouble I
  jmdn. dazu **bringen**, etw. zu tun *to make somebody do something II
Brite/Britin British I
britisch British I
Broschüre brochure I; leaflet III AC3, 91
Brot bread I
  belegtes **Brot** sandwich I
Brötchen bread roll III AC1, 34
Brücke bridge II
Bruder brother I
brüllen to roar III TS3, 87
brutal violent III TS2, 60
Buch book I
buchen to book II
Bücherei library III TS2, 56
Büchse can I
Buchstabe letter I
buchstabieren *to spell I
Bühne stage III U3, 68
bunt colourful I
Buntstift pencil I
Burg castle II
Büro office I
Bus bus I
Busbahnhof bus station I
Busch *(Buschlandschaft)* bush III TS2, 59
Business business III U1, 11
Butter butter III AC1, 34

C

Café café; snack bar I
Cafeteria cafeteria I
campen to camp II
Camping camping II
Cartoon cartoon III AC2, 62
Casting casting III TS4, 113
Cent *(Währung)* cent I
Center centre I
Champion champion III TS1, 32
Chance chance II
Chaos chaos III U3, 76
Charakter character I
Chat chat III U2, 40
Chatroom chat room II
Chatroom chatroom III U1, 12
chatten to chat I
Checkliste checklist II
Chef boss III U1, 20
China China I
Chipkarte smartcard II
nach **Christus** AD (= Anno Domini) III U3, 64
vor **Christus** BC (= before Christ) III U3, 64
circa about I
Clan clan III U2, 44
Clown clown II
Cola coke I
Comedian comedian II
Comedy Show comedy show II
Comic comic II; graphic novel III TS3, 84
Comicheft comic II
Computer computer I
Computerunterricht Technology II
cool cool I
aus **Cornwall** Cornish II
Couch sofa I
Cousin/Cousine cousin I
Cover cover III U1, 8
Creme cream I
Cricket cricket II
Curry *(Gewürz oder Gericht)* curry I

D

da because I
da there I
  da ist/sind there is/are I
dabei sein *to be in II
Dach roof II
Dachboden loft I; attic II
Ich habe nichts **dagegen** (zu) … I don't mind … III U1, 18
dahin there I
damals back then III U3, 64
Dame lady III U3, 76
Sehr geehrte **Dame**, sehr geehrter Herr Dear Sir or Madam II
Dampf steam III U2, 42
Dampfmaschine steam engine III U2, 42
danach then; after that I
dankbar thankful I
Dankbarkeit gratitude III AC1, 35
Danke! Cheers! III AC2, 62
Danke. Thank you.; Thanks. I
danken to thank II
  Nichts zu **danken**. You're welcome. I
dann then I
darauf zu towards II
das that I
  Das (hier) ist … This is … I
  Das macht … That's … I
  Das war knapp! That was close! I
dass that I
Datum date I
dauern *to take II
die **Daumen** drücken *to keep your fingers crossed I
davonkommen mit *to get away with II
Deck deck I
Definition definition II
definitiv definitely II
dein/-e your I
dein/-er/-e/-es yours II
Dekoration decorations *(pl)* I
dekorieren to decorate I
Delfin dolphin III TS1, 29
demonstrieren (für) to campaign (for) III U2, 39
denken *to think I
  Denke/Denkt an … Think of … I
  denken an to remember I
  denken über *to think of I
Denkmal monument II
dennoch still II
deprimierend depressing III U4, 103
deren *(Relativpronomen)* whose III U3, 72
der-/die-/dasselbe the same I
Desaster disaster II
deshalb that's why II
Design design III U3, 64
Designer/-in designer III U1, 12
dessen *(Relativpronomen)* whose III U3, 72
Detail detail II
  nach **Details** durchsuchen to scan II
Detektiv/-in detective III U3, 73
deutlich clear I
Deutsch German I
deutsch German I
Deutsche/-r German I
aus **Deutschland** German I
Dezember December I
Diagramm diagram I
Dialekt dialect II
Dialog dialogue I
Diele hall II
Dienstag Tuesday I
dies this I
diese (hier) these I
  diese dort those I
diese/-r/-s this I
Dilemma dilemma III TS4, 107
Ding thing I
Dinosaurier dinosaur II

direkt direct III TS1, 30
direkt right III U3, 72; straight III U4, 103
Diskussion discussion II
diskutieren to discuss I
Distanz distance II
Distel thistle III U2, 37
DJ DJ III U1, 21
doch after all I
Dollar *(Währung)* dollar III U1, 11
ein Gespräch dominieren to hog a conversation III AC2, 62
Domino dominoes III U4, 100
Donner thunder *(no pl)* II
donnernd roaring III TS3, 87
Donnerstag Thursday I
doof silly I
Dorf village I
dort there I
dorthin there I
Dose can I
aus der **Dose** tinned I
Drama drama II
dramatisch dramatic II
dran kommen to reach II
Du bist dran. Your turn.; It's your turn. I
draußen outside I
draußen bleiben *to keep out (of) III U2, 48
draußen halten *to keep out (of) III U2, 48
nach draußen out I
Dreck dirt III U3, 72
dreckig dirty II
Drehbuch script III AC2, 63
drehen to film II; to turn III TS3, 85
sich im Kreis **drehen** *to go round in circles III U2, 48
Drehort set III U3, 76
drei three I
dreizehn thirteen I
drin inside I
dritte/-r/-s third I
dröhnen to boom II; to roar III TS3, 87
dröhnend roaring III TS3, 87
Druck- print II
drücken to press II
die Daumen **drücken** *to keep your fingers crossed I
du you; u *(= you)* I
du/dir/dich/Sie/sich (selbst) yourself I
Du auch? You too? I
Du bist dran. Your turn.; It's your turn. I
Dudelsack bagpipes *(pl)* III U2, 37
duften *to smell III U3, 65
dumm silly I; stupid II
Zu **dumm**! Too bad! I
Dummkopf silly II
dunkel dark II
Dunkelheit the dark; darkness II
durch through I
durchdrehen *to go crazy II
Durcheinander mess II; chaos III U3, 76
etw. durcheinanderbringen to mess sth up III TS4, 106
schmaler Durchgang close III U2, 43
durchgehen to pass III U3, 72
Durchsage announcement II
nach Details durchsuchen to scan II
dürfen can I; may II; be able to (do sth) III U1, 20; be allowed to (do sth) III U1, 20
nicht **dürfen** mustn't I
durstig thirsty III TS2, 59
Dusche shower I
DVD DVD I

E

Ebbe low tide II
echt real II
Ecke corner II
Edelstein jewel III U3, 75
audiovisueller Effekt audio-visual effect II
Es ist egal. It doesn't matter. III U1, 8
Ehefrau wife, wives *(pl)* II
Ehemann husband III U3, 65
ehrlich honest III U1, 22
Ei egg I
Eiche oak III TS1, 30
Eichhörnchen squirrel I
eifersüchtig sein (auf) *to be jealous (of) I
eigene/-r/-s own I
Eigenschaftswort adjective II
eigentlich actually III U2, 44
eigentlich in fact III U2, 44
eilen to hurry I
Eimer bucket II
ein/-e a; an I
ein paar a couple of I
ein wenig a little I
ein/-e andere/-r/-s another I
noch **ein**/-e another I
einander each other I
einbiegen to turn I
Einchecken Check-in I
eindeutig definitely II
eindringen (in) to invade III U3, 68
eine/-r/-s one, ones *(pl)* II
Einerseits ..., (aber) andererseits ... On the one hand ..., (but) on the other hand ... II
einfach easy I; simple III TS1, 30
einfache Fahrkarte one-way ticket; single ticket II
einfach just I
Einfall idea I
sich etwas einfallen lassen *to think of II
einfallsreich imaginative III U1, 9
einfangen to capture III U3, 70
Einführung introduction II
Eingang entrance III U2, 48
eingängig catchy III TS1, 32
eingeklemmt crushed III U4, 102
eingequetscht crushed III U4, 102
eingießen to pour I
Einheit unit I
einige some; a few I; several II U2 40
sich einigen (auf) to agree (on) II
Einkäufe machen *to do the shopping III U2, 51
Einkäufe shopping I
Einkaufen shopping I
einkaufen gehen *to go shopping I
einladen to invite I
Einladung invitation I
Einleitung introduction II
einmal once I
einmarschieren (in) to invade III U3, 68
einpacken to wrap I
einprägsam catchy III TS1, 32
Einreise immigration III U4, 97
Einreisebewilligung visa, visas *(pl)* III U4, 93
einrichten *to set up I
eins one I
einsam lonely I
einschenken to pour I
einschlafen *to fall asleep I
einschließen to include II
Setze/Setzt ein ... Put in ... I
einst once I
einsteigen *to get into I
Einstellung shot II
Eintrag entry III TS2, 56
eintreten to enter III U1, 17
Eintritt entrance III U2, 48
Eintrittskarte ticket I
nicht einverstanden sein to disagree III U1, 9
Einwanderung immigration III U4, 97
Einwanderungsbehörde immigration office III U4, 97
einwickeln to wrap I
Einzelheit detail II
Einzelkind only child I
einzeln individual II
einziehen in to move in/into II
einzige/-r/-s only II
Eis ice; ice cream I
Eisbahn ice rink I
Eisbrecher *(Sätze, um mit jmdm. ins Gespräch zu kommen)* icebreaker III AC3, 91
Eiscreme ice cream I
Elefant elephant III TS2, 60
Elektrik electrics II
Elektriker/-in electrician II
elektrisch electric III U3, 73
Elektrizität electricity II
elektronisch electronic II
Element element II
elf eleven I
Elfenbein ivory *(no pl)* III TS2, 60
Elisabethaner/-in Elizabethan III U3, 72
elisabethanisch Elizabethan III U3, 72
Eltern parents *(pl)* I
E-Mail e-mail I

per **E-Mail** schicken to mail **II**
Empfang signal **III U2**, 48
empfangen to receive **II**
Ende ending; end **I**
am **Ende** at the back of **II**
Ende gut, alles gut. All's well that ends well. **III U3**, 72
enden to finish **I**; to end up; to end **II**
endgültig final **II**
endlich at last **I**; finally **II**
Energie energy **II**
eng close **I**; narrow **III U2**, 43
sich **engagieren** (für) to campaign (for) **III U2**, 39
Engel angel **III TS4**, 107
aus **England** English **I**
Engländer/-in English **I**
Ich bin **Engländer**/-in. I'm English. **I**
Englisch English **I**
englisch English **I**
englischsprachig English-speaking **I**
entdecken to discover **II**
Entdeckung discovery **III U2**, 42
auf **Entdeckungsreise** gehen to explore **I**
Entfernung distance **II**
entgegen allen Erwartungen against all odds **III TS3**, 84
eine Nachricht **entgegennehmen** *to take a message **I**
einen Anruf **entgegennehmen** to answer the phone **I**
entgegnen to reply **I**
Entgegnung reply **I**
enthalten to contain **III U4**, 99
entlang along **I**
entlanggehen *to go down **I**
entrümpeln to clear out **I**
(sich) **entscheiden** to decide **I**
Entscheidung decision **II**
eine **Entscheidung** treffen *to make a decision **II**
Entschuldigen Sie! Excuse me … **I**
sich **entschuldigen** to apologise **III U1**, 23
Entschuldigung! Sorry!; Excuse me … **I**
entsetzt horrified **I**
sich **entspannen** to relax **II**
entspannt laid-back **III U1**, 10
entsprechen to match **I**
enttäuscht disappointed **I**
entwerfen to design **II**
eine Geschichte langsam **entwickeln** to step into a story slowly **III TS3**, 89
Entwurf plan; draft **I**; design **III U3**, 64
er he **I**
Erdboden earth **II**; ground **III U4**, 103
Erde world **I**; earth **II**
die **Erde** earth **II**
Erdkunde Geography **II**
Ereignis event **I**
erfahren to experience **III U3**, 67
erfahren über *to learn about **III U1**, 9
Erfahrung experience **II**
erfinden to create **I**; to invent **III U2**, 42
Erfinder/-in inventor **III U2**, 51
Erfindung invention **III U2**, 42; fiction *(no pl)* **III TS3**, 84
Erfolg success **III U1**, 10
Erfolg haben (in/bei/mit) to succeed (in) **III U1**, 11
erfolgreich successful **III U1**, 12
erforschen to explore **I**
ergänzen to add **I**
Ergebnis result **II**
ergreifen to grab **II**; to capture **III U3**, 70
erhalten to receive **II**
sich **erheben** *to rise **III TS3**, 87
(jmdn. an etw./jmdn.) **erinnern** to remind (sb of sth/sb) **III TS1**, 31
sich **erinnern** (an) to remember **I**
Erinnerst du dich? Remember? **I**
Erinnert ihr euch? Remember? **I**
Erinnerung memory **II**
Erkältung cold **II**
erkennen to realise **III U2**, 48
erklären to explain **I**
Erklärung statement **II**
erkunden to explore **I**
erleben to experience **III U3**, 67
ernähren *to feed **II**
ernst serious **I**
etw. **ernst** nehmen *to take sth seriously **II**
ernsthaft serious **I**
erraten to guess **I**
erreichen *to get to **I**; to reach **II**
erschaffen to create **I**
erst only **I**
erst wenn until **II**
erstaunlich amazing **II**
erste/-r/-s first **I**
als **Erstes** first **I**
ertappt caught on camera **II**
ertränken to drown **III TS3**, 87
ertrinken to drown **III TS3**, 87
erwachsen werden *to grow up **III U3**, 69
Erwachsene/-r adult **II**
erwähnen to mention **II**
erwarten to expect **III TS4**, 112
entgegen allen **Erwartungen** against all odds **III TS3**, 84
erwidern to reply **I**
Erwiderung reply **I**
erzählen *to tell **I**
erzählen von to talk about … **I**
nochmals **erzählen** *to retell **I**
Erzähle mir von … Tell me about … **I**
Erzählliteratur fiction *(no pl)* **III TS3**, 84
Erzählung story, stories (pl) I
Erziehung education *(no pl)* **III U3**, 69
es it **I**
Es ist super zum/für … It's great for … **I**
Essen food **I**; meal **II**
(ein Bonbon) **essen** *to have *(a sweet)* **I**
essen *to eat **I**
etwa about **I**
etwas some; something; a little **I**
euer/eure your **I**
eure/-r/-s yours **II**
Euro *(Währung)* euro **I**
Europäische Union European Union (EU) **II**
ewig forever **II**
Examen exam **II**
Experte/Expertin expert **II**
extra extra **I**

F

Fabrik factory **III U3**, 67
Fackel torch **II**
Fahne flag **III U2**, 37
fähig sein zu to be able to (do sth) **III U1**, 20
Fähre ferry **III U4**, 93
fahren *to go **I**; to travel **II**; *to drive **III U3**, 77
Fahrer/-in driver **II**
Fahrgast passenger **III U4**, 93
einfache **Fahrkarte** one-way ticket; single ticket **II**
Fahrplan timetable **I**
Fahrpreis fare **II**
Fahrrad bike **I**
Fahrschein ticket **II**
Fahrt trip; tour; journey **II**
fair fair **I**
Fairplay fair play **III TS1**, 28
Fakt fact **II**
fallen *to fall **I**
fallen (lassen) to drop **II**
falls if **I**
falsch wrong **I**; fake **III TS4**, 111
fälschen to fake **II**
Familie family **I**
Fan fan **III AC3**, 91
fangen *to catch **II**
Fantasie fantasy **I**; imagination **III U1**, 9
fantasievoll imaginative **III U1**, 9
fantastisch fantastic **II**
Fantasy fantasy **III TS3**, 84
Farbe colour **I**
Welche **Farbe** hat …? What colour is …? **I**
farbenfroh colourful **I**
Farm farm **I**
Farmer/-in farmer **II**
aus der **Fassung** bringen *to upset **III AC1**, 35
fast almost; nearly **II**
Fastnachtsdienstag Shrove Tuesday **I**
faszinierend fascinating **III U2**, 46
faul lazy **III TS1**, 29
Favorit/-in favourite **III U3**, 68
Februar February **I**
Feder feather **III U3**, 71
Federkiel quill **III U3**, 71
Federmäppchen pencil-case **I**
Was **fehlt**? What is missing? **I**
fehlend missing **II**
Fehler mistake **I**
Feier party **I**

feiern to celebrate I
Feiertag holiday I
Feind/-in enemy III TS3, 84
Feld field II
felsig rocky II
Fenster window I
Fensterladen shutter III U4, 94
Ferien holidays *(pl)* I
fernbleiben von to stay away from II
(sich) fernhalten von *to keep away from II
Fernsehen TV (= television) I
fernsehen to watch TV I
Fernseher TV (= television) I
fertig finished II; ready III TS2, 57
Fertiggericht ready meal I
Fertigkeit skill I
fertigstellen to finish I
fesseln (an) to tie (to) III U2, 49
fesseln to hook III TS3, 85
Fest festival I
festhalten *to hold I
(sich) **festhalten** an *to hold onto III U2, 49
Festival festival I
festnehmen to arrest II
feststecken in … stuck in the middle of … III TS1, 31
Feuer fire III TS2, 59
Feuerwerk fireworks *(pl)* I
Fieber fever II
Figur character I; figure II
Fiktion fiction *(no pl)* III TS3, 84
Film film I
Filmemacher/-in filmmaker II
filmen to film II
finden *to find I
Finger finger I
Firma company III U1, 11
Fisch fish, fish *(pl)* I
fit werden *to get fit I
Fläche space; area II
Flagge flag III U2, 37
Flair flair II
Flamme flame III TS2, 59
Flasche bottle I
Flashback flashback III U3, 78
Fleisch meat *(no pl)* III U2, 41
fliegen *to fly III TS1, 30
Flohmarkt flea market I
Flöte recorder III U1, 14
Flucht escape III TS3, 84
Flüchtling refugee III U4, 104
Flug flight III TS1, 30
Flugbegleiter/-in flight attendant III U4, 93
Flughafen airport II
Flugsteig gate III U4, 99
Flugzeug plane III U4, 92
Flur hall II
Fluss river I
flüstern to whisper I
Flut high tide II
Flyer flyer I
Fokus focus III TS3, 88
Folge sequel II
folgen to follow II
folgende/-r/-s the following II
Form form I
in **Form** kommen *to get fit I
verneinte **Form** negative form I
formal formal II
formell formal II
formen to form II
förmlich formal II
Formular form II
sich fortbewegen *to get around II
fortfahren *to go on I
Fortsetzung sequel II
Forum forum II
Foto photo; picture I
auf dem **Foto**/den **Fotos** in the photo(s) I
Fotos machen *to take photos I
ins **Foto** laufen to photobomb III U3, 77
Fotoapparat camera II
Fotoaufnahmen photo shoot III U3, 74
Fotograf/-in photographer III U3, 76
Fotografie photo I
fotografieren *to take photos I
Fotoshooting photo shoot III U3, 74
Fotostory photo story I
Frage question I
fragen to ask I
Frage/**Fragt** nach … Ask about … I
fragen nach to ask for I
Französisch French II
französisch French II
Frau woman, women *(pl)* I
Frau *(Anrede)* Mrs I
Fräulein *(Anrede)* Miss III U1, 15
frei free I
Freiheit freedom *(no pl)* III U1, 20
Freiluft- outdoor II
Freitag Friday I
Freizeit free time; leisure I
Freizeitzentrum leisure centre I
fremd strange I; foreign III U4, 93
Fremdsprache foreign language III U4, 92
fressen *to eat I
Freude fun I
Freudenfeuer bonfire I
sich freuen an to enjoy II
Freund/-in friend I
Dafür sind **Freunde** da. That's what friends are for. I
Freundin *(in einer Paarbeziehung)* girlfriend II
freundlich friendly II
Freundschaft friendship II
Freundschaft schließen *to make friends II
frisch fresh I
froh happy I; glad III AC3, 91
fröhlich happy; fun I
Front- front II
Frucht fruit I
früh early I
so **früh** this early III AC1, 35
Frühgeschichte ancient history II
Frühling spring III TS2, 57
Frühstück breakfast I
frühstücken *to have breakfast I
Frühstückszerealie cereal *(no pl)* I
fühlen *to feel I
sich **fühlen** *to feel I
sich ausgeschlossen **fühlen** *to feel left out II
sich schlecht **fühlen** *to feel sick II
führen to guide III TS1, 31; *to lead III U2, 43
Führer/-in guide II
(sich) füllen to fill III U2, 42
Füller pen I
fünf five I
fünfzehn fifteen I
funktionieren to work II; to work out III U1, 23
für mich on my own III U4, 103
Für wen …? Who … for? I
Furcht fear II
furchtbar awful I; terrible III U3, 72
(sich) fürchten *to be afraid (of) III U4, 92
Fuß foot, feet *(pl)* I
zu **Fuß** on foot II
Fußball football I
Fußboden floor I
Fußbodenheizung underfloor heating *(no pl)* III U3, 64
Fußgelenk ankle II
Fußknöchel ankle II
Futter food III TS2, 57
füttern *to feed II

G

Gabel fork III AC1, 34
ganz all I
den **ganzen** Tag all day II
ganz quite III U3, 72
ganz whole I
Garage garage I
garstig nasty II
Garten garden I; backyard III TS3, 85
Gast guest III U1, 18
Gastfamilie host family III AC1, 34
Gaststätte restaurant I
Gate gate III U4, 99
Gattung genre III TS3, 84
Geächtete/-r outlaw II
Gebäude building I
geben *to give I
es **gibt** there is/are I
Gebiet area II
geboren werden *to be born III U3, 71
Ge- und Verbote dos and don'ts III AC3, 90
gebrauchen to use I
gebrochen broken I
Gebühr fee II
Geburtsdatum date of birth III U4, 97

Geburtstag birthday **I**
Alles Gute zum **Geburtstag**! Happy Birthday! **I**
Herzlichen Glückwunsch zum **Geburtstag**! Happy Birthday! **I**
Gedächtnis memory **II**
Gedanke thought **II**
Gedicht poem **I**
gedruckt print **II**
Sehr **geehrte** Dame, sehr **geehrter** Herr Dear Sir or Madam **II**
Gefahr danger **III U2**, 48
gefährlich dangerous **I**
Mir **gefällt** … I like … **I**
gefälscht fake **III TS4**, 111
Gefängnis prison **II**
Gefühl feeling **II**
gegen against **II**; versus (vs.) **III U2**, 51
Gegend region **II**
sich **gegenseitig** each other **I**
Gegenstand object **III U2**, 41
gegenüber stehen to face **III TS4**, 107
gegenüber opposite **I**
Gegenwart present **II**
Gegenwarts- present **III U2**, 46
Gehege run area **III TS2**, 57
geheim secret **III U3**, 75
Geheimnis secret **II**; mystery **III U3**, 76
geheimnisvoll mysterious **II**
aus dem Weg **gehen** to avoid **III TS2**, 57
ins Bett **gehen** *to go to bed **I**
nach unten **gehen** *to go down **I**
zu jmdm. nach Hause **gehen** *to go over to **II**
Wie **geht** es dir/euch/Ihnen? How are you? **I**
gehen *to go; to walk **I**; *to leave **II**
nicht **gehorchen** to disobey **III TS3**, 85
gehören (zu) to belong (to) **II**
zueinander **gehören** *to go together **I**
Geist ghost **II**; mind **III TS3**, 87
gelangweilt bored **I**
gelb yellow **I**
Geld money **I**
Geld sammeln to raise money **II**
Geld verdienen *to make money **I**
Gelegenheit chance **II**
Gemälde painting **II**
gemein nasty **II**; mean **III TS4**, 109
Gemeindezentrum community centre **I**
gemeinsam together **I**
gemeinsam haben *to have in common **III TS3**, 88
Gemüse vegetable **III U2**, 41
genannt werden *to be called **III U4**, 95
genau genommen in fact **III U2**, 44
genau exactly **II**
genau hier right here **II**
genauso wie the same way as **II**
Generation generation **III U3**, 67
Genie genius **II**
genießen to enjoy **II**
Gentleman gentleman, gentlemen *(pl)* **III U2**, 44
genug enough **I**
genügend enough **I**
Geocaching geocaching **II**
geöffnet open **I**
Geografie Geography **II**
Gepäck luggage *(no pl)* **III U4**, 92
gerade straight **III U4**, 103
gerade just; at the moment **I**; right now **II**
geradeaus straight on **I**
geradewegs straight **III U4**, 103
Gerät machine **I**; tool **II**; gadget **III U1**, 19
Geräusch sound **I**; noise **II**
gerecht fair **I**
Gern geschehen. You're welcome. **I**
gern haben to like **I**
gern mögen to love **I**
hätte/-st/-n/-t **gern** would like **I**
hätte/-st-/-n/-t sehr **gern** would love **I**
würde/-st/-n/-t **gern** would like **I**
würde/-st/-n/-t sehr **gern** would love **I**
Gerümpel rubbish **I**
Gesang singing **III U1**, 23
Geschäft shop **I**; business **III U1**, 11
geschehen to happen **I**
Geschenk present **I**
Geschichte story, stories *(pl)* **I**; History **II**
antike **Geschichte** ancient history **II**
eine **Geschichte** langsam entwickeln to step into a story slowly **III TS3**, 89
geschichtlich historical **I**
Geschick skill **I**
geschlossen closed **III U4**, 95
geschockt shocked **III TS4**, 113
Gesellschaft society **II**; company **III U1**, 11
Gesetzlose/-r outlaw **II**
Gesicht face **I**
Gesichtsausdruck facial expression **III AC2**, 63
Gespenst ghost **II**
Gespräch dialogue; conversation **I**
ein **Gespräch** dominieren to hog a conversation **III AC2**, 62
ein **Gespräch** für sich in Beschlag nehmen to hog a conversation **III AC2**, 62
das **Gespräch** am Laufen halten *to keep the ball bouncing **III AC2**, 62
gesprochen spoken **II**
Gestalt figure **II**
gestalten to design **II**
Gestaltung design **III U3**, 64
gestern yesterday **II**
völlig **gestresst** sein *to be stressed out **III U1**, 10
gesund healthy **I**
Gesundheit health **II**
Getränk drink **I**
getrennt separate **II**
Gewalt violence *(no pl)* **III TS3**, 84
gewaltig huge **II**
gewaltsam violent **III TS2**, 60
gewalttätig violent **III TS2**, 60
Gewerbe industry **III U2**, 41
Gewicht weight **III TS2**, 57
Gewinn prize **I**
gewinnen *to win **I**
Gewinner/-in winner **I**; champion **III TS1**, 32
Gewissen conscience **III TS4**, 107
Gewohnheit custom **III AC3**, 90
gewöhnlich usually **I**
gewohnt sein *to be used to **III AC1**, 35
gewöhnt sein an *to be used to **III AC1**, 35
Gig gig **III U2**, 40
Gipsverband plaster cast **III U3**, 76
Gitarre guitar **III U4**, 105
Gitter grid **I**
Glas glass **I**
glauben *to think; to believe **I**
gläubig religious **I**
der/die/das **gleiche** the same **I**
gleich right away **I**
jetzt **gleich** right now **II**
gleichmäßig regular **I**
gleichzeitig at the same time **I**
Glocke bell **II**
Glück haben *to be lucky **II**
noch mal **Glück** gehabt saved by the bell **III U1**, 14
Was für ein **Glück**! What luck! **III U3**, 72
glücklich happy **I**
Glücksbringer lucky charm **I**
Gold gold **III U3**, 70
goldenes Zeitalter golden age **III U3**, 66
grau grey **I**
grausam cruel **II**
greifen to grab **II**
Grenze limit **III U1**, 19
Griff knob **II**
groß big **I**; tall; high; large **II**
große Sache big deal **III U4**, 95
großartig great **I**; fantastic **II**
Großbuchstabe capital letter **I**
Größe size **I**
Großeltern grandparents *(pl)* **I**
Großstadt city **I**
großzügig generous **III TS1**, 28
grün green **I**
Grund reason **II**
Es gibt keinen **Grund** zu … There's no need to … **III TS4**, 112
Grund- basic **II**
gründen to found **III U3**, 66
gründen to start **III U2**, 42
grundlegend basic **II**
Grundschule primary school **I**
Gruppe group **I**; team **II**
Gruppenzwang peer pressure **III U1**, 22
gruselig scary **II**
Gruß greeting **I**
Grüße ausrichten (an) *to say hello (to) **I**
Herzliche **Grüße** Best wishes **II**
Herzliche **Grüße** *(am Briefende)* Love … **I**
Liebe **Grüße** *(am Briefende)* Love … **I**

Viele **Grüße** Best wishes **II**
Viele **Grüße** … *(am Ende von Briefen und Mails)* Yours … **II**
grüßen *to say hello (to) **I**
Günstling favourite **III U3**, 68
Gürtel belt **III U3**, 65
gut good; fine **I**
gut sein in *to be good at **I**
gute Leistungen erbringen *to do well **III TS4**, 110
Ende **gut**, alles **gut**. All's well that ends well. **III U3**, 72
Guten Morgen. Good morning. **I**
Mir geht's **gut**. I'm fine. **I**
Guthaben credit **II**
Gymnasium grammar school **II**

H

Haarbürste hairbrush **III U3**, 66
haben *to have got; *to have **I**
hätte/-st/-n/-t gern would like **I**
hätte/-st/-/-n/-t sehr gern would love **I**
nicht ganz Unrecht **haben** *to have a point **III U1**, 18
Hafen harbour **II**
Hafendamm pier **I**
Hähnchen chicken **I**
Hai shark **III U4**, 102
halb *(bei Uhrzeitangaben)* half past **I**
eine **halbe** Stunde half an hour **III U3**, 77
halb half **I**
Halbjahresferien half-term break **I**
Halbschwester half-sister **I**
die **Hälfte** half, halves *(pl)* (of) **I**
Halle hall **II**
Hallo. Hello.; Hi.; Hey! **I**
Halskette necklace **III U3**, 66
Halt stop **II**
halten *to hold; *to keep **I**
halten von *to think of **I**
Haltestelle station **I**; stop **II**
Hamburger burger **I**
Hand hand **I**
Klatsch/Klatscht in die **Hände**. Clap your hands. **I**
Handbuch planner **I**
sich **handeln** um *to be about **I**
Handgelenk wrist **II**
Händler merchant **II**
Handlung action **I**; plot **III TS3**, 84
Handlungsort location **II**
Handschuh glove **I**
Handy phone **I**; mobile **II**
jmdn. **hänseln** to tease sb **III U1**, 22
Happy End happy ending **III TS3**, 84
hart hard **II**
hassen to hate **II**
häufig often **I**
häufig gefragt frequently asked **I**
Haupt- main **I**; lead **III U1**, 10
die **Haupteinkaufsstraße** the high street **III U1**, 20
Hauptfigur protagonist **III TS4**, 106
Hauptrolle lead part **III U1**, 10
Hauptstadt capital **II**
Hauptwort noun **I**
Haus house **I**
nach **Hause** home **I**
zu **Hause** at home **I**
zu jmdm. nach **Hause** gehen *to go over to **II**
Hausarrest haben *to be grounded **III U1**, 20
Hausaufgabe(n) homework **I**
Haustier pet **I**
Haustür front door **II**
in jmds. **Haut** stecken *to be in sb's shoes **III TS3**, 86
He! Hey! **I**
Heim home **I**
heimlich in secret **II**
Heimweh haben *to be homesick **III U4**, 104
heiraten to marry **III U3**, 66
heiß hot **II**
heißen *to be called **III U4**, 95
Ich **heiße** … My name is … **I**
Wie **heißen** Sie? What's your name? **I**
Wie **heißt** du? What's your name? **I**
Heizung heating **III U3**, 64
Held hero, heroes *(pl)* **II**
Heldin heroine **II**
helfen to help **I**
heranzoomen (auf) to zoom in (on) **III U3**, 76
heraus out **I**
herausfinden *to find; *to find out **I**; to work out **II**
Herausforderung challenge **II**
herauskommen aus *to get out of **II**
herausschneiden to edit out **III U3**, 77
Es **stellte** sich **heraus**, dass … It turned out that … **III U4**, 100
Herberge hostel **III U4**, 94
Herd cooker **I**
herein in **I**
hereinkommen *to come in **II**
Herkunft origin **III U4**, 105
Herr lord **III U3**, 65
feiner **Herr** gentleman, gentlemen *(pl)* **III U2**, 44
Herr *(Anrede)* Mr **I**
Sehr geehrte Dame, sehr geehrter **Herr** Dear Sir or Madam **II**
herrisch bossy **III U1**, 14
Herrschaft reign **III U3**, 70
herrschen to rule **II**; to reign **III U3**, 71
die **Herrschenden** those in power **III TS2**, 60
herstellen to produce **III U2**, 39
um … **herum** around **I**
herumschleichen to sneak around **II**
sich **herumtreiben** (mit) *to hang out (with) *(infml)* **III U1**, 20
herunter down **II**
herunterfallen *to fall off **II**
herunterkommen *to come down **I**
herunterladen *(aus dem Internet)* to download **II**
herunternehmen *to take off **I**
herunterrollen to roll off **II**
Herz heart **II**
Herzliche Grüße Best wishes **II**
Herzliche Grüße *(am Briefende)* Love … **I**
heute today **I**
heute Abend 2nite *(= tonight)* **I**; tonight **III TS4**, 107
heute Nachmittag this afternoon **II**
heute Nacht tonight **III TS4**, 107
heutig present **III U2**, 46
Hi. Hi.; Hey! **I**
hier here **I**
genau **hier** right here **II**
Highlight highlight **II**
Hilfe help **I**
ohne fremde **Hilfe** alone **I**
hilflos helpless **I**
hilfreich useful; helpful **I**
hilfsbereit helpful **I**
Himmel sky **III U2**, 48
hinauf up **II**
hinaus out **I**
hinausfließen to flow out **II**
hinausgehen *to go out **II**
hinein inside **I**
hineingehen to enter **III U1**, 17
hineingelangen *to get into **I**
Hin- und Rückfahrkarte return ticket **II**
hinfallen *to fall over; *to fall **I**
wo ich **hingehöre** where I belong **III U4**, 102
hinkommen *to get there **I**
Lege/Legt … umgedreht **hin.** Put … face down. **I**
hinnehmen to accept **III U4**, 102
sich **hinsetzen** *to sit down **I**
hinten at the back of **II**
hinter behind **I**
Hintergrund background **I**
Hintergrund- backing **III U1**, 10
hinterhergehen to follow **II**
Hinterhof backyard **III TS3**, 85
hinüber over; across **I**
hinübergehen zu *to go over to **II**
hinunter down **II**
hinunterfallen *to fall off **II**; *to fall down **III TS1**, 32
hinuntergehen *to go down **I**
hinunterrollen to roll off **II**
Hinweis clue **II**; hint **III AC2**, 63
hinzufügen to add **I**
historisch historical **I**; historic **III U2**, 36
Hobby hobby, hobbies *(pl)* **I**
hoch tall; high **II**
hochleben lassen *to give the bumps **I**
Hochzeit wedding **I**
Hockey hockey **II**
Hofdame lady-in-waiting **III U3**, 76
hoffen to hope **I**

Hoffnung hope **I**
hoffnungsvoll hopeful **I**
höflich polite **I**
Sei/Seid **höflich**. Be polite. **I**
Höhepunkt highlight **II**
Höhle cave **II**
holen *to get **I**; to fetch **III U4**, 103
Holz wood **III U2**, 49
aus **Holz** wooden **III U2**, 48
hölzern wooden **III U2**, 48
Homepage homepage **I**
Honig honey **III TS1**, 29
Hoppla! Oops! **I**
Hör- audio **I**
horchen auf to listen for **I**
Hören listening **I**
hören *to hear **I**
Horn horn **III TS2**, 60
Horror horror **III TS3**, 84
Horrorfilm horror **III TS3**, 84
Horrorgeschichte horror **III TS3**, 84
Hör-/Sehverstehen viewing **I**
Hose trousers *(pl)* **II**
kurze **Hose** shorts *(pl)* **III U1**, 17
Hosentasche pocket **III U2**, 48
Hospital hospital **II**
hübsch beautiful **II**; pretty **III U1**, 21
Huch! Oops! **I**
jmdn. **Huckepack** nehmen *to give sb a piggyback **III U4**, 102
Hügel hill **II**
Huhn chicken **I**
Hülle wrapping **I**
Humor humour *(no pl)* **III U2**, 46
Sinn für **Humor** sense of humour *(no pl)* **III U1**, 23
Hund dog **I**
den **Hund** ausführen to walk the dog **I**
mit dem **Hund** spazieren gehen to walk the dog **I**
Ich bin **hundemüde**. I'm dog-tired. **I**
Hunderte (von) hundreds of **III U2**, 43
hungrig hungry **I**
hüpfen to bounce **III AC2**, 62
Husten cough **II**
Hut hat **I**
hüten to look after **I**
Hymne anthem **III U2**, 40

I

ich I; me **I**
Ich bin aus … I'm from … **I**
Ich bin Engländer/-in. I'm English. **I**
Ich heiße … My name is … **I**
Ich mache … nicht gern. I don't like … **I**
Ich mag … nicht. I don't like … **I**
Ich möchte … I'd like to … *(= I would like to)* **I**
Ich weiß (es) nicht! I don't know! **I**
Ich würde gern … I'd like to … *(= I would like to)* **I**
ich würde lieber I'd rather **III U3**, 79
Idee idea **I**
sich **identifizieren** mit to identify with **III TS3**, 84
Identität identity **II**
Idiot/-in idiot **II**
Igel hedgehog **III TS2**, 56
ignorieren to ignore **III U1**, 21
ihm him **I**
ihn him **I**
ihnen them **I**
ihr you; u *(= you)* **I**
Ihr/-e your **I**; yours **II**
ihr/-e her; its **I**
ihr/-e *(Pl.)* their **I**
illegal illegal **III TS2**, 60
im in; on **I**
im Innern inside **I**
im Moment at the moment **I**
im Weg sein/stehen *to be in the way **I**
Imbiss snack **I**
Imbissstube snack bar **I**
immer always **I**
für **immer** forever **II**
immer noch still **I**
immer wieder over and over again **III TS1**, 32
immerhin after all **I**
Immigration immigration **III U4**, 97
in in; on; at; to; into; inside **I**
in Cornwall Cornish **II**
in der Nähe von near **I**
in der Straße in the street **I**
in Not in need **II**
in … hinein into **I**
in Ordnung OK; fine **I**
indem as **I**
Inder/-in Indian **I**
indisch Indian **I**
individuell individual **II**
Industrie industry **III U2**, 41
Infinitiv infinitive **I**
Informatik IT *(= Information Technology)* **III U1**, 10
Information information *(no pl)* **I**
Informationen information *(no pl)* **I**
Informationsblatt leaflet **III AC3**, 91
Informationstechnik IT *(= Information Technology)* **III U1**, 10
Inlineskates fahren to skate **I**
Inlineskatefahren inline skating **I**
Inlineskates skates *(pl)* **I**
inmitten among **III TS3**, 85
innen inside **I**
inoffiziell unofficial **III U2**, 40
Insel island **II**
Installateur/-in plumber **II**
Instruktion instruction **I**
intelligent smart **III U1**, 9
interessant interesting **I**
Interesse interest **II**
sich **interessieren** (für) to care (about) **II**
sich **interessieren** für *to be interested in **II**
interessiert sein an *to be interested in **II**
international international **I**; multi-ethnic **II**
Internet internet **I**
Internetauftritt website **I**
Internettagebuch blog **III U2**, 44; **III TS2**, 59
Interview interview **I**
interviewen to interview **I**
irgendein/-e/-er any **I**
irgendjemand anyone else **II**
irgendwelche any **I**
irgendwo anywhere; somewhere **II**
irreal unreal **III U4**, 105
sich **irren** *to be wrong **I**

J

ja yes; yeah *(infml)* **I**
Jacke jacket **III U2**, 41
jagen to chase **I**
Jahr year **I**
Jahrbuch yearbook **II**
Jahrhundert century **II**
18-**jährig** 18-year-old **II**
11-**Jährige**/-r 11-year-old **II**
Januar January **I**
je … desto the … the **II**
jedenfalls anyway **II**
jede/-r/-s every; each **I**
jeder everyone **I**; everybody **II**
jede Menge lots (of) **I**
jedes Mal, wenn whenever **II**
jemals ever **II**
jemand somebody **I**; someone **II**
jemand anderes anyone else **II**
jene those **I**
jenes that **I**
jetzt now **I**
jetzt gleich right now **II**
Job job **I**
Joghurt yoghurt **I**
jubeln to cheer **II**
Jugend youth **III TS4**, 112
Jugend- teen **II**; teenage **III TS4**, 107
jugendlich teenage **III TS4**, 107
Jugendliche/-r teenager **I**; kid **III U3**, 73; teen **III TS3**, 84
Juli July **I**
jung young **I**
Junge boy **I**
Juni June **I**
Juwel jewel **III U3**, 75

K

Kaffee coffee **I**
Kaiser emperor **III U3**, 64
Kaiserreich empire **III U3**, 64
Kalender planner **I**; calendar **III U3**, 66
kalt cold **II**
kalt stellen *to leave it to cool **I**

Kamelrennen camel racing **II**
Kamera camera **II**
mit der **Kamera** festgehalten caught on camera **II**
Kameraeinstellung shot **II**
Kamin chimney **II**
Kampf fight **II**; battle **III U3**, 68
kämpfen *to fight **II**
Kaninchen rabbit **I**
Kapitän/-in captain **I**
Kapitel unit **I**
kaputt broken **I**; out of order **III TS4**, 112
Karneval carnival **II**
Karotte carrot **I**
Karriere career **III U1**, 10
Karte card **I**
Kartenschalter ticket office **III U2**, 48
Kartoffel potato, potatoes *(pl)* **III U2**, 42
Kartoffelchip crisp **I**
Kartoffelpüree mashed potatoes *(pl)* **III U2**, 42
Käse cheese **I**
Kasten box **I**
Katastrophe disaster **II**
Kategorie category **II**
Katze cat **I**
kaufen *to buy; *to get **I**
Käufer/-in buyer **I**
Kaufmann merchant **II**
Kaugummi chewing gum **III U4**, 99
kaum hardly **III TS4**, 110
keine Ahnung no idea **II**
Keine Sorge! Don't worry! **I**
kein/-e no **I**
kein/-e/-en not … any **I**
Keks biscuit **I**
Kelte/Keltin Celt **III U3**, 69
keltisch Celtic **II**
kennen *to know **I**
kennen lernen *to get to know **III U1**, 12
kennzeichnen to mark **II**
Kerl guy **II**
Kerze candle **I**
Kerzenlicht candlelight *(no pl)* **II**
Kfz-Mechaniker/-in mechanic **II**
Kilometer kilometre (km) **III TS3**, 87
Kilt kilt **III U2**, 37
Kind child, children *(pl)* **I**; kid **III U3**, 73
Kino cinema **I**
Kirche church **I**
Kiste box **I**
Klang sound **I**
klappen to work out **III U1**, 23
klar clear **I**
Klasse group; class **I**
Klasse *(in einer englischen Schule)* tutor group **I**
Ausstellung in der **Klasse** class display **I**
Klassenarbeit test **I**
Klassenkamerad/-in classmate **I**
Klassenlehrer/-in tutor **I**
Klassenposter class poster **I**
Klassenzimmer classroom **I**
klatschen to clap **I**
Klatsch/Klatscht in die Hände. Clap your hands. **I**
Kleid dress **III U3**, 68
Kleider clothes *(pl)* **I**
Kleidergröße size **I**
Kleiderschrank wardrobe **I**
Kleidung clothes *(pl)* **I**; outfit **II**
klein small; little **I**; tiny **III U2**, 46
Klempner/-in plumber **II**
Klettern climbing **II**
klettern to climb **I**
Klick click **II**
Klicken click **II**
Kliff cliff **III U2**, 46
Klima climate **III U4**, 104
Klimaanlage air-conditioning **III U4**, 103
klingeln *to ring **I**
klingen to sound **I**
Klippe cliff **III U2**, 46
klonen to clone **III U2**, 42
Klub club **I**
klug clever **II**; smart **III U1**, 9
Knacken crack **III U2**, 49
knackend cracking **III U2**, 48
knapp close **I**
Das war **knapp**! That was close! **I**
Knoblauch garlic **III U4**, 95
sich den **Knöchel** verrenken to twist your ankle **II**
Knopf button **III U4**, 103
Koala koala **III TS2**, 59
Koch-AG Cooking Club **I**
Kochen cooking **I**
kochen to cook **II**
Koffer suitcase **III U4**, 93
Kofferraum boot **III U3**, 77
Kokosnuss coconut **II**
Kollektion collection **II**
Kolonie colony **II**
komfortabel comfortable **III U3**, 65
Komiker/-in comedian **II**
komisch funny **III U1**, 14; odd **III AC3**, 90
jmdn. **komisch** anschauen *to give sb funny looks **III U1**, 14
kommen *to come **I**
kommen nach *to get to **I**
kommen zu *to get to **I**
Komm jetzt! Come on! **I**
Komm schon! Come on! **I**
Kommentar comment **II**
kommentieren to comment (on) **II**
Kommunikation communication **II**
kommunizieren to communicate **II**
Komödie comedy **III TS3**, 84
Komparativ comparative **II**
Kompromiss compromise **II**
Kompromisse eingehen to compromise **III U1**, 9
Konfitüre jam **III AC1**, 34
konfrontiert werden mit to face **III TS4**, 107
konfus confused **III U1**, 22
König king **I**
Königin queen **II**
königlich royal **I**
königlicher Leibgardist Beefeater **II**
konkurrieren (mit) to compete (with) **III U1**, 9
konkurrierend competitive **III U1**, 19
können can **I**; to be able to (do sth) **III U1**, 20
kann nicht can't **I**; cannot **II**
können nicht can't **I**; cannot **II**
(vielleicht) **können** may **II**
Es **könnte/-n** auch … sein. It might as well be … **III TS3**, 87
könnte/-n could **II**
konnte/-n could **III U1**, 20
Kontakt contact **II**
in **Kontakt** bleiben (mit) to stay in touch (with) **II**
kontaktfreudig outgoing **III U4**, 105
kontinuierlich steady **III U4**, 103
Kontrolle control **III U4**, 93
kontrollieren to check **I**
Kontrollpunkt checkpoint **III U4**, 102
Konversation conversation **I**
(sich) **konzentrieren** to concentrate **III U4**, 103
sich **konzentrieren** (auf) to focus (on) **III U1**, 10
Konzept draft **I**
Kopf head **I**
etw. aus dem **Kopf** bekommen *to get sth out of one's head **III TS1**, 32
Kopfhörer headphones *(pl)* **II**
Kopfschmerzen headache *(no pl)* **II**
Kopfweh headache *(no pl)* **II**
kopieren to copy **I**
Korbball netball **I**
Koreaner/-in Korean **II**
Koreanisch Korean **II**
koreanisch Korean **II**
Körper body **III U1**, 9
menschlicher **Körper** human body **II**
korrekt correct; right **I**
Korridor hall **II**
Korrigiere/Korrigiert … Correct … **I**
kosten *to cost **I**
Es **kostet** …/Sie **kosten** … It's …/ They're … **I**
Wie viel **kostet/kosten** …? How much is/ are …? **I**
kostenlos free **I**
Kostüm costume **I**; fancy dress **II**
Krachen crack **III U2**, 49
Kraft energy; power **II**; force **III U4**, 105
Krampf cramp **II**
Kran crane **III U2**, 43
krank sick **II**; ill **III TS2**, 57
Krankenhaus hospital **II**
Krankenpfleger nurse **III U3**, 77
Krankenschwester nurse **III U3**, 77
Krankenwagen ambulance **III U3**, 77

Kraut herb **III U4**, 95
kreativ creative **I**
Kreis circle **I**
sich im **Kreis** drehen *to go round in circles **III U2**, 48
kreischen to scream **II**
kreuzen to cross **II**
Krieg war **III U4**, 100
Krieger warrior **II**
Kriminalität crime **II**
Kriminelle/-r criminal **II**
Krone crown **III U3**, 68
Kronjuwelen crown jewels **II**
Küche kitchen **I**
Kuchen cake; pie **I**
Küchenschrank cupboard **I**
Kuh cow **II**
Kühlschrank fridge **I**
Kultur culture **I**
Kummerkastentante agony aunt **II**
sich kümmern (um) to care (about) **II**
sich **kümmern** um to look after **I**
sich um jmdn. **kümmern** *to take care of
sich um jmdn./etw. **kümmern** *to take care of sb/sth **III U3**, 76
Kunde/Kundin customer **II**
Kunst art **II**
Kunstunterricht Art **I**
Kurs course **II**
kurz short **I**
kurz vor on the brink of **III TS2**, 60
Kurzantwort short answer **I**
Kurzform short form **I**
Kurznachricht text (message) **I**
Küste shore; coastline **II**; coast **III U4**, 94
Küstenverlauf coastline **II**
Küstenweg coastal path **II**

L

Lächeln smile **I**
lächeln to smile **I**
lachen to laugh **I**
Laden shop **I**
Lady lady **III U3**, 76
Lage location **II**
Lage (aus) layer (of) **III TS2**, 57
Lagerfeuer bonfire **I**
Lamm lamb **I**
Lämmchen lamb **I**
Lampe light **II**
Land country, countries *(pl)*; land **I**; countryside **II**
landen to end up; to land **II**
landesweit national **I**
Landkarte map **I**
Landschaft landscape **II**
Landung landing **III U4**, 99
Landwirt/-in farmer **II**
lang long **I**
(nicht) **länger** (not) any longer **II**
... lang for ... **II**
langsam slow **I**
eine Geschichte **langsam** entwickeln to step into a story slowly **III TS3**, 89
sich langweilen *to get bored **II**
langweilig boring **I**
Laptop laptop **II**
Lärm noise **II**
lassen *to let **I**; *to leave **II**
Lass/Lasst uns ... Let's ... **I**
Lassi lassi **I**
Lauf run **II**
Laufbahn career **III U1**, 10
Laufen running **II**
laufen *to run; to walk **I**; *to be on **II**
ins Foto **laufen** to photobomb **III U3**, 77
Läufer/-in runner **II**
Laune mood **II**
laut loud **I**; noisy **III U3**, 67
laut vorlesen/vorsingen *to sing out loud **III TS1**, 29
läuten *to ring **I**
Layout layout **III U1**, 19
Leben life, lives *(pl)* **II**
leben to live **I**
lebendig lively **III TS4**, 112
Lebensmittel food **I**
Lebensstil lifestyle **III U3**, 67
leer empty **III U2**, 48
legen *to put **I**; to place **II**
Lege/Legt es in ... Put it in ... **I**
Legende legend **II**
jmdm. eine **Lehre/Lektion** erteilen *to teach somebody a lesson **II**
lehren *to teach **II**
Lehrer/-in teacher **I**; instructor **II**
königlicher **Leibgardist** Beefeater **II**
leicht easy **I**; light **III AC2**, 62
Leichtathletik athletics *(no pl)* **III U4**, 94
leid tun *to be sorry **I**
Tut mir **leid**! Sorry!; I'm sorry! **I**
leihen *to lend **III U1**, 21
leise quiet **I**
sich leisten to afford **III U3**, 79
gute **Leistungen** erbringen *to do well **III TS4**, 110
leistungsorientiert competitive **III U1**, 19
leiten to guide **III TS1**, 31
Lektion unit **I**
jmdm. eine Lehre/**Lektion** erteilen *to teach somebody a lesson **II**
Lernen studies *(pl)* **II**
lernen *to learn **I**; to study **III U1**, 10
auswendig **lernen** *to learn ... by heart **I**
Lesen reading **I**
vor dem **Lesen** pre-reading **I**
lesen *to read **I**
Leser/-in reader **I**
letzte/-r/-s last **I**; final **III U2**, 46
letztlich finally **II**
Leute people *(pl)* **I**
Licht light **II**
Lichtblitz flash **III U3**, 77
lieb nice **I**
Lieber ... Dear ... **I**
Liebe ... *(Anrede in Briefen)* Dear ... **I**
Liebe Grüße *(am Briefende)* Love ... **I**
Liebe love **II**
lieben to love **I**
Ich **liebe** dich. I love you. **I**
Ich **liebe** ... I love ... **I**
lieber better **I**
ich würde **lieber** I'd rather **III U3**, 79
Liebesfilm romance **III TS3**, 84
Liebesgeschichte romance **III TS3**, 84
Lieblings- favourite **I**
Mein/e **Lieblings ...** My favourite ... **I**
Was ist dein/-e **Lieblings**...? What's your favourite ...? **I**
Lied song **I**
Liedtext (song) lyrics *(pl)* **III TS1**, 28
Lifestyle lifestyle **III U3**, 67
lila purple **I**
Limit limit **III U1**, 19
Limonade lemonade **I**
Lineal ruler **I**
Linie line **I**
Link link **II**
linke/-r/-s left **I**
links on the left; left **I**
auf der **linken** Seite on the left **I**
Liste list **I**
Liter litre (l) **III U2**, 39
live live **III TS3**, 88
locker laid-back **III U1**, 10; easy-going **III U4**, 105
Löffel spoon **III TS1**, 29
Logik logic **III U1**, 9
lokal local **II**
Londoner/-in Londoner **I**
Lord lord **III U3**, 65
Los ticket **I**
löschen to delete **III U1**, 23
lösen to solve **II**
losgehen *to leave **II**
loslassen *to let go (of) **II**
Lösung solution **II**
Löwe lion **II**
Lücke gap **I**
Luft air **III TS1**, 30
Luft holen *to take a breath **III TS3**, 87
Lüge lie **III U1**, 22
lügen to lie **II**
die Lunge the lungs *(pl)* **III TS3**, 87
lustig funny; fun **I**

M

Maat mate **I**
machen *to do; *to make **I**
Fotos **machen** *to take photos **I**
sich Notizen **machen** *to take notes **I**
Machen wir uns doch nichts vor. Let's face it. **III TS4**, 108

Machst du so …? Is this how you (do) …? I
Mir macht es nichts aus (zu) … I don't mind … III U1, 18
Macht power II; force III U4, 105
mächtig powerful II
Mädchen girl I
Magen stomach II
Magie magic III U4, 105
magisch magical II
Mahlzeit meal II
Mai May I
mailen to mail II
Mal time II
malen to paint I
Malerei painting II
Mama mum I; mummy III U1, 21
Mami mummy III U1, 21
manchmal sometimes I
Mango mango I
Manieren manners *(pl)* III AC3, 91
Mann man, men *(pl)* I
Mannschaftsführer/-in captain I
Mäppchen pencil-case I
Mappe folder I
Marathon marathon II
markieren to mark II
Markt market I
Marmelade jam III AC1, 34
Marmelade aus Zitrusfrüchten marmalade III AC1, 34
marschieren to march III TS2, 60
März March I
Maschine machine I
Maske mask III U4, 102
Match match II
Material material II
Mathe Maths II
Mathematik Maths II
Matrose sailor I
Mauer wall I
Maus/Mäuse mouse, mice *(pl)* I
Mechaniker/-in mechanic II
Medien media II
Medikamente medicine *(no pl)* III TS2, 60
Medizin medicine *(no pl)* III TS2, 60
Meer sea I
Meerschweinchen guinea pig I
mehr more I
(nicht) mehr (not) any longer II
mehr … als more … than I
mehrere several III U2, 40
Mehrzahl plural I
meiden to stay away from II; to avoid III TS2, 57
Meile *(brit. Längenmaß)* mile II
mein/-e my I
Mein/e Lieblings… My favourite … I
mein/-er/-e/-es mine II
meinen *to mean II
Meinung opinion II
anderer Meinung sein to disagree III U1, 9
einer Meinung sein (mit) to agree (with) II
seine Meinung ändern to change one's mind III U3, 68
die meisten (the) most I
der/die/das meiste (the) most I
meistens usually I
melden to report II
Meldung report II; news report III TS2, 56
melken to milk II
Melodie tune III TS1, 29; melody III TS1, 32
eine Menge a lot of I
jede Menge lots (of) I
Mensch person, people *(pl)* I
Menschen people *(pl)* I
Menschenmenge crowd II
menschlicher Körper human body II
sich merken to remember I
merkwürdig strange I; weird II; funny III U1, 14
sich messen (mit) to compete (with) III U1, 9
Messer knife, knives *(pl)* III AC1, 34
Meter metre II
mich me I
mieten to rent (out) III U2, 47
Milch milk I
Milliarde billion III U1, 11
Million million II
Ich habe das schon eine Million Mal gemacht. I've done this a million times before. II
Millionär/-in millionaire III U1, 10
mindestens at least II
Mine mine II
Mini- mini II
Minute minute I
mir me I
Mir geht's gut. I'm fine. I
mischen to shuffle II; to mix (up) III U3, 76
misstrauisch suspicious III U4, 97
missverstanden misunderstood III U1, 18
mit with I
mit *(dem Fahrrad)* by *(bike)* I
mitbekommen *(ugs.)* *to catch III AC2, 62
mitbringen *to bring; *to take I
miteinander together I
Mitglied member II
mithalten (mit) *to keep up (with) II
mitkriegen *(ugs.)* *to catch III AC2, 62
Mitleid haben mit *to feel sorry for III U1, 23
mitmachen *to be in II
mitnehmen *to take I; to pick up III U3, 72
Mitschüler/-in classmate I
mitsingen *to sing along III TS1, 28
Mitspieler/-in player II
Mittagessen lunch I
Mittagspause lunch break I
Mitte middle I
mitteilen *to tell I
mittelalterlich medieval II
mitten in … stecken stuck in the middle of … III TS1, 31
Mitternacht midnight III U2, 41
Mittwoch Wednesday I
Mix mix III U1, 21
Mobiltelefon mobile II
Modalverb modal II
Mode fashion II
Model model I
Modell model I
Modeln modelling III U1, 10
Moderator/-in presenter I
modern modern II
mögen to like; *to be into; to want (to) I
gern mögen to love I
nicht mögen to hate II
Du magst … You're into … I
Ich mag dich. I love you. I
Ich mag … I like … I
Ich mag … nicht. I don't like … I
Ich mag … total gern. I love … I
Ich möchte … I'd like to … *(= I would like to)* I
Möchten Sie …? Would you like …? II
Möchtest du …? Would you like …? II
Möchtet ihr …? Would you like …? II
möglich possible I
möglicherweise probably II
Möglichkeit chance II
Möhre carrot I
Moment moment II
im Moment at the moment I
Monarch/-in monarch III U3, 66
Monat month II
Mondlicht moonlight III U2, 48
Monster monster I
Montag Monday I
montags on Mondays I
Monument monument II
Mord murder III U3, 72
Mörder/-in murderer III U3, 73
Morgen morning I
Guten Morgen. Good morning. I
morgen tomorrow I
morgens in the mornings I
Motiv motive III TS4, 108
Motivation motivation III TS4, 107
motivieren to motivate I
Motto theme I
Mountainbikefahren mountain biking II
müde tired I
sich Mühe geben to push oneself III U1, 14
Müll rubbish I
Müll herumliegen lassen to litter III AC3, 90
Mund mouth I
mit vollem Mund sprechen to talk with your mouth full III AC3, 90
Münze coin I
murmeln to mutter III U4, 94
Museum museum I
Museumsrundgang gallery walk I

Musik music I
Musik- musical III U2, 41
musikalisch musical III U2, 41
Musiker/-in musician II
Musikgruppe band III U2, 38
Müsli muesli III AC1, 34
müssen must I; *to have to II
(tun) müssen to need (to do) I
nicht **müssen** needn't I
Muster pattern III AC2, 62
mutig brave I
Mutter mother I
Muttersprache first language II
Mutti mummy III U1, 21
mysteriös mysterious II
Mysterium mystery III U3, 76

N

nach unten down II
nach to I
nach drinnen inside I
nach Hause home I
nach unten downstairs II
(**nach**) oben up II
nach *(bei Uhrzeitangaben)* past I
nach *(zeitlich)* after I
nach draußen outside; out I
nach oben upstairs II
Nachbar/-in neighbour *(BE)* I
Nachbarschaft neighbourhood III U2, 51
nachdenken *to think I
Warte/Wartet und **denk/denkt nach**. Stop and think I
nacherzählen *to retell I
nachjagen to chase I
Nachmittag afternoon I
heute **Nachmittag** this afternoon II
nachmittags *(Uhrzeit)* p.m. I
Nachricht message I
eine **Nachricht** entgegennehmen *to take a message I
eine **Nachricht** hinterlassen *to leave a message I
Nachrichten news *(sg)* II
Nachrichtenbeitrag news report III TS2, 56
nachschauen to look up I
nachschlagen to look up I
nachspielen to act out II
nachspüren to trace I
nächste/-r/-s next I
der/die **Nächste(n)** next I
als **Nächstes** next I
am **nächsten** Tag the next day II
Nacht night I
die ganze **Nacht** all night I
heute **Nacht** tonight III TS4, 107
über **Nacht** overnight III U1, 21
Nachtisch pudding I
Nachtwanderung night walk II
nackt bare III TS1, 29
Nahaufnahme close-up II
in der Nähe von near I
nahe near I; close II
Name name I
Namenstag name day I
Nase nose II
die **Nase** voll haben (von) *to be fed up (with) III U1, 17
Nashorn rhino III TS2, 60
nass wet II
national national I
Natur nature II
natürlich of course I
Naturwissenschaften Science II
neben next to I; besides; by II
(von) nebenan next door III AC2, 62
Nebenraum side room III U4, 97
Neffe nephew III U4, 97
negativ negative II
(ein Bonbon) nehmen *to have *(a sweet)* I
etw. ernst **nehmen** *to take sth seriously II
nehmen *to take I
neidisch sein (auf) *to be jealous (of) I
nein no I
benennen to name I
nennen to name; to call I
jemandem auf die Nerven gehen *to get on people's nerves I
nervös nervous II
nett nice I; friendly II
Netz net II; web III U2, 50
soziales Netzwerk social network II
neu new I
neueste/-r/-s latest III U2, 44
Neuigkeiten news *(sg)* II
neulich the other day III U4, 100
neun nine I
nicht not I
auch **nicht** not … either III U1, 16
nicht gehorchen to disobey III TS3, 85
nicht mehr not any more I
nicht mögen to hate II
noch **nicht** not … yet II
nicht- non- II
nichts nothing; not … anything I
Nichts zu danken. You're welcome. I
nie never I
niederbrennen *to burn down III U3, 71
niedlich cute I
niedrig low II
niemals never I
niemand nobody II
niemand anderes nobody else II
Nieselregen drizzle III U4, 103
nirgendwo nowhere II
nirgendwohin nowhere II
noch still I; yet II
noch ein/-e another I
noch einmal again I
noch mal again I
noch nicht not … yet II
noch mal Glück gehabt saved by the bell III U1, 14
Nomen noun I
Nord- north II
Norden north II
im **Norden** north III U2, 46
nördlich north III U2, 46
normal normal II
normalerweise usually I
Normanne/Normannin Norman III U3, 65
normannisch Norman III U3, 65
in Not in need II
Note mark III U1, 10
notieren to note down II
Notiz note I
Notizen machen *to make notes I
sich **Notizen** machen *to take notes I
Notlüge white lie III TS4, 108
November November I
Nudeln pasta I
null zero I
null *(bei Telefonnummern und Uhrzeitangaben)* oh I
Nummer number I
nun now I
nun well I
nur only; just I
Nuss nut I
nützlich useful I
nützliche Ausdrücke Useful phrases I
nutzlos useless III U4, 103

O

O! Oh! I
o.k. OK I
ob if I
oben on top I; above; upstairs II
(nach) **oben** up II
obendrauf on top I
oberer Teil top I
oberes Ende top I
im Obergeschoss upstairs II
Obst fruit I
obwohl although III U4, 97
oder or I
offen open I
offensichtlich obvious III U3, 74
öffentlich public II
offiziell official III U2, 40
offline offline II
öffnen to open I
oft often I
so **oft** whenever II
ohne without I
ohne fremde Hilfe alone I
Ohr ear III AC3, 90
Oje! Oh dear! II
okay okay III TS4, 107
Öko- Eco II
Oktober October I
Oma grandma; granny I

Onkel uncle **I**
Online-Pinnwand wall **III U1**, 23
  online stellen to post **II**
online online **II**
Opa grandad **I**
optimistisch optimistic **III U1**, 23
Orange orange **I**
orange orange **I**
Ordner folder **I**
Ordnung order **I**
  in **Ordnung** fine **I**
  in **Ordnung** bringen to tidy *(a room)* **I**
Organisation organisation **II**
organisieren to organise **I**
  sich **organisieren** *to get organised **II**
Ort place **I**; space **II**
örtlich local **II**
Ost- east **I**
Osten east **I**
Ostern Easter **I**
Outdoor- outdoor **II**
Outfit outfit **II**

P

Paar pair **I**; couple **II**
ein paar some; a few; a couple of **I**
Päckchen packet; parcel **I**
Packung packet **I**
Paket packet; parcel **I**
Palme palm tree **II**
panisch werden to panic **II**
Papa dad **I**
Papier paper **I**
  Stück **Papier** piece of paper **I**
Paradies paradise **II**
Paragraf section **II**
Park park **I**
Partei party **III U2**, 39
Partizip past participle **II**
Partner/-in partner **I**
Partnerarbeit pair work **II**
Party party **I**
Pass passport **III U4**, 93
Passagier/-in passenger **III U4**, 93
passen to fit **II**
  passen zu *to go with; to match **I**
  zueinander **passen** *to go together **I**
passieren to happen **I**
Pasta pasta **I**
Pastete pie **I**
Pause break **II**; pause **III U1**, 14
PC PC *(= Personal Computer)* **II**
Pech haben *to be unlucky **I**
peinlich embarrassing **II**
Pence *(brit. Währungseinheit)* penny, pence *(pl)* **I**
penetrant pushy **III TS4**, 109
Peng! Bang! **II**
Penicillin penicillin **III U2**, 42
Penny *(brit. Währungseinheit)* penny, pence *(pl)* **I**

perfekt perfect **I**
Periode period **III U2**, 39
Person person, people *(pl)* **I**
  berühmte **Person** celebrity **III TS2**, 59
  pro **Person** each **I**
persönlich face-to-face **II**
persönlich personal **I**
Persönlichkeit personality **III U1**, 9
Perspektive perspective; point of view **II**
Pfandhaus pawn shop **III U3**, 79
Pfandleihe pawn shop **III U3**, 79
Pfeife pipe **II**
Pfeil arrow **III TS1**, 30
Pferd horse **I**
Pfirsich peach **III TS1**, 29
Pfund *(brit. Währungseinheit)* pound (£) **I**
Picknick picnic **I**
Pick-up pick-up **I**
Pier pier **I**
Pille pill **II**
pink pink **I**
Online-Pinnwand wall **III U1**, 23
Pizza pizza **I**
Placemat placemat **I**
Platzdeckchen placemat **I**
Plan plan **I**
planen to plan **I**
Planet planet **II**
Plattform platform **II**
Platz place **I**; space; pitch **II**
Platz! *(Befehl für Hunde)* Sit! **I**
plaudern to chat **I**
plötzlich suddenly **I**
Plural plural **I**
Polizei police **II**
Pommes frites chips *(pl) (BE)* **I**
Pony pony **I**
Ponyreiten im Gelände pony trekking **II**
Popstar pop star **III U1**, 17
populär popular **I**
Porträt profile **I**
positiv positive **II**
Possessivform possessive form **I**
Post *(Eintrag im Internet)* post **I**
Poster poster **I**
Postkarte postcard **II**
prägnant to the point **III AC2**, 63
praktisch practical **II**
Präposition preposition **I**
Präsens present **II**
Präsentation presentation **I**
präsentieren to present **I**
Praxis surgery **I**
Praxisräume surgery **I**
Preis price; prize **I**; award **III U1**, 16
preiswert cheap **I**
pressen to press **II**
Privatdetektiv/-in private detective **II**
pro per **II**
  pro Person each **I**
  pro Stück each **I**
probieren to try **I**; to taste **III U3**, 68

Problem problem **I**
Probleme trouble **II**
produzieren to produce **III U2**, 39
Profil profile **I**
Profileinstellungen account settings **III U1**, 23
Programm programme **II**
Projekt project **I**
Prominente/-r celebrity **III TS2**, 59
Prosa fiction *(no pl)* **III TS3**, 84
Prospekt brochure **I**; leaflet **III AC3**, 91
Protagonist/-in protagonist **III TS4**, 106
Protest protest **III TS2**, 60
prüfen to check **I**; to test **II**; to check out *(coll)* **III AC2**, 62
Prüfung test **I**; exam **II**
Publikum audience **III U3**, 72
Pudding pudding **I**
Punkt point **II**
Punktestand score **II**
Puzzle puzzle **I**
Pyjama pyjamas *(pl)* **II**

Q

Qualifikation trial **II**
Qualität quality **I**
Quelle source **II**
quer durch across **I**
Quiz quiz **I**

R

Rabe raven **II**
  Herr der **Raben** raven master **II**
Rad wheel **I**
Radfahren cycling **I**
Radiergummi rubber **I**
Radio radio **II**
Rahmen setting; set **II**
am Rande von on the brink of **III TS2**, 60
Rap rap **I**
rappen to rap **I**
Raster grid **I**
Rat advice **II**
raten to guess **I**
Ratespiel guessing game **II**
Ratschlag tip **I**; advice **II**
Rätsel puzzle; quiz **I**; mystery **III U3**, 76
Ratte rat **I**
Räuber/-in robber **II**
Rauch smoke **III TS3**, 85
Raum room **I**; space **II**
Raumschiff spaceship **II**
rauschen to roar **III TS3**, 87
reagieren to react **III U1**, 23
Reaktion reaction **II**
realisieren to realise **III U2**, 48
realistisch realistic **II**
recht haben *to be right **I**
rechte/-r/-s right **I**
rechthaberisch bossy **III U1**, 14

rechts on the right; right **I**
auf der **rechten** Seite on the right **I**
Rechtschreibung spelling **I**
rechtswidrig illegal **III TS2**, 60
recyceln to recycle **II**
reden to talk **I**
reden mit to talk to **I**
Redensart saying **III U1**, 8
Redewendung phrase **I**
Redner/-in speaker **I**
Referendum referendum **III U2**, 37
Referenzartikel reference article **III TS2**, 56
Regel rule **I**
regelmäßig regular **I**
Regen rain **III U4**, 103
Regenbogen rainbow **III TS1**, 29
Regenmantel raincoat **III U2**, 42
Regieanweisung stage direction **III AC2**, 63
regieren to rule **II**; to reign **III U3**, 71
die **Regierenden** those in power **III TS2**, 60
Regierungszeit reign **III U3**, 70
Region region **II**
Regisseur/-in director **III TS4**, 106
regnen to rain **II**
Reich empire **III U3**, 64
reich rich **III U1**, 10
die **Reichen** the rich **II**
Reihenfolge order **I**
Reim rhyme **I**
(sich) **reimen** to rhyme **III TS1**, 28
rein in **I**
reinigen to clean **I**
Reise trip; travel; journey **II**
Reisebericht travel report **II**
Reisebüro travel agent's **II**; travel agency **III U2**, 47
Reisebus coach **II**
Reiseführer guide **II**
(das) **Reisen** travel **II**; travelling *(no pl)* **III U4**, 93
reisen to travel **II**
Reisende/-r traveller **III U4**, 99
Reisepass passport **III U4**, 93
Reiseziel destination **III U4**, 105
reizen to tempt **III TS4**, 107
Religion *(Schulfach)* RE *(= Religious Education)* **II**
religiös religious **I**
Rennen race; running; run **II**
rennen *to run **I**
reparieren to fix **II**
Reporter/-in reporter **II**
Requisite prop **II**
reservieren to book **II**
der **Rest** the rest **I**
Restaurant restaurant **I**
Resultat result **II**
retten to save **I**; to rescue **III TS2**, 59
Rettung rescue **II**
Rettungsboot lifeboat **I**
Rezept recipe **III TS2**, 56
Rezept *(für Arzneimittel)* prescription **II**

Rhinozeros rhino **III TS2**, 60
Rhythmus rhythm **I**
richtig correct; right **I**; real **II**
richtig beantworten *to get right **II**
Richtung direction **I**
in **Richtung** towards **II**
riechen *to smell **III U3**, 65
riesengroß huge **II**
riesig huge; large **II**
Ring circle **I**; ring **III U3**, 64
ein **Risiko** eingehen *to take a risk **III TS4**, 108
Ritter knight **II**
Rock skirt **II**
Rock *(Musik)* rock **III U2**, 48
Rock 'n' Roll rock 'n' roll **II**
Rohr pipe **II**
Rohrleitung pipe **II**
Rolle role **I**; part **III U1**, 10
Rollen tauschen to swap roles **I**
Rollenbesetzung casting **III TS4**, 113
Rollenspiel role play **I**
Rollschuhe skates *(pl)* **I**
Rollstuhl wheelchair **II**
Rolltreppe escalator **I**
Römer/-in Roman **II**
römisch Roman **II**
rosa pink **I**
rot red **I**
Route route **II**
Routine routine **III U4**, 102
Rückblende flashback **III U3**, 78
Rücken back **II**
Rücken an **Rücken** back to back **I**
Rückenschmerzen backache **II**
Rückenweh backache **II**
Hin- und **Rückfahrkarte** return ticket **II**
Rucksack backpack **III U2**, 38
Rückseite back **II**
rufen to shout; to call **I**; to cry **II**
Rugby rugby **II**
Ruhe silence *(no pl)* **III TS3**, 87
ruhig quiet **I**; silent **III U3**, 72
die Beine und Hände **ruhig** halten *to keep one's feet or hands still **III TS1**, 32
Rühr- sponge **I**
ruinieren to ruin **II**
Rumäne/**Rumänin** Romanian **II**
Rumänisch Romanian **II**
rumänisch Romanian **II**
rumhängen (mit) *to hang out (with) *(infml)* **III U1**, 20
Runde round **II**
Rundgang tour **II**
Rutschbahn slide **I**

S

Saal hall **II**
Sache thing **I**
große **Sache** big deal **III U4**, 95
Saft juice **I**

Sage legend **II**
sagen *to say; *to tell **I**
sagenhaft mythical **III U4**, 105
sagenumwoben mythical **III U4**, 105
Sahne cream **I**
Salat salad **I**
Salbe ointment **II**
sammeln to collect **I**
Geld **sammeln** to raise money **II**
Sammlung collection **II**
Samstag Saturday **I**
Sand- sandy **II**
Sandale sandal **III U3**, 66
sandig sandy **II**
Sandwich sandwich **I**
Sänger/-in singer **II**
Sanitärarbeit plumbing **II**
Satz phrase; sentence **I**
Satzstellung word order **I**
sauber clean **III TS2**, 57
säubern to clean **I**
sauer sein (auf) *to be fed up (with) **III U1**, 17
Säugling baby **I**
Saxofon saxophone; sax **I**
scannen to scan **II**
Schach chess **II**
Schachtel box **I**
Schade! Too bad! **I**
Schaf sheep ʃiːp, sheep ʃiːp *(pl)* **II**
schaffen to create **I**
Du **schaffst** es! You can do it! **III TS1**, 32
Wir haben es **geschafft**! We did it! **II**
Schälchen bowl **I**
Schale bowl **I**
Schalter switch **III U2**, 51; desk **III U4**, 93
scharf sharp **III TS3**, 86
Schatten shadow **III TS3**, 85
Schatz treasure **II**
Schau show **II**
schauen to look **I**
Schau/Schaut mal! Look! **I**
Schau(t) genau ... Look closely ... **II**
schaukeln to rock **III U4**, 102
Schauplatz setting; scene **II**
seinen **Schauplatz** haben (in) *to be set (in) **III U4**, 105
Schauspielen acting **II**
Schauspieler actor **II**
in **Scheiben** schneiden to slice **I**
scheinen to seem **III U1**, 19
schenken *to give **I**
scherzen to joke **II**
Schicht (aus) layer (of) **III TS2**, 57
schicken *to send **I**
schieben to push **II**
Schiedsrichter/-in official **II**
jmdn. **schief** anschauen *to give sb funny looks **III U1**, 14
schiefgehen *to go wrong **I**
schießen to kick **II**
schießen (auf) *to shoot **III TS1**, 30
Schiff ship **I**

Schiffsbau shipbuilding **III U2**, 41
Schiffsjunge cabin boy **I**
Schiffsoffizier mate **I**
Schild sign **II**
Schinken ham **III AC1**, 34
Schinkenspeck bacon **I**
Schlacht battle **III U3**, 68
Schlaf sleep **III U4**, 95
Schlafanzug pyjamas *(pl)* **II**
schlafen *to sleep **I**; *to be asleep **II**
Schlafzimmer bedroom **I**
schlagen *to hit; to whip **I**; *to beat **II**
Schläger racquet **II**
Schlagzeile headline **III TS2**, 56
Schlagzeug drums *(pl)* **III U2**, 40
Schlamm mud **II**
schlammig muddy **II**
Schlange queue **I**
schlau clever **II**; smart **III U1**, 9
der/die/das schlechteste the worst **II**
sich **schlecht** fühlen *to feel sick **II**
schlecht bad **I**
schließen to close **I**
Schließfach locker **I**
schließlich at last; after all **I**; in the end; finally **II**
der/die/das schlimmste the worst **II**
schlimm terrible **III U3**, 72
schlimm *(ugs.)* bad **I**
Schlittschuh laufen to skate **I**
Schlittschuhbahn ice rink **I**
Schlittschuhe skates *(pl)* **I**
Schloss castle **II**
Schluchtenklettern gorge scrambling **II**
Schluss end **I**
zum **Schluss** in the end; finally **II**
Schluss *(einer Geschichte)* ending **I**
Schlüssel key **II**
Schlüsselanhänger key ring **III U2**, 49
Schlüsselbegriff key word **I**
Schlüsselbund key ring **III U2**, 49
schmal narrow **III U2**, 43
schmaler Durchgang close **III U2**, 43
schmecken to taste **III U3**, 68
Schmerz pain **II**
Schmuck jewellery; decorations *(pl)* **I**
schmücken to decorate **I**
Schmuggler/-in smuggler **III U4**, 102
Schmutz dirt **III U3**, 72
schmutzig dirty **II**
Schnäppchen bargain **I**
schnappen to grab **II**
schnarchen to snore **I**
Schnee snow **III U3**, 70
schneiden *to cut (off) **II**
in Scheiben **schneiden** to slice **I**
schneidend sharp **III TS3**, 86
schnell fast; quick **I**
Schock shock **II**
schockiert shocked **III TS4**, 113
Schokolade chocolate **I**
schön nice; fine **I**; beautiful **II**
schon already **I**; yet **II**
schon einmal before **II**
Schornstein chimney **II**
Schotte/Schottin Scot **III U2**, 42
Schottenkaro *(bestimmtes Muster eines Clans)* tartan **III U2**, 37
Schottenrock kilt **III U2**, 37
karierter Schottenstoff tartan **III U2**, 37
schottisch Scottish **II**
Schrank cupboard **I**
schrecklich awful **I**; terrible **III U3**, 72
Schreiben writing **I**
schreiben *to write **I**
schreien to shout **I**; to scream; to cry **II**
Schritt step **I**
Schritt halten (mit) *to keep up (with) **II**
Schritt-für-**Schritt**- step-by-step **II**
Stück Schrott piece of junk **III U1**, 21
schubsen to push **II**
schüchtern shy **II**
Schuh shoe **I**
Schularbeiten schoolwork **III TS4**, 110
schuldig guilty **III TS4**, 113
Schule school **I**
Schüler/-in student **I**
Schüleraustausch student exchange **III AC2**, 63
Schulfach subject **II**
Schulgebühren school fees *(pl)* **III U3**, 79
Schulgeld school fees *(pl)* **III U3**, 79
Schuljahr year **I**
Schulklasse class **I**
Schulstunde lesson **I**
Schultasche schoolbag **I**
Schulter shoulder **II**
Schüssel bowl **I**
schütten to pour **I**
Schutz security **III U4**, 97
schützen to protect **II**
Schwanz tail **I**
schwarz black **I**
schwarz werden *to go black **II**
schwarzes Brett noticeboard **II**
Schweif tail **I**
Schweigen silence *(no pl)* **III TS3**, 87
schweigsam silent **III U3**, 72
Schwein pig **I**
schwer hard **II**; heavy **III U2**, 49
Schwerpunkt focus **III TS3**, 88
Schwester sister **I**
schwierig hard; difficult **II**
Schwierigkeit problem **I**
Schwierigkeiten trouble **II**
in Schwierigkeiten bringen *to make trouble **I**
Schwimmbecken swimming pool **III TS3**, 87
Schwimmen swimming **I**
Schwimmen gehen *to go swimming **I**
schwimmen *to swim **I**
Science-Fiction *(Zukunftsdichtung)* science fiction **II**
sechs six **I**
Second-Hand-Laden charity shop **I**
See lake **I**
See zum Rudern boating lake **I**
seekrank seasick **III U4**, 92
Seemann sailor **I**
Segelboot sailboat **II**
segeln to sail **III TS1**, 31
sehbehindert partially sighted **II**
sehen *to see; to look **I**
Sehenswürdigkeit sight; attraction **II**
sehr very; very much **I**; extremely **III TS2**, 59
Sehr geehrte Dame, sehr geehrter Herr Dear Sir or Madam **II**
Hör-/Sehverstehen viewing **I**
Seil rope **III U2**, 49
sein *to be **I**; *to be like **III U2**, 36
beeindruckt **sein** *to be impressed **II**
sein/-e his; its **I**
seit for *(+ Zeitraum)* **III U2**, 38
seit since *(+ Zeitpunkt)* **III U2**, 38
seitdem since *(+ Zeitpunkt)* **III U2**, 38
Seite page **I**; side **II**
auf der anderen **Seite** von across; opposite **I**
selber yourself **I**; himself; myself; yourselves **II**
das Selbst self, selves *(pl)* **III U1**, 9
selbst even **I**
du/dir/dich/Sie/sich (selbst) yourself **I**
ihr/euch/Sie/sich (**selbst**) yourselves **II**
er/sich (selbst) himself **II**
ich/mir/mich (selbst) myself **II**
selbstbewusst confident **II**
Selbsteinschätzung self-evaluation **I**
selbstkritisch self-critical **II**
selbstsicher confident **II**
selbstverständlich of course **I**
Selfie selfie **II**
seltsam strange **I**; weird **II**; odd **III AC3**, 90
senden *to send **I**
Sender station **II**
Sendung programme **II**
separat separate **II**
September September **I**
Serie series, series *(pl)* **III TS3**, 84
Sessel chair **I**
setzen *to put **I**
sich **setzen** *to sit down **I**
Shorts shorts *(pl)* **III U1**, 17
Show show **II**
Comedy **Show** comedy show **II**
sich each other **I**
sicher sure **I**; safe **II**
sicher sein *to be sure **II**
Ich bin mir (nicht) **sicher** … I'm (not) sure … **III AC1**, 35
Sicherheit security **III U4**, 97
Sicht view **II**
Sie you; u *(= you)* **I**
sie her; she **I**
sie *(Pl.)* they; them **I**
sieben seven **I**

siegen *to win I
Sieger/-in winner I; champion III TS1, 32
Sightseeing- sightseeing II
Signal signal III U2, 48
Signalwort signal word I
Silber silver II
simpel simple III TS1, 30
Singen singing III U1, 23
singen *to sing I
sinken *to sink III TS3, 87
Sinn meaning II; sense III TS3, 86
jmdm. in den **Sinn** kommen *to rise up in one's mind III TS3, 87
Sinn für Humor sense of humour *(no pl)* III U1, 23
Sippe clan III U2, 44
Sitte custom III AC3, 90
Situation situation I
Sitz seat III U3, 73
Sitzbank bench III U1, 23
Sitz! *(Befehl für Hunde)* Sit! I
sich gegenüber **sitzen** *to sit face to face I
sitzen *to sit I
Sitzplatz seat III U3, 73
Skandinavien Scandinavia III U2, 42
Skateboard skateboard II
Skateboardfahren skateboarding I
Skizze outline II
Sklave/Sklavin slave III U3, 70
Skript script III AC2, 63
Slogan slogan II
Smalltalk small talk III AC2, 62
Smartphone smartphone II
SMS text (message) I
eine **SMS** schicken to text II
Snack snack I
so like this; so; like that I; that's how II
so oft whenever II
so … wie as … as I
so viel that much III AC1, 35
so früh this early III AC1, 35
sobald as soon as II
Sofa sofa I
sofort right away I; right now II
sogar even I
Sohn son III U2, 38
solch such III U1, 15
solche/-r/-s such III U1, 15
Soldat/-in soldier III U2, 40
(tun) sollen **sollte(n)** nicht shouldn't II
sollte should II
sollten should II
solltest should II
solltet should II
Somali Somali III U4, 103
somalisch Somali III U4, 103
Sommer summer II
Sommerferienlager summer camp II
Sonderangebot special offer I
sonderbar weird II
Song song I
Sonne sun II
Sonnenblume sunflower III TS1, 29
sonnig sunny II
Sonntag Sunday I
sonst otherwise III U3, 74
sonst noch else III U1, 19
Sonst noch etwas? Anything else? I
Keine Sorge! Don't worry! I
sich Sorgen machen to worry II
für jmdn. sorgen *to take care of sb/sth III U3, 76
sorgfältig careful II
Sorte kind I
Soße sauce III U2, 42
Souvenir souvenir II
sowieso anyway II
soziales Netzwerk social network II
Sozialwissenschaften Humanities *(pl)* II
Spalt gap I
die Spanier Spanish III U3, 66
Spanisch Spanish III U3, 66
spanisch Spanish III U3, 66
spannend exciting I
Spannung suspense II
sparen to save II
Spaß fun I
Spaß haben *to have fun I; to enjoy oneself III U1, 14
Es macht **Spaß**. It's fun. I
spät late I
zu **spät** late I
zu **spät** kommen *to be late I
Wie **spät** ist es? What's the time? I
zu **spät** dran sein *to be late I
kleiner Spaten trowel II
später later I
mit dem Hund spazieren gehen to walk the dog I
spazieren gehen *to go for a walk II
Speck bacon I
Speer spear II
spektakulär spectacular III U2, 46
sperren to ban III U2, 42
speziell special I; specific III U4, 105
spezifisch specific III U4, 105
Spiegel mirror III U3, 66
Spiel game I; match II
spielen to play I
eine Theaterszene **spielen** acting a scene I
einen Streich **spielen** to play a trick (on) I
spielen (in) *to be set (in) III U4, 105
spielen *(Theater)* to act I
Spieler/-in player II
technische Spielerei gadget III U1, 19
Spielfeld field; court; pitch II
Spielkarte card I
Spielstand score II
Spielzeug toy I
Spind locker I
Spinne spider III U2, 50
Spinnennetz web III U2, 50
Spitze top I
spontan spontaneous II
Sport sport I
Sportart sport I
Sportunterricht PE *(= Physical Education)* II
Sprache language I
Sprachmittlung mediation I
Sprechblase speech bubble I
Sprechen speaking; talking I
sprechen *to say; to talk; *to speak I
mit vollem Mund **sprechen** to talk with your mouth full III AC3, 90
sprechen über to talk about … I
Sprecher/-in speaker I; talker III AC2, 62
Sprechgesang chant II
Sprichwort saying III U1, 8
springen to jump I; to bounce III AC2, 62
Spur clue II
Staatsoberhaupt head of state II
Stadion stadium II
Stadt city; town I
Stadtplan map I
Stadtteil part I
Stamm clan III U2, 44; tribe III U3, 64
Stammbaum family tree I
Standbild still II
ständig always I
Standort location II
Standpunkt point of view II
Star star I
stark strong; powerful II; heavy III U2, 49
Stärke power II
starren to stare I
Start start III U3, 72; take-off III U4, 99
starten to start I
Startpunkt starting place II
Station station I
stattdessen instead III U1, 20
stattfinden *to take place I
Steak steak I
stechen *to sting III TS3, 87
mitten in stecken stuck in the middle of … III TS1, 31
stehen *to stand I
gegenüber **stehen** to face III TS4, 107
jmdm./etw. im Weg **stehen** *to stand in the way of sb/sth III AC3, 90
stehen auf *to be into I
stehlen *to steal II
steigen to climb I; *to rise III TS3, 87
Stein stone III U2, 48
Stein- stone III U2, 48
steinig rocky II
Stelle place I
an Jays **Stelle** in Jay's shoes III U1, 12
an jmds. **Stelle** sein *to be in sb's shoes III TS3, 86
stellen *to put I
online **stellen** to post II
sterben to die III TS1, 32
Stern star I
Steuer wheel I
Steuerrad wheel I

Stichwort key word **I**
Stiefel boot **III U3**, 66
Stiefmutter stepmum **I**
Stil style **III U4**, 95
still quiet; still **I**; silent **III U3**, 72
Stille silence *(no pl)* **III TS3**, 87
Stimme voice **I**
Stimmung mood; atmosphere **II**; humour *(no pl)* **III U2**, 46
Stöhnen groan **III U4**, 94
stolz (auf) proud (of) **II**
stoppen to stop **I**
stören *to get in the way **II**; to bother **III U4**, 99
Story story, stories *(pl)* **I**
stoßen to push **II**
Stoßzahn tusk **III TS2**, 60
Strand beach **II**
Straße road **II**
auf der **Straße** in the street **I**
in der **Straße** in the street **I**
Straße *(in der Stadt)* street **I**
Strecke route **II**
Streich trick **I**
einen **Streich** spielen to play a trick (on) **I**
Streit fight **II**; argument **III U1**, 20
(sich) streiten *to fight **II**
streng strict **III TS3**, 86
streng mit jmdm. sein *to be hard on sb **III U1**, 15
strikt strict **III TS3**, 86
Strom electricity **II**
Stromausfall power cut **II**
Stück piece **I**
pro **Stück** each **I**
Stück für **Stück** bit by bit **III TS4**, 111
Stück Papier piece of paper **I**
Stück Schrott piece of junk **III U1**, 21
Student/-in student **I**
Studie survey **I**
studieren to study **III U1**, 10
Studium studies *(pl)* **II**
Stufe step **I**
Stuhl chair **I**
stumm silent **III U3**, 72
Stunde hour **II**
eine halbe **Stunde** half an hour **III U3**, 77
Stundenplan timetable **I**
Sturm storm **I**
stürzen *to fall down **III TS1**, 32
Such- search **II**
Suche search **II**
suchen (nach) to search for **III U4**, 98
suchen nach to look for **I**
Süchtige/-r addict **III U4**, 94
Süd- south **II**
Südafrika South Africa **II**
Süden south **II**
im **Süden** south **III U2**, 44
Südkoreaner/-in South Korean **II**
Südkoreanisch South Korean **II**
südkoreanisch South Korean **II**
südlich south **III U2**, 44
super great; cool **I**
Superlativ superlative **II**
Supermacht superpower **II**
Supermarkt supermarket **I**
Suppe soup **III U4**, 95
Surfen surfing **II**
süß cute; sweet **I**
Süßigkeiten sweets *(pl)* **I**
Swimmingpool swimming pool **III TS3**, 87
Symbol symbol **II**
Szene scene **I**; in-crowd **III U1**, 20

T

Tabak tobacco *(no pl)* **III U3**, 68
Tabelle grid **I**
Tablet tablet **II**
Tablette pill **II**
Tafel board **III TS1**, 28
die Tafelrunde the Round Table **II**
Tag day **I**
am nächsten **Tag** the next day **II**
den ganzen **Tag** all day **II**
ein **Tag** in ... a day out in ... **II**
eines **Tages** one day **II**
Tagebuch diary **II**
Tagebucheintrag diary entry **II**
Talent talent **I**
Talentwettbewerb talent show **I**
Talisman lucky charm **I**
Tante aunt **I**
Tanz dance *(no pl)* **II**; dance **III U1**, 10
Tanzen dancing **III U2**, 44
tanzen to dance **I**
tanzen zu to dance to **III TS1**, 32
Tänzer/-in dancer **III U1**, 10
Tanzveranstaltung dance *(no pl)* **II**; dance **III U1**, 10
tapfer brave **I**
Tasche bag **I**; pocket **III U2**, 48
Taschengeld pocket money **I**
Taschenlampe torch **II**
Tasse cup **III AC1**, 34
Tätowierung tattoo **III U1**, 18
Tatsache fact **II**
Tatsachenbericht news report **III TS2**, 56
tatsächlich actually; in fact **III U2**, 44
Tattoo tattoo **III U1**, 18
Rollen tauschen to swap roles **I**
tausende (von) thousands of **I**
Taxi taxi **II**
Team team **II**
Technik Technology **II**
technische Spielerei gadget **III U1**, 19
Technologie technology **II**
Tee tea **I**
Teebeutel tea bag **III U3**, 79
Teenager teenager **I**; teen **III TS3**, 84
Teil part **I**
im hinteren **Teil** at the back of **II**
teilen to share **II**
teilnehmen (an) *to take part (in) **II**
Telefon phone; telephone **I**
Telefon mit Wählscheibe rotary phone **III U2**, 51
Telefonanruf phone call **I**
telefonieren to phone **III TS4**, 107
Telefonzelle phone box **III U4**, 103
Teller plate **III AC1**, 34
Tennis tennis **I**
Test test **I**
einen **Test** machen *to take a test **II**
testen to test **II**
teuer expensive **I**
Teufel devil **III TS4**, 107
Text text **I**; lines *(pl)* **III TS4**, 106
Theater theatre **I**; drama **II**
Theaterstück play **III U3**, 66
eine Theaterszene spielen acting a scene **I**
Thema theme **I**; topic **II**; subject **III U1**, 9
Therme baths *(pl)* **III U3**, 64
Ticket ticket **I**
tief deep **II**
Tier animal **I**
Tierarzt/Tierärztin vet **I**
Tierheim animal shelter **III TS2**, 59
Tierpark zoo **II**
Tierwelt *(in freier Wildbahn)* wildlife **II**
Tipp tip **I**; hint **III AC2**, 63
Tisch table **I**
Titel heading **I**; title **II**
Titelblatt cover **III U1**, 8
tja well **I**
Toast toast **I**
Tochter daughter **III U3**, 66
Tod death **III TS3**, 84
Toilette toilet **I**
tolerant tolerant **III TS4**, 112
toll great **I**; amazing **II**
Tomate tomato, tomatoes *(pl)* **I**
Ton sound **I**
Tonmodell model **I**
Tonpfeife clay pipe **II**
Tonstudio recording studio **I**
Tor goal **I**
Torte cake **I**
tosend roaring **III TS3**, 87
tot dead **II**
töten to kill **III TS2**, 60
Tour tour **II**
Tourist/-in tourist **I**
Touristeninformation tourist information centre **I**; tourist board **II**
Tradition tradition **I**
traditionell traditional **III U2**, 36
tragen to carry **II**
tragen *(Kleidung)* *to wear **I**
Trainer/-in coach **I**
trainieren to practise **I**; to train **II**
Training training **II**; practice **III U1**, 8
Transport transport **II**
Ich traute meinen Augen nicht. I couldn't believe my eyes. **II**

Traum dream **II**
Traum- fantasy **I**
traurig sad **I**
treffen *to meet; *to hit **I**
sich auf halbem Weg **treffen** *to meet halfway **III U1**, 18
sich **treffen** *to meet **I**
sich **treffen** (mit) *to hang out (with) *(infml)* **III U1**, 20
treffend to the point **III AC2**, 63
Ich lasse mich **treiben**. I go wherever the wind takes me. **III U4**, 105
Treppe stairs *(pl)* **III U2**, 48
treten to kick **II**
Trick trick **I**
trinken *to drink **I**
Trip trip **II**
trocken dry **III TS2**, 57
trotzdem anyway **II**
Tschüss! Bye! **II**
T-Shirt T-shirt **I**
Tudor- Tudor **III U3**, 66
tun *to do; *to make **I**
tun als ob to act like **II**; to pretend **III U4**, 103
was man **tun** und was man nicht **tun** sollte dos and don'ts **III AC3**, 90
Tunnel tunnel **I**
Tür door **I**
Türklingel doorbell **III U1**, 14
Turm tower **III U2**, 48
Turnier competition **II**
Turnschuh trainer **III U1**, 20
Turteltauben lovebirds *(pl)* **II**
Tüte bag **I**
Typ guy **II**
Typ *(ugs.)* bloke *(fam)* **III U1**, 20
typisch typical **I**
typisch typically **III U2**, 37

U

U-Bahn underground **II**
die Londoner **U-Bahn** the Tube **II**
Übelkeit verspüren *to feel sick **II**
Üben practising **I**
üben to practise **I**
über about; over; across **I**
über Nacht overnight **III U1**, 21
überall everywhere **I**
überall (in) all over **I**
überall (egal, wo) anywhere **II**
überfallen to invade **III U3**, 68
überfliegen to skim **II**
überfüllt crowded **III AC3**, 91
sich **übergeben** *to be sick **III U1**, 17
überhaupt at all **I**
überladen overloaded **III U4**, 102
überleben to survive **III TS1**, 32
übernachten to stay **II**
Übernachtung sleepover **I**
übernatürlich supernatural **III U4**, 105
überprüfen to check **I**
überqueren to cross **II**
überraschen to surprise **II**
überraschend surprising **II**
überrascht sein *to be surprised **II**
Überraschung surprise **I**
überreagieren to overreact **II**
überreden to persuade **II**
Überschrift heading **I**; title **II**
übersetzen to translate **I**
Übersetzung translation **I**
übertreiben to exaggerate **III TS4**, 108
überzeugen to convince **III U2**, 50
überzeugend convincing **III U4**, 101
überzeugt convinced **III TS4**, 107
üblich usual **III U1**, 21
übrig left **I**
Übung exercise **I**; practice **III U1**, 8
Übungsheft exercise book **I**
Ufer bank; shore **II**
UFO UFO **II**
Uhr clock **I**
Um wie viel **Uhr**? What time? **I**
Wie viel **Uhr** ist es? What's the time? **I**
Uhr *(Zeitangabe bei vollen Stunden)* o'clock **I**
um *(bei Uhrzeitangaben)* at **I**
um halb acht at 7:30 **I**
um ... herum around **I**; round **II**
umarmen to hug **I**
umbringen to kill **III TS2**, 60
(sich) **umdrehen** to turn round **II**; to turn **III TS3**, 85
Umfrage survey **I**
Umgebung set **II**
Lege/Legt ... **umgedreht** hin. Put ... face down. **I**
umgehen mit *to deal (with) **II**
umher around **I**
umkehren to turn back **III U3**, 72
umkippen *to fall over **I**
Umriss outline **II**
sich **umschauen** to explore **I**
umsegeln to sail **III TS1**, 31
umsteigen (in) to change (onto) **II**
umziehen to move (house) **II**
unabhängig independent **III U2**, 37
Unabhängigkeit freedom *(no pl)* **III U1**, 20; independence *(no pl)* **III U2**, 37
unaufhörlich steady **III U4**, 103
unbekannt unfamiliar **III AC1**, 34
und and **I**
unehrlich dishonest **III TS4**, 110
unfair unfair **II**
Unfall accident **II**
unfreundlich unfriendly **II**
ungefähr about **I**
ungefährlich safe **II**
Ungeheuer monster **I**
ungehorsam sein to disobey **III TS3**, 85
unglaublich amazing **II**
Unglück disaster **II**
unheimlich scary **II**
unhöflich rude **I**; impolite **III AC1**, 34
Uniform uniform **I**
unkompliziert easy-going **III U4**, 105
unordentlich messy **III U1**, 14
Unordnung mess **II**
nicht ganz **Unrecht** haben *to have a point **III U1**, 18
unrecht haben *to be wrong **I**
unrechtmäßig illegal **III TS2**, 60
unregelmäßig irregular **I**
uns us **I**
unscharf out of focus **III U3**, 77
unser/-e our **I**
unsicher unsure **III TS4**, 107
unsichtbar invisible **III U4**, 103
unten downstairs **II**
nach **unten** down **II**
nach **unten** gehen *to go down **I**
unten below **I**
unter under **I**; among
untergehen *to sink **III TS3**, 87
im **Untergeschoss** downstairs **II**
unterhalb below **I**
unterhalten to entertain **III TS4**, 106
Unterhaltung conversation **I**; entertainment *(no pl)* **III U3**, 71
Unternehmen company **III U1**, 11
unternehmen wegen *to do about **II**
Unterricht lesson **I**
unterrichten *to teach **II**
Unterrichtsstunde lesson **I**
Unterschied difference **I**
unterschiedlich different **I**
unterstützen to support **III U1**, 10
unterwegs out and about **II**; on the move **III U4**, 92
unverschämt rude **I**
unwohl sick **II**
Update update **III U2**, 44
üppig lavish **III U4**, 105
Urlaub holiday **I**
Ursprung origin **III U4**, 105
ursprünglich originally **II**
usw. *(= und so weiter)* etc. *(= et cetera)* **II**

V

Vanillepudding custard **I**
Vanillesoße custard **I**
Vater father **I**
Vegetarier/-in vegetarian **III U2**, 41
vegetarisch vegetarian **III U2**, 42
etw. **verändern** *to make a difference **II**
Veränderung change **II**
Veranstaltung event **I**
verantwortlich responsible **III U4**, 102
die **Verantwortung** tragen (für) *to be in charge (of) **III U1**, 14
verantwortungsvoll responsible **III U4**, 102
jmdn. **verärgern** *to make sb angry **III AC1**, 35

verärgert angry **I**
Verb verb **I**
verbessern to improve **I**
sich **verbessern** to improve **I**
verbieten to ban **III U2**, 42
verbinden *to put through **I**; to join; to link **II**
Verbindung link; connection **II**
Ge- und **Verbote** dos and don'ts **III AC3**, 90
Verbrechen crime **II**
Verbrecher/-in criminal **II**
verbrennen *to burn **III U3**, 71
verbringen *(Zeit)* *to spend **II**
verdienen to earn **I**; to deserve **II**
Geld **verdienen** *to make money **I**
die Augen **verdrehen** to roll one's eyes **III U3**, 76
Verein club **I**; society **II**
Verfasser/-in writer **III U3**, 68
verfolgen to trace **I**
verführerisch tempting **III TS4**, 109
Vergangenheit past **II**
Vergangenheitsform simple past; past form **II**
vergeben *to forgive **II**
etw. **vergeigen** to mess sth up **III TS4**, 106
vergessen *to forget **I**
Vergleich comparison **II**
vergleichen (mit) to compare (with/to) **I**
verhaften to arrest **II**
Verhalten behaviour *(no pl)* **III AC3**, 90
sich **verhalten** to behave **III U1**, 14
sich **verirren** *to get lost **II**
Verkauf sale **II**
verkaufen *to sell **I**
Verkäufer/-in assistant **II**
Verkehr traffic **III U4**, 98
Verkehrsmittel transport **II**
öffentliche **Verkehrsmittel** public transport *(no pl)* **II**
Verkleidung fancy dress **II**
verlassen *to leave **II**
sich **verlassen** (auf) to rely (on) **III U1**, 10
verlegen embarrassed **II**
verleihen *to lend **III U1**, 21
verletzen *to hurt **II**
verletzt hurt **II**; wounded **III U2**, 48
Verletzung injury **II**
verlieren *to lose **II**
verloren gehen *to get lost **II**
vermeiden to avoid **III TS2**, 57
vermieten to rent (out) **III U2**, 47
vermischen to mix (up) **III U3**, 76
vermissen to miss **II**
vermuten to guess **I**
verneint negative **II**
verneinte Form negative form **I**
Vernissage gallery walk **I**
vernünftig sensible **III TS4**, 108
Verpackung wrapping **I**
verpassen to miss **II**
verraucht smoky **III U3**, 64

sich den Knöchel **verrenken** to twist your ankle **II**
verrückt crazy **I**; mad **II**
verrückt werden *to go crazy **II**
Versammlung assembly **II**
versäumen to miss **II**
verschieden different **I**; separate **II**
verschiedene several **III U2**, 40
verschmutzen to litter **III AC3**, 90
Verschmutzung pollution **II**
verschütten *to spill **III U4**, 94
verschwenden to waste **II**
verschwenderisch lavish **III U4**, 105
verschwommen blurred **III U3**, 79
verschwunden missing **II**
verschwunden sein *to be gone **II**
sich **versichern** *to make sure **I**
versorgen to supply **II**
Verspätung delay **III U4**, 99
versprechen to promise **II**
Verstand mind **III TS3**, 87
sich **verständigen** to communicate **II**
Verständnis understanding **II**
(sich) **verstecken** *to hide **II**
verstehen *to understand **I**
versuchen to try **I**
in **Versuchung** führen to tempt **III TS4**, 107
in **Versuchung** gebracht tempted **III TS4**, 107
vertrauen to trust **III U1**, 20
vertrauen (auf) to rely (on) **III U1**, 10
nicht **vertraut** unfamiliar **III AC1**, 34
verunreinigen to litter **III AC3**, 90
verursachen to cause **II**
verwenden to use **I**
verwirrt confused **III U1**, 22
verwischt blurred **III U3**, 79
verwundet wounded **III U2**, 48
verzeihen *to forgive **II**
verzieren to decorate **I**
Verzögerung delay **III U4**, 99
Video video **II**
Videochat video chat **II**
viel much **I**
so **viel** that much **III AC1**, 35
Viele Grüße Best wishes **II**
viel/-e lots (of); a lot of **I**
viel a lot **I**
viel zu lernen a lot to learn **I**
viele many **I**
vielleicht maybe **I**; perhaps **III U2**, 48
Vielvölker- multi-ethnic **II**
vier four **I**
Viertel nach/vor quarter past/to **I**
Viktorianer/-in Victorian **III U3**, 67
viktorianisch Victorian **III U3**, 67
violett purple **I**
Visum, **Visa** *(Pl.)* visa, visas *(pl)* **III U4**, 93
Vitamin vitamin **III U3**, 79
Vogel bird **II**
Vogelbeobachtung birdwatching **II**
Vokabular vocabulary **I**
Volksentscheid referendum **III U2**, 37

Volksstamm tribe **III U3**, 64
voll (von) full (of) **I**
Volleyball volleyball **I**
völlig completely **II**; quite **III U3**, 72
vollkommen perfect **I**
von from; about; of **I**; by **III U2**, 42
von ... bis from ... to **I**
vor in front of **I**
vor dem Lesen pre-reading **I**
vor *(bei Uhrzeitangaben)* to **I**
vor *(zeitlich)* before **I**; ago **II**
Voraussage prediction **II**
vorbei over **II**
vorbei (an) past **I**
vorbeigehen (an) to pass **III U3**, 72
vorbereiten to prepare **I**
Vorder- front **II**
Vorderseite front **II**
sich **vordrängeln** to jump the queue **I**
vorgeschichtlich prehistoric **II**
vorhaben *to be up to **II**
vorher before **II**
Vorhersage prediction **II**
laut **vorlesen** *to sing out loud **III TS1**, 29
Vormittag morning **I**
vormittags in the mornings **I**
vormittags *(Uhrzeit)* a.m. **I**
Vorschlag suggestion **I**
vorschlagen to suggest **III U4**, 99
Vorsicht! Be careful! **I**
vorsichtig careful **II**
Vorsingen audition **III U1**, 13
laut **vorsingen** *to sing out loud **III TS1**, 29
Vorsprechen audition **III U1**, 13
vorstellen to present **I**
sich (etwas) **vorstellen** to imagine **I**
Stelle/Stellt ... **vor**. Introduce ... **I**
Vorstellung introduction **II**; performance **III TS4**, 106
Vorstellungskraft imagination **III U1**, 9
Vortanzen audition **III U1**, 13
vortäuschen to fake **II**; to pretend **III U4**, 103
Vortrag presentation **I**
vorüber over **II**
vorüber (an) past **I**
vorwärts forward **III U3**, 72

W

Wachdienst security **III U4**, 97
Wache guard **II**
Wachs wax **II**
wachsen *to grow **II**
Wachsfigur wax figure **II**
Wächter/-in guard **II**
wackelig wobbly **II**
Waffe weapon **III U3**, 75
Wahl choice **II**
wählen choose; to vote **I**
Telefon mit **Wählscheibe** rotary phone **III U2**, 51
wahr true **II**

während *(+ Nomen)* during *(+ noun)* **II**
während while; as **I**
Wahrheit truth **III U4**, 97
wahrnehmen to notice **II**
wahrscheinlich probably **II**
Währung currency **III U4**, 93
Wald forest **II**; wood **III TS3**, 85
Wäldchen wood **III TS3**, 85
Waliser/-in Welsh **II**
Walisisch Welsh **II**
walisisch Welsh **II**
Wand wall **I**
Wandern walking; hiking **II**
wann when **I**
wann immer whenever **II**
warm warm **III TS2**, 57
warnen to warn **III TS4**, 110
(einen Augenblick) **warten** *to hang on **III U4**, 94
Warte/Wartet und denk/denkt nach. Stop and think **I**
Warte ab! Wait and see! **I**
warten (auf) to wait (for) **I**
Warteschlange queue **I**
warum why **I**
was what **I**
Was fehlt? What is missing? **I**
Was für ein Glück! What luck! **III U3**, 72
Was hast du? What's the matter? **II**
Was ist das? What's that? **I**
Was ist dein/-e Lieblings…? What's your favourite …? **I**
Was ist los? What's the matter? **II**; What's up? **III U1**, 14
Was ist mit …? What about …? **I**
was noch what else **I**
was sonst what else **I**
Was um alles in der Welt …? What on earth …? **II**
waschen to wash **I**
sich **waschen** to wash **I**
Waschmaschine washing machine **II**
Wasser water **I**
Wasserrutsche water slide **I**
Webdesigner web designer **III U1**, 14
Webseite site **II**
Website website **I**
Wechsel change **II**
wechseln to change **II**
Wechselt euch ab. Take turns. **I**
Weg way **I**
im **Weg** sein/stehen *to be in the way **I**
im **Weg** stehen *to get in the way **II**
weg away **I**
weg sein *to be gone **II**
wegen because of; for **II**
wegfahren *to drive off **III U3**, 77
wegführen *to lead off **III U2**, 43
wegnehmen *to take **I**
wegrennen *to run away **I**
wegwerfen *to throw away **I**
weh tun *to hurt **II**
Weide field **II**
Weihnachten Christmas **I**
weil because **I**
eine **Weile** a while **II**
Wein wine **I**
weinen to cry **III TS1**, 31
auf andere **Weise** in other ways **II**
weiß white **I**
weit far; wide **II**
weiter (weg) further **III U2**, 46
weitere more; other **I**
weiterführen *to go on **I**
weitergeben to pass (on) **I**
weitergehen *to go on **I**
weitermachen *to go on **I**
welche/-r/-s what; which **I**
Welche Farbe hat …? What colour is …? **I**
Welche … sind es? What are …? **I**
Welle wave **I**
Welt world **I**
Was um alles in der **Welt** …? What on earth …? **II**
wem who **I**
wen who **I**
Für **wen** …? Who … for? **I**
wenden to turn round **II**
sich **wenden** an to turn to **II**
Wendung expression **II**
weniger less **III U3**, 67
ein **wenig** a little **I**; a bit **II**
wenige a few **I**; few **II**
wenigstens at least **II**
wenn when; if **I**
wer who **I**
Wer ist es? Who is it? **I**
Wer macht mit? Who's in? **II**
Werbespot advert **III TS1**, 28
Werbespruch slogan **II**
werden *to become; *to get **II**
würde/-st/-n/-t would **III U1**, 9
werfen (nach) *to throw (at) **I**
Werk factory **III U3**, 67
Werkzeug tool **II**
wert sein *to be worth **I**
das **Wesentliche** gist **II**
West- west **I**
Westen west **I**
Wettbewerb contest **I**; competition **II**
in **Wettbewerb** treten (mit) to compete (with) **III U1**, 9
ich **wette** I bet **II**
Wetter weather **I**
Wettervorhersage weather forecast **II**
Wettkampf contest **I**
Wettlauf race **II**
Whisky whisky **III U2**, 39
wichtig important **I**
wichtig nehmen to care (about) **II**
wie like **I**
wie as **II**
wie how **I**
Wie viele …? How many …? **I**
Wie alt bist du? How old are you? **I**
Wie alt sind Sie? How old are you? **I**
Wie geht es dir/euch/Ihnen? How are you? **I**
Wie heißen Sie? What's your name? **I**
Wie heißt du? What's your name? **I**
Wie man … How to … **I**
Wie spät ist es? What's the time? **I**
Wie viel (kostet/kosten) …? How much is/are …? **I**
Wie viel Uhr ist es? What's the time? **I**
Wie war es? What was it like? **III U3**, 64
Wie wär's mit …? What about …? **I**
wieder again **I**
Wiederaufnehmen pick-up **I**
wiederholen to repeat **III TS3**, 31
Wiederholung revision **II**
auf **Wiedersehen** goodbye **I**
wiederverwerten to recycle **II**
wiegen to weigh **III TS2**, 57
Wiese field **II**
wild wild **II**
Wilderei poaching *(no pl)* **III TS2**, 60
Wildnis bush **III TS2**, 59
Willkommen! Welcome! **II**
willkommen heißen to welcome **II**
Wind wind **II**
Windsurfen windsurfing **II**
Winter winter **III TS2**, 57
Winterschlaf hibernation **III TS2**, 57
winzig tiny **III U2**, 46
wir we **I**
wirklich real **II**
wirklich really **I**; actually **III U2**, 44
wirr confused **III U1**, 22
wissen *to know **I**
Ich **weiß** (es) nicht! I don't know! **I**
Wissenschaftler/-in scientist **III U2**, 42
Witz joke **I**
witzig funny; fun **I**
WLAN wifi **III U4**, 94
wo where **I**
wo ich hingehöre where I belong **III U4**, 102
Woche week **I**
Wochenende weekend **I**
am **Wochenende** at the weekend **I**
Wochentag weekday **II**
Woher …? Where … from? **I**
wohin where **I**
Wohlfahrt charity **I**
wohltätige Zwecke charity **I**
Wohltätigkeitsverein charity **I**
wohnen to live **I**
wohnen bei to stay with **II**
Wohnung flat **I**
Wohnzimmer living room **I**
Wolke cloud **II**
wollen to want (to) **I**
Workshop workshop **I**
Wort word **I**
Wortbildung word-building **II**

Wörterbuch dictionary **I**
Wörterwolke word cloud **II**
Wortschatz vocabulary **I**
Wortschlange word snake **I**
Wortspiel play on words **III TS1**, 32
Wortstellung word order **I**
Wortverbindung collocation **II**
Worum geht es in/im ...? What is ... about? **I**
wunderbar beautiful; wonderful **II**
sich etwas **wünschen** *to make a wish **I**
Ich **würde** gern ... I'd like to ... (= *I would like to)* **I**
würde/-st/-n/-t gern would like **I**
würde/-st/-n/-t sehr gern would love **I**
Würfel dice **II**
Würfle/Würfelt mit zwei Würfeln. Roll two dice. **I**
Wurm worm **I**
Wurst sausage **III AC1**, 34
wusch whoosh **I**
Wut anger *(no pl)* **III U1**, 21
wütend angry **I**
jmdn. **wütend** machen *to make sb angry **III AC1**, 35

Z

z.B. *(= zum Beispiel)* e.g. *(= for example)* **I**
Zahl number **I**
zählen (auf) to count (on) **I**
Zauber- magical **II**
Zauberei magic **III U4**, 105
Zauberer wizard **II**
auf **Zehenspitzen** gehen to tiptoe **II**
zehn ten **I**
zehnmal ten times **I**
Zeichen sign **II**
Zeichentrickfilm cartoon **III AC2**, 62
zeichnen *to draw **I**
Zeichnung drawing **I**
zeigen to show **I**
mit dem Finger auf jmdn./etw. **zeigen** to point at sb/sth **III AC3**, 90
Zeile line **I**
Zeit time **I**; tense **II**
(**Zeit**) brauchen *to take **II**
zur selben **Zeit** at the same time **I**
die ganze **Zeit** all the time **II**
Es ist **Zeit** aufzustehen! Time to get up! **I**
Zeitalter era **III U4**, 105
goldenes **Zeitalter** golden age **III U3**, 66
Zeitform *(grammatisch)* tense **II**
Zeitpunkt point **II**
Zeitschrift magazine **I**
Zeitspanne period **III U2**, 39
Zeitstrahl time line **I**
Zeitung newspaper **III TS2**, 57
Zelten camping **II**
zelten to camp **II**
zentral central **II**
Zentral- central **II**
Zentrum centre **I**
zerbrechen *to break **I**
zerschlagen to smash **III U4**, 102
zerschmettern to smash **III U4**, 102
zerstören to ruin **II**
Zeug stuff **I**
Zeuge/Zeugin witness **II**
ziehen to pull **I**; *to draw **II**
Ziel goal **I**; purpose **III U4**, 97; destination **III U4**, 105
Ziellinie finish line **II**
ziemlich quite **III U3**, 72
Zimmer room **I**
Zimmergenosse/Zimmergenossin room-mate **I**
Zinn tin **II**
Zitrone lemon **II**
zögern to hesitate **III TS3**, 85
Zoll customs *(sg)* **III U4**, 93
zollfrei duty-free **III U4**, 93
Zoo zoo **II**
Zorn anger *(no pl)* **III U1**, 21
zornig angry **I**
zu closed **III U4**, 95
zu too **I**
Zu dumm! Too bad! **I**
zu to **I**
zu Hause at home **I**
zubereiten to prepare **I**
züchten *to grow **III U3**, 65
Zucker sugar **III AC1**, 34
zudecken to cover **III U4**, 103
zuerst first **I**; at first **II**
Zug train **I**
Zuhause home **I**
zuhören to listen (to) **I**
Zuhörer/-in listener **II**
zujubeln to cheer **II**
auf jmdn. **zukommen** *to come up to sb **III U1**, 21
Zukunft future **II**
zukünftig future **III U4**, 105
zum Beispiel for example **II**
zumachen to close **I**
zunächst at first **II**
zuordnen to match **I**
zupassen to pass **II**
(ein Foto) **zurechtschneiden** to crop (a photo) **III U3**, 77
zurück back **I**
zurückfahren to return **II**
zurückgehen to turn back **III U3**, 72
zurückgehen auf *to go right back to **II**
zurückkehren to return **II**
zurücklassen *to leave behind **III U2**, 43
zurückschrecken to jump back **II**
zurückspringen to jump back **II**
zurzeit these days **III U1**, 20
zusammen together **I**
zusammenstoßen to crash **III U3**, 77
zusätzlich extra **I**; additional **II**
zuschauen to watch **I**
Zuschauer/-in viewer **II**
zuspielen to pass **II**
zuständig sein (für) *to be in charge (of) **III U1**, 14
zustimmen to agree (with) **II**
Zutat ingredient **II**
zuvor before **II**
sich **zuwenden** to turn to **II**
Zweck purpose **III U4**, 97
zwei two **I**
Zweifel doubt **III U1**, 9
zweisprachig bilingual **II**
zweite/-r/-s second **I**
Zwickmühle dilemma **III TS4**, 107
Zwilling twin **II**
Zwillings- twin **II**
zwischen between **I**
zwölf twelve **I**

In the classroom

Tip

Die Wörter und Ausdrücke auf diesen Seiten musst du nicht auswendig lernen. Aber in vielen Situationen im Klassenzimmer wirst du sie nützlich finden!

Asking for help and information

Can you help me, please?	Kannst du / Können Sie mir bitte helfen?
How do you do this exercise?	Wie macht man diese Übung?
How do you spell …, please?	Wie schreibt man …, bitte?
Is this right? I'm not sure.	Ist das richtig? Ich bin mir nicht sicher.
Is it OK to …?	Ist es in Ordnung, wenn ich / wir …?
Is it true or false?	Ist das richtig oder falsch?
Sorry, I don't know. Ask …	Tut mir leid, das weiß ich nicht. Frag …
Sorry. Can you say that again, please?	Wie bitte? Können Sie das bitte wiederholen?
What does that mean?	Was bedeutet das?
What's for homework?	Was haben wir als Hausaufgabe auf?
What's that in English / German?	Was heißt das auf Englisch / Deutsch?

Vocabulary for instructions and activities

(Die mit * gekennzeichneten Begriffe werden im Bildungsplan als Operatoren definiert. Die Verwendung der geforderten Operatoren in Green Line beginnt in Band 1 und wird Band für Band ausgebaut.)

Act (out) one of the scenes. / Act (out) the dialogues.	Spiele eine der Szenen. / Spiele die Dialoge.
Add more words / ideas.	Füge weitere Wörter / Ideen hinzu.
Ask your partner questions.	Stelle deinem Partner / deiner Partnerin Fragen.
Answer your partner's questions.	Beantworte die Fragen deines Partners / deiner Partnerin.
***Check** your partner's text.	Überprüfe den Text deines Partners / deiner Partnerin.
Choose a character / one of the situations / options.	Wähle eine Figur / eine der Situationen / Optionen.
Collect ideas.	Sammle Ideen.
***Compare** English and German.	Vergleiche das Englische und Deutsche.
Complete the answers.	Vervollständige die Antworten.
Copy the grid / the mind map.	Schreibe die Tabelle / das Wörternetz ab.
Correct the wrong sentences.	Korrigiere die falschen Sätze.
***Describe** what you see / how it makes you feel.	Beschreibe, was du siehst / wie du dich dabei fühlst.
Decide who writes which part.	Entscheidet, wer welchen Teil schreibt.

***Discuss** different ideas.	Diskutiert verschiedene Ideen.
Divide your class up into two groups.	Teilt eure Klasse in zwei Gruppen auf.
Exchange your flyers / questions.	Tauscht eure Flyer / Fragen untereinander aus.
***Explain** your answer. / Explain why.	Erkläre deine Antwort. / Erkläre warum.
Fill in your grid / the form.	Fülle deine Tabelle / das Formular aus.
Find the rule / the right word order.	Finde die Regel / die richtige Wortstellung.
Finish your brochure.	Stelle deine Broschüre fertig.
Form expert groups.	Bildet Expertengruppen.
Get organised.	Organisiert euch.
Give reasons. / Give examples / feedback.	Nenne Gründe. / Gib Beispiele / ein Feedback.
Go back to your home group.	Gehe zurück zu deiner ersten Gruppe.
Guess the new words.	Errate die neuen Wörter.
Imagine you're one of the people in the story.	Stelle dir vor, du bist eine der Personen in der Geschichte.
Improve your text / part of the report.	Verbessere deinen Text / Teil des Berichts.
Learn your text by heart.	Lerne deinen Text auswendig.
Listen to the sentences / the dialogue.	Höre dir die Sätze / den Dialog an.
Look at the picture / the examples.	Schau dir das Bild / die Beispiele an.
***Look up** the words.	Schlage die Wörter nach.
Make a poster / a grid / a mind map / notes.	Fertige ein Poster / eine Tabelle / ein Wörternetz / Notizen an.
***Match** the sentence parts.	Ordne die Satzteile einander zu.
Note down what is missing.	Notiere, was fehlt.
Plan the scenes.	Plane die Szenen.
Practise your scenes / the dialogues.	Übe deine Szenen / die Dialoge.
***Present** the information from your text.	Präsentiere die Informationen aus deinem Text.
Put in the correct forms.	Setze die richtigen Formen ein.
Read your text aloud. / Read your text out loud.	Lies deinen Text laut vor.
Record your final report / dialogue.	Nehmt euren fertigen Bericht / Dialog auf.
Repeat the sentences / the dialogues.	Wiederhole die Sätze / die Dialoge.
***Report** what the people say.	Berichte, was die Leute sagen.
Say the words / the sounds.	Sage die Wörter / die Laute.
Scan the text for details.	Suche den Text nach Details ab.
***Share** the information with your partner.	Teile die Informationen mit deinem Partner / deiner Partnerin.
Skim the text for the gist.	Überfliege den Text und finde die wichtigsten Aussagen.
***Sum up / Summarise** what happens in the story.	Fasse zusammen, was in der Geschichte passiert.
Swap roles.	Tauscht die Rollen.
Take notes.	Mache dir Notizen.
Take turns.	Wechselt euch ab.
***Talk** with / to your partner (about …).	Sprich mit deinem Partner / deiner Partnerin (über …).
***Tell** your partner about your experiences.	Erzähle deinem Partner / deiner Partnerin von deinen Erfahrungen.

Think - pair - share.	Nachdenken - Paare bilden - teilen / austauschen.
Think about different problems.	Denke über die verschiedenen Probleme nach.
Think of ideas for ...	Überlege dir Ideen für ...
*Translate the words / sentences.	Übersetze die Wörter / Sätze.
Underline the words that change.	Unterstreiche die Wörter, die sich ändern.
Use the ideas / the vocabulary.	Verwende die Ideen / die Vokabeln.
Watch the film.	Sieh dir den Film an.
Work with a partner or in a group.	Arbeite mit einem Partner / einer Partnerin oder in einer Gruppe.
*Write dialogues / a short text / a reply / a summary.	Schreibe Dialoge / einen kurzen Text / eine Antwort / eine Zusammenfassung.
Write about your friends.	Schreibe über deine Freunde.
Write down your ideas / key words.	Schreibe deine Ideen / Schlüsselwörter auf.

Useful words

activity - Aktivität	presentation - Präsentation; Vortrag
answer - Antwort	prompt card - Rollenkarte
class display - Ausstellung in der Klasse	puzzle - Rätsel; Puzzle
collocation - Wortverbindung	pros and cons - Vor- und Nachteile
description - Beschreibung	question - Frage
dialogue - Dialog	quiz - Quiz; Rätsel
dice - Würfel	quote - Zitat
draft - Entwurf; Konzept	report - Bericht
drawing - Zeichnung	revision - Wiederholung
example - Beispiel	rhyme - Reim
fact - Tatsache; Fakt	role play - Rollenspiel
folder - Ordner; Mappe	rule - Regel
game - Spiel	scene - Szene
grid - Gitter; Tabelle; Raster	signal word - Signalwort
heading - Überschrift	slogan - Slogan; Werbespruch
information - Information(en)	speech bubble - Sprechblase
key word - Schlüsselwort	story - Geschichte; Erzählung
list - Liste	task - Aufgabe
mind map - Wörternetz	theme - Thema
order - Reihenfolge	title - Titel; Überschrift
perspective - Perspektive	unit - Lektion; Kapitel
phrase - Redewendung; Ausdruck	useful phrases - nützliche Ausdrücke
picture story - Bildergeschichte	vocabulary - Vokabular; Wortschatz
point of view - Standpunkt; Ansicht	word bank - Wortsammlung

Find more online:
nm6et5

Irregular verbs

■ ■ ■ Grundform, *simple past* und *past participle* sind identisch
■ ● ● Grundform unterscheidet sich vom *simple past* und *past participle*
■ ● ■ Grundform und *past participle* sind identisch, nur das *simple past* hat eine andere Form
■ ● ▲ Grundform, *simple past* und *past participle* haben alle eine andere Form

■ Grundform	■ simple past	■ past participle	Deutsch
cost [kɒst]	cost [kɒst]	cost [kɒst]	kosten
cut [kʌt]	cut [kʌt]	cut [kʌt]	schneiden
hit [hɪt]	hit [hɪt]	hit [hɪt]	schlagen, treffen
hurt [hɜ:t]	hurt [hɜ:t]	hurt [hɜ:t]	verletzen, sich weh tun
let [let]	let [let]	let [let]	lassen
put [pʊt]	put [pʊt]	put [pʊt]	legen, setzen, stellen
set up [set ˈʌp]	set up [set ˈʌp]	set up [set ˈʌp]	erbauen, errichten
upset [ʌpˈset]	upset [ʌpˈset]	upset [ʌpˈset]	aus der Fassung bringen

■ Grundform	● simple past	● past participle	Deutsch
bring [brɪŋ]	brought [brɔ:t]	brought [brɔ:t]	(mit)bringen
build [bɪld]	built [bɪlt]	built [bɪlt]	bauen
burn [bɜ:n]	burnt [bɜ:nt] / burned [bɜ:nd]	burnt [bɜ:nt] / burned [bɜ:nd]	(ver)brennen
buy [baɪ]	bought [bɔ:t]	bought [bɔ:t]	kaufen
catch [kætʃ]	caught [kɔ:t]	caught [kɔ:t]	fangen; mitbekommen
deal (with) [di:l]	dealt (with) [delt]	dealt (with) [delt]	sich befassen (mit), umgehen (mit)
dig [dɪg]	dug [dʌg]	dug [dʌg]	graben
feed [fi:d]	fed [fed]	fed [fed]	füttern, ernähren
feel [fi:l]	felt [felt]	felt [felt]	fühlen
fight [faɪt]	fought [fɔ:t]	fought [fɔ:t]	kämpfen, (sich) streiten
find [faɪnd]	found [faʊnd]	found [faʊnd]	finden
fit [fɪt]	fit [fɪt] / fitted [ˈfɪtɪd]	fit [fɪt] / fitted [ˈfɪtɪd]	passen
get [get]	got [gɒt]	got [gɒt]	holen, bringen, bekommen; werden
hang [hæŋ]	hung [hʌŋ]	hung [hʌŋ]	hängen
have [hæv]	had [hæd]	had [hæd]	haben
hear [hɪə]	heard [hɜ:d]	heard [hɜ:d]	hören
hold [həʊld]	held [held]	held [held]	halten
keep [ki:p]	kept [kept]	kept [kept]	(auf)bewahren, behalten
lead [li:d]	led [led]	led [led]	(an)führen
learn [lɜ:n]	learnt [lɜ:nt] / learned [lɜ:nd]	learnt [lɜ:nt] / learned [lɜ:nd]	lernen
leave [li:v]	left [left]	left [left]	(ver)lassen
lend [lend]	lent [lent]	lent [lent]	(ver)leihen
lose [lu:z]	lost [lɒst]	lost [lɒst]	verlieren
make [meɪk]	made [meɪd]	made [meɪd]	machen, tun
mean [mi:n]	meant [ment]	meant [ment]	bedeuten, meinen
meet [mi:t]	met [met]	met [met]	treffen
pay [peɪ]	paid [peɪd]	paid [peɪd]	(be)zahlen

read [ri:d]	read [red]	read [red]	lesen
say [seɪ]	said [sed]	said [sed]	sagen
sell [sel]	sold [səʊld]	sold [səʊld]	verkaufen
send [send]	sent [sent]	sent [sent]	senden, verschicken
shine [ʃaɪn]	shone [ʃɒn]	shone [ʃɒn]	scheinen, glänzen
shoot [ʃu:t]	shot [ʃɒt]	shot [ʃɒt]	schießen (auf)
sit [sɪt]	sat [sæt]	sat [sæt]	sitzen
sleep [sli:p]	slept [slept]	slept [slept]	schlafen
smell [smel]	smelt [smelt] / smelled [smeld]	smelt [smelt] / smelled [smeld]	riechen, duften
spell [spel]	spelt [spelt] / spelled [speld]	spelt [spelt] / spelled [speld]	buchstabieren
spend [spend]	spent [spent]	spent [spent]	ausgeben; verbringen
spill [spɪl]	spilt [spɪlt] / spilled [spɪld]	spilt [spɪlt] / spilled [spɪld]	verschütten, auslaufen
stand (up) [stænd]	stood (up) [stʊd]	stood (up) [stʊd]	(auf)stehen
sting [stɪŋ]	stung [stʌŋ]	stung [stʌŋ]	stechen
teach [ti:tʃ]	taught [tɔ:t]	taught [tɔ:t]	unterrichten, lehren, beibringen
tell [tel]	told [təʊld]	told [təʊld]	erzählen
think [θɪŋk]	thought [θɔ:t]	thought [θɔ:t]	(nach)denken, glauben
understand [ˌʌndəˈstænd]	understood [ˌʌndəˈstʊd]	understood [ˌʌndəˈstʊd]	verstehen
win [wɪn]	won [wʌn]	won [wʌn]	gewinnen, siegen

■ Grundform	● simple past	■ past participle	Deutsch
become [bɪˈkʌm]	became [bɪˈkeɪm]	become [bɪˈkʌm]	werden
come [kʌm]	came [keɪm]	come [kʌm]	kommen
run [rʌn]	ran [ræn]	run [rʌn]	laufen, rennen

■ Grundform	● simple past	▲ past participle	Deutsch
be [bi:]	was [wɒz] / were [wɜ:]	been [bi:n]	sein
begin [bɪˈgɪn]	began [bɪˈgæn]	begun [bɪˈgʌn]	beginnen, anfangen
bite [baɪt]	bit [bɪt]	bitten [ˈbɪtn]	beißen
blow (out) [bləʊ]	blew (out) [blu:]	blown (out) [bləʊn]	(aus)blasen, (aus)pusten
break [breɪk]	broke [brəʊk]	broken [ˈbrəʊkn]	(zer)brechen, kaputt machen
choose [tʃu:z]	chose [tʃəʊz]	chosen [tʃəʊzn]	(aus)wählen
do [du:]	did [dɪd]	done [dʌn]	machen, tun
draw [drɔ:]	drew [dru:]	drawn [drɔ:n]	zeichnen
drink [drɪŋk]	drank [dræŋk]	drunk [drʌŋk]	trinken
drive [draɪv]	drove [drəʊv]	driven [ˈdrɪvn]	fahren
eat [i:t]	ate [et]	eaten [i:tn]	essen
fall [fɔ:l]	fell [fel]	fallen [ˈfɔ:lən]	fallen
fly [flaɪ]	flew [flu:]	flown [fləʊn]	fliegen
forget [fəˈget]	forgot [fəˈgɒt]	forgotten [fəˈgɒtn]	vergessen
forgive [fəˈgɪv]	forgave [fəˈgeɪv]	forgiven [fəˈgɪvn]	vergeben, verzeihen
freeze [fri:z]	froze [frəʊz]	frozen [ˈfrəʊzn]	gefrieren, erstarren
give [gɪv]	gave [geɪv]	given[ˈgɪvn]	geben
go [gəʊ]	went [went]	gone [gɒn]	gehen, fahren
grow [grəʊ]	grew [gru:]	grown [grəʊn]	wachsen; anbauen
know [nəʊ]	knew [nju:]	known [nəʊn]	kennen, wissen
lie [laɪ]	lay [leɪ]	lain [leɪn]	liegen

→ Fortsetzung auf S. 286

→ Fortsetzung von S. 285 Irregular verbs

ring [rɪŋ]	rang [ræŋ]	rung [rʌŋ]	klingeln; anrufen
rise [raɪz]	rose [rəʊz]	risen ['rɪzn]	steigen, sich erheben
see [si:]	saw [sɔ:]	seen [si:n]	sehen
show [ʃəʊ]	showed [ʃəʊd]	shown [ʃəʊn]	zeigen
sing [sɪŋ]	sang [sæŋ]	sung [sʌŋ]	singen
sink [sɪŋk]	sank [sæŋk]	sunk [sʌŋk]	sinken, untergehen
speak [spi:k]	spoke [spəʊk]	spoken ['spəʊkn]	sprechen
steal [sti:l]	stole [stəʊl]	stolen ['stəʊlən]	stehlen
swim [swɪm]	swam [swæm]	swum [swʌm]	schwimmen
take [teɪk]	took [tʊk]	taken ['teɪkn]	nehmen
throw [θrəʊ]	threw [θru:]	thrown [θrəʊn]	werfen
wake up [ˌweɪk‿'ʌp]	woke up [ˌwəʊk‿'ʌp]	woken up [ˌwəʊkn‿'ʌp]	aufwachen; aufwecken
wear [weə]	wore [wɔ:]	worn [wɔ:n]	anhaben, tragen
write [raɪt]	wrote [rəʊt]	written ['rɪtn]	schreiben

Grammar solutions

Unit 1

G1 If I become a famous dancer, I'll earn a lot of money.

1. If we **don't leave** now, we'**ll miss** our train.
2. If we **miss** our train, we'**ll be late** for the film.
3. If we **are late** for the film, they probably **won't let** us in.
4. And I'**ll be** really upset if that **happens**, Shahid. …

G2 They wouldn't worry if they didn't care.

Jay: If Mum and Dad **tried** to understand me, we **wouldn't fight** so often.
Shahid: … You **wouldn't have** so many fights if you **worked** harder for school and **got** better marks.
Jay: The problem is that they don't believe in me, Shahid. If they **believed** in me, they **wouldn't worry** about my marks.
Shahid: … Maybe if you **weren't** so laid-back, they **wouldn't have to** worry so much.

G3 You have to push yourself.

Olivia: … **myself** … | Lucy: … **me** … | Olivia: … **yourself**.
Claire: … **yourselves**. … **each other**.

G4 An interview with Ayla

Lösungsvorschlag:
a) 1. Have you prepared for Sports Day yet?
2. Have you bought new sports shoes yet?
3. Have you already started eating healthy food?
4. Have you ever hurt your foot?
5. Have you found a name for your team yet?

b) 2. Have you bought new sports shoes yet?
- No, I haven't. I don't need any new shoes. My old ones/shoes are OK.
- Yes, I have. I've just bought some new shoes. Look, they are in this bag.
- Yes, I have. I bought them last week.

3. Have you already started eating healthy food?
- Yes, I have. I've already eaten two apples today.

4. Have you ever hurt your foot?
- Yes, I have. I've hurt my leg twice/two times. When I was little, I broke my leg at the ice rink. And last year I twisted my ankle.
- No, I haven't.

5. Have you found a name for your team yet?
- Yes, I have. But I'm not going to tell you.
- No, I haven't found a nice name yet.

Unit 2

G5 How long have they been chatting?

1. How long **has** Mr Wilson **been working** in a hotel? – He **has been working** there **since** 2012.
2. How long **has** Mrs Wilson **been teaching** English? – She **has been teaching** English **for** five years.
3. How long **have** their children Sam and Jack **been going** to school? – Sam **has been going** to school **for** three years, Jack **(has been going to school) since** last year.

G6 Is Haggis made with meat?

… **was invented** in Ireland … | … **was brought** to Scotland … | … **has been played** in Scotland … | … **is played** between two teams …

G7 What were they doing when Holly took the picture?

2. A: Were Will and Kate visiting Edinburgh when Holly and Gwen saw them?
   B: No, they weren't. They were visiting Glasgow.
3. A: Was Gwen running in the park when she fell over?
   B: No, she wasn't. She was running down the road.
4. A: Were Holly and Gwen walking through the field when the cows started to follow them?
   B: No, they weren't. They were walking past it.

Unit 3

G8 He hadn't finished his game

Henry VIII and the Church of England

In 1509, seven weeks after Henry VIII **had become** the new king of England, he **married** Catherine of Aragon. She had been the wife of his older brother Arthur, who **had died** in 1502. Together, Henry and Catherine **had** a daughter, Mary. But Henry **needed** a boy who could become the next king. So, in 1533, after Catherine **had become** too old to have any more children, Henry **decided** to marry Anne Boleyn, who he **had met** and fallen in love with in about 1525. When the Pope **said** "no", Henry **broke** with Rome and **founded** his own Church - the Church of England.

G9 The people who really knew how to have fun

Elizabethan England

1. **who** | 2. (which/that) | 3. **who** |
4. **whose** | 5. (which/that)

G10 All's well that ends well.

Tips for London visitors

1. **cheaply** | 2. **fantastic** | 3. **nice/great** | 4. **scary** |
5. **realistically** | 6. **extremely well**

G11 You can see London faster and more easily with a guide.

- Jamal paints beautifully, David paints more beautifully, but Peter paints most beautifully.
- Peter dances well, David dances better, but Jamal dances best.
- David jumps high, Peter jumps higher, but Jamal jumps highest.

Unit 4

G12 You told us there was free wifi!

A message from Jack

Jack's mother: Jack sent me a message this afternoon. He said that **he'd had** a good trip and that **he'd arrived** safely. **He hadn't had** time to look around yet, so **he couldn't tell me** much, but he said that the hostel **was** clean and the people **were** very friendly. He said **he'd call** again later, but **he didn't know** when because **they were going** into town for dinner and **he wasn't sure** when **they'd be back**.

G13 Steve's blog

Eddie: Steve sent me a message from France last week. He said that the athletics event **had started the day before** and that **their** team **was** doing well. But it **was** very cold **there**. He said that if **he** ever **came back** to **that** place, **he'd take** warmer clothes. **He wished he'd listened** to Ms W.

G14 He asked me what the purpose of my visit was

1. The man at passport control asked me **why I was** travelling alone.
2. He wanted to know **where I was from**.
3. He asked me **how long I planned** to stay.
4. He wanted to know **if I had** family in Bangladesh.
5. He asked **if I could speak** Bengali.
6. He wanted to know **if anybody was meeting me** at the airport.

G15 He told me to go into a side room

1. Rafiq's mum **asked him to say hello** to everyone from **them**.
2. She **told him to be careful** with his passport and **not to lose it**.
3. She **asked him to call her** as soon as **he got to** Dhaka.
4. She **told him to have fun** while **he was** there and **to take** lots of photos.

Unit solutions

Unit 1, Story: Alternative endings

→ page 22, ex. 4

Hang out with us instead!

Alternative ending 1:

Shahid was on his way home on the train when he received a text message from his best friend, Dan, who was also a DJ:

Hi Shahid. Hope your weekend went well. Just to say, that was a great idea you had last week to copy all of our music onto each other's hard drives. I've really enjoyed listening to all your tracks - and it's great to know that we don't have to worry about losing all our music! Dan

Alternative ending 2:

When Shahid arrived home the next morning, Jay said: "I've got something to tell you." Jay told his story while Shahid listened quietly - he never shouted but sometimes that made you feel worse. Finally, Shahid spoke. "You know how important my music is to me - without it I can't do my DJ work. So, you can guess how you're going to spend all your weekends for the next two or three months, can't you? I need you to record all my songs again. All of them!" How could Jay argue? He knew he had no choice. Shahid was really disappointed in him and now he couldn't go out for weeks! How much worse could life be?

Bildquellen:
U.1 YERMAN FILMS (Andrea Artz), London; **U.2** shutterstock (Richie Chan), New York, NY; **2.1; 33.1** 123rf (kotenko), Nidderau; **4.1; 57.1** Getty Images (Oxford Scientific), München; **4.2; 85.1** Corbis (Paul A. Souders), Berlin; **6.1; 106.2** Ullstein Bild GmbH (ArenaPAL), Berlin; **8.1** Corbis (KidStock/Blend Images), Berlin; **8.2** Corbis (Brian Mitchell), Berlin; **9.1** Getty Images (Matthias Hangst), München; **9.2** Thinkstock (Andrii_Oliinyk), München; **9.3** Thinkstock (arabes), München; **9.4** Thinkstock (Nixken), München; **9.5** Thinkstock (nuranvectorgirl), München; **9.6** Thinkstock (pking4th), München; **9.7** Thinkstock (nosopyrik), München; **9.8** Fotolia.com (alexghidan89), New York; **9.9** Thinkstock (comzeal), München; **10.1; 10.2; 12.1; 38.2; 38.3; 40.1; 41.1; 68.1; 77.1; 77.2; 78.1; 117.1; 123.1; 123.2; 161.1; 162.1; 168.1** YERMAN FILMS (Andrea Artz), London; **11.1** Getty Images (Bloom-berg), München; **12.2** Thinkstock (iStock/kadmy), München; **13.1; 67.3** shutterstock (George Dolgikh), New York, NY; **13.2** Getty Images (THOMAS COEX/AFP), München; **16.1** shutterstock (Glayan), New York, NY; **17.1** iStockphoto (PeopleImages), Calgary, Alberta; **18.1** Corbis (Sandra Hoever), Berlin; **20.1** Corbis (Mark Scoggins), Berlin; **21.1** YERMAN FILMS (Andrew Kemp), London; **26.1; 30.1** Avenue Images GmbH (Banana Stock), Hamburg; **27.1** www.CartoonStock.com (Madden, Chris), Bath; **27.2** www.CartoonStock.com (Farris, Joseph), Bath; **28.1** Weisshaar, Harald, Bisingen-Zimmern; **29.1** shutterstock (visionaryft), New York, NY; **31.1** Getty Images (Steve Jennings/WireImage), München; **32.1** Getty Images (GREG WOOD/AFP), München; **32.2** shutterstock (Syda Productions), New York, NY; **33.2** shutterstock (Joshua Resnick), New York, NY; **23.1; 23.2; 23.3; 34.1; 34.2; 35.1; 35.2; 51.1; 51.2; 63.1; 63.2; 63.3; 63.4; 79.1; 79.2; 91.1; 91.2; 91.3; 105.1** February Films, London; **36.1** plainpicture GmbH & Co. KG (Fancy Images), Hamburg; **37.2** Alamy Stock Photo (Ian Dagnall), Abingdon, Oxon; **37.4** iStockphoto (TT), Calgary, Alberta; **37.1** Getty Images (Panoramic Images), München; **37.3** iStockphoto (George Clerk), Calgary, Alberta; **38.1** iStockphoto (abzee), Calgary, Alberta; **39.1** Corbis (Kristian Buus/In Pictures), Berlin; **40.2** Corbis (BPI/Richard Lee/BPI), Berlin; **42.1** Corbis (Najlah Feanny/SABA), Berlin; **43.1** iStockphoto (code6d), Calgary, Alberta; **43.2** Alamy Stock Photo (John Peter Photography), Abingdon, Oxon; **44.5** iStockphoto (Gim42), Calgary, Alberta; **44.2** iStockphoto (Mnieteq), Calgary, Alberta; **44.3; 172.1** shutterstock (JASPERIMAGE), New York, NY; **44.1** Corbis (Adam Burton/Robert Harding World Imagery), Berlin; **44.4** Corbis (Colin McPherson/Sygma), Berlin; **44.6** Alamy Stock Photo (Thornton Cohen), Abingdon, Oxon; **45.1** iStockphoto (damircudic), Calgary, Alberta; **46.1** Getty Images (DEA/PUBBLI AER FOTO/De Agostini), München; **47.1** shutterstock (Ron Dale), New York, NY; **47.2** shutterstock (Gepardu), New York, NY; **47.3** shutterstock (Vectomart), New York, NY; **52.1** iStockphoto (miss_elli), Calgary, Alberta; **53.1** Ullstein Bild GmbH (Stiebing), Berlin; **53.2** Getty Images (Sean Gallup), München; **55.5; 55.4** shutterstock (Rainer Albiez), New York, NY; **55.3** shutterstock (Matyas Rehak), New York, NY; **55.1** shutterstock (chrisdorney), New York, NY; **55.2** Fotolia.com (zuzule), New York; **57.3** shutterstock (Elena11), New York, NY; **57.2** shutterstock (Denisa Doudova), New York, NY; **58.1** shutterstock (David Dohnal), New York, NY; **59.1** Corbis (Joel Sartore/National Geographic Creative), Berlin; **59.2** iStockphoto (PandaWild), Calgary, Alberta; **59.3** shutterstock (Adam Filipowicz), New York, NY; **59.4** Getty Images (Hulton Archive/James Pozarik/Liaison), München; **60.2** shutterstock (Catfish Photography), New York, NY; **60.1** shutterstock (Graeme Shannon), New York, NY; **60.3** Thinkstock (Stockbyte), München; **62.1** www.CartoonStock.com (McNeill, Geoff), Bath; **64.3** 123rf (Zvonimir Atletic), Nidderau; **64.1** Picture-Alliance (Becker & Bredel), Frankfurt; **64.2** Alamy Stock Photo (Lenscap), Abingdon, Oxon; **65.2** shutterstock (Sytilin Pavel), New York, NY; **65.1** shutterstock (Thomas Owen Jenkins), New York, NY; **66.1** Getty Images (Stapleton Collection), München; **67.1** Corbis (The Print Collector), Berlin; **67.2** Corbis (I Love Images), Berlin; **67.4** shutterstock (Monkey Business Images), New York, NY; **68.2** Imago (EntertainmentPictures), Berlin; **71.1** shutterstock (Anneka), New York, NY; **72.1** shutterstock (Kamira), New York, NY; **73.1; 119.1; 119.2** February Films (Andrew Kemp), London; **74.1** f1 online digitale Bildagentur, Frankfurt; **75.1** Getty Images (Fine Art Images/Heritage Images), München; **80.1** Thinkstock (Jupiterimages), München; **80.2** iStockphoto (miskolin), Calgary, Alberta; **80.3** iStockphoto (fcafotodigital), Calgary, Alberta; **80.4** shutterstock (Sergios), New York, NY; **80.5** shutterstock (CHANG JO-YI), New York, NY; **80.6** Thinkstock (Hemera Technologies), München; **82.1** iStockphoto (Chris Jackson/EdStock), Calgary, Alberta; **83.1** Getty Images (Corbis Historical), München; **84.1; 56.1** Corbis (Jim Craigmyle), Berlin; **85.2** Corbis (Kelly-Mooney Photography), Berlin; **87.1** shutterstock (Photobank gallery), New York, NY; **89.1; 89.2** Ernst Klett Sprachen GmbH, Stuttgart; **92.1** Thinkstock (brians101), München; **93.1** Getty Images (Marco Di Lauro), München; **93.2; 135.1** Getty Images (E+), München; **93.3** Thinkstock (Creatas), München; **98.1** iStockphoto (Tarzan9280), Calgary, Alberta; **100.1** shutterstock (Dave Allen Photography), New York, NY; **101.1** Klett-Archiv (Peter Niehoff), Stuttgart; **106.1** Fotolia.com (Katrina Brown), New York; **107.1; 108.1; 110.2; 112.1; 110.1** Clemens Weisshaar, Bisingen-Zimmern; **114.2** Fotolia.com (Christian Schwier), New York; **114.1** Corbis (Samantha Mitchell), Berlin; **115.1** shutterstock (javi_indy), New York, NY; **120.1** iStockphoto (DenisZbukarev), Calgary, Alberta; **124.1** Getty Images (Photolibrary), München; **125.1** Getty Images (Getty Images Sport), München; **125.2** akg-images (EON/UA/Album), Berlin; **127.1** Getty Images (Sonya Hurtado), München; **127.2** Getty Images (Digital Vision), München; **128.1** Getty Images (Cultura), München; **130.1** Corbis (Andreas von Einsiedel), Berlin; **130.2** Corbis (Jimmy Collins), Berlin; **130.3** shutterstock (marekuliasz), New York, NY; **130.4** Corbis (GraphicaArtis), Berlin; **133.1** Getty Images (LatitudeStock - Allan Hartley), München; **134.1** iStockphoto (Tracie Andrews), Calgary, Alberta; **138.1** shutterstock (In Tune), New York, NY; **138.2** iStockphoto (RF/Ischa Gast), Calgary, Alberta; **138.3** shutterstock (Bikeworldtravel), New York, NY; **144.1** Fotolia.com (Michael Rogner), New York; **149.1** PONS GmbH, Stuttgart; **152.1** shutterstock (Dmitry Kalinovsky), New York, NY; **153.1** shutterstock (Kues), New York, NY; **157.1** ddp images GmbH, Hamburg; **157.2** dreamstime.com (Edward Bartel), Brentwood, TN; **158.1** akg-images (Album), Berlin; **158.2** Getty Images (Matt Cardy), München; **158.3** Ullstein Bild GmbH (pwe Verlag GmbH), Berlin; **170.1** Getty Images (Lonely Planet Images/J. Smith), München; **171.1** shutterstock (Michaelpuche), New York, NY; **171.2** Thinkstock (Alan Crawford), München; **174.1** Ullstein Bild GmbH (CARO/Rupert Oberhäuser), Berlin; **176.1** iStockphoto (Duncan Walker), Calgary, Alberta; **177.1** Ullstein Bild GmbH (AP), Berlin; **177.2** Thinkstock (tupungato), München; **179.1** Alamy Stock Photo (Tony Cortazzi), Abingdon, Oxon; **181.1** iStockphoto (Monique Rodriguez), Calgary, Alberta; **181.2** iStockphoto (Cathy Yeulet), Calgary, Alberta; **181.3** Thinkstock (PaulSimcock), München; **195.1** shutterstock (Press-master), New York, NY; **199.1** Fotolia.com (konstan), New York; **199.2** iStockphoto (luoman), Calgary, Alberta; **199.3** Thinkstock (Vrabelpeter1), München; **199.4** iStockphoto (jeangill), Calgary, Alberta; **199.5** shutterstock (NemesisINC), New York, NY; **199.6** iStockphoto (blackjake), Calgary, Alberta; **203.1** shutter-stock (wallix), New York, NY; **203.2** shutterstock (Targn Pleiades), New York, NY; **212.1** Avenue Images GmbH (Ingram Publishing), Hamburg; **214.1** gemeinfrei, ; **221.1** shutterstock (Sentavio), New York, NY; **281.1** February Films (Elke Bock), London; **Timeline.1** Corbis (Stuart Forster/Robert Harding World Imagery), Berlin; **Timeline.2** Alamy Stock Photo (CJG - UK), Abingdon, Oxon; **Timeline.3** iStockphoto (Andrew Gosling), Calgary, Alberta; **Timeline.4** Corbis, Berlin

Textquellen:
Songtexte: 13 "Holiday" Text: Stevens, Lisa/Hudson, Curtis Lee © House of Fun Music Inc, Sony/ATV Music Publishing (Germany) GmbH, Berlin; **31** "Count on me" Text: Hernandez, Peter Gene/Lawrence, Philip Martin/Levine, Ari © BMG Gold Songs/Bughouse/Mars Force Music/Round Hill Songs/Toy Plane Music BMG Rights Management GmbH, Berlin Northside Independent Music/Roc Nation Music/WB Music Corp./Neue Welt Musikverlag GmbH, Hamburg; **40** "Flower of Scotland" Text: (OT) Williamson, Roy, Copyright Variena Music Inc./Edition AIM Publishing; **96** "Island in the sun" Text: CUOMO, RIVERS Copyright E O Smith Music, Melodie der Welt J. Michel GmbH & Co. KG Musikverlag, Frankfurt
Texte: 29 "Happy Poem": From *Time Travelling Underpants*, Macmillan Children's Books, 2007, 978-0-330-44709-6, p50; **30** "The Arrow and the Song": From *The Belfry of Bruges and Other Poems* by Henry Wadsworth Longfellow, 1846, public domain; **33** "A smile" (anonymous), public domain; **33** Untitled poem: "I loved my friend" by Langston Hughes, The Collected Works of Langston Hughes, University of Missouri Press, 2003; **57** Brent Lodge Wildlife Hospital, 2014; **60** Ben Pulsford, *First News*, 03.10.2014; **85** Reprinted with the permission of Simon & Schuster Books for Young Readers, an imprint of Simon & Schuster Children's Publishing Division from AMONG THE HIDDEN by Margaret Peterson Haddix. Copyright © 1998 Margaret Peterson Haddix.; **87** Excerpt from *Pig-Heart Boy* by Malorie Blackman, Doubleday, an imprint of Random House Children's Books, London, 1997 © Oneta Malorie Blackman, 1997; **102** From *Where I belong* by Gillian Cross, Oxford University Press, April 2010; **107–112** *Eight Plays for Teenagers* Kapitel 5, "Claire's Devil". EKS - First published in Sweden by Utbildningsstaden AB 1995

Sollte es in einem Einzelfall nicht gelungen sein, den korrekten Rechteinhaber ausfindig zu machen, so werden berechtigte Ansprüche selbstverständlich im Rahmen der üblichen Regelungen abgegolten.

Time line of British history

We don't know much about **the earliest people** who lived in the British Isles, but we can still see some of the famous stone rings they built, like Stonehenge. We also know that their priests were called Druids.

500 BC

A typical Celtic round house

From around 500 BC, the **Celts** came from Europe to live in the British Isles. They lived in round houses with fires in the middle and built high walls to keep out wild animals. They had many gods.

43–410 AD

After the **Romans** had arrived, the Celts moved north and west to Scotland, Ireland and Wales. The Romans built Hadrian's Wall to keep the Scots out of their part of the island of Britain.

5th, 6th cent.

After the Romans had left, Germanic tribes called **Saxons and Angles** conquered England. The Angles gave England its name: It means 'Land of the Angles'.

1066–1154

At the battle of Hastings, William, Duke of Normandy defeated Harold, King of the Saxons. The **Normans** ruled England for the next 88 years.

1485–1603

Henry VIII and his six wives, as wax figures at Madam Tussauds

The **House of Tudor** was important in English history. Henry VIII changed England from a Catholic to a Protestant country, and founded the Navy. His daughter Elizabeth was perhaps the biggest 'star' of the Tudor family. While she was queen, England became rich and powerful and started to colonise North America. It was a 'golden age' for music, literature and the theatre too.

18th, 19th cent.

Industrialisation started in England in the 18th century. Factories with machines were built all over Britain and the invention of the steam engine meant that people could travel much more than before.

Powerful symbol of the Industrial Revolution: the steam train

1837–1901

Queen Victoria reigned for almost 64 years

During the reign of **Queen Victoria**, Britain had so many colonies around the world that people said the sun always shone somewhere in the British Empire.

After 1945

After the two world wars, Britain rebuilt itself, and people started to enjoy themselves again. British music and fashion became popular around the world. Even today, the music of the Beatles and Rolling Stones still has a major influence.

1973

The UK joined the European Community (later the European Union), but the British kept their own money: the pound.

SCOTLAND
SHETLAND ISLANDS
Atlantic Ocean
ORKNEY ISLANDS
OUTER HEBRIDES
Highlands
Inverness
Loch Ness
ISLE OF SKYE
Aberdeen
Balmoral Castle
Ben Nevis
Dunnottar Castle
Tay
Dundee
Firth of Forth
Loch Lomond
Glasgow
Edinburgh
Edinburgh Castle
Clyde
Tweed
ARRAN
North Sea

THE BRITISH ISLES